THE LOST PROMISE

THE LOST
PROMISE

*American Universities
in the 1960s*

ELLEN SCHRECKER

The University of Chicago Press   CHICAGO

The University of Chicago Press, Chicago 60637
Published 2021
Printed in the United States of America

30 29 28 27 26 25 24 23 22 21   1 2 3 4 5

ISBN-13: 978-0-226-20085-9 (cloth)
ISBN-13: 978-0-226-20099-6 (e-book)
DOI: https://doi.org/10.7208/chicago/9780226200996.001.0001

Library of Congress Cataloging-in-Publication Data

Names: Schrecker, Ellen, author.
Title: The lost promise : American universities in the 1960s /
Ellen Schrecker.
Description: Chicago : The University of Chicago Press, 2021. |
Includes bibliographical references and index.
Identifiers: LCCN 2021027259 | ISBN 9780226200859 (cloth) |
ISBN 9780226200996 (ebook)
Subjects: LCSH: Education, Higher—United States—History. | Universities
and colleges—United States—History. | College students—Political
activity—United States. | Nineteen sixties.
Classification: LCC LA227.3 .S37 2021 | DDC 378.73—dc23
LC record available at https://lccn.loc.gov/2021027259

♾ This paper meets the requirements of ANSI/NISO Z39.48-1992
(Permanence of Paper).

For April and Mark

CONTENTS

INTRODUCTION

Universities in the Long Sixties

*The trouble with this college, the trouble with every college in this coun-
try, is that we really <u>are</u> at the center. All the slogans about the colleges
being the future of America, the poor bastards don't know how right
they are. . . . It was true. We were at the center of American consciousness. Our fantasies had finally caught up with us.*[1]

Once upon a time in the not-so-distant past, American higher education got a lot of respect. From the mid-1950s through to the early
1970s, colleges and universities were at the center of American life.
Even as many campuses were wracked by turmoil, they were also
experiencing what has come to be seen as a golden age—at least for
white men.[2] Faculty positions were considered prestigious, and the
academic community as a whole—faculty, students (both graduate
and undergraduate), researchers, administrators, and intellectual
hangers-on—seemed to be engaged in an exciting collective endeavor
to improve their institutions and perhaps even make the world a better place.

But it didn't last. The contradictions within the academic community ultimately brought that halcyon moment to a painful and confusing end—with consequences that haunt us to this day. By the mid-
1970s, colleges and universities no longer had the universal approval
they once possessed. How and why that happened is the subject of
this book.

It is a chronicle of declension, a sobering story of how a seemingly indispensable social institution attained a position of power and approbation—and then lost it. While today's colleges and universities, undermined by decades of disinvestment and disrespect, now struggle simply to survive, during the early 1960s the academy's influence extended far beyond its campuses. Especially after Sputnik, higher education emerged from the anti-intellectualism of the McCarthy era, where professors were scorned as eggheads (if not subversives) and students engaged in panty raids not politics. Many in the academic community believed that they and their institutions were not only crucial to America's national security, but also central to economic progress. Showered with money by foundations and governments at every level, universities entered an era of unprecedented expansion.

The period I'm calling the long sixties was also when the academy became the repository of the American dream, not only of upward mobility, but also for many of a more egalitarian society that would challenge the racial and gender intolerance and inequality that had for so long impeded human progress.[3] As the quintessential liberal institution during the heyday of American liberalism, higher education attracted idealistic people—students and faculty alike—many of whom still trusted the authorities and their promises. Others, however, sought to shake up their campuses and disciplines. Gravitating into what was to become the New Left, radicals and left-liberals wanted higher education to become a force for liberation available to all comers. Believing in the power of ideas, they felt that their intellectual efforts could influence the powers that be and move both the university and perhaps even the whole country toward justice and true democracy.

That did not happen, of course. In retrospect, it's clear that the university never had as much power and autonomy as its members and critics assumed. Its enormous expansion and its accompanying optimism, as well as the pervasiveness of its own ivory tower myth, blinded the academic community—left, right, and center—to its own limitations. As institutions doubled and tripled in size, they were transformed, attracting the academically ambitious and often the unconventional, while putting a new emphasis on research instead of teaching. The ensuing cultural conflicts and turf battles, not to mention the growing political disagreements over Vietnam, race, and other divisive issues, made it impossible for the academic community to develop a coherent response to the challenges it faced— from women, African Americans, and its own radicals as well as from conservative politicians and an increasingly hostile public. The situation was completely unprecedented. As in a recurring bad dream, the academic community was facing the final exam without having taken the course.

Even today American universities are still, by some measures, number one in the world.[4] It is a ranking built on misconceptions, or perhaps the realization that higher education elsewhere also has its defects. Even before COVID-19, the academic community was suffering. With the traditional liberal arts in decline, and underpaid and exploited part-time and temporary instructors supplying 75 percent of the teaching staff, only a handful of colleges and universities provided their graduates with much beyond technical training and considerable debt. But it didn't need to be that way.

I admit to overstating my case. Still, it was hard to lose a dream and to do so suddenly. At some point around 1965, the bright promise of an expansive and liberating system of mass higher education darkened. The war in Southeast Asia and the failure of the political establishment to grant real equality to its citizens of color disabused and radicalized an entire generation of students and professors. Although most of the problems of racism, sexism, the Cold War, and economic inequality could not have been solved by educational reforms, left-wing critics deemed the university complicit in them. As a result, when some academic leaders could not or would not satisfy the radicals' mostly reasonable demands, their campuses seemed to spin out of control, destroying much of the public's previous confidence in higher education. The university was soon hollowed out and assaulted by the right-wing enemies of liberal culture, and it never recovered.

* * * *

There are two interrelated strands to this story—growth and turbulence. In the sixties, colleges and universities expanded so exponentially that their traditional folkways simply imploded. Many institutions would have been disrupted even if the rest of the United States had been calm. But it was not. Despite—or perhaps because of—the country's relative affluence, the struggle to fulfill the democratic promise of higher education in the face of racism, sexism, and US warmongering ensured turbulence.

It is impossible to stress enough how thoroughly the Vietnam War permeated the waking lives of student and faculty dissidents during the long sixties. It was distressing to find out from newspapers every morning that our country had killed hundreds or perhaps thousands of men, women, and children the day before. Our shame, our anger, and ultimately our inability to stop the horror destroyed our trust in the liberal order. That disillusionment marked an entire generation. Whether it was biologists discovering that the US Army was using their research to destroy crops in Southeast Asia or professors refusing to flunk students who might then be drafted—the war ultimately forced faculty members of all political persuasions to face unwelcome, but unavoidable, moral choices.

The university's long sixties occurred in several phases, beginning in the mid-1950s when the academic community emerged from its encounter with McCarthyism to enter a decade of optimism and expansion. By the middle of the sixties, events off campus—the Vietnam War and the struggle for racial equality, in particular—were to politicize higher education, even as its explosive growth was creating unforeseen tensions. For the next five to ten years, confrontations took place at many, though by no means all, institutions. Finally, after one last burst of conflict, the unrest ended in the early 1970s as the war wound down and the buoyant economic expansion of the previous decade sputtered to an end, inaugurating a new era of austerity.[5]

But because so much change occurred so quickly during those years, there is no coherent narrative, no single story that traces how one thing led to another. Everything seemed to be happening at once. Though petering out, the trauma endured. The events of the long sixties hung over higher education for the next half century, while the backlash they incurred spilled over into the rest of society—poisoning its political discourse and paving the way for decades of neoliberal policies designed to shrink the public sector—its institutions of higher learning, in particular.

∗   ∗   ∗   ∗

My protagonists are the men, women, and institutions of the academic community. Across the approximately twenty-five hundred colleges and universities that flourished during the long sixties, that community comprised a congeries of students, professors, administrators, and ideologies sharing institutional connections—even if fragmented and all too often at odds.[6] The key component was the faculty: the men (they were overwhelmingly men) who planned and taught the courses, did the research, and constructed academic careers. Undergraduates cycled through this world in four-year cohorts of varying self-awareness, while a smaller population of graduate students—as allies and intermediaries—bridged their world and that of their teachers. Many administrators were also faculty members, who saw their service as temporary, even as their duties increasingly pulled them away from their original mindset and allegiances. Academia also housed public intellectuals and consultants, much of whose work life occurred off campus; clergy, including some of a radical bent; and such hangers-on as faculty wives, political activists, writers, and artists-in-residence.

The book begins with a quick survey of the institutional expansion that began in the 1950s and the changes that accompanied it, particularly the uneven sloughing off of the political repression of the McCarthy era that had so completely marginalized the Left. As seeds of political activity began to sprout, the academy's newly energized radicals became involved with the vibrant civil rights movement of the early 1960s. Initiated by students at the Black colleges and universities in the South, it offered the prospect of genuine social change.

Soon students demanding political freedom shook up the University of California, Berkeley. As faculty members and administrators struggled to deal with the protests, political divisions emerged. Berkeley's experience presaged a pattern. Almost all of the subsequent waves of student unrest broke out first at major universities and big-city campuses. Not only did those institutions attract politically engaged students and professors, but because of their size, they were able to produce a critical mass of activists who forced the academic community to respond—and the media to pay attention. These large urban and elite institutions were where the action was, at least until the end of the 1960s: UC Berkeley, the University of Michigan, the University of Chicago, the University of Wisconsin, CCNY, Columbia, Cornell, San Francisco State, and other major universities. Protests may have occurred later at lesser-known and smaller institutions, but the issues were the same as at the top-tier ones.

The Vietnam War, of course: radical and left-liberal professors and graduate students came to the issue first. The teach-ins they organized actually jump-started the antiwar movement. Although a minority at the time, their analyses of what was happening in Southeast Asia created the scenario about the conflict that most of their students and colleagues—as well as growing numbers of political leaders and ordinary Americans—were eventually to embrace. Later on, as both student and faculty radicals raised new questions about their institutions' collaboration with the national security state, the protests intensified. Frustrated by their failure to end the war, some increasingly desperate activists even turned to civil disobedience.

Today, after all the years of rhetoric about tenured radicals and Marxist professors, it might be a surprise to learn that the overwhelming majority of faculty members in the long sixties, even the liberal ones, opposed the student disruptions. Most academics were essentially apolitical—moderates who wanted nothing more than for everything to calm down. They definitely did not appreciate having to make what the political theorist Michael Walzer called the "harsh choices" the 1960s forced upon them.[7] Unfortunately, however, the university was confronting such polarizing issues that its members could not avoid taking sides, forming factions that split the community. Confusion reigned. Neither faculties nor administrations seemed able to offer coherent responses to their troubles—an unfortunate situation that could only encourage hostile outsiders to intervene.

Radical academics did not dominate the nation's faculties, but they did have an impact. They created their own organizations, appealed to audiences on and off campus, and, in many cases, worked with local and national left-wing peace and social justice groups. Though often marginalized and even repressed, they did bring new perspectives and somewhat more democratic practices into the university. That almost all of them were men certainly deserves mention. Although second-wave feminism got much of its early energy from within the academic community, it did not come into its own until the long sixties was near its end.

As political activism tapered off in the early 1970s, a financial crunch hit the academic community, forcing even the wealthiest Ivy League institutions to dip into their endowments for operating expenses and to admit women students to keep their enrollments up.[8] The fiscal plight of public institutions was even more alarming. Increasingly upset by the student unrest, the politicians who had so generously supported state colleges and universities reversed course. By the late 1960s, although enrollments continued to grow, the democratic vision of universal mass higher education evaporated. Within a few years, as tuitions rose rapidly and ballooning debt began to subvert the life chances of students, tenure-track jobs melted away, transforming most prospective faculty members into permanent temp workers without either economic security or academic freedom.

Obviously, the university's turmoil during the long sixties did not cause all these problems directly. Nonetheless, the inability of the academic community to meet the reasonable demands of its constituents for a more democratic campus meant that its members lacked the solidarity that an effective defense against the conservative onslaught required. If nothing else, the academic community's past problems should alert its current members to the urgent need for unity in the face of existential challenges.

* * * *

This is a big book. It could have been three times as long. I had to force myself to keep it within limits and did so by eliminating dozens of fascinating case studies. Every chapter, sometimes every paragraph, deals with subjects that deserve entire volumes of their own, some of which have already been written. I do not, for example, pay much attention to the development and activities of the student movement since many others have already done so. Nor do I give as much consideration as they deserve to events toward the end of the long sixties, like the early women's movement, the academy's structural reforms and pedagogical experiments, and the details of the backlash.

The book consists of four sections. The first deals with the massive expansion of higher education as well as the nascent political activities of academics during the early part of the long sixties. The second covers the growth of the antiwar movement and the development of opposition to war-related research. The third looks at the student unrest as well as at the ways in which faculties and administrators struggled to handle it. The final section deals with the radical academics, tracing their political work as well as their scholarship and, of course, the opposition they encountered.

My biggest challenge has been shaping all this into a coherent whole. It was not only an intellectual challenge, but a political one. I found my opinions about the events I had lived through complicated by having to rethink, if not necessarily revise, my original assessments. It's my fervent hope that, in light of the current threats to the university (and perhaps even to the American democratic system as a whole), I will not be alone in looking again at the long sixties and figuring out what lessons it can teach us.

PART I
EXPANSION AND ITS DISCONTENTS

"GOOD TIMES FOR SCHOLARS"

The Golden Age of American Higher Education

When E. Alden Dunham, Princeton's former director of admissions, visited the State University of New York at Brockport on a fact-finding mission for the Carnegie Commission on Higher Education in the late 1960s, he was both awed and horrified. Muddy, barren, and cluttered with cranes, the school seemed to be one huge construction site, an "instant campus" that Dunham considered architecturally "unimpressive . . . largely because the buildings look alike and are crowded together." Of course, aesthetics was hardly at issue for Brockport's ambitious leaders as they struggled to accommodate their school's exploding student body and growing faculty.[1]

Founded in 1835 by a group of Baptists as the Brockport Collegiate Institute to offer what amounted to a high school education with some teacher training on the side, it became the Brockport State Normal School in 1867, and then, in the early 1940s, the Brockport State Teachers College with a campus consisting of one building, a few hundred students, and less than fifty professors and administrators. After joining the State University of New York (SUNY) in 1948, Brockport really began to grow. By the mid-1960s, it had become the State University College of Arts and Sciences at Brockport with 2,500 students and 200 faculty and staff members. By the end of the decade, it was up to 5,500 students and 350 faculty members. The physical campus expanded as well, adding residence halls, a college union, library, and all the other buildings that Dunham had found so unappealing. The school's mission had also changed; SUNY Brockport was now the

FIGURE 1.1. SUNY Brockport under construction, 1965. © Drake Memorial Library, College Archives, SUNY Brockport, Brockport, NY 14420.

largest public institution of higher education in the Rochester area, offering both undergraduate and master's degree programs in education and the liberal arts.[2]

An Expanding Sector

Dunham saw the same transformation at most of the fourteen other mid-level state institutions of higher learning he visited. From Chico State in California to Western Michigan University to Ball State in Indiana to Missouri Southern State University, construction was booming, educational offerings were proliferating, and the schools were expanding in every way. Had he gone to Tampa, he would have seen the brand-new University of South Florida springing up on the site of a World War II bombing range. A similar sight would have greeted him in Bellingham, Washington, where a teacher's college was turning into the four-year Western Washington University. Everywhere, the same transformation—new residence halls, libraries, student centers, and ever-larger parking lots.

Public higher education expanded most extensively. As late as 1950, state colleges and universities accounted for less than 50 percent of the nation's college students; twenty years later, they were educating 75 percent of them.[3] This growth was most dramatic at the second-tier state schools like SUNY Brockport. The already large urban campuses like San Francisco State and the City College of New York (CCNY) were also growing—and running out of space. At City College, one faculty member recalled, "the school now resembled a subway rush hour that lasted from 8 a.m. until 4 p.m." Facilities had to be upgraded as well.[4] Similar transformations were taking place at flagship state universities like Berkeley and Wisconsin, and even at private schools. Stanford's enrollment surged from 3,000 students in 1945 to 11,500 twenty-five years later as the school morphed from a somewhat provincial home for well-heeled California playboys into a national academic powerhouse.[5]

Though we tend to associate the sixties on campus with student protest—with images of Mario Savio atop a police car in the middle of the Berkeley campus or the gun-toting members of Cornell's Afro-American Society exiting the student center after a day and a half of occupation—a more authentic portrayal might well show countless building cranes. For we simply cannot understand what happened to the academic community during the 1960s and early 1970s unless we realize that it was growing exponentially.

Numbers tell the story. Between 1959 and 1969, enrollments in higher education went from more than 3.6 million students to roughly 8 million, while the number of institutions also increased—from 2,004 to 2,525 during the 1960s and to 3,152 by 1979—and the size of those schools tripled.[6] California's grew first, fastest, and largest. The state's famous Master Plan for Higher Education of 1960 specified that its institutions would expand by 350 percent between 1958 and 1975.[7] Before World War II, its State College system consisted of seven schools with 13,000 students; by the late 1960s, it comprised twenty institutions and 170,000 students with more than 200,000 in 1970. The University of California system expanded as well—from seven campuses with 43,600 students in 1948 to eight with over 100,000 (and growing) in 1965.[8] And its community colleges also grew—massively. The younger SUNY system grew from 34,000 students in 1960 to 117,000 in 1970 with some twenty-eight separate units.[9] In New York City, the City University of New York (CUNY) system debuted in 1962 with nearly 100,000 students and increased to 160,000 by 1975.[10]

Individual schools grew as well—if they hadn't started from scratch. In the year that CCNY's open-admissions program began, its freshman class rose from 1,752 to 2,742.[11] UCLA, which already had 10,000 students before World War II, doubled by the end of the 1950s.[12] San Francisco State, established in 1956, had 18,000 students by the end of the 1960s. Private schools were also booming. During the 1960s, Hofstra, a commuter college servicing Long Island, grew from nearly 8,400 students to some 12,000, including a much higher percentage of students living on campus.[13] Even Harvard increased its freshman class from 1,000 to 1,500 in 1965.[14]

Significantly, Harvard raised the size of its graduate schools even more, as did most of the nation's other top universities. In the academic year 1949–50, American universities awarded 6,420 PhDs; ten years later, they granted 11,622; and in 1973, the peak year, they produced 34,790.[15] Two-thirds of Stanford's growth during the 1960s occurred in its graduate divisions.[16] At Berkeley by the end of the decade, two-fifths of its students were at the graduate level. Because the Master Plan had capped enrollment at 25,000, quite a few professors were talking about divesting the university of its responsibility for the first two years of college to allow for even more expansion at the graduate level.[17] Even many second- and third-tier schools developed vocational MA programs and other post-graduate courses of study. And the more ambitious regional universities began to offer PhDs.[18]

Expansion for What?

The best explanation for this enormous expansion is the simplest. American higher education's mission—or rather, missions—changed. The academy became newly central to the nation's economic growth and social stability. Until the 1940s the scholarship, research, and the civilizing polish of college were essentially peripheral for most Americans. Higher education was an elite phenomenon, required perhaps by those who pursued teaching, medicine, or the ministry, but indulged in otherwise by late adolescents of the leisure class while forging future business or marital connections. For most middle-class Americans, economic success did not require a bachelor's degree.

In the aftermath of the Second World War, however, the academy embraced a new democratic mission. It opened its doors to a much broader segment of the population. This was driven in part by the so-called GI Bill, which brought more than 2 million veterans right onto campus.[19] Originally designed to keep them out of the job market to avoid a postwar depression, the program provided unprecedented social mobility for working- and lower-middle-class men (again, there were few women). It also benefited the institutions. Faculty members were thrilled by the influx of so many serious students, while administrators rejoiced in larger enrollments.[20]

These positive experiences encouraged the academy to shed its upper-class identity and, in theory, welcome anyone with the ability to take advantage of its offerings. In the process, colleges and universities became the nation's main vehicle for economic mobility, certifying their graduates for positions within an increasingly bureaucratized and technologically complex society. Just as the frontier had supposedly provided a social safety valve for nineteenth-century America, so did higher education by the mid-twentieth century. A bachelor's degree, in other words, reinforced the American dream; it had become the passport to the middle class.[21]

But only for some. Not only have economic considerations priced a college education beyond the reach of many otherwise qualified students, but the stratification of institutions within the academic world has reinforced, if not aggravated, the social and economic inequities that higher education was supposed to alleviate. It has, in other words, propped up the traditional status quo. Built-in discrimination in the name of meritocracy has kept people of color and other marginalized groups from taking advantage of the networking and automatic status that accrue to graduates of selective institutions.[22] So, while the university did become more inclusive after the war, it did not overcome the barriers to social mobility that it supposedly had promised to do.

At the same time, universities took on another role: chief supplier of scientific research and technological advancement, supplanting individual entrepreneurs, private corporations, and government laboratories. Although some research had always taken place on some campuses, it did not become central to most until the 1940s. With the advent of World War II and then the Cold War, the military establishment required massive inputs of scientific expertise. As a result, by the time the Korean War broke out in 1950, federal funding had become a significant percentage of the budgets of the major research universities. As MIT's president James Killian put it, "Those were memorable and exciting times when government, industry, and the universities felt themselves in a symbiotic relationship and achieved a powerful creative collaboration."[23]

Working for Washington brought funding and prestige to individual academics, too. Specialized laboratories and research centers sprang up. Institutions like Stanford, Berkeley, and the Massachusetts Institute of Technology also coordinated their hiring and research agendas with private corporations. Stanford developed office parks to house defense industries, while MIT did so much Pentagon work that, one outside physicist quipped, it was hard to tell whether it "is a university with many government research laboratories appended to it or a cluster of government research laboratories with a very good educational institution attached to it."[24]

Especially for those professors who prized political influence, the late 1950s and early 1960s were heady, indeed. Scientists in particular got entrée to the White House and the highest levels of the defense establishment.[25] Sputnik brought those people closer to power. Within a month of its launch, Eisenhower had created the President's Science Advisory Committee (PSAC), whose eighteen members were the elite of the elite: Nobel laureates and senior professors at the top research universities.[26] They and their colleagues who served as high-level consultants for the national security state were very much of an in-group. A third of the early PSAC's members, including its first three leaders—James Killian, George Kistiakowsky, and Jerome Wiesner—came from Cambridge, Massachusetts. "Actually, we all know each other," the MIT physicist Jerrold Zacharias explained. "People always think that because the United States has a population of one hundred seventy million and there are a lot of people in the Pentagon, it all has to be very impersonal. Science isn't. It's just us boys."[27]

But it was not only those "boys" who got unprecedented access to the president. Prominent scholars in economics, political science, and area studies also gravitated to Washington, DC, especially in the early 1960s when the dean of Harvard's faculty, McGeorge Bundy, became the national security adviser and the Kennedy administration ostentatiously lured dozens of high-profile academics there. Whether it was the Ivy League and Big Ten economists on the Council of Economic Advisers or the Harvard historian and American ambassador to Japan, Edwin O. Reischauer, Kennedy's New Frontier gave these faculty members an often heady taste of power—or at least the sense that they had access to it.[28] And as the once-scorned "eggheads" of the McCarthy era became desirable political commodities, professors everywhere began to gain a new measure of respect and self-confidence.

Significantly, the increased affluence and status of the academy's elites motivated the denizens of less well-endowed institutions. Ambitious administrators and professors everywhere began to emphasize faculty publications and discoveries. As a result, research became de rigueur at almost every type of school. "Publish or perish" became a mantra that spread from the sciences to the humanities and social sciences, defining careers even as the profession enjoyed new levels of prestige and economic security.

As higher education adapted to its new missions, it embraced a new set of competitive values. The demographic explosion we call the baby boom had obviated Depression-era concerns about financial survival. Instead, the academic community became increasingly ambitious. Community colleges began to offer liberal arts courses; teachers colleges morphed into full-scale colleges; four-year schools provided graduate programs; and regional institutions strained to develop national reputations. That massive growth combined with these new pressures for status created considerable stress, as the institutions that University of California president Clark Kerr called the "multiversity" took on an ever-increasing load of missions.[29]

There was one surprising consequence of the competition for prestige. A group of aspiring private research universities in the South—

FIGURE 1.2. Clark Kerr, president of the University of California and propagandist for the "multiversity," at a press conference during the Free Speech Movement crisis at Berkeley, 1964. © The Bancroft Library, University of California, Berkeley.

Duke, Vanderbilt, Emory, and Tulane—found themselves under pressure to experiment with desegregation in order to get the federal grants, foundation support, and high-powered faculty members that signified the big time. As Duke's frustrated provost explained, "The inability to admit the small number of duly qualified Negroes has created barriers to the fullest development of Duke University and has resulted in a decline in its prestige." Sometimes, however, their ambitions brought professors and administrators at such schools into conflict with conservative trustees and politicians for whom maintaining the racial status quo was paramount. Even so, ambitious leaders of public institutions in the South—though even more vulnerable to such pressures from segregationist politicians—could sometimes prevail.[30]

Yet for all the problems that the expansion of higher education created, the 1950s and 1960s were, economically at least, a golden age.[31] The democratization of the academy coupled with the prestige of scientific research made business and political leaders more than willing to provide funding. And no group received as many benefits from this rising tide as the professoriate.[32] No surprise that its members took those opportunities—and then some.

A New Professoriate

Just as the boxy modernist structures of the 1950s and 1960s began to crowd out the ivy-covered Victorian buildings on the bulging campuses, so, too, a new cohort of academics poured onto those campuses. Faculties grew as exponentially as enrollments. In 1949, there were 246,722 faculty members; by 1969, there were 450,000, with 675,000 by the end of the 1970s.[33] At UCLA, the faculty grew from 200 members before the war to more than 900 by the early 1960s.[34] Stanford's almost doubled from 619 to 1,200 during the sixties, Hofstra's from a bit over 330 to more than 700.[35] As a result, by the mid-1960s, the majority of faculty members on thousands of campuses were newcomers. At SUNY Albany, 75 percent of its 950 faculty members in 1969 had arrived within the past eight years, 50 percent within the past three.[36]

Not only were there many more of those professors, but they came from different backgrounds, followed different career paths, and pursued different intellectual agendas than their predecessors. It would be a gross exaggeration to claim that the profession was completely transformed. Even among the new hires, many probably had no desire for change and would have wanted only to be left alone to handle their classes and scholarship in the traditionally unhurried way, leaving plenty of time for gardening, cocktails, and the occasional round of golf. But they were a diminishing proportion of the professoriate.[37] And, like their new students, many were not upper- and upper-middle-class WASPs. The most noticeable were the Jews who previously had been kept un- or under-employed by genteel anti-Semitism, ensuring their ghettoization in a few institutions like CCNY or, as a number of émigré scholars who fled Hitler discovered, in the historically Black colleges and universities (HBCUs).[38]

Some fields discriminated more than others. Humanities departments were considered particularly unwelcoming. It was a major event among the New York Intellectuals in 1939 when Columbia University's English department tenured its first Jew, the literary critic Lionel Trilling. Historians were equally bigoted. "You better go to law school," an aristocratic lecturer at Harvard told the future Yale historian John Blum in the late 1940s. "Hebrews can't make it in history."[39] The labor historian Herbert Gutman similarly recalled a mentor warning him that "being an historian was an Anglo-Saxon profession. . . . He urged that I do the safe thing and become an economist."[40] Not that economists were much better. In 1953, Cornell's economics department hired Douglas Dowd despite his radical politics rather than give the job to a brilliant candidate from Yale who was Jewish.[41] Scientists had an easier time, no doubt because the criteria for employment were less subjective. Blum, who taught at MIT in the early 1950s, recalls many more Jews on its faculty than at Harvard.[42]

By the mid-1950s, however, as anti-Semitism waned within society and the demand for college teachers increased, Jews were no longer barred from positions even at the top institutions. Nonetheless, a few vestiges of anti-Semitism lingered, mainly among the old guard. Perhaps its last gasp occurred during the Brown historian Carl Bridenbaugh's presidential address to the American Historical Association in 1962—what his former Berkeley colleague Carl Schorske called "that terrible speech." Bemoaning the inability of younger historians "to recapture enough of a sense of the past to enable them to feel and understand it," Bridenbaugh ascribed that deficit to the fact that "many of the younger practitioners of our craft, and those who are still apprentices, are products of lower middle-class or foreign origins, and their emotions not infrequently get in the way of historical reconstructions."[43] It was a sign of the times that this speech caused

Bridenbaugh considerable embarrassment and "a general drop in his reputation."[44]

Despite its postwar expansion, the academic community did not welcome everyone. Women, African Americans, and other people of color missed out on the party. Racial segregation ruled, in both the North and South. No matter what their qualifications, African American academics, including the major scholars with major-league credentials who had created the field of Black studies, were marginalized until the 1960s. Essentially barred from teaching in majority-white institutions, they could not publish in mainstream journals, get grants, or attend the meetings of the main professional organizations in their fields. Sometimes they couldn't even get access to the research materials they needed unless they found a friendly Black janitor to sneak them into the archives. The economically strapped HBCUs where they worked not only paid badly and lacked decent libraries, but, because they were under the control of white supremacists, had no academic freedom either. And, unlike their white colleagues, the HBCUs' Black teachers could not leave the South.[45] The discrimination against African Americans was so pervasive at majority-white institutions in the North that it hit the front page of the *New York Times* when Brooklyn College hired John Hope Franklin to chair its history department in 1956, the first such appointment in the country.[46]

Women were equally marginalized. Worse yet, the golden age marked a decline in their professional status. They had been pushed out of their previous niches at women's colleges and former teachers colleges when those schools bought into the postwar race for prestige. Upgrading their faculties apparently required hiring men. Women (who, it was assumed, were psychologically, if not intellectually, unfit for academic life) were supposed to marry, raise children, and stay at home—a disqualification that they all too often internalized. Female scientists who did find work rarely made it onto the tenure track or else were shunted off into minor fields and inferior positions. This discrimination was so pervasive that it was not even recognized. Accepted as natural, in the words of historian Margaret Rossiter, "it was just the way it was." The chill of McCarthyism kept those women who did understand why their careers were blighted from speaking out. It was not until late in the long sixties, with the advent of second-wave feminism, that academic women began to press for change.[47]

Women's research and scholarship was similarly sidelined. Denied grants and access to the networks of knowledge and power within their disciplines, their work was not taken seriously or was simply ignored. The eminent women's historian Gerda Lerner recalled being told, when she complained about the inability of female scholars to publish in the main journals in their fields, that "it was a sad 'fact' that no good articles by women were being submitted."[48] Time and again, well-qualified women would discover that they would be passed over for jobs or grants in favor of male colleagues with inferior records. Married women had the additional disadvantage of the nepotism rules that would not allow both spouses to be hired at the same place.[49] This discrimination was so widely accepted that even the most politically sensitive men seemed unaware of its existence. It took place, Carl Schorske recalled, within "a totally male-dominated profession and we simply didn't question it." Whenever a colleague suggested hiring a woman, he explained, "usually, somebody else would say, 'she's a young woman, she's going to get married, she'll never play a role. Why waste the time?' That real deep-seated male chauvinism was regnant in the entire society."[50]

Professors in the Making

But for young white men of an intellectual bent, the ivory tower was more than welcoming. Many saw the academy as "the ideal career." Even weak students considered becoming professors. One study in 1964 found that 87 percent of the college seniors in the top 20 percent of their class wanted to attend graduate school. But so, too, did 71 percent of those in the bottom half who did not think their mediocre grades an obstacle.[51] And, in fact, they may not have been. Graduate schools were expanding so extravagantly that they accepted almost anyone. The money was there; and departments gained status, it was believed, the more graduate students they enrolled.[52]

Outside support was crucial. In the late 1940s, many observers feared that the United States was not producing enough qualified faculty members to handle the projected tsunami of baby boomers.[53] The federal government and foundations like Ford with its Woodrow Wilson Fellowship program poured so much money into PhD programs that by the 1950s most full-time graduate students were fully supported. The federal government was especially generous to young scientists, not only the military, but also the National Science Foundation and the National Institutes of Health and Public Health Service. This patronage increased enormously after Sputnik when Congress rushed through the National Defense Education Act (NDEA). By 1966–67, the federal government was awarding sixty thousand graduate fellowships—four times as many as only five years before. Scientists and people in area studies got the most support, but graduate students in other fields profited as well.[54] The demand for future faculty was so prodigious that even women were recruited, even if they were not encouraged once they matriculated.[55]

My own decision to go to graduate school is illustrative. I had not thought about getting a PhD. As a thoroughly unenlightened pre-feminist, I was going to become a high school teacher and had lined up a student teaching position in a Boston suburb. Then, midway through my final semester at Radcliffe in the spring of 1960, my undergraduate thesis adviser nominated me for a Woodrow Wilson Fellowship. Since I loved history, I completed the application with the attitude that if the fellowship came through, I'd go to graduate school. It did and I did, even though I hadn't applied anywhere. Harvard took me in. Wilson money, it seemed, brought automatic admission.

Most of my academic cohort had similar experiences. We enjoyed school; we were good at it; and the academy courted us. A slightly earlier generation of students had also meandered into graduate school. Martin Oppenheimer took an MA in sociology at Columbia in the early 1950s, recalling, "I just sort of arrived." He had good letters of recommendation, tuition was cheap, and he got a day job. Drafted just as the Korean War ended, he served two years and then got a PhD at the University of Pennsylvania under the GI Bill.[56] "I couldn't imagine doing anything else," the Columbia sociologist Allan Silver explained. He enrolled in graduate school at the University of Michigan as soon as he got out of the army in 1953.[57]

By the late 1950s and early 1960s, with seemingly unlimited money available, graduate school became even more appealing. "What else would one do?" the economist William Tabb remembered. "For me, being a professor is like being a student. You get paid to do what you want." The sociologist Thomas Mayer also knew that he wanted to be an academic, but not in what field. Ultimately, he decided on sociology and "Stanford recruited me." Kate Ellis recalled her academic career as "extremely accidental. . . . In the sixties if you were a woman you didn't think of creating a path for yourself. . . . I drifted around." Then "somebody suggested I major in English and then somebody suggested I go to graduate school."[58] The Berkeley sociologist Troy Duster had a similar experience. He had so impressed his undergraduate professors at Northwestern that

> all of the sudden I'm being asked to be a teaching assistant. . . . And within about a week I get an invitation from UCLA to come out and be a graduate student. It was a different world. It wasn't about applications; it was about networks. It was about senior professors being able to write a letter or pick up a phone and say, "I have a student. I think you ought to take this student seriously." And then, . . . out of the blue, I get this note saying "You've been accepted."[59]

Money was not a problem.[60] Those were "good times for scholars," the historian Renate Bridenthal recalled; "money was raining down." After her Wilson funding ran out, she got a fellowship from Columbia as well as support for research in Germany. When Carl Riskin started graduate school in economics at Berkeley, he was offered even more money if he studied Chinese. "The government was trying to recruit a cadre of China experts," the NYU sinologist Moss Roberts explained. What with Columbia's then-low tuition, NDEA and Ford Foundation grants, his graduate training was completely covered.[61] The biologist Saul Slapikoff was recruited from Brooklyn College by the PhD program at Tufts Medical School that paid him the then-munificent sum of $4,000–5,000 a year during the next three and a half years.[62]

And graduate students didn't need much money in those days. William Chace, the future president of Emory, remembered arriving at

Berkeley's English department along with 120 other graduate students in the fall of 1961. With his $1,200 Wilson stipend, tuition an affordable $250 for an out-of-state student (reduced to $136.50 after a year in residence), and $60 a month for rent, it was possible to get by—especially if one adopted, as many did, a bohemian lifestyle.[63] In the college towns of the Midwest where living expenses and tuitions were also low, a graduate student in English at a school like Indiana University could support herself on a teaching assistantship.[64] Madison, Chicago's Hyde Park, Columbia's Morningside Heights, Ann Arbor—the graduate ghettos of America's leading research universities swarmed with thousands of future faculty members living on peanut butter and canned tuna.

Not all of them made it through. Berkeley's English department, according to Chace, had 412 graduate students in the fall of 1961 and 374 the following spring.[65] A special faculty committee chaired by English professor Charles Muscatine that was investigating the attrition rate decried the hurdles that were erected to "compensate for inadequate admissions procedures." Except in the sciences, these measures, Muscatine's report concluded, "harass the student with endless examinations whose primary purpose is to settle the question of competence which ought to have been decided earlier, and to compel him to arrange his course of study for the primary objective of passing exams."[66]

Ambitious departments at major research universities recruited indiscriminately. They then relied on such exigencies as language requirements, qualifying examinations, and dissertations to weed out the ranks. As a result, large numbers dropped out. As many as 75 percent of all PhD candidates in the humanities and 70 percent in the social sciences never finished their degrees. The figure in the natural sciences was a more manageable 40 percent. Some schools did have better records; at Princeton, with smaller, more intimate departments, 71 percent of graduate students made it through.[67] But, especially in large departments, personal attention was hard to come by. "The graduate school here was so big," the Harvard historian John Womack recalled. "Somebody like [H. Stuart] Hughes had fifty or sixty students doing theses. How could you possibly deal with that?"[68] Still, financial problems probably caused more dropouts than academic failure or the

impersonality of large departments. After the first few years of graduate work, many students scrambled for new sources of income, often
taking teaching jobs before they began their theses. And, as Muscatine's report noted, they could "never quite manage to carry a heavy
teaching load, raise a family, and finish a dissertation far from encouragement, supervision, and the resources of a university library."[69]

A Sellers' Market

Nonetheless, because of what seemed like an insatiable demand for
professors, one did not need a PhD in hand to get a job at a four-
year college or university. Moreover, because jobs were so plentiful,
horizontal mobility was also common. According to one study from
the mid-1960s, not only were 97 percent of all college teachers interested in other positions, but the turnover rate for all faculty was about
20 percent.[70] The market for qualified academics was so voracious
that even people who had lost their jobs for political reasons could
find new ones—something that would never have happened during
the McCarthy era. All they needed were connections.[71]

This was because, until the end of the 1960s, the job market, expansive as it was, relied almost exclusively on personal contacts rather
than open competitions. In 1965, according to one study, friends and
colleagues were behind the awarding of 65 percent of all academic
positions. These informal methods were especially important at high-
end schools. "If we go shopping for faculty," Schorske recalled from
his stint at Berkeley in the 1960s, "either we go for finished books or
through the old-boy network."[72] The editor of a volume of Yale historian C. Vann Woodward's letters described how one of the most powerful of those "old boys" operated:

> Academic jobs for a student, for example, might be secured by Wood-
> ward picking up a telephone, calling the chair of a department, and
> saying the right word in the right ear, with no bother about search
> committees, affirmative action, and whether graduate students ap-
> proved of a candidate. His correspondence is full of letters from
> chairmen—then, invariably, men—who would say, "We are looking

for a young married man in the field of American History with a secondary field in the Far East or Western Civilization," and promptly hire whomever Woodward suggested. Or someone from a Southern university in the late 1960s would ask if he knew of a presentable young Negro, who might cause no trouble, "a man who is level-headed, objective, and who, hopefully, could disregard somewhat the matter of race, as his colleagues are trying to do . . . [someone who would] not allow himself to be 'captured' by extremists of any color."[73]

Almost every white male I interviewed, if he hadn't alienated his thesis adviser, remarked on the ease of getting a job. Many, in fact, had several offers. When Jules Chametzky was finishing his degree in American studies at Minnesota in 1955, he didn't even consider going to the "boondocks" and so turned down offers from the Universities of Florida, Nebraska, and Texas to teach in the humanities program at Boston University. He finished his dissertation three years later and went back on the job market, ending up at the rapidly expanding University of Massachusetts. The following year he helped his department hire eight people.[74] So intense was the competition that, as the former president of Princeton William Bowen recalled, "at meetings of many professional associations in the fifties and sixties, department chairmen literally stood in line to interview job candidates."[75] Moreover, there was so much pressure on departments to "make a quick commitment," Christopher Jencks and David Riesman noted, "that in many cases a preoccupied department chairman hires a man he has never seen in action or only heard read a ten-minute paper to an audience at a professional meeting."[76]

With the appropriate credentials, people could often write their own tickets. When, for example, the historian Staughton Lynd decided he wanted to teach at a historically Black institution, all it took for him to get a job at Spelman College was for one of his professors to introduce him to his former student Howard Zinn.[77] Similarly, Bill Zimmerman opted for a position at Brooklyn College over a more prestigious institution because he preferred its political climate.[78] When my ex-husband was denied tenure at Princeton and went on to the job market in the early 1970s, he limited his search to either

Boston or New York—and received two good offers from each city. Thomas Mayer also got several "attractive" propositions after the University of Michigan refused to tenure him. "I was very interested in mountaineering and skiing," he recalled, so he went to the University of Colorado Boulder.[79] In 1968, William Chace rejected offers from Virginia, Yale, and MIT to take a position at Stanford, where his wife could teach as well.[80]

Research, Prestige, and Privilege

While professors enjoyed their teaching, their students, their colleagues, their summer vacations, and their ability to control their own work, prestige remained important.[81] Most of the men and women who entered the academic world between 1960 and 1975 sought positions that would enhance their status. It was the prospect of acclaim that kept faculty members in their labs or the library long after they had finished teaching for the day. For some, the intellectual pleasure of research was its own reward; for others, however, it also had a competitive and somewhat coercive component. They were expected to produce—and were compensated accordingly. The attention their work received enhanced their careers, of course, but it also benefited their colleges and universities.

By the 1960s, despite the enormous diversity of institutions, more and more of them were prioritizing research and graduate training. At the top of the pyramid were the major universities like Harvard, Berkeley, the University of Chicago, and the University of Michigan, as well as what Christopher Jencks and David Riesman called the "university colleges," wealthy, selective private schools like Swarthmore, Wellesley, and Williams. These were the schools that trained the new breed of faculty members who were driving the competitive culture of academic research. They valued research over teaching, graduate education over undergraduate, and the liberal arts over vocational training. They also featured selective admissions policies and residential student bodies.[82]

Whenever they could, schools tried to raise the supposed quality of their students—a less than egalitarian measure that later conflicted with their ostensible desire to recruit students of color.[83] When Stanford became more selective after World War II, applications to the former party school soared. The same thing happened at the University of Pennsylvania. When it started to recruit more academically inclined undergraduates, Penn's culture changed. Its fraternities no longer ruled the campus.[84] But even public institutions, especially the space-starved urban schools, raised their admissions standards. In 1940, New York City high school graduates had to have an eighty average to get into City College; by 1969, it was eighty-six.[85] The same situation prevailed in California, where the Master Plan mandated that the state college system admit only the top 30 percent of each high school class. Even Trenton State College in New Jersey had to be selective; in 1968, it took only 1,500 of the 5,400 people who applied.[86]

But, above all, the key to an institution's prestige was its high-powered professors. As early as the 1930s, Harvard's president James Bryant Conant had stressed the centrality of the faculty to reputation.[87] Accordingly, as Jencks and Riesman observed, "the typical president's greatest ambition for the future is usually to 'strengthen' his institution, and operationally this usually turns out to mean assembling scholars of even greater competence and reputation."[88] If they could afford them, ambitious administrators sought academic stars. But, except perhaps for Nobel laureates and Pulitzer Prize winners, not even the most talented administrators could assess the quality of professors in the dozens of disciplines their institutions covered. They had to rely on more subtle indicators of reputation, trusting their own faculty members to hire status-raising scholars and scientists.

The process therefore empowered individual departments to become the arbiters of value. Brand names mattered. It was tempting for ambitious chairmen and selection committees to recruit ABDs (all but dissertation) from the most prestigious schools rather than people with degrees from second- or third-tier institutions.[89] Senior professors at major universities, professional organizations, university presses—all helped to create the reputational system that structured the increasingly hierarchical academy.[90]

The rewards for the men at the top of the system were considerable—especially in hot scientific fields. Their ability to win research grants

as well as their unlimited mobility gave them the power to negotiate the higher salaries, reduced teaching loads, and better facilities
that would increase their productivity and, thus, add to their own as
well as their universities' stature.[91] From the institutional perspective,
however, as the University of California president Clark Kerr noted in
1963, there was a downside. These high-flying researchers tended "to
shift their identification and loyalty from their university to the agency
in Washington" that provided their research grants and to abandon
"their concern with the general welfare of the university. . . . [T]hey
become tenants rather than owners, taking their grants with them as
they change their institutional lodgings."[92] Their presence also created
serious imbalances, skewing the academic reward system away from
fields that brought in little cash. Physicists and electrical engineers
could attract big money; classicists and French professors could not.

Still, Kerr was not about to abandon the rat race. Berkeley was,
after all, a major contender, flaunting its reputation as the number
one public university. It ran some of the most important research
laboratories—and to this day designates coveted parking spaces for
Nobel laureates. It did not abandon the quest for more and more distinguished scholars and scientists; nor did it, as it once had done, automatically promote most of its junior faculty. As early as the 1930s,
Conant had upgraded Harvard's faculty by making tenure increasingly difficult to attain.[93] Kerr followed suit, rejecting 20 percent of
the candidates his faculty had approved—and not just in science. Every department, he insisted, had to be ranked among the top six in the
country.[94] By the late 1950s, administrators elsewhere were following
that example.[95]

The University of Pennsylvania jettisoned its local orientation. After raising the quality of its undergraduates, in the 1960s it built new
facilities and recruited faculty nationally.[96] MIT pulled off a similar
upgrade. Already a leading engineering school, after the war it transformed itself into a more diverse university whose faculty consisted
of scientists with PhDs instead of engineers with MAs. It even began
to expand into the social sciences and humanities.[97] Some recently
established institutions also aimed high. In the early 1960s, the University of California's new campus at San Diego recruited particularly

promising biologists.[98] It also sought out established stars, like the Nobel laureate Linus Pauling, the philosopher Herbert Marcuse, and the historian H. Stuart Hughes, who, for one reason or another, were unable or unwilling to stay at their current institutions.[99]

But no school pushed for preeminence as self-consciously—and as successfully—as Stanford. Even before the end of the war, Frederick Terman, the school's future provost, believed that Stanford had the opportunity to achieve "a position in the West somewhat analogous to that of Harvard in the East." He presciently steered faculty members toward areas that would attract corporate, foundation, and, especially, military funding, which would allow him to hire more people in those fields, attract more graduate students, and win even more grants.[100] Terman believed that his opportunistic approach—constructing what he called "steeples of excellence"—improved the institution's academic quality. He ruthlessly imposed his vision on the entire faculty, refusing to approve one-third of the tenure candidates that departments recommended. Those who resisted, Terman believed, were simply inferior. Actually, only a few resisted. As the author of the most insightful study of Stanford's ascent noted, Terman and his followers "may best be understood not simply as academic entrepreneurs but as administrators consciously working to make entrepreneurship the normative behavior of university professors."[101]

Martin Meyerson was another academic impresario. A city planner who had briefly served as Berkeley's chancellor in the aftermath of the 1964 Free Speech Movement, he was lured to the expanding campus of SUNY Buffalo by what Warren Bennis, its future provost, described as "the romance of taking a mediocre up-state university and creating—well—*the Berkeley of the East.*"[102] With Governor Nelson Rockefeller pouring money into the SUNY system, this vision was not totally unrealistic. Each of its four major universities had a specialty. Stony Brook was the science campus; Binghamton focused on the social sciences; Albany handled policy studies; and Buffalo got the humanities. And, for a decade or so, the dream almost worked.[103]

Meyerson went on a hiring binge, raiding scholars and writers from Harvard, Princeton, and Yale. During his first year, Bennis interviewed over three hundred candidates while recruiting nine new chairs, two deans, and forty-five new full-time faculty members.[104] The English department became legendary. For Bruce Jackson, it

> was the most interesting English department in the country. Other universities had the best English departments for history or criticism or philology or whatever. But UB was the only place where it all went on at once: hot-center and cutting-edge scholarship and creative writing, literary and film criticism, poem and play and novel writing, deep history and magazine journalism. There was a constant flow of fabulous visitors, some here for a day or week, some for a semester or year. . . . [T]here was not a better place to be.

The department sparkled with stars. When the chair, Albert Cook, initially tried to recruit Jackson by dangling the names of such future colleagues as the critic Leslie Fiedler and the poet Charles Olson, he turned up his nose. "I was at Harvard, and Buffalo was, well, Buffalo." The following year, Cook tried again, explaining that "since I talked to you we hired C. L. Barber. Lionel Abel. John Barth. Robert Creeley." Jackson took the bait, turning down offers from Pennsylvania, MIT, and UCLA for the glamorous colleagues, higher salary, and promise that he could teach whatever he wanted.[105]

Cultural Conflicts

Even at the time, however, Meyerson's ambitious blueprint ran into problems. "We are trying to change a sleepy, drowsy university with a very mixed faculty into a first-rate institution," Bennis explained. "The question is whether we will be kept from doing so by deadwood, by organizational dry rot, or by people who fear the future and hope the whole effort will collapse."[106] Administrators and faculty members elsewhere confronted similar problems. How to transform the culture of an institution without causing so much dissension that it becomes dysfunctional. How, in other words, to impose the research-intensive agenda of the new academic model on older faculty members who were accustomed to a less competitive teaching-oriented system. The problem was especially acute at the former teachers colleges. Unless all the parties were unusually sensitive and diplomatic, serious conflicts could—and did—arise.

SUNY Albany, for example, saw what some faculty members referred to as a "blood bath" when a newly recruited chair "simply told the old guard to do research or get out." He then forced them to share offices, took away their committee assignments, and made them teach introductory courses.[107] Usually, the pressure wasn't quite that brutal. But many older professors became uncomfortable with the new direction of their institutions, even if they kept their offices and upper-level courses.[108] The younger people, too, unless there was mutual respect, chafed at having to work under senior professors who, as the San Francisco State philosopher Arthur Bierman recalled, "weren't interested in publication, they were interested in their field [of education]. We all came in, we wanted to continue like our professors did at the university in the academic subjects."[109] At a number of schools, even before the student rebellion of the late 1960s, that cultural gap created so much mutual hostility that the newcomers left or were forced out.

Politics simply intensified the dissension, as did conflicts over unorthodox lifestyles and institutional governance. It is likely, therefore, that, even without the serious disagreements over the student protests of the 1960s and early 1970s, the problems caused by the near-universal adoption of the newly competitive model of academic success—along with the unprecedented expansion of the entire system of American higher education—would have produced serious internal disruptions and turf warfare on many a campus. Professors and administrators, in other words, had plenty of reasons not to get along.

2

"MEMORY OF AN EARLIER AGE"

Remnants of McCarthyism in the
Academic Community

The golden age of the American higher education had a dark side: the academic community had collaborated with McCarthyism. Even as colleges and universities adapted to their new mission of mass higher education and attracted thousands of bright young people into the professoriate, they were also administering anti-communist loyalty oaths, banning politically controversial speakers, and, most regrettably, purging their ranks of politically tainted faculty members. More than one hundred academics were fired during the late 1940s and early 1950s. Most were former communists who had taken the Fifth Amendment during a congressional investigation or else had been quietly fingered by the FBI. They were then blacklisted, forced out of the academy, or into exile until the witch hunt finally petered out in the mid-1960s.[1]

None of the professors who lost their jobs had proselytized in class or done anything illegal. They had simply refused to cooperate with the congressional inquisition because they did not want to become informers and so invoked the Fifth Amendment's protection against self-incrimination in order to avoid prosecution for contempt of Congress. Although the leaders of the institutions that housed these unfriendly witnesses knew they had done nothing wrong, they were deemed too much of a threat to remain on the campus. Both the administrators and faculty committees involved with their dismissals rationalized their actions by claiming—without any evidence—that communists were unfit to teach and that the people who refused to reveal their past affiliation with the party might still be in it.

The purges—reinforced by the Supreme Court's refusal to rule against them and the failure of the American Association of University Professors, the quasi-official guardian of academic freedom, to intervene—discouraged faculty members and an entire "silent generation" of students from taking political risks. Self-censorship was the order of the day, both on and off campus. Professors pruned their syllabi and avoided controversial research. An important survey of social scientists at the height of the anti-communist furor in 1955 revealed a professoriate composed largely of timid liberals who feared standing up against the witch hunt and, significantly, might not support those of their colleagues who did.[2] Still, by the 1960s, the academy—and much of American society as well—began to recover its political nerve. The academic victims of the witch hunt were returning to the classroom, and their once-passive colleagues were insisting on their rights and those of their students, while the still-stodgy AAUP was reentering the picture. McCarthyism, in other words, had begun to recede.

But it did not disappear altogether.

Academic Freedom in Transition

Although Joseph McCarthy died in 1957, the movement he gave his name to lingered on. After all, J. Edgar Hoover remained in control of the FBI and had never abandoned his war on the remnants of American communism even as the civil rights movement, the New Left, and the Black Power movement rendered the traditional Communist Party passé. He viewed the turmoil of the 1960s as inspired by the Kremlin. As a result, throughout the sixties, the Bureau secretly intervened on many campuses, planting informants, provocateurs, and misinformation, while seriously harassing left-wing faculty members. Other conservatives, like the southern segregationists, found anti-communism a useful tool for cracking down on dissenters and movements that they could not otherwise suppress.[3]

Yet by the late 1950s and 1960s, the Supreme Court was not always justifying violations of civil liberties in the name of national security. And within the academic community, the anti-communist loyalty oaths and speakers bans that had been ubiquitous during the Red

Scare were not always enforced—and when they were, resistance sometimes developed. The fear that kept professors so quiescent during the 1950s had faded—at least within most mainstream institutions. Moreover, because of the enormous demand for warm bodies with higher degrees, it had even become possible for fired political dissenters to find new jobs.

The experiences of Clinton Jencks show just how much the times had changed. A World War II veteran, union organizer, and lifelong radical who had worked with hard-rock miners in southwestern New Mexico during the early 1950s, Jencks had been under FBI surveillance for years. He had been convicted of perjury for falsifying an anti-communist affidavit, but when the Supreme Court had reversed his conviction on procedural grounds in 1957, the Justice Department dropped the case. But the FBI continued to hound Jencks. He would get one blue-collar job after another, only to have Hoover's agents show up and convince his employers to let him go.[4]

The academy rescued him. He received a Woodrow Wilson Fellowship in April 1959.[5] Though the FBI then put the House Un-American Activities Committee (HUAC) on his case and he took the Fifth Amendment, there were few repercussions.[6] He got a PhD in economics from Berkeley, won a Fulbright fellowship to Europe, and ended up on the faculty at San Diego State. In the fall of 1965, the chair of his department told the school newspaper that "Jencks was a well-qualified economics instructor and . . . his past had no real bearing on his qualifications to teach here. . . . We really don't care much about that sort of thing as long as he is willing to sign the loyalty oath."[7] The power of California's McCarthy-era loyalty oath, like others, had eroded so significantly, that even radicals were now willing to sign it.[8] Yet such oaths and other anti-communist regulations were still on the books.

Dismissing "Communists"

Jencks's date with HUAC had been preceded by the appearances of Elias Snitzer and David Fine, two Lowell Technological Institute professors, in March 1958. Both men refused to cooperate with the committee: Snitzer invoked the First Amendment, Fine the Fifth.[9]

Snitzer had been in the Communist Party but had left along with most of its members after Soviet premier Nikita Khrushchev's 1956 revelations about Stalin's crimes. When he was hired at Lowell Tech, Snitzer, an electrical engineer, told the dean about his past.[10] Fine, a mathematician, had never been a communist, but, as he told the school's trustees, he had participated in the CP's youth movement and in a number of the so-called "front groups" in the party's penumbra.

From the start, the university cooperated with the inquisition. Lowell Tech's president had allowed representatives of the state police to question the men; and he suspended them a few days before their date with HUAC. But the administration prepared no formal charges, organized no faculty hearings, and made no attempt to present evidence of wrongdoing. Instead, an assistant state attorney ran a cursory hearing before the board of trustees, which quickly fired the two scientists. Although the AAUP censured Lowell Tech for its blatant violation of academic freedom, neither man tried to rejoin the faculty. Fine had been planning to leave the academy in any event, and Snitzer was hired by an optical company, where he helped to invent the laser.[11]

Richard Reichard was another academic who had a belated brush with the Red Scare. Hired by George Washington University for the academic year beginning in September 1959, he took the Fifth Amendment before HUAC in July. A month later, the acting president of George Washington notified the young historian that the university was "reconsidering your qualifications and suitability to join the faculty." Reichard was no more forthcoming about his politics with the GWU authorities than he had been with HUAC. And so, after several "informal" hearings, the trustees fired him, insisting that they couldn't tell whether his claim of conscience was sincere or just a communist ploy. Although Reichard soon found another teaching position, the AAUP investigated and censured the university. Most disturbingly, the AAUP intimated that the initial move against Reichard came from his departmental colleagues.[12]

Although the AAUP did not intervene when Paul Sporn lost his job, his colleagues in SUNY Buffalo's English department were more supportive. He had been there for several years before he was publicly identified as a former communist at a HUAC hearing in April 1964. A feisty character who became active in the Maoist Progressive Labor Party after being expelled from the CP, Sporn had grudgingly signed the university's anti-communist affidavit. The product of the Mc-Carthy era, the 1949 Feinberg Law required all SUNY faculty members to deny party membership and, if they were former members, discuss it with the president. When HUAC prodded him about the Feinberg certificate, Sporn not only availed himself of the Fifth Amendment, but added the First, Sixth, Ninth, Tenth, and Fourteenth Amendments, as well as Article III of the Constitution for good measure.[13]

SUNY Buffalo's president Clifford Furnas had already warned the faculty that he would suspend anyone who did not cooperate with the House committee. In a press release, Furnas referred to Buffalo's policy of suspending Fifth Amendment witnesses—a policy adopted during an earlier brush with McCarthyism when the university had been one of the few institutions of higher learning *not* to fire an unfriendly witness.[14] Now, the administration canceled Sporn's summer school classes. The state authorities then suspended him without pay and filed formal charges. His failure to inform SUNY's leaders that he had been in the Communist Party at the time he signed his Feinberg certificate probably constituted "a willful, false representation to the University" and was, thus, "grounds for dismissal for cause."[15]

Protests began even before the official action. Faculty members and students complained to the president, held meetings, and circulated petitions around the campus and beyond. Despite an open letter from a full complement of academic civil libertarians that included such distinguished individuals as the educator Alexander Meiklejohn, the theologian Paul Tillich, the Nobel Prize winner Linus Pauling, and the Columbia University art historian Meyer Schapiro, Sporn lost his job.[16] Though the SUNY system, unlike Lowell Tech and George Washington, did observe the niceties of academic due process, a faculty committee (none of whose members came from Buffalo), recommended that the young radical be fired—and he was. He soon joined the English department at Wayne State in Detroit.[17]

Eli Katz's colleagues were more successful than Sporn's in protecting his job. Katz had come to Berkeley in 1963 as a one-year visiting professor to teach Yiddish. He was to receive a tenure-track appointment once he completed his dissertation. Though Katz had signed non-communist affidavits at Berkeley and other California schools, he had refused to cooperate with HUAC more than five years before. A ban on communist faculty members was on the books, and the school's leaders operated on the McCarthy-era assumption that unfriendly witnesses were still in the party.[18] Katz did not want to risk his career fighting the shadows of the Red Scare, so he accepted a job at Western Reserve and left for Cleveland.

His case did not end there. Serendipitously, his cousin's husband, the biologist Leon Wofsy, was just then considering an offer from Berkeley and alerted his soon-to-be colleague Howard Schachman about Katz's situation.[19] A veteran of the loyalty oath wars of the early 1950s, Schachman enlisted a few allies and prodded Berkeley's academic senate to take up the young Yiddish scholar's case. Before long, a packed faculty meeting voted overwhelmingly to condemn the administration. A few years later, acting chancellor Martin Meyerson brought Katz back to the campus.[20]

Angela Davis and the Last Gasp of Anti-Communism

One would think that after Berkeley's faculty had so roundly repudiated the administration, the University of California would have been more reticent about a repeat performance. But such was not the case. In 1969, when the board of regents tried to oust the controversial UCLA philosophy instructor Angela Davis, the university had been in what the AAUP termed a "highly developed state of tension" for years.[21] Ronald Reagan had won the statehouse in 1966 by attacking the Berkeley Free Speech Movement, and he and his conservative allies among the regents had little sympathy for left-wing politics—or academic freedom. Certainly none for Davis.

Actually, almost everything about Angela Davis was controversial—including her Afro hairstyle and her PhD thesis adviser at the University of California, San Diego, the Marxist philosopher Herbert Marcuse. A gifted student who spent several years in Europe working with the philosophers of the Frankfurt school, Davis had been recruited by UCLA the spring of 1969. At no time did Davis hide her left-wing politics, including her membership in the Che-Lumumba Club of the Communist Party in Los Angeles. Not surprisingly, she had also been targeted by the FBI, which quickly orchestrated the exposure of that membership.[22]

As a result, Davis had not even begun to teach when the regents, citing a raft of official anti-communist policies dating back to 1940, called on UCLA's chancellor to initiate proceedings against her. The board's demand infuriated the faculty. What followed were repeated attempts to eliminate Davis. First, it was because of her party membership, and when that action was voided by the California Superior Court, it was the inflammatory language of her speeches, which a UCLA investigation found to be "distasteful and reprehensible," but not sufficiently "intemperate as to justify disciplinary action."[23] Finally, the regents vetoed her reappointment on the ground that she had made insufficient progress on her dissertation. It was a flimsy pretext, but, they insisted, it was necessary to avert "great harm to the University."[24]

Two months later, a shoot-out at the Marin County courthouse in which four people were killed led to criminal charges against Davis as an accessory. Understandably, as she fought for her freedom, Davis's academic troubles faded into the background. Ultimately acquitted, she then returned to the academy, at the University of California's brand-new campus at Santa Cruz.

In one very important way, the academic freedom cases of the late fifties and early sixties differed considerably from those of the early Cold War. There was no blacklist. The expansive job market not only enabled the protagonists to find new academic positions, but it also removed the fear that had previously constrained their colleagues from making a fuss. Now, more professors and the AAUP stood up for their sanctioned colleagues, refusing to countenance violations of academic freedom and professional autonomy. Even when faculty members—and, we should note, aroused students—could not save the jobs of their politically vulnerable teachers and colleagues, the days when they would collaborate in ousting them had definitely passed.

Academic Freedom Violations in the South

The situation was different in the South. Although communism had never been much of an issue within an academic system so thoroughly permeated with white supremacy, *Brown v. Board of Education* changed things. Not because there were former communists and unfriendly witnesses on southern faculties, but because leading segregationists believed they could win more respectability by Red-baiting the proponents of integration than by openly promoting Jim Crow. As a result, charges of communist infiltration surfaced as southern politicians and their allies pressed colleges and universities to eliminate supposedly subversive professors.

Often, however, there were no charges of communism. The merest whiff of support for integration could cost people their jobs. That happened in 1957 when the trustees of Texas Technological College dismissed three professors without telling them why. Since one was active in the liberal branch of the Democratic Party, another studied racial discrimination, and the third organized adult education seminars on current events, the AAUP's investigators surmised that they were simply too liberal for Lubbock.[25]

Perhaps the most egregious case of southern Red-baiting took place in South Carolina, where Governor George Bell Timmerman tried to force two HBCUs—Allen University and Benedict College—to fire six of their most highly credentialed faculty members. Equating academic quality with subversion, Timmerman had earlier opposed the regional accreditation authority's requirement that department chairs hold earned PhDs as "opening doors to infiltration by incompetents, and undesired and highly trained Communist workers." He brushed off criticism of his attack on Allen and Benedict by describing academic freedom as "an instrumentality of treason" and claiming "that

the presence of Communists at these two Negro institutions is in fur-
therance of a long-range program to promote racial hatred among
young and impressionable Negro students." At first the African
American clergymen who served on both schools' boards of trustees
hoped to resist. But when the state board of education threatened to
withhold teaching certificates from their graduates, the trustees had
to backtrack. "There was no other way of saving Allen University," the
chair of its board explained.[26]

Purges also occurred when southern politicians took on the NAACP.
Equating that moderate organization with the Communist Party,
segregationist legislators in Mississippi and Arkansas modeled laws
against it on other states' anti-communist legislation. Thus, just as
New York required its public servants to sign the Feinberg certificates,
Mississippi and Arkansas imposed similar disclaimer requirements
on their teachers. As they debated the measure, the Arkansas lawmakers took testimony from J. B. Matthews, a professional witch-hunter
and former associate of Joseph McCarthy, who informed them that
their flagship university was swarming with Reds.[27]

While Mississippi's educators were too frightened to resist their
state's requirement, a handful of Arkansas public school teachers and
professors defied theirs and were promptly fired. Backed by the AAUP,
the University of Arkansas professors sued and were vindicated by the
Supreme Court in December 1960. The Arkansas authorities resisted,
nonetheless, forcing the ousted teachers to spend years trying to get
reinstatement and back pay. Governor Orval Faubus actually rejoiced
when the AAUP officially censured the university in 1964. The organization's sanction would stop "the wrong kind of teachers [and] . . .
undesirables cold at the state line."[28]

As the civil rights movement picked up in the early 1960s, faculty
activists elsewhere in the South came under fire. The Spelman College historian Howard Zinn was one of them. Dismissed arbitrarily in
1963 by the authoritarian president of that all-Black women's college
in Atlanta, Zinn had been arrested many times as he and his students
engaged in the nonviolent civil disobedience that challenged the city's
racial status quo. But as the dismissal of Lawrence Reddick, the chair
of Alabama State College's history department, reveals, a sympathizer

with the civil rights movement did not have to sit-in at a segregated cafeteria to lose his job. Reddick, a University of Chicago PhD and the former curator of the New York Public Library's renowned Schomburg Collection of Negro Life and History, had been involved with Martin Luther King Jr. and the Southern Christian Leadership Conference ever since the 1955 Montgomery bus boycott.[29] Though Reddick tried to keep a low profile, when a few dozen ASC students launched the Deep South's first lunch counter sit-in at the Montgomery County Courthouse in the spring of 1960, the Alabama State Board of Education, pressured by the governor and influenced by a secret FBI report on his record of supposed pro-communist activities, summarily fired Reddick and put the college's president on leave. Twenty other faculty members quit in protest.[30]

There were similar incidents throughout the South where intense racism contributed to a much higher level of political repression than elsewhere. About one-third of the academic freedom violations that the AAUP reported on in the 1960s occurred below the Mason-Dixon Line. No doubt there would have been more, but the threat of repercussions usually silenced even the mildest critiques of the status quo from both Black and white academics. Most usually tried to avoid the conflict, mainly by not even mentioning the issue of race. As one University of Georgia mathematician explained, "It wasn't a subject that was taught. It had been dangerous if you were a professor and talked about it too much." Thus, when Georgia finally admitted Black students in 1961, only the bravest faculty members dared to risk the hate mail, death threats, and other forms of harassment they received for eating lunch with them. When they could, many of these liberal white Southerners fled the region.[31]

The repression was most extreme in Mississippi. In 1957 the board of trustees at the all-Black Alcorn A&M dismissed the school's president and expelled the entire student body after a boycott of a racist professor; three years later, a dozen Alcorn faculty members were fired for supporting their students' civil rights activities.[32] When lethal rioting broke out as James Meredith integrated the University of Mississippi in 1961, a group of its professors produced a document blaming the local press for helping to create a "general state of confusion, alarm, and misdirected wrath." After the overtly racist White Citizens' Council responded by publishing their names and addresses, the statement's sixty-four signers got hate mail, death threats, and midnight phone calls. Professors who sat with Meredith at the school cafeteria were similarly harassed. And the university's administration did nothing to stop it.[33]

In such an atmosphere, academic freedom was a mirage. According to James Silver, the chair of Mississippi's history department, "Through one means or another freedom of speech had long since been curtailed." Professors who could not stomach the repression were already gone. Within a few years, 20 percent of the Ole Miss faculty had fled what one departing chemist called "the breakdown of moral and professional responsibility on the part of the university's administrative officers."[34]

A little over a year later, in November 1963, Silver gave his presidential address to the Southern Historical Association. It was a blistering attack on Mississippi's racist establishment and the "totalitarian society" it created that "has eliminated the ordinary processes by which change may be channeled."[35] Silver's strong language drew national attention. As he no doubt expected, Mississippi's leading segregationists called for his dismissal, and the university's trustees charged him with making "provocative and inflammatory speeches calculated to increase racial tension and provoke racial violence." Silver turned his speech into a best-selling book—and never returned to Ole Miss.[36] Yet Silver was no rebel. For years, like all the other faculty members at Mississippi's institutions of higher learning, he had complied with the state's loyalty program.

Loyalty Oaths: A Remnant of the Red Scare

In the North, academics were beginning to contest such regulations. In 1963, when the SUNY Buffalo dissident Paul Sporn signed his Feinberg affidavit, he appended a four-page statement describing how it violated his constitutional rights. But he, like countless others at the time, signed anyhow. Most of them treated the matter as an empty ritual—which it usually was—but by the sixties, civil libertarians and radicals like Sporn were beginning to challenge that requirement.*

Teachers' oaths originated in the 1920s and 1930s. Most were rather innocuous statements in which the individuals affirmed their support for the state and federal governments and disapproved of any movement advocating their overthrow. There was some opposition, but only a tiny handful of faculty members (mainly Quakers) resisted signing.[37] With the advent of the Cold War, the demand for loyalty programs intensified. By the end of the 1950s, thirty-two states and the District of Columbia had some kind of oaths on the books. Many tended to differ from the earlier ones in that signers had to swear allegiance to their state and nation, but also deny that they were communists.[38]

The most notorious of these oaths was that imposed upon the faculty of the University of California by the board of regents in 1949. It polarized the Berkeley campus. Two years of bruising struggles led to the dismissal of thirty-one non-signers—though dozens of others had already resigned rather than sign. Nearly fifty outside scholars— among them the UN official Ralph Bunche, the H-bomb physicist Edward Teller, the inventor of cybernetics Norbert Wiener, the poet and novelist Robert Penn Warren, and the future Berkeley activist Carl Schorske—turned down otherwise tempting offers because of the oath.[39]

California's faculty was split—and bitterly so. After all, there was no way a professor could avoid taking a stand.[40] For months, hundreds of people held out against signing, but ultimately gave in, albeit with considerable reluctance and guilt. The Berkeley historian Kenneth Stampp was typical. "I battled with myself and finally signed the oath, I think for purely personal reasons. I had two small kids, and I just didn't want to get fired." Howard Schachman refused to sign until he was finally convinced by his colleagues that otherwise his career would be destroyed.[41] When the California Supreme Court ruled in

---

* I recall signing such an affidavit when I took my first job as a TA at Harvard in the early sixties. I was completely surprised by the requirement and too flustered to resist, which in retrospect I probably would have done had I known about that requirement in advance.

1952 that the loyalty oath imposed on all state employees during the Korean War superseded the university's one, some of the non-signers returned to Berkeley. But the episode left scars. People did not easily forget their colleagues' behavior during the crisis and how vulnerable even such a prestigious faculty had been. "In the department," Stampp recalled, "one knew who was for and who was against."[42] Still, within a few years, the campus had calmed down. And for newly appointed faculty members, signing the 1950 loyalty oath seemed, the political scientist Sheldon Wolin recalled, "just pro forma."[43]

The academy's response to the disclaimer affidavit incorporated into the National Defense Education Act (NDEA) of 1958 showed how much the political climate had changed. That massive program of grants and loans was a response to the post-Sputnik fear that American higher education was lagging behind that of the Soviet Union. At the last minute, Senator Karl Mundt, whose anti-communist credentials stretched back to his HUAC service in the late 1940s, inserted a loyalty oath into the package. No one questioned the proviso's inclusion.[44]

The academic establishment, however, resisted. A number of prestigious institutions simply refused to enroll in the program. Though professors and graduate students had been signing similar statements for years, the NDEA required the universities, rather than the federal agencies, to administer the disclaimer. And given the increasingly liberal climate within higher education, academic authorities did not want to be put into the position of enforcing a measure with which they disagreed. University administrators were also upset that their students and faculty members were the only recipients of federal funds required to take such an oath.[45] In addition, it is likely that many leading educators were, at least in part, trying to assuage a lingering sense of guilt over the academy's gutless behavior at the time of the California loyalty oath.

Thus, for example, the AAUP denounced the disclaimer and called for Congress to revise the law. Until the disclaimer was finally rescinded in 1962, every issue of the *AAUP Bulletin* carried a list of the institutions that were boycotting or opposing the NDEA's programs. Nearly 150 colleges and universities made that honor roll, including the entire Ivy League, all the Seven Sisters, most of the Big Ten, as well as the University of Chicago, UMass Amherst, Swarthmore, and, more surprisingly, Notre Dame, Boston College, and the Newton College of the Sacred Heart. Even a few southern schools came out against the oath, including the Universities of Florida, North Carolina, Tulane, and Tougaloo College in Jackson, Mississippi.[46]

Harvard's president Nathan Pusey led the campaign against the NDEA loyalty oath, alerting his peers to its "deeply un-American" nature. It was, he charged, not only "contrary to the kind of educational practice the Act seeks to promote," but also "wasteful of time and energy." His students, he explained, were barred from the program because the faculty had voted "by a large margin . . . against the use of the funds so long as the disclaimer provision is in the Act." Even more significant was the opposition displayed by President Eisenhower and his successor, John F. Kennedy. Eisenhower, after all, had been the president of Columbia from 1948 to 1953 and understood why the academy found the disclaimer so distasteful, while Kennedy was a Harvard man with good Harvard connections. In a 1959 article in the *AAUP Bulletin*, the then-senator blasted the oath as "a futile gesture toward the memory of an earlier age which threatens to defeat the very purposes of the bill." After several attempts, Congress finally voted unanimously for repeal in October 1962.[47]

What is so surprising is that even after this campaign revealed how strongly the academic establishment opposed loyalty oaths, they remained on the books and, in many cases, continued to be enforced. We have no complete record of how many men and women refused to sign disclaimers and were then either let go or not hired during the 1960s. Still, the cases that we do know about reveal considerable confusion and bureaucratic incoherence at institutions of higher learning, an early portent perhaps of the academy's later inept handling of political issues.[48]

Since the loyalty oaths were, indeed, a political issue, it helped their opponents to have powerful friends—as the biologist Leon Wofsy did. The former leader of the Communist Party's official youth group, he had embarked on a scientific career after leaving the party in 1956. By the early 1960s, Wofsy's research in immunology had become, in his words, "pretty hot" and he received "a flood of offers." He accepted

SUNY Buffalo's. "They were anxious to have me. I was anxious to go." He was, however, appalled by the Feinberg certificate. He informed the Buffalo authorities that, like Paul Sporn, "I would sign it, and . . . I would do everything in my power to get rid of the oath." That opposition combined with Wofsy's past convinced the skittish administration to withdraw the position.[49]

He then accepted an offer from the University of Pittsburgh, where the same thing happened. Meanwhile, Berkeley was also wooing him. Though Wofsy had already signed the state employees' loyalty oath when he was a postdoctoral researcher at the University of California, San Diego, it was clear that getting the regents to approve his appointment to the Berkeley faculty would be difficult. Ultimately, Wofsy recalled, his eminent mentors and colleagues "all ganged up on Kerr" and even threatened to resign if the controversial biologist was not hired. The California president, to his credit, pushed the appointment, and Wofsy came to Berkeley in the summer of 1964—just in time for the Free Speech Movement.[50]

By then, a number of other Berkeley academics had decided to challenge the loyalty oath. When the mathematician Charles Aronson refused to sign the affidavit in 1964, they joined him in a lawsuit. Within a few years, the litigation had attracted a varied and eminent collection of plaintiffs, including, among others, Barbara Garson, the author of the satirical antiwar play *McBird*, the Americanist Henry Nash Smith, the Nobel Prize–winning physicist Owen Chamberlain, Sheldon Wolin, Howard Schachman, Kenneth Stampp, and Suzanne Goldberg, the future wife of the Free Speech Movement's leader, Mario Savio. They won their case in 1967.[51] Even so, because the oath's language was so anodyne, it remained on the books. In 1973, because she added the phrase "under duress" to her signature on the oath, the author Jessica Mitford was denied an adjunct position at San Jose State. But, then, she had also refused to be fingerprinted.[52]

Academics elsewhere mounted similar lawsuits. The one from the University of Washington eventually reached the US Supreme Court. An initial suit, filed at the time the disclaimer was adopted in 1955, was thrown out on a technicality. In 1962, when the board of regents demanded that the UW administration actually enforce the oath, the case was revived by a mixed group of sixty-four tenured and non-tenured academics all offering different reasons why the disclaimer interfered with their professional obligations and First Amendment rights. On June 1, 1964, the Supreme Court in its 7–2 decision on *Baggett v. Bullitt* ruled that the Washington oath was "unconstitutionally vague." Significantly, the decision avoided dealing with the substantive issues involved in requiring college teachers to take a political test for employment.[53]

The Keyishian *Case and After*

The Feinberg certificates in New York State were among the academy's most expansive loyalty oaths. Although the program had been in existence since 1956, it did not apply at the University of Buffalo until that school was absorbed by the SUNY system in 1962. By the end of 1963, the Buffalo administration decided to enforce the oath. The faculty was not happy, but was told by a panel of law school professors at a packed special meeting of the AAUP that it would be hard to fight. Accordingly, the chapter did not recommend noncompliance, although it did pass several resolutions against the oath and asked the administration to grant due process to non-signers before firing them.[54]

It could have been a fluke, but of the five dissidents whose suit ultimately went to the Supreme Court, three—Harry Keyishian, George Hochfield, and Ralph Maud—belonged to Buffalo's lively English department and a fourth, George Starbuck, was an established poet with an appointment as a librarian. The fifth, the Quaker philosopher Newton Garver, had spent a year in prison during World War II as a draft resister. For Hochfield, who had already lived through several attacks on academic freedom, first at Berkeley as a graduate student and then at Ohio State during a struggle over outside speakers, he had come to Buffalo "determined that I would never let it happen again." The others felt the same way. "I've signed the damn things for the Army," Starbuck wrote to a friend, "but I'm just not going to sign one more sweeping general promise about what I will forbid myself to think, discuss or condone." The youngest plaintiff, Harry Keyishian, had a personal investment in the case. He had encountered the academic Red Scare in the early 1950s when several of his professors at Queens College were fired. He recalled his "sense of frustration and impotence" watching "these very decent, intelligent, talented teachers vanishing from the system, being driven out and being unable to do anything about it."[55]

Perhaps because of their nonconformist ways and perhaps because they assumed that McCarthyism was on the ropes, these men were willing to risk their careers. They actually believed they might prevail. Although most of the Buffalo faculty opposed the oath, with the exception of the English department, its members kept their distance from the non-signers. At best, as Starbuck noted, his colleagues expressed "sympathy of the sick-room variety" that viewed the non-signers "as terminal cases of quixotism." They were, Hochfield recalled, "not especially brave" and "essentially careerist."[56]

It took several years for the case to make its way through the legal system. Finally, on January 23, 1967, the Supreme Court rendered its 5–4 decision against the Feinberg Law. Writing for the majority, Justice William Brennan agreed with the ruling in the University of Washington case that the law was simply too vague. But he then decried its violation of the First Amendment's right to free expression. And, in what still stands as the nation's most expansive legal justification for academic freedom, Brennan declared:

> Our Nation is deeply committed to safeguarding academic freedom, which is of transcendent value to all of us and not merely to the teachers concerned. That freedom is therefore a special concern of the First Amendment, which does not tolerate laws that cast a pall of orthodoxy over the classroom.[57]

It would be gratifying to report that Brennan's magisterial formulation provided the death knell for loyalty oaths within higher education. But quite a few such oaths remained on the books (and do so to this day). For the most part, colleges and universities stopped enforcing them, politicians made no effort to repeal them, and the judiciary simply believed they were too trivial to bother about—in the words of

Justice John Marshall Harlan, "no more than an amenity."[58] But even at liberal institutions in liberal parts of the country, being expected to sign a loyalty oath during the 1960s could still shock an unsuspecting academic.

Joseph Pedlosky was one such individual. A mathematician who joined the MIT faculty in 1964, Pedlosky considered himself a liberal, but not a serious political activist. When he received a copy of the oath that all Massachusetts teachers had been required to sign since 1935, he figured that if he just threw it away, nothing would happen. He certainly had no intention of signing it. "I felt this was an act of intimidation—making teachers sign a loyalty oath. . . . just a message to teachers, to stay in line, don't do anything out of the ordinary." But the administration persisted and in December 1964 it warned him that he would be fired if he didn't comply. So, along with another professor, Pedlosky hired a civil liberties lawyer and sued the school.[59]

Most of his older colleagues were liberals and had signed the oath. According to Pedlosky, they regarded his behavior as "eccentric." MIT's leaders were not eager to dismiss Pedlosky, but they felt constrained to enforce the law. Although the dean, Jerome Wiesner, a high-level science adviser to the Kennedy and Johnson administrations, disliked the loyalty oath, he made it clear that he was much too busy saving the world from a nuclear holocaust to give Pedlosky's "little oath issue" any attention. The provost, Charles Townes, who had just won a Nobel Prize for inventing the laser, was more helpful. Not only did he encourage the young mathematician to seek an injunction so that he could continue to teach while his case was being litigated, but he also promised that if the courts sustained the law, he would give Pedlosky a research appointment that did not require the oath.[60]

Meanwhile, a few miles up the Charles River at Harvard, another junior faculty member was also refusing to take the oath. Samuel Bowles was the son of the ambassador to India, Chester Bowles, and an instructor in the economics department. Like Pedlosky, he, too, found the measure "a politically inspired . . . invasion of the teacher's privacy of opinion and an inhibition of his freedom of speech." Yet despite President Nathan Pusey's leadership in the fight against the NDEA disclaimer, Harvard's authorities, like MIT's, believed, that the university "must simply comply with all the laws of the Commonwealth." Since Bowles decided to piggyback his case onto Pedlosky's, when Massachusetts's highest court threw out the oath as "altogether too vague a standard to enforce judicially," he was able to stay at Harvard—at least until he was denied tenure.[61]

Significantly, both Bowles and Pedlosky emphasized their disappointment with their colleagues. Professors at both institutions helped with legal expenses, but, with only a few exceptions, they also advised capitulation.[62] In fact, Pedlosky later admitted, he would have signed the oath if the MIT authorities had publicly denounced it. Bowles, too, found himself "surprised that the President [Pusey] has not made a general statement opposing this oath." He recalled, "I found it disappointing that people whom I admired as liberals, as people who believed in liberty, would so easily, not only sign, but also urge others to do the same."[63] In many ways, this disillusionment prefigures the similar disenchantment with liberalism that many more academics were to experience during the second half of the sixties when the Vietnam War and the radical student movement disrupted their campuses.

Speakers Bans in Transition

At the same time as the Buffalo authorities were confronting the complications of the Feinberg Law, they were also facing the challenge of hosting politically controversial outside speakers. In 1962, the university organized a lecture series to highlight its tradition of academic freedom. The program featured a range of potentially incendiary speakers, from the communist historian Herbert Aptheker to the British fascist Oswald Mosley. Despite massive protests against Mosley's appearance, Buffalo's president refused to cancel the event. But he could not prevent a local politician from obtaining a last-minute injunction against Aptheker. A group of students and faculty members challenged that injunction, though it took more than a year before New York's highest court threw it out. When Aptheker finally did get to speak on campus, he drew a much larger crowd than he would have two years before.[64]

Although Aptheker's open identification as a communist denied him a regular faculty position until late in his career, his Columbia PhD and specialization in Black history at a time when few whites studied it, gave him a modicum of intellectual legitimacy. As a result, he became the poster child for the civil libertarian campaign against restrictions on outside speakers: a token communist, whose appearance (or non-appearance) on a campus offered student and faculty liberals and radicals a chance to contest an irritating remnant of the McCarthy era.[65] Thus, despite the FBI's covert efforts to get his appearances canceled, during the early 1960s Aptheker spoke at dozens of schools while being blocked at others.[66]

Like loyalty oaths, speakers bans predated the Cold War. In 1922, for example, the president of Clark University personally stopped a lecture by the radical economist Scott Nearing by turning off the auditorium's lights. Most of the rejected speakers were on the left, though some schools—the Universities of Washington and California among them—sought to mitigate political harassment by refusing to let outsiders discuss any kind of partisan politics on campus. Public colleges and universities were especially vulnerable. The restrictions ranged from state laws and trustees' resolutions to ad hoc decisions by presidents and deans. For example, in the immediate aftermath of the loyalty oath controversy in January 1952, the University of California regents explicitly barred communists from speaking on campus. And as the Cold War intensified, other schools, both public and private, followed suit.[67]

But by the late 1950s and early 1960s, students and professors started to challenge such restrictions. In 1956, for example, a Princeton debate club's invitation to Alger Hiss hit the front pages. And, in California, under pressure from the faculty, Clark Kerr slowly edged away from the restrictions on outside speakers.[68] Even so, because he felt compelled to humor the regents and the state legislature, the directives he issued in 1959 not only failed to satisfy his liberal critics, but also produced contradictory results.[69]

Finally, in the spring of 1963, as Berkeley's campus was becoming increasingly politicized, an invitation to Aptheker by the History Club prompted Kerr and the regents to revise their speakers' policy. The history department had voted 27–1 to co-sponsor Aptheker's talk, but the chancellor, Edward Strong, refused to let it take place on university property. Accordingly, the lecture was moved to the YMCA across the street from the campus. There were no fireworks. In fact, as Kenneth Stampp—who along with the history department chair Carl Schorske was one of the main supporters of the talk—recalled, the event was "rather disappointing":

> He spoke for fifty minutes or so about Reconstruction historiography. . . . Frankly, it was an awfully dull speech. He had a bunch of three-by-five cards with titles on them, and he sort of flipped through them and said, "This is a good book, this is a bad book," and a little more, but not much more than that.[70]

A few months later, Kerr convinced the regents to rescind the speaker ban—with the caveat that the president could still require "controversial" programs to provide opposing speakers and be moderated by a tenured faculty member.[71] By arguing that communists could speak at Harvard, the University of Michigan, and Stanford, Kerr was reflecting the drive for status that fueled so much of the academy's transformation during the 1960s. He also revealed the pervasiveness of the anti-communist mindset. As he explained to the regents, the speakers' policy had to change because it "permitted American Communists to pose as civil liberties martyrs denied the 'right' to speak on the campus, rather than presenting them as the puppets which in reality they are."[72]

Yet for all its defects, California's revised speakers policy did symbolize a new openness on campus. At its 1964 annual meeting in St. Louis, the AAUP awarded Kerr and the regents its seventh Alexander Meiklejohn Award for academic freedom. In retrospect, it was ironic, for within a few months, the Berkeley administration precipitated higher education's first major confrontation with the nascent student movement when it cracked down on its students' political rights and stimulated the formation of the Free Speech Movement.

As students and professors at many other schools began to shake off their passivity, they used invitations to Aptheker and similar speakers

FIGURE 2.1. The Red Menace: Herbert Aptheker and Angela Davis. Angela Davis © Daily Worker and Daily World Photographs Collection / Tamiment Library, NYU.

to push against their institutions' political constraints. Accordingly, quite a few administrators found themselves, like Kerr, caught between the demands for censorship by trustees and/or local politicians and the call for freer speech by students and faculty members. Some institutions eased their restrictions; others intensified them.

Ohio State's experiences were illustrative. An aspiring research university located in the state capital in a deeply conservative region of Ohio, the school's notorious "gag rule" had officially barred communist speakers since 1951. In 1963, two years after OSU's president canceled a public forum critical of HUAC and the legislature extended the gag rule to all the state's public colleges and universities, a student group, with considerable faculty support, invited Aptheker to the campus.[73] He came but did not speak. Instead, in a clever ploy devised by the organizers, he sat quietly on the stage while a political science professor read passages from his books—all readily available in the university's library. By the following semester, the pressure to rescind the gag rule was so intense that Ohio's governor, unwilling to risk a Berkeley-style free speech confrontation, liberalized the board of trustees and in September 1965 repealed the measure. A month later, Aptheker returned to Columbus (along with two carloads of FBI agents)—and this time he spoke.[74]

Southern colleges and universities, by contrast, instituted and toughened their speakers bans. In 1955, the University of Mississippi's board of trustees ruled that all invited speakers had to "be investigated and approved by the head of the institution involved." The president then canceled a talk during "Religious Emphasis Week" by an Episcopal priest who had donated money to the NAACP.[75] A few years later, the board revised its policy to make it even easier to ban speakers "who will do violence to the academic atmosphere." It is hard to tell exactly what kind of "violence" the moderate civil rights leaders Aaron Henry and Charles Evers were planning to inflict on anything other than the racial status quo.[76]

Racial issues were also responsible for the nation's most notorious speakers ban—in North Carolina.[77] The measure, which prohibited communists and Fifth Amendment witnesses from speaking at public colleges and universities, was a move by conservative lawmakers to strike against the relative liberalism of the state's flagship university. In the summer of 1963, that liberalism was on display during the nightly civil rights marches by UNC students, professors, and others through the streets of the state capital, Raleigh. As he fulminated against the demonstrations, television journalist and future US senator Jesse Helms successfully invoked the specter of communism to urge legislators to keep their schools and colleges free of Reds.

The university's moderate leaders opposed the act and worked to get it revised to let the board of trustees do the vetting. They assured the legislature that they would keep controversial speakers off the campus. And they did. Within the faculty and the larger academic community, the law encountered the kind of opposition provoked by the California loyalty oath nearly fifteen years before. Professors sought outside offers, while job candidates and professional groups boycotted the state and its institutions of higher learning. The Southern Association of Colleges and Schools even threatened to withhold the University of North Carolina's accreditation unless the law was repealed—a measure that would have made it impossible for graduates to teach in the state's public schools.

Once the trustees and administrators promised to ensure "that no Communist of the type of Gus Hall [the party's chair] . . . or Herbert Apthecker [*sic*] will speak on our campuses," the law was revised, giving the university's leaders the authority to keep such undesirable speakers away. For North Carolina's civil libertarians, the trustees' policy was as restrictive as the original legislation. Nonetheless, once the faculty voted to approve that policy, the legislature amended the law.[78]

By the end of 1965, as the Vietnam War intensified, UNC's recently formed Students for a Democratic Society (SDS) chapter decided to test the ban by inviting Aptheker and the anti-HUAC campaigner Frank Wilkinson to Chapel Hill. Fearful of what the state's politicians might do, the UNC president arranged for the men to deliver their speeches from the sidewalk just outside the university grounds. Thus, on March 9, 1966, Aptheker, who had actually lectured at the university a few years earlier, stood before the low stone wall bordering the campus to address an audience of two thousand students. He then gave a more formal presentation entitled "The Negro Movement—Reform or Revolution?" at a nearby church. Three weeks later, Aptheker, Wilkinson, and a dozen students sued UNC's top administrators and trustees to eliminate the ban. It took nearly two years before the federal district court threw out the regulations—predictably, on the grounds of "vagueness."[79]

By then the communist issue had lost its bite. The Vietnam War and the growing student movement convulsed campuses, provoking a massive political backlash. Ironically, that backlash resulted in several states adopting measures against communist speakers as well as laws against radical students and professors. In February 1966, for example, just as the UNC authorities were dithering about Aptheker and Wilkinson, Michigan's legislature called on their state's university presidents to ban communist speakers. The presidents of Wayne State and Michigan State Universities announced that they would not comply. Aptheker spoke to a student group at Wayne State two hours after the resolution passed. He spoke at MSU the following day. Of course,

by early 1966, it was not Aptheker's communism but his opposition to
the war in Vietnam, including a highly publicized December 1965 trip
to Hanoi, that had spurred the resolution. By letting Aptheker speak,
the Michigan university presidents revealed that, at least in some parts
of the country, the McCarthy era on campus really was over.[80] And,
even in the South, that anti-communist furor was receding. In February 1970, Angela Davis gave a talk at the University of Alabama.[81]

3

"THE PRE-SIXTIES"

The Liberal Moment on Campus

By the spring of 1961, the civil rights movement and John F. Kennedy's New Frontier were energizing thousands of young people, but all was quiet at the Brockport State University College of Education. Neither the newly formed Peace Corps nor the sit-in movement seemed to rouse its "lethargic" student body. So when he came across an ad in the *New York Times* opposing the House Un-American Activities Committee, the Brockport political scientist Edward Cain seized upon it as a way to spark some political excitement. He quickly rounded up thirty colleagues to sign a one-sentence petition to their congressman calling for the committee's abolition. Though some of the signers worried about getting in trouble, they did not think they were making a particularly radical gesture. Such, however, was not the case with the conservative congressman, who forwarded the petition to the district commander of the American Legion in Rochester. Soon the Brockport president's office was flooded with phone calls from patriotic Legionnaires wanting to know what he was planning to do about the "Reds" on his faculty. Worse yet, two officers from the New York State Bureau of Criminal Intelligence showed up as well, demanding to see the signers' personnel files.

Eventually, Cain placated his worried superiors by explaining to the congressman and the Legion that his use of college stationery for the petition did not mean that the faculty officially endorsed its contents. The AAUP wrote a letter to Governor Nelson Rockefeller decrying the intervention of the state police as a "threat to the whole concept of academic freedom." And, in what seems to have been a conciliatory gesture, the Legion invited Cain to debate a HUAC supporter at the local post's showing of *Operation Abolition*, a controversial film about the committee's raucous May 1960 hearings in San Francisco. Because they claimed to fear that Brockport's students might start the same kind of riot the movie supposedly portrayed, the Legion's authorities refused to admit any outsiders. This exclusion finally aroused the students, and soon the incident was the talk of the campus.[1]

Cain was no radical. He identified as a liberal Democrat of the Adlai Stevenson persuasion, a profile that was typical of academics concerned about politics during the period one social scientist has labeled "the pre-sixties."[2] That Cain could recruit so many other professors for a protest against HUAC shows how much the political atmosphere had lightened since the height of McCarthyism. The academic community was rediscovering its political voice. These were years of intellectual as well as political ferment. On many campuses, people were raising questions and then realizing that the answers might require them to act. Racial inequality, nuclear weapons, and the removal of institutional constraints on political freedom all demanded their attention. And as faculty members and students studied, wrote, and began to organize around these issues, the McCarthy-era chill began to dissipate.

Nothing revolutionary happened. Everybody obeyed the rules. Men still dressed for demonstrations in jackets and ties, women in skirts, stockings, and heels. They believed—or at least hoped—that the system might work. The late 1950s and early 1960s were in many ways the high point of American liberalism, years of optimism and of confidence in the power of knowledge—a moment when it was still possible to believe that ignorance and misinformation caused most of the nation's problems. Once the powers that be understood what was at stake, they would take the necessary actions to clear things up—or so most liberal academics assumed. As a result, it made sense to mobilize the nation's still-prestigious college and university teachers, to circulate petitions, and to make their opinions heard. They were not always wrong.

Remnants and Nodules of the Left

Although McCarthyism had marginalized the academic Left, it had not entirely destroyed it. Even in the 1950s, a few Marxists and independent radicals were able to slip past the blacklist and hold faculty positions. Some even continued their political activities or else served as role models and mentors. Accordingly, when the anti-communist furor abated, some of these radicals emerged.

One was the tenured Marxist economist Paul Baran at Stanford.[3] The sociologist Hans Gerth also made it through the McCarthy years, as did the philosopher Herbert Marcuse.[4] Significantly, both Gerth and Marcuse were teaching at universities—Wisconsin and Brandeis, respectively—that during the 1950s housed some left-wing scholarship and student activity. Those schools and a few others—Berkeley, Cornell, and University of Michigan among them—by fostering a more hospitable climate for unorthodox politics, allowed left-wing professors and their students to experiment with unconventional ideas and question the status quo. Especially at some of the nation's largest universities, it was possible for individual departments to harbor nodules of radical thought and action.

Wisconsin housed the most well-known of these nodules. The university prided itself on its long tradition of academic freedom and public service. It tolerated more radicalism than most other institutions; and despite its location in Joseph McCarthy's home state, it had emerged largely unscathed from the Cold War witch hunt. In the early fifties, Wisconsin was the only major university that did not ban the Communist Party's student group. Herbert Aptheker and other communists could speak on campus. Seen as "comfortable for radicals," Wisconsin attracted a critical mass of already politicized undergraduates and graduate students. Many were "Red diaper babies," the intellectually serious and politically precocious offspring of communist parents, New York Jews who knew that they would feel at home in Madison.[5] In fact, when the historian and Red diaper baby Joan Scott arrived in Wisconsin from Brandeis for graduate school, eager to experience what to her was the exotic *goyische* world of the Midwest, she remembered, "the first people I meet are the people I went to summer camp with."[6]

By the late 1950s, Wisconsin undergraduates, graduate students, and professors had created a unique political culture that was both activist and scholarly and not particularly sectarian. Although it embraced card-carrying communists (who, nevertheless, concealed their membership), it also contained socialists, Trotskyists, and left-liberals of all varieties. If they disagreed violently about the Soviet Union, they still congregated in the same quasi-bohemian hang-outs, listened to the same folk music, and worshipped the same professors.[7] Dedicated to civil liberties, civil rights, and peace, these radicals took part in anti-nuclear demonstrations, picketed businesses that did not hire Black workers, and cavorted at the anti-military balls that spoofed the ROTC's annual formal event. They also believed, the women's historian Elizabeth Ewen recalled, "that your political and intellectual work didn't have to be separate. The fight for the mind was as important as the action in the street. This wasn't true in other places."[8]

Wisconsin's history department embodied that aspiration. It housed a cohort of independent radicals who challenged the Cold War consensus within their field. William Appleman Williams was perhaps the most influential. Not only did he develop a revisionist interpretation of American expansion, but he also imbued his students with "an intellectual excitement that," historian Warren Susman explained, "would not otherwise have existed. He made intellectual work *seem* very important."[9] Madison's left-wing professors also imposed high intellectual standards. They also introduced those students to the cutting-edge work of the British social historians and continental theorists. And to Karl Marx. Williams and the European historian George Mosse taught an entire course on Marxism.[10]

The intellectual vitality of those years was contagious. History classes were packed; in the fall of 1961, 25 percent of all Wisconsin students took at least one course in the department.[11] The dynamic Europeanist Harvey Goldberg drew seven hundred students; George Mosse attracted five hundred. The faculty was as energized as its students. It was, Mosse recalled, a terribly exciting period from the point of view of teaching. The students read a great deal, they took their history seriously, and they were eager for intellectual discussion. I have never witnessed their kind of intellectual excitement on campus before or since.[12]

Perhaps the most visible product of all this intellectual ferment was the journal *Studies on the Left*. Founded in 1959 by a group of Williams's graduate students, it established, in Paul Buhle's words, "a public presence for the new history."[13] It was surprisingly inclusive, featuring a piece by Herbert Aptheker in its first issue, as well as a translation by Hans Gerth of Walter Benjamin's iconic essay, "The Work of Art in the Epoch of Mechanical Reproduction." Its most important contribution, however, may well have been the development of the concept of "corporate liberalism" by the editorial board member Martin Sklar, a concept that, along with Williams's "open door" interpretation of American imperialism as the permanent core of US foreign policy, offered *Studies*' readers new intellectual tools for analyzing the American state and society.[14]

Although the journal left Wisconsin for New York in 1963 and folded in 1967, it introduced a new world of critical scholarship and political activism to an entire cohort of graduate students and young faculty members at more conventional campuses. Its first issue sold three thousand copies; by the mid-1960s its circulation reached ten thousand.[15] "I can't tell you how important I found *Studies* even when I was upset with it," the former editor Susman explained. "*Studies* sought to make scholarship activist without making it vulgar."[16] Williams's desire for a "useable past" shaped the journal. He wanted to convince his readers and students of "the visceral importance for the Left of *creating a general social consciousness* of the true nature of advanced capitalism as a necessary precondition for socialism."[17] Even without having read Gramsci, whose work had yet to be readily available in English, Williams and his acolytes were waging the Gramscian struggle for ideological hegemony. At the same time, the graduate students and young faculty members involved with *Studies* were also trying to realize their professional ambitions. They recognized "the possibility," one of them explained, "that they can pursue a successful academic career by making a radical political contribution."[18] As we shall see, the tension between activism and scholarship that such a goal created was to confound the academic Left for the next decade and a half. The *Studies'* circle simply grappled with it sooner.

Brandeis's political culture was more diffuse—and more hooked into the world of the New York Intellectuals. Brandeis was founded in 1948, when the establishment of a secular Jewish university seemed like a useful precaution in case the academy's prewar anti-Semitism returned. It was liberal, experimental, and, as the political theorist and graduate Michael Walzer recalled, a place "where the sixties started in the fifties." The school's founding president, Abram Sachar, created a first-rate faculty by "giving jobs to people who couldn't get jobs elsewhere," refugees from the Red Scare among them. The atmosphere, as Joan Scott remembered, was "very political, very exciting." If *Studies* was Madison's contribution to the world of intellectual journals, *Dissent* was Brandeis's. Its founders, Lewis Coser and Irving Howe, brought a polemical brand of social democracy to a campus inhabited by an eclectic mix of intellectuals and radicals who included Marcuse, Max Lerner, Philip Rahv, Philip Rieff (and his then-wife Susan Sontag), Abraham Maslow, Kurt Wolff, Alan Grossman, and Maurice Stein—all, another graduate recalled, "afraid of fascism and McCarthyism."[19]

As at Madison, many of these professors encouraged their students to push themselves intellectually. Marcuse, who came to be considered the intellectual godfather of the New Left, was already a local "culture hero." According to the Brandeis graduate Martin Peretz, he delivered his "elegantly prepared" lectures to "packed and rapt classrooms," but was also rigorous with regard to "the standards of mental discipline and honesty." The historian Ronald Aronson recalled, "Something was happening in Marcuse's classes. . . . [W]e were learning how to read, to think." They were also encouraged to be politically active. Scott recalled Marcuse running up to her in the middle of the 1962 Berlin crisis, thrusting a ten-dollar bill in her hand, and saying, "Go, organize!" The philosopher Angela Davis, whom Marcuse considered his best student, credited him with making it clear "that I did not have to choose between a career as an academic and a political vocation that entailed making interventions around concrete social issues."[20]

Cornell's was a different milieu, a major research university in rural upstate New York. It housed a first-rate and politically involved physics department whose most energetic activist, Philip Morrison, a former communist and Manhattan Project alumnus, specifically went to Ithaca so that he could work in the peace movement without arousing too much attention from the media.[21] By the late fifties, a small cohort of graduate students had come under his influence. One, the mathematician Charles Haynie, became politicized after learning from Morrison about the deleterious impact of McCarthyism on the physics community. Soon he and his fellow graduate students were on the front lines of the local anti-nuclear movement.

> We didn't start out as radicals; we started out as "enlightenment liberal intellectuals." We were all slowly, and, I must say, reluctantly, radicalized by this dialectical process of engagement with the issue, trying desperately to remain in graduate school and forging ahead with our careers, careers that often (as mine had) required continual security clearances and jobs in military-related laboratories.[22]

Other Cornell activists, including Haynie's "Red diaper baby" roommate David Kotelchuck, were already on the left when they arrived in Ithaca. Douglas Dowd, who emerged as a major figure in the antiwar movement, joined the faculty in 1953. Within a few years, he recalled, the campus saw "substantial organized activities" against nuclear tests. By the early 1960s, Cornell's radicals were not only heavily involved with the civil rights movement, but were also running the campaign of a peace candidate for Congress.[23]

The University of Michigan was another school with a collection of political activists, mainly in its well-regarded social science departments.[24] In 1955, when William Gamson, who was to become one of the key activists in the antiwar teach-in movement, began graduate work in sociology at Ann Arbor, he had already been radicalized by his undergraduate years at Antioch, an alternative institution whose

history and innovative work-study curriculum fostered an activist oppositional culture that, he recalled, reminded him of "Berkeley's in the
sixties." In 1955, Michigan's faculty was still recovering from the traumatic firing of two professors the year before for refusing to cooperate
with HUAC. That event spurred the organization of "an energetic liberal caucus," galvanized by resistance to McCarthyism and bolstered
by its proximity to Detroit's powerful labor movement.[25]

Among Michigan's early activists were eminent scholars and social
scientists like the Quaker economist Kenneth Boulding, the mathematician Anatol Rapoport, and the philosopher Arnold Kaufman. As at
Cornell, these professors focused most of their efforts on the nascent
anti-nuclear movement—but with a strong educational component
that took students and their idealism seriously. Boulding and his wife,
Elise, held weekly meetings about nuclear issues; Kaufman developed
the theory of political participation that strongly influenced the New
Left's concept of "participatory democracy"; and a non-credit seminar
on conflict and civil rights drew a hundred students. Within a few
years, the work of these faculty activists was to inform the nation's first
teach-in as well as the language and ideas of the New Left's influential
"Port Huron Statement," written by Tom Hayden, Michigan '61.[26]

In truth, activist professors of both the liberal and the radical persuasions existed on campuses throughout the country. Not far from
the University of Michigan, for example, Wayne State was the home
base for the energetic political scientist and educational reformer Otto
Feinstein and his leftist academic journal *New University Thought*. By
the mid-1950s, Washington University in St. Louis was to become a
leading site in the struggle against atmospheric nuclear testing.[27] And
in Boston, a cluster of worried academics began to meet occasionally
to discuss the nuclear arms race. Organized primarily by the MIT biologist and Nobel laureate Salvador Luria, by 1962 its roughly ninety
members included many active and eminent professors—mostly
scientists—like the linguist Noam Chomsky, the biologists Matthew
Meselson and John Edsall, the physicist Bruno Rossi, and the Manhattan Project chemist George Kistiakowsky. They called themselves the
Boston Area Faculty Group on Public Issues, or BAFGOPI.[28]

Elsewhere, individual professors were quietly organizing on their campuses. The Quaker schools like Swarthmore and Haverford as well as such progressive liberal arts colleges as Antioch and Oberlin tended to attract political activists. Many of these people, like the Haverford College physicist William Davidon, carried out most of their political work off campus, collaborating with peace groups and the pacifist American Friends Service Committee.[29] But when the Vietnam War escalated in the mid-1960s and student protests erupted, these faculty activists took on more public roles as organizers, speakers, mentors, and mediators within their increasingly politicized institutions.

Foreign Influences

Herbert Marcuse, Salvador Luria, George Mosse, Hans Gerth, Anatol Rapoport, Lewis Coser, and many other concerned professors were not native-born Americans. They were part of the important, largely Jewish, cohort of politically sophisticated intellectuals who had fled European fascism before World War II. The contributions of these and other foreign-born scholars and scientists to America intellectual life are well known.[30] But they also influenced the conventional political culture of their schools. For many of the academics who were to become politically and professionally active in the 1960s, the exposure to such a different worldview was transformative.

Perhaps nowhere was that outsiders' perspective as unsettling as in the South, where a small cohort of foreign-born academics contributed to the growth of the civil rights movement. Because of the anti-Semitism endemic to the American academy in the 1930s and 1940s, these Jewish refugees had ended up at historically Black institutions that welcomed them. As victims of the Third Reich's peculiarly lethal form of racism, these professors felt a special bond with their students. Some even participated in the early civil rights movement. The historian Georg Iggers, at Philander Smith College in Little Rock, for example, assisted the NAACP's campaign to integrate that city's Central High School in the mid-1950s. Not all the émigré teachers were political activists, but most sought to broaden their students' lives and, like their African American colleagues, usually supported those students' involvement in the struggle for racial equality.[31]

On campuses outside the South, foreign students sometimes jolted future faculty members into questioning their view of the world. At Brandeis, the historian Temma Kaplan recalled, European leftists and "others with strong political commitments" ensured that "contemporary events permeated almost every class," while her African and other Third World student friends "tutored me in their views of history."[32] Norma Stoltz Chincilla found that her conversations with the left-wing Latin American graduate students at the University of Wisconsin opened up radical alternatives to mainstream sociology. And for the already radicalized Red diaper baby Rosalyn Baxandall, her contacts with Madison's African and other politically sophisticated foreign graduate students exposed her to "a well-articulated, anti-imperialist interpretation of the American empire, which we incorporated."[33] A similar process occurred at such HBCUs as Howard University, where hundreds of African students shared the insights from their own struggles for decolonization, providing future Black Power activists with an enduring internationalist mindset.[34]

For other graduate students and young faculty members, going abroad—whether to Europe, Latin America, or, in a few cases, Southeast Asia—forced them to reassess their political and intellectual commitments. It is important to realize how marginalized Marxism and other forms of oppositional thought and scholarship were during the 1950s and early 1960s. As a result, some of these future activists came into contact with a living Left tradition only when they went overseas.[35] It was in Paris in 1964, for example, that the future sociologist Hester Eisenstein discovered Marx, "met my first Marxist, and by the end of the year had fallen in love with Marxism."[36] John Womack remembered that "two years in England, 1959–61, mainly reading Hegel and Marx with teachers who took them seriously" transformed him from a naive American populist into a much more sophisticated social critic.[37] Equally transformative was the new social history being done by British scholars. "It is difficult," the historian Eric Foner explained, "to recapture the sense of intellectual excitement produced by the works of E. P. Thompson, Eric Hobsbawm, and other British practitioners of 'history from below.'"[38] Thompson's *The Making of the*

English Working Class, in particular, was de rigueur among graduate students and junior faculty. "We read all the new social history as it was published," Joan Scott recalled. "This was a moment of disciplinary reformation and we were eagerly participating in it." The excitement was more than intellectual, however, since the British Marxists were also political activists who, in the words of historian John Gillis, "had come to history not by way of graduate study but through a realization of the importance of history to their engagement with the great issues of the day."[39]

Political Activism Returns

By the late 1950s, those "great issues of the day" brought increasing numbers of faculty members as well as students out of their classrooms and laboratories and into the political arena. Some of those issues (racial equality and freedom of speech, for example) had been around for decades, while others (nuclear weapons, in particular) were more recent. At the same time, as we shall see in chapter 5, more and more professors and future professors became increasingly critical of American intervention overseas, first in Cuba, then in Southeast Asia. The academics in all of these movements espoused a wide variety of views. Some were classic Cold War liberals, hostile to communism and supportive of US foreign policy, even as they championed civil liberties and civil rights. Others were more radical—not only Red diaper babies and other remnants of the Old Left, but also left-liberals who were moving toward the New Left as they found themselves increasingly alienated by what the "system" was doing.

The paralysis that McCarthyism had imposed had definitely receded. Professors and graduate students became more assertive, especially in defending the right to dissent. At Berkeley, for example, the faculty's civil libertarians not only challenged the university's restrictive speakers' policies, but they also opposed attempts to crack down on the incipient student movement.[40] In Ithaca, some younger scientists formed a Committee to Abolish HUAC and publicized their campaign by staging theatrical performances of its hearings. Their presentations drew hundreds of people and were so successful that, one of the organizers remembered, "We didn't have to give a political lecture."[41]

There was also the 1961 newspaper ad against HUAC that brought controversy at Brockport. It garnered nearly 350 signatures, roughly a third of them from the academy, the rest clergy and a mixed collection of writers, lawyers, union officials, and others, including Eleanor Roosevelt, Alexander Meiklejohn, and Martin Luther King Jr. Among the academic signers were Paul Baran, William Appleman Williams, Kenneth Stampp, William Davidon, H. Stuart Hughes, Kenneth Boulding, and the Nobel Prize–winning chemists Linus Pauling and Harold Urey.[42] Admittedly, most of the signers were people who had already been involved in the struggle for civil liberties during the McCarthy era.

But for the first time, these people's activities were having an impact. One signer, Arthur Bierman, a San Francisco State philosopher, had already spearheaded a movement that thwarted HUAC's proposed investigation of Bay Area teachers in the summer of 1959. Calling themselves San Franciscans for Academic Freedom and Education (SAFE), Bierman's group managed to put together a coalition of labor leaders and politicians that forced the committee to postpone its hearings.[43] A year later, when HUAC did hold hearings in San Francisco, things were less decorous. Hundreds of students showed up for several days of demonstrating, culminating in a melee that ended with the police using fire hoses to wash the protesters down the steps of city hall.[44] As was to happen throughout the following decade, the students' confrontational behavior grabbed attention; the more decorous conduct of their teachers did not.

Academics and the Civil Rights Movement

The anti-HUAC protests had not taken place inside a political vacuum. The struggle for racial equality had already reached northern campuses. Reinvigorated by the sit-ins that began in Greensboro, North Carolina, a few months before, the civil rights movement was to energize many previously quiescent students and faculty members. Almost all the radicals I interviewed for this book had been involved in some way or another with the struggle for racial equality, even if they didn't directly brave Mississippi's racist mobs. For the Red diaper baby Richard Flacks, the picket lines supporting the sit-ins in front of the Ann Arbor Woolworth's were an encouraging sign that "it was possible to have progressive action in this country." Similar demonstrations took place in other college towns. The former Cornell graduate student Charles Haynie recalled marching outside the Woolworth's in Ithaca with about fifteen people, "most of whom I knew personally." In Philadelphia, Madison, Berkeley, Los Angeles, New York City, and dozens of other places, undergraduates, graduate students, and even some professors were out on the street, many for the first time.[45]

Soon they were demonstrating against racial injustice much closer at home. There had been sporadic campaigns against racial discrimination in cities and college towns throughout the 1950s. Housing and jobs were the main issues—though there were also protests against barbershops that would not cut the hair of African Americans. One of the first political actions the international law expert Richard Falk took part in was a lawsuit against trustees of Ohio State who, as landlords, would not rent apartments to Black people. Eric Foner was involved in a similar campaign near Columbia.[46] By the early 1960s, much of this activism took place under the auspices of the Congress of Racial Equality (CORE), the main direct action civil rights group in the North. The Michigan psychologist Richard Mann recalls that, as co-chair of the Boston CORE chapter, he and his colleagues became involved in housing struggles, sometimes picketing the offices of realtors who would not show the same rentals to African Americans as to whites.[47]

People in Madison participated in a successful (and, some recalled, fun) CORE-run "shop-in" at the local Sears to demand that the store hire Black salespeople.[48] CORE activists at Berkeley also held shop-ins at supermarkets as well as sit-ins at automobile dealerships and sleep-ins at a San Francisco hotel.[49] Kenneth Stampp recalled participating in the picketing that fellow historian Charles Sellers organized at a drugstore. "I don't know how much good it did, but it made us feel good doing something and carrying a sign, and I was very pleased that one of my daughters was there with me carrying a sign."[50]

Sellers, then the acting chair of the Berkeley chapter of CORE, also took his children to massive demonstrations that, he remembered, "broke the color line" of that city's retailers. Then Sellers, a southerner, went to the South in the spring of 1961 to participate in the Freedom Rides that CORE was organizing to fill the jails of Jackson, Mississippi. Arrested for trying to integrate the waiting room in the Jackson airport, Sellers was only one of several northern academics to join their Black colleagues and students to put their bodies on the line during that campaign.[51] After organizing a Cornell group that provided the Freedom Riders with money and other support, Charles Haynie also headed south with a contingent from Ithaca. Arrested with an interracial delegation in a whites-only waiting room in the New Orleans railroad station, Haynie spent two weeks in jail, the last six days on a hunger strike.[52]

Yale's chaplain William Sloane Coffin also went south. Along with John Maguire, the future president of SUNY Old Westbury, Coffin organized an independent, more establishment-oriented Freedom Ride. "Quickly over the phone," Coffin explained, "we drew up a list of professors and clergy we knew, Northern and Southern, black and white, who could not be typed and dismissed as agitators or mere students." Coffin apparently believed that his Ivy League connections would convince the Kennedy administration to give the unconditional support to the civil rights movement that the Freedom Riders were seeking. He lost that illusion when he and his colleagues were arrested in the Montgomery, Alabama, bus station. They spent two days in jail before being bailed out by Coffin's Yale colleagues, not all of whom were happy with his activism. Along with scores of alumni, the provost demanded that Coffin resign for damaging Yale's reputation. He told Coffin, "It's damned undignified for the chaplain of the university to go to jail."[53]

Though Coffin may have raised some important eyebrows in New Haven, his job was not at issue. For civil rights activists on the faculties of southern colleges and universities, the situation was quite different.

FIGURE 3.1. Howard Zinn at "Freedom Day," voting rights demonstration, Selma, Alabama, October 7, 1963. © Danny Lyon/Magnum Photos.

Like Gloria Wade Bishop, an African American instructor of English and education at Spelman College arrested for picketing an Atlanta delicatessen along with her students and then summarily fired, they could be—and were—dismissed for participating in sit-ins and other forms of nonviolent civil disobedience.[54] Both Black and white academics were affected, though their fates differed considerably. A few were progressive whites who, like Howard Zinn and Staughton Lynd at Spelman, had sought positions at HBCUs specifically to participate in the freedom movement. Zinn was the most well-known. Arrested many times, he not only helped his students desegregate both Atlanta's public library and its largest department store, but also served as a key adult adviser to the Student Nonviolent Coordinating Committee (SNCC), while his prolific publications provided an early and sympathetic introduction to the Black student movement.[55]

These white activists were taking considerable risks. Zinn was fired in the summer of 1963. Until it became too dangerous for him to stay in Mississippi, the Tougaloo College sociologist John Salter, who helped a large NAACP youth group organize boycotts and demonstrations, endured repeated beatings and arrests.[56] And after the Ford

Foundation rather patronizingly loaned a number of its Woodrow Wilson Fellows to several HBCUs, some of these young white teachers were let go when their support for and participation in their students' campaigns against segregated facilities antagonized their more cautious colleagues and administrators.[57] Native white southern professors who supported the freedom struggle, if they hadn't already fled the region, tended to keep a low profile.

Black academics in the South faced an even more unpleasant situation if they participated in the civil rights movement. Since northern institutions of higher education were also segregated, they lacked the white professors' option of leaving the region. They were thus exceptionally vulnerable to and dependent on the South's racist white power structure and their institutions' sometimes authoritarian administrations.[58] Even so, most opposed Jim Crow and some actively fought against it. Tuskegee political scientist Charles Gomillion spent decades pursuing the right to vote until he was vindicated by the Supreme Court in 1960.[59] On the day Rosa Parks was arrested, Alabama State College English professor Jo Ann Robinson borrowed the school's mimeograph machine and with a few students produced and then distributed fifty thousand flyers urging Montgomery's Black residents to boycott the city's buses.[60] With the covert support of Alabama State's president, Robinson managed to keep her job until she quit a few years later to protest the dismissal of her colleague Lawrence Reddick.[61]

Robinson, like many of her Black colleagues, also used her classroom to fight for racial equality. At HBCUs throughout the South, these teachers had spent years preparing their students for action by discussing human rights and democracy in their classes and developing a sense of Black consciousness. While a student at Alabama State in the 1940s, for example, the civil rights leader Ralph Abernathy recalled "being taught all sorts of useful and subversive ideas by our faculty members, some of whom were openly urging us to make a difference in our people's struggle for freedom."[62] When their students took to the streets in the 1960s, those faculty members supported them as best they could. They loaned them their cars, refused to mark them absent when they had been arrested, raised bail money, and testified at their trials. Some college presidents, mainly at private institutions in the upper South and urban centers, also supported their student activists. But on other Black campuses, the picture was much bleaker as segregationist politicians and trustees cracked down on protesting students and their faculty allies.[63]

The situation of the HBCUs' leaders during the long sixties was particularly complicated. Only a few were so satisfied with their own comfortable position within the segregated system that they resisted all change. Most others, like their faculty members, genuinely opposed Jim Crow and sought to build Black institutions that would provide their students with genuine educational opportunities. But they had little autonomy and feared that open support for racial equality might simply provoke the white supremacists who controlled their institutions. They sought instead to win more resources for their institutions by relying on those authorities' last-ditch plan to avoid integration by upgrading the HBCUs. That strategy, however, often led these Black college presidents to pander to their racist superiors, while suppressing their students' and faculty members' participation in the civil rights movement. The outcome was discouraging. Token integration occurred, but the desired improvements never materialized and the once-vibrant Black culture of the HBCUs began to dissipate.[64]

Nonetheless, as the struggle for racial equality reached its peak in the mid-1960s, it drew both liberal and radical white academics into the South for short periods of time. It had become so respectable that quite a few establishment figures took part in it. In the spring of 1965, for example, many joined Martin Luther King Jr. for the Selma to Montgomery march. Kenneth Stampp, Richard Hofstadter, C. Vann Woodward, and John Hope Franklin were among the forty or so eminent and emerging historians who chartered a bus for the final lap. Others went to Alabama as individuals.[65] In retrospect, that moment probably constituted the apogee of political unanimity within the nation's faculties.

A more radical cohort of younger academics had already gone south the year before, for the Mississippi Summer Project. Designed by SNCC's leaders to attract attention to the horrific repression that denied Mississippi's African Americans their civil rights, the project brought elite white students and teachers to the nation's most racist state in the hopes that the media coverage of the violence against those volunteers' efforts to register voters would force the federal government to intervene. That did not happen. Instead, the Kennedy administration's failure to protect them led many Mississippi Summer veterans to jettison whatever illusions they had about the good faith of mainstream liberals.

A less dramatic, though equally important, component of the Mississippi Summer Project was its Freedom Schools. They were created to give Mississippi's Black students some of the education their inadequate public schools did not provide as well as to train future leaders for their communities. According to Charles Cobb, the SNCC staff member who conceptualized them, the Freedom Schools were designed "to challenge the student's curiosity about the world, introduce him to his particularly 'Negro' cultural background, and teach him basic literacy skills in one integrated program."[66] Headed by Staughton Lynd, who had left Spelman for Yale after Zinn was fired, the project ended up with about fifty schools and two thousand students.

According to many of the volunteers who taught at them, the innovative pedagogy of the Freedom Schools contributed, albeit indirectly, to their own later educational experiments.[67] Students themselves decided what they wanted to learn. The feminist scholar Florence Howe recalled her surprise at discovering that her Freedom School students demanded courses in chemistry and French; these were, they explained, subjects that were available only in Mississippi's white public schools. Classes featured "open questions" without answers designed to "unlock students' ability to think rather than to accept teachers' words as law."[68] And, apparently, they succeeded. The Tougaloo historian John Dittmer claimed that he could always tell the Freedom School alumni in his classes because "they thought for themselves, they asked questions."[69]

So, too, did their teachers; and, in the process, they became radicalized. For many of the female Mississippi Summer volunteers, their encounters with racist repression so sensitized them to injustice that, like Florence Howe, they were primed to conceptualize their own oppression—and to help found the women's liberation movement.[70]

Other veterans of the civil rights movement of the early 1960s, both male and female, Black and white, brought their experiences into the antiwar and other movements of the era, shaking up the nation's colleges and universities in the process.

The Scientists Mobilize

But not all the activists of the early 1960s were to be found at a demonstration. A movement inspired by some well-known scientists was already pressing to end the atmospheric testing of nuclear weapons. These people had worried about the bomb from before Hiroshima. In the immediate aftermath of the war, a group of Manhattan Project physicists mounted a successful drive to put the control of atomic energy in civilian hands. Some then continued to organize in the hopes of preventing an arms race. Believing that they were the only people who understood what nuclear weapons could do, these scientists came to feel they had a mission—actually, an obligation—to educate people about the bomb and its dangers.[71] Good liberals, most of them, they claimed to believe that once the facts about nuclear weapons were known, the powers that be would do the right thing. In the words of the future editor of the *Bulletin of the Atomic Scientists*, they were going to "preserve our civilization by scaring men into rationality." They were both liberal and optimistic—and eager to reach an international agreement to ban the bomb.[72]

The Cold War soon cut short the scientists' campaign. Not only had the growing antagonism between the US and the USSR destroyed all hopes for averting a nuclear arms race, but the domestic anti-communist crusade was wreaking havoc within their community. Nearly half the professors who lost their jobs for political reasons during the McCarthy years were physicists or biologists. Accordingly, by the late 1940s, the scientists' main peace group, the Federation of Atomic Scientists, had abandoned its commitment to internationalism, purged its staff, and monitored its members.[73]

Individual academics retreated as well. Even as committed an activist as the future Nobel laureate Linus Pauling, who had, he admitted, "associated myself in a smaller or larger way with every peace movement that has come to my attention," pulled back. Beginning in 1951, when faced with the demand for his dismissal by a group of Caltech trustees, an investigation by the California version of HUAC, the denial of a security clearance, and the State Department's refusal to issue him a passport, Pauling resigned from all his left-wing organizations and refrained from the political activity to which he had been devoting over half his time.[74]

Tainted Science, Moral Scientists

Although Pauling had never worked on the bomb, many other top scientists had. They had, as J. Robert Oppenheimer famously remarked in 1947, "known sin, and this is a knowledge they cannot lose." For years that knowledge and their guilt was to plague American scientists. Some, as we have seen, responded by trying to influence public policy. Others felt that, whatever their personal views, scientists should not intervene in political matters outside the areas of their expertise. Still others viewed the threat of nuclear warfare as a moral challenge.

Some dealt with that ethical dilemma by refusing to work on weapons-related projects. Among the most prominent were the physicist-turned-biologist Leo Szilard and the MIT mathematician Norbert Wiener, who would no longer take money from the military.[75] Other lesser-known scientists made similar decisions, risking serious career consequences.[76]

Encouraged by the examples of Szilard and Wiener, Victor Paschkis, a Quaker engineer at Columbia, organized a conference on the ethical problems of military-related research at Haverford College in June 1948. A year later, many of its participants joined Paschkis in founding the Society for Social Responsibility in Science (SSRS), a group designed to "witness . . . our refusal to engage in activity that appears individually to us to be destructive."[77] The SSRS was never large or influential. By 1955 it had dwindled to some thirty-five to forty members, some of whom chafed at its emphasis on individual morality rather than collective action. Eventually, perhaps under the prodding of Haverford's William Davidon, the organization did support at least one demonstration, a 1959 peace vigil against the US Army's research on chemical and biological warfare at Fort Detrick in Maryland. Yet as small as it was, the organization did stimulate debate about the moral responsibilities of scientists at a time when little else was disturbing their quiet campuses.[78]

The moral approach of the SSRS was very much in accord with the work of such pacifist organizations as the Fellowship of Reconciliation and the American Friends Service Committee (AFSC), which attracted many scientists and others, especially in the Philadelphia area, where Quakers were prominent. During the McCarthy years, the AFSC provided the cover of religious respectability for faculty activists who wanted to work for peace and other causes without being Red-baited. In the early 1960s, for example, the sociologist Martin Oppenheimer and the literary scholar Paul Lauter staffed the AFSC's educational outreach efforts, trying to encourage historians and others to study the peace movement.[79]

Fallout and the Campaign against Nuclear Testing

By then, the peace movement was being resuscitated by some of its original advocates. As before, these scientists were using their expertise to promote a political campaign—this time against atmospheric nuclear testing.

For most ordinary citizens, that testing became problematic on March 1, 1954, when the United States detonated its first hydrogen bomb in the South Pacific. The unexpected size of the blast astonished its makers. Eighty-five miles away, outside of the designated danger zone, a heavy coating of radioactive ash rained down upon the Japanese fishing boat *Lucky Dragon*. By the end of the day, all twenty-three members of the crew were feeling nauseous. By the time they reached their home port, they had full-blown radiation sickness. Their radio operator died in September. Thus did the world learn that nuclear fallout was bad for humans.

Scientists already knew something about that danger. The Nobel

Prize–winning geneticist Hermann Muller had discovered that radiation caused mutations; the University of Montana biologist E. W. Pfeiffer had found the damaging by-products of aboveground atomic tests in the air and soil of North Dakota. And in 1953, researchers discovered that one of those by-products, the radio-isotope strontium 90, had a much longer half-life than originally thought; and, because it behaved chemically like calcium, could enter the human food chain through the fallout-tainted grass cows ate and the milk they produced, going directly into the bones of growing children. By 1956, there was enough information to convince Adlai Stevenson, the Democratic candidate for president, to call for a ban on atmospheric nuclear tests.[80]

The *Lucky Dragon* mobilized the scientific community. Linus Pauling, no longer intimidated by McCarthyism, decided to publicize the issue. He won the Nobel Prize in Chemistry in 1954 and thus felt relatively safe in resuming his political activities. By 1956, Pauling was giving two or three speeches a week and again devoting more than half his time to the dangers of nuclear weapons.[81]

His most useful allies were a group of scientists at Washington University in St. Louis. Two, in particular—the environmentalist Barry Commoner and the Manhattan Project veteran E. U. Condon—had long been concerned about the social responsibility of scientists. In May 1957, Pauling delivered a major lecture at the university. As he recalled, the audience's response to his demand for an end to the atmospheric testing of nuclear weapons was so "tremendous" that he, Commoner, and Condon decided to circulate a petition. "We mimeographed it," Pauling recalled,

> and sent it out to twenty-five scientists that we knew. They all sent it right back, signed. So then I got back to Pasadena and my wife and I and some of our students and others in the lab got busy and sent out hundreds of copies with the names of these first twenty-five signers. And within a month or two I had two thousand signatures.

Released in June 1957, it was the first public statement by the scientific community since the postwar campaign against military control of the bomb. "As scientists," the petition explained, we have knowledge of the dangers involved and therefore have a special responsibility to make those dangers known. We deem it imperative that an immediate action be taken to effect an international agreement to stop the testing of all nuclear weapons.

The document was soon circulating among scientists worldwide, ultimately obtaining over eleven thousand signatures from more than forty countries.[82]

The Atomic Energy Commission and its scientific supporters opposed the petition, claiming that Pauling and his allies were exaggerating the dangers of nuclear fallout.[83] Because the government released little information about the effects of the bomb tests, obtaining that information became one of the key demands of the anti-nuclear movement—a demand that resonated among scientists with their traditional commitment to maximum communication and the sharing of research. In order to increase the impact of their crusade, Commoner and his allies created a citizens' committee in St. Louis that not only disseminated the latest scientific evidence to the general public, but also pressed the government for greater openness. Soon similar groups sprang up in cities and college towns from Philadelphia to Palo Alto. To maintain their effectiveness in a political atmosphere still tainted by McCarthyism, the scientists stressed that they were not conducting a partisan campaign, but simply publicizing the results of the best available research. The committee, a 1962 brochure explained, took "no position on political or military issues except the position that a free people must be an informed people."[84]

The St. Louis activists' most effective gambit was inspired by a 1958 journal article suggesting that if strontium 90 was as ubiquitous as so many scientists believed, it could be measured by examining baby teeth. Thus was born the St. Louis Baby Tooth Survey, a local, and eventually national, call for parents to send their children's baby teeth to be tested for radioactivity. Soon St. Louis's dental schools were deluged with tiny teeth, some 25,000 by 1960; ultimately 200,000 by 1966. As anticipated, the lab results showed that a massive rise in the presence of strontium 90 in the teeth coincided with the onset of the atmospheric testing of nuclear weapons. Children born in 1963 had fifty times as much strontium 90 in their teeth as those born in 1950.[85]

The campaign against nuclear testing had spread far beyond its small community of politically active physical scientists. Now, the peace movement reentered the political arena. Although it was not a primarily academic endeavor, the largest and most influential peace group of the late 1950s and early 1960s, the Committee for a Sane Nuclear Policy (known as SANE), had ties to the scientists' movement. Many of its members and, as of 1963, both its co-chairs—the Harvard historian H. Stuart Hughes and the Case Western Reserve pediatrician Benjamin Spock—were academics. The organization's political orientation was ambiguous. Its original leaders were Cold War liberals who, when the group came under fire from the right, purged its staff and chapters of their supposedly communist members. But many of its affiliates in places like Ithaca and Philadelphia resisted anticommunism; they felt their campaigns against nuclear testing and, after 1961, fallout shelters were too important for them to worry about leftist infiltrators. And, in any event, the organization's rapid growth showed how respectable the anti-nuclear movement had become.[86]

"Insider" Scientists and Arms Control

At the same time as Pauling, Commoner, and their allies in SANE and other peace groups were building their public campaign against nuclear testing, many of the nation's top physicists were quietly pursuing the same goal. After all, most scientists shared a basic consensus about the problems that nuclear weapons presented and the possible solutions to them. Differences were mainly about tactics, not goals. Should they rock the boat or pull strings from inside? These disagreements were not unique to the scientific community either then or later; all political activists within the academy operated across a spectrum that ranged from networking with cabinet officials to destroying draft board records. What was unique was that in the aftermath of World War II, because of the technical issues that nuclear weapons introduced, scientists had gained access to the government's top policy makers. As a result, many of those who had that access believed they

FIGURE 3.2. Benjamin Spock in a SANE ad run in the *New Jersey Herald*, May 24, 1962. © DG 058, SANE, Inc. Records and Ephemera, Newspaper Advertisement collection, Swarthmore College Peace Collection.

could be more effective working from within the power structure than organizing a movement from below.[87]

Oppenheimer was the quintessential scientific insider, privy to the highest levels of nuclear decision making until he lost his security clearance in 1954 due to a policy disagreement and personal conflict with the head of the Atomic Energy Commission. His downfall revealed that even the nation's most eminent academics risked serious consequences for taking difficult positions especially if, like Oppenheimer, they had once consorted with the Left. As a result, those scientists who hoped to influence policy debates pulled back from controversy. They were concerned above all with eliminating the threat of a nuclear holocaust, but they shrank from using moral arguments to make their case in the hopes that a more "realistic" approach would increase their credibility. And, to a certain extent, that approach worked. They were able to use their technical expertise to convince Kennedy and his advisers that it was safe to sign a limited test ban treaty.[88]

In a sign of how the times had changed, in May 1963 the scientific luminaries Hans Bethe and Freeman Dyson also gave their names to a petition calling for an end to atmospheric testing.[89] Such an action showed that for mainstream liberals, during the academic golden age in the early 1960s, a combination of public education, newspaper ads, and insider access produced considerable confidence in their ability to influence American policy.

Vietnam destroyed that cozy illusion.

4

"THE BERKELEY INVENTION"

The Student Movement Begins

In 1970, the President's Commission on Campus Unrest, chaired by the former governor of Pennsylvania William Scranton, noted that most of that unrest consisted of "entirely peaceful and orderly manifestations of dissent." It also explained that, basically, it had all begun at Berkeley.[1] Student protests had shaken up American campuses since the eighteenth century, but the 1964 Free Speech Movement (FSM) at the University of California received extraordinary attention.[2] What happened there affected the entire academic community—and not just because, as *The Report of the President's Commission on Campus Unrest* noted, it "became the prototype for student protest."[3] Those events also determined how the rest of the nation came to think about higher education for decades to come.

According to the Scranton Commission, the "Berkeley Invention" was "an authentic political invention—a new and complex mixture of issues, tactics, emotions, and setting."[4] For the first time, students engaged in nonviolent civil disobedience on their campuses, applying the tactics of the civil rights movement to their own local issues. At Berkeley specifically, students were opposing the university's peculiarly repressive regulations on expression and demanding the right to engage in political activities on and off campus. But it seemed like a harbinger of something more.

Universally considered the leading US public university, Berkeley had been propelled to eminence by California's postwar boom and the energetic empire building of its ambitious presidents Robert Sproul and Clark Kerr.[5] In a famous series of lectures at Harvard in the spring of 1963, Kerr had touted his institution as a "multiversity," a driver of economic progress that was to dominate the upper echelons of higher education.[6] The school's stature was such that, Harvard dean McGeorge Bundy actually maintained, "every day the sun shines in Berkeley is a dark day at Harvard."[7] California's faculty glittered with stars—Nobel laureates as well as many prolific public intellectuals whose response to the Free Speech Movement helped to shape how the rest of the nation came to view it.

Perhaps because the FSM caught them by surprise, most Berkeley professors tried to remain uninvolved during the early stages of the crisis. Of course, they noticed what was going on. "You couldn't avoid it," the political scientist Robert Scalapino explained.[8] On the morning of October 1, 1964, hundreds, then thousands, of students sat down around a police car in the middle of the campus to keep it from taking an activist to jail. For thirty-two hours a succession of speakers stood on the roof of the car debating the restrictive speech policies. "I stayed to watch," a graduate student and future university president recalled, "but I did not stay long. I recall thinking: 'This is happening and it is important. But it's not happening to me. I have my work to do.'"[9] Others felt the same way. "I'd gone by it and I'd gone to it," the sociologist Neil Smelser noted. "But I wasn't inclined to do anything about it." The most common faculty response was, in Scalapino's words, "astonishment."[10]

Yet Berkeley's professors were hardly political virgins, as shown by the battles over the anti-communist loyalty oath in 1949. Though very much an artifact of McCarthyism, the oath was also a product of the University of California's specific vulnerability as a liberal institution in a politically volatile state whose powerful conservatives were determined to eliminate dissent from their flagship campus.[11] By 1964 the issues had changed, but to keep those external forces at bay, the administration had essentially banned all political activity on campus. The University of California was, in fact, much more repressive than comparable institutions.[12]

By the late 1950s and early 1960s, a small, but active, handful of professors—"the civil-libertarian left-wing of the faculty" the histo-

rian Carl Schorske called them—had been working to eliminate constraints on outside speakers and student political activities. "Long before the students were activists in these matters," Schorske explained,
"the faculty was activated." A few of its members—the historians
Charles Sellers, Kenneth Stampp, and Lawrence Levine, and the sociologist John Leggett among them—took leadership roles in the local
civil rights movement.[13] On the Berkeley campus, they rolled back the
ban on communist speakers by sponsoring a lecture by the party's historian Herbert Aptheker.[14] They also bombarded the administration
with letters and petitions protesting its harassment of SLATE, the left-
wing student organization formed in 1957 to bring such real-world
issues as racial discrimination and freedom of speech into student
government.[15] And they provided support for the students arrested at
the raucous protest against the San Francisco HUAC hearings in April
1960.[16] But at no point did these faculty civil libertarians drop their
moderate tone or adopt a confrontational posture.[17]

Edward Strong, the chancellor of the Berkeley campus, was a well-
liked former philosophy professor who had been an outspoken opponent of the loyalty oath. As an administrator, however, he felt compelled to uphold the regulations.[18] The president, Clark Kerr, had a
national reputation as an innovative educator and had, in fact, been
appointed largely to reassure the faculty that the bad old loyalty oath
days were gone.[19] A former labor mediator, he considered himself an
expert conciliator.[20] But as the campus unraveled during the fall of
1964, relations between the two leaders, never good to begin with,
deteriorated to such an extent that the chancellor privately admitted, "My trust in the President has been shaken. I don't know where
I stand."[21]

Strong's distrust was well placed. Kerr's behavior was, if nothing
else, erratic. Kerr was under so much pressure from conservative regents, politicians, alumni, and the media that the measures he did take
to open up the institution remained rather narrow, imposing substantial limitations on outside speakers, while letting serious restrictions
on political activities remain. Kerr also came under attack for trying
to centralize the university; not consulting the faculty about a major
change in the academic calendar; and—shades of McCarthyism—for

firing Eli Katz in 1964 for taking the Fifth Amendment before HUAC several years before.[22]

Yet even as Kerr was limiting free speech, he was also protecting it. Not only did he refuse demands to punish the students arrested in the HUAC fracas, but he also convinced the regents to approve the appointment to the faculty of the ex-communist biologist Leon Wofsy.[23] He even managed to lift the ban on communist speakers. Thus, because the institution appeared to be shedding its repressive past, the American Association of University Professors conferred upon Kerr and the board of regents its Alexander Meiklejohn Award for Academic Freedom in April 1964.[24]

By that spring, the school had a not-undeserved reputation for political exuberance. "Things are happening at Berkeley," the political scientists Sheldon Wolin and John Schaar announced in the *New York Review of Books*. "This reputation acts as a magnet, drawing young people with activist yearnings from all over the nation."[25] In the spring of 1964, those activists threw themselves into the Bay Area's struggle for racial equality—demonstrating, sitting-in, and shopping-in to force businesses to hire African Americans. Dozens of Berkeley students, including the future FSM leader Mario Savio, who was soon to join the Mississippi Summer, were among the 167 protesters arrested at a sleep-in at the San Francisco Sheraton Palace Hotel.[26]

As the fall term got under way, the prospect of continued demonstrations worried the administration. The presidents of the nation's leading research universities had been warned that student activists in the civil rights movement might create trouble. Berkeley, Chancellor Strong recalled, was considered specifically endangered.[27] But as the free speech crisis unfolded, the university's response couldn't have been worse, exacerbated by what the sociologist Nathan Glazer called the school's "both rigid . . . and fragile" administration.[28] Toward the end of September, in the first of its several missteps, Strong's office banned political action on the strip of land bordering the campus, where student organizations had long recruited people for political activities.[29]

The ban seemed arbitrary at best. Activists assumed it had been prompted by local conservatives and defied the order.[30] The authorities suspended eight students. On September 30, several hundred peaceful demonstrators surged into the administration building demanding to be charged as well. The next day, the campus police arrested the former student and civil rights activist Jack Weinberg for refusing to budge from his suddenly illegal table. But a group of students blocked the police car Weinberg was in, and two and a half months of crisis began.[31]

Soon several thousand students surrounded the car while Savio and dozens of other speakers clambered onto its roof. The protesters represented a coalition that ranged from the Young Republicans to the Communist Party's Du Bois Club. Charles Sellers was one of the first and staunchest of the faculty members to support the students. From atop the police car, he explained that the administration's actions contravened the university's core educational values.[32] Other professors, both radicals and not-so-radicals like the sociologists Nathan Glazer and Seymour Martin Lipset, also climbed onto the police car to discuss the pros and cons of Berkeley's restrictions on political activity and the students' resort to direct action.[33]

Meanwhile faculty members and administrators scrambled to find some way out of the impasse before the police took action. Chancellor Strong threatened to sanction the student activists. "Freedom of speech by students on campus is not the issue," he declared. "The University cannot and will not allow students to engage in deliberate violations of law and order on campus."[34] Kerr took a softer line, fearful of violence. (Governor Edmund G. Brown had warned him to avoid another Mississippi or Alabama.) He was willing to meet with the students and to listen as well to the senior professors who were eager to broker a settlement.[35]

Known as the "group of 15," the would-be mediators were prominent and politically sophisticated people like Lipset, Glazer, and the philosopher Lewis Feuer.[36] Another key participant was the future dean of Harvard, Henry Rosovsky, who, while not sympathetic to the student protesters, was committed to conflict resolution and, as a fellow economist, had a direct line to Kerr. Several other faculty members

were also involved, among them Schorske, Smelser, the political scientists Scalapino and Paul Seabury, the philosopher Joseph Tussman,
and the sociologists William Petersen and William Kornhauser.[37]

Significantly, few, if any, of these professors supported the limitations on political expression. The regulations "seemed," one of them
recalled, "sort of out of touch with the evolving times."[38] Though no
friend of the FSM, Lipset strongly believed that those restrictions
were "irrelevant and destructive to the purposes of the university."[39]
In one area, at least, consensus reigned. Accordingly, while the so-
called "Pact of October 2," drafted by the faculty mediators and agreed
to by Kerr and the FSM leaders, obligated the students to "desist from
all forms of their illegal protest against University regulations," it also
contained provisions for a faculty-student-administration committee
to "conduct discussions . . . into all aspects of political behavior on
campus" and for a faculty committee to handle the cases of the eight
suspended students.[40]

That faculty committee concluded that although the eight students
had disobeyed the authorities, the regulations they defied were illegitimate. Accordingly, the committee recommended no action against
them, and that was that. But the newly formed Campus Committee on
Political Action that was to revise the regulations on political speech
and activity had a harder time. The FSM's leaders initially considered
it illegitimate because the administration, instead of the academic
senate, had appointed its faculty representatives.[41] Reconstituted, that
committee got down to work, only to reach an impasse within a few
weeks. The students insisted that the university had no right to sanction them if they broke the law off campus, while the administration
refused to waive proceedings against dissidents who recruited students for actions that resulted in their arrests. The students were correct. For the university to punish them for their "advocacy" of illegal
action would, in fact, have violated their First Amendment rights. But
since the courts had yet to completely resolve the constitutional issues, the university authorities would not budge.[42]

Worse yet, Kerr came to view the FSM's criticism of his position as
a personal attack:

By changing the definition of free speech to include advocacy, they were engaged, with great success, in transforming me overnight from a courageous and successful defender of free speech and winner of academe's most prestigious award into a reactionary opponent of free advocacy.[43]

A number of faculty members who, like Glazer, had originally supported the students agreed. Alienated by the FSM's strident language and disruptive behavior, they could not condone what they considered the students' demand to break the law with impunity. No compromise was possible and the committee simply "fell apart."[44]

Meanwhile, an informal group of the left-liberal professors who had long been pressing for greater political freedom were meeting in Charles Sellers's office and each other's private homes to plan how to rally the rest of the faculty to the students' cause. They had closer ties to the Free Speech Movement's leaders than most of their colleagues, and thus felt positioned, as one of them put it, "to hammer out a policy that the faculty could believe in" that would also be acceptable to FSM and that the administration and regents could then adopt without losing face.[45] The membership of the group fluctuated. There may have been about fifteen or twenty of them. They had, the biologist Howard Schachman recalled, "no divisions, . . . no pride of authorship. Charlie [Sellers] was always at the typewriter, always writing what we were working out." The group's most junior members, the historians Reginald Zelnik and Lawrence Levine, became its main contact with Mario Savio and the FSM Steering Committee because, as Zelnik put it, "we could, to various degrees, speak the same political language."[46]

Persuading their colleagues to support the students' position, however, was a challenge. Though almost all the Berkeley professors who took a position on the issues disapproved of the FSM's resort to civil disobedience, they were just as hostile to the university's repressive bungling. That ambivalence made it hard for the academic senate to act. At its meeting on October 12, for example, the senate passed contradictory resolutions both supporting and opposing the Free Speech Movement. The following month's meeting produced an equally equivocal result. Many faculty members were, according to Smelser, more "confused and perplexed" about the issues than anything else.[47]

The Bust and Beyond

The logjam ended abruptly in early December. On November 28, without consulting Kerr or heeding the warnings of his faculty advisers, Chancellor Strong deferred to the regents' desire to discipline the student activists and sent letters to four of the FSM's top leaders citing them for their activities in the police car incident.[48] The students were outraged, and the faculty were not much happier. "While this was not technically a breach of faith," the moderate historian Henry May explained, "it seemed to be contrary to the agreement of October 2 and subsequent negotiations."[49]

On the afternoon of December 2, about a thousand people including a few faculty members and the folksinger Joan Baez marched into the administration building, Sproul Hall, demanding that the administration rescind the threatened sanctions. The occupation was peaceful. The students sang songs, played cards, did their homework, celebrated Hanukkah, spoke with sympathetic professors, and mulled over their options. Though Kerr hoped to negotiate a settlement, he was overruled by the governor. At about three o'clock in the morning, 367 local and campus police officers, sheriff's deputies, and members of the State Highway Patrol began to clear the building. They arrested 773 people. Some walked out; others went limp and had to be carried out. The whole operation took nearly twelve hours. Despite some complaints, the police were much more restrained than they would be later on.[50]

Although a few professors, among them the mathematician Stephen Smale and the sociologist John Leggett, had been inside the administration building, all but one left before the police arrived.[51] Along with dozens of their colleagues, they went to the Santa Rita prison farm to bail out their students and bring them back to the campus. The bust became a wake-up call for a number of previously uninvolved professors. The East Asia scholar Franz Schurmann probably spoke for most of those individuals: "I have not been an active participant, but events of the last few days have changed my mind."[52] The recently arrived young English professor Morton Paley was a similar convert. He had not been concerned until, as he recalled, "I saw the police covering the windows in Sproul with newspapers" so that "you couldn't see what they were doing." It was "so appalling," he could not remain uninvolved. As he stood in line with his colleagues at the local courthouse to vouch for their arrested students, the eminent Americanist Henry Nash Smith apologized to him: "Mr. Paley, when we had our interview, we didn't tell you you would have to do this."[53]

As the arrests continued throughout the morning, a crowd of several thousand gathered outside Sproul to hear the usual speakers and figure out what to do. It was clear that it was no longer possible to conduct business as usual. The graduate student TAs within the Free Speech Movement had called a strike, hoping to force the faculty to act. Caught between their dislike of the FSM's civil disobedience and their outrage at the mass arrests, Berkeley's professors could either cancel their classes in sympathy with the students or else hold them and, thus, support the administration. Even for someone like Carl Schorske, whose support for the FSM was never in doubt, it was an agonizing dilemma. "I will cooperate with the strike against the policy of the university," he explained, "but I will not stop my teaching function come hell or high water, because that's not what I'm here for." He moved his classes off campus.[54] Other faculty members did meet their regular classes, only to talk about the issues and then dismiss the students.[55]

In the meantime, a number of faculty heavies inserted themselves into the action. They felt that the university had lost control by calling in the police and that it was up to them to save it. The head of the political science department, Robert Scalapino, was already in touch with Kerr. He planned to organize the department chairs into an alternative administrative body that would, in Scalapino's words, "end the turmoil" by creating "a kind of centrist position that would bring the bulk of students and the administration together."[56] Nathan Glazer called an impromptu faculty meeting right after the bust. Castigating both the administration and the students as "inept, obstinate, impossible to bring to reason," Glazer told eight hundred or so faculty

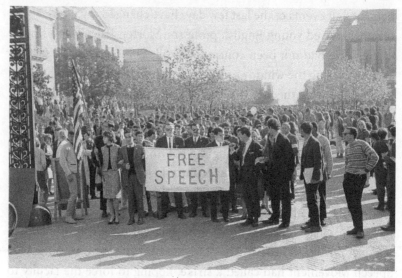

FIGURE 4.1. Berkeley professors supporting the Free Speech Movement, November 20, 1964. Morton Paley, in sunglasses holding up the sign (*center*), John Leggett to his right, John Searle to his left. © The Bancroft Library, University of California, Berkeley

members, "We are here, not to take sides, but to protest the action of today."[57] In the discussion that followed, the history chairman Henry May then offered a resolution recommending amnesty for the students, the immediate implementation of new regulations for political action, and the creation of a faculty committee to take disciplinary action out of the hands of the regents. Professors from all sides proposed additional measures. There was one from the political scientist Herbert McClosky representing the Sellers group of civil libertarians that demanded "that no student be prosecuted by the university for participating in any off-campus activity." There was also an abortive one from the campus AAUP chapter, calling for the replacement of Chancellor Strong as well as a resolution by the philosopher John Searle pleading for a suspension of classes until things cleared up, since "the presence of mass police destroys the atmosphere of teaching." Though Glazer adjourned the meeting before a vote on Searle's proposal, all the others were overwhelmingly adopted.[58]

The emotional turmoil that pervaded the two-hour meeting—which had no official standing—revealed how deeply the faculty had been affected. The language of speakers from both the Right and the Left smacked of the apocalypse. One maintained that "the university is dead today." Others talked about "disaster," "the collapse of the university," "the desperate situation now confronting the University," and so on.[59] Significantly, despite their serious differences of opinion, most of the professors there had lost patience with the administration's ineptitude. They would take matters into their own hands.

Over the next few days, Berkeley's professors scrambled to develop proposals for the official faculty meeting scheduled for December 8. "The whole campus," Smelser recalled, "was beginning to form into groups of lone rangers and small groups who all thought they had something to say about the settling of the big developing controversy."[60] There were two key issues: how to deal with off-campus illegal activities and how to handle future disciplinary cases.[61] Scalapino's more moderate and conservative group wanted, according to May, "to support authority of a sort and to leave things as they were rather than radically change." Most of them recognized, however, that, as May put it, "No settlement is possible which does not take account of the strong emotions now influencing our students and many of our faculty."[62]

If Berkeley was to be pacified, May et al. believed, the authorities would have to accept student amnesty and grant more power to the faculty. Although reluctant, Kerr apparently acquiesced. On Sunday, December 6, he canceled the next morning's classes to allow each department to discuss the issues in advance of an all-campus meeting at the outdoor Greek Theatre in the afternoon, where he and Scalapino would present the chairmen's solution.[63]

Meanwhile, on the left, the FSM's faculty supporters were busily organizing. Two members of the Sellers group also belonged to the academic senate's Committee on Academic Freedom (CAF). That committee, its member Kenneth Stampp recalled, "began meeting and meeting and meeting"—with other professors, administrators, legal experts, and the steering committee of the Free Speech Movement.[64] The CAF and the Sellers circle met informally on Sunday to discuss a draft proposal that they felt would satisfy the student activists as well as the faculty. That meeting resulted in the formation of the "Committee of 200" (the seating capacity of the auditorium in which they met). With the help of some law school professors, especially the young constitutional law authority Robert Cole, the faculty's main FSM sympathizers hammered out the 200's resolution. It called for the "reasonable regulation of political activity to prevent interference with the normal functions of the University," but stipulated that, in accordance with the First Amendment, there would be no restrictions on the content of that speech or advocacy. At the last minute, to avoid future confusion, the drafters modified "reasonable regulation" to specify that such regulation could apply only to an activity's "time, place, and manner." They also included provisions for giving the faculty control over "future disciplinary measures in the area of political activity."[65]

Two sets of proposals confronted the Berkeley faculty: the pro-administration one produced by Scalapino's Council of Department Chairmen and the pro-student one developed by the Committee of 200.[66] At some of the meetings of humanities and social science departments before the Greek Theatre conclave, serious opposition to Scalapino and Kerr's solution emerged, as radical professors and graduate students felt it inadequately protected free speech. Philip Selznick, the chair of the sociology department, disagreed so strongly with the Scalapino committee that he refused to join the other chairmen on the stage.[67]

Somewhere between twelve and twenty thousand students, professors, and interested outsiders packed the Greek Theatre that Monday afternoon. Beforehand, the FSM's Savio had asked Scalapino if he could speak or at least make an announcement at the end of the program, but Scalapino refused. He and Kerr were to be the only speakers. Nevertheless, just as Scalapino was officially adjourning the meeting, Savio strode to the microphone, only to be pulled roughly off the stage by two university police officers. Pandemonium ensued. A few minutes later, Savio was allowed to return to the podium, where he announced a rally to follow.

That one short episode, May recalled, resulted in "the complete and permanent collapse of anything like this compromise program."[68] The moderate liberals who dominated the faculty lost confidence in

FIGURE 4.2. Robert Scalapino, chair of the political science department and pro-war East Asian specialist, supporting the University of California administration at the Greek Theatre, Berkeley, December 7, 1964. © The Bancroft Library, University of California, Berkeley.

the administration. They were so upset that, at least temporarily, they were willing to side with the Free Speech Movement.[69] The denouement came the following afternoon when the academic senate voted 824–115 to accept the resolution drawn up by the Committee of 200. Thousands of students milled around outside Wheeler Hall, listening to the debates over loudspeakers and responding with boos and cheers. Afterward the exuberant crowd greeted the professors with applause, tears, and hugs.[70]

There was, however, more opposition within the faculty than the lopsided vote indicated. It coalesced around an amendment presented by Lewis Feuer, who wanted to specify that the content of speech or advocacy would not be restricted "provided that it is directed to no immediate act of force or violence." In an overblown and somewhat incoherent argument, Feuer not only invoked the specter of the Nazi students of the 1930s, but also envisioned a student Ku Klux Klan chapter that could "advocate . . . defacing Jewish synagogues, Negro and Catholic churches," unless the faculty insisted that there would be no "university sanctuary for these acts of speech, advocacy, and organization." It was clear that Feuer and his supporters, including Glazer, believed that the FSM's "nonviolent uncivil disobedience" was a direct threat to the university—and even perhaps to democracy itself.[71]

In opposition, the FSM's supporters referred to the Constitution as well as to the need to abolish the kind of paternalism that had originally spawned Berkeley's restrictive policies. One philosopher noted that the students would interpret that amendment as a hostile reimposition of "the same kind of punitive threats and actualities as has led to this miserable situation in the first place." It was a powerful argument, especially to an audience that wanted the unrest to stop. The atmosphere was so "highly charged," business school professor Earl Cheit recalled, that "by this time people were in no mood for amendments." Feuer's amendment went down to defeat, 737–284.[72]

Quite a few faculty members were unhappy about their own support for what the Russian historian Martin Malia called "the sacred resolutions." He had voted for the Committee of 200's proposal, he explained, but "I genuinely did not understand what was involved in this. I was concerned with getting the university back on its feet."[73]

Cheit also voted for the resolutions despite his strong opposition to the "terrible idea" of having the faculty handle student discipline.[74] Neil Smelser was similarly distressed. "As we emerged from Wheeler," he later recalled,

> there was this huge clapping and applauding and yelling and cheering and whistling for the faculty. I remember feeling almost nauseated at this. I wasn't opposed to the students, but I was sufficiently alienated from some aspects of that whole episode that I didn't want to be given credit for supporting it.[75]

That ambivalence was probably common. His colleagues wound up in broad agreement with the FSM's demands because "nothing else could bring peace to the University."[76] That pattern of accommodation and regret recurred repeatedly during the next few years at Berkeley and elsewhere, helping to undermine the stature and credibility of the entire academic community.

Evidence of those regrets emerged a week later when the faculty named the emergency executive committee that was to provide temporary leadership for the university. The Committee of 200 put together a slate of the usual suspects—Schachman, Schorske, Searle, Selznick, and Tussman among them.[77] Their colleagues on the right organized as well. Lipset seems to have been the most active political operator, joined by the economists Dale Jorgenson and Walter Galenson as well as Feuer and Malia. They sought a restoration of traditional authority. They worried that the "SLATE slate" would allow, in Malia's words, "a takeover of the senate apparatus by a left group, a politically motivated group that wanted to reorganize the university."[78]

As large as the margins of victory had been on December 8, only half the faculty had been there, most of them from the College of Letters and Science. The mail ballots in the committee election may have provided a more representative sample. Schorske was the only member of the 200—as well as the only representative of the liberal arts departments—to be elected. Everyone else came from the professional schools: business administration, law, and agriculture. They were political moderates who, Schorske recalled, "had not spoken out . . . or taken strong positions." Instead, they were well-known, competent, experienced "people with a long campus history of committee work," the kind of established faculty leaders who normally ascended into deanships and other high administrative positions.[79]

Actually, the group worked well together. "As a committee," Schorske explained, ". . . our major responsibility was and had to be to the faculty, making sure it held together in practical pursuit of proper academic principles."[80] Only with a united faculty would it be possible for the committee to defuse the conflict. This was not an easy task. Not only had there been enormous hostility to the FSM in the press and the general public (generated in part by the FBI's COINTELPRO counter-subversive campaign), but neither Kerr nor, especially, Strong was happy with what the faculty had done on December 8.[81] Nevertheless, when Schorske and his colleagues lobbied the regents before and during their meeting on December 18, they succeeded—in part.[82]

Although the regents accepted some of the academic senate's resolutions, they refused to surrender their ultimate authority over student discipline. They did, however, promise to delegate that authority to the president and chancellors, "who will seek advice of the appropriate faculty committees in individual cases." That language was sufficiently vague for both sides to claim a sort of victory and postpone further divisive discussions.[83] The faculty's representatives had more success with eliminating the university's restrictions on political speech and activity. A carefully drafted memorandum by Robert Cole and two other legal experts explained that recent court decisions had ruled against imposing restrictions on the "content or substance of expression."[84] It convinced the regents to issue a statement that they "do not contemplate that advocacy or content of speech shall be restricted beyond the purview of the First and Fourteenth Amendments to the Constitution."[85]

The next day, Berkeley's Christmas vacation began and the campus calmed down. Soon Chancellor Strong was on his way out; and his temporary replacement, Martin Meyerson, was making conciliatory statements about the rights of dissenters and need for educational reform.[86] The faculty's intervention had saved the day, providing political cover for both the administration and the regents. For the partisans of the FSM, this was the faculty's "finest hour," producing, in the words of Sheldon Wolin and John Schaar, "a climate of respect and concern that offers more promise than has been present in a long time that the future of this University can be a noble one."[87] For President Kerr, it was "the ultimate triumph of conciliation." The mollified students would go back to their classrooms, and the Free Speech Movement would melt away.[88]

In the immediate aftermath of the crisis—and for the next fifty years—scholars, pundits, and veterans of the Free Speech Movement tried to figure out what had happened and why. As the educational historian Robert Cohen has pointed out, much of the FSM's impact came from its success: it did bring political freedom to the Berkeley campus.[89] It did so largely because its goal was universally shared. What self-respecting academic could oppose free speech?[90] Adding to the FSM's legitimacy in the faculty's eyes was its connection to the civil rights movement—at that time a source of unquestioned moral authority within the liberal mainstream.[91] Equally important was that, despite its civil disobedience, the FSM was not a radical group. Almost all the students involved, as well as their faculty supporters, were moderates or liberals of one sort or another. They did not want to change society; they simply wanted their institution to live up to its stated mission of broadening minds and seeking the truth.[92]

Significantly, the faculty also shared an aversion to the administration's ineptitude.[93] One of Kerr's main tactical errors had been demonizing the students. Indirectly fed misinformation by the FBI, Kerr actually engaged in Red-baiting, blaming Berkeley's troubles on a "hard core group of demonstrators" that "contained . . . persons identified as being sympathetic with the Communist Party and Communist causes."[94] That tactic not only destroyed the student activists' respect for Kerr, but alienated the faculty veterans of the loyalty oath struggle without mollifying the conservatives, who couldn't understand why the president didn't just, as one irate citizen put it, "expel all the rebels."[95] In addition, Kerr had the unseemly habit of blaming others, including the faculty and, especially, Chancellor Strong. Strong "was made the fall guy," Vice Chancellor Lincoln Constance recalled. "No question about it."[96]

The Aftermath

Although the free speech crisis officially ended on December 18, the university's troubles were far from over. Even as he urged his colleagues to support the resolution, the physicist Charles Zemach had warned them, "Let no one believe that questions of law and order and discipline are being solved by the motion before us. . . . [L]et's not kid ourselves that the future is all peaches and cream."[97] A few weeks later, in *Commentary*, Nathan Glazer noted, "I—and many other faculty members—are filled with foreboding." Seymour Martin Lipset had a similar response, claiming that he had "reacted to the seeming 'solution' of the Berkeley crisis in December 1964 . . . with pessimism."[98]

Glazer and Lipset were right. They soon decamped for Harvard, joining a handful of colleagues who, modeling themselves on the so-called White Russian opponents of the Bolshevik Revolution, actually referred to themselves as the "White Berkeleyans."[99] "I know personally of five or six faculty members who are leaving," the economic historian David Landes wrote to the *New York Times*, "not because of lack of sympathy with 'free speech' or 'political action,' but because, as one put it, who wants to teach at the University of Saigon?" Landes, too, soon took off for Cambridge.[100]

Lipset had been approached by Harvard in the spring of 1964, but postponed going for a year so that it wouldn't look as if he was fleeing the scene.[101] A confidant of Clark Kerr's, Lipset had opposed the students' use of direct action, arguing publicly "that civil disobedience is only justified in the absence of democratic rights."[102] He had even mounted the roof of the captured police car to tell the students why they should work through regular channels. But his response revealed how little he understood about the students' position. According to two former graduate students, Lipset was on the police car "trying to expound his theory about pluralism" and

> telling the students that they should resolve their problems through voting and people shouted back at him, "But we can't—." You know, he said, "The university is pluralist," and blah, blah, blah, blah. And then,

people shouted, "But we can't vote!"∗ . . . And then he said, "Well, but you've committed violence." And people said, "What violence?" And then he said, "Well, you've destroyed property." And people shouted, "What property? We haven't destroyed any property?" . . . And he said, "Well, this police car. You've done at least a thousand dollars-worth of damage." And people shouted, "You're standing on it!" . . . He's probably the heaviest person who stood on the police car all afternoon. And he looked down at the police car. . . . And then— . . . Then he climbed off, I think.[103]

The future dean of Harvard, Henry Rosovsky, also abandoned Berkeley for Cambridge, albeit reluctantly. "I was very much out of sympathy with the student movement," he explained.

I just felt very strongly that the university was not a legitimate target. I loved universities, I felt these were illegitimate and cheap attacks. . . . The FSM . . . for people like me who were politically astute . . . really ruined things. . . . It was impossible to work and I started looking for other jobs from the belief that wherever I went there would be harmony and peace.[104]

Harvard was the main, though not the only, refuge. Among others, Lewis Feuer went to the University of Toronto, the political scientist William Petersen to Ohio State, and the economist Walter Galenson to Cornell. They had all strongly opposed the students, viewing the FSM and its leaders as irrational, if not manipulative and totalitarian.[105]

Yet some of their colleagues on the left eventually departed as well, Carl Schorske among them. "I was not outraged by the defiance of legal authority," Schorske explained, "because authority was violating rights. I didn't favor disorderly behavior, but it didn't bother me so deeply." He did, however, become upset about "the cultural deterioration" of Berkeley, the hippies and dropouts on Telegraph Avenue, "really sick people, Berkeley counterculture, students and others of wasted lives."[106]

∗ The voting age at the time was still twenty-one.

When Schorske left in 1969, however, it was because he felt unable to balance his desire to participate in the antiwar movement and university governance with his commitment to scholarship. After serving on the emergency executive committee, he did a stint as an administrator. He "was feeling to some degree eaten up. . . . My work suffered greatly." The fevered atmosphere of the late sixties did not help. It was hard to operate politically when

> you have somebody at your right who thinks you're a Maoist, and you have somebody at your left who thinks you're a fascist. And you're in the middle between these two, and every man in the whole community has exactly the same experience. No matter if he's way over to the right, or way over to the left.

Finally, he was upset about the failure of his colleagues to establish a new interdisciplinary program in cultural history. Thus, when "an enormously tempting" offer came from Princeton and the Institute for Advanced Study, he reluctantly took it.[107]

After December 8, underlying tensions within the faculty had begun to surface. "From here on," Henry May explained, "in the Academic Senate there were two sides approximately equal in numbers, and . . . equal in academic distinction."[108] There was also a small cadre of professors on the far right who had been opposed to the students from the start. Though they had little influence on their colleagues, they had connections to the FBI and to the more conservative regents.[109] May identified with the so-called Faculty Forum, an organization formed in late December under the leadership of Glazer, Martin Malia, and the Japanese historian Delmer Brown that explicitly sought to counter the influence of the Left. They hoped to recruit those of their colleagues who disliked the FSM, but "had not identified themselves with either the right or the left." Most of these people considered themselves moderates, even liberals, but within the Berkeley context they were on the right.[110] Their trajectory foreshadowed an increasingly common one, as self-professed liberals shed some of their liberalism in the face of student unrest.

The main fathers of the Faculty Forum came from the history department, which by the end of the academic year was splitting in half. While Sellers, Schorske, Zelnik, and some others remained on the left, May, Stampp, and a number of others moved to the right. Nonetheless, May, as chair, was determined to hold the department together.[111] And he succeeded, creating what even someone as conservative as Malia called "a very civilized atmosphere." Schorske agreed, noting that history was "such an intellectually loose discipline" that historians did not feel that colleagues with a different approach were challenging the foundations of their scholarship.[112]

Such was not the case within Berkeley's social science departments, where acrimonious disputes led to open warfare that deformed personnel and curricular decisions as well as destroyed individual friendships. In most cases, the more politically and historically oriented professors tended to be on the left, while the quantitative ones, like demographers, veered right. The sociology department, one well-informed observer noted, "practically blew apart."[113] Old friends stopped talking to one another.[114] Within a few years, those dissenters who didn't leave the university deserted the department. The chair, Philip Selznick, ended up in the law school, while Reinhard Bendix and some other sociologists found niches in political science and even psychology.[115]

Things were just as fraught among political scientists. Although Robert Scalapino claimed that the department weathered the crisis without too much damage, its left-wing members felt under siege.[116] "It was awful, terrible," Norman Jacobson recalled. "People not speaking to each other, hating each other. . . . And by the spring of 1965, the department was wracked." Locks were being changed.[117] The fissures were as much methodological as political. "There was that division between behaviorists and theorists." The quants and hard-science types moved right, along with those who had ties to the government like Scalapino and Paul Seabury.[118] The then-untenured Michael Rogin recalled:

> If you had a radical critique of American politics, that was seen as methodologically illegitimate. They claimed that it wasn't a matter of the politics, it was a matter of the methods. So people who were try-

ing to work on American politics in historical and theoretical ways were running into trouble.[119]

Sheldon Wolin, a traditional political theorist and the only political scientist within the leadership of the Committee of 200, felt increasingly marginalized. Personnel decisions became politicized as the department's more conservative leaders sought to hire "apolitical" candidates. As elsewhere, people began to leave. David Apter went to Yale, John Schaar to Santa Cruz, and Wolin himself, first to Santa Cruz and then to Princeton. Jacobson went half-time into the psychiatry department and then into the experimental college.[120]

Significantly, most of the internecine struggles occurred within the university's largest unit, the College of Letters and Science. The most prominent activists came from the history, sociology, political science, philosophy, English, and mathematics departments. Most scientists were seemingly uninvolved, as were the engineers, and the business and law school professors.[121]

Pundits and Protesters: Professors Assess the FSM

Because the events at Berkeley received so much national attention and because a number of the university's most politically active professors were public intellectuals who wrote for the mainstream media, their assessments of their experiences with the FSM influenced the way many outside academics and ordinary citizens came to view both the Berkeley troubles and later outbreaks of student activism elsewhere.[122]

Upheaval, rebellion, turmoil, chaos, crisis, and, especially, revolution—whatever language they used and whatever views they held about the student movement, almost all the professors emphasized its unprecedented nature. They believed that they had just lived through a world-shaking event. It was, for Wolin, "truly a revolutionary moment; there had been nothing like it before." Others described it as "a kind of small-scale revolution . . . that . . . overthrew a whole structure of authority" and "a small-scale but genuine revolution."[123] They wrote books and articles titled "Rebellion at Berkeley," "Berkeley Revolt," "The 'New Left' Uprising at Berkeley," "Revolution at Berkeley," and so on.[124]

Few championed the students' resort to direct action. Even Reginald Zelnik, perhaps the faculty member closest to Mario Savio and the FSM, could be critical.[125] The literary scholar Charles Muscatine, a key member of the Committee of 200, recalled that he felt "horrified" when Savio rushed onto the stage at the Greek Theatre.[126] The FSM's faculty supporters were much more impressed by its members' earnestness and commitment. "These are among our very best students," Philip Selznick declared.[127] Not only were they intellectually gifted and serious, but they were also idealistic.[128] Moreover, most of them were not radicals.[129] Their "radicalism," Wolin and Schaar explained, "consisted in little more than devotion to some traditional principles which their elders had taught them." They were political novices who subscribed to no overarching ideology. "With few exceptions," Wolin and Schaar reported, "they behaved with dignity and restraint."[130] Not only did they take off their shoes when they mounted the police car, but, as another observer noted, most of the demonstrators "wore jackets and ties, or skirts and blouses and spoke in respectful terms to administrators." They were not going to destroy the university.[131]

The movement's critics conceded most of these points. Savio, in particular, evoked considerable respect from his opponents.[132] Nonetheless, there was no mistaking the anger and, particularly, the paternalism that dominated the response of the administration and its faculty supporters to the FSM. Time and again, the students asked to be taken seriously as political actors, and time and again they were brushed off as immature.

The traditional culture of American higher education seems partly at fault here. Based on the doctrine of in loco parentis, the university denied students the power to control their own social and personal lives, treating them as less than adults in areas they were perfectly competent to handle. Because that paternalistic attitude rendered the students powerless, the administration seemed unable to concede the legitimacy of their demands for political freedom. As a result, the authorities paid insufficient attention to the *content* of those demands, while seriously overreacting to their *style*. In particular, the administrators were so offended by the students' disrespectful behavior and their "language of the gutter," that they felt personally attacked—and responded in kind.[133] The biologist Lincoln Constance, the vice chancellor for academic affairs, recalled wanting to "smack Savio right in the face because he was insolent and brash, and frankly I thought he was off his rocker."[134]

It is easy to understand why the embattled Clark Kerr came to develop "increasingly negative" feelings about Savio and his colleagues' stubborn refusal to abandon their First Amendment rights.[135] But it is harder to account for the overt enmity of the faculty. Vice Chancellor Constance observed:

> Most faculty members had some group of students they felt very close to particularly in the social sciences and they believed they could with their special knowledge, special relationship, put a quietus on it, and get the thing somehow in some kind of normal channels.
>
> What happened was that, okay, so they worked out something with this particular group of students, and then wham, the whole thing had moved down the street. They were just left talking to themselves. A lot of social science faculty, particularly, lost face over this, and quite a number of them left, I think, primarily for that reason because they had felt, indeed, that they could command the situation. But it was a very fluid situation, one that kept changing all the time.[136]

Henry May's assessment was the same. He viewed these disappointed faculty members as people who "think they can control the situation but get burned."[137] Most of these professors, still identifying as liberals and even socialists of a sort, had initially sympathized with the students' quest for political freedom and expected to mentor them in achieving it. But for people like Nathan Glazer, who were not only brushed off by the young people they had cultivated, but were then, in his words, "denounced orally and in print as 'finks' and stooges of President Kerr," it was understandable why they may have turned against the FSM.[138]

Nevertheless, the sheer hostility evinced seems disproportionate for a group of twenty-year-olds whose main crime was to use offensive language and occupy the administration building. "Irresponsible true believers," "a bunch of rowdies," "amoral," "anti-intellectual," 'totalitarian," "undemocratic," "extremist" were only some of the epithets hurled at the student protesters.[139] Perhaps the most extreme articulation of this antipathy came from Lewis Feuer, who claimed that the movement's tactics "sometimes remind one unpleasantly of young German students talking in a similar vein in the early 30s." His evidence: Savio's "seizure of the microphone at a meeting organized and conducted by a faculty group" was "a reversion to the tactics of Nazi and fascist students in Europe."[140]

These paternalistic diatribes brushed off the students' activism as the product of their immaturity. Lipset offered a classic example of that condescension, defining students as "socially irresponsible" and asserting that they

> have generally not established a sense of close involvement with adult institutions; experience has not hardened them to imperfection. Their libidos are unanchored; their capacity for identification with categories of universal scope, with mankind, the oppressed, the poor and miserable, is greater than it was earlier or than it will be later in life. Their contact with the articulated mores and political standards of their society is abstract.[141]

Such an interpretation justified trivializing the students' political agenda.

So, too, did the vision of the FSM as a bit flaky, in May's words, "a romantic movement, . . . based on emotions, individual feelings, and so forth."[142] May's assessment, as well as Wolin and Schaar's portrayal of the students' ideas about education as "somewhat romantic and wooly," was not unsympathetic. But, for opponents like Kerr, the FSM's style could be viewed more negatively as stemming from "passion and irrationality." Henry Rosovsky called it "California craziness, the kind of rootlessness of people in California."[143]

Another paternalistic cliché was that the students were acting out personal and psychological problems. They were, if not mentally ill, at least as disturbed as disturbing. As one early supporter-turned-critic claimed, many leading student radicals were "people who are themselves messed up psychologically."[144] Lipset added a sociological twist, speculating that anxiety about "their situation as socially 'marginal' individuals, . . . whose status and future are not yet established," propelled student activists to "seek a socially acceptable explanation for their fear of possible personal failure . . . in the ideologies of radical social movements."[145]

And then there was Feuer's widely circulated conception of "generational revolt." Even before the crisis, Feuer had been studying the notion that student movements "are the product of selfless, altruistic idealism combined with the resentment and aggression of one generation against another." He also contended that "all the activists" at Berkeley "were sons against the father."[146] Lipset offered a similar explanation. As students come into contact with new ideas and ways of life that differed from those of their parents, they "seek a new certainty in beliefs opposed to those taught at home. Radical movements give young people an idealistic rationale for breaking with their families."[147] The fact that contemporary research provided little evidence for such allegations did not prevent them from being taken seriously in some university circles as well as among non-academics.[148]

Feuer also maintained that these unmoored young radicals sought out Berkeley "precisely because they want to have the experience of generational revolt." The university's size, impersonality, and reputation for political activism "acts as a magnet for the morally corrupt." Worse yet, "intellectual lumpen-proletarians, lumpen-beatniks, and lumpen-agitators wend their ways to the university campus to advocate a mélange of narcotics, sexual perversion, collegiate Castroism, and campus Maoism."[149] While not too many Berkeley professors and administrators bought into Feuer's portrayal of the FSM as thrill-seeking, drug-addled revolutionary misfits, some students managed to find personal fulfillment in the FSM.[150] The movement did, in fact, provide psychological benefits to its adherents, who discovered that demonstrations were exciting, enabling them to develop friendships and find new meaning in their lives, and, even at times, experience what one of them called "an ecstasy of community bonding."[151]

And, finally, there was the charge that outside agitators had instigated the turmoil, a time-worn trope that has traditionally surfaced whenever movements for social change threaten the status quo.

Clearly, the Berkeley activists were more than capable of running their own show, but the notion that professional revolutionaries, including some real live communists, had subverted the university had considerable appeal for the FSM's academic opponents (not to mention right-wing politicians and journalists). Many of these professors simply could not conceive of their politically naive students mounting such an articulate and well-organized campaign. Kerr and others also noted, "Many of the 'demonstrators' are not university students."[152]

The FBI helped disseminate those allegations—mainly through the vice chancellor for student affairs Alex Sherriffs, later to become Governor Ronald Reagan's top adviser on higher education—persuading quite a few administrators and right-wing professors that they were confronting a well-planned insurgency.[153] Chancellor Edward Strong, according to one of his colleagues, became "convinced that there was a strong Communist-radical block [*sic*] in this."[154] Kerr was so concerned about the university's vulnerability to charges of communist activities on campus that he labeled "some elements" of the FSM as practitioners of the "tactics of Fidel Castro and Mao Tse-tung."[155] A few faculty members echoed that charge, Glazer among them. He viewed the FSM as dominated by civil rights activists, "identified with direct action, and . . . leaders of groups in a direct or indirect line of descent from the Communist and Trotskyist student political groups of the past."[156]

Others zeroed in on that "direct . . . line of descent," citing the supposedly malign influence of the FSM's token Communist Party member, Bettina Aptheker, Herbert's daughter.[157] According to one of his colleagues, "Lipset always tried to poison my ear about her." Her presence "lurking" next to Savio at the Greek Theatre was proof positive "of how the far left was manipulating this meeting."[158] The equally dogmatic Martin Malia agreed. "It was Bettina who put Mario [Savio] up to going out on the stage and getting tackled. . . . [S]he is experienced in agitation."[159] Ironically, most of the professors who actually dealt with Aptheker felt that, perhaps because of her party discipline, she was more sophisticated, pragmatic, and easier to get along with than the other FSM leaders.[160] (That her gender may have contributed seems never to have crossed these gentlemen's minds.) In any event, what then remained of the local Communist Party kept its distance from the rather untidy Free Speech Movement.[161]

Even so, many members of the Berkeley establishment subscribed to the thesis that a hard core of seasoned radicals had subverted the campus. Robert Scalapino contended that the FSM's leaders "had already been involved in other movements. Some of them had come from the East Coast very recently, and they had been involved in the Civil Rights Movement and they relished this kind of activity."[162] Other faculty members found the FSM's competence suspicious. Their "efficient, almost military, organization" as well as their "walkie-talkies" and the "endless stream of propaganda" from the group's "public information center," one conservative explained, reeked of "skilled personnel and money" from outside.[163]

Berkeley's professors were also at fault—or so the administration and its faculty supporters contended. Although it was common for outside politicians, journalists, and private citizens to blame the faculty for leading their students astray, the academic critics who were closer to the action realized that their colleagues who had backed the resolution of December 8 did not incite their students—but they did facilitate their antics. They gave in to "hysteria," terrified by what Glazer called "the terrible power of the students."[164] They were "Munichmen," another colleague called them, academic Neville Chamberlains eager to appease the students. By abandoning their own "moral commitment to legality" and condoning the protesters' defiance of the law, the professors' "capitulation" was teaching the students, in Glazer's words, "that extreme tactics could be used without censure."[165] During the next few years, the contention that spineless professors encouraged trouble at their universities was to become ubiquitous within conservative circles, undermining public support for the nation's faculties.

Against the Multiversity

Just as there was a consensus within the faculty that the University of California's political restrictions were both unfair and unwise, so, too, a consensus emerged that the institution's size and impersonality had contributed to the student unrest. Clark Kerr bears some responsibility here. In 1963 he coined the term "multiversity" to describe the assorted functions of a major research university.[166] As the key institution within what he called the "knowledge industry," it would stimulate innovation and economic growth. At the same time, Kerr recognized the serious downside of that mission: It encouraged faculty members to focus primarily on their research. They would compete to obtain the lowest teaching loads and identify more with their professional colleagues and off-campus funders than their own universities. In the process, undergraduates would no doubt suffer. In fact, Kerr even predicted that unrest might break out over the impersonality of such an institution.[167]

The Free Speech Movement's leaders, especially Mario Savio, amplified these issues, articulating a wider-ranging critique of the multiversity's sins.[168] As did quite a few faculty members.[169] Significantly, however, Berkeley's professors and administrators seem to have paid more attention to the problem than did the students. The undergraduates were much more upset about restrictions on their personal and political activities than about "endless bureaucratic routines, gigantic lecture courses," and the fact that, as Sheldon Wolin and John Schaar pointed out, "it is possible to take a B.A. at Berkeley and never talk with a professor."[170] For graduate students, however, that lack of contact was more serious. One TA in the political science department who taught under a well-known professor recalled that for an entire semester she "never met the man. Never met him."[171] And for a generation of future academics, that impersonality—at Berkeley and elsewhere—was toxic. Although it is unclear to what extent the critique of the multiversity contributed to the Free Speech Movement, it attracted considerable attention at the time. And as the academy's troubles deepened over the next few years, that cultural and educational condemnation of its operations was to become increasingly influential.[172]

If nothing else, the Free Speech Movement did intensify the preexisting concerns about academic culture. As they demanded more of a say over their own social lives and political activities, Berkeley's students also began to call for more control over their own educations. Relevance was their mantra. They wanted the curriculum to deal with current social problems and to be more sensitive to their moral and cultural concerns. Within a few years, as the demands for student power shook up the academy, faculty members not only had to confront calls for programs in fields like Black studies and women's studies, but also for such pedagogical reforms as pass-fail courses and even in some cases the abolition of grades.

While some professors had already been thinking about updating the curriculum and changing their teaching methods, the FSM challenged others to reevaluate what they were doing in class. Although most of the reforms that resulted from this ferment were short-lived, for a number of professors, both junior and senior, the free speech crisis produced a moment of intense intellectual activity and pedagogical experimentation.[173]

That crisis also prompted the Berkeley faculty, already upset about the university's growing bureaucratization and centralization, to rethink governance.[174] They might well have sought to increase their power within the university, but their students' demands for greater participation in educational decision making jump-started the process. If nothing else, the turmoil had made it clear that it was necessary to streamline Berkeley's traditionally languid governance procedures. Even if poorly attended, "faculty meetings that went on and on and on and on" where "every faculty member had to talk. And talk. And talk," as one economist put it, were not conducive to amplifying the faculty's voice within the university.[175]

And, as we have seen, it was a muddled voice, indeed. Within a few months, as the war in Vietnam ramped up, Berkeley's professors were to confront a new and—again—unprecedented situation. This time, however, the University of California was no longer alone; other institutions of higher education also came to experience the kinds of student unrest that had so flummoxed Berkeley. Guided in part by the misleading narratives that California's public intellectuals had disseminated, they all too often responded to their own campus troubles with much the same ambivalence, fear, and confusion. The rest of the nation watched all of this with alarm, in the process losing their unconditional respect for the world of higher education.[176]

PART 2
RESPONDING TO VIETNAM

5

"NOT ONLY POLITICALLY DISASTROUS BUT INTRINSICALLY WRONG"

Early Opposition to American Intervention in Cuba and Vietnam

At the same time as the free speech drama was playing out on the Berkeley campus, faculty members and students there and elsewhere were becoming concerned about what Washington was doing in Southeast Asia. Their critique was part of a small but growing movement within the academy that had begun to question the benign intentions of their own government. Radicals, of course, had long viewed the United States as a bastion of racism, imperialism, and economic exploitation. But there were few of those. Their ranks expanded during the early sixties as liberal academics, who had originally harbored the belief that the United States could be a force for progress, lost that illusion.

For those who had been involved with the Black freedom struggle, that reckoning had begun, as we have seen, when the Justice Department failed to protect civil rights workers in the Deep South. For others, Washington's early hostility to the Castro regime, especially the CIA's disastrous Bay of Pigs invasion in the spring of 1961, was a turning point. Within a few years, as knowledge about their country's intervention in Southeast Asia began to spread, many future radicals and left-liberals came to feel that the government harbored an imperialist, rather than a democratic, agenda for the Third World. That transition is the subject of this chapter.

Cuba

At first even the establishment embraced the Cuban revolution. At a moment when C. Vann Woodward was complaining to his fellow historian Richard Hofstadter about "the great rush . . . among all & sundry to get as near to the middle of the road as possible," who could resist the romance of the brave and bearded rebels fighting their way down from the mountains to topple the brutal and corrupt Batista dictatorship?[1] In April 1959, only a few months after his triumphant march into Havana, Fidel Castro visited the United States. Although the Eisenhower administration kept its distance, thousands of students came to hear him at Harvard and Princeton.* He presented himself and his government as something new and exciting, politically on the left, of course, but consciously not aligned with either the United States or the Soviet Union. And for a few months, Castro was something of a mainstream darling. That love affair ended abruptly with the large-scale executions of Batista's supporters and expropriations of American-owned businesses and plantations.[2]

But on campus, at least within left-wing precincts, support for and curiosity about the new regime remained. It provided, after all, a contemporary model of a revolutionary society, opening up previously unimaginable social and political possibilities. Though most of the academy's activists were still more concerned with the anti-nuclear and civil rights movements than with the developments in Cuba, they did want to see what a revolution looked like from the inside.[3] Since tourism was still allowed, quite a few graduate students, undergraduates, and faculty members took the trip. For many, it was an eye-opening experience, not only to find themselves amid such a profound transformation, but also to discover how distorted a picture of that transformation the US government and mainstream media were purveying to the American public.

---

* I was among the 10,000 people who heard Castro speak from the balcony of the field house at Harvard. Officially introduced by Harvard's dean of the faculty, McGeorge Bundy, Castro spoke in English with a fairly heavy accent, but we could make out most of what he was saying. One thing was somewhat puzzling, however; he kept talking about how much his revolution owed to the "Jews" of Cuba and his hope that the "Jews" of America would continue to support it. After he finished, Bundy very conspicuously thanked him for his remarks to the "youth" of America.

The year 1960 was the high point of that political tourism. In July 1960, my late husband, Marvin Gettleman, then an instructor at CCNY, and the Berkeley graduate student Robert Scheer put together a delegation of students and others for a three-week tour of the island. Marvin recalled his determination to ensure that he would get testimony from as many sides of the revolution as he could, both pro and con. He was impressed—especially by an unscripted visit to a local meeting in the countryside where he had "the experience of seeing people totally powerless taking their own lives in their own hands." The 1960 Christmas break saw hundreds of students and teachers also taking advantage of cheap tours, while others traveled on their own.[4] The economist William Tabb hitchhiked to Miami and then flew to Havana. The Russian historian Louis Menashe and his wife, Sheila, actually drove there, by way of a ferry from Key West.[5]

These trips were transformative. The playwright Barbara Garson went there for her honeymoon and recalled:

> I guess what really made Cuba make me political is that when I got back—we all know that newspapers lie, but to know it is one thing, and to have black and white in front of your face is just—you know, you're walking around spluttering.[6]

For Garson, as for so many of the other political tourists, realizing how much their own government was distorting information was profoundly upsetting. Many became involved with the recently organized Fair Play for Cuba Committee and began to speak out.

Much of this activity occurred in places like Madison, Berkeley, and New York City. The *Studies in the Left* crowd quickly adopted the Cuban revolution as the harbinger of a new political possibility. One of its editors, the history graduate student Saul Landau, came back from Havana so convinced that he had seen "a revolution that answered the dreams of the New Left without abandoning the Old Left" that he became the Fair Play committee's official campus representative, speaking and organizing chapters at about forty colleges and universities.[7] His colleagues on the magazine devoted their third issue to Cuba. They reprinted pieces by Jean-Paul Sartre and Che Guevara, while explaining that they "consider the Cuban Revolution to be the most important and least understood social development in the recent history of the Western Hemisphere." They also pointed out that the official US policy, guided as it was by the "devil theory of communism," bears "no relation to world reality" and was, thus, bound to result in disaster.[8]

Avoiding that disaster required disseminating a more nuanced and sympathetic portrayal of the Cuban scene. Landau was only one of the left-wing journalists, intellectuals, and academics who took up the challenge. The Columbia sociologist C. Wright Mills was the most prominent. A trip to Cuba in the summer of 1960 led Mills to write *Listen, Yankee*, a best-selling, though much criticized, exposition of the new regime's history, practices, and goals in the form of first-person narratives by fictitious Cuban revolutionaries.[9]

The early academic supporters of the Cuban revolution had trouble even getting a hearing. The Michigan State Latin Americanist and Fair Play activist Samuel Shapiro contributed favorable pieces to the *New Republic*—and was denied reappointment.[10] Encouraged by the success of *Listen, Yankee*, Scheer and Maurice Zeitlin, a fellow graduate student, decided to also write a book. They approached seventeen publishers, only to be turned down by editors who claimed that "we don't feel comfortable" about the project. They finally got a contract from Delacorte, only to have the publisher back out when the White House made its disapproval clear. Ultimately published by the slightly unorthodox Grove Press, it sold a respectable five to ten thousand copies.[11] But a favorable view of Cuba was a hard sell. And college teachers who were particularly vocal about their support for Castro could lose their jobs.[12]

Many of the Cuban revolution's most active campus supporters had already been active in the left. Paul Baran, Stanford's Marxist economist, visited the island and returned as one of the Bay Area's most vocal and energetic advocates of the Cuban cause.[13] Before Zeitlin became the individual who many considered "the central person" in the Cuban support movement at Berkeley, he had been involved as a Wayne State undergraduate with the Green Feather movement against the Detroit school system's banning of Robin Hood.[14] Mathematician Stephen Smale, the faculty adviser for Berkeley's Fair Play for Cuba chapter, had been a communist during his undergraduate days at the University of Michigan. Like Smale, many of the group's faculty advisers and main supporters soon became leading antiwar activists on their campuses, among them Douglas Dowd at Cornell and Arnold Kaufman at Michigan.[15]

The Bay of Pigs invasion in April 1961 escalated the opposition to American foreign policy. The mathematician Michael Marcus may have been typical of the liberals for whom this was a turning point. He had been somewhat sympathetic toward Castro, but unhappy with his takeover of American-owned businesses. Marcus was working at RAND at the time, so he had access to classified information and knew what the government was up to. "I had a conversion," he explained, and moved to the left.[16] There had been a few sporadic protests on such campuses as Yale, Columbia, and CCNY.[17] Suddenly, there were protest meetings and demonstrations in dozens of cities and college towns. Some large, some small. But, as the historian Van Gosse noted, these rallies produced "the first publicly visible dissent over imperial policies since the beginning of the Cold War."[18] It was particularly galling that the white paper justifying the invasion had been written by the former Harvard historian Arthur Schlesinger Jr., the Kennedy administration's resident intellectual. In a message read at a big Fair Play for Cuba demonstration in San Francisco, C. Wright Mills not only denounced the Kennedy administration's "barbarism," but added that "Schlesinger and Co. have disgraced us intellectually and morally."[19]

The main protests within the academic community took the form of newspaper ads. After a public meeting at Harvard on April 23 drew four hundred people, a group of faculty members produced "An Open Letter to Kennedy on Cuba" that forty-one of them signed, among them H. Stuart Hughes and David Riesman. Published in the *New York Times* on May 11, it opposed support for the Cuban counter-revolutionaries, called for a stronger diplomatic effort to keep Castro from aligning his country with the communist bloc, and urged Kennedy to improve conditions elsewhere in Latin America to counter the attraction of the Cuban revolution.[20] In Berkeley, Carl Schorske organized another ad, this one from 181 historians representing forty-one different schools.[21] A similar open letter went out from thirty-eight Princeton faculty members, denouncing the US policy toward Cuba as "not only politically disastrous but intrinsically wrong." That document elicited a counter-statement from forty-three other Princeton professors invoking the specter of Munich and claiming that "those who would have us adhere, without exception, to a unilateral position of nonintervention condemn us to a steady erosion of the free world."[22]

If nothing else, a debate had begun. Most of the signatories of the petitions against the invasion were not radicals. They had no ties with Fair Play for Cuba, nor were they fans of Fidel. As one of the Harvard organizers put it, "All of us share a dislike for Castro and would prefer to see a more democratic leader, [but] it is not possible to achieve this aim through any kind of American intervention."[23] In many ways, the position these people took, decrying the US government's crude tactics but hoping for some third force, was to prefigure mainstream liberals' positions on the Vietnam War in its early stages. That such a position bore little relation to reality did not undermine its popularity among campus moderates.[24] In any event, within a few months, Cuba seemed to recede from the academy's attention, replaced by the civil rights movement and the campaign against nuclear testing—especially since the Bay of Pigs made it clear that the United States was not going to repeat that fiasco any time soon.[25]

The Cuban Missile Crisis reopened the debate. Though the overwhelming majority of academics rallied around the president, a few did not. Terrified by the prospect of nuclear warfare, Stephen Smale drove to Mexico, but then turned right around.[26] William Davidon contemplated moving to New Zealand. There were a few tiny protests. The biologist Jonathan Beckwith recalls marching around Nassau Square in Princeton along with Maurice Zeitlin, the philosopher Robert Nozick, and about a dozen other people. Staughton Lynd participated in a similar demonstration in downtown Atlanta, and at least one college teacher lost his job for protesting in his small Illinois town.[27] At the University of Wisconsin, William Appleman Williams responded to the missile crisis by delivering what one former student remembered as "incredible powerful lectures" that explained what was happening.[28]

At Harvard, I was one of hundreds of students and faculty members at an overflow meeting on October 24, 1962, who heard both H. Stuart Hughes and the political scientist Barrington Moore excoriate the Kennedy administration's handling of the crisis.[29] Hughes was running as an independent peace candidate for the US Senate "to challenge the bipartisan consensus" by stimulating a "debate on the life-and-death issues of the nuclear age." In his campaign speeches, he claimed that the president "had unnecessarily stirred up an atmosphere of national emergency." This was not a popular position; because of it, Hughes recalled, his support outside of the academy "appeared to be melting away."[30] Within two years, he and many other academic leftists were taking similarly unpopular positions on Vietnam.

Vietnam: The War Begins

Although the United States had been involved with Vietnam for years, it did not emerge as a major issue on campuses until early 1965 when the Johnson administration escalated the US government's commitment. Until then, while some academics recognized that there were serious problems in Southeast Asia, only a tiny handful seriously concerned themselves with them. Few radical activists seemed to care about what was happening in Vietnam, focusing instead on the antinuclear, Fair Play for Cuba, and civil rights movements.[31] Lynd recalls his surprise in August 1964 when the SNCC leader Robert Moses excoriated Lyndon Johnson for sending troops "to the other side of the globe to fight a war that nobody understands" instead of sending federal marshals to protect civil rights workers in the Deep South. "I was blown away," Lynd explained, "because if there had ever been a moment to focus on civil rights, here's Bob making a connection to the war."[32]

Washington's involvement with Southeast Asia had developed gradually. A former French colony, Vietnam had enjoyed a brief moment of independence immediately after World War II until the French, with Washington's help, returned to power. Nearly a decade of revolutionary warfare ensued. After the communist victory in China in 1949 and the outbreak of the Korean War in 1950, Washington increased its assistance to the doomed French. The Vietnamese rebels, known as the Viet Minh, may have been nationalists, but they were also communists. That was enough to convince most American policy makers that the Vietnamese struggle for national liberation was simply another front in the Soviet campaign to impose communist regimes on vulnerable countries throughout the world. Therefore, when the French withdrew from Southeast Asia in 1954, temporarily splitting Vietnam between a communist government in the North under Ho Chi Minh and a non-communist one in the South, the United States stepped in. It imposed a pro-American regime in Saigon under the authoritarian Catholic Ngo Dinh Diem. When Diem then began to crack down on the remnants of the Viet Minh, an insurrection broke out.

As the former nationalist fighters, now known as the Vietcong, increased their control over the largely Buddhist countryside, Washington increased its commitment to Diem. By the summer of 1963, however, Diem's authoritarianism—especially his brutal crackdown on an opposition movement headed by Buddhist monks—and the ineffectiveness of his army had so alienated his American sponsors that they countenanced a military coup against him. Though the coup succeeded, the Vietcong guerrillas continued to gain support throughout the countryside. By the spring of 1964, the situation within South Vietnam was so chaotic that Johnson was edging toward the major military effort that his advisers convinced him was needed to keep Saigon from falling to the communists.

The 1964 presidential campaign delayed the escalation. Johnson was running as a peace candidate against the hawkish Republican Barry Goldwater. Early in August, LBJ defused Goldwater's criticism of his supposedly toothless Vietnam policy by ordering a bombing raid on North Vietnam in retaliation for an alleged attack on some US destroyers in the Gulf of Tonkin. Although the administration used the incident to get congressional passage of a resolution authorizing military action against North Vietnam, Johnson held back from further escalation. Instead, as he campaigned, he hammered away at Goldwater's recklessness, promising repeatedly: "We are not about to send American boys nine or ten thousand miles away from home to do what Asian boys ought to be doing for themselves."

With the election behind him, however, Johnson abandoned that promise. The South Vietnamese government was about to collapse, and his advisers hoped that American airpower would bolster Saigon's morale as well as cut off what they claimed was an invasion by the North Vietnamese. But the bombing campaign was only a first step. At the end of March 1965, ground forces arrived, initially to defend the airbases, but then to take on the Vietcong directly. By the end of the year, there were over 150,000 American troops in South Vietnam.

American Academics and Vietnam before 1965

Perhaps if American politicians, academics, and the public had known more about what was going on in Southeast Asia, the Kennedy and Johnson administrations might have abandoned their disastrous agenda there. Or not. But such knowledge was not readily available. There was essentially no American scholarship about that part of the world. Whatever background information existed was almost entirely in French—and about the French.[33]

In fact, there were at most a handful of people within the full-time faculties of American colleges and universities who even knew how to speak Vietnamese. Even as late as 1970, there was no tenured full professor teaching Vietnamese studies anywhere in the United States and, outside of the military, fewer than thirty students of the language.[34]

Bernard Fall, a Howard University political scientist and former French Resistance fighter who may have been the nation's leading expert on Vietnam, could barely speak Vietnamese, if at all.[35] Even among the two dozen or so Michigan State University faculty members who staffed a government-funded research and consulting project in Saigon from 1955 to 1962, only a few knew French and only an anthropologist had learned enough Vietnamese to use it in his work.[36] One college teacher who did have what he called "some facility with the language" was the economist Robert S. Browne. He had advised the US government in Vietnam and Cambodia from 1955 to 1961 and had married into a Vietnamese family.[37] But at the time Browne became a fixture on the antiwar lecture circuit, he had yet to finish his dissertation and was teaching part-time at Fairleigh Dickinson University. Moreover, just about all the French scholarship on Vietnam was about the French colonial period and the French war.[38] It was several years before a small American cadre of specialists emerged, many of whom studied the language while in the US military.

Despite the limitations on information, it was possible in 1965 for American scholars—especially if they knew French—to learn enough about Vietnam to realize that Washington's intervention there would lead to disaster. As early as the mid-1950s, the independent journalist I. F. Stone had been critiquing US policy in Vietnam.[39] By the early 1960s, there were mainstream journalists in Saigon, like David Halberstam and Homer Bigart of the New York Times and the UPI's Neil Sheehan, reporting on the worsening crisis under Diem and his successors. And a handful of American academics had either been in Vietnam or were educating themselves enough to write about it. Not all of them opposed American policy. The Michigan State professors provided an early cadre of apologists for the South Vietnamese regime. The project's leader, political scientist Wesley Fishel, was particularly close to Diem, having befriended him in 1950 while Diem was in exile in Tokyo. The following year, Fishel managed to get him an academic appointment at Michigan State, while bringing him to the attention of the right circles in Washington. When the Americans placed Diem at the helm of the South Vietnamese government three years later, he immediately summoned Fishel to Saigon to help organize his administration.[40]

With the financial backing of the US government, that relationship blossomed into the Michigan State University Group, a research and training program that brought more than one hundred American educators and advisers to Saigon between 1955 and 1962. Few of its members were actually MSU professors.[41] Most, in fact, were law enforcement professionals whose work, according to a quasi-official report, consisted primarily of "instructing local police and security agencies in the use and maintenance of the revolvers, riot guns, tear gas, handcuffs, motor vehicles, and other equipment provided them through American aid."[42] It was also common knowledge, in Lansing as well as Saigon, that a detachment of CIA agents used the project

FIGURE 5.1. Wesley Fishel, leading pro-war scholar at Michigan State at national teach-in, Washington, DC, May 15, 1965. © Rowland Scherman Collection. Special Collections and University Archives, University of Massachusetts Amherst Libraries.

for cover.[43] Educationally, the Michigan State program was a wash. Except for a handful of French speakers, the instructors shared no common language with Saigon's aspiring bureaucrats. A few MSU staffers, including the only one who knew Vietnamese, did produce some empirical research on Vietnamese society. But, like the similar studies generated by the RAND Corporation later in the 1960s, that perfectly respectable work had no impact.[44]

On the contrary, even though Fishel breakfasted with Diem at the presidential palace three times a week, the muted criticism that emerged from some of his project's reports angered his host. Diem was even more upset by the more overt criticism appearing in articles by former MSU staffers in the *New Republic* in 1961. The Michigan State authorities apologized, explaining that academic freedom prevented them from attempting "to censor returning scholars." They did, however, promise to hire only those faculty members in the future who were likely to "write scholarly, scientific studies and not sensational, journalistic articles." Nonetheless, such assurances could not save the project, which was winding down anyhow as the widening insurgency brought a demand for military, rather than civilian, advisers.[45] Because the program had produced the largest contingent of academics with knowledge of Vietnam, its alumni contributed disproportionately to the early discussions about the war. They were to grace the podiums of the nation's teach-ins for several years—both in opposition to and support for the conflict.

Most of the academics who publicly supported American policy in Vietnam during the early 1960s did so because they believed that the Cold War demanded it. They were propounding the official line about the need to keep the dominoes from falling: The US government had to prop up South Vietnam in order to prevent Communist China (always "*Communist* China") from taking over the rest of Asia. Communism, in their eyes, was both monolithic and expansionist; thus, Ho Chi Minh's campaign for national liberation was identical to Stalin's seizure of Eastern Europe, not to mention Hitler's takeover of Czechoslovakia. And all of Western civilization was at stake.

The apologists also struggled to make Ngo Dinh Diem's repressive regime palatable to American audiences. Fishel's patronizing 1959 article in the *New Leader*—"Vietnam's One-Man Democratic Rule: A Far Eastern Specialist Questions Accepted Western Views on Asia's Road to Freedom"—claimed that the Vietnamese were not yet sophisticated enough to appreciate Western-style democracy. Fishel predicted that Diem, through "strong leadership and considerable political flexibility and manipulative skill," would "bring increasing benefits, happiness and freedom to his countrymen."[46] Those supporters of the official line on Vietnam who lacked Fishel's credentials rationalized their position by exaggerating their own ignorance and that of others. Loyal citizens, they claimed, simply had to trust the government; Washington had much better sources of information than any of its critics possibly could.[47]

From Realism to Morality: Bernard Fall and Hans Morgenthau

But by the early 1960s, that argument was becoming threadbare. There were enough scholars writing about Vietnam for concerned individuals to question the government's story. Perhaps the two most persuasive early academic critics of America's actions in Vietnam were the political scientists Bernard Fall and Hans Morgenthau. Fall, a former French soldier, probably knew more about Vietnam than anyone else in the United States, and Morgenthau was arguably the nation's most influential international relations specialist. Ironically, though perhaps not coincidentally, they were both Central European Jewish refugees with outsiders' perspectives.[48]

Fall had escaped from Austria to France after Hitler took over in 1938. A teenager when Paris surrendered to the Third Reich, Fall joined the Resistance in the South of France. After the war, he served in the French army, worked for the Americans at the Nuremberg Tribunal, and won a Fulbright fellowship to Syracuse University in 1951. He decided to write his dissertation on Vietnam and went there for the first time in 1953. Suspicious of the optimistic assessments coming out of headquarters, Fall soon discovered that the French had much less control over their colony than they claimed. "From the general point of view this place is a hotbed," he wrote to his fiancée in 1953,

> and a more likely spot to start a general war than ten Koreas. Any knowledge we get out of it soon might help a few bigger people than you and I keep things on an even keel, and I happen to be one of the guys trained to present such knowledge intelligibly.[49]

Soon Fall was writing for both scholarly and popular publications. From the mid-1950s on, he taught seminars about contemporary Southeast Asia at schools like Cornell and Howard, where he was on the faculty. He was also in demand as a speaker—especially to military audiences who found his analysis of the French fiasco enlightening. His 1961 book, *Street without Joy*, was, he was told, "on *every* MAAG [Military Assistance Advisory Group] officers' desk in Vietnam, who say it is 'the Bible.'"[50] Not surprisingly, his critical examination of the policies of the Diem government and its American sponsors made him persona non grata within official circles. The FBI, which put him under surveillance, considered him a French agent, while the Pentagon gave orders that he was not to be used for lectures or briefings—

FIGURE 5.2. Bernard Fall in Vietnam, 1963. © Courtesy of Dorothy Fall.

orders that the head of the Special Forces School at Fort Bragg, North Carolina, ignored, because, he explained, "we've learned more from him than from any half a dozen other guests that I can remember."[51]

In the early 1960s, Fall did not consider himself hostile to the American desire for a non-communist South Vietnam. Rather he saw himself as a realist, understanding the nature of revolutionary guerrilla warfare and wanting to help the United States avoid the errors of the French. His initial lesson was straightforward: the war in Vietnam was unwinnable. The solution had to be political. As Washington escalated the conflict, he eventually came to regret his earlier relationship with the government.[52]

Hans Morgenthau shared Fall's tough-minded assessment. No left-winger, Morgenthau was, in fact, a founder of the realist school of international relations. His 1948 treatise, *Politics among Nations*, had become the standard textbook in the field. Its message—and the core of Morgenthau's opposition to Washington's military venture in Vietnam—was that national interest, not some abstract ideology, had to be the basis for foreign policy. By the early 1960s, as the Kennedy administration was inching ever deeper into Southeast Asia, Morgenthau could see no vital national security interest involved. On the contrary, in articles in such mainstream publications as the *New York Times, New Leader, Commentary,* and the *Washington Post,* he argued that policy makers were increasingly dominated by an irrational fear of communism and divorced from a realistic appreciation of the actual issues.[53]

Ultimately, although both Morgenthau and Fall (who was killed by a land mine in February 1967) never abandoned their essentially pragmatic assessments of American policy in Southeast Asia, they also came to oppose that policy on moral grounds. What the United States was doing in Vietnam was not just counterproductive—it was wrong. That evolution from realism to morality occurred among many other liberal critics of the war.[54]

Coming to that realization and then acting upon it took time. As they became aware of what the American government was doing in Southeast Asia, quite a few scholars opposed it, but did not yet feel strongly enough about it to speak out in public. Even so, mainstream liberals who had previously supported Washington's anti-communist efforts began to have serious doubts.[55] "Are we being as stupid in Vietnam as it seems?" the historian and public intellectual Henry Steele Commager asked in October 1963. Within a year, he was writing to the head of the Senate Foreign Relations Committee to express his growing concern. By the following year, when the bombing began, he went public.[56]

Another scholar who viewed American policy in Vietnam initially as a mistake was the international law professor Richard Falk. His conversion from supporter to critic occurred during the day he spent at the Ohio State University library reading about the French in Vietnam. "Just that one afternoon in the library," he recalled, gave him an "early predisposition to oppose the war." Though he became much more radical later, Falk was originally "a little left of center liberal with a more or less realist view of international politics."[57] The China scholar Joseph Esherick was another Cold War liberal whose initial critique of American policy focused on its misguided conduct of the war. A Berkeley graduate student learning Chinese in Hong Kong, Esherick went to Saigon "out of curiosity" during his spring vacation in 1965. He wrote several articles for the *San Francisco*

Chronicle about how badly the war was going, but he did not consider himself opposed to the American presence.[58] He, like many liberals, thought the war was just a "mistake." Some elite academics—Ivy League professors as well as Yale's president Kingman Brewster—who opposed the war for pragmatic reasons had close ties to the administration. Like the top scientists who hoped to gain a hearing for their views on nuclear weapons within the ruling circles, these prestigious professors felt that they would have more influence by cultivating their connections with McGeorge Bundy, W. W. Rostow, Arthur Schlesinger Jr., and the other well-placed former Ivy League professors in the government than by speaking out in public.[59]

The initial target of those critics who did go public was Diem.[60] A September 1962 article in *Harper's* by Stanley Millet, who had spent 1961–62 as a visiting professor of political science at the University of Saigon, was typical. His demoralized Vietnamese friends, Millet explained, "had few illusions about the nature of communism and dreaded the Communist victory which the policies of the Diem regime seemed to make inevitable." If the country was to be saved, the United States had to find other leaders, "more sane and moderate than Diem," who "can revive the energy and resolve that Diem has stifled."[61]

By then, Diem had become so authoritarian that even his strongest supporters were becoming disillusioned. In June 1963, the American Friends of Vietnam—a group of former officials, businessmen, politicians, and academics cofounded in 1955 by Michigan State's Wesley Fishel (and supported by such eminent individuals as Schlesinger and the then-senator John F. Kennedy)—sponsored an academic conference on the crisis that proposed replacing Diem. Within a few months, Fishel himself had composed a memo at the State Department's request that recommended a coup against the man whom he had helped put in power.[62] Later, after Diem's removal brought South Vietnam no closer to salvation, many Cold War liberals still dreamed of a third force, an indigenous political grouping that could somehow produce a democratic, but non-communist, government.[63] It took several years of bloodshed for those critics to realize that such a solution was as unrealistic as official Washington's belief that bombing North Vietnam would create stability in the South.

Even before the Buddhist crisis of 1963 brought Saigon's troubles to the nightly news, a number of academics and others were becoming concerned about South Vietnam. Robert S. Browne's papers for the early sixties bulge with speaking invitations, most from campus activists and community peace groups.[64] At the same time, a few already radicalized faculty members had been circulating petitions, organizing meetings, and making clear their opposition to American policy.[65] Many, like the academic signers of a March 1963 open letter to President Kennedy, were McCarthy-era survivors and veterans of the Old Left.[66] Their small protests were easy to brush off.[67] But these people were there, aware of the problems, and ready to be called upon.

Because so many academics moved to the left on account of Vietnam, it is hard to make distinctions about the politics of the early critics of the war. Certainly, almost all the remnants of the Old Left who made it through the McCarthy years like Leon Wofsy and Paul Baran ended up in the antiwar movement. There were also a number of left-liberal, but anti-communist, academics, who, like H. Stuart Hughes, took strong positions against the war early on but, refusing to work with any groups or individuals tainted by communism and disliking the radical rhetoric of the emerging New Left, urged a strategy of restraint and "respectability."[68]

Hughes, as the co-chair of SANE, had been pushing the group's more skittish leaders to come out against the war. Finally, in 1964, after an agonizing debate, SANE did.[69] The group then supported a petition that, in the name of "5000 college and university educators," called for a neutral Vietnam. It appealed to Johnson "not to enlarge the scope of the war, but instead to work for a neutralized North and South Vietnam, as separate, federated, or reunified states, protected by international guarantees and peacekeeping forces against all outside interference." The document, published as an ad in the *Washington Post* on July 11, listed twenty professors as its original sponsors. Besides Hughes, Benjamin Spock, and SANE activists like William Davidon, they included the Columbia economist Seymour Melman, the psychoanalyst Erich Fromm, and Harvard's well-known sociologist David Riesman.[70]

At a Washington press conference, where they released all five thousand signers' names, Morgenthau, Browne, and a former Agency for International Development official then at Princeton talked about Vietnam. Morgenthau's message—that a victorious Ho Chi Minh would remain neutral in the Cold War—finally got attention, if not always favorable attention. Despite the criticism, the petition was, SANE's political director claimed, "the first real publicity break-through."[71] It alerted the White House to the potential for resistance from the academy. But, as the Tonkin Gulf incident less than a month later revealed, the prospect of angry professors hardly deflected the administration from escalating the war.

Given the growing unease of many academics about Vietnam, it is surprising how little attention they paid to that incident. No doubt it was the presidential campaign, as much as the summer vacation, that kept campuses quiet. The Pakistani political scientist Eqbal Ahmad organized a protest at the University of Illinois, but there seemed to be little other opposition on campuses.[72] As we now know, the incident itself had been greatly exaggerated, and the Democratic Party leaders who rushed the so-called Tonkin Gulf Resolution through a nearly unanimous Congress stifled their doubts in order to ensure that Johnson would win in November.

For the academy's liberals, who did not want to criticize an administration whose Great Society reforms they strongly supported, the election offered an additional reason not to go public with their concerns about Vietnam. On the contrary, they sought to mobilize their colleagues to back LBJ. "Do you think there is a place for a committee of intellectuals for Johnson, or professors for Johnson, or historians for Johnson?" C. Vann Woodward asked one of LBJ's top aides. "Some of us at Yale are interested in this."[73] Elite scientists signed on as well. Terrified by Barry Goldwater's loose talk about nuclear weapons, they organized Scientists and Engineers for Johnson, a nonpartisan group that recruited thousands of members, among them ten Nobel Prize winners as well as Eisenhower's top science adviser George Kistia-kowsky and his successor, Jerome Wiesner. "It was never really for Johnson," Wiesner recalled, "it was against Goldwater."[74]

Even Benjamin Spock, though publicly identified with the call for a neutral Vietnam, loaned his name to the Physicians Committee for the Re-election of Johnson.[75] Four years later, Spock would be running for president on an antiwar platform. But in 1964 the academic opposition to Goldwater was so strong that, as Staughton Lynd recalled, "When I got to Yale, none of my colleagues could understand why I wasn't going to vote for Johnson."[76] Lynd may have been unique here. Other activists, who had become disillusioned with the administration, still viewed LBJ as essentially progressive and grudgingly gave him their vote, hoping for the best.[77] "We voted for him last November," the Marxist historian Eugene Genovese explained, "because we didn't want the war in Vietnam escalated."[78]

6

"THE MOST WORTHWHILE ALL-NIGHTER"

Teach-Ins and the Antiwar Movement's Pedagogical Moment

Although the United States' involvement in Vietnam had been going on for years, opposition to it did not emerge as a major issue on the nation's campuses until early in 1965 when the Johnson administration began to bomb North Vietnam on a regular basis. At that point, concerned faculty members decided to act. They felt compelled by a sense of professional obligation to use their research skills and expertise to alert the country to the disaster that lay ahead. Their activity could not have been more academic. They were going to teach their students, colleagues, and the broader public the truth about Vietnam.[1]

While some of these people were convinced from the start that Washington was motivated by imperialism, most others were liberals who operated on the assumption that if the powers that be really understood the situation, they would get out of Vietnam. As a result, for the next few years, thousands of college and university teachers gave speeches, organized conferences, circulated petitions, took out ads in the local and national press, and published books, articles, and letters to the editors—all in what the University of Chicago political scientist Hans Morgenthau later came to view as "the naïve assumption that if power were only made to see the truth, it would follow that lead."[2]

From early 1965 to sometime in 1966, these lectures, teach-ins, petitions, and publications constituted what the historian David Schalk called the "pedagogic" phase of the intellectuals' antiwar movement, "composed of calm, rational, frequently scholarly writings." These critiques also predicted what would probably happen if the government continued its misguided policy. "In an extraordinarily large number of cases," Schalk noted, "these predictions were proved correct."[3]

A striking characteristic of the professoriate's initial opposition to the war was that many, if not most, of these antiwar faculty members had already been active in other social and political movements. Staughton Lynd and Howard Zinn had participated in the civil rights struggle in the South; Linus Pauling and William Davidon had campaigned against nuclear weapons.[4] Many of the Berkeley faculty's most prominent opponents of the war had recently defended the Free Speech Movement (FSM). His support for the FSM, English professor Frederick Crews recalled, "really oriented me toward activism when the Vietnam issue came up the following year."[5] Similarly, for biologist Leon Wofsy, "just as the civil rights movement in a sense was a launching pad for FSM, the FSM was a launching pad for the anti-war movement."[6] In other words, almost all the academic activists during the "pre-sixties" gravitated into the antiwar movement after 1965.[7]

The First Teach-In

The escalation of the war brought about the creation of a new form of protest—the teach-in. It was so effective a vehicle for dissent that the academic community quickly became the main source of opposition to the war. Though it was later eclipsed—notably in the media and, thus, the popular mind—by younger noisier protests, for about a year and a half the nation's faculties, with the assistance of graduate students and some undergraduates, provided the leadership and the intellectual framework for the growing challenge to the escalating conflict. An initially small group of professors literally taught the rest of the country why the war was wrong.

For many academics, recalled the anthropologist Marshall Sahlins, a central figure in the University of Michigan teach-in, Johnson's escalation was

a personal as well as a political betrayal. . . . [J]ust three months before they had been campaigning to an unprecedented extent in the presidential election for the so-called peace candidate, Mr. Johnson—and all the more urgently because his jingoist opponent Barry Goldwater was running on a pro-escalation platform. Now they found themselves double-crossed by Operation Rolling Thunder, the massive bombing of North Vietnam.[8]

At first, these faculty members resorted to traditional methods of dissent. Benjamin Spock, whom Johnson had personally thanked for supporting his reelection, wrote directly to the White House.[9] Less well-known professors turned to collective action, gathering names for petitions and ads in newspapers. On February 19, calling on the government to "Stop the Widening of the War, Seek a Cease-Fire," and "Negotiate an International Settlement," SANE ran an ad in the *New York Times*. Among the eighty-seven professors, clergymen, and intellectuals it listed besides Spock, Browne, Morgenthau, and the other usual suspects were such activists and luminaries as MIT's Nobel laureate Salvador Luria, Nathan Glazer, and John Roche, the Brandeis political scientist and head of the quintessential Cold War liberal organization, Americans for Democratic Action, who would eventually join the Johnson administration as its intellectual-in-residence.[10] Eleven days later, an ad hoc group called the University Committee to Protest the War in Vietnam placed an "Open Letter to President Johnson" in the same paper, this one signed by nearly six hundred faculty members from more than twenty schools in the New York City area.[11] A small group of Berkeley people put a similar ad in the *San Francisco Chronicle*.[12]

The most important action, however, took place in Ann Arbor, where on the evening of March 11, 1965, about two dozen University of Michigan faculty members gathered in the living room of political scientist Arnold Kaufman to decide how to oppose the war. Most assumed that the meeting would result in some kind of petition for the local paper. William Gamson, however, wanted "a more dramatic alternative."[13] Along with the social psychologist Richard Mann, he suggested that the faculty group declare a moratorium on business as usual, cancel classes for the day, and "focus all our attention on what was happening in Vietnam." Within a day, Gamson recalled, thirteen people had signed onto the moratorium and released a call for it to the student newspaper. Within a week, forty-six faculty members and teaching fellows had given their names, including a few major figures like the economist Kenneth Boulding and the mathematical biologist Anatol Rapoport. Most, however, were junior social scientists without tenure.

That the teach-in movement should have originated at the University of Michigan was no accident. Most of the faculty activists were located within its well-regarded social science departments—including some of the institution's most distinguished professors.[14] They had been politically involved for years—signing petitions against nuclear weapons, for a fair housing ordinance, and in support of Johnson's reelection. Trained at Michigan, both Gamson and Mann had recently returned to Ann Arbor from Harvard, where they had been co-chairs of the Boston chapter of CORE. At Michigan, Gamson worked with the Center for Research on Conflict Resolution, a kind of think tank for the peace movement, while Mann had become involved with Vietnam through a fellow graduate student who had lived there. A further influence in Ann Arbor was the presence of the Students for a Democratic Society (SDS), then emerging as the iconic New Left organization, whose early leaders—Tom Hayden, Richard Flacks, Carl Oglesby, Bob Ross, and Paul Potter among others—were close to Gamson and other faculty activists.[15] Finally, there was the sense within Ann Arbor's progressive circles that the university had to atone for firing two professors who had refused to cooperate with the House Un-American Activities Committee in 1954.[16]

The moratorium would not be a strike; the protest was against the war, not the university. Rather it was an educational venture, modeled on the Boston Freedom Schools of the early 1960s, where parents protesting de facto segregation boycotted the public schools and provided alternative classes on Black history and the civil rights movement. Even so, the moratorium encountered serious opposition. Michigan's president Harlan Hatcher urged the rest of the university to trust the nation's leaders. "There is a time and place for making protests," he stated, "but dismissing classes is not an acceptable one." Michigan's governor George Romney was equally dismissive, calling the idea "about the worst type of example professors could give to their students."[17] The Michigan State Senate also chimed in, calling on Hatcher to discipline the moratorium's sponsors. "The action of the twenty instructors at the University of Michigan who have threatened cessation of classes," the senate resolution declared, "is not only totally ill-advised but represents a clear violation of their duties as instructors at a State University to their students and to the people of the State of Michigan, and hereby is condemned."[18]

The organizers began to consider alternatives. Arnold Kaufman and the anthropologists Marshall Sahlins and Eric Wolf proposed that instead of calling off classes, the faculty dissidents should offer an all-night educational program on Vietnam—a teach-in, according to Sahlins, who apparently coined the phrase.[19] The symbolism of invoking the sit-ins and disruptions of the civil rights movement was, Gamson later realized, "perfect." Plus, it had the advantage of avoiding a battle with the university that would divert attention from the war in Vietnam. It also eliminated the risks to their careers that concerned some of the non-tenured faculty members. Still, the debate raged for hours; and it wasn't until four o'clock in the morning of March 17 that the group abandoned the moratorium. Gamson was one of the last holdouts until he finally realized that a teach-in would fulfill his main objectives of disrupting business as usual and serving an educational function. "Instead of a work moratorium we would stage a sleep moratorium."[20]

The Michigan administration embraced the March 24 teach-in with enthusiasm, arranging for lecture halls, providing sound equipment, and waiving parietal hours to allow undergraduate women to stay out all night. The event itself surpassed the most optimistic predictions of its organizers. More than three thousand students showed up—and stayed, even after a bomb scare. Besides an opening plenary featuring Robert Browne, historian Arthur Waskow from the Institute for Policy Studies, and a dissenting Michigan State anthropologist named John Donoghue, there was a rally on the library steps. The planners also scheduled a series of smaller workshops and seminars led by Michigan professors, graduate students, and SDS leaders. There were films, folk songs, and food provided by a local women's peace group as well as a final session that was supposed to figure out what to do next.

Significantly, the organizers did not invite anyone to speak in support of the government's Vietnam policy; they believed the Johnson administration possessed ample opportunities for making its case.[21]

At the six a.m. closing plenary, with five hundred students still around, the organizers asked the audience what they had learned from the night's activities. Significantly, the most striking feature of the evening was the rapport that it had created between the students and their professors. According to an observer, students overwhelmingly reported that "this is what a university should be; this has been the most important experience in their years at Michigan; they see the faculty as human beings." The students interviewed by the school newspaper offered similarly glowing assessments. Of course, the stated content of the teach-in had an impact, as well. "I'd never really thought very much about this," one young man told the *Michigan Daily*, "but, after tonight, I think we should get out of Vietnam."[22]

The Teach-Ins Go National

The teach-in got "an enormous amount" of publicity, Gamson noted, both locally and nationally. The organizers realized that they could extend their impact far beyond Ann Arbor with similar programs on other campuses. One of the organizers recalled:

> We took to the telephones and to the media. . . . We expected to sell the plan at Wisconsin and Berkeley and Columbia. But Flint Junior College and the University of Miami in Coral Gables were not to be outdone. By T-Day, March 24, we knew of thirty-five other teach-ins that were in the works, and these proved to be only a beginning.[23]

At least a hundred teach-ins took place that spring. Actually, Michigan's was not the first. Marist College, a small Catholic men's school in New York's Hudson Valley, had that honor on March 22, with an impressive program that reached beyond the university and across the political spectrum; speakers included two congressmen, the former ambassador to South Vietnam Henry Cabot Lodge, the pacifist leader A. J. Muste, Staughton Lynd, and the Jesuit priest and poet Daniel

Berrigan, who was to become the most high-profile religious opponent of the war.[24]

There was no standard template. Each teach-in was organized locally, usually by a small group of faculty activists, sometimes in co-
ordination with graduate and undergraduate students. On less active
campuses, community groups sponsored the events.[25] Some had ties
to Michigan. For example, the key figure at the University of Oregon,
the anthropologist David Aberle, had previously taught at Michigan
and had been contacted directly by Marshall Sahlins.[26] Similarly, Richard Flacks had just begun to teach at the University of Chicago, where
his politics and connections to his former teachers and SDS comrades
quickly propelled him into a leading role in the Chicago teach-in,
along with Morgenthau and Gilbert White, an eminent geographer
who had done research in the Mekong Delta. "The fact that Morgenthau would lend his weight to antiwar protest," Flacks observed, "was
very significant at Chicago." But on other campuses, faculty leaders
emerged spontaneously—and then contacted Michigan.[27]

Ann Arbor was buzzing. As it became clear that a national movement was, in fact, developing, the Michigan organizers pondered their
next move. They had already decided that if other campuses signed
on, they would put on a national teach-in in Washington, DC, that
would feature a debate with a high-ranking administration official.[28]
To give that ambitious endeavor the credibility and support it needed,
the Ann Arbor people created a national organization. They hoped
to assuage the doubts of their more moderate colleagues by giving it
an anodyne name: Inter-University Committee for Debate on Foreign
Policy (IUC). It was to be "the national and coordinated component
of what is and should remain a diverse collection of groups across the
country."[29]

The IUC also planned to operate as a clearinghouse for people
looking for speakers and literature for teach-ins of their own. Richard
Mann served as the IUC's initial executive director, handling the lo-
gistics for the Washington event. An early June meeting in Ann Arbor
of some fifty antiwar faculty activists from around the country established a more formal organization with a national board, an executive
committee, and a biweekly newsletter.[30] Money was no problem. The

group had a few angels, while some of its members made substantial loans to float the project. Later, when the committee ran an ad in the *New York Times*, checks as well as signatures poured in from academics around the country.[31]

Robert Browne, Noam Chomsky, Barry Commoner, William Davidon, Douglas Dowd, David Kotelchuck, Staughton Lynd, Stanley Millet, Hans Morgenthau, Stephen Smale, Benjamin Spock, William Appleman Williams, Howard Zinn, and the Michigan organizers—the names on the IUC's constantly evolving letterheads are familiar ones with a few surprises like Irving Howe, who soon quit. There were all of three women—Mary Wright, the Yale historian of China; the Wisconsin graduate student Joan Scott, elected to the board as its student representative; and the Cuba activist Sandra Levinson, then at CUNY.[32] When the Cornell economist Dowd replaced Sahlins as president after the Washington teach-in, many of its activities moved to Ithaca, where a graduate student in chemistry, Joseph Griffith, and his wife, Patricia, owned an offset press and became the IUC's de facto staff.[33] Cornell was hardly a backwater; on the contrary, it was one of the top American sites for academic research on Southeast Asia.

From the start, the movement confronted an identity crisis—one with serious political implications that mirrored the tensions between the academic community's liberals and its radicals. Should a teach-in be a protest against the war or a debate that presented all sides of the issue? The inaugural event at Michigan was clearly the former. "To be sure, the meeting had the format of academic discourse," Anatol Rapoport explained. "But there was no question about the *basis* of the discussion. The point of departure was our conviction that the present U.S. policy in Southeast Asia was dangerous, ineffective, illegal, and immoral." The organizers explicitly did not invite any government spokesmen or advocates for the administration's policy.[34]

On many other campuses, however, teach-in sponsors sought more balance and genuine debate. Their rationale was partly professional and partly political. As academics, they felt obliged to maintain the objectivity that was then considered obligatory for legitimate scholarship. They also viewed a balanced program as a political necessity since opposition to the conflict was far from widespread on American campuses. The liberal academics who put together the teach-ins felt that impartial panels would be more effective in reaching wavering or uninformed students and colleagues than what one organizer called "an anti-Government diatribe."[35] The San Francisco State political scientist Marshall Windmiller agreed, insisting that it was better to provide information than, as Scott urged, establish "the validity of a moral basis for dissent."[36]

Both sides were correct, of course. There were many ways to build an antiwar movement. Righteous outrage was appropriate; but so, too, was the provision of information. Ultimately, a teach-in's format probably depended more on the political and academic culture of the institution than on anything else. On a conservative campus like Princeton, for example, where the faculty prided itself on its intellectual distinction, its May 5 teach-in had no outside speakers. Though the auditorium was packed, the program was actually rather dull and extremely academic. It ended at two o'clock in the morning with two junior philosophers arguing about an arcane problem in epistemology.[37]

At Michigan State, on the other hand, with its cadre of former advisers to the Saigon regime, the school's first teach-in on April 11 was put together by a faculty group headed by John Donoghue, a disillusioned alumnus of the MSU project. The program's organizers explicitly refused to let Wesley Fishel or the other local apologists for the South Vietnamese regime share the platform.[38] Two months later, Fishel, with the covert assistance of the Johnson administration, mounted his own pro-war event at MSU, featuring Vice President Hubert Humphrey and a State Department spokesman, the African American journalist Carl Rowan.[39]

And then there was Berkeley. Though clearly against the war, the organizers of the school's massive May 21–22 teach-in invited some pro-war speakers. There had already been a thousand-student demonstration with a handful of faculty speakers. A group of activists under the leadership of the mathematician Stephen Smale and the soon-to-be notorious former graduate student Jerry Rubin then formed a coalition, the Vietnam Day Committee, to mount a larger event. "Our mode was one of continually doing things," Smale explained, all kind of things, which would make Vietnam Day into a bigger and sharper antiwar protest. . . . It was more of an exciting challenge. How to make something that would be the greatest teach-in, the biggest Vietnam War protest. How to make Johnson cringe.[40]

They got logistical support from the administration, still shell-shocked from the previous semester's Free Speech Movement and anxious to avoid another crisis. "We made big demands," Smale explained, "outdoor loudspeakers and everything. They opposed it at first, but timidly. We got the essentials."[41]

As befitting the nation's most highly politicized campus, Berkeley's was the biggest teach-in of the season, lasting for thirty-five hours with crowds of between 10,000 and 12,000 at its peaks and as many as 25,000 to 30,000 overall. The program featured an exhaustive assortment of local, national, and even international antiwar and countercultural celebrities and intellectuals ranging from the poet Allen Ginsberg and the folksinger Phil Ochs to the novelist Norman Mailer and Ernest Gruening, one of the two senators to vote against the Tonkin Gulf Resolution. I. F. Stone spoke twice; and Staughton Lynd, an increasingly forceful critic of the war, called for escalating the protests into a

> nonviolent revolution . . . not the violent overthrow of the United States government, but the non-violent retirement from office of the present administration. And, further, that the way to bring this about is the creation of civil disobedience so massive and so persistent that the Tuesday Lunch Club that is running this country—Johnson, McNamara, Bundy and Rusk—will forthwith resign.

Only one speaker supported the war, although two others—Eugene Burdick and Robert Scalapino—pulled out very publicly at the last minute.[42]

To a certain extent, the organizers of such seemingly one-sided events were not to blame. It was hard to recruit people—whether faculty members or outside experts—to defend the administration.

Charles Haynie, who was helping to organize teach-ins in the Cornell area in the fall of 1965, had trouble finding pro-war speakers. The ones he recruited "were often ill-informed and could only plead that we are already at war, we must support our boys in uniform."[43] The Columbia professors who organized a March 26 teach-in had invited six supporters of the war; none were available.[44] Nor could the professors who sponsored the all-nighter at Rutgers on April 22–23 persuade the State Department to provide any speakers. They were able to recruit two administration supporters from their own faculty; the rest of the program consisted of nine antiwar professors.[45]

As at many of these programs, the students who attended the Rutgers teach-in were enthusiastic: "the greatest event presented on the campus in memory," "the faculty and student body's finest hour," and "probably the most worthwhile all-nighter I've ever experienced."[46] Audience members recall a particularly dramatic moment when the historian Warren Susman nearly assaulted a pro-war English professor for making racist comments about Asians.[47] Separating the combatants was another historian, Eugene Genovese, whose own remarks generated the most serious threat to academic freedom produced by the teach-in movement. Genovese, who had just gotten tenure a few weeks earlier for his brilliant scholarship on American slavery, announced: "Those of you who know me know that I am a Marxist and a socialist. Therefore, unlike most of my distinguished colleagues here this morning, I do not fear or regret the impending Viet Cong victory in Vietnam. I welcome it."[48] That statement ignited a political storm. Wayne Dumont, the Republican candidate for governor, demanded Genovese's dismissal. Academic freedom, Dumont insisted, "does not give to a teacher in a state university, supported by taxpayers' money, the right to advocate victory of an enemy in war, in which some of his own students may very well lay down their lives in the cause of freedom."[49]

These were not idle threats. Thirteen years before, Rutgers had been the first American university to fire faculty members for taking the Fifth Amendment before a congressional investigating committee. Rutgers's president Mason Gross had been the provost at the time and so was well aware of the problems that ousting Genovese might create.

Backed by Governor Richard Hughes, who was Dumont's real target, Gross stoutly defended his controversial professor's right to speak. As long as he did not impose his political beliefs on his students—and his colleagues assured the administration that he did not—Genovese could keep his job. To dismiss him would, Gross explained, "result in censure and probably loss of accreditation. This in turn would result in loss of faculty and great difficulty in recruiting new faculty." Governor Hughes's overwhelming victory in November revealed that, at least at that time, antiwar activities at their state's flagship university did not seem to disturb New Jersey's voters.

Such was not, however, the case within the Johnson administration, whose members were more concerned about the teach-ins than they let on in public. At a speech before the American Society of International Law on April 23, Secretary of State Dean Rusk lashed out:

> I continue to hear and see nonsense about the nature of the struggle there. . . . I sometimes wonder at the gullibility of educated men and the stubborn disregard of plain facts by men who are supposed to be helping our young to learn—especially to learn how to think.[50]

McGeorge Bundy, the former Harvard dean who served as the national security adviser under both Kennedy and Johnson, was equally dismissive. Many years later he admitted that he had been "somewhat surprised by the level of student and academic protest in the spring and summer of 1965."[51] But at the time, he responded sarcastically to an invitation to address a teach-in at Washington University, St. Louis, noting how "strange" he found the invitation's assumption "that a public official is somehow especially accountable to the profession in which he worked before coming to the Government" and concluding "that if your letter came to me for grading as a professor of government, I would not be able to give it high marks."[52]

This did not mean that the administration ignored the teach-ins. According to George Reedy, LBJ's press secretary, one of the reasons why Johnson made a conciliatory gesture toward negotiations in an April 7 speech at Johns Hopkins University was to deflect the growing criticism on campus. The government also decided to present its case on campus, sending out three- and four-man "truth teams"—officially entitled the Inter-Departmental Speaking Team on Viet-Nam Policy—to several universities in the Midwest. Consisting of articulate young military officers and civilian officials just back from Southeast Asia, their mission was to give their campus audiences "the facts of life in Vietnam."[53]

The project was not a success. "Perhaps we have, for the first time in our experience," the director of the Voice of America mused, "a non-packageable commodity."[54] One of the truth teams' members, Daniel Ellsberg, quit in disgust over the lies he felt the government was purveying. Though most of the schools gave the government delegations a respectful hearing, they encountered an unfriendly reception at the University of Iowa. And then, when they reached Madison on May 6, they were met by more than two hundred students and faculty members who stood in the back of the auditorium, wearing black armbands, carrying placards, and asking hostile questions about torture and napalm.[55] That episode ended the experiment. At the big Berkeley teach-in two weeks later, the organizers set up two empty chairs on the stage for the State Department officials who had been invited but did not show up.[56]

The National Teach-In and Beyond

Bundy did agree to appear at the Inter-University Committee's National Teach-In on May 15. There were some conditions, of course. He would not debate directly with Senator Wayne Morse, who along with Alaska's Ernest Gruening had voted against the Tonkin Gulf Resolution, nor with Hans Morgenthau, whom he claimed bore a personal grudge because Bundy had once refused to appoint him to the Harvard faculty.[57] Instead Bundy wanted the confrontation to take place within the context of a panel of experts both for and against the administration's Vietnam policy, to show that not every academic opposed the war.[58] There were to be three sessions: a morning panel consisting of Morgenthau; Isaac Deutscher, a European Marxist scholar who would place the war in a broader context; and Arthur Schlesinger Jr., who would present the official case. In the afternoon,

Bundy would face Cornell's Southeast Asian expert George M. Kahin, each backed up by a panel of sympathetic academics: Fishel, Scalapino, Columbia's Zbigniew Brzezinski, and Michael F. M. Lindsay of American University for the government, and for the antiwar side, Mary Wright, Morgenthau, William Appleman Williams, and Stanley Millet. The evening program consisted of eight smaller sessions where antiwar professors and government experts would debate such topics as China policy, the domino theory, "Civil War and Aggression from the North," and "Can the War Be Won?"—the last featuring Daniel Ellsberg for the administration.[59]

The event got all the publicity its organizers craved, including serious attention in the mainstream press, telephone hookups to public address systems and radio stations at 122 college campuses, and live coverage by National Educational Television, with segments aired on the commercial networks. An audience of three thousand students, professors, federal officials, and ordinary citizens attended the morning session and five thousand the afternoon one.[60] But Bundy never showed. Lyndon Johnson had been unhappy about his national security adviser's willingness to engage with the war's opponents. At the last minute, he sent him on an official mission to the Dominican Republic, which US Marines had just occupied. Scalapino presented the government's case instead.[61]

Despite Bundy's absence, most of the Michigan organizers considered the National Teach-In, in Richard Mann's words, "a great success." It had provided an "intellectually responsible" forum where, for the first time in a decade and a half, thoughtful questions could be raised about the anti-communist assumptions and global interventionism undergirding American foreign policy. A debate had begun and, according to Anatol Rapoport, "The nation listened."[62]

A month later, Bundy and Morgenthau finally had their face-off. Broadcast on CBS television on June 15, it echoed, in shortened form, the original format of two debaters backed up by teams of experts. When confronted by difficult questions, Bundy claimed that secret information he could not divulge supported the government's position. As the Pentagon Papers and other sources later revealed, it was a weak (and essentially dishonest) argument, but Bundy was a skillful

FIGURE 6.1. Arthur Schlesinger at national teach-in, Washington, DC, May 15, 1965.
© Rowland Scherman Collection. Special Collections and University Archives, University of Massachusetts Amherst Libraries.

FIGURE 6.2. Mary Wright at national teach-in, Washington, DC, May 15, 1965. © Rowland Scherman Collection. Special Collections and University Archives, University of Massachusetts Amherst Libraries.

debater and Mann was not the only IUC activist to feel that "Bundy and Scalapino talked circles around us." As academics, the antiwar panelists were simply too attached to nuance to make a persuasive case in the face of the government's lies and oversimplifications.[63]

By the fall of 1965, even as many schools were still organizing teach-ins, the movement began to lose momentum. "I think the format of the Teach-in is no longer fruitful on a national scale," Joe Griffith reported from Cornell. It "has also lost its national publicity value."[64] While the first wave of teach-ins got front-page coverage, the *New York Times* report on the big Berkeley one appeared on page 26. In explaining the decline, Douglas Dowd noted

> that our natural foils—the State Department and the Pentagon—wouldn't have anything to do with us, because they just kept losing. . . . By the time that had gone on for a year or so the State Department didn't want to send people out any more. The teach-in really got its energy from the clash. That's what made us look good, was the other guys. . . . So we realized that . . . the teach-ins really couldn't go on any more, that it took two to tango.[65]

The novelty had worn off.[66]

Nevertheless, the next few years saw hundreds (maybe thousands) of smaller teach-ins, conferences, congressional hearings, demonstrations, and other forms of antiwar protests both on and off campuses. With some help from the IUC and other antiwar groups, a cadre of experienced faculty members filled the demand for speakers at these events.[67]

Staughton Lynd was among the most ubiquitous of these activists. He chaired the program at the first major antiwar demonstration in April 1965 that brought an unprecedented twenty-five thousand protesters under SDS auspices to Washington, DC; and he quickly became a fixture on the antiwar circuit.[68] Especially after his return from Hanoi at the end of 1965, he became, he recalled, "one of the most sought-after Movement speakers in the United States. . . . In those days I felt an obligation to accept almost any invitation to speak against the war." He finally pulled back in May 1966 when he sensed that he was becoming "a platform personality." He was on the road so often that he rarely saw his family and feared that his marriage—not to mention his career—was in danger.[69]

Lynd's speaking schedule was extreme, but he was by no means unique. Howard Zinn was another gifted orator who rarely turned down a speaking engagement.[70] Nor did Noam Chomsky. "My first talks about the war," he explained, "were in churches (with maybe four people: the organizer, some drunk who walked in, the minister, and some guy who wanted to kill me) or someone's living room, where a few neighbors were gathered." Later on, as he gained a national reputation, his appearances drew thousands.[71] Browne, Spock, Morgenthau, Millet, Williams, Dowd, and the other antiwar academic stars also worked the national scene, while dozens of lesser-known, but just as dedicated, college and university teachers spoke at local events. And they did so for years.

The Literature of Protest

As befitting academic events, there was usually a literature table at the teach-ins. Not that it was initially loaded with items; there was little published material about Vietnam available in English. There were occasional articles in the *New Republic*, *The Nation*, *Commentary*, and a few similar journals, including the new left-wing muckraking magazine *Ramparts*. Probably the most important source of information in those days was the four-page weekly bulletin put out by I. F. Stone. But it was clear that there was much more to know about the situation in Southeast Asia. Within a few months, several antiwar publications began to appear, most written by professors, graduate students, or former graduate students, some of whom had dropped out of school to work full-time in the antiwar movement.

The most ambitious was *Viet-Report*, which called itself "An Emergency News Bulletin on Southeast Asian Affairs." John McDermott, who became one of its first two associate editors, recalls going to a February 1965 meeting of local academic antiwar activists in a crowded Upper East Side apartment. The group quickly decided to put out a magazine focused on Vietnam. Its changing roster of editors and staff members were mainly New York City–based junior faculty members and graduate students. Carol Brightman, a charismatic graduate student pursuing a PhD in English at NYU, became its editor. Martin Nicolaus, who was studying with Herbert Marcuse at Brandeis, was the other associate editor. Its original four-person advisory board consisted of Browne, Lynd, Millet, and the Wayne State activist and political scientist Otto Feinstein. Early funding came from New York City's University Committee to Protest the War in Vietnam, as well as three angels: Dr. Spock, the retired US appellate judge and civil libertarian Henry W. Edgerton, and George Rawitscher, a physicist at the University of Connecticut. There was also some overlap with editors from *Studies on the Left*.[72]

Viet-Report's founders viewed the publication as an appendage of the teach-in movement. "The business plan of the magazine," Nicolaus recalled, "was to produce informational articles about the Vietnam war, to print it in an inexpensive format, and to distribute it in bulk to antiwar groups on college campuses for them to hand out in connection with campus antiwar teach-ins." Orders of one hundred or more copies sold for six cents an issue. From early runs of about 40,000 copies, *Viet-Report*'s circulation was up to 120,000 copies before the magazine fell victim to sectarianism and folded in 1968.[73]

Realizing how little they knew about the area they were covering, and encouraged by their funders, the editors made one of their first projects a short history of Vietnam. McDermott took on the assignment. Experts like Bernard Fall, Browne, and Millet were generous with advice, reading lists, and collections of documents. McDermott's history, published in three installments, was then put out as a separate booklet. Because of its success, McDermott recalled, "I was on the road all the time, with bundles of *Viet-Report*."

My main occupation then was as an itinerant preacher against the Vietnam War and the Cold War perspective which animated it. . . . I was invited to visit and speak at 124 different US college campuses, often more than once, the whole encompassing perhaps 200 visits spread more or less evenly over the 8 year period.[74]

He earned enough from honoraria for those appearances that for a few years after he lost his teaching job at Long Island University for refusing to sign New York State's 1949 Feinberg Law anti-communist affidavit, he could work full-time on the magazine.[75]

McDermott and his fellow editors were determined to provide coverage that the mainstream media did not. At the same time, they wanted *Viet-Report* to be perceived as a "reliable" source of information.[76] Accordingly, the magazine's contents were a mixture of official documents (from all sides), commentary and articles by the editors and other authors, and translations—mainly from the French—of useful articles and reports.

Its first issue, for example, in July 1965, featured the translation of a report of his visit with the Vietcong by a French journalist, the first part of McDermott's history of Vietnam, as well as articles by Fall, Millet, Nicolaus, and a book review by Lynd. The second issue printed the entire text of the Geneva Agreement of 1954 that ended the French presence in Southeast Asia, with the most important passages rendered in boldface type. The third had a report by Browne on his trip to Saigon in the summer of 1965. Later issues expanded the magazine's purview to the Dominican Republic, Thailand, and finally, in the summer of 1968, to a double issue on "Colonialism and Liberation in America," containing articles by Tom Hayden, Michael Klare, and the sociologists Frances Piven and Richard Cloward, among others on the urban situation—with a Bronx street scene on the cover. The magazine also paid attention to the universities with which so many of its authors and staff members were connected. Carol Brightman provided an important early piece on chemical warfare research at the University of Pennsylvania; and in January 1968, *Viet-Report* came out with a double issue, "The University at War," that contained an exhaustive survey of the military-related secret research then under way on the nation's campuses.[77]

The magazine carried no advertising, though it ran occasional announcements about such projects as draft counseling and provided information about other literature useful to the antiwar movement. One book that it did promote was *Viet Nam: History, Documents, and*

VIET REPORT

AN EMERGENCY
NEWS BULLETIN
ON SOUTHEAST
ASIAN AFFAIRS
OCT., 1965   50c

**POSTSCRIPT TO VIETNAMESE HISTORY
LETTER TO AMERICANS
Jules Roy
AN EYEWITNESS IN THE NORTH
Christopher Koch**

FIGURE 6.3. *Viet-Report*, October 1965. © Courtesy of the Tamiment Library, New York University.

Opinions on a Major World Crisis by the historian Marvin Gettleman, an original member of *Viet-Report*'s research staff.[78] That book, rushed into print in the summer of 1965, another historian observed, became "the Bible of the anti-war movement."[79] It contained nearly 450 pages of official documents from all sides and reports from the field, as well as Robert Scheer's essay about how the United States came to back Diem and pieces by Fishel, Fall, Morgenthau, Stone, and others. It went through many printings and editions, ultimately selling some 600,000 copies—and is still in print.[80] Bernard Fall produced a similar volume with Marcus Raskin of the Institute for Policy Studies. Entitled *The Viet-Nam Reader*, it, too, contained a mélange of official texts and interpretive essays, more policy-oriented than Gettleman's historically focused volume.[81]

Teach-in organizers relied as well on such iconic documents as Stone's April 1965 analysis of the Johnson administration's "White Paper on Vietnam" and Scheer's pamphlet *How the United States Got Involved in Vietnam*, underwritten by the Center for the Study of Democratic Institutions. Local activists produced their own studies and bibliographies. During the summer of 1965, while he was at Cornell ostensibly finishing his PhD, Charles Haynie took a seminar about Vietnam with the French scholar Philippe Devillers, who encouraged him to write a pamphlet. Like McDermott's similar oeuvre, Haynie's hundred-page essay got wide circulation. When the Inter-University Committee placed an ad in the *New York Times* promising assistance in mounting teach-ins, it was overwhelmed with requests for help. Its staff sent out copies of Haynie's pamphlet along with reading lists and the names of prospective speakers.[82]

On the West Coast, three key activists in Berkeley's Faculty Peace Committee (FPC)—the China scholar Franz Schurmann, the English professor Peter Dale Scott, and the historian Reginald Zelnik—produced *The Politics of Escalation*, an early analysis of US policy in Vietnam.[83] That same peace group was also, at least indirectly, responsible for introducing Noam Chomsky to a broader audience when Chomsky asked the literary scholar Frederick Crews, whom he had met through the FPC while spending a semester at Berkeley, to help him publish an article in the *New York Review of Books*. The piece, "The Responsibility of Intellectuals," was Chomsky's devastating critique of the Cold War liberals' contribution to the Vietnam conflict. Crews, who had been writing for the *NYRB* for a few years, recalled, "I sent it off to Robert Silvers in New York and he said, 'My god, I'm publishing it.'" And so he did, launching the political career of one of the most influential public intellectuals and academic critics of the war.[84]

Traveling to War

When Robert Scalapino declined the Vietnam Day Committee's invitation to address the big Berkeley teach-in, he explained that it was purveying "propaganda, not knowledge," in part because "only a handful of the performers have ever been to Vietnam."[85] It was true, of course. But given some of the fine reporting that Vietnam-based journalists like David Halberstam and Homer Bigart were producing, one did not have to spend a semester in Saigon to know that the war was a disaster. Still, there was something to be said for firsthand experience. Over the course of the conflict, nearly one hundred academics made the journey, most to Saigon, but a few to Hanoi as well. Some, like *Viet-Report*'s John McDermott, went as individuals, quasi-journalists who wanted to see what the war actually looked like.[86] Others, like Robert S. Browne, went with delegations to meet with South Vietnamese intellectuals, religious figures, and politicians or, for those who went to the North, to assess the damage done by American bombs and see if they could help broker peace negotiations.

Though Staughton Lynd was not the first academic to visit Hanoi— that honor belonged to the Berkeley political scientist and women's peace activist Frances Herring, who went in the summer of 1965— the young Yale historian may well have been the most controversial.[87] He was invited by the communist historian Herbert Aptheker, who had been asked by the North Vietnamese government to bring two non-communist colleagues. After some hesitation because of Aptheker's party affiliation, Lynd agreed to go, as did the SDS leader Tom Hayden.[88] Lynd made sure that the trip would take place over the Christmas holidays so that he would not miss any classes. His scrupulousness did not, however, save his job. Not only had the US government banned travel to North Vietnam, but it also hinted that the trio risked possible prosecution under the 1798 Logan Act prohibiting private citizens from engaging in diplomatic negotiations.[89] Moreover, for Lynd to visit a communist country in the company of as controversial an individual as Aptheker was to risk losing legitimacy—and not just in the eyes of supporters of the war. There was a serious debate among the leaders of the IUC about the trip. Even though they all agreed that it should be supported on the grounds that Americans needed as much information about Vietnam as they could get, some feared that Lynd's association with Aptheker might taint the mission.[90]

Both Lynd and Hayden were fully aware that they were getting a Potemkin village view of North Vietnam. "Our interactions with 'ordinary Vietnamese citizens' were carefully arranged by our hosts," they later explained, "and we have no reason to believe that the enterprises we toured or the workers and peasants with whom we spoke were typical."[91] Although their trip coincided with an American bombing pause that Johnson touted as a measure to encourage the North Vietnamese to begin peace negotiations, they did see enough bomb damage to counter the government's claim that its planes did not hit civilian targets, an assessment the *New York Times* correspondent Harrison Salisbury confirmed a year later. When Lynd and his colleagues met with Prime Minister Pham Van Dong, he told them that his government was ready to begin talks, but that the Americans never approached them. He was lying; but so, too, was LBJ. Neither side wanted peace at that point.[92]

Even before Lynd reached North Vietnam, the trip drew enormous attention—and condemnation. Yale's president Kingman Brewster, nonetheless, defended Lynd's "conscientious effort" and claimed that it would be "unthinkable" for the university to penalize him for it. Lynd had been warned beforehand "to keep my mouth shut while in Hanoi." But, without his knowledge or consent, Radio Hanoi released the transcript of his remarks at a cultural event in which he had excoriated the Johnson administration's "lies to the American people" and attacked US policy in Vietnam as "immoral, illegal, and antidemocratic."[93] Suddenly, politicians and pundits talked of treason, the State Department revoked Lynd's passport, and Brewster, swamped by alumni demands for the controversial historian's ouster, was soon backtracking. Calling Lynd "naïve" and "irresponsible," he claimed that his comments had given "aid and comfort to a government engaged in hostilities with American forces."[94] Within a few months,

John Blum, the chair of Yale's history department, made it clear that Lynd would not be receiving tenure. At the time, Blum told Lynd that his non-reappointment was a technical budget issue; it wasn't, as Blum later admitted. His superiors at Yale could no longer stomach Lynd's uncompromising opposition to the war. Blum viewed him as "excessively emotional, hyperbolically emotional, not subject to rational discourse about either urban racial issues or/and the war in Vietnam."[95] So, of course, he had to go.

William Davidon was another academic whose trip to Vietnam got front-page attention. The Haverford physicist was part of a delegation, organized by the Committee for Non-Violent Action and headed by the eminent pacifist A. J. Muste. The group arrived in South Vietnam in mid-April 1966, planning "to establish more direct contact with whatever democratic anti-war elements exist in Saigon."[96] For their first five days, they met with a variety of antiwar Buddhists, Catholics, and intellectuals. But when they tried to hold a press conference at their hotel, the local police barred reporters from the building and forced the group to hold the event at the city hall, where it was disrupted by hired thugs and South Vietnamese security forces posing as "students." Davidon and his colleagues then set off for a planned demonstration outside the American embassy, but were immediately rounded up, whisked to the airport, and put on a plane for Hong Kong. As both Davidon and the columnist Nat Hentoff noted, the media seemed interested only in the rowdy demonstrations and not in the group's report about the widespread opposition to the war that they had found. Since Haverford, as a Quaker school, was more tolerant of antiwar activism than Yale, Davidon's only penalty—if you want to call it one—was losing his position as chair of the physics department.[97]

Later trips by other academics got less attention. Washington's attempts to take away people's passports—though ultimately overturned by the courts—discouraged visits to Hanoi in 1966 and 1967.[98] Moreover, the logistical problems of hosting American delegations made it difficult for the North Vietnamese to invite more than a handful of visitors. In addition, because many of those people were strongly identified with the Left, they lacked mainstream credibility and, thus, drew less media attention in the United States than more moderate travelers might have received.[99]

The Impact of the Teach-Ins

In a letter to his former colleague Howard Zinn at the end of June 1965, the eminent American historian Carl Degler discussed his opposition to the war, but claimed to have reservations about the rhetoric of the antiwar movement. Even so, he supported the teach-ins. "You, as a participant in one of them," he told Zinn, "can take pride, I should think, in having helped to change the climate of opinion in the country." He then expressed the opinion that the movement would gradually force Washington to pull back.[100] While Degler's optimism was misplaced, his assessment of the impact of the teach-ins was correct. They did, indeed, "change the climate of opinion in the country." Not only did they bring the war to the attention of thousands of students and faculty members, but they also offered a coherent narrative that explained why the war was both unwinnable and wrong. Even more important, they began the process of educating the rest of the country as well.

Congress was perhaps the most important group that the academic critics of the war wanted to reach—and to some extent did reach. Senators Gruening and Morse were not the only politicians who opposed the Johnson administration's Vietnam policy. Others slowly began to question what was going on. The antiwar professors pushed them to act. Wayne State's Otto Feinstein, as the executive secretary of a preexisting academic peace group, was particularly eager to encourage congressmen to hold informal hearings in their districts during the summer of 1965. He helped two Michigan representatives organize such a session in Detroit. On Manhattan's Upper West Side, Representative William Fitts Ryan held a two-day teach-in in August featuring over twenty speakers, including such key figures as Wesley Fishel, Mary Wright, Robert Browne, and Hans Morgenthau.[101]

The antiwar activists, however, wanted official platforms, not unofficial ones. Their biggest catch was William Fulbright, chair of the Senate Foreign Relations Committee, who mounted the first major congressional investigation of the war early in 1966. "Something . . . is wrong," Fulbright noted, "or there would not be such a great dissent, that is evidenced by teach-ins and articles and speeches by various responsible people." Accordingly, he convened a formal set of hearings that not only questioned the administration's highest officials and former officials, but also brought in the nation's top China scholars to discuss the risk that the administration's Vietnam policy posed for a broader war with China. Covered live on CBS television, it was the grandest teach-in of them all and legitimized, as only the political establishment could, the opposition to the war that the teach-ins had done such a formidable job of developing.[102]

"TO TAKE A STAND"

*The Academic Community Wrestles
with the War, 1965–67*

By 1966, the pedagogical phase of the antiwar movement was essentially over; providing information was no longer the movement's main thrust. At a time when the TV networks and mainstream press bombarded readers and viewers with dispatches from Saigon, one did not have to know French or subscribe to *I. F. Stone's Weekly* to find out what was happening in Southeast Asia. Almost every day, the front page of the *New York Times* carried at least three stories about the conflict. For politically aware Americans, Vietnam was impossible to ignore.

Rendered respectable, if not necessarily effective, by the teach-ins and Fulbright hearings, the antiwar movement grew, especially on campuses. Increasing numbers of faculty members and their students came to view the conflict as misconceived, horrifically destructive, and repugnant to all their political and moral values, and sought, in one way or another, to bring it to an end. From 1966 to 1968, as the war ground on and on, antiwar academics faced a variety of tactical choices that usually reflected their position on the political spectrum. Most were liberals of one stripe or another, and most were also in the core liberal arts disciplines, in the humanities, natural sciences, and social sciences.[1]

Significantly, however, college teachers were no longer as central to the movement as they had been—even at their own institutions. Student activists, often with faculty support, grabbed the headlines, disrupting their campuses and forcing their professors to confront issues that they would otherwise avoid.

Divided Minds in Divided Campuses

The sometimes disorderly protests of the next few years intensified the debate about the war, creating fissures that were to affect American higher education for decades to come—and undermine its support within the larger society as well. It is quite possible that serious divisions would have surfaced even without Vietnam. On many campuses, faculties had been struggling with the generational and other professional conflicts produced by their institutions' explosive growth, while student radicals were already active in the civil rights struggle and the Berkeley Free Speech Movement. But Vietnam became an omnipresent specter that troubled academe for nearly a decade.

At the same time, it is important to understand—as most antiwar academics did—that even on their own campuses, until the late 1960s opponents of the war were still a minority. Support for the Johnson administration's Vietnam policy, though shallow, was widespread. The rowdy groups of frat boys who showed up to protest the early teach-ins, carrying signs and heckling speakers, were only the most vociferous expressions of that support.[2] There were also some outspokenly pro-war (or at least pro-administration) professors who gave speeches, wrote articles, and circulated petitions. Admittedly, those petitions drew fewer and, according to one historian, less eminent signers than the antiwar ones.[3] But that may have simply meant that the war's supporters felt less intensely about the conflict than their antiwar colleagues, not that they were outnumbered.[4] Within a few years, however, openly pro-war professors had lost their constituencies and, in at least once instance in the fall of 1967, relied on covert assistance from the Johnson administration to organize a conference and get media attention.[5]

Moreover, just as the early academic critics of the war supplied the intellectual ammunition for the antiwar movement, so, too, did their faculty opponents develop arguments to bolster the government's position. Besides the standard rationalizations—the dominoes, the

Munich analogy, the fear of a postwar bloodbath, the need to keep our word to our ally, and, above all, the refusal to countenance the expansion of communism—pro-war academics added a new scenario, one that presaged a later stab-in-the-back narrative. They insisted that the teach-ins and antiwar demonstrations were themselves responsible for prolonging the conflict by encouraging the North Vietnamese to believe that they could triumph simply by waiting until the peace movement forced the US government to capitulate.[6] Moreover, as the campus unrest intensified, it became easier for administration supporters to get a hearing by attacking the movement's "extremist clamor" than by defending the war.[7]

By the late 1960s, more than a few moderate and liberal opponents of the war were to become as hostile to antiwar radicals as their more hawkish colleagues. Like the Yale historians who could no longer tolerate Staughton Lynd's uncompromising moralism, some liberals pulled back.[8] Though they remained opposed to the war, many of these liberals, at elite schools and elsewhere, seemed more concerned about the bad behavior of their allies on the left than the continued bloodletting in Southeast Asia.[9]

For liberal academics who had originally supported the war, changing their positions was no easy process. Arthur Schlesinger turned against the Vietnam conflict less than a year after he had defended it at the May 1965 National Teach-In in Washington. As a public intellectual, Schlesinger could hardly avoid taking a stand on the war. But he did so cautiously, explaining in March 1966 that "it is a damned complicated and difficult issue and consequently one on which men of good will, equal in patriotism and liberalism, can reach opposite conclusions."[10] Further heightening his ambivalence was his aversion to "displays of emotion, however virtuous," which he found "not only unworthy" but also "ineffectual." By the end of 1966, however, Schlesinger identified with the Democratic Party's doves and became, according to the historians Louis Menashe and Ronald Radosh, "a leading critic of the Administration," though what that opposition consisted of remains unclear, since as late as the spring of 1967, he was still claiming that the United States had to keep troops in Vietnam to force the communists to negotiate.[11]

Most academics shied away from taking sides on the war. In addition, like the historian Carl Degler, many clung to the Cold War consensus. The US intervention in Vietnam, Degler like many others believed, was a necessary part of "the general effort of the U.S. and the west in general to prevent the forcible expansion of communist power."[12] It was to take two more years of bombing, casualties, and protests for the academy's liberal and moderate majority to turn openly against the war. Even then, they were guarded.

Nonetheless, by the middle of 1967, it would have been hard to find even a seemingly apolitical faculty member, apart from the war hawks, who did not disapprove of at least some aspects of the Vietnam venture, if only privately. As early as May 1966, for example, ten eminent Columbia historians and social scientists, portraying themselves as "responsible" citizens who had "refused to join with our colleagues in public criticism of the government's policy," sent a four-page single-spaced letter to Lyndon Johnson. In it, they urged him to prepare the public for the realities of an unfavorable outcome in Vietnam, while offering nine specific recommendations for refraining from further escalation, negotiating a political settlement, and stepping up economic assistance to the rest of Asia. Surprisingly, the president replied a month later in an even longer, single-spaced letter, reiterating the administration's standard defense of the need to "prevent the take-over of South Vietnam by force," while observing that "it is always good to hear from gentlemen." The "gentlemen" conveyed their disappointment in a short letter to Johnson on August 3, though they also rejected their colleague Daniel Bell's invitation to publish the correspondence in his magazine, *The Public Interest.*[13]

A year later, sixteen of Harvard's equally eminent and rather conservative senior faculty members (the dean of the faculty of Arts and Sciences, the president of Radcliffe College, and four present and future Nobel laureates among them) also sent a private message to LBJ. In it, they also explained that they had never taken any public stance on the war, but that they believed that military escalation was no longer useful. Accordingly, they offered to assist him quietly in de-escalating the fighting and finding a political solution. Johnson, who had little love for the Ivy League, nonetheless agreed to meet with the group, no doubt hoping to co-opt them into helping him sell the war. The mission failed. As Harvard dean Franklin Ford later wrote to Johnson, "We came home with our misgivings about America's present course in Vietnam undiminished and, indeed, in some respects sharpened."[14] But, as promised, they never went public with their concerns. Even so, the fact that such a distinguished group felt compelled to do something, however cautiously, indicates that the academic establishment had pretty definitively turned against the war by the summer of 1967—six months before the Tet Offensive made it clear that an American military victory was not in the offing.

In the meantime, most of the openly antiwar professors continued to circulate petitions, place ads, hold teach-ins, and march in demonstrations.[15] These activities spanned the political spectrum from SANE's decorous protests to manifestos encouraging civil disobedience.[16] Ad hoc organizations proliferated. Seemingly every institution hosted some kind of faculty peace group, with a name like the Committee to End the War in Vietnam and often with ties to community antiwar groups and even a vague connection to a short-lived National Coordinating Committee to End the War in Vietnam founded by Lynd and a few others in the summer of 1965.

Most such groups espoused a variety of political positions. In SANE, for example, co-chair H. Stuart Hughes remained wedded to conventional politics. He planned to rely

> solely on the spoken and the written word, on disciplined marches and advertisements in newspapers as evidence of our existence and our respectability. We aimed to extend our following bit by bit from its original base among intellectuals until finally it would include the majority of our countrymen. One day they would elect a Congress that would vote the country out of the war.[17]

SANE's other co-chair, Benjamin Spock, however, followed a more radical trajectory from lending his name to letters and ads to courting arrest at a draft board sit-in.

Signing public statements and sending checks was probably the most common and earliest of the academic community's antiwar

activities. The number of petitions was, historian David Schalk admitted, so "enormous" that "I cannot even begin to imagine approximate
totals or how to arrive at them, as there were so many different sponsors, both regional and national, preparing texts that were directed to
a wide variety of authorities and potential supporters."[18] Such statements attracted hundreds and sometimes thousands of signers.[19]
They came from local and regional groups, individual institutions,
specific disciplines, and thousands of ordinary college and university
teachers. And they appeared in hundreds of outlets from left-wing
magazines and the student press to the leading newspapers. The *New
York Times* was the venue of choice. An ad there on June 5, 1966, contained more than sixty-four hundred signatures of academics and
other professionals, filling three pages.[20] The sociologist Everett Carll
Ladd counted more than twenty thousand names in the Sunday *New
York Times* between October 1964 and June 1968. Most signers came
from such core liberal arts disciplines as psychology, biology, sociology, and English, but every field was represented, even if sparsely
from agriculture, business, engineering, and education schools.[21]

These ads dealt with international law, bombing halts, chemical
warfare, negotiations, draft resistance, and just about every moral or
political issue connected to the conflict. Early ones tended toward
moderation, urging the administration not to escalate the conflict. As
some sectors of the antiwar movement became more militant, their
manifestos did as well, demanding immediate withdrawal and encouraging civil disobedience. Most, however, were vague and somewhat tepid. There was, for example, a petition circulated by a "straight
arrow liberal" colleague at Wesleyan in 1965 that, the literary scholar
Richard Ohmann recalled, "said something like 'Mr. President, please
stop the bombing.'"[22]

As the opposition to the war spread, signing a mild petition was
no longer risky. In fact, by the spring of 1967, as one of LBJ's main
advisers told him, among academics and "intellectuals . . . [n]ot only
is it fashionable for them to be against the war, it is *un*fashionable
to be for it."[23] By then, establishment liberals like Schlesinger, Kenneth Galbraith, and Clark Kerr, who only a few years before would

never have openly criticized the administration, were sponsoring an ad in several papers under the rubric "Negotiations Now!"[24] A similar statement elicited more than a hundred signatures from the full professors at Yale—though as C. Vann Woodward, one of its chief sponsors, noted, it did not propose any policy other than an unconditional bombing halt.[25]

These petitions entailed considerable effort, requiring an often hectic round of holding meetings, writing and revising statements, gathering signatures, raising money, and rushing to meet newspaper deadlines. Most of the time it was easy to collect both signatures and checks, especially on the elite campuses and other schools in New England and the rest of the Northeast, though by 1967, signers could even be found in Texas. The Boston Area Faculty Group on Public Issues (BAFGOPI) was particularly energetic about sponsoring petitions.[26] When the recently radicalized biologist Jonathan Beckwith returned to the Harvard Medical School from a postdoc in France in the fall of 1965, he immediately threw himself into BAFGOPI's petition campaigns. Assigned to canvass the medical school, Beckwith got his entire department to sign.[27]

Demonstrations

It required little more courage, though more physical effort, for college teachers to join a demonstration than to sign a newspaper ad. As early as the summer of 1965, protest marches began to replace teach-ins as the tactic of choice. Unlike the teach-ins, however, the main demonstrations did not take place on campus but on the streets of cities like New York, Boston, San Francisco, and Washington, DC, usually under the aegis of an antiwar coalition. Even so, academics were disproportionately involved in their planning—at least in the early stages.

The marches and rallies came in many flavors, with often competing goals and tactics. Those organized by the centrist liberals and moderates emphasized respectability, hoping that rational arguments and orderly demonstrations would eventually bring an end the war.

Thus, for example, because they feared that participation by communists and radicals would alienate middle-class citizens, SANE's leaders refused to let Linus Pauling and Staughton Lynd become sponsors of their November 1965 demonstration in Washington. They were also careful to ensure that no Vietcong flags or offensive slogans would undermine their decorous image. "The tone of the March will be affirmative and creative," a leaflet explained.

> There will be no civil disobedience. All signs will be provided in Washington except those indicating cities and schools of origins, which should be brought by the marchers. There will be no organizational signs or literature.[28]

At the other end of the political spectrum were those Berkeley professors who had actively supported the Free Speech Movement (FSM). Leon Wofsy, Carl Schorske, and the China scholar Franz Schurmann, among others, formed the Faculty Peace Committee, a loose collective that promoted a wide range of legal and illegal protests and intellectual projects.[29] Their more militant colleagues worked directly with FSM alumni in what became the Berkeley Vietnam Day Committee (VDC), an overtly radical New Left organization that not only mounted the massive thirty-six-hour teach-in but also engaged in a series of actions and demonstrations that gave the Bay Area antiwar movement a distinctively confrontational identity.[30]

One of the earliest and most militant of the VDC's faculty radicals was the mathematician Stephen Smale. A major figure in his field who in 1966 would receive the mathematicians' equivalent of the Nobel Prize, Smale was also a veteran leftist. Disappointed by the fact that coverage of the enormous teach-in had been relegated to the back pages of the *New York Times*, Smale and his colleagues turned to more militant tactics. Not only did they organize several demonstrations, including two large and occasionally disruptive marches from Berkeley to the Oakland Army Terminal during the so-called "International Days of Protest" in October 1965, but they also, at Smale's suggestion, made an abortive attempt to stop the troop trains that ran through Berkeley to Oakland, carrying recruits bound for Vietnam.[31] "We certainly didn't prevent any troops from going to the front lines," he admitted, but

> the shock of a militant confrontation constituted an important victory. . . . With the extended news coverage of this and subsequent troop train clashes, the country was beginning to see the cost of the War in terms of the threat to its institutions. . . . We were warning Johnson and the government that if they continued the War, then the fabric of American society would be threatened.[32]

Smale's stint with the antiwar movement was brief. Disappointed by the VDC's lack of enthusiasm for further direct action, he left the organization after the October protests and returned to his mathematical pursuits. Still, his six months of activism did have an impact.[33] "He laid out the whole direction of the antiwar movement," his fellow co-chair, Jerry Rubin, explained.

> He was almost like the Lone Ranger. He came in on his horse and gave us the message, and then dropped the silver bullet and went off.
> What happened in Berkeley with the Vietnam Day and with the .troop train protests . . . was the script for the whole decade. Steve Smale wrote that script, and then he left the others of us to carry it out.[34]

While Smale embodied the professorial New Left's emerging embrace of nonviolent civil disobedience, Sidney Peck, a sociologist at Case Western Reserve, led its more pragmatic sector's shift to mass demonstrations. Involved from the start with the teach-ins and the Inter-University Committee for Debate on Foreign Policy, Peck soon became concerned about the limitations of the pedagogical approach.[35] But rather than disrupt the war machine, he wanted to build a mass movement. Accordingly, after creating a local antiwar coalition, he invited representatives of the nation's main peace and New Left organizations to Cleveland in the summer of 1966 to create a national body to coordinate future demonstrations.[36]

Peck had caught the movement's zeitgeist. "I don't think any of us—

certainly not I—were conscious of the fact that we were on a ladder or path," recalled Cornell's Douglas Dowd, who was to become the chair of the National Mobilization Committee to End the War in Vietnam, or the Mobe as the group that emerged from Peck's invitation came to be called.

> I remember when we got together in Cleveland to start the Mobe that it was just taken for granted by everybody that we had to do something more than just getting up in an auditorium with some speeches. I can't remember even talking about it. It was as though you'd been sort of petting around, necking with somebody, and all of sudden you begin to fuck, you know. You don't say, "Let's do it." It just happens. That's how the Mobe came to be.[37]

In order to avoid the factionalism that was already surfacing in the antiwar movement, the Mobe's early leaders, Peck and, especially, the revered pacifist minister A. J. Muste, insisted that it be non-exclusionary. It would not bar communists or any other political group and would let each member organization do its own thing as long as it supported the overall movement against the war.[38]

After encouraging its constituent groups to mount local protests at the time of the national elections in November 1966, the Mobe turned to organizing major demonstrations for the following April in New York and San Francisco. The Mobe then followed those events, the largest of their kind until then, with the more controversial demonstration at the Pentagon in November 1967, where Jerry Rubin, perhaps channeling Smale, encouraged a confrontation with the military. Though the arrests of Noam Chomsky, Norman Mailer, and dozens of other academic and intellectual civil disobedients received the most coverage, the event also featured a massive and perfectly respectable demonstration. I can recall marching for hours on a cold, gray day from the Lincoln Memorial over the Potomac to Virginia only to end up on the outskirts of the Pentagon's gigantic parking lot in a huge crowd unable to hear or see a thing, completely unaware that civil disobedience was taking place, and eager to get back onto the bus for Princeton.

Electoral Activities: The Peace Candidates

The Pentagon demonstration turned out to be the Mobe's last fling. By the end of 1967, that phase of the movement had run out of steam. Although the teach-ins, demonstrations, and growing student unrest—along with the unabated resistance of the Vietnamese communists and nationalists—were, in fact, having a cumulative impact on increasing numbers of politicians and policy makers, there was no public indication that the government's position on Vietnam was about to change. While some of the more frustrated radicals within the academy began to contemplate civil disobedience, most of its liberals were turning to electoral politics.

It was not a particularly controversial move. After all, ever since the political scientist Woodrow Wilson left the presidency of Princeton for the New Jersey governor's mansion in 1911, professors had run for office. No form of dissent could be more all-American than an electoral campaign designed to influence official policy. Especially for left-liberal academics, such campaigns had considerable appeal. To begin with, they were thoroughly respectable undertakings that attracted mainstream attention and support in the way that the peace movement's more disruptive or innovative tactics did not. As a congressional candidate from Indiana University explained, "You can best present people with new, minority or unconventional ideas by clothing them in conventional dress."[39]

Few, if any, of the activists who embraced electoral politics expected to win. They were also divided over whether to run inside or outside the Democratic Party. They viewed their campaigns, as the organizers of an independent campaign on Manhattan's Upper West Side for the *Studies on the Left* editor James Weinstein explained, as "an important organizing and educational tool."[40] In particular, they hoped that electoral politics could help build a larger movement.[41] Quite a few academics ran as antiwar candidates, but I have no idea how many. If there is any scholarship specifically on the subject, I did not encounter it.

What I did find, however—to my surprise—was how many of the leading doves had taught college before they reached the US Senate.

Among the most prominent were two former law school professors: Wayne Morse of Oregon and William Fulbright, the chair of the Senate Foreign Relations Committee. The senate majority leader Mike Mansfield taught East Asian and Latin American history at the University of Montana before entering politics. Other such senatorial doves included LBJ's 1968 challenger Eugene McCarthy, South Dakota's George McGovern, Idaho's Frank Church, and Oregon's Mark Hatfield.[42] None of these former academics had originally campaigned as single-issue candidates. Most were certified New Dealers who wanted to win elections, not bring political alternatives into mainstream debates. Still, it is tempting to think that their academic backgrounds may have propelled them toward opposing the Vietnam War sooner than their congressional colleagues.

Even before the Vietnam War escalated, however, other academics were running for office specifically to bring new perspectives into the political arena. "Of course I had no realistic possibility of getting elected," H. Stuart Hughes confessed, in describing his campaign as a peace candidate for the US Senate from Massachusetts in 1962.

> But this *was* a chance to challenge the bipartisan consensus in a highly visible campaign and to lift that campaign above the level of a local clan battle by redirecting it toward debate on the life-and-death issues of the nuclear age.

Hughes's patrician eloquence, Ivy League imprimatur, and political pedigree as the grandson of the US Supreme Court Chief Justice and presidential candidate Charles Evans Hughes ensured the Harvard historian considerable media attention, especially since he was running against two other political scions, Edward Kennedy and George Lodge.[43] At the peak of the campaign, three thousand people worked for Hughes—students, faculty members, suburban housewives, and me. He ended up with fifty thousand votes, some 2 percent of the total, but felt, nonetheless, that the undertaking was a success. "I had been taken seriously as an equal candidate; the press coverage had been good; minds had been opened. I had prodded the other candidates to talk about *my* issues."[44]

Hughes was not the only professor to run for office as a peace candidate that year. In upstate New York, Cornell's anti-nuclear activists were also eager to mount such a campaign. Because of their earlier communist connections, neither of the group's main faculty leaders, Douglas Dowd and the physicist Philip Morrison, could realistically run, so the activists enlisted Harrop Freeman, a Quaker law professor who had written a book about the "insanity" of nuclear weapons. The campaign turned out to be a disappointment. Not only did Freeman lose as expected, but, as Dowd recalled, at some point he became convinced that he stood a chance of winning and stopped talking about nuclear weapons.[45]

As far as I can tell, no faculty members ran as peace candidates in 1964. Instead, they rallied to Lyndon Johnson—or, rather, against the hawkish and conservative Barry Goldwater. Even left-wing academics overcame their hesitations and went, as the slogan put it, "part of the way with LBJ."[46]

Within two years, however, Johnson had become the enemy, and quite a few academics were running as or working for peace candidates. Many of the leading antiwar organizations urged their supporters to involve themselves in electoral campaigns. The sputtering Inter-University Committee for Debate on Foreign Policy, for example, published an ad in the March 6, 1966, *New York Times* explaining that all supporters of "reasoned dissent" must "try to promote the candidacy of opponents to this war, in the political party of their choice" and promising to "send documents to help candidates organize effective campaigns."[47] SANE, too, decided to enter electoral politics, by organizing a "Voter's Peace Pledge Campaign" co-chaired by William Sloane Coffin that ultimately got seventy-three thousand signers to promise to support and vote for congressional candidates in 1966 "who agree to work vigorously" for de-escalation, negotiations, and a ceasefire. Under its auspices, Benjamin Spock traveled around the country campaigning for the peace candidates in the Democratic primaries.[48]

There may have been one hundred such candidates.[49] Probably the most successful, certainly the most well-known, was Robert Scheer, the University of California graduate student turned journalist who ran for Congress in the district comprising Berkeley and much of Oakland. Largely because of his articles in *Ramparts*, where he exposed Michigan State University's ties to the CIA in Vietnam, Berkeley's Faculty Peace Committee and other Bay Area activists enlisted him as an antiwar candidate. The incumbent congressman, Jeffrey Cohelan, had a progressive voting record but backed the war. Scheer and his supporters wanted to challenge the centrist establishment that Cohelan represented, not only because of its stance on Vietnam, but also because of its failure to devote serious resources to the War on Poverty. As Scheer later explained, the campaign was designed to "raise issues in the community" and force its members "to take a stand on the war in Vietnam." Though the Berkeley faculty played a minor role in the campaign, over a thousand volunteers turned out, a veritable cross-section of that mixed community—students, housewives, businessmen, welfare mothers, preachers, and high school teachers. The campaign also received considerable publicity as politicians, academics, and celebrities recognized its symbolic importance.[50]

Scheer almost won. He got 45 percent of the vote—taking Berkeley with 54 percent and Oakland's Black neighborhoods with 57 percent. California's other antiwar candidates, including the former Michigan State Vietnam adviser, Stanley Sheinbaum, also won more than 40 percent of their districts' votes in the Democratic primaries.[51] Both local and national academic activists mounted congressional campaigns, among them Robert Browne and Stanley Millet. These races took place across the country in cities and college towns like Lancaster, Pennsylvania, New Haven, Cleveland, and Ann Arbor. Typically, as Indiana University psychologist James Dinsmoor explained, they wanted to inject antiwar issues into "normal, local politics." Dinsmoor lost the Democratic primary, but he did carry the university's county and had, he felt, "encouraged people to think of the issue as a legitimate one." As expected, none of these peace candidates won, though the pacifist scholar Elise Boulding's Ann Arbor write-in campaign pulled so many votes from the Democratic incumbent that he lost to his Republican opponent.[52]

Toward the McCarthy Campaign and Beyond

Some antiwar activists became engaged in related political activities—especially antiwar referenda campaigns, which allowed activists to canvass from door to door bringing their message to ordinary citizens.[53] Most, but not all, took place between 1966 and 1968 in cities and college towns like Ann Arbor, Berkeley, Cambridge, Ithaca, Madison, and San Francisco. Though the San Francisco effort lost by a two-to-one margin as did the Madison one, the balloting was closer in the other towns, with the antiwar forces usually garnering about 40 percent of the votes.[54]

A more ambitious undertaking, and one that fed directly into the presidential challenge of Eugene McCarthy at the end of 1967, was the Vietnam Summer project. Conceptualized by the historian Gar Alperovitz, then at Harvard, its faculty and other sponsors called on students to "consider repeating the Mississippi Summer precedent—this time not by going South, but by staying in their own university areas to organize the community. Door-to-door."[55] The goal was to develop a base of antiwar activists and sympathizers upon which to build electoral challenges at every level. It caught on at once, especially after Benjamin Spock and Martin Luther King Jr. endorsed it following the Mobe's big April 1967 demonstration in New York City. By the end of August, Vietnam Summer had expanded to a staff of 500 full-time workers and more than 26,000 volunteers working at some 700 local projects.[56]

As the student volunteers were gaining political experience, talk about a direct challenge to LBJ began to surface. There was a move among some left-liberal and radical members of the academy to run a third-party campaign, perhaps an antiwar and social justice ticket headed by King and Spock. Organized under the rubric of the National Conference for a New Politics, it enlisted the likes of Spock, Coffin, and Herbert Marcuse, but aborted when a counterproductive combination of Black nationalism and white guilt destroyed the NCNP at its first national conference in Chicago over Labor Day weekend.[57] The remnants coalesced around the loosely organized campaign by the

Peace and Freedom Party that ran the Black Panther Eldridge Cleaver for president and Douglas Dowd for vice president.[58]

The most important electoral challenge to the war emerged within the Democratic Party with the presidential campaign of Minnesota senator Eugene McCarthy. The peripatetic liberal organizer Allard Lowenstein, then teaching at CCNY, was deeply engaged in drumming up support for a "Dump Johnson" movement to run a moderate, yet liberal, antiwar politician who would, coincidentally, head off any more radical candidates.[59] A group of establishment academics including Arthur Schlesinger, the Yale historian John Blum, David Riesman, and Kenneth Galbraith had similar plans. Although they could no longer support the Johnson administration's Vietnam policy, they were regular Democrats accustomed to working within the system. Galbraith, for example, headed the Americans for Democratic Action, the quintessential Cold War liberal organization, while Blum had actually been asked by Johnson to edit a volume of his state papers to be used during the 1968 presidential campaign. After their first choice, Robert Kennedy, declined to run, these people turned to Eugene McCarthy.[60]

The McCarthy campaign had considerable support among liberal professors.[61] It gave opponents of the war a suitable outlet for their opposition to the war that did not require an alliance with what they considered the more disreputable elements of the antiwar movement. "I bitterly opposed the war," Blum explained,

> but I also believed that opposition should flow through available political channels. . . . Success in that endeavor seemed unlikely, but the effort would at least set an example for my students, an example that would contrast with the demonstrations of the SDS on other campuses, where agitators of the New Left had trashed libraries or seized buildings and destroyed academic records.[62]

One didn't even have to "bitterly" oppose the war to support McCarthy. Martin Malia, the Berkeley Russian historian who had organized a petition denouncing the Vietnam Day Committee's confrontational tactics in the fall of 1965, was, he claimed, "moderately against the war in Vietnam, I supported Gene McCarthy."[63]

Students, Professors, and the Draft: The Class-Rank Controversy

Meanwhile, the war intensified. The body counts—both Vietnamese and American—kept growing, as did the demand for additional American soldiers. From nearly 30,000 troops in March 1965, when LBJ escalated the conflict, to 184,300 at the end of the year, to nearly 390,000 in December 1966, to 463,000 a year later—the Pentagon was pouring ever-larger numbers of young men into the conflict. As draft calls began to rise, student opposition to the war grew as well. Until then, college students had been exempted from the conflict. As long as they remained in good standing at their college or university, the Selective Service System granted them a 2-S student deferment. Less privileged young men, African Americans and working-class and rural whites, served instead. By the beginning of 1966, however, the military decided to draft students at the bottom of their class. In order to head off complaints from the elite colleges and universities that their weaker undergraduates deserved to rank above the young men at less selective institutions, the Selective Service System also offered students the option of retaining their 2-S classifications if they did well in a national aptitude test scheduled for the spring.[64]

That measure brought the war home to previously quiescent campuses. For the first time since LBJ escalated the conflict, the demand for class rank fueled serious internal debates and major student protests that forced the entire academy to confront the Vietnam War not just as concerned citizens, but as policy-making faculty members. Moreover, as professors argued about whether to cooperate with the Selective Service System, it became clear that the issue also raised questions about the university's broader relationship to the federal government.

Class rank was determined by grades; and grades were traditionally under the faculty's control. Suddenly, however, an otherwise routine academic procedure became a matter of life and death. To a certain extent, that was already the case. Since students who flunked out automatically lost their 2-S deferments, once the war escalated it became common on some campuses to view grades as "A, B, C, D, and Nam"; and some professors marked their students accordingly. "It's a rotten, stinking war," one antiwar instructor explained, "and I'll be damned if I'll help it along by sending over more cannon fodder. Unless he's clearly an idiot, . . . I intend to pass every able-bodied man in my class."[65] Failing a student had become a moral issue and one that for some academics could engender considerable guilt. "I never had forgotten turning in those final grades," the historian Dan Carter recalled of the summer course he taught at East Carolina University in 1966,

> looking at the list of students with "F" beside their names, and asking myself: what if one of these young men—most of them only three or four years younger than me—dies in Vietnam because they confused Charlemagne with Pepin the Short?[66]

Thus, when class ranking came to determine draft status, the moral dilemma intensified. "A difference between a B and a C," William Gamson explained, "could determine whether a student will be drafted out of college and sent to kill—and, perhaps, to die—in an unjust war."[67]

Few faculty members or high administrators had ever given much thought to their students' military deferments, much less developed a policy for submitting grades to draft boards or offering exemption examinations in university buildings. In fact, many schools, among them SUNY Buffalo and the University of Chicago, had never even ranked their students.[68] At Columbia, President Grayson Kirk had assumed that rank lists were a simple bureaucratic matter that the registrar would deal with. President Clifford Furnas at SUNY Buffalo had the same response, explaining that holding the Selective Service System's tests on campus was "a routine decision, like hundreds made every day."[69]

Many faculties were similarly unaware of the implications of that system's demand for student grades. But that was not the case at a few larger institutions that housed a critical mass of politically active students and professors.[70] The protests that they organized against the rank lists were to bring the draft to the nation's attention as well as to raise questions about their institutions' collaboration with the war effort. For the first time, administrators and faculty leaders had to deal with the large-scale student unrest that was to inflame so many campuses for the next few years. Their often confused responses were all too typical, contributing significantly to the overall decline of the academic community's stature within the rest of the country.

It is unclear how many such protests took place. There were seven major confrontations—at SUNY Buffalo, Chicago, CCNY, Cornell, Stanford, Wayne State, and Wisconsin. Less disruptive demonstrations also occurred at Harvard, Brandeis, UCLA, the University of Michigan, San Francisco State, and Indiana University—and probably elsewhere.[71]

As they urged their institutions to refuse to send class rankings to the military or host the exemption exams, antiwar professors tailored their arguments to a variety of constituencies. They appealed to their colleagues' consciences: college teachers should not be put into what one professor at Los Angeles State College called "a morally intolerable position."[72] Moreover, just as individual faculty members should not be making life-and-death decisions about their students, neither should their schools, especially when those decisions bore no relationship to their educational missions. Universities, in other words, should not be in the business of selecting soldiers.

In addition to their moral compunctions, many antiwar faculty members opposed class ranking on the grounds that the entire system of student deferments was unjust. Although the concrete evidence did not emerge until 1967 when SDS publicized a 1965 memo by General Lewis Hershey describing how the Selective Service System "channeled" recruits into the military, it was already clear that the system was skewed against the poor. Student deferments kept middle-class young men out of the military, while those who could not afford college were drafted.[73] "It strikes us as implausible," a group of Harvard professors noted in December 1966, "to suppose that it is in the national interests that students, regardless of their fields, should be deferred while the disadvantaged are compelled to enter military service."[74]

Others objected that the request for class ranks posed a threat to the political independence of the university: the military's demand interfered with the autonomy of the faculty.[75] Even faculty members who had no desire to actively oppose the war had qualms about implementing a policy that originated in the manpower needs of the armed forces.[76]

Antiwar professors also argued that the military's demand for grades would have a deleterious impact on the classroom. A widely circulated "Educators' Statement of Principle on Selective Service" signed by 142 Chicago-area faculty members in the spring of 1966 laid out the main argument against the rank list's "corrosive effect on education." Besides exacerbating the already "negative effects of excessive emphasis on grades" and the unnecessarily competitive atmosphere that it encouraged, basing student deferments on class rankings would involve professors in an "intrinsically arbitrary decision" that has "no ultimately just criteria" and will "impede the educational enterprise of all college and university students."[77] In addition, as the San Francisco State College Senate noted in its resolution against the tests and class rankings, "These criteria will discourage students from exploring academic areas and activities in which they are unsure of abilities to receive high grades."[78] When the Yale sociologist Robert Cook refused to submit his grades, he did so not only to protest their use by the Selective Service System, but also because grading created an "authoritarian" relationship between teachers and students that was "incompatible with real education."[79]

Prescient observers also warned of grade inflation. Professors might well decide not to give any bad grades at all—as indeed happened.[80] The Long Island University historian Joseph Dorinson recalled a colleague who was a "sucker" for hard-luck stories from students who insisted that he had to raise their grades or they would go to Vietnam.[81] There were more than a few individual faculty members and TAs who quietly withheld grades or gave all their students A's.[82]

It was, of course, much more effective for such teachers to mount a collective protest, even if their administrations did not approve, which often they did not. When William Gamson discussed the matter with Michigan's vice president for academic affairs on behalf of antiwar faculty members and graduate students, he was told: "Grading students is part of the requirements of the job. . . . When people can't meet the requirements of the job, they quit and find another." Gamson and twenty or thirty of his colleagues decided instead to "withhold grades for the courses we teach and place them in escrow, to be released only when they are not being used to decide who is drafted." They also held a weeklong fast to publicize what they were doing. Because they worried that their students would suffer, however, they did create an "escape clause," releasing the grades if they got a written request from the student to do so. Not only did the administration threaten to replace the missing grades with F's in their students' transcripts, but a large majority of the faculty senate condemned the grade strike as well.[83]

Richard Flacks was part of a small group at the University of Chicago that had a similar confrontation, this one with the provost and future president Edward Levi. When Flacks and a few of his colleagues presented a list of suggestions for dealing with the issue and tried to explain why "we couldn't allow the grades we were giving as faculty to be used for that purpose," Levi was unsympathetic: "You want this institution to commit civil disobedience?" Undeterred, students and faculty members continued to organize against the class-ranking system. Flacks helped draw up and publicize the Chicago-area "Educators' Statement of Principle on Selective Service."[84] When he released the statement, he intimated that as many as fifty college teachers might withhold their grades if their institutions did not abolish the class rankings.[85]

His position was not, however, shared by most of his colleagues at the University of Chicago. The senior professors on the powerful Faculty Senate Council, after spending several months secretly considering the antiwar faculty's list of suggestions, decided to support the administration's cooperation with the draft. Its rationale, which reflected a near consensus within the academic community at the time, was that universities had long collaborated with the federal government and that, whatever one felt about the war in Vietnam, it would be wrong to end that relationship under pressure from student protests. Ironically, the policy that Chicago's faculty leaders ultimately adopted was the same one that Gamson and his colleagues had devised and that many other institutions were to embrace as well. The university would rank its students, but would send out the result only if an individual student requested it. Wisconsin did the same. Yale's policy was the converse: the registrar would deliver a student's class ranking to his draft board unless the student asked him to withhold it.[86]

The rationale for holding the exemption exams on campus was similar. Again, administrations stressed the routine nature of cooperation with the government; and again, they presented the exam as a matter of individual choice and, even, academic freedom. "The test is being given here and in many other locations in the United States," Buffalo president Furnas explained,

> as a convenience for those students who wish to take it. No one has to take the test. It is not mandatory. But certainly this would be a gross infringement on the personal freedom of the individual. As a matter of fact, it would definitely be an infringement on the rights of those students who desire to take the test if they were to be denied the opportunity by the actions of another group of students.[87]

And since students were signing up for the examinations by the thousands—6,000 at CCNY for the first exam on May 14, and 750,000 overall in 1966 and 1967—even the most militant students and faculty members refrained from interfering with the exam. Instead, SDS and the IUC prepared their own test, the "National Vietnam Examination," a set of questions about the history of Vietnam and the war that antiwar students handed out at the exam sites. Both tests went off without a hitch, the government's at nearly four thousand campuses and the antiwar movement's at several hundred.[88]

Before the exams were given, however, students at a few campuses occupied university buildings in protest. These were—the Free Speech Movement excepted—the first major episodes of nonviolent civil disobedience directed against American colleges and universities during the 1960s. It was a sign of the newness of the situation and the professoriate's still ambivalent attitude about the war that faculties varied in their responses to those sit-ins, even though the actions their schools took were often much the same.

FIGURE 7.1. Students taking Selective Service exam, ca. 1966. © Rowland Scherman Collection. Special Collections and University Archives, University of Massachu-setts Amherst Libraries.

Significantly, however, when professors at institutions like Wisconsin, Chicago, and Buffalo faced militant students for the first time in 1966, many based their responses less on the substantive issues of the war and the draft than on their relationship to their administrations and, even more important, their attitude toward what the students were doing. At those schools, like Chicago, where professors had close ties to the administration and did, in fact, have the final say on educational policies, they tended to support their institution's collaboration with the Selective Service System. But where those ties were strained and it appeared as if the administration had acted in an arbitrary manner, the faculty was more willing to sympathize with the students. Significantly, although the radical academics were closer to the students than their more moderate colleagues, only a tiny handful of professors actually took part in the sit-ins—among them, Hans Gerth at Wisconsin, Georg Iggers at SUNY Buffalo, the mathematician Robert Greenblatt at Cornell, and some junior people at Chicago, including Richard Flacks and the historian Jesse Lemisch. Moreover, those who did side with the students, like Flacks, often worked as mediators.[89]

Like professors and administrators, the students were also in uncharted waters. Though viewed by right-wing professors and outside politicians as what one Chicago conservative called a "step in a power play by SDS to get more say in the operation of the university," that was not the case. SDS did play a role, but a much smaller one than was commonly believed. The organization's central leadership actually delayed coming out officially against the draft until December 1966, although chapters, at Chicago and Cornell, for example, took up the issue sooner.[90] Other campus antiwar groups were equally, if not more, important. Like the faculty activists, the antiwar students were sincerely repelled by the draft and its inequities and wanted their universities to extricate themselves from such an immoral system.[91] These students' demands differed slightly from campus to campus and were often, as even they admitted, vague and confused. Some simply opposed class rank, while others questioned their school's willingness to host the exemption exams. At CCNY, for example, the main demand of the roughly two hundred students who had taken over the administration building was simply a "binding" student-faculty referendum on the issues.[92]

By the beginning of May 1966, the antiwar students had been negotiating with their administrations for several months with no success. Their decisions to engage in direct action were the result of their frustration.* At Cornell, one student activist recalled, it was President James Perkins's "evasive and unsatisfactory" response to the SDS chapter's request that the school not sponsor the exam that nudged him and his comrades to occupy a building.[93] When, in the first sit-in of the season, thirty undergraduates, graduate students, and teaching assistants took over the SUNY Buffalo president's office on May 2, they did so because he refused to meet directly with them. When he agreed to call a university-wide meeting to discuss the issue, the two-day sit-in ended.[94] Stanford's antiwar students took over the president's office for much the same reason.[95] At Chicago, once the four hundred or so student demonstrators understood that the faculty and not the administration had the final say with regard to the draft, they ended their two-day occupation.[96] It was the same at the largest of these demonstrations at Wisconsin, where such left-wing faculty stars as William Appleman Williams, Harvey Goldberg, Maurice Zeitlin, and the historian William Taylor offered to convince their colleagues to oppose the rank list and exam once the students left the administration building.[97]

These protests were nonviolent on both sides. The students did not rifle the president's files or trash any offices. Nor, with only a few exceptions, did the authorities call in the police or inflict more than token punishments on the demonstrators.[98] At Chicago and Wisconsin, in particular, the sit-ins shared something of the aura of the previous year's teach-ins. Student leaders, faculty members, and administrators entered the occupied buildings and addressed the student protesters on a variety of issues. In Madison, the connection was explicit. When the students vacated the administration building, they took over historic Bascom Hall for a teach-in. Dozens of professors, one student leader recalled, "had climbed through the windows to Bascom Hall to

---

* It has been all but impossible to find definitive estimates for the numbers of students involved in these sit-ins. I have seen numbers for the University of Chicago, for example, that range from 200 to 450, while those for the University of Wisconsin are from one to two thousand, many of them fraternity brothers who, with reason, were worried about their grades. Estimates of the length of these sit-ins vary as well, though most seem to have lasted about two days.

join us, just watching and sharing their own stories," participating in a discussion "about the sort of society, education, or life we wanted." It was, he noted, "a type of sociological talk it would never have occurred to us to have in class."[99]

The protests at the University of Chicago caught the institution's administrators and most faculty members by surprise. Chicago, after all, was not a huge and impersonal operation like Berkeley or Wisconsin. On the contrary, as the historian Jesse Lemisch noted, the university had an "intensely intellectual environment" where students "had immense respect for learning," while the senior professors were close to the administration and enjoyed "a highly collegial atmosphere."[100] Almost as soon as the sit-in began, some faculty conservatives circulated a petition to their colleagues calling on them to support the administration if it called the police to clear out the protest. It got two hundred signatures. While the rest of Chicago's professors probably did not want to call the cops, most were equally unsympathetic toward what they viewed as the "coercive" behavior of the students. Accordingly, at the faculty senate's meeting a few days after the occupation ended, 85 percent of the senior professors voted to maintain the rank-list policy.[101]

Ironically, the Chicago sit-in may have had a bigger impact than was apparent at the time. Even before the students ended their sit-in, the administration announced that it would sponsor a conference on the draft.[102] And so for three days in early December, seventy-four invited participants came to a consensus on scrapping the current Selective Service System. For the conservative economist Milton Friedman, who as a libertarian opposed the draft and later served on the presidential commission that dealt with the issue, that conference "was the key event that started the ball rolling decisively toward ending the draft."[103]

Like Chicago's professors, most of the faculty members at Wisconsin considered the main problem to be the students' "coercive" behavior, not the university's cooperation with the Selective Service System. They would not accede to the demonstrators' demands to meet "under duress." Even someone as radical intellectually as William Appleman Williams did not support the building takeover. Nor was he alone.

As one former Wisconsin graduate student recalled, "A number of Old Left intellectuals declined to participate or were inconspicuous. They did not see their role as offering leadership to a generation of student radicals."[104] Although there were a few arrests, there was no violence and the administration acted quickly, facilitating the teach-in at Bascom Hall and agreeing to establish a student-faculty committee to study the issue. Meanwhile Wisconsin would continue to let the tests be given and the class ranks compiled, "but with the understanding that the university is not endorsing the rank-in-class concept."[105] The faculty went along. As the only student on the eventual committee, the future Latin American historian John Coatsworth recalled, the group only had two or three meetings before it recommended continued cooperation. He was the lone dissenter but was surprised by how close the faculty's vote on accepting the committee's report turned out to be.[106]

Since it has long been common within academe for administrators and faculty members to deal with sensitive situations by appointing committees, Wisconsin's response was not exceptional. Even schools that did not experience student protests over the issue established such bodies.[107] Even more common were the various referenda, both at institutions that had experienced sit-ins and those that had not. The results reflected considerable confusion among both students and faculties. On such elite campuses as Cornell, Michigan, and Harvard, for example, the students voted against the class-rank system, often by two-to-one margins, but they also supported their 2-S deferments and the exemption exams.[108] At City College, the students voted 3,192 to 1,832 against class ranking; they also opposed the exemption exam, but by a much smaller margin. And at institutions where the war itself was on the ballot, the respondents seemed to support LBJ, but not all the way. At Cornell, for example, the students voted against immediate withdrawal but did favor a ceasefire and free elections in Vietnam.[109] On campuses still untouched by the antiwar movement, support for the war remained strong.[110]

Because the issue of the draft had become so entangled with that of the student protests and institutional governance, it is hard to tell exactly what the positions that faculties took reflected, especially on campuses where no clear majority emerged or where they endorsed contradictory policies. Stanford's professors were typical. At a well-attended faculty meeting in June, the participants, in the words of Richard Lyman, the school's provost and future president, "spent four hours finding ways to touch all the bases on the draft controversy." They opposed the class-ranking system, but also "expressed general approval of the university's present Selective Service policies." They nevertheless asked President Wallace Sterling "to join with other university presidents in urging the government 'to explore alternative arrangements for meeting the nation's military requirements.'" For good measure, the council applauded Sterling's "tactful and patient" handling of the sit-in.[111]

The binding referendum that the CCNY sit-in had spawned—and that the school's professors supported—revealed a faculty essentially split down the middle. Its members voted, but by very close margins, in favor both of class ranks and the exam.[112] At Cornell, the faculty also split, voting 1,300–480 to offer its "strong approval" of the exemption exam, but opposing the rank lists two to one.[113] Columbia was something of an outlier, perhaps because the issue caused few problems in 1966. In the spring of 1967, the students voted four to one against class ranks, the University Council voted unanimously to abolish the rank lists, and the trustees went along.[114]

Because they were, after all, confronting the most divisive political issues of the day, many academics were unhappy about having to take any kind of position. Harvard's faculty, for example, simply refused to deal with the issue. It voted 141–88 to table an anti-draft resolution drawn up by the political philosopher John Rawls, even though its conservative members agreed that the 2-S exemption was unjust. According to the antiwar political scientist Stanley Hoffman, the majority of his colleagues did not want to discuss the resolution because of the "honest feeling that the Faculty would be split wide open."[115] A moderate liberal at the University of Chicago revealed the extent of his own ambivalence when he told a researcher that he agreed with his radical colleagues on the injustice of the Selective Service System. "There's just no way you can calculate these things," he admitted.

Therefore a draft which pretends that a student's life is worth more, that an A student's life is worth more than a B student's life, that a student's life is worth more than a laboring man's life, is an immoral system.

At the same time, however, he explained, he so valued the university that if

> I see it possibly destroyed by my pursuing a particular moral line, then I have a moral conflict and have to make a choice. . . . And since I put such a very high value on this oasis of an effort to preserve human reason and the free act of inquiry in a world that has never known many such institutions and never will have very many, then I would sacrifice all kinds of things in order to preserve it.[116]

In other words, for such professors, institutional loyalty took precedence over their opposition to the war and the draft.

On the other hand, at schools where that loyalty had been undermined by perceptions of insensitive or authoritarian behavior by the administration, professors were much less willing to collaborate with the Selective Service System. At SUNY Buffalo, for example, the Executive Committee of the Faculty of Arts and Sciences recommended that the university not submit class ranks unless the student asked for it. President Furnas, though promising to appoint a special task force, nonetheless acted unilaterally in offering the exam and sending students' class ranks to their draft boards. To a certain extent, he was vindicated when two-thirds of the students later voted in favor of holding the exam on campus.[117]

San Francisco State, a school whose location and massive expansion attracted a particularly iconoclastic group of professors, was to my knowledge the only school where the academic senate actually took a stand against cooperating with the Selective Service. In April 1966, it passed a resolution asking the acting president to order the registrar not to compute the class rankings. Instead he sat on the resolution; and the senate let the matter slide. The following year, however, the faculty again passed the resolution by "an overwhelming margin." Eric Solomon, an English professor, senate member, and president of the AFT local, recalled experiencing "the end of innocence" when he transmitted that action to the school's new president, John Summerskill.

> And then this nice sweet man . . . simply said "I can't do it." He said, "I work for the Chancellor and the Chancellor has ordered me that we will give these grades." And we said, "But we voted." And he said, "Sorry, boys."

Though the faculty as a whole did nothing, a group of militant students disrupted Summerskill's inauguration, while the unionized professors mounted an "informational picket" at a trustees' meeting.[118]

As these episodes reveal, the class-rank crisis involved more than just an institution's position on Vietnam. When it became clear, as it did at San Francisco State and Buffalo, that professors did not have the power to make decisions about such educational matters as grades, conflicts over governance arose. This was new. Complicating the situation was the emergence of another key player in these internal debates; students were also demanding a say in decisions about academic policy. These were issues that, as we will see, would soon tear apart the nation's campuses.

8

"EVERYTHING FELT ILLEGAL"

Academics and Direct Action

By 1967, the most committed antiwar professors had been demonstrating, teaching-in, speaking out, and writing against the escalating conflict for two years with little apparent impact. "It had become increasingly evident," the Temple University theologian John Raines recalled, "that nonviolent protest was not working and we wanted to go to nonviolent resistance."[1] While only a tiny percentage of the nation's faculty members were to engage in civil disobedience, because some of those who did were prominent—like Benjamin Spock and Noam Chomsky—their efforts could not be ignored. If nothing else, those efforts signaled a new stage in the opposition to the war. The academics who opted for open resistance engaged in both concrete and symbolic actions that skirted or even broke the law. They helped young men defy the draft; they stopped paying their taxes; they got arrested at demonstrations; and a very few even considered violence. All were ready to put themselves on the line to shut down the war machine.

Opposing the Draft

For most of these antiwar academics, as William Sloane Coffin put it, "aiding and abetting students in draft resistance" during 1967 and 1968 was their main form of civil disobedience.[2] Though they participated in other illegal actions as well, supporting draft resisters allowed these activists both to dramatize their opposition to the war and to initiate debates about its cost and morality. This was especially the case because the most committed student activists at that time were openly resisting the draft. The moral and material support they received from their faculty mentors significantly sustained their organizing efforts and, they believed, legitimized their individual acts of civil disobedience.[3]

The class-rank protests of 1966 and 1967 had been effective. The military's attempt to conscript weaker students ended in 1967 when the Selective Service System changed course, restoring the 2-S exemption for all students in good standing. But the draft remained, hanging over the lives of the young men who had no desire to go to Vietnam.[4] And, in fact, few did. Out of the Harvard class of 1970, for example, only fifty-six graduates went into the military and only two served in Vietnam. But that outcome was not apparent at the time. As a result, many students made determined efforts to avoid induction. And quite a few faculty members tried to help them—both legally and not.[5]

Some of that assistance took the form of draft counseling. It is important to recognize the distinction between openly defying the draft—and thus risking a criminal prosecution—and avoiding the draft by taking advantage of every loophole the law allowed. The antiwar academics involved with the latter activity were just as opposed to the war as those who broke the law. Many of them applied strategies that they knew relied on deceiving draft boards and medical examiners. Because he knew that some of his advice might be illegal, for example, Charles Freehof, a draft counselor at Brooklyn College, explicitly refused to keep records.[6] The historian David Schalk, who counseled dozens of young men in the Hudson Valley, also never wrote down his clients' names. He and his colleagues around the country were remarkably successful. Just about every young man who availed himself of counseling was able to avoid both prison and Vietnam.[7]

Becoming a draft counselor was a major commitment. Not only did it involve intensive training (usually by Quakers from the Central Committee for Conscientious Objectors in Philadelphia or by some other pacifist instructors), but it also necessitated keeping up-to-date on the Selective Service System's evolving regulations and legal parameters. Thus, for example, although it was originally almost impossible for draftees to become conscientious objectors unless they belonged to a pacifist denomination like the Mennonites or the Society of Friends, as the war intensified the courts so expanded the definition of conscientious objection that ultimately an applicant no longer had to believe in God. In theory, he simply had to convince his draft board of his sincerity.[8] Proving that sincerity, however, required expert assistance. Potential COs had to heed appropriate legal doctrines to ensure that even if they were initially rejected they might succeed on appeal or prolong the proceedings until they reached the magical age of twenty-six when their draft eligibility would expire. As the war dragged on, the demand for that kind of assistance grew exponentially.

By the late 1960s, there were draft counseling centers in most cities and college towns where academics, clergymen, lawyers, and such well-educated women as Staughton Lynd's wife, Alice, helped their clients craft credible CO applications as well as find other legal ways to avoid military service.[9] The indefatigable activist and literary scholar Paul Lauter became involved with draft counseling in 1965 as the peace secretary for the American Friends Service Committee in Chicago. While there, he began to cooperate with the SDS national office, eventually writing its thirteen-page "Guide to Conscientious Objection."[10]

David Schalk began his career as a draft counselor after he and seventeen other MIT faculty members took a training course in the fall of 1967. So many students took advantage of their services that MIT eventually hired five full-time draft counselors. The following year Schalk moved to Vassar and immediately began doing draft counseling in nearby Poughkeepsie, where from 1968 to 1970 he headed the Dutchess Country Draft Counseling and Information Service. He remembered the work as "very, very time consuming. You had to be very careful." The FBI was watching and, he believed, tapping his phone.[11] The historian Georg Iggers, who had left the South for a job at SUNY Buffalo, was also under surveillance. He had, he claimed, "counseled hundreds of war objectors in my office, at home, and in the Friends [Quakers] Meeting House."[12] Though successful in gaining CO status for the men he advised, Iggers regretted that most of them were middle-class whites. "We tried very hard to reach out to the black community, but with almost no success."[13]

Despite the FBI's determined efforts, it never caught counselors like Lauter, Schalk, and Iggers doing anything illegal. As they prepped their clients for interviews with draft boards, found sympathetic doctors to describe supposedly incapacitating physical and psychological problems, and enlisted antiwar clergymen to attest to their clients' moral convictions, they were careful to stay within the law. They also worked with attorneys to handle—and drag out—the multiple appeals that CO applicants often had to file. Other antiwar academics, while not officially draft counselors, also helped students and others avoid the draft. Many, including myself, wrote letters to draft boards, while more prominent individuals testified at trials of draft resisters and other antiwar students. As a leading authority on international law, for example, Princeton's Richard Falk served as an expert witness in conscientious objector cases throughout the sixties. He explained that because the "war was being carried on in violation of international law, it was reasonable for a person to perceive it as illegal," and that, as a result, such an individual had a "Nuremberg obligation" not to participate in it. Howard Zinn's testimony in similar cases supplied the historical background for such a claim.[14] And the psychologist Bill Zimmerman actually taught one of his students how to give a psychotic response to a Rorschach test.[15]

While most of the young men who avoided the draft did so for personal reasons, several thousand sought to make their defiance of the draft a weapon in the antiwar movement.[16] These were the resisters. They did not try to obtain medical exemptions or become conscientious objectors. Instead, they publicly burned or turned in their draft cards and encouraged others to do the same; when called up, they refused induction. Since Congress had passed a law in August 1965 against burning or mutilating one's draft card, these young men knew they might go to prison. But in their more optimistic moments, they envisioned their audacity inspiring so many others that the military would run out of recruits and the war would end. "It was the hope," Staughton Lynd and the Harvard graduate student and anti-draft activist Michael Ferber explained,

that acts of returning a draft card and refusing all subsequent cooperation with the draft would multiply as the example became known un-

til there were too many for the draft and court systems to handle. . . .
Eventually, perhaps when ten thousand acted, perhaps when fifty, the
prisons would fill, courts would clog, and the resulting bureaucratic
flap would bring pressure on the federal government to end the war,
or at the very least the president would have to ask Congress for legislation to make new courts and prisons and so risk a reexamination
of the war and its rising costs.[17]

That didn't happen, of course. But by the spring of 1967, these young
men's defiance of the Selective Service System did signal a new phase
in the antiwar movement.[18]

Most of these draft resisters had already been working with antiwar professors. Supporting these students' defiance provided a way
for committed faculty members and other dissidents to engage in civil
disobedience. Though most of these professors were beyond draft age
and so could not resist the draft directly, it was also against the law to
"aid, abet, and counsel" someone else to do so. At the end of 1964, a
group of early antiwar activists—Lynd, Linus Pauling, William Davidon, and the brothers Daniel and Philip Berrigan among them—
circulated the draft of an explicitly radical "Declaration of Conscience
Against the War in Vietnam." It announced that its signers would not
only refuse "to cooperate with the United States government in the
prosecution of the war in Vietnam," but would also encourage others
not to join the armed forces or do any military-related work. Despite
its acknowledgment that such encouragement was illegal and might
lead to "serious consequences," it attracted about five thousand signatures by the beginning of August 1965. It was the first of what came
to be known as "complicity statements"—and it got little attention.[19]

At that early stage, few, if any, radical academics actually broke
the law. True, Lynd had advocated nonviolent direct action at the big
Berkeley teach-in in May 1965, but aside from Lynd's own arrest at a
Washington, DC, demonstration in August 1965 and Stephen Smale's
attempt to obstruct the Oakland-bound troop trains at the same time,
most academic opponents of the war eschewed civil disobedience.[20]
They remained in the pedagogical mode, seeking to build a movement by providing information.

Still, a few dissenters including Noam Chomsky and the Lynds did defy the law: they refused to pay their income taxes. The IRS responded by seizing their bank accounts and deducting the delinquent payments plus penalties and interest.[21] Withholding his income tax, Chomsky explained, not only symbolized "a refusal to make a voluntary contribution to the war machine," but it also indicated "a willingness . . . to take illegal measures to oppose an indecent government." By 1967, he was involved with a broader tax resistance movement led by Boston-area faculty activists.[22] There were other anti-tax groups as well, gathering names and circulating petitions, sometimes with hundreds of signatures.[23] There were individual tax resisters as well. The Brandeis physicist Robert Lange, for example, listed forty-nine dependents on his tax returns—and was prosecuted for his efforts.[24] But although I've found considerable evidence of professorial tax resisters, it is impossible to know how many faculty members actually did this.[25]

Ultimately, for somebody like Chomsky, that gesture, though symbolically useful, seemed toothless. It could not impede the war effort since the government took the money anyhow. Accordingly, he had become increasingly willing to engage in direct action—and to risk repression.

> I knew that signing petitions, sending money and showing up now
> and then at a meeting was not enough. I thought it was critically necessary to take a more active role, and I was well aware of what that
> would mean. It is not a matter of putting a foot in the water, now and
> then, getting it wet and then leaving. You go in deeper and deeper.
> And I knew that I would be following a course that would confront
> privilege and authority.

Understandably, he assumed the government would strike back. "Confidently" expecting "that I'd be in jail in a few years," he encouraged his wife to get her PhD so that when he did go to prison, she would be able to support the family.[26]

Ironically, of course, his main contribution to the antiwar movement was not his direct action—though having such an important figure get arrested certainly lifted the morale of us more timid folks. Rather, it was his—completely legal—ability to speak truth to power. In February 1967, he published "The Responsibility of Intellectuals" in the *New York Review of Books*, considered by many to be "the single most influential piece of antiwar literature" of the 1960s.[27] In it, not only did Chomsky excoriate such former professors as Arthur Schlesinger, McGeorge Bundy, and W. W. Rostow for betraying their calling, but he also articulated the case for intellectuals to resist the war effort. Academics had a special responsibility, he explained, because they are the people who, more than anyone else, have the ability

> to expose the lies of governments. . . . In the Western world at least, they have the power that comes from political liberty, from access to information and freedom of expression. For a privileged minority, Western democracy provides the leisure, the facilities, and the training to seek the truth lying hidden behind the veil of distortion and misrepresentation, ideology, and class interest through which the events of current history are presented to us.

Especially for academics, who have the "unique privileges" of working within a protected environment, not to confront "the butchery in Vietnam" is to renounce the responsibility that comes with those privileges—and ultimately to reenact the moral collapse of the good Germans.[28] The juxtaposition of such blunt, even snarky, language with a plethora of historical evidence gave the piece its power—especially within an academic community where most opposed the war, even if they did nothing to stop it.

Chomsky's timing could not have been better. By the spring of 1967, quite a few other antiwar academics and intellectuals were also talking about direct action. For those faculty activists who had become disillusioned by the apparent failure of their pedagogical campaign to stop the war, supporting the draft resistance movement seemed an obvious step. As he watched some young men destroying their draft cards at a protest meeting in San Francisco where he was one of the speakers, Frederick Crews "felt that I would go to jail. I felt more and more drawn into draft resistance."[29] As had been the case with the teach-ins, most of the early initiatives occurred at such high-profile institutions as Cornell, Stanford, and Yale, but, as the response to the growing number of complicity statements was to reveal, antiwar faculty members throughout the nation were becoming increasingly militant—as, of course, were their students.

Cornell was an early center of draft resistance. The faculty housed a number of antiwar activists including Douglas Dowd and the mathematician Robert Greenblatt, both of whom held leadership positions within the Inter-University Committee for Debate on Foreign Policy (IUC) and the National Mobilization Committee to End the War (the Mobe) in Vietnam. In the fall of 1967, they were joined by Daniel Berrigan. His appointment as the associate director of Cornell's religious ministry, Dowd recalled, "was like kerosene arriving at a fire." By then, a small but politically effective group of antiwar students had already ignited the campus.[30] In December 1966, SDS had tried to set up a table in the Willard Straight student center to solicit draft-card-burning pledges. When the administration banned their recruiting on the grounds that they were advocating illegal action, the students occupied the building's lobby. A group of sympathetic professors tried to place their bodies between the SDS table and the campus police and then mounted a two-day teach-in on the moral and legal issues surrounding the draft.[31] A few days later, just as the faculty was voting to support the administration's decision to hold the draft exemption exam on campus, the charismatic local SDS leader Bruce Dancis tore up his draft card before an audience of some three hundred people, while a group of twenty-one other students placed an ad in the *Cornell Sun* headlined "WE WON'T GO," stating that they would refuse military service and encourage others to do the same.[32] Within a few months, not only had several other Cornell students destroyed their draft cards, but they had also organized a well-publicized protest in Central Park's Sheep Meadow during the Mobe's massive April 15, 1967, antiwar demonstration where some 175 young men burned or tore up their draft cards.[33]

By the spring of 1967, the draft resisters' "We Won't Go" campaign had spread throughout the academy. Yale students meeting in the Lynds' living room formulated and then published their "We Won't

Go" statement in the fall of 1966. A national "We Won't Go" conference took place in Chicago in December (at exactly the same time as
the University of Chicago was hosting its official symposium on the
draft). Soon there were "We Won't Go" groups on some sixty campuses ranging from Stanford, Harvard, and Wisconsin to Wooster
College, a small church-related school in Ohio. By the summer of
1967, as many as two thousand students had signed pledges to resist
the draft and, under the leadership of the Stanford student government president David Harris and a few others, started The Resistance,
an anti-draft organization that was planning a nationwide draft-card
burning in October 1967.[34]

Faculty members had been involved s from the start. Staughton
Lynd was ubiquitous, as was Dowd, who personally supported Dancis
to the tune of $100 a month after he dropped out of Cornell to orga-
nize draft resistance full-time. On both coasts, clumps of academics
were forming support groups. In New York City, for example, Paul
Goodman and the writer Grace Paley, then teaching at Sarah Lawrence, created an outfit called Support-in-Action to back up the draft
resisters. Richard Ohmann recalls participating in the "little support
groups" that accompanied a "few, very few" Wesleyan students to the
induction center in Providence where they took their stand against
the army.[35]

Some faculty members remained ambivalent about encouraging
young men to break the law. Chomsky was not alone in expressing a
certain measure of guilt about advocating actions that were risky for
others. Berkeley's Crews had similar reservations. "It was fraught with
moral questions," he explained.[36] Many academics decided that the
young men were sufficiently mature and politically aware enough to
understand the consequences of their actions. As Chomsky put it in
another *New York Review of Books* article, "Resistance must be freely
undertaken."[37]

There was less ambivalence among academics about their own decisions to break the law. A few burned their own draft cards, while
some courted arrest by joining student sit-ins or occupying induction centers. The Columbia economist Robert Zevin recalled that, although over the draft age, he had wanted to burn his draft card, only

to discover that it had been in a wallet stolen several years before. When he explained to the Selective Service office that he needed a new card so that he could destroy it, he was called in for a physical.[38]

Even among the more sober faculty radicals, there was a certain frisson about operating beyond the law. Wesleyan's Ohmann recalled, "Everything felt illegal at the time." He became involved with a kind of "underground railroad" to get deserters and draft evaders to Canada. "I would call the War Resisters League and say 'I've got a friend who's interested in traveling.' They'd understand. It was a little bit of cloak-and-dagger stuff, just enough to make me feel more radical than I was."[39] A few years later, a group of academics organized by Howard Zinn and Eqbal Ahmad created the network of safe houses that hid Daniel Berrigan from the FBI for a few months after he had been sentenced to prison for destroying draft records in Catonsville, Maryland.[40]

Resistance and Its Supporters: The Complicity Statements

For most of the antiwar academics, however, their main form of civil disobedience consisted of openly declaring their support for draft resisters. In the summer of 1966, Lynd and the former SDS president Carl Oglesby had drawn up such a complicity statement, but got only a few signatures. By the following spring, however, the nearly defunct Inter-University Committee for Debate on Foreign Policy had picked up their statement and was soliciting signers, though warning them that, according to the civil liberties attorney Leonard Boudin:

> This statement could be construed as violating the Selective Service Act (maximum 5 years and $5000); Espionage Act, counseling insubordination, (maximum 10 years or $10,000); Military Assistance Act (not less than 10 years or $5,000); and as an act of Treason (maximum capital punishment).[41]

It attracted few signers and was soon dropped by the IUC in favor of a statement composed by Robert Zevin, who modeled his draft on the influential 1960 manifesto of Jean-Paul Sartre and 120 other French intellectuals opposing their country's war in Algeria. "I tried it out on some of my colleagues at Columbia," Zevin recalled. "Jim Shenton was enthusiastic, so were Eric Bentley and Seymour Melman." So he spent "months and months . . . drumming up support" from the usual suspects as well as a group of Greenwich Village intellectuals around Grace Paley and the critic Dwight Macdonald and Donald Kalish, the chair of UCLA's philosophy department who was to hire—and defend—Angela Davis a few years later.[42]

Similar documents were already floating around the West Coast. At Stanford, Mitchell Goodman, a teacher and poet then in residence, circulated a statement among his colleagues calling for "acts of mass civil disobedience." To his surprise, fifty professors, including a number of eminent ones, signed the radical pledge. Published in May, the Stanford manifesto revealed how frustrated these academics had become. They declared:

> We do not want to protest the war any longer, we want to stop it. We are prepared, through mass civil disobedience to say NO to our government. . . . We can not be certain that such acts will stop the war. We do believe, however, that nothing else has any chance of stopping it. If only 10% of those who marched against the war on April 15th will involve themselves in such an action, we might realistically hope to reverse the escalating murder and suffering.[43]

Some six hundred West Coast academics signed a similar "Declaration of Conscience" that was published in the May 25 issue of the *Daily Californian*. Citing the "We Won't Go" statements of students at Berkeley, Harvard, Princeton, Stanford, and Wisconsin, it pledged the signers' "full and active support" to all young men "who determine that they will not participate in this war."[44] Paul Lauter and the feminist literary scholar Florence Howe had also written up a similar statement.[45]

By the middle of 1967, these complicity statements were flooding faculty mailboxes. It is hard to tell how many of these documents there were or how many people signed them. The files of RESIST, the group that eventually coordinated most of the faculty support for the student refuseniks, contain dozens of such manifestos with hundreds and, eventually, thousands of signatures.

What ultimately became the most important of these statements was drafted that spring by Marcus Raskin and Arthur Waskow of the Institute for Policy Studies. Raskin had been collaborating with Bernard Fall on a Vietnam reader. As the war intensified, Fall had become increasingly troubled by the seeming passivity of the American intelligentsia. Prompted by Fall's concern, Raskin and Waskow decided to emulate the same French "Manifesto of the 121" that had inspired Zevin.[46] They circulated a statement to their networks of antiwar teachers and writers, including Zevin, who agreed, with a few suggestions, to meld his text with theirs. By the summer of 1967, the Raskin-Waskow-Zevin draft had attracted considerable support from dozens of eminent and not-so-eminent academics, writers, and members of the main antiwar religious group, Clergy and Laity Concerned About Vietnam (CALCAV).[47]

"A Call to Resist Illegitimate Authority" was addressed "To the young men of America, to the whole of the American people, and to all men of goodwill everywhere." It cited the "moral outrage" that its signers shared with the draft resisters, explaining in some detail that the war was violating the Constitution and international law and asserting that "every free man has a legal right and a moral duty to exert every effort to end this war, to avoid collusion with it, and to encourage others to do the same." It then listed the different "courageous and justified" actions that young men were taking to resist the war and gave specific suggestions for how to support them. Recognizing that its signers "might all be liable to prosecution and severe punishment," the "Call" ended with an appeal to

> all men of good will to join us in this confrontation with immoral authority. Especially we call upon the universities to fulfill their mission of enlightenment and religious organizations to honor their heritage of brotherhood. Now is the time to resist.[48]

Meanwhile, Mitchell Goodman continued to work in the same vein with his wife Denise Levertov and some other poets and writers to fashion yet another complicity statement, soliciting support for The Resistance's October draft-card turn-in.[49] Then, sometime in the middle of September, Goodman became aware that a group around Chomsky and Dwight Macdonald was circulating the Raskin-Waskow-Zevin "Call." It made sense, Goodman believed, to combine their efforts, and he volunteered to coordinate the project. "I went to New York and got tremendously involved," he recalled. "I worked about fourteen hours a day, seven days a week." The group decided to release "A Call to Resist Illegitimate Authority" and then participate in The Resistance's October sixteenth protest by collecting the draft cards that the young resisters were planning to turn in. They would then show up in Washington on October 20, the day before the Mobe's long-planned march on the Pentagon, and turn those cards over to the Justice Department.[50]

Published with 158 names in the October 7 *New Republic* and the October 12 *New York Review of Books*, "A Call to Resist Illegitimate Authority" was, according to many observers, "almost definitely the single most important petition to be circulated during the Vietnam years." Richard Fernandez, the executive secretary of CALCAV, the main religious antiwar organization, recalled that it "gave a lot of resisters a lot of courage" and was "a *huge* influence. . . . Not only for what it said, but for the [political] cover and the sense of energy, synergism it created within the resistance movement."[51] Its main sponsors, who would soon formally organize themselves as RESIST (not to be confused with the student group, The Resistance), held a press conference at the Hilton hotel in New York City on October 2. It was an elite bunch: Chomsky, Coffin, Spock, Paul Goodman, the poet Robert Lowell, the anthropologist Ashley Montagu, Raskin, and Waskow.[52]

At a meeting in the Columbia faculty club afterward, the organizers discussed future actions "to capitalize on the unique position of the signers as prominent intellectuals and clergymen." After delegating Mitchell Goodman to coordinate with The Resistance's October sixteenth event, a group formed a temporary steering committee. It was a fluid organization, part letterhead names and part worker bees. Its members included, among others, Chomsky and his MIT colleague Louis Kampf, Davidon, Richard Flacks, Kalish, Ohmann, as well as the Chicago geographer Gilbert White, and a slightly reluctant Frederick Crews, who admitted "there was no way I could get around not lending my name to the cause."[53] The organization soon moved its headquarters to Cambridge, where Lauter became its national director and Kampf ran the office. "I was working two jobs," Kampf recalled, "one the academic one, and the other the office. I'd begin there around four or five p.m. and stay in the office until midnight. I was young and had lots of energy. I became more and more involved, and was seriously thinking about quitting the academy."[54] Meanwhile, the group's "Call to Resist" continued to circulate; by the middle of 1968, it would garner thousands of signatures, two-thirds of them from academics.[55]

On October 16, at eighteen different sites across the United States, somewhere between 1,200 and 1,500 young men turned in or burned their draft cards. In retrospect, because it figured so prominently in the later criminal prosecution of Coffin, Spock, Raskin, Mitchell Goodman, and Michael Ferber, the Boston ceremony got the most attention. After Howard Zinn addressed a crowd of 3,000 on the Boston Common, the resisters and their supporters walked a few blocks to the Arlington Street Church, where Coffin and Ferber, among others, spoke. Then 214 men gave their draft cards to a handful of clergymen and academics, including the Harvard philosopher Hillary Putnam, who had been designated to collect cards from the non-believers, while sixty-seven more men burned their cards.[56] In San Francisco, The Resistance leaders collected some 400 draft cards on the steps of the federal building, plus the ashes of about sixty others that had been burned the week before at Berkeley.[57] At Cornell, thirteen students and one professor surrendered their draft cards to the local draft board accompanied by a cohort of fourteen professors and six ministers pledging to support them.[58] In New York City, the protest and draft-card turn-in took place in front of the Foley Square Courthouse, and there were similar ceremonies at equally symbolic locations throughout the country.

The follow-up occurred in Washington a week later. A group of resisters and their academic supporters massed at the Department of Justice to turn the collected draft cards over to the attorney general. As they marched up the building's front steps to deposit the cards in a fake-leather briefcase that Dr. Spock was holding, each individual gave his name and that of the place or institution he represented.[59] Coffin's speech there could not have been clearer about the determination of the resisters' adult supporters to share their fate.

> We hereby counsel these young men to continue in their refusal to serve in the armed forces as long as the war in Vietnam continues, and we pledge ourselves to aid and abet them in all the ways we can. This means that if they are now arrested for failing to comply with a law that violates their consciences, we too must be arrested, for in the sight of the law we are now as guilty as they.[60]

Attorney General Ramsey Clark had no intention of accepting the cards. The assistant attorney general he assigned to greet the delegation gave its members coffee, but refused to take the briefcase. So Coffin put in on a table and, he recalled, "We said thanks for the coffee, and out we went."[61] The event got some, though not a lot of, attention, overshadowed as it was by the next day's more dramatic demonstration and arrests at the Pentagon.

A week later, the FBI showed up at Yale and many of the other campuses housing the students whose draft cards had been submitted to the Justice Department. Agents questioned these young men and, in some cases, their parents as well. At the same time, under pressure from President Johnson, General Lewis Hershey sent a letter to local draft boards advising them to revoke the deferments of anybody who had interfered with the military's recruiting. But that was all. Though some resisters did receive induction notices, the huge wave of expected arrests did not occur.[62]

Instead, on January 5, 1968, a federal grand jury in Boston handed down an indictment charging Spock, Coffin, Ferber, Raskin, and Mitchell Goodman with "a continuing conspiracy to aid, abet, and counsel violations of the Selective Service law." Attorney General Clark, who later claimed to have already turned against the war, explained that he had decided not to prosecute the young and vulnerable draft resisters, but to focus on the ringleaders, who, he believed, were in a better position to defend themselves.[63]

The five defendants were certainly activists, even if not conspirators. To begin with, not all of them knew each other; they met for the first time when they began to plan their legal defense.[64] Because of its legal plasticity, conspiracy is the indictment of choice for many a political prosecution. It requires neither evidence of collusion among the perpetrators nor the commission of an overt act, successful or not. Each member of the conspiracy is guilty of everything the other members said or did. Thus, despite an all-star legal team, the malleable nature of the charge plus an unsympathetic judge and unfriendly jury ensured not only that the Five would be convicted, but also that they would be frustrated in invoking the "Nuremberg defense" that the war was illegitimate. Ultimately, none of the defendants went to prison.[65] Once the 1968 Tet Offensive showed that the war was probably unwinnable, the political atmosphere shifted and public support for prosecuting antiwar activists dwindled. Several defendants won on appeal, but it took two years of litigation before the Justice Department finally dropped the remaining case against Spock and Coffin.

If the Spock indictment was intended to stamp out the resistance movement, it failed. True, it did worry some of the activists who assumed that they would be next. Crews sought a speaking engagement at Simon Fraser University in British Columbia to assess the prospect of moving to Canada.[66] But, in fact, the Spock case energized the antiwar movement. Hitherto silent faculty emerged to protest both the war and the prosecution. Thus, for example, a petition supporting the defendants received 600 signatures from the Yale faculty, while some 28,000 people signed a complicity statement during the trial, declaring that "if they are sentenced, we will take their places."[67] Meanwhile, according to Ohmann, "money was pouring into the RESIST office," enabling the group to support other antiwar organizations and to circulate yet other petitions.[68]

There were problems with RESIST, however. It was hard to build a long-term movement around a single symbolic act. As a result, especially after the 1968 Tet Offensive and after Johnson and Nixon began to pull ground troops from Vietnam and address the inequities in the Selective Service System, the draft resistance effort began to run out of steam. Antiwar academics and students then turned to other forms of nonviolent civil disobedience.

There was, for example, the sanctuary movement that tried to shield military deserters and draft resisters. This movement had developed within the religious community, which was resuscitating the medieval practice of using churches as asylums. Richard Mumma, the Presbyterian chaplain at Harvard and RESIST board member, was eager for universities to provide refuge as well. There was opposition, of course. When Coffin tried to turn the Yale Chapel into a sanctuary, President Kingman Brewster and the Chapel's faculty deacons demurred. "Bill," he was told, "on this issue we're not as certain as you and the students are that your wills are that clearly aligned with the will of the Lord."[69]

Harvard was more welcoming. On September 22, 1968, a group of theology students set up the first academic sanctuary at the Divinity School, where they sheltered an AWOL marine, with, if not the blessing, at least the neutrality of the dean and faculty. A similar sanctuary was formed a few weeks later at Boston University's chapel, where about 1,300 students and faculty members gathered to protect a military deserter. For three days, until some 120 FBI agents stormed the chapel and seized the deserter, supportive faculty members taught their courses and encouraged, in Zinn's words, an "ongoing free speech exercise . . . sort of like a twenty-four-hour-a-day teach-in."[70] At MIT, students from The Resistance established a fully secular sanctuary in the student center that saw 1,200 people protect a nineteen-year-old army deserter. For six days, the sanctuary "just galvanized the whole campus" and, Chomsky recalled, "completely changed the mood of the whole university."[71] There were also sanctuaries at Brandeis, Chicago, and a short-lived one at City College that resulted in 170 arrests of students, faculty members, and community people.[72] At the same time, individual academics, like Haverford's William Davidon and his wife, Ann Morriset, were sheltering AWOL servicemen in their homes.[73]

To a certain extent, the sanctuary movement was a turning point within the antiwar movement as it began to shift its emphasis from the young men opposing the draft to resisters within the military. Robert

Zevin and Paul Lauter, for example, while still connected to RESIST, began to put their energies into the United States Servicemen's Fund, an umbrella organization that funded such resistance activities within the armed services as underground newspapers and GI coffee shops near military bases.[74]

Civil Disobedience Continues

By the late 1960s, as more and more academic (and non-academic) opponents of the war turned to nonviolent civil disobedience, they openly courted arrest. Even before the Justice Department indicted him, Dr. Spock got himself arrested, for the first time, along with 263 other protesters at a sit-in outside the Whitehall induction center in downtown New York during "Stop the Draft Week" on December 5, 1967. While compared to activists like Staughton Lynd or Davidon, Spock was late to the party; his willingness to go to jail signals how widely the move toward resistance had spread.[75] After all, as Noam Chomsky pointed out, "It's a big step to say I'm going to be arrested."[76]

Again, there is no way to tell how many college and university teachers got arrested while protesting the war. Many of the radical activists I interviewed, as well as those who wrote memoirs, seemed rather casual about their run-ins with the law. Younger faculty members may have been more willing than their elders to go to jail; some had already been arrested during the civil rights movement. Still, until the late sixties, it was unusual for professors to openly defy the police. Those who did were among their schools' most radical faculty activists and often acted alone.[77]

Based on anecdotal evidence, it seems likely that by the later stages of the war the most prominent academic radicals had been picked up by the police at least once. "I was in and out of jail," Chomsky explained, noting that the only reason he wasn't indicted along with the Boston Five was that "when the draft cards were being carried into the Department of Justice, I was outside haranguing the crowd." He was, however, arrested the next day at the Pentagon and immortalized for it in Norman Mailer's *Armies of the Night*.[78] Among the less eminent jailbirds, Robert Zevin was arrested for trespassing when he went with a group of his Columbia students to recruit for the antiwar movement in the Dow Chemical Company's offices in Rockefeller Center. The University of Massachusetts English professor Jules Chametzky spent four hours in jail when he was arrested at a nearby airbase along with fifty other faculty members from UMass and other nearby campuses.[79] Faculty draft resisters also faced prosecution, including several Cornell professors and James Douglas, a professor of Catholic theology at the University of Hawaii, who spent a month in prison.[80] By the spring of 1971, even someone as non-radical as my ex-husband got himself arrested with a group of other Princeton professors in the big Mayday demonstration where the Washington, DC, police rounded up some seven thousand protesters.[81] A year later, the historian Carolyn Eisenberg managed to recruit twenty-five of her Dartmouth colleagues to get arrested while trying to block a bus bearing draftees to the induction center in Lebanon, New Hampshire. Civil disobedience, she recalled, had become "fashionable" at that point.[82]

At the very fringes of the academic antiwar movement were the few radicals whose illegal activities went further. These were people like the Catholic peace movement's ultra-resisters whose actions, though obviously symbolic, nonetheless included the destruction of property. Six days after the Pentagon bust where Daniel Berrigan had been arrested, his brother Philip broke into the Baltimore Selective Service office and poured blood on its files. Then, on May 17, 1968, the Berrigans and seven other Catholics, a few college teachers among them, raided the draft board in Catonsville, Maryland, and burned its records with homemade napalm—all in front of the forewarned media.[83] Other draft board raids followed including some whose perpetrators did not surface publicly because they wanted to continue their break-ins.

The Temple University theologian John Raines was one of those culprits. As part of the clandestine East Coast Conspiracy to Save Lives, he had helped destroy the records of a draft board office in North Philadelphia. Then, at some point during the fall of 1970, he and his wife, Bonnie, were approached by William Davidon about participating in what was to become the movement's single most successful act of civil disobedience: the March 1971 raid on the FBI's field office in

FIGURE 8.1. William Davidon under arrest at antiwar demonstration, December 29, 1965. © Theodore B. Hetzel Photograph Collection, Swarthmore College Peace Collection.

the Philadelphia suburb of Media, Pennsylvania. Long convinced that the Bureau had been suppressing dissent, Davidon realized that he needed evidence. The stakes were high, but Davidon and his seven fellow conspirators—four of whom including Raines and Davidon were academics—had planned carefully. They were lucky as well. Not only did they find and then disseminate documents definitively proving that the FBI was, indeed, trying to disrupt political dissent, but they also managed to avoid exposure for over forty years. They surfaced in 2013, revealing their identities to Betty Medsger, the *Washington Post* reporter who had first broken the story of their burglary in 1971. Ironically, because Davidon was an unindicted conspirator in the Berrigan-related case of the Harrisburg Eight, the FBI had him under surveillance during much of the time he and his colleagues were plotting their heist.[84]

By the late 1960s and early 1970s, the academic presence in the antiwar movement was no longer as central as it had been in the early days of the US escalation. Yet the nation's institutions of higher learning were seething with unrest, as students and some faculty members raised troubling questions about their schools' complicity with the military-industrial complex. As the focus of the unrest shifted, student protests erupted and previously uninvolved faculty members, often reluctantly, had to address the other war-related issues that their own institutions' complicity with the military-industrial complex had brought to the fore. Unfortunately, the most disruptive of those protests disturbed the rest of the country as well, undermining the positive image of higher education most Americans traditionally held.

9

"AN INESCAPABLE RESPONSIBILITY"

Universities and the War Machine

Summit and Spicerack: Military Research
at the University of Pennsylvania

The orders looked fishy to Robin Maisel, a University of Pennsylvania undergraduate working at the school's bookstore during the summer of 1965. Why would the scientists at the Institute for Cooperative Research (ICR) be interested in books on rice diseases, Vietnam, and aerosol dispersion? A politically sophisticated member of the Young Socialist Alliance as well as the Philadelphia Area Committee to End the War in Vietnam (CEWV), Maisel took his suspicions to Gabriel Kolko, his main history professor, who felt equally queasy about the ICR's activities. A bit more poking around confirmed their doubts. The Institute's offices had combination locks on its filing cabinets and other security features that no ordinary academic unit would have. Moreover, a copy of the ICR's annual catalog from 1962 revealed that its Summit and Spicerack projects under contract to the US Army and Air Force were looking into "the feasibility of the use of temporarily incapacitating chemical and biological agents, including psychochemicals, in specified military situations."[1] Its 1964 report noted that its members were also studying "the total systems concept including munitions, delivery vehicles, and statistical-mathematical predictive models, etc." Piecing these clues together made it pretty clear that some of Penn's scientists were carrying on secret research in chemical and biological warfare (CBW) that had military applications in Vietnam.[2]

In early October, Maisel and his colleagues in the CEWV described their findings in a document that they sent to Penn's president Gaylord Harnwell as well as to the International Red Cross, the United Nations, and to Richard Mann, the Michigan psychologist then running the Inter-University Committee for Debate on Foreign Policy. If the Summit and Spicerack projects were indeed involved with chemical and biological warfare in Vietnam, they wanted Penn to shut them down. "By accepting this research, the U. of P. has closely tied itself to our government's war machine," the document stated.

> The most likely immediate application of the research of the ICR and similar institutes is against the civilian populations of North and South Vietnam, poisoning both the people and their staple foods. As long as the ICR remains on the University campus, the University is culpable in the murderous uses to which the results of this research will be put. . . . [C]enters for the development of more effective means of mass destruction do not belong on the college campus, or anywhere else.[3]

Philadelphia's antiwar community took up the issue as well, sponsoring talks by well-known activists and mounting a demonstration outside the ICR offices as part of the broader movement's "International Days of Protest" in mid-October.[4]

To its credit, Penn's administration did not deny that the Army Chemical Corps had been funding the Institute for Cooperative Research. Established at the height of the early Cold War in 1951, the ICR had become a major center for chemical and biological warfare research. As the Vietnam War escalated, so, too, did the Pentagon's support for the ICR's classified operations. In 1960, it received $948,000 from the military; in 1964, it got $2.4 million; and in 1966, $4 million.[5] Although some Penn officials, including the provost, became concerned about allowing so much secret research on campus, the president, the trustees, and, of course, the faculty members who did that research had no such qualms. Even as the administration admitted that the ICR's scientists had been developing "dispersal systems for defoliants" in Vietnam, the ICR director insisted that its work was purely defensive. For Kurt Kreiger, the chemistry professor running the Summit-Spicerack projects, that research was a patriotic obligation. "If the University depends for its freedom on a free society, it has some responsibility to defend the free society. . . . I like to believe that we are making some small contribution to the national defense."[6]

The Summit-Spicerack controversy emerged in 1965, two years before the bulk of the academic community turned against the Vietnam War; even so, most Penn professors opposed the project. They did so, however, not because the ICR's work was, as the antiwar activists maintained, "immoral, illegal, and inhuman," but because it was secret.[7] The conduct of classified research at American universities had been problematic for years. This, however, was the first time that it had surfaced in connection with the conflict in Southeast Asia. Without the antiwar movement, questions about such work would probably have simmered quietly within the scientific community for several more years without gaining wider attention.

By focusing on the classified nature of the ICR's research, professors avoided challenging the standard contention that the university was politically neutral. Secrecy was safer to confront. The university's physicists, whose field had been grappling with security constraints since World War II, were especially upset. Their department unanimously reaffirmed a 1953 statement against "the imposition of restrictions on publication of research" that violate "the basic concept of a university."[8] Then, on November 3, at what the chair of the faculty senate called its "best" and "largest meeting in recent history," its members voted 193–57 to ban classified research from the campus.[9]

Admittedly, that resolution, which had been drawn up in collaboration with the administration, contained a few loopholes. It emphasized that faculty members should be free to pursue whatever research they wanted to, "except when a national emergency has been declared by the President of the United States."[10] However, such an "emergency" had been in effect from the start of the Korean War and had never been repealed. "A statement like this," Kolko complained, "can be applied to justify just about any action."[11] Still, the administration decided to move the CBW research to an ostensibly independent laboratory at the newly created University City Science Center—and, of course, set up a special committee to study the matter.[12]

A few months later, both *Ramparts* and *Viet-Report* ran articles about the Summit-Spicerack projects. As a result, by the middle of 1966, the nation's academics, some of whom had been drawn into debates about student draft deferments, were now having to confront some of the other ways in which their institutions were cooperating with the military-industrial complex. Some of the issues they dealt with were not new, but Vietnam gave them new saliency. And when student protests targeted the Reserve Officers' Training Corps (ROTC), the military research units, and the recruiters for defense industries, the armed services, and the CIA, many universities began to fray. What made these issues so divisive was the desire of most academics to maintain the political neutrality of their institutions even as their radical colleagues and students were insisting that such "neutrality" was a sham.

Academics and the State: A Long-Term Relationship

American higher education had long been involved with the armed forces and the government at every level. A year after he founded the University of Virginia, for example, Thomas Jefferson required its students to have military training. The 1862 Morrill Act that established the land-grant institutions made "military tactics" required for their male students.[13] During the early twentieth century, universities and faculty members became involved in the municipal, state, and federal reforms of the Progressive movement. World War I increased the ties between the academy and the state. Chemists made poison gas and explosives, while historians and others were enlisted in propaganda campaigns.[14] Though academics largely left Washington after the war, quite a few returned in the early 1930s, among them the three Columbia faculty members who served in Franklin Roosevelt's "brain trust."[15] Other professors staffed the New Deal's booming alphabet agencies and expanding bureaucracies.

But it was World War II that consolidated the relationship between the academic community and the government. Even before Pearl Harbor, the former president of MIT Vannevar Bush, who was to head the wartime Office of Scientific Research and Development (OSRD), was determined to incorporate the academic establishment into the coming war effort.[16] As a result, most of the 5,000 scientists who eventually worked for Washington during World War II did so under the aegis of a major university in what came to be known as "federal contract research centers."[17] The Manhattan Project was the most famous such center. Its 1,500 civilian scientists produced the atomic bomb in laboratories at Columbia, the University of Chicago, and, most importantly, Los Alamos, New Mexico—an installation that Berkeley was to oversee for more than sixty years. MIT ran an equally important project at its Radiation Laboratory, where 1,200 scientists developed radar and other guidance systems. Other universities—Johns Hopkins, Michigan, Penn, and the California Institute of Technology (Caltech), among them—also worked on weapons.[18] Although many of the academic scientists attached to these projects chafed at the military's restrictions on their research, they did not refuse to participate. Patriotism and a desire to defeat the Nazis even drew people like Caltech's Linus Pauling into developing explosives.[19]

Nor was it only scientists who worked for the military. The US Army's Office of Strategic Services (OSS), the precursor of the CIA, recruited large numbers of historians, anthropologists, economists, and area specialists for its Research and Analysis Branch under the Harvard historian William Langer—most from the Ivy League and other elite institutions. Carl Schorske, Herbert Marcuse, Arthur Schlesinger Jr., Carl Kaysen, H. Stuart Hughes, and, in fact, nearly all my graduate school professors in the Harvard history department worked for the OSS. So, too, did the China scholar John Fairbank, who then went to Chongqing with the Office of War Information, while the MIT economist W. W. Rostow ended up selecting bombing targets in Europe.[20] Among the many other economists working for the government were the future Nobel laureates Tjalling Koopmans, who formulated statistical methods for the allocation of scarce shipping, and Simon Kuznets, who along with Robert Nathan developed the national income accounting method used to mobilize the economy. Kenneth Galbraith served as deputy director of the Office of Price Administration.[21]

That relationship—both of individuals and institutions—continued after the war. Manhattan Project veterans proffered advice on the weapons they had created, while the economists in the recently established Council of Economic Advisers sought to prevent a new depression.[22] In fact, even before the war was over, the military had decided to farm out much of its research and development to the universities.[23] It became common for professors to do consulting work under contract for the Defense Department, Atomic Energy Commission, CIA, and similar agencies. For larger projects, universities created special units like Penn's ICR specifically to conduct classified military research. The intensification of the Cold War in the late 1940s followed by the outbreak of the Korean War ensured that there would be no letup in defense spending.

Money poured into dozens of institutions, sometimes for large collective projects, sometimes as individual research grants. At the behest of scientists in the New York City area, the AEC established a major facility at Brookhaven, Long Island, while it also funded the Argonne National Laboratory near the University of Chicago and the Lawrence Livermore National Laboratory to develop nuclear weapons under Berkeley's auspices.[24] Other faculty members did defense-related research at literally dozens of special laboratories that ranged from Columbia's Electronics Research Laboratory to Kent State's Liquid Crystals Institute.[25]

The military spigots flowed indiscriminately from the start. Until the early 1950s, the US Navy's Office of Naval Research (ONR) not only underwrote much of the basic research done within the academy, but it also asked no questions about the military applicability of that research, and it even offered money to politically tainted scientists at the height of the McCarthy era and after.[26] Nor was the ONR unusual. The biologist Richard Lewontin was supported for years by the Atomic Energy Commission and its successor agencies, even though, as he recalled,

I worked with the Black Panther Party, gave public speeches attacking the war policy of the government, was on the committee, together with officials of the Socialist Worker's Party and the Communist Party, that organized peace marches through downtown Chicago, had open relations with the representatives of the Vietnamese National Liberation Front, and helped to organize scientific support for them.[27]

Similarly, for years, the air force underwrote the linguistics research of Noam Chomsky at MIT's Research Laboratory of Electronics.[28]

Cold War Military Research

Until Vietnam, most professors and graduate students had few qualms about taking Washington's money. The Pentagon made it easy and attractive for them, creating several new institutional arrangements specifically for elite scientists. Among them were the Defense Department's Advanced Research Projects Agency (ARPA), the Institute for Defense Analyses (IDA), and the Jasons. ARPA farmed out defense-related work to individual researchers as well as to the clusters of professors at the IDA sites that were set up at a dozen major research universities.[29] The Jasons was an independent collection of some forty younger scientists tasked with working together on specific Defense Department projects for six or seven weeks in the summers. Though the group's founders initially envisioned their project as a full-time research unit like the US Air Force's RAND Corporation, few of the brilliant young men they wanted to recruit were willing to abandon their faculty positions.[30]

The civilian scientists in these groups originally had no misgivings about working on weapons.[31] In fact, three-quarters of the physicists who were asked to join the first class of Jasons in 1960 accepted. At the time, consulting for the Defense Department conferred a lot of status, as well as a hefty stipend and the appeal of spending summer vacations with their families and close colleagues at an attractive seaside community like La Jolla, California, or Woods Hole, Massachusetts.[32] A research appointment at the Institute for Defense Analyses was, at least for a while, a mark of attainment in theoretical physics.[33]

As Berkeley physicist Charles Schwartz recalled of his 1962 stint with the Jasons: "There was a sense of glamour attached to it. I had to get a security clearance, go to Washington, get paid, have a bunch of briefings . . . the headiness—wow, you were really getting into it!"[34]

Besides such perks as the rapid promotions, reduced teaching loads, higher salaries, and larger labs that ambitious administrators like Stanford's Frederick Terman showered upon the scientists and engineers who took on military projects, the work itself conveyed prestige.[35] Weapons research was still permeated by the aura of the outstanding chemists and physicists in the Manhattan Project and MIT's Radiation Laboratory.[36] In fact, military research had become so attractive that, as one observer reported, "if the memos and reports you wrote weren't stamped 'secret,' they just weren't important; they didn't involve 'real' science or engineering."[37] According to Stuart Leslie's influential account, "The military-driven technologies of the Cold War defined the critical problems for the postwar generation of American scientists and engineers. Indeed, those technologies virtually defined what it meant to be a scientist or an engineer."[38]

Much of this weapons research was done in partnership with industrial corporations. Although chemists and agricultural scientists, in particular, had long worked closely with corporations, defense work now produced new forms of institutional collaboration.[39] The Stanford administration was particularly eager for such connections. It not only persuaded the Lockheed Corporation to pay part of the salary of an engineering professor the school recruited, but also hired industrial engineers without academic backgrounds onto the faculty.[40] It also developed an early research park that encouraged defense-related industries to build facilities on Stanford land and work with faculty members and their students.[41] It also helped those faculty members set up their own companies. MIT did the same, indirectly creating the Route 128 belt of technology-rich firms that encircled Boston. By the late 1960s, MIT's faculty and alumni had formed over 160 such companies, while similar, if less numerous, spin-offs developed near other research universities, the University of Michigan and Georgia Tech among them.[42]

As the economic benefits of the military's investments in academic research became better known, political pressure mounted to spread those benefits more widely. For years, the big money had been going to a handful of major research universities. By the mid-1960s, the Pentagon was encouraged to disperse the bounty more widely. Such a measure might also avoid the student protests against military research that were disrupting elite institutions. Accordingly, the Defense Department inaugurated Project THEMIS in the fall of 1967, awarding more than forty grants to second-tier schools that ranged from Dartmouth and Georgetown to Louisiana State and Texas Christian—but not necessarily dodging student unrest.[43]

Though scientists were the main beneficiaries, social scientists also won contracts from the defense establishment. In 1951, the CIA provided a $300,000 grant to establish an institute "to research worldwide political, economic and social change for the defense and intelligence community." Housed at MIT because Harvard banned classified research, the Center for International Studies posted armed guards at the entrance and required all its members to have security clearances.[44] Five years later, the similar Foreign Policy Research Institute (FPRI) was set up at the University of Pennsylvania.[45] Economists also received military support, sometimes at separate institutions like the RAND Corporation and sometimes at their own institutions, for research in such areas as game theory and systems analysis.[46]

Defense-related funding also flowed into the multidisciplinary field of area studies. Harvard's Russian Research Center produced non-classified studies that were coordinated with—and sometimes subsidized by—the CIA as well as the State and Defense Departments. Some of that work had direct military applications, as when the air force mined the Center's interviews of Russian émigrés to select future bombing targets in the Soviet Union.[47] By 1968, there were some 191 international studies centers, most, though not all, at Research I institutions. It may not have been such an exaggeration to consider them, as one radical critic did, "extension schools for the State Department."[48] As we have seen, the Michigan State Advisory Group received some $25 million from the government between 1955 and 1962 for training police and other security forces in the Philippines, Colombia, Taiwan, and South Korea as well as South Vietnam.[49]

Another funder of the social sciences was the army's Special Operations Research Office (SORO), based at American University in Washington, DC.[50] In 1964, SORO sponsored the highly controversial, though unclassified, "Project Camelot," designed to be "the Manhattan Project of social science." It planned to award an unprecedented amount of money to a massive interdisciplinary effort that would develop "Methods for Predicting and Influencing Social Change and Internal War Potential." By studying the roots of "internal war" (a euphemism for revolution) in several Latin American countries and elsewhere, the eminent behavioral scientists of Project Camelot would, it was hoped, create effective programs of counter-insurgency.[51]

But it never got off the ground. Critics noted that its mission was not only overly vague, but also seemed designed to bolster an authoritarian status quo. In Chile, where the project's military backing was first exposed, it became a public scandal, damaging American-Chilean relations and undermining the research of several scholars. The government even confiscated the notes of an American graduate student. Other social scientists in Latin America and elsewhere found their work impeded by the backlash against Project Camelot. Within the academic community, there were reasonable fears, especially among anthropologists, that people and governments worldwide would view their research as a cover for American imperialism and refuse to cooperate. The bad publicity and a turf war between the State and Defense Departments led to the cancellation of the project in the spring of 1965. Though the Pentagon continued to finance similar work, it did so on a smaller scale and, unlike Project Camelot, in secret.[52]

Questions Arise

Clearly, military-sponsored research could create serious problems for scholars and scientists, not least when they were required to keep their work secret. Allowing an outside agency to decide what could be published conflicted with the most basic practices of a community where progress depended upon sharing results and building upon one another's work—and where people's careers and reputations rested upon their publication records. The situation worsened during the mid-1950s, when the military began to tighten up its security restrictions, barring people from certain kinds of research because of their politics or foreign citizenship.[53] The Public Health Service, the forerunner of the National Institutes of Health, imposed similar political barriers.[54]

Government sponsorship raised additional ethical issues, especially once researchers realized that their work could be used in the Southeast Asian conflict that many considered pointless and immoral. A few scientists were also beginning to worry about the impact of defense funding on the very nature of scientific inquiry. These issues became particularly troubling by the mid-1960s as campus militants and radical scientists began to demand serious answers.

But even moderates worried about secrecy—and had for years. During the war, the chemist James Bryant Conant, on leave from his position as Harvard's president, had been greatly disturbed by what he considered the excessive concern with security in the Manhattan Project and elsewhere. In a December 1946 speech to the American Association for the Advancement of Science (AAAS), he announced that it was "highly inadvisable for universities which are dedicated to free investigation" to do the kind of classified work they had done "for patriotic reasons" during the war. Though he was more than willing to let Harvard take the Pentagon's money and would even allow individual professors to do secret work on their own, secret research under institutional auspices was beyond the pale. The university, he announced in 1949, "will accept no contracts which involve classified work."[55]

Harvard was a wealthy institution and could afford to pass up that tainted largesse.[56] Elsewhere, the poisoned fruit was hard to resist, even at other top-tier institutions. The men who ran Stanford and MIT, for example, evinced no qualms about secret research and welcomed classified work. One scholar noted that the people at MIT's Instrumentation Laboratory considered its security requirements "part of the cost of doing business with the military." Indeed, many considered it a patriotic obligation. On some campuses, scientists even let their graduate students participate in secret projects and write classified dissertations.[57] Universities had, according to MIT's president James Killian, "an inescapable responsibility in this time of crisis, to undertake research in support of our national security which under normal circumstances we would choose not to undertake."[58]

There were other reasons why academics began to question the place of military research. Even if they did not worry about how the Pentagon might use their work, questions about its intellectual legitimacy arose. Was it basic or applied science? Since the latter lacked the status of the former, at some institutions working on a military project could be professionally damaging. This was especially the case when that research was being conducted in collaboration with industrial corporations that might place so many commercial restrictions on the work and its dissemination as to make it unacceptable as an academic enterprise. Still, given the direction that scientific research was taking by the 1950s and, in particular, the growing size of its projects, quite a few scientists felt that the traditional distinction between applied and basic science was out-of-date.[59]

There was also the fear that defense-related research—whether classified or not—might distort an institution's academic mission. Military projects diverted attention and, more importantly, money from research and education in other fields. Even during the golden age of the late 1950s and early 1960s, university resources were not unlimited. All too often, hiring a faculty member in microwave electronics took precedence over replacing a retiring classicist.[60] Here again, Frederick Terman was the point person. His devotion to what he called "steeples of excellence" meant, in practice, putting Stanford's resources into the fields he was interested in—which tended to be ones that also interested the military. But even within a single department, subfields that could attract federal funding sometimes flourished to the detriment of ones that Washington ignored, even if equally rewarding intellectually.[61]

Naturally, administrators and scientists on defense contracts justified that research and its restrictions in the name of national security. But they also defended it in terms of academic freedom. Terman, for example, argued that Stanford's professors should be allowed to select problems to study without any interference from their colleagues,

their institution, or external authorities. Accordingly, banning classified research might "deny to many scholars in the university the opportunity to carry on effective investigation in their chosen fields of
inquiry." Worse yet, it might have "the consequence of driving a group
of scholars from the university" to more accommodating institutions.
Terman et al. avoided the charge of hypocrisy by explaining that accepting the constraints imposed by the military-industrial complex
was a voluntary decision of an individual researcher and, therefore,
did not infringe on that person's academic freedom.[62]

The Insiders: Elite Professors Advise the Government

Just as the late 1950s and early 1960s had been the golden age of feder-
ally sponsored research, it was also the moment when certain top professors gained access to the highest circles of the government. Political
leaders seemingly valued academic knowledge and eagerly recruited
faculty members not just because of their specific expertise, but also
because, as Lyndon Johnson was wont to say, they wanted to surround
themselves with "the best minds" in the country.[63] Under McCarthyism, that had not been the case.[64] Sputnik, however, turned professors
into national assets. Their brains were now essential to success in the
Cold War. As the historian Richard Hofstadter noted, "The national
distaste for intellect appeared to be not just a disgrace but a hazard to
survival."[65] Even non-scientists were in demand. They could be enlisted as ghostwriters, speechmakers, and overall legitimizers, making politicians, one author explained, "appear to be men of vision and
conviction."[66]

John F. Kennedy recognized their value early on.[67] Even before he
announced his candidacy for president, Kennedy and his main assistants were meeting regularly in Cambridge with an academic advising committee composed primarily of such Harvard notables as
Schlesinger, Galbraith, and the economist Carl Kaysen. Besides supplying policy recommendations, those well-known liberals worked
to overcome the reservations about Kennedy held by their colleagues
who were more inclined to support Adlai Stevenson or Hubert
Humphrey.[68]

Kennedy's victory brought many of these academics to Washington—some at a fairly high level. Harvard dean McGeorge Bundy not only served as the national security adviser, but also recruited a Cambridge-centric network of social scientists including Kaysen and MIT's Rostow. Galbraith became the ambassador to India, while his colleague Edwin O. Reischauer went to Tokyo. Schlesinger became the administration's "intellectual-in-residence," a brand-new position that made him Kennedy's unofficial ambassador to the worlds of high culture and academe.[69] Scientists also felt empowered by the New Frontier. As leading members of the President's Science Advisory Committee, elite academics like Harvard's George Kistiakowsky and MIT's Jerome Wiesner became insiders.

After Kennedy's death, many of his academic advisers stayed on, serving the Johnson administration until the Vietnam War made them too uncomfortable to remain. Schlesinger left first, replaced early in 1964 by the less well-known Princeton historian Eric Goldman. His tenure resulted in disaster a year later when the poet Robert Lowell publicly rejected an invitation to the "White House Festival of the Arts" because of his opposition to the bombing of North Vietnam and the invasion of the Dominican Republic. "Although I am very enthusiastic about most of your domestic legislation and intentions," Lowell wrote Johnson in a letter he published in the New York Times, "I nevertheless can only follow our present foreign policy with the greatest dismay and distrust." Lowell's protest ruined Goldman's party and soured the president considerably on the intellectual establishment.[70]

Vietnam was to ruin many a party, as increasing numbers of the government's academic advisers began to question the conflict.[71] As early as 1961, Galbraith had been warning JFK against intervening in Southeast Asia, but both he and Johnson ignored him.[72] Over the next few years, most of the academic advisers, like their colleagues back on campus, moved from initial support for the war to gradual disillusionment and then to the loss of whatever influence they had.[73]

Not all these professors were ambivalent about the war. Some, in fact, supported it and may well have been instrumental in escalating and prolonging it. McGeorge Bundy definitely bore some responsibility.[74] W. W. Rostow may have had even more. During his tenure at MIT's CIA-backed Center for International Studies in the 1950s, Rostow had produced his "Non-Communist Manifesto," *The Stages of Economic Growth*, an influential but deeply flawed book that claimed the only path to modernization for an underdeveloped nation was to emulate America's liberal capitalism.[75] Rostow had been a Vietnam hawk from the start, even advocating intervention to help the French. In fact, he was such a fervent advocate of escalation that Kennedy kicked him off the National Security Council. Johnson, however, chose him to succeed Bundy. Rostow's loyalty and absolute certainty that bombing North Vietnam would eventually lead to victory had enormous appeal to the more and more isolated president.[76] Nor did Nixon's open hostility to the Ivy League prevent him from relying on the Harvard professors Henry Kissinger and Daniel Moynihan.[77]

Scientists and Weapons

Scientists never reached the same policy-making heights, but they did have some influence in Washington. Most were physicists, motivated above all by their desire to prevent nuclear armageddon. They were determined to develop mechanisms to control the terrifying weapons they had created. Their record as advisers was mixed. It was initially assumed that super-geniuses could solve any problem after having smashed the atom. The White House and the military sought their advice not just about nuclear weapons, but also about intercontinental ballistic missiles, supersonic aircraft, pesticides, and, ultimately, Vietnam. Until they fell out with LBJ over the war, the nation's leading scientists did get a respectful hearing, even if their advice got shunted aside or misrepresented.[78]

Much of the early work of the Jasons and the other elite consultants had to do with the nuclear test ban treaty and a projected anti-ballistic missile (ABM) system. In both cases, the scientists, who in fact viewed almost everything related to nuclear weapons as a moral and political issue, used technical arguments to present their advice. Otherwise, they feared, they would not get a hearing.[79] They had some success with nuclear testing, where the technical problem of differentiating between underground tests and earthquakes proved soluble. They could cite the latest advances in seismology to show that a partial test ban would not endanger American security.[80]

The advisers were less successful with regard to the ABM system, which they feared would only exacerbate the arms race. They made their case against it, however, by arguing that its technological problems were insurmountable (as they still may be). Yet, despite convincing Secretary of Defense Robert McNamara, they could not prevail against the political pressures from Congress and the military. In 1967, McNamara, on the defensive within the administration because of his growing skepticism about Vietnam, decided to appease his hawkish critics and back a "thin ABM." That decision for scientists like Kistiakowsky and Wiesner, who were already estranged from LBJ because of Vietnam, ended their advising careers. Both men quit their positions and reluctantly came out against the war and the ABM.[81]

Their hands were hardly clean. Because of their overriding concern about nuclear weapons, Kistiakowsky and his colleagues had been pressing the government for years to diversify its arsenal. In particular, they urged greater attention to counter-insurgency, to chemical and biological warfare, and to the deployment of such new or underdeveloped weapons as helicopters, tear gas, defoliants, night-vision technology, and napalm.[82] Anything but nukes. Since their concerns meshed with those of the government's other academic advisers like Rostow and Bundy, they got their wish. As the war in Southeast Asia escalated, countless researchers conducted technical studies of individual weapons systems and their applications in Vietnam.

The Jasons became involved in the spring of 1964, when a few of them decided to inform themselves about the situation in Southeast Asia. They brought in such political scientists as Bernard Fall and MIT's Ithiel de Sola Pool to provide expertise and, as one member noted, "we came out knowing more about the sociology of Vietnam than of Georgia." They also produced two studies: "Night Vision for Counterinsurgents" and "Working Paper on Internal Warfare."[83] Despite their early interest in Vietnam, the Jasons (like the other scientific advisers) were still devoting most of their efforts to other weapons systems and arms control. While much of the Jasons' output remains classified, the historian Sarah Bridger estimates that less than 5 percent of the group's studies in 1965–66 dealt with Southeast Asia.[84]

Ironically, much of these scientists' Vietnam-related work stemmed from their desire to de-escalate the conflict. Calling themselves the Cambridge Discussion Group, Kistiakowsky, Wiesner, and MIT's Jerrold Zacharias, along with Kaysen, Galbraith, and the political scientist and former White House aide Richard Neustadt, began to talk about what Kistiakowsky called "an acceptable way of stopping the war."[85] Zacharias then sent a letter to colleagues proposing a summer session to find a technical fix that would enable the United States to stop the bombing, yet bring the war to an end. They joined forces with the Jasons. With McNamara's blessing, the advisers devised two studies: one on the efficacy of the bombing and the other on the feasibility of constructing a barrier to stop infiltration from North Vietnam. If, as Kistiakowsky and his colleagues hoped, the barrier proved effective, McNamara was willing to stop the bombing.[86]

It turned out that assessing the air war required little technical know-how. Under the leadership of Kaysen and the Harvard chemist E. Bright Wilson, the panel produced a report whose opening sentence was blunt: "As of July 1966 the U.S. bombing of North Vietnam (NVN) has no measurable direct effect on Hanoi's ability to mount and support military operations in the South at the current level." From the start, the authors had been skeptical about the assumptions underlying the air war. They were, as Kistiakowsky wrote McNamara, "forcibly impressed by the extraordinary unreliability and uncertainty of [the military's] data," as well as by the way the military brass misrepresented intelligence from the field to support their preconceptions.[87] They pointed out that, given North Vietnam's subsistence agricultural economy and the assistance it was getting from China and the Soviet Union as well as the impossibility of assessing its "will to resist," it was unlikely that even a massively intensified bombing campaign would bring Hanoi to its knees.[88] Augmented by a similar RAND study and a second IDA report with the same conclusions at the end of 1967, the advisers' 1966 analysis did convince McNamara that the bombing should end.[89] Johnson, however, did not agree, telling Rostow in March 1968, "I basically do not regard bombing as a matter of science."[90]

The Jasons also reported on the prospect of a barrier to stop the infiltration of troops and supplies into South Vietnam. In their report, they described an electronic minefield stretching across the Ho Chi Minh trail from North into South Vietnam seeded with a variety of tiny aspirin-, gravel-, and ravioli-sized explosives and sensors that would alert nearby airplanes to the presence of the enemy. Two future Nobel laureates, Val Fitch and Leon Lederman, to their later chagrin, actually designed little mines that could be dropped from the air. Though the project was never fully implemented, some pieces of what came to be called "McNamara's wall" were used during the war. It had little impact on the military situation, though whether that was because of the US commanders' lack of enthusiasm for the project or the ability of the enemy to counter it is hard to tell. However, the Pentagon did become intrigued by the sensors and the prospect of an electronic battlefield that would replace combat troops with computers and unmanned drones.[91]

Meanwhile, the bombing continued. By the middle of 1967, many scientists were pulling away from the government, upset about the war and their inability to influence it.[92] "I now think it was a con job," the Berkeley Nobel laureate Donald Glaser confessed. "They used us technically but didn't listen to us."[93] Marvin Goldberger, the Jasons' first director, agreed. The military, he believed, just "looked on us as an *add-on*. . . . They would bomb the North, *and* they would do this. So I quit after a while." So, too, did Kistiakowsky. Early in 1968, he sent a letter to about one hundred colleagues explaining why he would no longer advise the government. "At the end of '67," he later told a journalist,

particularly after seeing that Mr. McNamara was essentially fired from his job, I reached the conclusion that it was completely futile to continue. At that point, I resigned, and resigned in what might be called a tactless way. In other words, I didn't claim illness or family business or fatigue. I just wrote that I vehemently opposed the present Vietnam policy and could not be even a minor party to it anymore.[94]

That Kistiakowsky considered it "tactless" to disagree publicly with the Johnson administration reveals how seriously compromised so many decent, thoughtful professors had become. They were crippled by what came to be called "the adviser's dilemma." They knew the war was wrong, but they feared that public opposition would destroy their access to policy makers.[95] Kistiakowsky's letter simply added to the angst-ridden discussions among his colleagues about whether to engage in internal or external dissent.[96] Some, like Freeman Dyson, refused to work on Vietnam-related projects while still advising on nuclear arms control.[97] Others simply agonized. "Perhaps half the PSAC was clearly and vocally *though always in private* [italics mine] opposed to the war," physicist and ARPA leader Herbert York explained. "Some of us would even caucus occasionally about whether or not there would be any value in some sort of loud resignation." That gesture never occurred; but by the late 1960s, most of the advisers had quit. But quietly.[98] New people were recruited, —most, however, were no longer eminent professors but applied scientists and engineers working for the military or private industry.[99]

Vietnam to one side, there is little evidence (the test ban treaty excepted) that the nation's top policy makers heeded their scientific advisers' recommendations on other issues, especially those with political ramifications. Johnson, for example, pushed for a manned spaceflight despite the consensus among his advisers that it lacked scientific value. Similarly, although Nixon's scientific advisers realized that a supersonic transport plane would be unworkable, rather than heed them, he simply dissolved the President's Science Advisory Committee.[100] Even when the administration seemed to accept the findings of its scientists, as Kennedy did with a 1963 report by Wiesner on the damaging impact of pesticides, it did not implement its suggestions.[101]

Economists also found their advice ignored. In particular, LBJ's refusal to heed his advisers' recommendation to raise taxes to pay for the war in Vietnam contributed to an economic crisis.[102] That crisis undermined the credibility of academic economists, for the White House advisers involved did not admit publicly that their advice had been rejected. As a result, they and their field got blamed for a mess they tried to avert. But because they feared losing their access to power, the high-powered academics on the Council of Economic Advisers refused to engage in public debate. They did not even want to send a memo to Johnson describing the cost of the conflict in Southeast Asia. There was one dissenter, the-far-from-radical Harvard economist James Duesenberry, who believed that he and his colleagues had failed to fulfill their professional responsibilities. But he neither resigned nor went public. "I figured they weren't going to stop [the war]," he later explained,

> so I thought I might as well stay in the meantime and work for the most stable financial policies. What good would it have done if I had resigned? There would have been an article on page three of the *New York Times* one day and forgotten the next. . . . At least I got the tax program and some housing legislation through. As an economist I was not concerned with the big picture.[103]

That pragmatic silence was endemic among the academic advisers in every field—and it was disastrous. High-level advisers kept quiet to preserve their influence, but some also did so because they viewed themselves like lawyers, professionally bound to preserve confidentiality.[104] They also feared that, given the intense emphasis on security, they might face criminal sanctions if they revealed what they had been working on.[105] In retrospect, many of the former advisers admit that the secrecy was counterproductive. Maintaining confidentiality, combined with the military's compartmentalization of information, meant that the advisers often had only incomplete information. Interviewed in 1971, Wiesner noted that he still had to maintain confidentiality about some of his advice. His overall assessment was grim:

> The nation has paid a much higher price for its secrecy than it would have paid through a policy of complete openness. We've done many things on the basis of inadequate information, not only in the Viet-

nam war: I question whether the arms race would have taken the extreme form it did if the intelligence fellows had been forced to say what the bases of their estimates were and to defend them.[106]

The demand for secrecy also legitimized actions that many advisers opposed. But by keeping unfavorable reports secret, Washington could claim it had the approval of the leading experts—even if it didn't. Moreover, because the government released few reports about its controversial decisions, there was little debate about their wisdom or morality. After all, with the academic advisers on board, as one disillusioned physicist put it, the public could only assume "it's in good hands."[107]

Few, indeed, were the academic consultants willing to breach confidentiality. One did not become a high-level adviser by advocating a kind of civil disobedience. By the late 1960s, however, Vietnam eroded that gentility. As Kistiakowsky explained:

We thought of ourselves as what might be referred to as His Majesty's Loyal Opposition. We were working through the channels, within the organization, as yet. In my case it was a bitter experience, and it led me outside the channels.[108]

In retrospect, Kistiakowsky and some of his colleagues regretted that they had not spoken out sooner and more forcefully. But they had been co-opted. "If you know inside information," the former PSAC member Marvin Goldberger explained,

you think everyone who is on the outside doesn't know what they were talking about. And the sad fact of it was, they knew what they were talking about and I didn't. And I've always been ashamed at how slow I was in making that realization.[109]

Eventually, a few academic advisers did go public with their critiques. Some contacted people in Congress and the press.[110] Insiders had become outsiders, but because of how much Vietnam and the student uprisings had poisoned the atmosphere, academic scientists as well as their colleagues in other fields were beginning to lose much of their authority.

Insiders and Outsiders

By the late 1960s, as more and more academics turned against the war, it was sometimes hard to distinguish the insiders from the outsiders. Often it depended on the issue. Thus, for example, the Jason physicist Richard Garwin was, along with a few other scientists, instrumental in helping to kill the supersonic transport (SST) in 1970. When Nixon overruled the advice of Garwin's scientific panel, he joined a public campaign against the SST. Along with other opponents of the project, including fifteen eminent economists, Garwin and his allies triumphed. Congress killed the venture.[111] Yet Garwin continued to work for the military. He defended his affiliation with the Jasons into the 1970s even in the face of militant demands for the group's dissolution.[112]

Harvard biologist Matthew Meselson was similarly both an insider and an outsider. Brought to Washington in the summer of 1963 by a senior professor in his department, Meselson decided that he didn't know enough about nuclear weapons to offer useful advice to the Arms Control and Disarmament Agency (ACDA) that he was assigned to. He noticed, however, that no one was looking at chemical and biological warfare and, as a biochemist trained by Pauling, he decided to study it. "I wanted to know more about this issue than anyone else," he explained. His Harvard connections fostered high-level contacts with people like Bundy and Kissinger, which gave him access to information. What he found convinced him that CBW should be banned. Although the military supported chemical and biological weapons because they were both cheaper and easier to produce than nuclear ones, Meselson opposed them on just those grounds: they could encourage dangerous proliferation. Moreover, because such weapons had been outlawed in international treaties, deploying them in combat could well be considered a war crime.[113]

What had begun as a matter of curiosity for the young biologist soon became a crusade. The United States was already conducting

FIGURE 9.1. Matthew Meselson in his office at Harvard, 1963. © Harvard University Archives.

chemical warfare by using herbicides in Vietnam. Beginning in 1961, the military had expanded its application of defoliants into Operation Ranch Hand. Until 1971, Americans sprayed tons of chemicals, including Agent Orange, on the countryside of South Vietnam to flush out guerrillas by destroying their food supplies as well as their jungle cover. But, as Meselson and other critics discovered, the Pentagon knew very little about how its defoliants affected the ecology and population of the area or, as became apparent years later, the American troops who handled those chemicals.[114]

Soon Meselson was spending half his time on the issue, following a three-pronged strategy of working within the government, mobilizing the scientific community, and finally appealing to the public. Initially he did not want to disseminate information about these chemicals for fear that it would encourage proliferation. By the end of 1965, however, Operation Ranch Hand had reached the press, spurring a campaign against it within the scientific community. One of Meselson's most effective allies in that campaign was the Yale biologist Arthur Galston, who had inadvertently discovered defoliants while working on his dissertation more than ten years before. Learning that the military was using his research to destroy vegetation in Southeast Asia, Galston explained, "violated my deepest feelings about the constructive role of science, and moved me into active opposition to official US policy."[115]

Other scientists were speaking out as well. Along with the chair of his department, Meselson had begun to organize within the academy, recruiting twenty-two eminent scientists to write an open letter to President Johnson calling for more study and a halt to the use of chemical weapons in Vietnam. Its release at the end of September 1966 hit the front page of the *New York Times*. Forced to respond, the military cited some inside studies showing that the weapons were harmless "weed killers." In the spring of 1967, Meselson and his allies resubmitted that letter, this time with five thousand signatures. They got the same brush-off.[116] By this point, these scientific gadflies were pressing the government to release whatever information it had on the effects of defoliants in the war. They also urged their major professional organizations to conduct their own research. They met considerable resistance—from scientists as well as the military. In 1967, for example, the American Society for Microbiology voted 600–34 to continue its advisory role in the army's biological warfare laboratory at Fort Detrick, Maryland.[117]

Even so, evidence was piling up—and being very reluctantly released—about the probable connection between birth defects and the chemicals in Agent Orange, as well as the ecological damage it was causing. After a few inconclusive studies appeared, Meselson finally persuaded the American Association for the Advancement of Science (AAAS) to sponsor a research trip in the late summer of 1970. He and his colleagues found what they had expected to find—definitive evidence of the toxic effects of dioxin throughout the sprayed areas. Paradoxically, their mission got significant support from the local American commanders, who had come to believe that the defoliation campaign was not only militarily ineffective, but was, in fact, counterproductive since it alienated the farmers whose crops were being destroyed.[118]

By the time Meselson and his associates submitted their findings in December 1970, the program was about to end. Meselson had also been briefing the White House and State Department and had, he felt, supplied the information that Kissinger used when he and Ellsworth Bunker, the American ambassador to South Vietnam, urged the president to stop the spraying. Within a few years, Nixon had not only ended Operation Ranch Hand, but the United States finally ratified the 1925 Geneva Protocol banning chemical and biological warfare.[119] Though the military's desire to abandon CBW may have been crucial to those decisions, it is, nonetheless, likely that the insider/outsider campaigns of academic scientists like Meselson's had at least some impact. If nothing else, their public advocacy, in addition to the student and faculty pressures to ban military research from their campuses, contributed to the growing and increasingly bitter debate about the responsibility of scientists for the consequences of their work.

"TO CONFRONT CAMPUS MILITARISM"

Opposing the War Machine

By the late 1960s, as many academic scientists navigated the tricky balance between insider and outsider status, some younger and more radical academics were mounting a frontal attack on the universities' collaboration with the military-industrial complex. They found the antiwar activities of their liberal colleagues commendable but inadequate. Signing petitions or refusing to participate in defense-related research constituted an essentially individualistic response to the academy's collaboration with the national security state; a broader, more drastic approach was needed. These radicals adopted a variety of strategies for combating that collaboration. Some challenged the status quo within their disciplines. Others worked with students and other campus groups to sever their institutions' ties to the war machine. While still others counted on public exposure and education to mobilize popular opposition to the corporate state's misuse of science.[1] And a few, convinced that they could no longer work within the system, moved to disrupt it.[2]

Their actions were part of a nationwide student-led surge of political activity that challenged the academic community to redefine its relationship with the military-industrial complex.[3] At MIT, where work for the Pentagon had never been a secret, antiwar graduate students proposed a research strike. Though MIT boasted several major military research centers, its faculty also harbored an eminent contingent of peace activists. Toward the end of 1968, these people—Noam Chomsky, Victor Weisskopf, Philip Morrison, and Salvador

Luria, as well as such outside luminaries as Hans Bethe and George Kistiakowsky—joined the students in planning a strike for March 4, 1969. Tensions surfaced between the more radical students and the "well-intentioned but timid" liberal professors that led to the formation of a separate faculty group, the Union of Concerned Scientists. Even so, the project quickly took off. The UCS's founding statement, signed by forty-eight MIT faculty members, was surprisingly strong.

> Misuse of scientific and technical knowledge presents a major threat to the existence of mankind. Through its actions in Vietnam our government has shaken our confidence in its ability to make wise and humane decisions. There is also disquieting evidence of an intention to enlarge further our immense destructive capability.
>
> The response of the scientific community to these developments has been hopelessly fragmented. There is a small group that helps to conceive these policies, and a handful of eminent men who have tried but largely failed to stem the tide from within the government. The concerned majority has been on the sidelines and ineffective. We feel that it is no longer possible to remain uninvolved.[4]

But the notion of a "strike" encountered significant opposition. Accordingly, the event was renamed a "Day of Reflection." As at the first University of Michigan teach-in, once it was clear that the program would not be a direct attack on the university, the administration canceled classes for the day and offered the use of its facilities. The event developed into an expanded teach-in; it lasted for three days and featured discussions about the ethics of scientists and their institutions by dozens of students and professors. The MIT organizers also reached out to other schools. As a result, dozens of campuses—Stanford, NYU, SUNY Buffalo, Fordham, Brooklyn Polytechnic, Stony Brook, Cornell, UCLA, UC Irvine, and UC San Francisco among them—hosted similar events focused on the responsibilities of scientists. The University of Pennsylvania canceled classes, the University of Chicago held a series of conferences, and several hundred Columbia students and professors staged a research strike. As one of the MIT organizers noted, the March 4 event got more publicity "than any other campus activity unmarred by violence."[5]

The disquiet that created those meetings did not disappear. At MIT, continued student agitation forced the administration to form a committee to look at the campus-based Instrumentation Laboratory that was developing guided missiles and the more remote Lincoln Laboratory that was doing some Vietnam-related projects as well. As the panel—which included top administrators, electrical engineers, a Manhattan Project veteran, student radicals, and Noam Chomsky—mulled over the ethical, scientific, political, and economic issues involved, the administration imposed a temporary ban on classified research.[6] Eventually the committee recommended that the laboratories remain under MIT control, but with a faculty-student panel enforcing restrictions against developing weapons. It was an unstable compromise, and by 1973 the university had divested itself of its Cambridge facility, now renamed the Charles Stark Draper Laboratory, while retaining its ties to the supposedly more "academically-oriented" Lincoln Laboratory. The war-related research continued.[7]

Against the War Machine: Student Protests and Faculty Responses

MIT was hardly the only institution to face such demands. By the late 1960s, the student antiwar movement had become a visible and often disorderly presence. As it grew and radicalized, its most militant members engaged in sit-ins and other forms of civil disobedience that disrupted normal campus life. Those protests—usually directed against a group or activity that symbolized the university's complicity with the Pentagon—brought the war home, as a common slogan put it. Through their direct action, the student radicals set the agenda for much of the political debate on their campuses, making it impossible for professors and administrators to avoid dealing with the issues the protesters had raised.

By 1967, student and faculty activists had zeroed in on the academy's collaboration with the war effort. Specifically, they targeted three issues: (1) contract research centers on their campuses, (2) the use of their schools' facilities for recruiting by the armed forces, the CIA, and defense industries, and (3) the military training provided by the Reserve Officers' Training Corps (ROTC). All these activities raised uncomfortable but inescapable questions about the missions of their institutions. Individual professors could not avoid becoming involved.

Around the same time as the 1965 campaign against the Summit and Spicerack projects at the University of Pennsylvania, dissidents at Stanford, Columbia, and elsewhere were also exposing the defense-related research on their campuses.[8] Between 1965 and 1970, left-wing students and faculty members demonstrated against the buildings and laboratories housing military research at about ten major campuses and a number of smaller ones. Until the protests expanded at the very end of the decade, most of these actions occurred at the elite institutions housing the bulk of the Defense Department's academic research.[9]

The year 1967 was pivotal. That fall, the previously quiescent Princeton campus made it to the front page of the *New York Times* because of a sit-in at the Institute for Defense Analyses' on-campus facility.[10] When Princeton Students for a Democratic Society (SDS) activists discovered that the university not only had nine Jason physicists on the faculty, but also housed the IDA's Communications Research Division in a secret computer laboratory protected by armed guards, the local chapter delivered a letter to President Robert Goheen demanding that the university oust the IDA. Goheen, who served on its board, refused. The IDA was a separate body, "independent of Princeton University," and provided "our Government" with "access to the latest and best scientific thinking . . . from independent and impartial people."[11]

On October 23, after announcing that they would take direct action if the administration did not act quickly enough, a group of SDS members and sympathizers took over the IDA building. Declaring, "I find myself appalled by this kind of demonstration," Goheen called in the police, who calmly arrested thirty-one of the demonstrators for trespassing. The faculty went into action as well, holding several unusually well-attended meetings on the issue. Its left-leaning members circulated a petition that got about a hundred signatures urging the university to cut its ties to the IDA. But other professors, including at least one Nobel laureate, sided with the administration and the IDA's "vital" research. Yet another group of faculty members, who claimed

FIGURE 10.1. Princeton police officers arresting student demonstrators at the Institute for Defense Analyses building, Princeton University, October 23, 1967. © Princeton University Archives.

that they took no position on the issues, formed the Student Legal Defense Fund to aid the arrested demonstrators. Faced with a divided constituency, Goheen resorted to the academy's usual response to a political controversy: he appointed a faculty committee.[12]

Chaired by the political scientist Stanley Kelley Jr., the committee eventually recommended that Princeton break its connection to IDA—not because of its contributions to the war in Vietnam, but, as their colleagues at Penn had concluded, because it engaged in secret research. Goheen and the trustees acquiesced, but also decided to let the president continue to serve on the IDA board "in a personal relationship." Within a few years, as the turmoil on campus increased, even that limited connection had become so unpopular that Goheen appointed yet another Kelley-chaired committee to explore the issues of governance and student power.[13]

Outside Recruiters on Campus

Princeton was not unique. Student antiwar protests were spreading, especially at elite institutions and those in major cities. The IDA, with its coterie of eminent scientists working on weapons-related research, was an ideal symbol of the academy's collaboration with the war; but it operated at only a dozen universities. Elsewhere, antiwar activists mounted demonstrations against outside speakers and public officials who supported the war. As early as 1963, campus protests disrupted the speaking tour of the notorious sister-in-law of South Vietnam's president Ngo Dinh Diem. In March 1966, Berkeley demonstrators forced the former Supreme Court justice and current delegate to the United Nations Arthur Goldberg to debate an antiwar professor; in November, Harvard students blocked the car of Secretary of Defense Robert McNamara for several hours. By the end of the decade, such demonstrations had become so ubiquitous that top officials could not visit most campuses.[14]

Among the most common protests were those aimed at recruiters from the military, the CIA, and defense industries. The Dow Chemical Company was a key target. Because it supplied US forces with napalm, a form of jellied petroleum that produced horrific burns, it came to symbolize the worst aspects of an inhumane war machine. By the fall of 1967, there were demonstrations against Dow at dozens of schools—Harvard, Berkeley, UCLA, Boston University, Emory, Penn, Brandeis, University of Wisconsin–Milwaukee, MIT, San Jose State, SUNY Buffalo, NYU, Marquette, Northeastern, Notre Dame, Wayne State, Williams, and the Universities of Chicago, Connecticut, Illinois, Indiana, Iowa, Maine, Michigan, Minnesota, and Rochester among them. Many consisted of leafleting and picket lines, but at some students blocked access to the recruiters. Most of these protests were nonviolent, but a few, including a serious confrontation at the University of Wisconsin–Madison in mid-October, turned nasty when local law enforcement agencies cleared demonstrators from university buildings. Similar actions were taking place against military recruiters and the CIA.[15]

No one was prepared for the unprecedented scale, extent, and turbulence of these demonstrations. As the head of the campus police at the University of Wisconsin later admitted, "We had no model; we were unrehearsed and unprepared for what followed, not only here, but at Columbia, Berkeley and other places."[16] Faculty members were as stunned by the turmoil as anyone else. Determined to restore some kind of order to their campuses, they struggled to resolve the issues that had precipitated the unrest. But their schools had never adopted regulations to deal with on-campus recruiters or government-sponsored research, not to mention the slightly later demands for student participation in governance and Black studies. As a result, at institutions where faculties participated in decision making, these often shell-shocked academics were devising policy on the fly. The confusion they displayed began to eat away at the public's respect for them and their institutions.

As these professors came together at the largest faculty meetings their schools had ever experienced, the proposals they haggled over and the rationales for them differed little from one campus to another.[17] To begin with, while it was clear that Vietnam was the underlying cause of most of their troubles, faculty members, even if they opposed the war, usually avoided discussing it. Instead, they tended to talk about technical issues like regulating recruiters and managing student protests. Otherwise, taking a stand would have "politicized" them. It would have undermined their schools' "institutional neutrality," creating fissures within the faculty and exposing it to attacks from hostile trustees and politicians.[18] On the other hand, they believed that it was perfectly legitimate to discuss outside recruiters. "While the placement service is not central to the functions of the University," a special faculty committee at Columbia explained, "it does perform a desirable and useful service for both students and faculty."[19]

Some faculty members had a direct interest in promoting on-campus interviews. Most were in chemistry departments or schools of agriculture, business, and engineering that had always worked closely with private corporations to help their graduates get jobs.[20] For other supporters of continued recruiting, the issues were more abstract; they tended to invoke patriotism, claiming that by providing well-educated employees to the military, the CIA, and corporations their universities were serving the national interest. It was an argument, elitist to its core, that conservative academics made in defending what Caltech president Lee DuBridge called their institutions' "wholesome influence" on war-related research.[21]

The most common defense of unrestricted recruitment, however, cited the flabby notion of academic freedom.[22] The principle, as articulated by proponents of the "open campus," was simply that barring military, CIA, and defense industry recruiters would violate the individual rights of the students who wanted to meet with them.[23] It was also claimed that by keeping only certain companies and agencies from its campuses, the academic community would be discriminating. These were arguments that liberals found hard to resist. In a 1968 statement, the American Civil Liberties Union likened the banning of defense-related recruiters to the anti-communist speech codes that had flourished only a few years before. "The barring of accredited outside agencies strikes against the concept of the open university and the right of students to hear all points of view," the ACLU declared. "Moreover, selective exclusions . . . are discriminatory in their application and suggest a possible infringement of the spirit of the equal protection clause of the Constitution."[24]

Those opposed to the recruiters denied these framings. There was, as Howard Zinn pointed out in a widely reproduced statement, "no absolute right of recruitment." The Bill of Rights did not protect Dow Chemical's job interviews. Though Dow recruiters could certainly express their opinions on campus, interviewing job candidates was not an exercise of free speech but a business operation.[25] Moreover, as the historian Henry Steele Commager contended, "The university is not an employment agency. . . . It is under no obligation whatsoever to make its facilities available to what is not educational." For these faculty members, the overriding issue was one of morality. For the university to facilitate the hiring practices of a corporation that made napalm was to support—indirectly, to be sure—an unconscionable war that ran counter to the humane values that institutions of higher learning professed. As Commager saw it, the inconvenience for students of having to leave the campus for certain job interviews could hardly be balanced against the "legitimate moral sentiments of its students and its faculty" no matter how "convulsively" they were expressed.[26]

Still, few if any professors welcomed those convulsions.[27] They were, in fact, so averse to confrontation that, whenever they could, they overwhelmingly supported postponing recruiters' visits.[28] When we look at how the faculties at the University of Wisconsin and SUNY Buffalo responded to demonstrations against Dow Chemical, we can see how discomforting the situation had become.

Buffalo's president in 1967 was Martin Meyerson, the city planner who had served with some success as the temporary chancellor of Berkeley in the aftermath of the free speech crisis before coming to Buffalo, with the mission of elevating the formerly provincial private university. As the school attracted a new cohort of intellectually active and politically sophisticated students, many of them Jews from New York City and its suburbs, the tenor of the student body became more volatile.[29] Wisconsin, by contrast, was a major research university with a long-standing progressive tradition. When the police arrested seventeen protesters at the school's first big Dow demonstration in February 1967, Chancellor Robben Fleming put up over $1200 of his own money to bail them out.[30] Fleming's successor, the sociologist William Sewell, had helped to organize Madison's first teach-in.[31] It was clear that if any major institutions were to sympathize with the anti-Dow demonstrators, it would be Buffalo and Wisconsin. But they did not.

At both schools, overflow faculty meetings condemned the disorderly students by considerable margins. In October 1966, after antiwar protesters had disrupted an appearance by Senator Edward Kennedy, Wisconsin's professors reaffirmed their commitment to free speech. Though students "may support causes by lawful means," the faculty declared, they may "not disrupt the operations of the university, or organizations accorded the use of university facilities." Then, when the February 1967 Dow sit-in did indeed disrupt the university's operations, the professors gave the chancellor power to "use whatever measures necessary to protect the continued operation of the university." At that same meeting, the faculty also voted overwhelmingly, 249–63, against sociologist Maurice Zeitlin's proposal to ban all recruiters from companies that make war materials. Among the minority supporting Zeitlin's resolution was the future chancellor Sewell. Like pragmatic liberals at other schools (including Richard Hofstadter of Columbia), Sewell felt that they could avoid trouble if the military and defense industry recruiters would simply move their interviews off the campus.[32]

Despite the faculty's left-wing reputation, none of its members—not even Zeitlin—supported the students' takeover of the building that housed the Dow recruiters on October 18, 1967. But neither were Wisconsin's professors happy with the violence that occurred after Sewell called the police to clear out the protesters. Even an antiwar faculty member like the historian George Mosse who opposed Sewell's decision to bring in the cops felt that obstructing the recruiters was an equally "terrible mistake." At a hastily called meeting the next day, more than thirteen hundred professors spent six hours wrangling over the wisdom of that decision. There was no consensus. While a resolution supporting the chancellor passed, 681–378, a more critical one that acknowledged Sewell's "good faith" but also condemned the "indiscriminate violence" of the police was defeated 562–495. Sewell, who was apparently devastated and soon resigned as chancellor, insisted that he was simply carrying out the policy the faculty had endorsed only a few months before: "You haven't had guts enough to admit that my reaction [to the sit-in] was an exact interpretation of what you intended." Ultimately, the crisis wound down with a few disciplinary actions against the student leaders—and, of course, an investigating committee.[33]

There was no violence at Buffalo; the administration had wisely postponed Dow and CIA interviews when the local SDS warned that it would disrupt them. Instead, President Meyerson called a special meeting of the faculty senate on November 13 to discuss the issue. After unanimously approving the postponement of the recruiting, the senate then voted 197–72 to support Meyerson's demand for an open campus. A month later the faculty, while unanimously endorsing the development of guidelines for dealing with student unrest, nonetheless tabled a proposal for creating a special student-faculty committee on "Placement and Recruitment Practices."[34] Meanwhile, a student referendum on bringing the recruiters back to the campus got a lopsided result: 1734–424 in favor. The Dow people came a few days later, cleverly smuggled into a distant building so early in the morning that by the time the protesters showed up the recruiters were gone.[35]

Dozens of other colleges and universities faced similar confrontations that fall—and their faculties tended to respond in similar ways as well. Whether it was the military, the CIA, or Dow, they supported the concept of an institution open to all recruiters, although sometimes expressing a desire to keep them from the most heavily trafficked areas of the campus. They also approved of punishing students who obstructed interviewers. At Harvard, for example, after the university put more than seventy students on probation and admonished over 170 more for blocking the Dow recruiter, the school's largest faculty meeting voted by a margin of five to one to support those sanctions.[36]

Other institutions raced to handle the demonstrations against recruiters by formulating guidelines for placement interviews. In the beginning of October, for example, after fourteen Columbia professors petitioned to end military recruitment on campus because of "an atmosphere of endemic crisis at this university," the Committee on Instruction banned all recruiting by Dow, the CIA, and the armed services until the undergraduates could be polled. That referendum, like others, produced an unequivocal 67 percent vote in favor of unrestricted recruiting.[37] Meanwhile a special faculty committee came to a similar conclusion. As its chair, the untenured sociologist Allan Silver, recalled, "We couldn't find a principle to prohibit recruiting by any lawful agency." The committee did, however, admit that placement interviews were not a core educational function and recommended that another committee tackle "the formulation of principles that would govern the relationships between the University and outside agencies."[38] Faculty committees elsewhere were coming to similar conclusions.[39]

There were complications, however. On October 26, the Selective Service director Lewis Hershey told local draft boards to rescind the deferments of protesters who interfered with military recruiters. For many academics, Hershey's order constituted an unwarranted intervention into internal matters.[40] The AAUP immediately demanded that the order be rescinded.[41] At Oberlin, when a draft board revoked one undergraduate protester's 2-S deferment, the faculty voted 130–0 to cancel all recruiting until the student was reclassified.[42] At the request of Columbia's faculty, President Grayson Kirk immediately suspended military recruiting until "positive assurances are received . . . that actions and speech by students concerning any University activity will play no role whatever in determining their draft status."[43] A month later, the eight Ivy League presidents sent an open letter to President Johnson reiterating that point. LBJ acceded to that demand. His response reassured the academic community that "the Selective Service System is not an instrument to repress and punish unpopular views." Hershey's directive would not be enforced.[44]

Over the next few years, as disturbances over recruiting spread from elite campuses to second- and third-tier institutions and special committee reports piled up, it became clear that no academically respectable solution would satisfy everyone. Worse yet, as those divisions contributed to the academy's failure to stem the unrest, the public's support for higher education began to ebb.[45] Meanwhile, although military and corporate recruiters began to move their interviews off campus, new conflicts arose.[46] In 1967, the Defense Department had instituted Project THEMIS to help disperse its academic funding to "underdeveloped" institutions. Not only did THEMIS have the obvious advantage of appealing to politicians from areas without major research universities, but its sponsors hoped it would avoid conflicts by working with less-volatile institutions.

Of course, it didn't. CCNY students demonstrated against it, as did the local SDS unit at SUNY Buffalo, whose members destroyed the construction shacks for the project's new building. By the spring of 1970, student demands for ousting THEMIS had even reached the campus of Florida State University in Tallahassee. The project also drew opposition from faculty members. At Buffalo, a group of younger instructors organized a Radical Faculty Caucus specifically to oppose THEMIS, while AAUP chapters at the University of Montana and Rutgers urged cancellation of their school's participation.[47] Though THEMIS petered out within a few years, what really killed it was not the opposition of radical students and scientists but the simple fact that the Pentagon no longer needed academic scientists to develop its weapons systems. Technological advances made it possible for such work to be done by scientists and engineers already employed by the military and defense industries.[48]

Military Training on the Campus

As the antiwar movement spread, student and faculty activists also began to focus on the Reserve Officers' Training Corps. There were only a dozen IDA centers and some fifty THEMIS projects, but there were over 360 ROTC units on campuses—from the Ivy League to the historically Black colleges in the South. By 1968, they were providing 65 percent of the army's newly commissioned officers and 55 percent of the navy's, and had been doing so since World War I.[49]

ROTC programs were initially popular with almost every group on campus. What better way to display patriotism and contribute to the war effort than to enlist in and support the training of military leaders? Administrators viewed the program as a source of prestige as well as moral guidance and character building. The first main controversy it provoked was its compulsory nature. Most schools with ROTC units required all their male undergraduates to take two years of military training. Opposition began to emerge, and by the end of the 1920s, a number of schools—Harvard, Princeton, Johns Hopkins, CCNY, and the University of Wisconsin among them—had transformed their compulsory ROTC units into voluntary ones. ROTC expanded along with the rest of the academy's ties to the defense establishment during the early years of the Cold War. Ironically, university presidents and other administrators were sometimes more enthusiastic supporters of the program than the Pentagon. They saw hosting an ROTC unit as part of their mission to prepare their students for careers, viewing the military as just another vocational opportunity. They did not want to eliminate that option nor deprive their students of the full scholarships or small monthly stipends some ROTC cadets received. And, of course, they sought to maintain good relations with the Defense Department.[50] A certain elitist idealism was also operative. Many academics thought that, as one Harvard Law School professor explained, "the more people like our graduates and graduates of our sister universities and colleges throughout the country, who will have responsibility for our young men the better it will be."[51] Maintaining ROTC, its defenders claimed, would prevent the development of an overly narrow officer corps focused on discipline and loyalty rather than rational thought.[52]

By the end of the 1950s, students had begun to mount a few mild protests, primarily against the program's compulsory nature. That opposition surfaced mainly at flagship state universities from California to Oklahoma and Wisconsin.[53] Since the military was not strongly committed to keeping ROTC compulsory, most of these schools dropped that requirement. By 1965 sixty army units had become voluntary, as had fifty-nine air force ones. Their enlistments declined precipitously. At the University of Illinois in 1963, for example, enrollments went from 2,195 students to 350. Yet many institutions, still required at least two years of military training, particularly in the South and at Catholic schools, second- and third-tier public institutions, and HBCUs.[54]

Meanwhile, there was a growing realization at the more elite institutions that the instruction ROTC was providing was not on a par with the rest of the curriculum. But no one was eager to disturb the status quo.[55] Nor was the military, though the Pentagon did try to upgrade its offerings as enrollments dwindled. In February 1960, for example, the army announced that it would let its advanced cadets take 20 percent of their required ROTC credits in regular college courses.[56] Congress made additional changes with the 1964 ROTC Vitalization Act, which among other reforms sought to attract students by requiring fewer credits. Unfortunately, because of the influence of the powerful (and reactionary) southern Democrats on the House Armed Services Committee, the measure also required ROTC to provide citizenship training and to stress old-fashioned outdoor drills to develop "order and discipline."[57]

The law also required that ROTC instructors be given faculty appointments, including a professorship for the unit's commander.[58] That proved hard to swallow for many faculty members, since the instructors had little, if any, academic training or teaching experience. Some did not even have BAs. They were regular army, air force, and naval officers, often nearing retirement.[59] During the 1960s, the military did send better trained officers to the campus and encouraged them to get MAs. Even so, some schools balked at putting them on the faculty. In 1970, for example, the University of Michigan refused to appoint two ROTC instructors because they could not qualify for admission to its graduate school.[60]

The quality of the ROTC curriculum was no better than that of its faculty. Prescribed by the Pentagon, it consisted of specialized training that was often of little use even to the military. Besides drills and marksmanship, its cadets took courses on "Map and Aerial Photo Reading," "Crew-Served Weapons," and political science offerings that many critics viewed as right-wing propaganda.[61] In opposing Yale's Naval ROTC program, historian John Blum, who had served in the navy during World War II, noted, "My experience as a midshipman had persuaded me forever that instruction in such things as seamanship, gunnery, navigation, and fire control had little intellectual content. Close-order drill offended adult sensibilities."[62]

Other academics agreed. A 1969 University of Michigan faculty report called the ROTC's courses "shockingly bad . . . simply inappropriate to a liberal arts education . . . appalling . . . conjectural, nonanalytical, cheaply moralistic, and often blatantly propagandistic." One Harvard philosopher characterized them in 1969 as, "narrowly vocational or preprofessional. . . . They have always been anomalies, and by now they are anachronisms." In 1967, not only did the unit at the University of Washington receive a secret briefing on the "subversives" in such organizations as SNCC and SDS, but its members were encouraged to spy on dissidents within the faculty and student body. It also inflated their cadets' grades, granting A's and B's to 72 percent of their students, while the figure for the regular Arts and Sciences classes was 44 percent. At Yale, the ROTC refused to let its cadets major in anthropology.[63]

The Campaign against ROTC

As the antiwar movement spread, ROTC units came under sustained attack. In 1966, Berkeley experienced what may well have been the first episode of civil disobedience aimed at ROTC when several dozen activists entered the student center to demonstrate against marine corps and naval recruiters. When the protesters refused to disband, the authorities called in the police, who arrested six of the group's leaders, Mario Savio and Jerry Rubin among them.[64] Within a few years, radicals elsewhere were engaging in similarly confrontational actions, their protests often evolving from orderly demonstrations to sit-ins to vandalism as the ROTC became the preeminent symbol of the connections between the academy and the war.

Many of the early protests were more political theater than guerrilla warfare. In the late fifties and early sixties, leftist students at the University of Wisconsin combated the ROTC by holding "Anti-Military Balls" at the same time as the unit was holding its annual prom. Ten years later, it was the radicals at Southwest Missouri State College who organized a similar "Peace Ball" during their "Week to Confront Campus Militarism."[65] Even as conservative an institution as the University of Mississippi saw a mild anti-ROTC demonstration.[66]

Over time these protests increased in size and disruptiveness. Although only one student showed up at Fordham's first such demonstration in 1965, the following year a hundred did. And in 1968, a few students actually interfered with the ROTC's annual parade.[67] In May 1968, the Alfred University historian M. L. Michael Kay, who had taken part in sit-ins against military recruiters and Dow Chemical, joined a dozen students in a picket line to protest compulsory ROTC. He was ejected by the campus police and fired two days later.[68] A similar fate befell the mathematician Edward Dubinsky at Tulane the following year. Like Kay, he was the leading faculty radical on the campus and, also like Kay, his participation in disruptive actions against ROTC cost him his job.[69]

From Florida State and San Francisco State to Harvard, Howard, and Hofstra, these sit-ins reached their height between 1968 and 1970.[70] Lasting anywhere from a few hours to a few days, they usually targeted either the ROTC facilities or the administration building. Most were peaceful. Sometimes the protesters left on their own; sometimes they left when the authorities threatened to call in the police or when the police came or when they were arrested. Sometimes, however, they fought back and even vandalized the premises. By 1969, some incidents had turned nasty, occasionally because of agents provocateurs. ROTC buildings were bombed and set on fire at dozens of schools, among them Harvard, Tulane, SUNY Buffalo, the Universities of Alabama and Wisconsin, and, most tragically, Kent State.[71]

The Faculty Decides

As the campus opposition to the Vietnam War intensified and increasingly zeroed in on ROTC, college teachers could not duck the issue. Many chose to focus on the military's demand that its courses receive regular academic credit. After all, at most schools the faculty still determined the curriculum and hired teachers. Letting the Pentagon do so seemed an unconscionable abdication of its professional responsibilities. By focusing on the issue of credits, professors could treat the ROTC presence as a technical academic, rather than political, matter. It wasn't, of course. It was clear that a vote to deny credits to ROTC courses was in effect a vote to dismantle the program.[72] But the obvious inferiority of the military's offerings provided an educational fig leaf for the many academics who were loath to openly question their institutions' relationship with the Pentagon.

Moreover, because so many professors had been critical of ROTC's offerings for years, they could also deny that their opposition to awarding credits had anything to do with the conflict in Southeast Asia.[73] It did, of course. In fact, had colleges and universities withdrawn credit a few years earlier, it might have affected the war effort. With ROTC supplying a large percentage of junior officers, its abolition might have caused a serious manpower crisis.[74] Or not. The military establishment wasn't *that* stupid, and it was willing to negotiate. The army, for example, implied that it could be flexible. Similarly, Nixon's Secretary of Defense Melvin Laird might well have abandoned the demand for credits if by doing so he could keep the Big Ten schools in the program.[75]

It is unclear how many colleges and universities that housed an ROTC unit debated its fate. As of June 1970, forty-six of the ninety institutions belonging to the National Association of State Universities and Land-Grant Colleges had mounted some kind of official investigation of the program.[76] At almost every college and university I've looked at, when confronted with actually having to make a decision about the ROTC, the faculty waffled. Its members were seriously split.[77] There were committees and subcommittees, reports and more reports, and delay after delay. Votes were close—with one exception.[78] Decisive majorities at just about every institution rejected the radicals' demand for the immediate ouster of the program. When the Harvard faculty finally voted on the issue, in February 1969, so few professors supported the SDS-initiated resolution for immediate abolition that no one bothered to count. Even so, the faculty did vote to withdraw credit from the ROTC's classes, as well as deny faculty rank to its instructors and eject it from its rent-free offices and classrooms—a decision that essentially had the same impact as quitting the program right away. But many of these professors seemed to assume that the Defense Department would somehow adjust to Harvard's restrictions.[79] Surprisingly, even San Francisco State's rather radical faculty voted 282–250 to retain the program, a tally that may have reflected its unhappiness with a recent student sit-in over the issue.[80] Only at Dartmouth, as far as I can tell, did the faculty vote explicitly to terminate the program.[81]

Most college teachers sought solutions that would both retain and reform the ROTC. The various committees recommended making the program academically respectable.[82] They would award credit only to classes that met their educational standards. "As long as the ROTC courses contain material of University caliber and are taught at University level by properly qualified individuals," the University of Texas faculty explained in 1969, "they will continue to receive our maximum support." At Fordham, the Faculty Senate Committee on the ROTC recommended awarding credit to courses taught by regular faculty members, as did the University of Michigan, whose faculty required a ROTC offering to be cross-listed by a regular academic department. Tulane's Curriculum Committee also ruled against allowing military officers to teach anything with "substantive political or policy content."[83] Elsewhere professors agreed to accept ROTC courses on an individual basis once they were approved by a faculty committee.[84]

At a few institutions, faculty committees toyed with more grandiose projects. They would develop special courses that would incorporate military subjects into intellectually exciting programs that would, the Buffalo committee explained, fulfill the university's "responsibility" to shape the "military toward the values of the broader society." Thus, at the same time as they were voting 229–92 to phase out the Air Force ROTC program, Buffalo's faculty decided to study replacing the Air Force's existing curriculum with a bundle of interdisciplinary courses that would deal with "military phenomena as they relate to mankind in war and in peace." The University of North Carolina considered a similar proposal to integrate ROTC into a new Curriculum on War and Defense. It would be "concerned with war not as a vocational specialty, governed by technical principles and experience, but as a paramount human problem, a phenomenon that is social, political, psychological, and ethical." As the Buffalo and UNC committees used identical language to describe their reforms, it is likely there was some intercampus cooperation.[85]

As for the program's technical instruction and required drills, many faculties treated them as extracurricular activities that carried no credits and could be incorporated into a few weeks of summer training at a military base off campus.[86] Further, Harvard, Michigan, and the University of Illinois at Chicago Circle, for example, withdrew their academic titles from the ROTC instructors. Other schools changed the program's name. At Princeton and Cornell, ROTC was no longer a "Department" but a "Program."[87]

Who Rules the Campus? ROTC and Governance

However they packaged and rationalized their willingness to eliminate or restructure their ROTC programs, faculty members were obviously responding to the upheavals of the moment—in particular the nationwide student strikes that broke out after Nixon's invasion of Cambodia and the shootings at Kent State in early May 1970.[88] At one school after another, professors sympathized with many of their students' demands. They felt enormous pressure to meet those demands and thus end the turmoil. But faculties did not always have the power to enforce their decisions, especially with regard to ROTC.

What happened at Harvard is instructive. Its radical students had been pushing to eliminate ROTC for years. In November 1968, upset that they were barred from attending the faculty meeting that was to deal with the issue, they took over the auditorium. Although the faculty reversed itself in January and voted to let students into future meetings, it didn't revisit the ROTC question until the following month, when it voted to turn the program into an extracurricular activity. But President Nathan Pusey and Dean of the Faculty Franklin Ford opposed this. Ford had wanted the professors to make a general statement and then let a committee negotiate the program's status with the Pentagon. And the Harvard Corporation (as the trustees were called), while approving the decision to deny academic credit and faculty status to ROTC, refused to evict it from its rent-free quarters or provide financial assistance to the students who would lose their ROTC fellowships. Such decisions were not, the Corporation claimed, academic matters over which the faculty had jurisdiction. Finally, when SDS led a takeover of the administration building early in April to force the administration to act, Pusey called in the police. The faculty, appalled by the violence that accompanied the bust and furious that the administration had not carried out its February resolution, called an emergency meeting to demand the complete severance of ROTC from the university.[89]

Trustees and administrators at other institutions overruled their faculties' decisions to limit or eject ROTC. Early in the 1960s, when Michigan State's professors had voted 400–248 against requiring military training, the board of trustees voted 4–2 to retain its compulsory status. The local AAUP chapter not only voted to censure the trustees for overriding the faculty vote, but it also rebuked the university's president for failing to support the faculty.[90]

Apparently because Rutgers was, like MSU, a land-grant university, its board of governors was as reluctant as Michigan State's to tinker with its ROTC unit. When, in the immediate aftermath of Cambodia and Kent State, the faculty voted 132–108 to eliminate ROTC, the board refused to accept that decision, claiming that the university could not simply break its contract with the Pentagon. As the dean explained, ROTC had provoked a struggle over governance, a dispute about "who has the power of decision about curriculum in the College." For the next few years, the issue festered, with the faculty reversing itself several times, until it finally rescinded its decision to deny credit to the program.[91]

What emerges from these conflicts was the radioactive nature of the ROTC issue and the enormous reluctance of almost all the key players to take any action on it. Moreover, despite student polls that invariably supported some kind of voluntary ROTC presence on campus, as well as most professors' clear preference for retaining and reforming the program, it seemed almost impossible to reach a consensus about what to do. Yet during moments when it seemed as if abolition was the only option that would pacify their campuses, and faculties were voting for its de facto abolition, even administrators and trustees were willing to go along. At the University of Massachusetts, the trustees were determined not to risk a confrontation with the teaching staff. "On all matters concerning academic standards and the quality of the curriculum," the chair of the board's committee on Faculty and Educational Policy explained, "the University must listen to the voice of the faculty above all others." It listened by delaying its decision—a classic academic solution.[92]

By the early 1970s, the issue disappeared. When the Nixon administration decided to undermine domestic opposition to the war by withdrawing American troops from Vietnam, implementing a lottery, and ultimately eliminating the draft altogether, ROTC lost its saliency on campus. Students had joined the program to give themselves better options for what had seemed to be inevitable military service. When the draft no longer hung over their heads, ROTC enlistments plummeted. Total enlistments in the Air Force ROTC fell from 25,966 in 1968 to 8,147 in 1972.[93] And at many of the institutions where faculties had reluctantly pushed their units off the campus, the authorities quietly renegotiated their return. There was little opposition.[94] Throughout the academic community's endless deliberations over its relationship with defense industries and the military, one theme predominated: its members did not want to deal with the issue. As in so many other contentious issues of the 1960s, its internal confusion and disunity undermined the university's ability to protect itself from radical militants and hostile outsiders.

PART 3
HANDLING STUDENT UNREST

II

"WE HAVE NO POWER"

What the Students Wanted

"I do not believe that the situations at Berkeley and in Cambridge are at all comparable," Harvard president Nathan Pusey assured a worried member of the Board of Overseers. "The events at Berkeley," Pusey continued, "amounted to a real revolution on issues which have largely been resolved here over the years." Harvard's vaunted house system, where undergraduates lived and ate with graduate students and faculty members, immunized them against the impersonality of the massive and atomized multiversity that, it was commonly believed, contributed so heavily to the student unrest at Berkeley.[1]

The University of Chicago's faculty and administration were equally complacent. The school's relatively small size and the intense intellectuality of its undergraduate student body, it was claimed, ensured against any such attack on the tightly knit community—although, in fact, the living conditions for undergraduates were abysmal.[2] Elsewhere as well, the consensus was that Berkeley's troubles were sui generis, the product of California's unique political environment and its students' understandable discontent. Such outsiders generally felt that Berkeley's students' disruptive behavior had no bearing on their own campuses.

They were wrong, but not entirely. True, the specific issues that prompted student radicals to take over administration buildings in Cambridge and Chicago were their own. Yet every protest—whether it was to end mandatory ROTC, obtain a Black studies program, or eliminate parietal hours for women—did share a common demand for students to have a say over their own lives and educations: "student power."

Almost all of the substantive demands that precipitated a conflict dealt with one of three issues: the Vietnam War, the struggle for racial equality, or the conditions of student life.[3] Berkeley excepted, the earliest confrontations tended to focus on the draft and the universities' collaboration with the military and defense industries. But it was race that led to some of the most disruptive and widely publicized sit-ins and strikes.[4] Surprisingly, however, the conflicts that engaged the broadest range of colleges and universities were not about national politics, but about local campus issues. They ranged from Berkeley's Free Speech Movement to the demonstrations against speaker bans and parietal rules at previously quiescent southern schools.[5] One survey of some 850 institutions found that opposition to dress codes was "the paramount issue in terms of proportions of student bodies activated."[6]

Bringing the War Home

Still, we cannot imagine the political upheavals of the 1960s on American campuses without the Vietnam War. Beginning in 1963, the nascent antiwar movement mounted a few demonstrations at a handful of mainly elite campuses. Some of the earliest took place at Princeton, Columbia, Wisconsin, and the University of North Carolina, where dozens and sometimes hundreds of demonstrators tried to disrupt the speaking tour of Madame Nhu, the garrulous sister-in-law of South Vietnam's president Ngo Dinh Diem.[7] In 1964, there were sporadic attempts to interfere with ROTC and military recruiters at such schools as Columbia and Stanford.[8] Then, after the war escalated, the student protests targeted top policy makers. Defense Secretary Robert McNamara and Vice President Hubert Humphrey encountered heckling and other forms of disruption on campuses like Harvard, Berkeley, and Cornell.[9] By 1969, such demonstrations were so pervasive that the only school where President Richard Nixon felt he could give a commencement address was General Beadle State College in Madison, South Dakota. The following year he could not even attend his own daughter's graduation at Smith College.

The institutions and their faculties that confronted antiwar demonstrations found little guidance from Berkeley's experiences during the free speech crisis; the substantive issues involved were different—and divisive. Until the middle of 1967, many, if not most, academics were still ambivalent about Vietnam and conflicted about their schools' connections to the defense establishment.[10] In fact, until 1970, most professors deemed it too divisive for their institutions to take a public stand on the war. Accordingly, when confronted with disruptive protests, they focused on the disobedient behavior of the students—not the substance of their demands. Often, when they had to devise some kind of policy to deal with the questions the students were raising, they either refused outright (as Harvard's faculty did with regard to the class-rank issue) or else evaded it by appointing a committee.[11]

Thus, for example, after Columbia's radicals disrupted a Naval ROTC awards ceremony in the spring of 1965, the university formed a student-faculty-administration committee to look at the school's "policies governing student rights and responsibilities." Two years later, when its SDS chapter demonstrated against the Institute for Defense Analysis, President Grayson Kirk appointed another committee to recommend guidelines for the university's relationships with outside agencies.[12] Wisconsin did the same in the wake of the violence accompanying the Dow protests in October 1967. Since it often took months, if not years, for these committees to render their reports, it is clear that many educational leaders were hoping to defuse the immediate crisis long enough for the issues that precipitated it to become moot.[13]

Racial Matters in the Age of Segregation and Tokenism

Such was not, however, the case with racial issues, connected as they were to the nation's most intractable economic, political, and social problems. By 1966, as it became clear that the civil rights movement had not eliminated racism or greatly improved the lives of most

African Americans, Black student and faculty activists turned to the nascent Black Power movement. In the San Francisco Bay Area, for example—which, thanks to the California Master Plan, housed the highest percentage of African American college students in the United States—Berkeley graduate students formed study groups to educate themselves and their fellows about their own history and culture. They absorbed the works of W. E. B. Du Bois, Carter G. Woodson, Malcolm X, Frantz Fanon, and other Black writers and then reached out to the growing numbers of African American students in the Bay Area's many campuses and beyond. As the proselytizing efforts of these organic intellectuals fed into the burgeoning Black Power movement, its adherents adopted a multifaceted cultural and political program that rejected assimilation, while seeking to encourage the African American community to achieve political power and economic progress on its own.[14]

Much of the Black Power movement's key organizing took place on the nation's campuses. By demanding that their schools not only recognize their situation as Black students in a white institution, but also provide them with the resources for their broader struggle, the African American activists were—albeit in a symbolic fashion—asking the academic community to address the unfulfilled promise of the civil rights movement. Understandably, these militant students did not always conceal their anger and frustration. By 1968 and 1969, as the Black Power movement gained momentum, its supporters mounted demonstrations at nearly two hundred institutions. According to several contemporary surveys, the concerns of African Americans, although only about 6 percent of the college student population, were central to over 50 percent of the protests.[15]

Whether at HBCUs or at previously white colleges and universities in the North, Black activists made roughly similar demands. Above all, they called for educational programs in Black studies that would recognize and, thus, validate their own history and culture. They also repudiated the goal of assimilation that an earlier generation of African Americans had embraced, objecting to what a group of Vassar women viewed as "becoming socialized to fit a white dominant cultural pattern."[16] At the HBCUs, Black Power activists also rejected

Eurocentric curricula and pedagogy, as well as the political and personal censorship that marked their institutions' accommodation to the white supremacist power structure. Some even demanded that those schools transform themselves into "Black Universities" that would, a leading proponent of Black Power explained, "*deliberately* strive to inculcate a sense of racial *pride* and *anger* and *concern* in its students."[17] In addition, at both the Black and the majority-white institutions, student activists sought to connect with the off-campus African American community.[18]

Nonetheless, differences among campuses did exist. The most obvious one was that the HBCUs' students still lived in a largely segregated society and so had no need of the separate social and cultural facilities that the Black students at traditionally white institutions like Cornell or the University of Illinois were demanding.[19] Instead, just as in the early 1960s, the HBCU activists continued to demonstrate against the nearby bowling alleys, restaurants, movie theaters, and other public facilities that still refused to serve them.[20] They also continued to protest the restrictive social and political regulations that so many of their institutions had traditionally imposed. Conscious of those institutions' educational inadequacies, they also pressed for more highly qualified faculty members and better facilities.[21]

The issues were different on campuses outside the South, where, as a result of the civil rights movement, increasing, though still small, numbers of Black students now matriculated. They forced the entire system of higher education to confront its own racist practices. After all, until the mid-1960s, de facto segregation had been the norm. At every level and at every kind of school, higher education, outside of the HBCUs, was essentially lily-white. As of 1954, only about four thousand Black students had attended white colleges and universities.[22]

Tokenism prevailed. Until the late 1960s, there were rarely more than a handful of Black students at selective institutions. When I went to Radcliffe in the late 1950s, to my knowledge, my class contained two Black students; one came from the Caribbean, the other was passing for white. Kenyon College, during the early 1960s, had all of two Black students.[23] In 1963, there were only five Black students at Princeton and eight at Cornell.[24] Most Black students on traditionally white campuses, if they weren't elite foreigners, were either athletes or the children of educated professionals.[25] Of the twenty-six Black students at Northwestern in 1964, twenty were athletes.[26]

During the sixties, their numbers rose, but slowly. By 1964, there were between fifty and seventy American-born Black students among Harvard's 4,600 undergraduates, and around fifty at Columbia.[27] There were more at the big state universities, even if the percentages were still tiny. Drawing from the large African American community in Chicago, the University of Illinois at Urbana-Champaign had 223 Black students in 1967, but that was still only 1 percent of the student body.[28] There were not many more at other flagship schools.[29] And in the middle of the largest Black and Puerto Rican community in the United States, the City College of New York in the fall of 1968 enrolled 565 Black and 431 Puerto Rican undergraduates out of an overall student body of 10,867. Significantly, at both CCNY and San Francisco State, measures to raise their academic profiles during the early 1960s led to an actual decline in the percentage of African American students.[30]

Conspicuous but isolated because there were so few of them, most of the Black students at the traditionally white institutions during the 1950s and early 1960s kept a low profile. Even so, they experienced discrimination both on campus and off. Not only were they harassed by campus police and barred from most fraternities and sororities, but they often had trouble finding a place to live. Many colleges and universities would not house them in the dorms or else would put them in segregated facilities, while local landlords frequently refused to rent to them. When confronted by students and civil rights groups demanding that they oppose this discrimination, all too many institutions of higher learning took no action. The University of Chicago was particularly egregious in this regard. While mouthing platitudes about its support for racial equality, it not only, as we shall see, aggressively engaged in gentrification, but also went along with the restrictive covenants in its neighborhood that barred sales and rentals to African Americans. It was not until a group of students that included Bernie Sanders sat-in at the administration building in January 1962 that the university finally changed its policy.[31]

At other schools, even when Black students did get on-campus housing, they experienced discrimination. In the mid-1950s, for example, despite having requested roommates, all of Amherst College's few Black freshmen were given single rooms, while as late as 1966 at Northwestern, the administration refused to let any of its incoming African American women room together.[32] In addition, with so few other Black students on these and other majority-white campuses, social isolation was a serious problem. While the African Americans who went to urban colleges and universities could find friendship and support in a neighboring Black community or HBCU, those who ended up in small towns and rural areas found themselves on their own and unwelcome. Tensions increased everywhere if the Black men tried to date white women.[33]

Worse yet, they sometimes encountered overt hostility. The Ku Klux Klan, which had long operated in southern Indiana near that state's flagship university, threatened to march against Indiana University's new Black students. Oshkosh, Wisconsin, was similarly inhospitable. When he arrived at the University of Wisconsin campus in 1966, one of the nine Black students there came under physical attack. To avoid getting beaten up, he recalled, he and his friends "kept in top shape, fighting condition. For self-protection we stuck together just like a little army. We went to class together, showered together, ate together, and met at certain times in the Union."[34]

But when, as at Oshkosh, Black students tried to create their own organizations for safety and companionship, they were accused of being racists. At Columbia, for example, administrators objected to what they termed the "separatism" inherent in the students' desire to organize their own fraternities and Black history reading groups—even though white fraternities had discriminated for years. Similarly, in 1963, Harvard's Council for Undergraduate Affairs vetoed the formation of a proposed African and Afro-American Club on the grounds that it was "discriminatory." A faculty committee reviewed and supported that decision, explaining that it was "unwilling at this critical time to put the weight of Harvard's approval behind the principle of racial separatism and exclusion." The dean actually reprimanded groups of Black students for sitting by themselves in the dining halls instead of joining whites.[35] The pressures for conforming to white culture were intense. "We didn't feel we had a choice," one former student explained. "The implication was plain that we were being let into the university on the condition that we become white men with dark skins."[36]

A New Black Cohort on Campus

Change came in the late 1960s, as the civil rights movement stimulated the leaders of northern white campuses to go beyond "genteel liberal integration." Beginning in the early sixties with pressure from the Kennedy administration and accelerating after the passage of the 1965 Higher Education Act, administrators, faculty members, and foundation officers consciously sought to increase minority enrollments.[37] As a result, many more African American students suddenly appeared on traditionally white campuses. And, empowered by their new numbers, they began to demand greater consideration there.

Within four years, the number of African American students at MIT rose from ten to more than two hundred. By 1970, a tenth of the freshmen at fifteen elite institutions in the East were Black: 10 percent at Harvard, 12 percent at Yale, 16 percent at Princeton, 17 percent at Radcliffe, and 22 percent at Barnard.[38] But there were more Black students at *all* institutions of higher learning. Between 1964 and 1967, the number of African Americans in college more than doubled, from 234,000 to almost 500,000, with almost 50 percent of them at traditionally white schools. And the percentages continued to rise. By 1980, only 34 percent of the nation's Black undergraduates were attending HBCUs.[39]

On some campuses African Americans now formed a critical mass of potential activists. Not all of them joined the Black Power movement. Many were as apolitical as their white classmates, concerned with their grades, their social lives, and their future careers.[40] And, of course, at working-class schools like CCNY and San Francisco State, many had families and/or were holding jobs that gave them little time for their studies, let alone demonstrations and sit-ins.[41] Still, they could no longer be ignored.

Even so, the new recruits did not have an easy time of it. Besides the normal problems of adjusting to college life, they had to deal with the special burdens of integration. Moreover, unlike the earlier cohort of largely middle-class African Americans, many of these new Black students came from working-class backgrounds and inner-city high schools that left them unprepared for the academic rigors of higher education. Not only were many the first members of their families to attend college, with all that situation's attendant personal and psychological baggage, but they were also struggling to find their place within an unfamiliar and often uncomprehending white world. "How does one make the transition," George Royal, a recent arrival at the University of Pennsylvania, asked in a letter to the college newspaper in October 1968,

> from studying eight hours a week to do well in high school to studying five and six hours a day in college? Our confusion was intensified by a lack of meaningful counseling on the part of the University. No one paid any particular attention to us until each found himself on probation.

Admitting that "the problem of academic adjustment is not limited to Black students," Royal continued,

> the difficulty of transition is amplified for us by a sudden immersion in a white community. School is no longer a six hour-a-day association with whites. There is suddenly a tremendous almost overwhelming self-consciousness about being Black. We are no longer individuals, but representatives of our race. This self-consciousness distorts everyday life in a manner that it is impossible to fully explain.[42]

That such pressures should have affected Black undergraduates is no surprise. When he integrated the University of Mississippi in 1962, James Meredith experienced so much stress during his first semester that he nearly flunked out. Though Meredith was rescued with intensive tutoring provided by a network of supporters, less well-known Black undergraduates were often left to flounder.[43] Whether because of inexperience, insensitivity, inadequate resources, or their own unacknowledged racism, many institutions did not provide African Americans with the special services and facilities they needed for success. This was as much the case at Yale as it was at the City College of New York. At best, these schools hired a few African American administrators and counselors, but rarely created an effective infrastructure that would not only give academic assistance, but also enable the Black students to overcome the social isolation that led so many to drop out.[44]

Retention, thus, became a major problem. The University of Illinois had expected only a small percentage of their recruits to get their BAs within four years and were actually surprised to discover that a third of them had done so. (Another 42 percent either transferred or graduated later.)[45] Clearly, despite their stated desire to diversify their student bodies, liberal administrators and faculty members did not give that project a high priority—or enough money. At the University of Connecticut in the early 1960s, as Homer Babbidge, the school's president, confessed to a friend, "We were not doing anything here for the higher education of Negroes that I can say is worth emulating." Not only was the number of Black students "disappointingly small," but the school simply had no idea how to handle them. They came from "an alien subculture," Babbidge explained, and efforts to help them were essentially "the things we already do to help the foreign student."[46]

Nonetheless, by the late 1960s, some institutions had developed special remediation and support programs. Outside grants provided resources, and they were often staffed by dedicated and gifted Black and white teachers and administrators, who, like Mina Shaughnessy of City College's SEEK program, respected their students while developing new pedagogies for the teaching of basic skills.[47] Such programs could be exciting venues for radical instructors. When Robin Dizard, an adjunct teaching remedial English at Oakland's Merritt Junior College in the late 1960s, got bored by the textbook she was supposed to use, she recalled, "I ordered the speeches of Malcolm X and all of a sudden my classes were jammed." Merritt may have been unusual. The birthplace of the Black Panther Party, it allowed leftists like Dizard and some of her colleagues to supply their radicalized Black students with the relevant political background and skills that they sought.[48] Remedial programs elsewhere, however, had trouble overcoming the patronizing attitudes of the conventional liberals who created them.[49] To refer to their African American students as "culturally deprived," "at risk," "disadvantaged," or from "an alien subculture" smacked of paternalism, creating considerable antagonism among the Black students who felt stigmatized. That so many of the instructors were white only increased that stigma.[50]

It was no wonder, then, that these students began to demand more control over their own educations. Beginning in 1966 and 1967, a critical mass of Black students formed their own political organizations, some inspired by former SNCC activists who, while resuming their own college careers, were also spreading the new Black Power ideology.[51] By the end of the 1960s, almost every institution that housed a significant cohort of African Americans also had some kind of organized Black student group. From Princeton's Association of Black Collegians and Vassar's Students' Afro-American Society to the Black Student Unions at San Francisco State and Fresno State, there were dozens, if not hundreds, of them.

The Black Students' Demands

Significantly, however, though the radicalized Black students maintained informal networks, no effective national organization emerged. These activists were too busy at home. The issues they pushed varied, although they made four basic types of demands. They sought special facilities and services for Black students. They called for admitting more minority-group students and hiring more African American faculty members and administrators. They demanded Black studies programs. And, depending on their location, they challenged their institutions' relationships with nearby Black communities. Another set of demands, to become important by the 1980s, arose at those few universities with significant endowments where Black students and their allies called for divesting from corporations with ties to the then-apartheid country of South Africa. Most of the schools where the Black students made such demands gave in to them—though not always without a struggle. And those struggles included many of the most disruptive campus encounters of the late 1960s and early 1970s.[52]

Especially at colleges and universities where there were few outlets for undergraduate socializing besides traditional (and traditionally discriminatory) fraternities and sororities, African American undergraduates sought their own student centers. They conceived of these centers as providing facilities for cultural activities, individual counseling, academic tutoring, and outreach to Black communities. At some schools, the student activists also demanded special housing, either in separate buildings or separate floors in dormitories.[53]

And, in many cases, the students accompanied those demands with actions. In 1967, for example, it took the peaceful occupation of the Duke University administration building before the authorities agreed to establish an all-Black dormitory.[54] A somewhat less peaceful Black student strike that brought the National Guard onto the campus at the University of Wisconsin in February 1969 forced the administration to set up an African American student center.[55] And, at Cornell, where protests against discrimination by a white fraternity led to the creation of an all-Black male off-campus house in 1967, demonstrations resulted in the establishment of similar housing for Black women as well.[56]

Because establishing a separate facility for African American students could be seen as a violation of the Civil Rights Act of 1964, legal issues sometimes became roadblocks. When Cornell established Wari House, the Black women's dorm, the New York Civil Liberties Union threatened to sue.[57] Antioch College nearly lost its federal funding when it set up an all-Black student center, while the University of Pennsylvania responded to the prospect of similar sanctions by buying a nearby building and renting it to a nonprofit organization run by students and community members. These centers sponsored outside speakers, tutored neighborhood schoolchildren, formed reading groups in Black history, and, in some cases, published journals and newsletters.[58] Arguably, the most important outreach activity by African American students was recruiting potential undergraduates from their home communities.[59]

As the Black students pressed to increase their numbers and provide better facilities and services for the new recruits, they encountered problems. Not only were most of the programs they sought seriously underfunded, but opposition developed among students and professors (as well as within the broader community) to the prospect of granting special treatment to supposedly less-qualified applicants.[60] Michigan's professors, for example, complained that the admission of more Black students would create "soft degrees" that would water down the quality of their school.[61] At Cornell, one proponent of greater access explained:

> The faculty would find ways of dragging its feet, . . . all kinds of questions about standards, about fairness would be raised—why should black students with lower scores receive scholarship aid when white students with equivalent scores weren't receiving scholarship aid, and so forth. The general questioning would be such that essentially we would get no program at all.[62]

The administration therefore maneuvered around the faculty. In an ironic twist that created future problems, in their drive for racial justice, Cornell's leaders had knowingly snubbed their professors.

Additional problems arose when urban campuses began to expand into neighboring Black communities. As early as 1957, the presidents of sixteen universities—among them, Harvard, Yale, MIT, Temple, the University of Pennsylvania, and NYU—met at the University of Chicago to discuss how they could deal with the supposed deterioration of their immediate surroundings. Gentrification (though the term had yet to be conceptualized) would be the answer. Universities would push out the poor African American residents who, they feared, threatened their institutions.[63]

Chicago was an innovator here. It had confronted such problems early on. Located in the multiracial neighborhood of Hyde Park, which had experienced an influx of southern Blacks in the late 1940s and early 1950s, the university's leaders panicked at the prospect of declining enrollments and the loss of faculty members if they could not maintain the area's attractiveness to white students and professors.

"We are fighting for our lives," Chicago's president Lawrence Kimpton explained. "We simply cannot operate in slums." But instead of trying to combat the racial discrimination responsible for the overcrowded living conditions of their Black neighbors, the university embarked on a massive campaign of what it advertised as "urban renewal." It sought federal and foundation support to buy up nearby housing, while displacing most of its residents. As one high-level administrator admitted, that effort succeeded—"saving the community and preventing its becoming another Negro slum."[64] A later attempt by the university to expand into the nearby Woodlawn neighborhood in the early 1960s was less successful. The local community, which had not been organized enough in the 1950s to prevent the university's encroachments, fought back, forcing Chicago's administrators to include community residents in their planning.[65]

The University of Pennsylvania was also planning to redevelop a supposedly blighted area near the campus by upgrading its housing stock and locating a high-tech science center there. By the mid-1960s, the university had displaced some 2,600 African American and white residents, and was well on its way to creating an upscale neighborhood for cosmopolitan liberals and college students. At that point, its new cohort of Black, as well as radical, students was working closely with the community to press the university to rein in that gentrification. In a synergy of protests, they called for a ban on classified military research in the new science center as well as compensation for the displaced residents. When 800 Black and white students peacefully took over the administration building for six days in February 1968, Penn's leaders gave in to most of their demands.[66] Similar issues arose at Harvard, Yale, and Northwestern.[67]

But nothing drew as much attention as Columbia's plan to build a gym in the park that separated the university from the rest of Harlem. Like Penn and Chicago, Columbia had been expanding physically for years. It bought up large numbers of single-room occupancy hotels and other low-cost housing units near the campus, and then used such tactics as denying heat to push out nearly ten thousand mostly Black and Puerto Rican residents. Columbia's provost, the eminent literary critic Jacques Barzun, was quite explicit about his desire to eliminate the neighborhood's "uninviting, abnormal, sinister and dangerous elements" so that Columbia could, like the University of Chicago, attract and retain students and faculty members who, he explained, "must not be subjected to an environment that requires the perpetual *qui vive* of a paratrooper in enemy country."[68]

No surprise, then, that an institution whose leaders held such an unflattering view of its neighbors might find itself on a collision course with them. According to the social scientist Daniel Bell, then on Columbia's faculty, his colleagues had few qualms about their institution's expansion. They shared Barzun's concerns about street crime; and when someone tried to introduce a resolution against the gym during a faculty meeting, no one seconded it.[69] But other local residents resented the university's failure to consult with them—and began to mobilize against the planned facility. In response, the university agreed to allot 17 percent of the space in the proposed facility for the community's use—albeit only at certain times and through a separate entrance. Harlem was not appeased.[70]

Nor were Columbia's African American students, who readily joined the struggle against "Gym Crow." It soon became one of the key issues in the 1968 student uprising that did, in fact, stop construction on the gym. (Powerful New York City politicians as well as many faculty members also opposed the project.)[71] But the Black students do not appear to have received such other concessions as Black studies or more Black faculty members. As late as 1984, the university had only three tenured Black professors, and it did not set up an independent Black studies program until 1987.[72]

The call for such programs was the demand that encountered by far the most resistance from the nation's faculties. There were several reasons for that obstruction. To begin with, because the call for Black studies tended to rely on the revolutionary rhetoric of Black nationalism, it was seen as separatist—and thus sometimes denounced by more moderate African American faculty members and civil rights leaders. Even more distressing for many professors was the demand by Black students to participate in and even control decisions about curriculum and academic personnel.[73]

An additional problem was finding qualified instructors. For years, the mainstream academic community had ignored the history and culture of African Americans, thus effectively sidelining Black scholars and their work. As a result, when the majority-white colleges and universities sought to appease their militant Black students, they found themselves struggling to find the African American academics with the mainstream credentials they sought. As Vincent Harding, the chair of Spelman College's history department, noted in 1969, "Every black Ph.D. who has his name mentioned twice, or has published in the slightest review, is besieged by Northern as well as Southern white institutions." Not only did these majority-white schools raid the HBCUs, but they also hired graduate students and high school teachers, while all too often complaining that bringing in such instructors would force them to lower their academic standards. On many campuses, faculty committees simply dug in their heels and refused to act.[74]

That opposition, though clearly an example of the insensitivity and institutional racism that suffused so much of academe, was also a manifestation of many faculties' hostility to "student power." Professors who said they supported civil rights and civil liberties often balked when confronted by their students' call for greater control over educational decision making. They were no more willing to cede their professional prerogatives to their students than they were to any other outsiders. Even radicals, it turned out, could become unsympathetic to the demand for student power when it threatened their own academic values and practices.[75]

In Loco Parentis and Student Life Issues

Faculty opposition to student power was hardly monolithic. Even when they were ambivalent about student demands for all-Black dormitories or the expulsion of military recruiters, not to mention control over tenure decisions, many professors, as at Berkeley in 1964, supported protests against restrictive political and social rules. By the late 1960s, the regime of in loco parentis had become a major target. Because those rules directly affected almost every student, such matters as dress codes, parietal hours, student governments, outside speakers, and the censorship of publications could at times mobilize students more readily than more divisive political issues like Black Power and Vietnam. Sometimes circulating petitions against curfews or joining picket lines against the failure to reappoint a popular teacher turned out to be a precursor of later, more overtly political, demonstrations. Thus, for example, two years before two hundred students disrupted Northwestern's annual ROTC ceremony in May 1969, its undergraduates demonstrated against the limits on men's visiting hours in women's dormitories.[76]

Of course, there had been protests against campus regulations and living conditions ever since Harvard students rebelled against rancid butter in 1766.[77] The Berkeley Free Speech Movement revealed not only how disruptive such demonstrations could be on twentieth-century campuses, but also how they could become vehicles for genuinely important issues. Such was especially the case at institutions where student social and political activities were seriously restricted. Southern colleges and universities were among the worst offenders, the HBCUs in particular. Because they feared offending segregationist trustees and politicians, Black institutions were scrupulous about policing their students. Many required chapel and class attendance. The rules for African American women were especially puritanical, seeking to counter racist stereotypes of Black female promiscuity. Their curfews were so rigid, in fact, that the students from Spelman, Atlanta's prestigious women's college, often had to rush out of movies before the end to get back on campus in time. And if they failed to attend the Sunday concerts, they could not sit on the porch or leave their rooms.[78] Women everywhere were under similar, if less stringent, regulations. Curfews rankled, particularly the obvious hypocrisy of a system that left men alone.[79]

There were dress codes designed to produce carefully groomed candidates for the middle-class marriage market.[80] In the early sixties, for example, Kent State's women had to wear "conventional dress" for dorm meals, including high heels on Sunday.[81] Spelman required stockings at all times, no socks, and, of course, no slacks. At Radcliffe, we could not wear pants below the second floor of the dorm, except on snow days. Nor, except for a few days per semester, were men ever allowed above the first floor and then only in rooms with the door open, and, when alone with a woman, the rule was that there must be three feet on the floor.[82]

Men also experienced constraints. They could, for example, bring women into their dorm rooms only for limited amounts of time.[83] Male students faced dress codes as well: business attire that marked its wearers as members of the professional middle class. In 1965, Michigan State men had to wear ties in the dorm cafeterias; and, as late as 1967, one former Columbia radical recalled he wore "sports jackets, even ties."[84]

Perhaps these were trivial, though symbolic, matters. A more serious constraint on students was political censorship. Until the mid-1960s, most of the nation's students, like their professors, were apolitical. The fraternity-dominated student governments engaged almost entirely in "sandbox politics," concerned with homecoming queen elections and similar lightweight fare. At Ohio State, where a stringent gag rule kept controversial speakers off the campus, the student government held at least three beauty contests a year.[85] When more politically aware students tried to bring up substantive matters like racial equality or civil liberties, as the members of SLATE did at Berkeley by the early 1960s, they could encounter official hostility.[86]

On some campuses, especially at southern colleges and universities, student governments were actually barred from engaging in controversy. In 1957, for example, when the student government at Mississippi's Alcorn A&M boycotted a segregationist professor, the trustees fired the school's president and expelled all the students, allowing them to return only after pledging never to protest again. Seven years later, when Alcorn's students rose up again, demanding a student government free from administration control, the new president had them all arrested. At Jackson State, Mississippi's largest HBCU, the president dissolved the student government because, he claimed, its support for the civil rights movement "embarrassed" the college.[87]

Student journalists were especially vulnerable, though most, no doubt, censored themselves. The editorial policy of the paper at Southeastern Louisiana State College, for example, explicitly stated: "Because of its explosive nature, columns, editorials, and other types of articles on the race issue should be avoided."[88] When students ignored that advice, administrators cracked down. In 1957, when the paper at South Carolina's all-Black state college in Orangeburg ran sympathetic articles about a local NAACP boycott, the paper's editors were expelled and its faculty adviser fired.[89]

Sexuality was as dangerous as politics. Sometimes, as at the University of South Florida in the early 1960s, they could be linked. Local conservative citizens and politicians, upset about the "extreme, liberal, atheistic teaching" at the new institution, forced the suspension of an English professor who had assigned an article by the New York Intellectual Norman Podhoretz that quoted some scurrilous language from the Beat Generation poets that Podhoretz was actually attacking.[90] Similarly, in January 1969, the administration at Georgia's Armstrong State College refused to reappoint an assistant professor of sociology who had been arrested for "furnishing lewd and obscene literature to minors"—specifically, copies of the Atlanta underground newspaper *Great Speckled Bird*.[91] At about the same time, the president of Florida State University overruled both the English department and the faculty senate to ban the publication of a short story in the literary magazine that, he claimed, contained too many four-letter words "considered by most people then to be unsuitable for a campus publication."[92]

But not every affront to modern literature and the First Amendment took place in the presumably benighted South. In the spring of 1960, the president of the University of Illinois fired a biology professor for defending premarital sex in the student newspaper.[93] Seven years later, at what many considered the most "swinging" campus in the country, President John Summerskill of San Francisco State suspended a student publication and its board because it had published a frontal photo of a nude woman, though by then the campus was in such turmoil that Summerskill's action aroused more chuckles than indignation. The following semester, however, when Summerskill suspended an author and the editor of that publication, he was forced to back down by a crowd of five hundred angry demonstrators and the threat of an ACLU lawsuit.[94]

By the late 1960s, protests against almost all manifestations of in loco parentis had become common even in the South, constituting what the historian Robert Cohen has called "a second kind of freedom struggle."[95] At Florida State, when the president censored the literary magazine in May 1968, two hundred students responded with a weeklong vigil and nearly forced him to resign.[96] At the University of Georgia, there was a three-day sit-in against in loco parentis. Similar protests took place at the University of Alabama as well as at South Carolina State.[97] And at Troy State in Alabama, where the president punished faculty members who had criticized his censorship of the paper, students circulated a petition opposing his actions. They were especially upset about the dismissal of an instructor in the English department.[98]

In Defense of Popular Teachers

So, too, were the denizens of an otherwise placid campus in New Haven. As early as the spring of 1965, at a time when most of Yale's rather conservative undergraduates still supported the war in Vietnam, they were nonetheless willing to protest over local issues. Accordingly, when they learned in the spring of 1965 that Richard Bernstein, a popular young philosopher, had been denied tenure, hundreds of students mounted a three-day vigil to call for his reinstatement. They viewed Bernstein as a victim of the university's "publish or perish" syndrome that, by seeking the increased prestige a prolific faculty would confer, ignored the educational needs of its students. By disrupting the campus, those students were determined to make Yale take their desire for better teaching seriously.[99]

Similar demonstrations in support of popular faculty members were occurring elsewhere as students began to make connections between broader social and political issues and what was (or was not) happening in their classes. No longer passive consumers, they began to call for greater control over what was being taught and who was teaching it. Along with the related demands of African American students for more Black professors and Black studies programs, these newly energized students disrupted dozens of campuses from Tufts to Vassar to Howard University by calling for greater "relevance," while opposing the dismissals of radical and not-so-radical teachers.[100]

Although many of the fired academics were left-wing activists, some were not. Unlike his radical colleague Staughton Lynd, Bernstein did not lose his job at Yale for political reasons. He had been unanimously recommended for tenure by his department, but was turned down at the next level by a faculty committee on the grounds that his scholarship was substandard. A popular teacher who offered a wide variety of courses and was always available to students, Bernstein had compiled a perfectly respectable publication record: several monographs and essay collections, as well as the editorship of a journal in his field.[101] Days after learning of Bernstein's fate, his outraged graduate and undergraduate students held several public meetings and mounted a major demonstration. For three full days, twenty-four hours a day, groups of twenty to one hundred respectably clad students marched in front of the administration building singing and carrying signs proclaiming, among other slogans, "Escalate Bernstein," and "Homer Was a Two-Book Man."[102]

The university had not seen so much activism since the 1930s. Although one professor denounced "the chanting, protesting, bellicose demonstrators," others were pleased, as one explained, that their students "are not merely interested in sex, sports, and motorcycles, . . . and that they insist on an individual education, rather than the processing through any mold."[103] Symbolic of the developing linkages between issues, Mary Wright, Yale's East Asian historian (and one of the very few tenured women in the Ivy League), addressed two campus meetings on the evening of March 4, 1965. At one, she excoriated the Johnson administration's escalation of the war in Vietnam, and at the other, she praised the students' support for Bernstein's tenure, as did the president of Yale's AAUP chapter, Arthur Galston, the biologist who had become an antiwar activist when he discovered that the military used his research to produce Agent Orange.[104]

President Kingman Brewster, who was to gain considerable praise for his skill at handling student protests, defused the situation by asking the faculty committee that had nixed Bernstein's tenure to reconsider the case. He did so, however, in the context of a brand-new requirement that tenure committees should have a "reasonable expectation" that a faculty member would be promoted to full pro-

fessor within five years. Brewster knew that the philosophy department's unanimous vote for Bernstein had been qualified by its refusal
to guarantee him rapid promotion, so his request was actually disingenuous. The committee heard the president's dog whistle and quickly
voted 5–2 against tenure, a verdict Brewster readily accepted. At the
same time, however, he sought to appease the students by appointing
an ad hoc committee to reassess the role of teaching in future tenure
decisions.[105]

Brewster's deft sloughing off of responsibility to the faculty for an
unpopular decision that he probably supported may well have been
exceptional. But in most other respects, the outcome of the Bernstein
case was little different from the way more authoritarian administrations dealt with similar student demonstrations. In 1967, for example,
students at the all-Black and considerably less liberal South Carolina
State in Orangeburg boycotted classes for two weeks in a wide-ranging
protest that included a call for the reinstatement of three instructors
who had complained about the institution's educational inadequacies.
Though the students did gain some of their demands, the three faculty
members did not return.[106] The Student Liberation Front's occupation
of the student center at Tulane in April 1970 was equally unsuccessful
in restoring the job of the mathematician summarily fired for disrupting an ROTC drill.[107] Though there were a few instances where student protests did restore people's jobs, most of the time they could not.

Left-wing faculty members were particularly vulnerable, and because they often had ties with the student radicals, their dismissals,
whether justified or not, sometimes set off sit-ins and demonstrations.[108] That is what happened at the University of Chicago, where
in January 1969 some four hundred SDS-led students occupied the
administration building for sixteen days to protest the sociology department's refusal to reappoint a radical activist and feminist named
Marlene Dixon.[109] An extremely popular teacher especially with the
radical students, Dixon had received a joint appointment in sociology and human development and, while renewed by the latter department, was turned down by the eminent and conservative senior
professors in sociology, who had never even bothered to assess her

teaching. Her very public participation in campus demonstrations and her gender in an all-male department unaccustomed to treating women as intellectual equals, as well as what seem to have been some severe psychological problems, certainly did not help her. When the well-known public intellectual Edward Shils responded to the student sit-in with a widely circulated four-page assessment of what he called Dixon's "at best unqualifiedly mediocre" scholarship, it was clear that her career at Chicago was over. A faculty committee, appointed by the administration at the height of the crisis—and chaired by the university's future president Hanna Gray, one of the few tenured women on the faculty—did admit that "Mrs. Dixon is an energetic, warm, dedicated, open and compelling teacher." But it then supported the sociology department's decision, though recommending a temporary one-year stay on humanitarian grounds. Dixon rejected the offer and left Chicago.[110]

Meanwhile, the administration under President Edward Levi, while refraining from calling the police, nonetheless adamantly refused to negotiate with the students. When it became clear that the occupiers would gain none of their "non-negotiable" demands for Dixon's reinstatement as well as for control over future faculty appointments and a general amnesty for the occupying students, they left the building. The faculty's disciplinary committee then cracked down, expelling forty-two of them and suspending more than eighty others. A few months later, when the sociology department denied tenure to another radical faculty member, Richard Flacks, the campus remained quiet.[111]

Similar protests occurred elsewhere. Often, as at Chicago, opposition to the dismissal of popular teachers was part of a larger package of demands. Vassar's Student Committee on Faculty Firings mounted a peaceful two-week sit-in the spring of 1971 to protest the dismissal of six faculty members, including an extremely popular radical economist. The students called for the reinstatement of the six pending the installation of "a just procedure of faculty evaluation," and also decried their own "disenfranchisement." "We have no power," they complained; and, facing the "evasiveness and disrespect of the administration and the faculty toward student opinion," they "felt compelled to seize some power 'illegitimately' in order to force those in power to listen." The sit-in ended quietly and a few changes were made.[112]

San Francisco State

When racial issues muddled the scene, student protests over faculty firings could become intense. The most notorious such troubles rocked the already turbulent campus of San Francisco State, where the trustees forced the suspension of a radical Black instructor in the fall of 1968. The upheaval that followed—while longer lasting, more violent, and more highly publicized—contained elements common to similar crises at institutions that had a politically volatile student body, a divided faculty, and power struggles at every level.

An upgraded teachers college not too far from Berkeley, SFSC's urban location and lively bohemian scene attracted non-traditional students and professors, who, as one historian recalled, kept the campus "just bubbling" with leftist politics and the counterculture. Another faculty member noted its "first-rate and original eccentricity," while still others prided themselves on their commitment to educating Black and white working-class students.[113] Besides housing an active cohort of antiwar students and teachers who staged demonstrations against Dow, ROTC, and similar targets on and off the campus, the school was also a magnet for Black nationalists, including former SNCC activists and members of the Black Panther Party. San Francisco State's administration was remarkably liberal and willing to accommodate its students' demands. By 1967, after offering some of the nation's first courses on African American subjects through its student-run Experimental College, SFSC was poised to become the first four-year traditionally white institution to create a full-fledged Black studies program.[114]

What made the situation at San Francisco State so incendiary was that at the same time as the well-meaning liberals who were running the school were trying to work with the college's student activists, they were also contending with California's fraught politics of higher education. Not only did they face a hostile governor in Ronald Reagan and a public still upset about the Berkeley Free Speech Movement, but they also had to deal with an increasingly centralized state college system headed by a rigid chancellor and board of trustees dominated by Reagan appointees who were dead set against sharing power with students and faculty members. A further complication was that the state college system had raised its admission requirements in the mid-1960s. In the process, African Americans had fallen from 10 to less than 4 percent of San Francisco State's student body. That combination of volatile students and an unsympathetic central administration turned out to be toxic. No wonder, then, that the institution churned through five presidents between 1966 and 1973.[115]

Beginning with a short occupation of the administration building to protest the submission of class rankings to the Selective Service System in the spring of 1967, SFSC's campus remained in near-constant turmoil for over two years, its restive African American and antiwar activists affected by (and affecting) the racial and political strife then coursing through so many cities and institutions of higher learning. The militant and politically sophisticated leaders of the Black Student Union (BSU) pressed for the usual demands: a student-run Black studies program, more Black faculty members, and a greatly expanded admissions policy that would accept and nurture every African American who applied. They had support from the campus leftists and, more importantly, from the local Black community that viewed San Francisco State's Black students as its future and was willing to fight for their educations.[116]

The administration, though not unwilling to implement much of the BSU's program, stressed the need to gain faculty support for it, which the impatient students saw as a sign of bad faith and underlying racism. The so-called "*Gater* incident" in November 1967 increased the racial tension. During the course of a protest against racist comments in the school newspaper, the *Daily Gater*, a group of BSU activists beat up the paper's conservative editor. Several were suspended and half a dozen arrested, including George Murray, a graduate student instructor in English who was also the Black Panther Party's minister of education. Over the next few months, the racial discord intensified.

Instead of calling the police, the president temporarily shut down the school, calming the campus but provoking an outraged response from San Francisco's conservative politicians, media, and citizens.[117]

By the spring of 1968, President Summerskill was ready to quit, caught between the student dissidents and the obdurate chancellor and board of trustees. The conflict escalated in May when a coalition of some four hundred Black radicals, white leftists, and students of color from the newly formed Third World Liberation Front mounted a weeklong demonstration demanding the elimination of ROTC, more minority student admissions, and the reappointment of the only Chicano professor on the faculty. After the protesters occupied the administration's offices for several hours, the police cleared the building. Despite nearly thirty arrests, there was none of the physical violence that had just marred Columbia and several other campuses.[118] Even so, the president's supposed permissiveness was too much for the chancellor and trustees. They forced Summerskill out, appointing in his stead Robert Smith, a respected former dean of the School of Education.[119]

Meanwhile, the San Francisco State administration was moving—slowly—to implement a Black studies program. Smith acceded to the BSU's suggestion that he hire as its director Nathan Hare, a radical Black sociologist with a University of Chicago PhD, who had been fired from Howard University for disrupting a speech by the Selective Service director Lewis Hershey.[120] Hare's task of putting the program together was not made any easier by the limited resources allotted him and his own inflammatory rhetoric and that of the Black student leaders and their allies.

Such rhetoric put President Smith in the middle of an insoluble conflict caused by the English department's decision in the fall of 1968 to rehire George Murray. Despite his participation in the *Gater* fracas, Murray was reputed to be an excellent teacher. He was also a Black Panther and a fiery speaker who called for guns, "killers, [and] political assassins" as the prelude to "an armed revolution." Naturally, that kind of provocative language attracted the media, intensifying demands from trustees, politicians, and ordinary citizens for the militant Black instructor's removal. Nonetheless, Smith resisted as long as he could, explaining that Murray had "done a competent teaching job" and there was no academic reason to fire him. To do so, the president repeatedly warned his superiors, would so inflame the campus as to be "irresponsible." The chancellor, however, ignored Smith's entreaties and suspended Murray. As predicted, San Francisco State blew up.[121]

The firing of Murray set off the school's biggest conflict. The Black Student Union called a strike for November 6, unless the administration satisfied its ten (soon-to-be fifteen) "nonnegotiable" demands, most of them familiar ones, as well as Murray's reinstatement.[122] The BSU adopted a strategy that its chair called "the war of the flea." They would make the campus ungovernable by occupying offices, invading classes, and engaging in such petty vandalism as blocking toilets and starting fires in wastebaskets.[123]

When the police arrived, they kept a low profile at first. But a few days into the strike, some students threw rocks and taunted the lawmen; the San Francisco Tactical Squad retaliated with billy clubs and arrests. After closing the campus temporarily, the administration organized an all-college convocation to discuss and thus defuse the strike. But chaos reigned. Protesters were beaten, bombs went off, windows were broken, and the main faculty critic of the Black studies program was ferociously hounded. Though some classes continued to meet, many did not. The administration, the students, much of the faculty, and the mayor of San Francisco wanted to close the campus until the strike ended. But Governor Reagan and the trustees were determined to keep it open, even, in Reagan's words, "at the point of a bayonet, if necessary."[124] Helpless to prevent the madness, President Smith resigned, unable to cope with the toxic combination of the Black students' fury over the dismissal of George Murray and the stubborn refusal of his reactionary superiors to let him deal with it.[125]

His replacement was S. I. Hayakawa, a best-selling popularizer in the field of semantics who had been teaching part-time at SFSC for several years. As the crisis escalated, the formerly liberal Hayakawa became the spokesman for those faculty members who advocated a hard line against the strikers. Appointing an ostensibly liberal non-white colleague with a national reputation, Reagan and his allies apparently believed, would appease the faculty and perhaps even the rampaging students.[126] They were wrong.

From the start, Hayakawa boasted about his toughness, playing to the politicians, the media, and the general public. San Francisco State's students and teachers were not appeased. The unrest continued, alleviated only temporarily by Hayakawa's decision to begin the Christmas break a week early. Ultimately, it took hundreds of arrests, an unprecedented faculty walkout, and several months of negotiations before the demoralized and embittered students and professors went back to class. At that point, San Francisco State, as two outside sociologists put it, was "not a viable educational institution."[127]

Amnesty as a "Non-Negotiable" Demand

Among the demands presented by San Francisco State's student strikers was "that no disciplinary action will be administered in any way to any students, workers, teachers, or administrators . . . as a consequence of their participation in the strike."[128] The call for amnesty had become a standard feature of academic protests.[129] Campus militants refused to accept the legitimacy of their institutions' disciplinary procedures—especially if they did not have a voice in their creation or enforcement. While rarely the only issue, the imposition of sanctions against leading activists could sometimes trigger trouble, as it did during Berkeley's free speech crisis. Then the demand for amnesty took on a life of its own, diverting attention from the issues that had actually inspired the unrest.[130] Significantly, although they may have disagreed among themselves about Vietnam or Black studies, almost all faculty members believed that disruptive students should be punished.

Though the demand for amnesty was near universal, the outcome varied. The situation at San Francisco State was particularly bleak. Since Hayakawa sloughed off the faculty's recommendation against punitive measures, hundreds of the students who had been arrested faced double jeopardy from the university and the courts. The faculty's disciplinary panel administered mild sanctions, but the outside criminal justice proceedings were more arduous—time-consuming, costly,

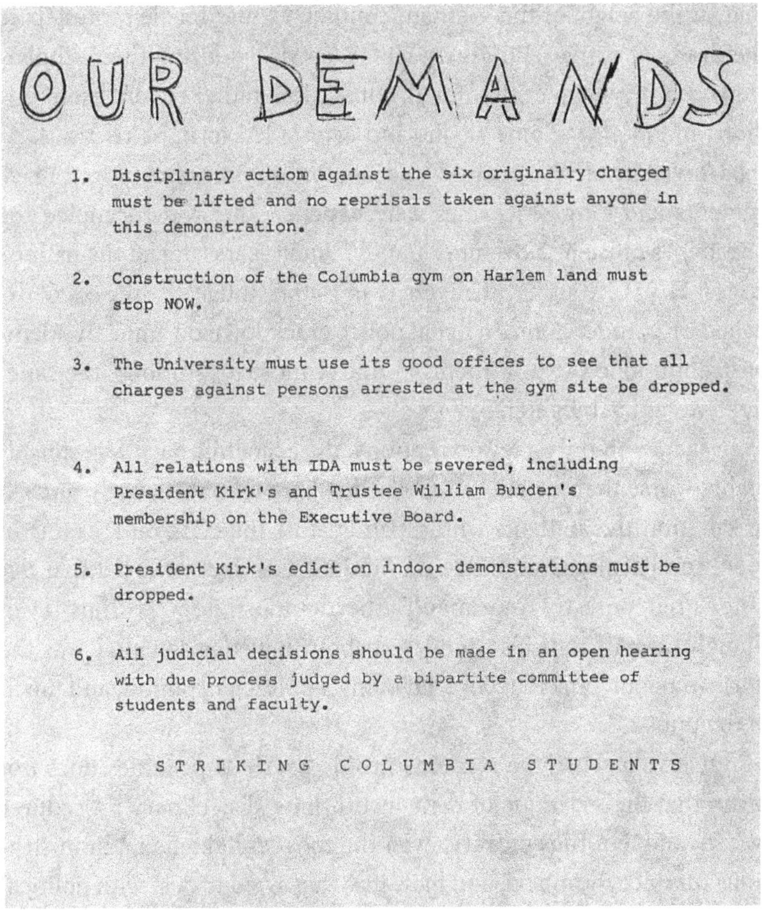

OUR DEMANDS

1. Disciplinary action against the six originally charged must be lifted and no reprisals taken against anyone in this demonstration.

2. Construction of the Columbia gym on Harlem land must stop NOW.

3. The University must use its good offices to see that all charges against persons arrested at the gym site be dropped.

4. All relations with IDA must be severed, including President Kirk's and Trustee William Burden's membership on the Executive Board.

5. President Kirk's edict on indoor demonstrations must be dropped.

6. All judicial decisions should be made in an open hearing with due process judged by a bipartite committee of students and faculty.

STRIKING COLUMBIA STUDENTS

FIGURE 11.1. Flyer with student demands, produced during Columbia crisis, April 1968. © University Archives, Rare Book & Manuscript Library, Columbia University Libraries.

and presided over by hostile judges. Though a few defendants, George Murray among them, went to prison, most received suspended sentences and probation. Nonetheless, their legal travails exacted a stiff personal toll of high anxiety, lost jobs, and academic setbacks—in most cases, simply for having been caught up in police crackdowns on demonstrations.[131]

Elsewhere, student protesters typically contended only with their own institutions. The penalties they faced ranged from mild warnings, probation, and letters in their files to suspensions and expulsions that, at the height of the Vietnam conflict, exposed male protesters to the draft. At some schools, students also risked losing their scholarships, a policy that, critics noted, constituted rather blatant economic discrimination.[132] Some sit-ins and arrests led to mass reprisals. At the University of Wisconsin–Oshkosh, for example, ninety-four Black students and four white ones were expelled after they occupied the president's office in November 1968.[133] Four years later, at the nation's largest HBCU, Southern University in Baton Rouge, the president expelled fifty students after a lethal police crackdown on a massive demonstration killed two of them.[134] But at most institutions, the sanctions were much lighter.

In fact, with only a few exceptions, the academic bark was considerably worse than its bite. At Cornell, where an official body refused to sanction the students who sat-in against the class-rank exams in 1966, the Faculty Committee on Student Conduct reversed that decision, but only to "reprimand" the demonstrators.[135] Thus, even though campus radicals thundered about injustice, leniency was the norm—an outcome that enraged many a politician, pundit, and much of the public.

But just because the students avoided serious penalties does not mean that their critique of their institutions' disciplinary procedures was invalid. On the contrary, even the most enlightened administrations fumbled, bumbled, and blew it as they tried to deal with political dissenters, all too often behaving in an inconsistent, undemocratic, and authoritarian manner. In the process, significant governance issues emerged, as well as legitimate demands for student participation in decision-making processes.

The main reason the academic community handled the disciplinary aftermath of its political conflicts so inconsistently was simply that the issue was completely new. Whatever arrangements had existed for student discipline dealt either with academic matters or else with parietals and other vestiges of in loco parentis. None of the academic administrators involved had ever confronted civil disobedience over broader social and political issues. "This is not the panty-raid era," one frustrated San Francisco State administrator remarked. He was hardly the only official who had no idea what to do.[136]

In addition, the ultimate locus of authority was not completely clear. Legally, trustees had the final say, but rarely intervened. At some smaller and/or more authoritarian institutions, presidents and their top aides usually enforced the rules. At other schools, however, student discipline was theoretically in faculty hands. But few professors sought that responsibility. Especially at institutions that prized research and publication, most faculty members paid little, if any, attention to students' problems outside of class.[137]

As a result, the actual work of handling drunken fraternity boys or first-year students who failed chemistry devolved upon a cadre of second-level bureaucrats. These deans of students and their professional assistants were perfectly capable of administering what a former editor of the Columbia newspaper called "family-type justice." But their institutions had never developed either the policies or the quasi-judicial structures that would guarantee due process and fair treatment to political dissenters. In addition, even when universities were reforming their disciplinary procedures, the process was sometimes too slow to head off trouble. The committee revising San Francisco State's disciplinary code, for example, was still mired in disputes when that school's big strike took place.[138]

As a result, when faced by building takeovers and other acts of civil disobedience, academic administrators had neither precedents nor guidelines; and they were often ambivalent or scared. They were also under considerable outside pressure to be tough. As a result, they sometimes inflamed already tense situations, as Chancellor Edward Strong did at Berkeley when he suspended the main leaders of the Free Speech Movement. At Howard, the administration's decision in the spring of 1967 to discipline a group of radical students and faculty members for disrupting an appearance by Lewis Hershey prompted weeks of demonstrations and a boycott that sought, among other demands, the creation of an effective student-faculty judicial system.[139]

At a number of schools, officials believed they lacked the authority to act. Thus, when eight hundred Harvard students blocked the car of Secretary of Defense Robert McNamara in the fall of 1966, Dean John Munro decried it as "mob rule," but then announced that there would be no punishment.[140] And at the University of Wisconsin, where the

National Guard had been summoned to deal with the 1969 student strike, the protesters were scrupulous about not breaking any major rules, so the authorities could not bring charges against them, despite considerable pressure from the trustees to do just that.[141]

There were also instances where administrators did not sanction students because they, in fact, supported them. This was especially the case with racial issues. Thus, in 1962, when a group of University of Chicago students (Bernie Sanders among them) sat-in to demand the integration of apartment buildings owned by the university, the authorities took no action because they, too, opposed that discrimination. In the spring of 1969, the Penn administration was similarly lenient toward the students who mounted an eight-day sit-in to oppose classified research and the university's expansion into a Black neighborhood. The moderate liberals running such schools as Cornell and Columbia seem to have been deterred from cracking down on Black student unrest by what their critics identified as "liberal guilt" and the realization that the protests against "institutional racism" may well have been, at least in part, justified. They were also, as we shall see, afraid of violence.[142]

Especially where there was violence, it could be hard to identify specific culprits—a problem that created considerable inconsistency in punishments. Smashed office equipment, broken windows, arson, fistfights, harassment, and death threats—even the most radical teachers could not condone that kind of behavior. But whom to charge? And with what? With hundreds of young people on the rampage, how were the authorities to identify the ones responsible for the worst offenses? After all, they didn't know most of the students. Faculty members were equally at a loss. "Are you going to turn the university into a bunch of informers?" the political scientist Dankwart Rustow asked his colleagues during the Columbia crisis of 1968. "How are you ever going to find out which students actually rifled which files?"[143] At some schools, administrators tried to solve that problem—and also suppress the unrest—by lopping off its leaders. They brought charges against the leading radicals on campus, people like Berkeley's Mario Savio or Mark Rudd of Columbia, a counterproductive move that simply undermined the already shaky legitimacy of the student disciplinary process.[144]

Elsewhere, administrators enlisted faculty members and others to identify the militants. At the University of Chicago, which had made no attempt to punish the students who sat-in against the class-rank system in 1966, the authorities were determined to crack down on the participants in the Marlene Dixon sit-in three years later. They hired a photographer to document the event and then asked faculty members to identify their students.[145] During the Third World Liberation Front strike of 1969 at Berkeley, deans and financial aid officers also singled out the students they knew. Even so, as one of them admitted, "It was still impossible to identify everyone and it's the kind of thing that will make students shy away from the dean's office for regular counseling. They'll figure being known by the dean is a political liability." It was, in fact, so hard to figure out whom to punish that one Berkeley administrator, perhaps not in jest, suggested spraying future protesters with a radioactive substance and then using a Geiger counter to pick them out.[146]

Ultimately, even the most obtuse academic administrators realized that the inequities of their judicial proceedings contributed significantly to the unrest. Most recognized the need for reform and for giving both faculty members and students voices in the process. Yet few institutions reformed in time to avoid trouble. At Howard, where protests against in loco parentis and the war were punctuated by calls for new disciplinary procedures, the students blew up at the seemingly endless delays in implementing them and the president's resistance to their demand for representation. Finally, in the spring of 1968, after a five-day sit-in and the prospect of an invasion by the police and National Guard, a group of trustees negotiated what one scholar called the "modest campus reforms" that "the procrastination of the administration and senior faculty" had thwarted.[147]

At schools like Penn, where more agile administrators managed to involve both students and professors in dealing with student demands, the campus was able to avoid serious disruptions. On more troubled campuses, faculty members, trapped between militant students and obdurate administrators, were caught up in power struggles shaped by the relative strength and political dexterity of combatants both on and off the campus. But the issues were confusing; and many academics believed, if not that the fate of Western civilization was at stake, then that of their own institution certainly was. They were not wrong. As the public's outrage over the disorders grew, its earlier support for higher education was melting away.

12

"DISORDERLY BEHAVIOR"

Students Disrupt the Academy

The Buffalo Forty-Five

They held a few informal meetings, but the nearly fifty SUNY Buffalo faculty members who carried their sleeping bags into Hayes Hall, the administration building, a little past noon on Sunday, March 15, 1970, were not completely sure what they were doing. Though they realized they might be violating an injunction against disrupting the normal functions of the university, they did not expect to go to jail. But within a few hours, forty-five of them had been picked up by the police and booked for contempt of court. That the university's top administrators could call for the arrest of faculty members for the quiet takeover of an unused conference room on a Sunday afternoon reveals how seriously the student movement had disrupted the nation's campuses. Admittedly, what happened at Buffalo was extreme. No other institution authorized widespread arrests of professors. Still, Buffalo's fears and frustrations were typical.

On the night of March 7, a week earlier, Peter Regan, the university's acting president, brought more than four hundred police and sheriff's deputies onto the campus to put down a disruptive student strike. Then, while rock-throwing radicals and edgy armed officers of the law taunted each other, Regan disappeared into an office building downtown, where he remained inaccessible to students, professors, and even some of his own staff. The faculty members who were to occupy Hayes Hall were desperate to have the police removed from the campus before something terrible happened. "We wanted to break the cycle of violence and counter-violence and draw attention to the continued police presence on campus," the historian Michael Frisch recalled. "We decided a sit-in would be more effective than a strike. . . . The university was unraveling, the administration had evaporated, and we were under a form of military government."[1]

They had no program, no leaders. "We really didn't know what we were doing," admitted Raymond Federman, one of the two full professors among the forty-five. "It was an 'experiment,'" an assistant professor of English explained. They wanted "to see what would happen when previously uninvolved faculty took such an action. We thought it would be perceived as so absurd that the administration would be forced to re-evaluate its rigid stance." When they entered Hayes Hall, they told the flustered administrators who greeted them that they wanted to see the acting president. As they were ushered into an empty conference room, they handed out a short statement:

> Peter Regan and his administration have defied the will of the Faculty
> Senate expressed Wednesday, March 11, for the immediate removal
> of police from the campus, thereby making themselves responsible
> for Thursday's events [student-police confrontations on March 12].
> Hence, we members of the faculty will occupy these premises until
> (1) the police are removed from the campus and (2) the injunction
> is lifted.
>
> We are in sympathy with the general principles of the strike and
> will be formulating new structures of university governance—to
> follow Regan's resignation—for the consideration of the university
> community.
>
> We call on all faculty members to join us here.[2]

The vice president for operations and systems soon arrived to assess the situation. He later testified that he was afraid the sit-in might get out of hand if other teachers and students joined. Accordingly, after conferring with Regan by phone, he warned the "assembled faculty members . . . that if they did not leave the premises in five minutes, they would be subject to arrest for trespass."[3] A few left, Georg Iggers among them. He had been persuaded by a sympathetic policeman who, hearing his foreign accent, feared that he might be deported if he were arrested.[4] As two, in fact, were.*

The forty-five who remained after Iggers left were then calmly escorted to a paddy wagon by campus security guards and Buffalo policemen and taken to the local precinct. At first Federman "couldn't believe what was happening," but then realized, "Shit, this is the real thing. . . . You are abruptly caught in the machinery and really lose control of events around you. You are fingerprinted, hear the gates close, and suddenly you are a criminal." They were soon released without bail.[5] Charged with criminal contempt, they also faced the prospect of an indictment for trespassing. A month later, a hostile judge sentenced them each to thirty days in the Erie County Penitentiary. They appealed and won, but not before enduring hate mail, death threats, and financial problems.[6]

Even at the time, it was clear that the administration had goofed. The Buffalo 45 had done nothing to disrupt the university's business. Regan himself admitted as much, stating: "Those members of our university who conducted the sit-in in the president's office Sunday were acting in the long and highly respected tradition of civil disobedience. While I disagree with their specific purpose, I recognize that they bore witness with their bodies and their liberties, and that they did so peacefully."[7] Indeed, despite the notoriety they accrued, the Buffalo 45 were typical of their peers at other troubled institutions: They were trying to pacify their campus.

Buffalo in Turmoil

SUNY Buffalo, the product of an uneasy merger of New York's rapidly expanding state university system with a somewhat undistinguished local private institution, was splintered from the start. Many of its older faculty members and administrators were suspicious of their

---

* One of the deportees was John Coetzee, a young assistant professor in the English department, who had his visa revoked the following year. He then returned to his home country of South Africa, wrote a number of well-received novels, won the Nobel Prize for literature—and received an honorary degree from SUNY Buffalo. Siggelkow, *Dissent and Disruption*, 219.

new academically ambitious colleagues, a suspicion that reflected the widening cultural gap between the university's largely white ethnic local constituency and the more cosmopolitan outsiders who were flooding in.[8] In addition, as an urban university in a declining industrial city with a Black neighborhood that endured several days of rioting during the summer of 1967, SUNY Buffalo also experienced racial tensions.

Within a few years of the arrival of its energetic president, Martin Meyerson, in 1966, SUNY Buffalo had doubled in size and was pushing all sorts of educational innovations. The place was "exploding with young faculty," Frisch recalled. "The year I came, there were seven new people in the history department alone." That many of these recent additions flirted with the New Left and adopted its countercultural lifestyle only intensified the faculty's internal divisions. The students were new, as well, many of them intellectually high-powered Jews from New York City and its suburbs.[9] Their long hair, sexual freedom, recreational drug use, and radicalism disturbed Buffalo's staid citizens, press, and power structure, including the conservative businessmen and professionals who made up the University Council, aka the board of trustees.[10]

Those new students were as prone to sit-ins, demonstrations, and vandalism as their peers elsewhere. In May 1966, they took over the administration building during the class-rank controversy. The following year, they threatened to block recruiters from Dow and the CIA. Then, in the spring of 1969, several hundred again occupied the administration building, this time in response to the sentencing of a local draft resister. Meanwhile, thanks in part to the historian Gabriel Kolko, who had been instrumental in the struggle against the classified military research at the University of Pennsylvania before he came to Buffalo, antiwar activists began a campaign against the university's arrangement to conduct biological research under the Defense Department's Project THEMIS. On April 16, two shacks at the project's construction site were firebombed (though by whom remains unclear).

There was more property damage in October when students ransacked the offices of the Air Force ROTC program. Bands of radicals also tried to disrupt classes. Black student organizations agitated for Black studies, financial aid, and increased admissions to the medical school, as well as for more African American construction workers on the school's new campus.[11] By the time the Black students declared a strike in the beginning of November, the campus had become so turbulent that Acting President Regan, a medical school psychiatrist who had taken over when Meyerson went on leave for the 1969–70 academic year, announced that he would call the police if things got out of control.[12]

As at other universities, the majority of Buffalo's professors tried to stay clear of the trouble. When pressed, as during the 1966 protest against class rank, they tended to support the administration, despite its failure to consult either students or professors.[13] When student radicals threatened to disrupt recruiters in the fall of 1967, the faculty also backed the administration. Though some conservative professors called for more punitive action, the administration held back. Richard Siggelkow, the vice president for student affairs and a professor in the School of Education, explained why he and his colleagues would not call in outside police. Their presence on other campuses "did not serve effectively as either a deterrent or as an effective solution" and, in fact, tended to create "additional strife, confusion, and mutual distrust."[14]

Despite the obvious desire of the decidedly liberal administrators and faculty members to mollify the students, the disruptions continued.[15] After some five hundred protesters took over the administration building in early March 1969, Meyerson convened a university-wide assembly, while encouraging every unit to cancel classes and hold teach-ins about educational and structural reforms. There were more than 125 such sessions dealing with everything from grading policies, curricular changes, and new governance structures for individual departments and entire schools to "Poetry as Transformation," "Latin American Economic Relations with American Corporations," and, my favorite, "Talk on Anything."[16]

The university was under considerable pressure—and not just from the radicals. For several years, locals had been critical of Meyerson's supposed leniency. Members of the city council demanded his ouster, while hate mail poured into his office. "If you do not have the courage to manage our university, please resign," one anonymous critic wrote. "It is positively unthinkable to allow a couple hundred young, wet nosed communist punks to dictate the operative policies at any institution owned by the people of the state."[17] Meyerson was walking a fine line. Ultimately, he quit, accepting an offer to head the University of Pennsylvania early in 1970.[18]

The Buffalo Meltdown Begins

The big crisis began on February 24, 1970, when a group of Black basketball players sat down in the middle of a game to draw attention to what they felt was unfair treatment by the coaching staff. The game was canceled, the police were called, but nothing much happened. The next day, protesters invaded the administration building. In the melee with campus security forces that followed, rocks were thrown, windows were broken, and the university police and members of Buffalo's Tactical Police Unit chased the crowd into the nearby student center, where they arrested half a dozen people and beat up dozens more, demonstrators and bystanders alike, while sustaining injuries themselves. The following day saw more of the same: protests, fighting, and vandalism directed against the usual targets as well as the local lawmen. The next day, the student militants declared a strike. Their evolving demands, besides calling for removing the police from campus and the resignation of Acting President Regan, touched on all the issues that had already disrupted many a university—ROTC, THEMIS, open admissions, curricular reform, and amnesty for student protesters.[19]

Regan responded by appointing a three-man ad hoc committee to investigate and report on the violence at the student center. Its twenty-page report, released less than two weeks later, the same day the Buffalo police and sheriff's deputies began their occupation of the campus, gave an excruciating blow-by-blow account of the evening's events, castigating the school's top administrators for having "accepted the risks of police actions too readily.... [W]e find their anticipation of a peaceful outcome to police intervention ... to have been, at best, naïve."[20] As in the conflicts at Berkeley, San Francisco State, Wisconsin, Columbia, and South Carolina State, bringing outside police forces onto an already troubled campus was to invite disaster. A few Buffalo administrators knew that, but their voices were ignored.[21]

As were those of the faculty, many of whom had become extremely upset and ready to act. At a hastily convened Sunday faculty meeting, the chair of the linguistics department suggested forming a faculty-student peace patrol to keep the violence under control. By ten o'clock that night, he had reached enough people to begin operating. By the next day there were some 150–200 volunteers; within five days, 600. They strove to be neutral. "We seek to be peacekeepers," an early leaflet explained. "Our primarily object is to keep campus order in the hands of campus people. We want to keep outside authority off campus—We want to keep the peace ourselves."[22]

Though Acting President Regan claimed to be supportive of the peace patrol's efforts, he did nothing to pacify the campus. Thus, for example, in a televised statement on Sunday, March 1, he blamed the student center melee on "a bunch of vicious vandals roaming the campus, destroying property, deliberately provoking . . . a kind of riotous situation in which physical injury was imposed on the police, on the bystanders, on the guilty ones."[23]

Despite the best efforts of the peace patrols, students and outsiders continued to occupy buildings, disrupt classes, and destroy property. On Thursday, March 5, Regan obtained an injunction making it a criminal offense for anyone "to disrupt the lawful educational function of the university."[24] On the same day, with dozens of unruly protesters blockading its offices in Hayes Hall, the administration suspended twenty students, two of whom were not even in Buffalo at the time. That action—which had to be rescinded a few days later because there was so much opposition to its arbitrary nature—simply added to the conflagration. Worse yet, despite pleas from students, professors, and even some of his own subordinates, Regan refused to negotiate directly with the student strikers on the grounds that it would legitimize their actions.[25] As on other campuses where administrators remained obdurate, the turbulence only increased. But Regan was under enormous outside pressure. He was in the running for the institution's presidency and felt unable to ignore the demands for toughness from the local notables who controlled that appointment.[26]

The Campus Occupation

As the unrest continued, tensions mounted within the faculty. The head of the peace patrols resigned and announced that he would support the strike.[27] Many other professors stopped teaching their classes, some because they sympathized with the strike, others because they could not handle the chaos. Thomas Baumer, the incoming vice president of the faculty senate, claimed that he was so endangered by the protesters that "he felt he was in need of a sidearm." Throughout the crisis, the executive committee of the faculty senate was in continuous session, deeply split over the growing possibility that Regan would again call in the police. Some of its more liberal members quit. The rest, its chairman recalled, "felt they had to stick it out." Then, after Regan did recall the police, its members issued a statement supporting their presence: "It was important to show that some sort of an institutional structure remained. The decision had been made, it became important to show a unified front."[28]

Meanwhile, Buffalo faculty members were going to all kinds of meetings, at every level, from ad hoc groups to individual departments to the full faculty senate. The university archives bulges with their records: formal minutes and resolutions, position papers, and personal appeals. Some took an ostensibly neutral stance, denouncing both the insensitive administrators and the radical students. Others took sides. Many called on the acting president to resign, while others supported the decision to bring in the police. Quite a few of these manifestos contained elaborate proposals for restructuring the university.[29]

Then, on Saturday, March 7, as Buffalo's increasingly stressed and weary professors were debating and drawing up proposals and resolutions, Acting President Regan, without consulting representatives of the student body or the faculty or even many of his own top administrators, formally asked the police commissioner to send his men to the campus. Accordingly, in the early hours of Sunday morning, a contingent of more than four hundred Buffalo policemen and sheriff's deputies marched in formation onto the campus. They were there, Regan announced, to deal with the "intimidation, threats, and destruction of property" caused by "the revolutionaries among us who are less concerned with the substantive issues than with the destruction of our 'system.'"[30]

Though some professors did support calling the police, most of the university's moderate and liberal faculty members and administrators opposed it. By the afternoon of March 8, some four thousand students and faculty members had mounted a demonstration against the occupation.[31] Over the next few days, that opposition intensified. The executive vice president for academic affairs and two other administrators resigned in protest, while individual professors and whole departments canceled their classes. At an emergency meeting of the history department's students and professors, the faculty members voted 13–7 for a resolution that

> the existence of city and county policemen on this campus is utterly incompatible with an academic institution. So long as they are present on this campus we are unable to meet our classes, and the removal of policemen is a precondition of normal teaching.[32]

As the week wore on, increasingly violent confrontations took place. Powerless, the peace patrols disbanded. "It was an intolerable situation," one of the Buffalo 45 recalled. "Armed cops were patrolling the campus and could beat up kids at night. The kids were playing Vietcong guerrillas, taunting the police and throwing snowballs with rocks inside. We were afraid it would lead to killings."[33] At an emergency meeting on March 11, the faculty senate overwhelmingly demanded the removal of the police. At the same time, however, a measure calling for the immediate resignation of Acting President Regan was defeated, 418–263. According to one respected faculty member, many professors,

sensing that he had tried hard in an impossible job and that he might
be followed by someone who might do a worse job, voted against the
motion or abstained. Had the question been put, "Do you approve of
the way Peter Regan has been doing his job?" the answer would have
been an overwhelming "no."[34]

Regan promised to cooperate with the faculty. Then he disappeared,
but not before appointing a Temporary Hearing Commission on
Campus Disruption under a hard-line former vice president for facilities, to handle the cases of the students he had suspended the week
before. He left behind a leaderless campus and an increasingly distraught faculty.[35] Two days after he ordered the police to arrest the
Buffalo 45, the faculty held another special meeting. First, it voted to
reform the ROTC program; then it called for Regan's resignation by a
two-to-one margin.[36]

The Buffalo 45 were not the only faculty members to have taken
matters into their own hands. For several weeks, a group of about
thirty-five professorial heavyweights and administrators had been
meeting informally, seeking to mediate between the warring parties.
On the morning of March 13, after a violent confrontation on the campus, they decided to form a temporary organization that would by-
pass the faculty senate executive committee and the administration,
provide more information to the campus community, and "deliberate
on possible actions to mobilize a faculty in disarray." Calling themselves the University Survival Group, they unsuccessfully pressed Regan to resign. They then began to think seriously about providing an
alternative source of governance to the university. The arrest of their
forty-five colleagues galvanized the group. They issued a press release,
announcing their formation and their desire to "restore some sense of
trust and direction in the University community."[37]

They also went to Albany to establish a dialogue with the SUNY authorities, the Rockefeller administration, and state legislators in order
to provide them with a more balanced account of the situation than
they were getting from the hostile media and their "one-sided sources"
in Buffalo.[38] They did not succeed. Though Regan did finally resign,
the University Survival Group's efforts to obtain an important role for

the mainstream faculty in the search for a new president got nowhere. Instead, the University Council, assisted by a group of conservative professors from the pre-Meyerson regime, forced through the candidacy of the hard-line head of the Temporary Hearing Commission on Campus Disruption. The old guard returned to power and, within a few years, many of the faculty superstars and administrators that Meyerson had recruited were gone.[39]

Seasons of Violence and Fear

Ultimately the violence abated with the early start of the spring vacation, but the bitterness remained. Even at a time when student unrest seemed to be breaking out on one campus after another, Buffalo's troubles were unique. With the possible exception of San Francisco State, whose structure and culture resembled Buffalo's, no other institution experienced quite as intense and prolonged a series of crises. Even so, the faculty's collective response there was strikingly similar to that of professors elsewhere: upset, impotent, and seriously split. The moderates and liberals who formed the majority of most faculties almost always tended to vacillate, unable to formulate coherent or effective responses to the upsetting and unprecedented events. Unfortunately, however, that all-too-obvious confusion was to undermine the popular respect that the academic community had once enjoyed.[40]

That confusion was understandable. As the student unrest mounted, everything seemed to be happening at once. Take the spring of 1968. In the beginning of April, just as a massive student strike that had closed down Howard University was petering out, students at Tuskegee took the board of trustees hostage. That same day Martin Luther King Jr. was assassinated. A few days later, the Black students at Ohio State took their school's vice president hostage. There were disruptive demonstrations and building takeovers at, among other places, Alfred University, Boston University, Bowie State College, Brooklyn College, Colgate, Columbia, Chicago, Duke, Northwestern, San Francisco State, Stanford, and the Universities of Georgia, Michigan, and Wisconsin.

The unprecedented nature of the situation unsettled everyone involved.[41] What particularly struck two University of Chicago scholars who studied the unrest there was "the debilitating effect of uncertainty for all parties when physical force was used on any side—as though a game were being undertaken without any understanding of what the signals meant or of what plays would lead to winning or losing." Even such a self-confident intellectual as Columbia's Daniel Bell confessed that he found the upheaval at his institution "extremely puzzling."[42]

He was not alone. The students who had precipitated the unrest also seemed confused. The leaders of Columbia's Students' Afro-American Society and the university's SDS chapter had no specific plans to attack the gym or occupy a building when they organized the protest rally that sparked Columbia's big crisis in April 1968.[43] Although Harvard's SDS had been planning an action in the following spring, its two main factions were still negotiating about its timing when one of them took over University Hall.[44] Elsewhere, there was often a similarly impromptu quality to the student actions—and even to their demands.[45]

Faculty members, especially when they felt caught between unruly students and obdurate administrators, were also at a loss. They usually felt a responsibility to intervene, but were blindsided by their own lack of preparedness and failures of communication. Columbia's professors were a prime example. As one somewhat unsympathetic graduate student noted, during the 1968 crisis, the faculty "was running around in circles flapping its wings, wringing its hands in naïve collective guilt and confusion, producing a great deal of unconstructive noise both orally and in writing."[46]

Ironically, however, more often than not, the students eventually got most of what they had been calling for. ROTC disappeared from many campuses along with some war-related research; Black studies programs were established. There were committees, studies, reports, and a flurry of curricular and student-life reforms—though rarely ones that let students hire or fire faculty members. The demand for student power had never been unreasonable; the activists who made it had finally forced the people who ran their institutions to pay attention to their concerns.[47] For many of these students, gaining a hearing may well have been their main goal.[48]

Yet despite the cleavages and indecisiveness within the academic

community, there were a few issues on which there was a near consensus. Above all, its members wanted the disruptions to stop. In addition, almost all of them deplored the students' behavior, viewing it
as coercion that some even claimed was interfering with their academic freedom. The eminent Columbia historian Richard Hofstadter
probably spoke for the majority of his colleagues when he confessed,
"I'm in the rather awkward position of one who feels the students had
a few good issues, very good issues, and a number of minor grievances that we ought to attend to—and yet is outraged by the methods
they resorted to."[49] The intensity of that outrage varied. The most fer-
vid opposition came from conservatives and some traditional liberals.[50] Radicals, too, deplored the students' unruly behavior.[51] Stanley
Hoffman, a leader of the Harvard faculty's Liberal Caucus, castigated
the students trying to shut down a faculty meeting for their "self-
indulgence, mock heroics, playing at revolution."[52]

At the same time, there was an analogous consensus about the
presence of outside police forces on the campus. Even those professors who would have agreed with Buffalo's acting president that student radicals were "vicious vandals" did not want to compromise the
autonomy of their institution. That had been the case as early as the
Berkeley free speech crisis.[53] The situation was the same at Columbia,
where, as the economist and administration supporter Peter Kenen
explained, "A call to the police would be an admission that we had lost
control of our own campus."[54] When that happened and policemen
and sheriff's deputies beat up students, many professors at Columbia
and elsewhere turned against the administrators who had brought on
the bloodshed.[55]

In sum, the student unrest had forced faculty members to take
sides—in full view of an increasingly hostile public. No longer able
to remain uninvolved, they were angry; they were tense; they were
frightened—and with good reason.

Some Conflagrations

Although the overwhelming majority of the student demonstrations of the 1960s and early 1970s were peaceful and law-abiding, the

violence that accompanied some of the student protests cannot be ignored and, because of the media, was not.[56] People were killed—disproportionately at HBCUs like Jackson State, Texas Southern, Southern University, North Carolina A&T, and South Carolina State, but also at Berkeley, Kent State, Wisconsin, UC Santa Barbara, and the University of Kansas—and mainly by local police officers, sheriffs' deputies, and National Guardsmen. Most of the bloodshed occurred between 1967 and 1972.

Even when no one died, people got hurt. At the University of Wisconsin, Madison police used billy clubs against bystanders as well as protesters during the Dow demonstration of October 1967. San Francisco State endured months of violence; more than eighty protesters were injured during arrests and hundreds more beaten, as well as thirty-two policemen hurt.[57] Nearly 150 people were injured during the Columbia bust, including administrators, professors, and journalists; forty-five were wounded during a riot at Duke in February 1969 after police were called to oust Black students from the administration building.[58] When the state police entered the Tuscaloosa campus of the University of Alabama in May 1970 to put down a melee, they attacked students on both sides of the fray—frat boys and sorority girls well as SDS members. They even assaulted a former all-state basketball star who was just trying to keep them from hitting his date.[59]

But not all the brutality came from the police. Although some of the campus violence originated with agents provocateurs, most was the work of student and non-student radicals.[60] On August 23, 1970, a bomb that a group of local revolutionaries planted at the University of Wisconsin's Army Mathematics Research Center killed a physics postdoc. A similar explosive at the Bank of America near the University of California, Santa Barbara, killed a worker. And another at San Francisco State went off prematurely, maiming the graduate student who was handling it.[61] Dozens of other bombs along with arson damaged classroom buildings, administrative offices, and, especially, ROTC headquarters. That violence peaked during the protests against the invasion of Cambodia in May 1970, when, as one study noted, "ROTC buildings were exploding or igniting at the rate of more than four a day." The air force reported that fifty-five of its units experienced injuries or major damage during the academic year of 1969–70. Arson destroyed or damaged buildings at all types of schools, from Princeton and Berkeley to DePauw and Whitewater State.[62]

Other kinds of property damage occurred. Windows were the main casualties, as rioters at dozens of colleges and universities threw stones and other objects at offices, classrooms, and other facilities. Berkeley historian William Bouwsma remembered the "mobs going through Dwinelle Hall, smashing all the windows out of all the offices and so on, including mine. I recall pulling my secretaries in further so they wouldn't be cut by the glass."[63] Administrative offices were trashed, furniture and desks destroyed, and files looted.[64] In a particularly academic form of destruction, rampaging students pulled books from shelves and dumped the contents of card catalogs onto library floors at Berkeley, Brandeis, Cornell, and the University of Illinois, among other institutions.[65] In just the first six months of 1969, one survey found $8 million of property damage at some seventy schools, though some early reports proved to have been exaggerated.[66]

Still, there was enough actual damage to put faculty members and administrators on edge. Normally rational individuals panicked. At Harvard, during the tumultuous spring of 1969, the Byzantine historian Robert Lee Wolff organized a group of senior professors to mount a cordon around Widener Library, while the chair of Stanford's English department, according to one former junior faculty member, "recruited members into round-the-clock protective vigils at our buildings."[67] Cornell's political scientists and historians did the same, as did faculty members at Berkeley, especially during an explosive minority student strike in 1969.[68]

Scientists were particularly worried. A Buffalo biologist organized a group of faculty members to patrol the laboratories during its student strike.[69] And at the University of Alabama, rumors in the spring of 1970 that one of the labs had been booby-trapped led the chair of the chemistry department to call for increased security. "One brick through one glass door would destroy a $75,000 piece of research equipment in chemistry," an administrator explained. "The same would hold true for the computer center."[70] Computers, which in the early days of the digital era often occupied entire buildings, were particularly at risk. In January 1969, Brandeis's Black students occupied both its computer center and its main telephone switchboard; UC Santa Barbara's Black students did the same, as did those at Northwestern.[71] Following the invasion of Cambodia, a group of SDS students and their faculty adviser took over the structure that housed NYU's computer, threatening to blow it up unless the university gave $100,000 to the Black Panthers' defense fund.[72]

Even after more than fifty years, it is easy to imagine how distressing such episodes must have been. If nothing else, people lost their peace of mind. Though it is clear in retrospect that many overreacted to the turmoil, it was not unrealistic to be afraid. Students, as well as police officers, could get out of control. People did get hurt. There were well-publicized incidents like the Black students' death threats against Cornell conservatives or the bomb planted outside the office of John Bunzel, the main critic of San Francisco State's Black studies program. But there was also violence (and threats of violence) directed against well-known faculty radicals.[73] Douglas Dowd, Cornell's most prominent gadfly, recalled, "I was pelted with eggs, tomatoes, and on one occasion stones, while giving public talks on the campus and off the campus in Ithaca. . . . I was frequently harassed in and out of the classroom, receiving threatening letters, had my office broken into, and had my car damaged—inter alia." He also received death threats and middle-of-the-night phone calls that escalated from intermittent to once an hour every night as the campus heated up in 1969.[74]

Especially after an unknown assailant, posing as a journalist, almost killed the University of Chicago's most prominent radical Richard Flacks with an ax, faculty activists, who had been receiving death threats for years, got scared as well. At the University of California, San Diego, Herbert Marcuse was so unnerved that he holed up at a friend's house, while a radical economist at nearby San Diego State had his house shot up and a friend seriously injured.[75] Yale's chaplain William Sloane Coffin received so many death threats that he had to be protected by both the New Haven police and the university's security forces.[76]

Conservative undergraduates from fraternities and football teams were also a problem.[77] During the 1968 troubles at Columbia, a group of right-wing students, calling themselves the Majority Coalition, threatened to empty the occupied buildings by force.[78] At Cornell the following year, a dozen fraternity brothers from Delta Upsilon invaded the Willard Straight student center and fought with the African American students who were occupying it.[79] There were similar incidents on other campuses, where jocks and other conservative students broke up protests, heckled, and sometimes physically attacked demonstrators.[80]

Still, most of the trouble did come from the left. There were enough instances of militant Blacks as well as SDS members and other white radicals assaulting or threatening professors and administrators to give substance to faculty members' fears. At a stormy symposium about South African investments at Cornell, an infuriated Black student grabbed President James Perkins by the collar and yanked him away from the podium. (The student was immediately expelled from the Afro-American Society.)[81] Sometimes protesters scuffled with occupants of university offices as they evicted them. Occasionally, they held them as hostages, as at Columbia, where militant Blacks and SDS members detained the acting dean of the college Henry Coleman and two other people in his office for over a day.[82] After a group of African American students kept a vice president of Ohio State captive in his office for eight hours, the local authorities charged them with kidnapping. The most dramatic case of hostage taking occurred in early April 1968 at Tuskegee when hundreds of students took over the guesthouse where the board of trustees was meeting. They forced its members to negotiate with them, releasing the trustees twelve hours later just before the state police and National Guard arrived. There were similar incidents at other schools: Berkeley, San Fernando Valley State College, Trinity College, and Cornell among them.[83]

Guns upped the ante. Rumors about armed students, African Americans in particular, intensified fears on already edgy campuses.[84] Even the radicals got scared, as Columbia's SDS leaders did when the Black students they were cooperating with in the early occupation of Hamilton Hall implied that they had weapons, though they soon got rid of them.[85] There were guns as well at San Francisco State in the possession of people like former SNCC field-workers and Black Panthers. Although I haven't found evidence that they were ever used (at least at SFSC), two Black Panthers were shot and killed in the beginning of 1969 in the UCLA cafeteria, the apparent result of a power struggle among factions within the Black student movement aggravated by the FBI's COINTELPRO program.[86]

The most notorious episode involving firearms occurred when the African American students who had taken over Cornell's student center on April 19, 1969, displayed shotguns and rifles as they left the building. At that point, the panic level on the Ithaca campus went through the roof. The occupying students were themselves terrified. They had brought in the weapons after hearing rumors that armed vigilantes were on the way and that the fraternity boys who had been repulsed when they had invaded the student center the day before might return with guns. "Then we were thinking they might set us on fire," one of the Black students recalled. "We got kind of paranoid then." The administration, equally terrified, banned firearms on the campus and set up a rumor clinic to combat inflammatory stories.[87]

Such rumors were especially intense on the urban campuses where African American student groups engaged in direct action.[88] Columbia's administrators, faculty members, and students were panicked, as one young English professor recalled, that Harlem residents would "burn Columbia to the ground" if the police were to harm the Black students who had taken over Hamilton Hall on April 23, 1968.[89] The historian Walter Metzger recalled being warned by an African American law student "that if the Negroes were hurt by the police there would be a response from Harlem." That warning occasioned, in Metzger's words, "some very apocalyptic imaginings at this time, which, as I remember, no one tried very hard to dispel."[90] Accordingly, the administration called on the mayor and the leaders of the African American community to persuade the students to end their occupation, only to be disappointed when the city's top Black politicians, state senator Basil Paterson and Manhattan Borough president Percy Sutton, came out publicly on the students' side—as was to happen at other institutions where community leaders supported the demands of the Black student protesters.[91]

There were similar fears at San Francisco State, where the mayor and local politicians also became involved. The institution's authorities sought the advice and assistance of San Francisco's Black leaders only to discover that the politicians, journalists, and clergymen supported the students. The future congressman Ronald Dellums, then a Berkeley City Council member, explained, "These are our black students, these are our finest, these are our future, these are our hope." The publisher of the Bay Area's main African American newspaper made the same point: "We were not going to permit the black students to be isolated on this campus. . . . If non-violent tactics fail, I and the other black community leaders will bear in mind the constitutional provision which gives citizens the right to bear arms."[92]

Similar threats emerged during the crisis over Harvard's Black studies program in the spring of 1969, when some African American students released a statement warning that if the administration responded "in the same brutal fashion" as it had against the white radicals a few days before, "Black students would be forced to call on their brothers in the greater Boston area for moral-and-other support. Should storm troopers be used against us, we must retaliate in kind."[93] Fortunately, no such invasions occurred on any campus. And the Black students' leaders knew that they would not. But the threat of them may well have deterred the authorities (outside the South, that is) from using unnecessary force against African American protesters. Certainly that was the case at Columbia, where mediators arranged peaceful evacuations and arrests for the Black students in Hamilton Hall, while leaving the white students occupying the other buildings to the mercies of New York City's finest.[94]

Harassment on Campus

Even if the threat of physical violence had been exaggerated and there were no police on campus, it was still no fun to teach at an institution undergoing major student unrest. Direct confrontations between students and professors were often disagreeable, occurring most frequently during strikes when militants disrupted classes or tried to keep professors from meeting their students.[95] At San Francisco State, organized groups of six to ten strikers mounted "classroom visitations," during which they would "ask students whether they support us, and if so, why are they attending classes?" Sometimes the instructors were sympathetic and invited the visitors to present their case or else simply canceled the class. But at other times the strikers encountered resistance, leading occasionally to fistfights and property damage.[96]

Crossing a picket line could also subject a faculty member to unpleasantness. The historian Dan Carter recalled "a striking graduate student spitting on me after I reluctantly crossed the teaching assistants' picket line to go to my class" in 1969 at the University of Wisconsin.[97] But even sympathetic faculty members were harassed. At San Francisco State, when the local chapter of the American Federation of Teachers called a strike in early January 1969 to prevent further violence on the campus, some of its members held informal classes while they walked the picket line, only to be hassled by militant Black students who claimed that any kind of teaching undermined their strike.[98]

Conservative teachers, especially those who openly opposed the student protests, received especially nasty treatment.[99] At San Francisco State, the chair of the political science department, John Bunzel, was the main target. He had published an article in the fall of 1968 attacking his school's proposed Black studies program. As a result, sometimes as many as seventy-five Black and white radicals flooded his classes, interrupting lectures and making it impossible for him to teach. Bunzel also endured death threats, an attempted bombing of his office, slashed tires, and the epithet "fascist scab" painted on his car. Other San Francisco State teachers unpopular with the strikers found that nobody would sign up for their courses.[100] At Harvard in 1969, when a group of SDS leaders disrupted the class of the political scientist Samuel Huntington, he threatened to call the police.[101] Similar heckling interrupted the economics classes of the Nobel laureate Milton Friedman at the University of Chicago, as well as those of a Wayne State psychologist whose work blamed the problems of Black children on their inability to fantasize.[102] Friedman brushed off the harassment, but others were more disconcerted.[103]

A particularly distressing form of harassment was endured by

FIGURE 12.1. San Francisco State faculty members on strike. Arthur Bierman with raised fist, January 1969. © Courtesy of Phiz Mezey.

the white instructors who, because of the paucity of qualified African American academics, taught the early Black studies classes.[104] They found themselves, in the historian Eric Foner's words, "pretty freaked out" to be considered the enemy or worse. While still in graduate school, Foner had been drafted to teach Columbia's first African American history course in 1967. "Inevitably and understandably," he recalled, "many of Columbia's black students felt that the first such course in the College's 200-year history ought to be offered by a black scholar." Within a month, a group of students began to disrupt his classes, staging walkouts and "denouncing the course, in the idiom of the day, as a racist insult (although, as they told me privately, they actually liked my lectures and had nothing 'personal' against me)."[105] Dan Carter, recruited to teach "Negro" history, had the same experience at the University of Maryland.

I struggled to navigate through the sometimes angry reactions of newly radicalized black students. At the end of my first lecture, a distressed black student walked past me and said, very loudly, to one of his friends, "My God, he's not only a honky, he's a cracker, too."[106]

Similar protests occurred at the University of Illinois, Harvard, and elsewhere.[107]

According to the Berkeley sociologist and Black activist Harry Edwards, many of the most disruptive students were middle-class African Americans who were acting out fantasies of racial militance. The "cornbread mafia," he called them, immersed in "the style of the times . . . conforming to expectations, playing the role, cultivating the image—often out of all proportion to the actual realities involved."[108] But for many white faculty members and administrators, who had rarely, if ever, encountered African Americans in any but a subordinate role, these seemingly tough young people with their deliberately offensive language, Black Power rhetoric, and intimations of violence could be scary, indeed.[109] One former Brooklyn College teacher recalled how his colleagues panicked in April 1969 when a group of two hundred Black students, upset by delays in implementing a Black studies program, stormed into a faculty meeting, took over the podium, barred the doors—and read out their not-very-radical demands.[110] By the late 1960s, therefore, it was not irrational for many faculty members to feel, as the Columbia economist Peter Kenen did, "very distraught, very tense," when students, both Black and white, began to disrupt the campus.[111]

Cultural Conflicts

At Columbia and elsewhere, those students were not only defying the traditional authority of their institutions' administrators and faculty members, but also cultural norms. As one Wisconsin observer noted, the crisis was in part the result of the students' repudiation of what had been until then "an implicit regard for the faculty's privileges and, more important, for their sensibilities." They were expected to display the appropriate "manners that were at once obedient, deferential, and respectfully distant."[112] But as the sixties progressed, that deference dwindled, a development that turned many academics against the radical students.[113] "We were ordinary faculty members," Berkeley's William Bouwsma explained, "whose contact with students had always been one of mutual respect and so on, and these characters didn't know the meaning of the word 'respect.'" His fellow historian Carl Schorske recalled how much that lack of deference upset his colleagues. "They didn't know how to deal with an assault on cultural mores, either personally or institutionally. So it was something beyond academic discipline or insubordination. I think it was psychological subversion." Though Schorske himself was never seriously upset by the Berkeley students' "disorderly behavior," he did recognize that it created problems. "What do you do with a guy who's walking around stark naked . . . or is calling you a mother-fucker? What are you supposed to do with that?"[114] What, indeed.

On some campuses, that cultural dissonance seriously impeded efforts to settle confrontations. After a number of students who had been occupying the administration building at Stanford in 1968 invited a group of faculty members to discuss the situation, some of those professors were so outraged that the students had addressed them by their first names that they walked out.[115] Columbia's faculty members were equally nonplussed by the students' disrespect. "I didn't know how to negotiate with anyone who called you a mother-fucker," the historian William Leuchtenberg later admitted.[116] During the 1968 crisis, as Leuchtenberg and his colleagues tried to mediate between the students and the administration, they invited the SDS leader Mark Rudd to address them. Not only did Rudd insist that there could be no settlement without amnesty, but he then described his earlier negotiations with the faculty's representatives as "exploratory talks . . . very exploratory, more in the line of bullshit." Rudd's expletive stunned his hearers. "It was at that moment," Peter Kenen recalled, "that I realized that we were dealing with people who were determined not to negotiate. The violence of Rudd's remark suddenly shattered my confidence that we were dealing with reasonable people."[117]

The key word here is "reasonable"; it had become a linguistic marker for those who insisted that the main value of an academic community was rationality.[118] Underlying much of the rhetoric about rationality was the unstated assumption that because the students were irrational, their demands did not deserve a hearing. The Russian historian Martin Malia, a conservative faculty leader at Berkeley, stated that position succinctly. He likened the protests to a "fever ready to break out at any time. . . . There was no point in reasoning with these people."[119] In fact, the only student language that some faculty members and administrators took seriously was the insistence that demands were "non-negotiable," an unfortunate rhetorical posture that allowed some authorities to justify their refusal to bargain.[120]

Faced with antagonists who seemed to repudiate their deepest values, many professors despaired. They felt unable to communicate with the disruptive students and sought above all to end the turmoil and restore their university's legitimate authority. Most of the time, therefore, they tended to support their administrations.[121] Unless the leadership behaved in an utterly outrageous fashion, it could count on the support of a majority of its faculty members.[122] In fact, even when the faculty adopted measures the administration opposed, as happened during a sit-in at Stanford, its members nonetheless voted "overwhelmingly" for a resolution of confidence in the administration.[123] But rarely could such a consensus restore calm to the campus. Conflicted about the turmoil, faculties possessed neither the self-confidence nor, as we shall see, the power to defend their institutions against their assailants both internal and external. As the unrest continued, public support for higher education rapidly melted away.

"INTELLECTUALS FALLING APART"

Divided Faculties Confront the Students

As student unrest intensified in the late 1960s, although most faculty members supported their administrations, serious divisions emerged within their ranks. As many as one-third of the professors at schools like Wisconsin and Harvard opposed a hard line against the students.[1] In many cases, such dissension occurred at institutions where earlier conflicts had already split the faculty—by politics, of course, but also by age, discipline, and professional orientation.[2] Factionalism was particularly intense at institutions where the expansion of the postwar years grafted a sudden influx of younger, more highly credentialed, intellectually ambitious, and cosmopolitan academics onto an older teaching-oriented faculty with strong local allegiances.[3] These divisions existed at every type of school—not only at SUNY Buffalo and San Francisco State, but also at Wisconsin, Ohio State, CCNY, and at many of the second- and third-tier state schools where more than half the faculty in the late 1960s consisted of recent arrivals—"a fact," one observer noted, "that creates problems in maintaining institutional coherence and unity of purpose."[4]

Many of the most serious conflicts occurred within departments. As we shall see, just at the moment that the City College of New York was introducing a controversial open-admissions policy, its history department was mired in personal feuds and struggles over curriculum and pedagogy. Similar conflicts occurred at other schools, ranging from Vassar to the University of Georgia. Politics were central to many of these disputes—especially when some of the younger people were so frustrated by the seemingly endless war in Vietnam that they began, in the words of the former Stanford English professor Bruce Franklin, "zooming to the left at the speed of light." A tiny handful of those faculty members, Franklin among them, mounted the barricades, aligning themselves with the revolutionary movements of the day.[5] Needless to say, their more traditional colleagues were horrified—as they were by the radicals' dabbling in the counterculture. At the University of Michigan, for example, the sociologist Richard Mann recalls how his cohort of political radicals on the faculty "lightened the emotional burden of being a leftie by joining the hippie movement . . . we had sort of gone native, closer to the student types, left the world of rationalism, argument, decorum."[6]

But these younger academics were not rebelling just for the hell of it. Like their students, they had real grievances and little power. At elite universities, for example, traditional departmental practices created barriers to the rational discussion of serious issues. Some departments were oligarchies, controlled by senior professors. When the sociologist Allan Silver came to Columbia in 1964, he recalled how "miserable" he and the other junior faculty members were.

> I was kind of shocked by the intensely hierarchical nature of the department. You didn't know anything that was going on. The place was run by mandarins. . . . Assistant professors were way down. You didn't know what the funding opportunities were.

One of Silver's colleagues, a young German historian, told Silver about a department meeting where the senior professor in his field sat next to him and didn't even know who he was. Silver hadn't met some of his senior colleagues either.[7]

At the University of Chicago, the distinctions of rank within the faculty were even more rigid. Assistant professors could not become members of the university senate until their third year on the faculty. In 1968, there was a move to expand that eligibility by a year; in 1969, that item was still on the agenda—undiscussed.[8] At Harvard, instructors on tenure-track lines, even with their PhDs in hand, did not receive regular faculty appointments. And at both Chicago and

Columbia, professors in the liberal arts departments were themselves split between college and graduate school faculties, with the latter enjoying a higher status and more privileges. Similar discrimination existed at less prestigious institutions as well. "Us, junior people," the soon-to-be fired Queens College medievalist Sheila Delaney recalled, "had no voice or vote in department meetings."[9] As the American Council on Education reported in 1970, younger faculty members deplored "the seeming fogyism of their elders" and chafed at their lack of power; at the same time "senior faculty are genuinely shocked by the seeming disrespect for 'objective scholarship,' the indifference to scholarly detachment, and the incivility being manifested within their own ranks."[10]

During quieter times such divisions could, and did, provoke conflicts over curricula and personnel. But when the upheavals of the late 1960s brought politics into the mix, these long-standing tensions prevented most faculties from developing a coherent collective response. Caught between unruly students and nervous administrators, many professors saw themselves as the disinterested third parties whose rational interventions would end the impasse. Unfortunately, as should have been obvious, these people were not disinterested parties, but deeply involved ones who were much too splintered to speak with a single voice. And when they did take a stand, it was usually (and correctly) perceived by the students as being close to that of the administration.[11]

Still, faculty members may well have been more invested in ending the disruptions than any other group on campus. Not only had they devoted their entire careers to higher education, but many had spent most of their adult lives at a single institution, identifying their own professional well-being and perceived status with their school's. In fact, for many of these people, loyalty to their institutions was the key factor that determined how they responded to the student troubles.[12]

Unsurprisingly, their first response was to call a meeting. As at Berkeley during the free speech crisis, concerned faculty members believed they had to take some kind of collective action to defuse the crisis. Accordingly, they formed groups of all sizes and political proclivities.

At Columbia, where there was no faculty senate or representative governing body, informal organizations quickly emerged. Within a few hours after the students took over Hamilton Hall to demand an end to the proposed gym in Morningside Park, the elimination of the Institute for Defense Analyses, and the removal of sanctions against a handful of SDS leaders, a small group of influential professors came together at Lionel Trilling's apartment. Opposing both amnesty and a call to the police, they consulted with the administration and wrote up proposals that Daniel Bell would present at an emergency faculty meeting the next day. Another larger group, mainly of more junior people, met in a classroom building and created what came to be known as the Ad Hoc Faculty Group. It met continuously from then until the bust, as its fluctuating membership—from 200 to 700 people at a time—struggled to find a way out of the impasse. Both groups were well represented at the following day's unprecedentedly large faculty meeting.[13]

And so it went everywhere. Professors sought out like-minded allies and then showed up at meetings in record numbers. At MIT, where no more than sixty people attended regular faculty meetings, six hundred came out during its crises. Cornell's 1969 upheaval brought out more than eleven hundred professors; Harvard's broke records as well and, beginning in 1967, repeatedly had to be moved to ever-larger venues. Same thing at CCNY, where there was a "huge" faculty meeting the day after the students shut down the campus in April 1969. In addition, official bodies of every kind—faculty senates, departments, unions, standing committees, and special committees—seemed to be in constant session throughout the late 1960s. At the University of Chicago, during the Marlene Dixon sit-in, the faculty's most important committee reported that it "has met daily, usually at far more than traditional length, for several weeks, and I suspect we shall continue to do so."[14] Or to take another example, in the academic year 1965–66 before the University of Wisconsin's troubles began, its English department met four times; two years later it met a dozen times.[15] One San Francisco State faculty activist recalled that during the height of that institution's unrest, "I seemed to be doing nothing but going to meetings."[16] At Berkeley, as well, the historian William

Bouwsma recalled that he and most of his colleagues felt the threat to "the future of the Berkeley campus" was so serious that "one did anything that one could to calm things down, and I became involved with sensitive committees that were supposed to straighten things out." But the unending meetings "just took so much time and so much patience" that he gave up and left for Harvard.[17]

Political disagreements only complicated matters. That professors should be so polarized at a time when they probably agreed about the key issues owed as much to the previous few years of debates about Vietnam and race as it did the need to pacify the campus in the face of the student unrest.

As the crises intensified, organized political factions emerged. CCNY had its Faculty for Action on the left, its local chapter of a conservative group called the Universities Committee for Rational Alternatives on the right.[18] Harvard's professors split into two caucuses. According to the political scientist Michael Walzer, the co-chair of what came to be known as the Liberal Caucus, the relationships between his group and the more conservative faculty members were "very bitter. . . . Some of my colleagues were very, very angry with me and the whole Liberal Caucus."[19] At Cornell, left-wing junior faculty members formed the Concerned Faculty to support the Black and radical students.[20] The University of Wisconsin also had a Liberal Caucus, as well as a more established body called the University Committee composed of the old-timers who had long been accustomed to handling faculty affairs and were so out of touch with their junior colleagues that some of them did not even know the Liberal Caucus existed.[21]

That lack of information was problematic.[22] Since the most eminent senior professors at major research universities usually taught large lecture courses or graduate seminars, they had little, if any, personal contact with the radicalized undergraduates. Yet they were usually more involved in negotiations and policy-making than their lower-ranking colleagues. As a result, the main protagonists—students, professors, and administrators—simply did not know one another.

Those faculty members who did know the student protesters tended to have more sympathy and respect for them, often because they were among their best students. Most of these sympathizers, however, were TAs and junior faculty members with little clout. There were also a handful of more well-known local activists like Douglas Dowd at Cornell and Immanuel Wallerstein at Columbia, who had taught or worked with the student radicals and were trusted enough by them to serve as intermediaries.[23] Unfortunately, they had little success, in part because the students did not realize that their faculty contacts were more radical than most other professors and, thus, overestimated how much support they had within the faculty.[24]

More importantly, however, faculty members themselves overestimated how much influence they wielded on their campuses—or over the students.[25] Despite their relative lack of power, the professors who tried to mediate often came under attack. Critics on the right viewed them as complicit with the protesters or worse, while the militant students felt betrayed when their teachers could not deliver.[26] Other observers, both on and off the campus, believed that faculty members were just too feckless and prone to interminable speechifying to negotiate realistically. "Their minds were too fine," one outside negotiator at Columbia explained, while an aide to New York's Mayor John Lindsay criticized the Ad Hoc Faculty Group's

> endlessly debated compromises. Several of their meetings lasted over fifteen hours without a break. Stoned on good intentions, high moralism, and lack of sleep, they were the least coherent individuals we dealt with on Morningside Heights. . . . Their only resource was moral fervor, and they ended up not only inadvertently prolonging the strike, but looking like fools. . . . They became one faceless aggregate of intellectuals falling apart.[27]

While there certainly was a lot of blather at Columbia and elsewhere, a more convincing explanation for the collective failure of the nation's faculties was simply that they lacked the power. That power, it turned out, was almost always in the hands of the presidents and trustees, who had little, if any, contact with faculty members, let alone students, but were also, as at Buffalo, under considerable pressure from outside politicians, alumni, and the media.

Trustees, in particular, could be surprisingly uninformed about the colleges and universities they ostensibly governed. Until the late 1960s, however, except for choosing their schools' presidents, these people rarely involved themselves with campus affairs. They wrote checks, went to football games, and rubber-stamped whatever the administration asked of them. Depending on the size and prestige of their institutions, they were nationally or locally prominent citizens—businessmen, attorneys, public officials, newspaper publishers, and religious or other community leaders—many of them political appointees. Harvard's five-man board of trustees, called the Corporation, for example, traditionally drew Boston Brahmins from financial institutions and white-shoe law firms. At SUNY Buffalo, the council was chaired by the CEO of the Buffalo Pipe and Foundry Company and comprised three other corporate executives, a banker, a newspaper publisher, two physicians, and one dentist.[28]

Rarely did trustees have contact with students or professors or get information from sources outside the administration.[29] Nor were they well informed about or sympathetic to the culture and values of their institutions. When the Berkeley philosopher John Searle dealt with the University of California Board of Regents in the late 1960s, he had to tell its members how tenure functioned. Nonetheless, when trouble occurred, they felt compelled to intervene; and, because they misunderstood the situation, they tended to respond with "uncoordinated repressiveness." Then, as Searle observed, they were "more likely to act as conduits for public pressure into the university than as buffers against it; and the times when they are most needed to act as buffers are precisely the times when they are most likely to act as conduits."[30] It was the same at many institutions. Especially, but not only, at public colleges and universities, trustees' lack of information made it hard for them to overcome their gut instincts to crack down, as so much of the public seemed to demand.

Outcomes, therefore, usually depended on the political wisdom or lack thereof of an institution's top officials—and on their desire or ability to fend off external pressures. It also depended on how well they were able to communicate with their faculties and students. Though a few leaders, Yale's Kingman Brewster, most conspicuously, did try to keep lines open to the campus radicals, most remained distant, if not overtly hostile.[31] An additional factor was the secrecy that administrations often maintained about their major policy decisions.[32] In sum, presidents of those colleges and universities where the worst confrontations took place all too often wanted to crack down on the protesters and so refused to bargain with them, a position that militated against working successfully with groups and individuals seeking a less drastic solution.

Such was the case at Columbia, whose nearly weeklong crisis in April 1968 was perhaps the most notorious student convulsion after Berkeley's free speech crisis.[33] The university's president Grayson Kirk was unyielding from the first. He was not a major presence on the campus, having long since delegated the day-to-day decision making to the eminent political scientist and provost David Truman. Neither man ever been much concerned about students. "I was never allowed to meet President Kirk, even as the spokesman for the officially recognized voice of the students," the former head of the Columbia University Student Council explained. "This does not mean that he was meeting with groups other than CUSC. It simply means that the president of Columbia University had no contact with the student body."[34] Thus, for example, when a joint student-faculty-administration committee, appointed to study "student rights and responsibilities" after a fracas over Naval ROTC recruiters in 1965, submitted its report a year and a half later, Kirk simply sat on it. When he finally released it in 1968, his only comment was: "I am not at the present time prepared to support certain of the committee's proposals."[35] Other top administrators were similarly dismissive of student concerns. In 1967, a graduate school dean famously stated that he was as interested in student opinions on a given issue as he would be "if they were to tell me they like strawberries."[36]

Kirk, it is true, was also unusually rigid about his own prerogatives. In particular, he would not cede his responsibility for student discipline, insisting that he was bound by a 1754 regulation.[37] The board of trustees made things worse by announcing four days into the crisis that it not only "wholeheartedly" supported the president's opposition to amnesty, but that it also ordered him to keep disciplinary power in his own hands "as required by the Charter and Statutes of the University."[38] Similarly, even though the university was willing to abandon the planned gym in Morningside Park, Kirk refused to say so in public.[39] That intransigence annoyed even his supporters. Probably reflecting the views of most of his liberal and moderate colleagues, Peter Kenen recollected, "I was taking a fairly pro-administration stand on many of the substantive issues, but expressing extreme irritation at the way in which the administration was saying things."[40]

Although the president's rigidity led to disaster at Columbia, it did have support outside the university. According to both Kirk and the provost Truman, they were under pressure from the presidents of hundreds of other institutions who believed, as Yale's Kingman Brewster told New York City mayor John Lindsay, "the very future of the American university depended on punishing the strikers. If Columbia gave amnesty to students who had occupied buildings, willfully destroyed records and defied every authority, it would be impossible to run any university."[41] Such appeals stiffened the spine of Columbia's administrators. As Truman put it, "This thing is far bigger than Columbia. . . . [W]e do not intend to betray our sister institutions."[42]

Meanwhile, as a total of five buildings came under occupation, members of the Ad Hoc Faculty Group began to worry about the possibility of violence from an increasingly likely police intervention as well as from football players and other conservative students (the future US Attorney General William Barr among them). As elsewhere, they decided to interpose their bodies between the protesters and their opponents. "Until this crisis is settled," they declared, "we will stand before the occupied buildings to prevent forcible entry by police or others."[43] And they did. The historian Walter Metzger recalls rushing to the campus where, "along with some rather pouchy types like myself," he put on a white armband and stood guard in front of one of the occupied buildings. Although the faculty group's action did cause the administration to postpone summoning the police, it was no impediment to New York's finest four days later.[44]

Dramatic as these actions were, not all of Columbia's professors opposed calling the police. Quite a few conservative and moderate academics came to believe, in the words of the Nobel Prize–winning physicist Polykarp Kusch, "this would have to be done." As Richard

FIGURE 13.1. Columbia professors with white armbands protecting students occupying a building, April 1968. © University Archives, Rare Book & Manuscript Library, Columbia University Libraries.

Hofstadter put it, "I then had come to the conclusion that the coming of the police was inevitable and it might as well be now." When the bust finally took place, however, neither the administration nor the faculty was prepared for its brutality or for the student strike that followed. To all extents and purposes, the university stopped functioning and did not return to anything like normality until the next academic year.[45]

*"One, Two, Many Columbias"**

Columbia's meltdown received enormous attention, but the academic community was so mired in confusion that its members could draw

---

* This was the slogan on a banner hung out of a window during the Columbia strike. It was a variant on a statement attributed to the Latin American revolutionary Che Guevara, "two, three, many Vietnams."

no useful lessons from it. Despite everyone's awareness of what was happening on other campuses, their responses to issues on their own were primarily determined by their schools' political cultures and specific problems. Some administrations and faculties managed to negotiate settlements with the insurgent students, while others would not even meet with them. Some brought in the police at the first sign of trouble; others sought to avoid doing so at all costs. Still others, like Buffalo and San Francisco State, simply spun out of control. The key decisions were invariably made by presidents, trustees, and even, as most tragically in California and Ohio, governors, either with or without the support of the schools' often seriously divided faculties.

Perhaps the most influential assessment of what happened at Columbia was the report of a quasi-official Fact-Finding Commission of eminent outsiders chaired by the Harvard Law School professor Archibald Cox (soon of Watergate fame). The Cox Report, as it was called, firmly opposed the building takeovers, but qualified its judgment by blaming the "catastrophe" in part on the "authoritarianism" of the Kirk administration, its insufficient concern for undergraduates, and its failure to pay attention to the special problems of its new Black students. The report also condemned the faculty's ill-fated efforts to negotiate, claiming that "the delay in calling the police . . . which the Ad Hoc Faculty Group forced upon the University officials . . . increased the likelihood of violence and magnified the reaction by lending an air of legitimacy to use of the tactics of physical disruption."[46] In other words, Columbia should have called the cops sooner.

Probably no institution took the Cox Commission's findings as seriously as Cox's own. Harvard's administration was jolted by Columbia's troubles. By the spring of 1968, there had already been several confrontations over Dow Chemical, ROTC, and Black studies. Even so, President Nathan Pusey did not think his institution would face a serious uprising. Unlike Columbia, he explained, Harvard had "no widespread 'alienation' of the student body, no breakdown in communications between students, teachers and administrators." Nor did he take the radical students seriously. They were, he noted in a widely circulated statement, "dreaming of glory—Walter Mittys of the left (or are they left?)—they play at being revolutionaries and fancy them-

selves rising to positions of command atop the debris as the structures of society come crashing down."[47] Still the administration began
to develop contingency plans.[48] It consulted with the trustees in the
Corporation as well as the deans, the chief of the campus police, and,
of course, Archibald Cox. After Brandeis's African American students
mounted an eleven-day occupation of their university's computer and
communications center in January 1969, Franklin Ford, the dean of
Harvard's Faculty of Arts and Sciences, moved sensitive files out of his
office, and the Corporation gave the president the authority to sum-
mon the police.[49]

Thus, when about two hundred SDS members took over University
Hall on April 9, the administration wasted no time in calling the cops,
who showed as little mercy as New York City's police had at Columbia the year before. At no point were faculty members or students
consulted—despite the establishment of a special Student-Faculty
Advisory Council a year and a half earlier to deal with just such an
eventuality.[50]

That was a serious mistake. Many of Harvard's most influential professors had already been losing respect for Pusey because of his aloof-
ness and resistance to what they believed were essential educational
reforms. Thus, while the faculty opposed the occupation of University
Hall, its members were also upset by the president's failure to seek
their advice. Their antagonism was reinforced when documents that
the students found in the dean's files revealed that the administration
had tried to keep ROTC on campus despite an earlier faculty vote
to eliminate it. Accordingly, the faculty's conservative caucus decided
not to push for an obviously divisive vote of confidence in the president, especially since it might fail. Over the next few weeks, Harvard's
leading professors sidelined Pusey as they tried to calm the campus.
They dealt directly with the Corporation, while developing temporary
governance structures to handle the most pressing issues.[51]

Though Harvard's top administrators had acted unilaterally in calling the police, at San Francisco State the administration had so little
power that its liberal president, Robert Smith, could not keep the police off campus during the explosive student strike. He resigned; and
his hardnosed successor, S. I. Hayakawa, only intensified the chaos.[52]

Arson, arrests, beatings, and roving bands of students enforcing the strike turned SFSC into a war zone. As at Buffalo, the faculty became terrified that there might be more serious bloodshed. As one sociologist put it, she felt "unsafe" on a campus that

> became a no man's land of battling students and police. The terrain was scarred and trampled by police movements, student sorties, the tracks of paddy wagons and horses, broken tree branches, foliage and litter—obliterating any possible impression that a college existed there.

Desperate, the San Francisco State local of the American Federation of Teachers unprecedentedly voted to strike in the beginning of January 1969. Given the violence and what they perceived as the breakdown of legitimate authority, they felt there was no other way to shut the school down. As far as I know, at no other college or university did faculty members try this. In order to get support from the rest of the San Francisco labor movement, the professors had to make traditional union demands for higher pay and better working conditions, but their main reason for walking off the job was to prevent violence— and in that they succeeded. For over a month, they maintained a relatively peaceful picket line in front of the main entrance to the campus that kept the conflagration under control. Once the students ended their strike two weeks later, Hayakawa and the central administration began to roll back many of the liberal reforms the previous San Francisco State presidents had instituted. But no one had been killed.[53]

No one was killed at Cornell, either—although not because the faculty intervened.[54] In order to persuade the armed Black students to leave the Willard Straight student center they had taken over in the early morning of Saturday, April 19, 1969, a pair of top administrators negotiated a seven-point agreement that met many of the students' demands—including amnesty for half a dozen African American students reprimanded for an earlier demonstration. But that agreement had to be ratified by the faculty, and it balked. Its members had been appalled by the sight of the Black students marching out of Willard Straight Hall Sunday afternoon draped in bandoliers and carrying guns. As a delegation informed President James Perkins that evening, the faculty would not act under duress. Accordingly, on Monday, after what one participant recalled as "a confused four-hour debate in the largest faculty meeting ever held at Cornell," the faculty voted 726–281 for a substitute proposal that President Perkins had hastily written up. It accepted most of the students' demands but did not nullify the sanctions on the earlier protesters. The faculty wanted more time to deal with that issue separately. But, as one critical professor explained, the language of the resolution was "totally confusing, and in many instances evasive to the point of nearing falsehood." That lack of clarity was to prove unfortunate.[55]

Understandably, the students felt betrayed by their professors, and both Black and white radicals threatened drastic action. As rumors of vigilantes swept the panicky campus, the Black student leaders escalated the violence of their rhetoric. "Cornell has three hours to live," one declared on the radio; "before this is over," President Perkins, a few other administrators, and the political scientists Allan Sindler and Clinton Rossiter "will die in the gutter like dogs." Sindler and his family fled their home for a local motel.[56] Meanwhile SDS was mobilizing thousands of students who, it was assumed, were itching to take over a building. Perkins was desperate to ward off any incident that might compel him to bring outside police onto the campus. So, too, were most professors, administrators, and even the campus police, all of whom feared what might happen if the sheriffs' deputies who were mustering in a parking lot off campus lost control. As one security official explained, "These guys had sawed-off shotguns. They were completely riot-equipped police, and if they had gotten the word to go in and arrest these people, I'm sure that there would have been bloodshed."[57]

The denouement came quickly. Two days after refusing to rescind the sanctions against the Black students, the terrified faculty members reversed themselves and voted for nullification. "I didn't find it easy," the Southeast Asian expert George M. Kahin admitted in a public speech. "I resented deeply having to act under the threat of violence, and that action cost me . . . some of my self-respect. Not simply because I was capitulating under force, but because I felt in doing so

I was further undermining the foundations of academic freedom at Cornell." He realized, however, that the Black students had seen the original rejection as a racist attack on the reforms they were seeking rather than as a condemnation of their use of force. Another professor made a similar confession.

> When I saw two to three thousand students ready to move out of Barton Hall to seize a building I reversed my position. I decided that we should nullify as an act of prudence. It was clear that the faculty position had been completely misunderstood. The faculty thought it was drawing a clear line of principle, but there was no point standing by that line when nobody even saw it as a line.[58]

"Prudence" won out, by a margin of three to one.[59] The campus was saved, but the trauma continued.

Many professors felt miserable. "I went off by myself and cried," one confided to a friend, while another said, "It was one of the saddest days of my life."[60] They viewed their support for nullification in existential terms. It was necessary if the university, if not all of civil society, was to survive. In the *New York Times*, the legal scholar Milton Konvitz characterized changing his vote as "a very bitter pill to swallow," and sought to justify what the outside world viewed as "a craven capitulation" as an effort to rescue Cornell from plunging into

> the wilderness, the state of nature as described by Hobbes. . . . The students were ready to nullify the social contract if we did not nullify the reprimands. Under these circumstances the majority voted to nullify—but, in fact, to refresh the social contract.[61]

Konvitz was far from the only Cornell professor who held such an apocalyptic view. In fact, even during the second faculty vote, two senior professors, Sindler, the chair of the government department, and the philosopher Allan Bloom, openly resigned from the university, while the antiwar activist Walter LaFeber quit as chair of the history department. They blamed the administration's habitually weak responses to student threats for undermining their ability to function as teachers and scholars. A dozen other professors soon followed.[62] In an article in the student paper, Sindler and his soon-to-resign colleague Walter Berns argued that the institution's capitulation to its students revealed that "the Cornell environment is no longer supportive of the kind of academic freedom a first-rate faculty requires."[63] Another dissident, the historian Donald Kagan, who had already accepted an offer from Yale, simply ran away. "I was absolutely so miserable that I just couldn't bear being there. And so I packed my family into the car and we just drove off to New York to get the hell away from it." He returned a few days later to join his colleagues in a campaign to oust the president.[64]

Kagan and his allies had been hostile to Perkins for years. They were historians, political scientists, and other scholars who considered the president to be an ambitious bureaucrat determined to increase Cornell's national influence, while ignoring his responsibility for protecting the academic freedom of the faculty. They were especially upset by the way in which the administration disregarded the faculty's prerogatives as it scrambled to placate its restive Black students.[65] They saw all their worst fears encapsulated in the willingness of the administration to rescind the earlier sanctions against the Black students. That Perkins and his supporters might have prioritized saving lives over saving face seems not to have factored into these professors' analysis.

In the aftermath of the crisis, many of these critics sought the president's removal. Not only did they contact selected trustees directly, but, in a totally unprecedented action, they also announced publicly that Perkins had lost the confidence of his faculty and that dozens of senior professors would leave if he remained in office. They had important support within the media, specifically Homer Bigart of the *New York Times*, who had hung out in the history and government departments during the crisis and whose one-sided articles about the faculty's antipathy to the president, according to Walter Berns, had "a helluva lot to do with Perkins's demise."[66] Perkins had his defenders, scientists in particular, but ultimately they could not counter the enormously unfavorable publicity produced by the faculty, not to mention the picture of the gun-toting Black students emerging from the student center. Thus, when a group of law professors who had previously supported Perkins criticized his failure to maintain academic freedom and law and order, he decided to resign.

Cornell was unique here in that the faculty's opposition forced the president out. At other institutions where the top administrators tried to maintain peace in the face of outside pressures to crack down on students, they were usually forced to resign *despite* support from the faculty. At CCNY, for example, President Buell Gallagher quit his post in April 1969 when the New York City Board of Higher Education caved in to the demands of conservative politicians for a crackdown on the Black and Puerto Rican students who had taken over the South Campus. Gallagher had been trying to avoid violence, but outside intervention made a peaceful solution impossible.[67]

Still, there were institutions whose leaders did manage to weather the turbulence by fending off calls for a crackdown, while treating their students with sensitivity and respect. We know much less about these successful individuals than about their less-flexible peers. One we do know about, Yale's Kingman Brewster, was by most accounts one of the most effective, if not *the* most effective, major university president of the period.[68] To begin with, he recognized the validity of his students' demands and was genuinely willing to give them a real say. Although he had little sympathy for civil disobedience and would have called the police if he felt it necessary, he conscientiously kept the lines of communication open with the Black and radical students from the start. Accordingly, even the campus Left respected him. As the head of the local SDS chapter acknowledged, Brewster

> would never do the stupid thing that would put everybody on our side. He wouldn't call the cops to smash our heads. . . . I spent a lot of time trying to fathom this guy in order to be able to embarrass and defeat him. And I really did come to admire his cleverness.[69]

The faculty's radicals were equally impressed by Brewster's political skill. He was, one explained, "a really brilliant liberal, I admired him." During a threatened confrontation over a Black Panther trial in the spring of 1970, he formed a special committee of activist students and professors and then managed to persuade the rest of the faculty to

support the Black students' demands for, among other things, the suspension of the university's "normal functions" until the crisis ended.
Though the governor of Connecticut had called out the National
Guard, Brewster insisted that the tanks and other military hardware
stay out of sight off the campus.[70]

There were other institutions whose administrations were similarly able to defuse student protests without alienating their faculties.
Wayne State, for example, was one such school. It could easily have
blown up, given its location in a working-class Black neighborhood as
well as its relatively large group of well-organized African American
students. Wayne's liberal president, William Keast, was, as one faculty
member noted, "haunted by the examples of Berkeley and Columbia"
and consciously sought to avoid serious confrontations. Like Brewster, he was determined to maintain cordial relations with the radicals, even going so far as to hold a weekly public coffee hour in the
student center cafeteria with the Black revolutionary who edited the
school newspaper. There were outside pressures for a tougher policy,
but Detroit's strong labor union culture—as well, no doubt, as the bitter memories of the city's 1967 riot—buffered the institution enough
to enable Keast to retain control. Like Brewster, he managed to ensure that the National Guard did not invade the campus.[71] NYU was
another institution that avoided serious trouble. When its Black and
radical students occupied the library and student center in October
1968, to protest the firing of a controversial African American faculty
member, the president overruled his provost at the last minute to cancel a police intervention. After prolonged negotiations, the demonstration fizzled out, with no subsequent sanctions.[72]

There were no sanctions as well after a group of African American students took over the communications center and computer at
Brandeis University. The newly installed president, Atlanta attorney
Morris Abram, initially wanted to call the police. But, influenced by
senior faculty members and reluctant to create "a symbolic confrontation of blacks and Jews . . . black kids bloodied at a Jewish institution," he decided to wait the demonstrators out. The occupation lasted
for eleven days while the administration negotiated for the students
to leave in peace.[73] On other campuses as well—Vassar, Boston Uni-

versity, Williams, and Penn among them—the authorities, often with the help of faculty mediators and even, at times, trustees, were able to negotiate successful settlements that ended building occupations without bloodshed or serious sanctions.[74]

Such was not the case at the University of Chicago, however. When its student radicals took over the administration building in the beginning of 1969 to protest the firing of Marlene Dixon, the university's president Edward Levi adamantly refused to negotiate. And he stuck to that position for the entire sixteen-day occupation, strongly supported by his faculty, who went so far as to deliver daily public statements praising Levi's tough stand and "wisdom of Solomon." Of course, it is possible that the president got such support because he made it clear he would not call the cops. Five months after the Chicago police riot at the Democratic National Convention and under pressure from senior administrators and professors to avoid a similar debacle, how could he?[75]

Still, even before the students left the administration building, the university began to punish them, with the faculty helping to identify the culprits. A hastily assembled disciplinary committee interrogated them about their political views, expelling forty-two hard-core radicals who refused to repudiate their actions, while exonerating those who had just been swept up by the transient passions of the moment. At that point, however, the faculty's unanimity broke down. With hundreds of students launching new actions against the punishments, about eighty professors held a one-hour vigil to emphasize their opposition to "the irregular procedures of the disciplinary committee and the harshness and inconsistency of the sentences imposed."[76] But the administration and its supporters did not budge. Levi's intransigence toward the students combined with his willingness to wait them out without calling the police earned him near-universal acclaim within the academic community and beyond.[77] When he left Chicago's presidency six years later, it was to become attorney general of the United States.

It may not have been a coincidence that Levi, Abram, and Brewster, were lawyers, trained to handle adversarial negotiations as well as rely on delay as a tactic. They were also open to using injunctions to tamp down campus unrest.[78] Obtaining an order from a local judge banning disruptive behavior on the campus was a convenient way to deflect responsibility for bringing in law enforcement officials. It seems to have been employed by quite a few administrations—among them Stanford, MIT, SUNY Buffalo, and the University of Connecticut—though not always effectively.[79] It did not, for example, deter the Buffalo 45 from courting a charge of contempt. Nor did it force campus rebels to pause and reflect on the legal consequences of their actions. Moreover, once an academic administration actually asked the authorities enforce an injunction, it ceded control over the campus. And there was always the prospect that the dissidents might contest an injunction's legitimacy—and win.[80]

In other words, there was no magic bullet. As a result, few, if any, of the protagonists drew any useful lessons from the varied reactions to the student protests of the late sixties and early seventies. Colleges and universities got sucked into a political struggle that could not be won. Whether or not faculty members and administrators supported the students' disorderly actions (and most did not), on campus after campus, all sides found themselves caught up in events that were unprecedented, disorienting, and scary. No wonder they responded with confusion.

PART 4
THE ACADEMIC LEFT AND RIGHT CONFRONT THE SIXTIES

"THE STRUGGLE FOR A DEMOCRATIC UNIVERSITY"

Radicals Challenge the Disciplines

Sometimes, something you've planned turns out better than you could ever have anticipated. That was certainly the case for a handful of left-wing academics at the Modern Language Association's annual meeting in New York City at the end of December 1968. For several months, Louis Kampf, Richard Ohmann, Florence Howe, Paul Lauter, Frederick Crews, and Noam Chomsky had been thinking about establishing a radical presence at the MLA. They had sent notices to some five hundred people and published a letter in the *New York Review of Books* announcing that they would "stir things up" at the convention.[1]

They were all, in the parlance of the day, movement "heavies." Chomsky had become one of the antiwar movement's main apostles of resistance. The others, although not as well known, were equally engaged. Slightly older than most sixties' radicals, they had entered the academy during the early 1950s and became active in the civil rights and antiwar movements. Crews was an eminent English professor at Berkeley. Howe, then at Goucher College, was to become a central figure in the new field of women's studies. Kampf chaired MIT's literature department while running the RESIST office, and Ohmann taught English literature and did administration at Wesleyan. Lauter, despite his Yale PhD and many publications, bounced from one teaching job to another throughout the 1950s and 1960s largely because he kept dropping out to work as a full-time political organizer. With his soon-to-be wife, Howe, he went to Mississippi in the early sixties; a few years later, after organizing against the draft for the American

Friends Service Committee, he helped Kampf run RESIST. And most of them had recently been involved with founding the radical New University Conference, or NUC.[2]

As they planned their action for the MLA, they modeled them-selves on their NUC comrades who had just formed a radical caucus within the American Sociological Association. Meanwhile, the con-ference staff offered them space at a convention hotel and a spot on a plenary panel. With the help of some local graduate students, the radicals held an open meeting at Columbia the night before the MLA conference began. They were planning to spend the next few days distributing literature, putting on workshops, holding public meet-ings, and submitting a handful of antiwar and other political resolu-tions to the business meeting. The unexpected turnout of about 450 people at Columbia enabled them to set up committees to handle tactics, throw parties, and organize task forces on issues like gradu-ate education and the position of women in the university. If all went well, they hoped to "activate and recruit" a few like-minded academ-ics into a radical caucus and expand their mailing list.[3] Instead, they took over the MLA convention.

Because the space the MLA had assigned them was in an obscure corner of the Americana Hotel, Howe had put up directional posters in the lobby. One, captioned "I Found My Job Through the MLA," had a picture of Eldridge Cleaver; another had a quotation from William Blake: "The Tygers of Wrath are Wiser than the Horses of Instruc-tion." Kampf had been standing before the posters handing out leaf-lets when a hotel detective stormed up and tore down "The Tygers of Wrath." Kampf put it back up, whereupon the detective shoved him and threatened to call the police. Lauter rushed off to get MLA of-ficials, but they claimed it was up to the hotel management. Soon the NYPD Tactical Squad arrived, demanded that Kampf relinquish the poster, and arrested him and two younger colleagues for defacing pri-vate property.

The contretemps galvanized the convention. As Kampf was being led out in handcuffs, a group of radicals invaded the plenary session. Some thirty or forty formed "a standing line, in silent vigil and pro-test, across the front of the meeting room," while the session's chair and incoming MLA president, the eminent Berkeley Americanist Henry Nash Smith, turned the podium over to Howe to explain what had happened and to raise money for bail. The next morning Stanford's Bruce Franklin led a sit-in at the hotel lobby to demand that the charges against Kampf and the others be dropped. That evening, over six hundred people showed up at an open meeting on "Student Rebellion and the Profession of Literature." The next day, a hastily improvised teach-in by Chomsky on Vietnam attracted some four hundred people.[4] Kampf's arrest had made the *New York Times*—albeit accompanied by a cranky editorial accusing the radicals of an "adolescent public display."[5]

At the end of the conference, for nearly five and a half hours, between six and eight hundred people crammed into the normally poorly attended business meeting. Most were hardly revolutionaries, nor had most of them been in contact with each other before the meeting. But the members were infuriated by the organization's failure to put the radicals' proposed antiwar and other resolutions on the agenda—not to mention its delay in pressing the hotel to drop the charges against Kampf et al. Accordingly, despite the MLA leaders' attempt to maintain a traditionally "apolitical" stance, not only did the business meeting pass all but one of the radicals' resolutions, but it also voted 292–187 to elect Louis Kampf as a write-in candidate for second vice president, putting him in line for the presidency two years hence. With even more support, the radicals got the organization's council to establish a Commission on the Status of Women, soon to be co-chaired by Florence Howe.[6]

The Learned Societies and Their Critics

"The Little Bourgeois Cultural Revolution of MLA 1968," as Kampf and Lauter termed it, far exceeded its organizers' expectations. Their critics assumed the radicals had choreographed the entire convention, but as Kampf recalled, he and his allies were "flabbergasted. We didn't plan this or pack this meeting. Apparently, we all underestimated the resentment boiling here against the system."[7]

Though Kampf no doubt exaggerated, since most academics refrained from overt politics, dissatisfaction had been building up—first on account of Vietnam and then in response to student pressures.[8] But by 1967, the academic dissenters were also looking more closely at their own profession. Although a tiny fraction of the broader professoriate, no overview of the academy during the long sixties can ignore the radicals' challenge to their universities and their disciplines. As the leading edge of a movement to democratize higher education, they did make an impact, even if not as transformative as they had hoped.

Spurred in part by the growing student demands for "relevance" in their educations, radical and left-liberal academics began to critique their disciplines. This was especially the case for younger faculty members and graduate students who had been socialized during the 1950s and early 1960s to identify more with their own areas of knowledge than with the colleges and universities where they worked.[9] They soon focused on the learned societies that not only constituted the academic community's main job markets, but also provided the institutional structure for awarding much of the status that determined the trajectory of most academic careers.

There were dozens of these organizations ranging from the American Association for the Advancement of Science with its more than 130,000 members and the MLA with its 33,000, to many smaller and more specialized subgroups and regional bodies, as well as a handful of groups for the Black and female scholars who were rarely, if ever, represented in the mainstream societies. All the major fields had associations, most of them founded along with the modern research university in the late nineteenth and early twentieth centuries.[10] Their official functions were to hold the annual conventions that became "flesh markets" for networking and job interviews and to publish peer-reviewed journals that served as gatekeepers for scholarship.[11]

The competition for the status that these organizations conferred attracted its most professionally ambitious members. Those who bestowed that status typically belonged to old-boy networks of the middle-aged, white, male professors from elite institutions who wrote the most important books, staffed the largest departments, attracted and placed the most graduate students, won the most grants and prizes, did the most outside consulting, and dominated their fields. But they did not run the learned societies in a democratic manner. From the start, these organizations relied on self-selection, subscribing to an informal consensus that promoted men (and at that time, they were almost always white men) with similar credentials and values.[12] Elections were usually uncontested. Though formally major policy issues had to be decided at business meetings during the annual convention, in reality a small group of elected officers and staff members actually ran the associations. After all, what normal academic would forgo a convention's boozy networking to sit through an hour and a half of reports about the book review editor's budget? At times, in fact, it was hard to round up a quorum.[13]

To some extent, the dullness of the business meetings reflected the determination of the leaders to present their organizations—and, by extension, their fields—as politically neutral and scientifically objective, ostentatiously remaining aloof from polarizing issues. They had provisions in their constitutions that limited their activities to professional and scholarly issues—measures that they assumed would protect them from outside intervention.[14] McCarthyism reinforced that assumption. For the moderate and liberal professors who had lived through the anti-communist witch hunts of the 1950s, taking positions on divisive political issues risked retaliation from right-wing politicians. Their organizations might even lose their tax-exempt status.[15] Yet as the largely liberal academic establishment's apolitical identity came under attack from the left, it had to confront its own internal conflicts over Vietnam, race, feminism, and the student movement. Neutrality was no option.[16]

Left Academics Organize: The Socialist Scholars Conference

By the mid-1960s, radical scholars had begun to organize. Their two most important early ventures were the Socialist Scholars Conferences (SSC) and the New University Conference (NUC). Except for their leftist political orientation and desire to transcend disciplinary boundaries, the two groups had different, though overlapping, missions and constituencies. The SSC drew from the remnants of the Old

Left and a variety of independent Marxists, including a group of historians with ties to the journal *Studies on the Left*. Started in 1965, it aimed to showcase previously marginalized socialist scholarship. The NUC, on the other hand, came out of the New Left. It was a militant political organization created in 1968 by younger faculty members and graduate students, many of them former SDS activists who envisioned it as, in one of its founders' words, "the prologue to the university section of a revolutionary socialist party."[17]

The main impetus for the Socialist Scholars Conference came from the historian Eugene Genovese and a group of his colleagues in the Rutgers history department and the social sciences department at Brooklyn Polytechnic University. They wanted the conference

> to inform the American public, including our fellow academicians, that socialist scholarship not only exists but that it extends in many directions and that it has contemporary relevance to many of the problems facing this country today. We wish to show . . . that alternative socialist interpretations have a validity, a vitality, and an integrity which have unfortunately been underestimated for too long.[18]

Because of the flap over Genovese's pro-Vietcong speech at Rutgers's April 1965 teach-in, the organizers decided that moving the meeting from Rutgers to Columbia would be in "the best scholarly interest" given "the present atmosphere."[19] The two-day conference in September 1965 was an unexpected success. Nearly nine hundred people showed up. A second conference the following year, held in a New York City hotel, attracted two thousand people. And the third, at the New York Hilton, drew nearly three thousand. Louis Menashe, the Polytechnic historian who chaired the steering committee in 1966, recalled the excitement of the packed sessions. "We felt the tide of socialism rolling across the land."[20]

Nonsectarianism was the order of the day. "No one's ideological credentials will be scrutinized," the organizers announced.[21] Though there was grumbling within the steering committee that some of the speakers were insufficiently radical, the SSC's "socialism" stretched from the orthodox communism of Herbert Aptheker to the main-

stream liberalism of the Yale historian (and soon-to-be president of
the American Historical Association) C. Vann Woodward, both of
whom appeared at a 1966 session on "The Legacy of American Slavery."[22] Other sessions dealt in one way or another with contemporary
issues, many addressed by the leading public intellectuals and activists
of the day. Among them were "The Welfare State," with Irving Howe;
"The Working Class in the World Arena," with a Soviet scholar from
Moscow's Institute of the World Labor Movement; "Poverty in America," with Michael Harrington, who had just published an influential
book on that subject; and a session on "Radicals and Hippies," with
the countercultural icon Abbie Hoffman packing a toy pistol. There
were also a few less jazzy panels, as if to show that socialist intellectuals could be as concerned about technical scholarly issues as their
more conventional peers.[23]

Though the conferences petered out within a few years, these eva-
nescent gatherings had an impact.[24] Not only did they introduce
thousands of academics to new scholarship in such fields as women's
studies, social history, and Marxist theory, but they also demonstrated
the value of interdisciplinary work. The historian Eric Foner, then a
graduate student at Columbia, recalled how the "tremendously exciting" sessions "opened up intellectual life in a very dramatic way."[25]

The New University Conference

At the time of the first Socialist Scholars Conference in the summer
of 1965, the antiwar movement was in its early stages and most campuses were quiet. Nearly three years later, when the New University
Conference was officially organized, the academy seethed with unrest.
The founders were veteran activists in what they called "the Movement."[26] In fact, just about every NUC member I interviewed mentioned that he or she had picketed Woolworths in the spring of 1960
to support the southern student sit-ins. Some, like Florence Howe and
Paul Lauter, later went to Mississippi. Others, like the *Viet-Report* editor John McDermott, became antiwar activists. While still others—
Richard Flacks, Bob Ross, and Bart Meyers among them—had joined
SDS and had actually participated in its 1962 Port Huron conference,

an event usually seen as the unofficial debut of the New Left.[27] But by 1967, these people were no longer comfortable in a student organization. They had graduated from college, embarked on academic careers, and wanted to find a more appropriate outlet for their political work within the university.[28]

During the late summer of 1967, in the aftermath of an abortive attempt to form an adult unit within SDS, a handful of graduate students and junior faculty members at the University of Michigan organized a conference called "Radicals in the Professions." Two hundred fifty people showed up. Besides academics, they were doctors, lawyers, social workers, city planners, journalists, and ministers. They shared a desire to combine their continuing political commitment with their responsibilities of spouses, children, and the need to earn a living in a personally satisfying way. Almost as important, there was the promise of an organization that could create a community to counter the morale-sapping political isolation that radicals at small or far-flung institutions all too often experienced.

In "Getting by with a Little Help from Our Friends," a widely circulated paper summing up the Ann Arbor conference, two SDS founders, Barbara Haber and Al Haber, described the "essentially personal crisis" they and their fellow radicals faced as they figured out how to "prepar[e] realistically for the long haul." The original SDS model—full-time students and organizers drifting from one movement hot spot to another while living on peanut butter and sleeping on couches—no longer fit. Yet these activists would lose their effectiveness, the Habers claimed, if they could not pursue their political vocation in their profession. "We cannot be radicals on weekends and evenings if all day, five days a week, we function as hacks, or cynics, or apologists." If they were to avoid either burnout or co-optation, these older New Leftists would have to find some kind of work "that would be personally viable," yet would also contribute to the political struggle.[29]

It was an uneasy balance. "The major unresolved tension at the conference," another participant noted, "centered around the degree to which a radical must choose professional work largely by criteria based on its strategic value to the movement, or whether 'personal satisfaction' should be a larger factor."[30] Unfortunately, that "unresolved tension" never got resolved. To begin with, quite a few radical academics experienced discomfort, if not actual guilt, about their relatively privileged economic position when they left graduate school and discovered, among other surprises, that, as the economist Michael Zweig noted, "for those of us who are young and just entering the profession, incomes rise very rapidly to levels none of us experienced."[31] These young scholars also found out that their professional identity threatened to subvert their political one. As Richard Rothstein, the NUC's second national secretary, observed, focusing so heavily on transforming the disciplines risked

> a new kind of cop-out by radical professionalism, legitimizing the elevation of "socialist scholarship" to unjustified priority, and allowing people to define themselves as historians (literati, sociologists, psychologists, etc.) who happen to be radicals rather than (what is our greatest need) revolutionaries who happen to be in the historical (etc.) profession.[32]

Yet for all its political disadvantages, higher education beckoned. After all, the university offered these leftists a tempting target for political activity because it could be considered a central prop of the unjust system they hoped to overthrow.[33] Transforming—but by no means destroying—their institutions thus gave these radicals an important role in the struggle for a better world. If they did not get co-opted by careerism, left-wing academics could use universities, one explained, "as crucibles for creating a revolutionary class that would ultimately gain access to influence and power."[34] And if they didn't feel that disrupting their institutions was a productive tactic at the time (as many of them did not), they could still rely on what Richard Flacks called "the Port Huron vision of the university as a resource and a base for democratic social change."[35]

After the Michigan conference, small groups in New York, Chicago, Ann Arbor, and elsewhere—Flacks, Howe, Kampf, Lauter, Jesse Lemisch, John McDermott, Bart Meyers, Bob Ross, and Naomi Weisstein among them—continued the conversation. They planned to follow up "Radicals in the Professions" with a conference explicitly focused on the academy.[36] Along with a few senior figures, including Tom Hayden, Noam Chomsky, Howard Zinn, and Berkeley's Franz Schurmann, they put out a "Call to Action" for a meeting in March 1968 in Chicago. "We are committed to the struggle for a democratic university," they proclaimed,

> one within which we may freely express the radical content of our lives and one which will be the antagonist and not the ally of pacifiers, domestic and international.
>
> We are prepared to act on this now and in the future just as we have acted throughout the freedom struggles at home and the Movement to end the war in Vietnam. The **New University Conference** is not the beginning of the struggle for a democratic university; it is merely the beginning of the intensification of that struggle.[37]

Three hundred fifty people came—most of them graduate students and junior faculty members with a small sprinkling of older leftists. They all shared the perception that the university had become a deeply corrupt institution, thoroughly embedded in the social system they wanted to replace.[38] There was, however, no consensus about how to effect that transformation. Instead, the conference featured a debate between Flacks and Staughton Lynd, who offered competing visions of an academic Left. Lynd, then struggling with a blacklist that eventually forced him out of the academy, claimed that it was useless for a radical to remain within such a compromised institution. Instead, he urged his audience to go out into the community to organize the revolution. "Disgorge the bait of tenure," he proclaimed, "and the problem of making a living can solve itself year-by-year." A charismatic figure, Lynd's call appealed to those younger NUC activists who shared his suspicion of the presumably corrupting bourgeois lifestyle of the academy.[39]

Flacks offered a more positive assessment of the ability of radicals to work within their institutions. He believed that they could "turn the universities into a major arena of struggle against imperialism, against militarism, against capitalist culture and ideology, and for the creation of an alternative culture and ideology, and a new class to carry that alternative into the rest of society."[40] A third position, articulated by the historian Jesse Lemisch, opposed both Lynd's revolutionary romanticism and Flacks's more pragmatic instrumentalism. Instead, in a widely circulated polemic that was later published as "Who Will Write a Left History of Art While We Are All Putting Our Balls on the Line?," Lemisch argued for the value of serious scholarship. Though a committed activist, he refused to subscribe to the notion that all professors had to dedicate "their research to the needs of the movement." He agreed that most academic work is "trivial," but he also admitted, "I do not dislike scholarship. I think that the idea of finding out how things actually work and have worked is an extremely radical idea. I do not share Staughton's disdain for truth-seeking. . . . [D]isciplined thought is an indispensable part of making a better world."[41]

For the next few years, this debate preoccupied the NUC—and the rest of the academic Left as well. In keeping with its commitment to openness and nonsectarianism, the fledgling organization took no official position on the issues involved, though it did turn down the suggestion that it transform itself into an auxiliary unit of SDS and let the students run the show.[42] Instead, the men and women at the Chicago conference drafted a provisional constitution, chose a temporary steering committee, and appointed Bob Ross, an early SDS activist and soon-to-be expelled University of Chicago graduate student, as their first national secretary. They gave the NUC a deceptively bland name in the hope that, with the word "conference" in its title, members might be able to get their schools to subsidize their travel to its meetings.[43] They also adopted a five-point program that would (1) organize local chapters, (2) create radical caucuses within the disciplines, (3) defend the jobs of campus radicals, (4) start a new magazine, and (5) form alliances with student activists and local Black and white critics of the universities.[44]

A second meeting in October finalized a structure with a Chicago-based national office and a full-time staff. At its peak in 1970 and 1971, the NUC had between one and two thousand members, about sixty chapters, and nearly a dozen paid staff members.[45] Again, in keeping with its New Left orientation, the central office tried to maintain a low profile and let the chapters do whatever their members wanted.

Nonetheless, it was impossible to avoid conflicts between the center and the periphery—over tactics, programs, and charges of miscommunication and elitism.[46]

At the same time as the NUC was building a network of radical academics, its leaders developed a national program of political campaigns. One, called "Open Up the Schools" (OUTS), demanded that the system of higher education provide, among other desiderata, universal access, affirmative action for under-represented minorities, the elimination of tracking, Black and women's studies, as well as such pedagogical reforms as the abolition of grades and the creation of politically relevant interdisciplinary curricula.[47] Another NUC campaign, the People's Peace Treaty, was a utopian effort to end the war in Vietnam by mobilizing ordinary citizens to subscribe to an unofficial peace treaty with the people of Vietnam. Ultimately, the NUC's two most important ventures were its support for the radical caucuses in the disciplines and the creation of a largely autonomous Women's Caucus that brought a left perspective to the emerging feminist movement of the late 1960s and early 1970s.

NUC activists recruited sympathetic colleagues at scholarly conferences and in their local antiwar and other political groups, hoping, as Florence Howe put it, to "get those who perceive themselves as radicals to participate actively and those who have thought of themselves as liberals to reevaluate their political commitments."[48] In pitching the new organization, they stressed that what distinguished it from the rest of the Left was its academic focus, interdisciplinary nature, and broad nonsectarian program. As its main mission statement put it, the NUC was

> a national organization of radicals who work in, around, and in spite of institutions of higher education. We are committed to struggle politically to create a new, American form of socialism and to replace an educational and social system that is an instrument of class, sexual and racial oppression with one that belongs to the people.[49]

Individual chapters emphasized different elements of that mélange. On many campuses, the NUC focused on support for student militants. Bertell Ollman, the political scientist who chaired the NYU chapter, recalled spending "most of our time defending students in whatever way we could."[50] Other chapters participated in anti-racist activities, taking care when they did so, however, to defer to the leadership of community groups like the Black Panthers.[51] Elsewhere, chapters supplied speakers to other groups and organized dozens, if not hundreds, of conferences and teach-ins on American imperialism and Vietnam as well as on such local issues as housing and public education.[52]

On some campuses, chapters sought to join the labor movement, despite considerable ambivalence about working with an institution whose leaders not only backed the war in Vietnam, but were also viewed as racists. Yet some NUC people supported strikes by the blue-collar workers on their campuses. They also helped organize graduate student unions, worked with AFT locals in community colleges, and sometimes even toyed with starting collective bargaining units for faculty members at four-year colleges and research universities.[53]

Chapters also immersed themselves in "internal education"; they set up study groups, sometimes assisted by bibliographies distributed by the national office. At Brooklyn College, the thirteen items on the NUC chapter's summer reading list included Frantz Fanon's *Wretched of the Earth*, William Appleman Williams's *Tragedy of American Diplomacy*, and the feminist tract "Notes from the Second Year: Women's Liberation," as well as Marx and Lenin.[54] On other campuses, NUC activists spearheaded antiwar and other "anti-militarism" work. At NYU, for example, the NUC chapter released a report in 1970 on the university's participation in the development of chemical and biological warfare.[55] The kind of intellectual and technical research that went into such a report was, one NUC leader explained, the uniquely valuable service that the organization could provide to the rest of the movement.[56]

And then there was feminism. From the first, the New University Conference committed itself to the women's liberation movement. Not only were such powerful early feminist intellectuals as Heather Booth, Marlene Dixon, Florence Howe, and Naomi Weisstein involved in the NUC, but they quickly created a separate Women's Caucus.[57] "Without an explicit commitment to engage also in the struggle against the oppression of women," a resolution at the 1969 National Convention stated, "NUC cannot be taken seriously as an organization working to bring about a radical transformation of American society and to combat the most pernicious manifestations of American corporate capitalism."[58] By the following year, the NUC's feminists had forced the group's male members to pay attention—at least verbally—to their demands for equal treatment. They even received a commitment to allocate 50 percent of the seats on the national executive committee to women, even if, as NUC activists of both genders admitted, there remained plenty of male chauvinism within the organization. Still, many of the men did struggle with the issue. "We are discovering that often our customary ways of doing things are oppressive to our sisters," one NUC activist remarked as he reprimanded a prospective member for using the salutation "Dear Sirs" in a letter.[59]

What is important to realize here is that NUC women were deeply involved with developing the analysis that produced the women's liberation movement at exactly the same time they were pushing for recognition within the NUC. As they took part in what came to be known as consciousness-raising and began to identify the sexist oppression they had been facing all their lives, they struggled to integrate their radical politics with their feminism.[60] "I was never a feminist separatist," the NUC activist Roberta Salper explained,

> and I enthusiastically supported the opportunity to work for both women's liberation and socialism. . . . For me, "socialist feminist" meant that sexism, racism, capitalism, and imperialism could, in different contexts be of equal importance. I was committed to an autonomous women's movement, but I also wanted to make sure women's liberation was included in the core of the New Left.[61]

That double commitment forced Salper and her female allies to fight on two fronts. On the one hand, they struggled with mixed success inside the NUC to bring a feminist sensibility to their male comrades; on the other, they worked alongside non-radical women in the broader women's movement, while also trying to infuse it with their left-wing agenda.[62] What they discovered, Salper explained, was that "the zeal with which we set about consciousness-raising, speaking to as many women as possible, . . . to alert them about the oppression and second-class status of women in America[,] did not leave time for the discovery of potential political differences among us." Other women in the New University Conference had similar experiences. Within a year or two, they were to find the NUC "redundant"—and so they left.[63]

Others did as well. By the middle of 1972, the NUC had disbanded. Several factors brought about that collapse, which was happening elsewhere in the New Left with factionalism rising and the Vietnam War seemingly winding down. The NUC was not immune to the craziness of the rest of the movement. Some of its younger members saw themselves as, in Louis Kampf's words, "instant revolutionaries who wanted us to mount the barricades."[64] In the beginning of 1970, for example, the organization parried an apparent takeover attempt by the Progressive Labor Party (PL), a Maoist sect, whose members had been disrupting meetings. The NUC's leaders rushed an "incompatibility resolution" against PL through the National Committee in an admittedly undemocratic way. That action, though widely believed to be necessary, was not well received by the NUC rank and file.[65]

Money also became an issue.[66] The academic expansion of the 1960s had begun to falter, precipitating a serious and unexpected job crisis. NUC people suffered a disproportionate number of political dismissals. Chapters threw themselves into self-defense campaigns, even as they touted the "educational" value of the repression they were facing since "it serves to smash the myth of the university's apolitical and pristine nature."[67] The national office set up a job bank, announcing: "Come to us if you are trying to find a place where you can be fired from next." As one discouraged (and soon-to-be sacked) activist put it:

What I would like to see NUC doing is achieving high visibility on campus by way of attractive program in motion. What I think we do now is achieve visibility by getting offed with painful frequency, so that most motion seems to be around the process of losing jobs.[68]

That focus on self-defense was a symptom of the organization's decline. So, too, was the growth of personal and political conflicts within its national office and top leadership. As its women deserted, its debts mounted, and its membership dwindled, many of the NUC's key "heavies" gave up. "We blew it" was the way Paul Lauter described the NUC's demise.[69]

Lauter may have been too hard on himself and his comrades. It is possible that the NUC may have been too ambitious. Had it concentrated mainly on the women's movement and its work within the disciplines, as Lauter had wanted it to, the organization might have fulfilled more of its promise. Or not. Still, as the saga of the radical caucuses reveals, it did have an impact.

The Radical Caucuses: Beginnings

Unlike the NUC, the radical caucuses usually took on narrow campaigns, directed against what they saw as the worst defects of their own disciplines and professional associations. Above all, they opposed the nominally apolitical stances of those organizations, challenging the contention that legitimate scholarship must be "unbiased" and "objective."[70] They also sought to expose and then rein in the academy's collaboration with the military-industrial complex.

These groups operated much as the NUC had, emphasizing recruitment, self-education, and outreach to the public while also arranging conferences and participating in local campus actions.[71] They also put out publications—newsletters initially, then books and more polished scholarly journals that their founders hoped would gain enough credibility to count toward people's tenure. If the intellectual thrust of the caucuses and their publications was not explicitly Marxist, it at least evinced a greater involvement with contemporary social and political problems than the mainstream of their disciplines and a desire for a more humane and enlightened scholarship. A few are still around, including the MLA Radical Caucus, the Union for Radical Political Economics, and the Caucus for a New Political Science. Journals of some others, like the Middle Atlantic Radical Historians Organization's *Radical History Review*, actually outlasted the groups that founded them, often under new names—as when *The Insurgent Sociologist* became *Critical Sociology* and the *Bulletin of Concerned Asian Scholars* became *Critical Asian Studies*.

Unfortunately, we don't know how many of these groups existed nor what all of them did. One scholar claims to have identified eighteen such organizations.[72] I've found at least seventeen but have probably missed some ephemeral ones, as well as local and regional bodies and those in smaller fields. But that's not counting the separate Black and women's caucuses, those involved with area studies, and the radical groups in areas like law, medicine, social work, and city planning, many of whose members belonged to the faculties of professional schools.[73]

The Radical Caucuses

Anthropologists for Radical Political Action (ARPA)
Caucus for a New Political Science (CNPS)
Committee of Concerned Asian Scholars (CCAS)
Eastern Union of Radical Sociologists
Mathematicians Action Group
Middle Atlantic Radical Historians Association (MARHO)
Psychologists for a Democratic Society
Psychology Liberation Movement
Radical Caucus of the American Historical Association
Radical Caucus of the American Philosophical Association
Radical Caucus of the Modern Language Association
Science for the People (SftP)
Scientists and Engineers for Social
and Political Action (SESPA)
Sociology Liberation Movement (SLM)
Union of Radical Criminologists
Union for Radical Political Economics (URPE)
Western Union of Radical Sociologists

These caucuses emerged between 1967 and 1969, many in response to the refusal of the learned societies to allow resolutions about Vietnam to come before their annual meetings. Except for the American Anthropology Association and the Eastern and Western divisions of the American Philosophical Association, which adopted fairly strong antiwar statements in 1966, leaders of one society after another rejected such resolutions as "political" and, therefore, contrary to their organizations' missions.[74]

Already reeling from the revelation that their discipline's executive secretary headed a foundation that served as a conduit for the CIA, political scientists were the first to create a radical organization in their field: the Caucus for a New Political Science (CNPS).[75] The group formed during a plenary session at the 1967 annual meeting of the American Political Science Association (APSA) in Chicago, when the moderator turned off the microphone to silence the repeated requests by members to discuss taking a stand on the war. "I was an unknown, sitting in the audience, and raised my hand," Marvin Surkin, one of the CNPS's founders recalled. "Then, without a mike, I announced that everybody who opposed that action should meet in the next room. That is when the caucus started."[76] It was ironic that the Caucus for a New Political Science, which turned out to be the most moderate of all such groups, should have been the first to organize.

The year 1967 saw similar incidents in many other fields. At the American Sociological Association's annual meeting in San Francisco, for example, a group of antiwar scholars mounted a vigil outside the convention hotel. Then, during what Richard Flacks and others recalled as "a rather stormy business meeting," they also submitted a number of unsuccessful resolutions, including one demanding "an immediate end to the bombing of Vietnam and the immediate withdrawal of American troops from South Vietnam."[77] By the time of the ASA's next convention in early September 1968, Flacks and his colleagues were ready for action, working with a group of Columbia graduate students "to inject some of the spirit of the Columbia revolt into the ASA sessions." Calling themselves the Sociology Liberation Movement (SLM), they planned to protest at the plenary session where Secretary of Health, Education, and Welfare Wilbur Cohen was scheduled to speak.[78]

Philip Hauser, the University of Chicago demographer who was the ASA's president, apparently considered Flacks a threat, warning him and his associates that if they tried to disrupt the meeting, they'd be arrested. But all the radicals wanted was to set up a literature table, offer a few sessions of their own, and place a representative on the panel with Secretary Cohen—all of which they got. Their most controversial action occurred when a hundred of them showed up at the plenary session wearing black armbands and buttons that read: "Knowledge for Whom?" Then, when Cohen began to speak, they rose, turned their backs, and quietly walked out.[79]

That demonstration worked. The nascent Sociology Liberation Movement's literature table was, one of its main organizers recalled, "swamped," while hundreds of people showed up at SLM events and signed up for its mailing list. The moment was ripe; the meeting took place at exactly the same time as the Democratic National Convention in Chicago. With the conference-goers transfixed by the omnipresent TV images of Mayor Daley's police attacking demonstrators, the ASA's business meeting overwhelmingly voted to cancel annual conventions in Chicago for the next ten years.[80]

The radical economists also organized themselves. After spending "two years of soul sessions" grousing about "the irrelevancy of modern economics," a group consisting mainly of graduate students at the University of Michigan and junior faculty members at Harvard put together a four-day conference at Ann Arbor in September 1968 and decided to form a separate organization rather than create a caucus within the American Economic Association. The Union for Radical Political Economics, or URPE as it was called, was to become the longest lasting and most intellectually ambitious left-wing counter-organization within the academic profession. Its official launch took place at a December 1968 alternative economics job conference in Philadelphia that had split off from the AEA then meeting in Chicago.[81]

Like the economists of URPE, the graduate students and junior faculty members who formed the Committee of Concerned Asian

Scholars (CCAS) at the Association for Asian Studies annual meeting in 1968 also created a separate organization.[82] Because their field of study was directly involved with the conflict in Southeast Asia, the founders of the CCAS believed they had a special responsibility to serve the antiwar movement. "We came together," their mission statement said, "in opposition to the brutal aggression of the United States in Vietnam and to the complicity or silence of our profession with regard to that policy." Their organization would not only oppose the war, but also "create alternatives to the prevailing trends in scholarship on Asia" that they believed had contributed to the devastation.[83]

Although the CCAS attacked mainstream scholarship, it did not encounter the same hostility from the field's leaders as some of the other radical caucuses. Harvard's John K. Fairbank, considered to be "the very embodiment of (Modern) Chinese studies in the United States" and whose graduate students were among the CCAS's lead organizers, not only chaired the group's inaugural meeting, but also continued to maintain respectful relationships with its leading activists even as they sought to dismantle his oeuvre.[84]

The day-to-day operations of the CCAS were similar to those of the other radical caucuses. The group provided speakers and resources for the antiwar movement. It also became involved in exposing and opposing universities' contracts with the government, such as the attempt by the State Department to set up a Vietnamese Studies Center at Southern Illinois University in the early 1970s.[85] The CCAS also critiqued the mainstream's paradigms and provided the alternative interpretations.[86] And although the organization folded in 1978 with the winding down of the Vietnam War, its publication lives on as *Critical Asian Studies.*

The path to radical organizing in the natural sciences differed from that in the humanities and social sciences. To begin with, conservatism prevailed in a number of disciplines like chemistry, agricultural science, or electrical engineering, where professors had long worked closely with corporations and the Pentagon. Even among more liberal scientists who opposed the war in Vietnam, there was considerable distaste for politicizing their disciplines. Or, as one self-identified leftist put it, the American Physical Society "should remain pure."[87] The radicals in science also differed in that they organized across their disciplines. Accordingly, the main left-wing organizations that emerged, Scientists and Engineers for Social and Political Action (SESPA) and Science for the People, tended to criticize the entire scientific establishment rather than any one branch of it.[88]

The first stirrings of resistance within the scientific community occurred in 1967 when Berkeley's Charles Schwartz became upset about the refusal of the American Physical Society's newsletter to publish his letter calling on fellow physicists to oppose the war in Vietnam. After the APS's ruling council turned down his appeal on the usual grounds—that the organization could not discuss political issues—Schwartz called for a constitutional amendment to allow the APS to consider resolutions "on any matter of concern to the society." Although a mail ballot rejected the "Schwartz Amendment" by a margin of nearly three to one, the debate dominated the physicists' 1968 meeting and beyond.[89]

A year later, the APS council allowed the creation of a division on "the problems of physics and society" to discuss such issues. By then, however, Schwartz and three other colleagues, including the future Nobel laureate Martin Perl, had issued a call for their version of a radical caucus. Scientists (and, later, Engineers) for Social and Political Action, or SESPA, was an umbrella organization. Even so, it soon split when Perl and its more moderate members rejected Schwartz's more radical agenda.

SESPA then merged with a group called Science for the People and turned its newsletter over to that organization's Boston chapter. Described by one historian as "the most important radical science group in the United States in the mid-twentieth century," Science for the People was interdisciplinary from the start.[90] It was also more eclectic than the other radical caucuses. And more decentralized. Though some of its founders were NUC activists from Chicago, it had no national organization aside from its bimonthly magazine. Its four thousand members—subscribers to *Science for the People* and others on its mailing list—were technicians and K–12 teachers as well as academics, while the activities of its more than thirty loosely affiliated chap-

FIGURE 14.1. *Science for the People*, December 1970. © Courtesy of the Tamiment Library, New York University.

ters ranged from disruptions of military-funded research centers to the publication of pamphlets and newsletters.[91]

The Radical Caucuses at the Learned Societies

From about 1967 to 1972, the radical caucuses debated, demonstrated, splintered, and produced often brilliant, though sometimes overwrought, analyses. They were typical representatives of the New Left: suspicious of authority, eager for action, and convinced that they were right. No doubt, they would have encountered hostility no matter how decorous they tried to be. But they belonged to a radical movement that did not seek respectability or buy into what some of the MLA's leftists called "the false standards of professional gentility."[92] In many cases, their hair was long, their language coarse—and even sectarian. They had a proclivity for the counterculture, some even forming "collectives" rather than "chapters." And a number of them had a penchant for dramatic action, a controversial tactic that some otherwise sympathetic supporters criticized as "guerrilla theater" and "the sort of mindless activism that has been so destructive of radical organizations."[93]

In 1969, for example, besides using the facilities of the American Sociological Association's convention to recruit members and present papers, the Sociology Liberation Movement, led by Marlene Dixon among others, also commandeered the presidential panel to demand a memorial tribute for the Vietnamese leader Ho Chi Minh.[94] Two years later, the insurgent sociologists struck again, with a feminist demonstration that flaunted an eight-foot-high red-white-and-blue plastic penis.[95] URPE's radicals disrupted the American Economic Association's business meeting in December 1969, demanding to make a presentation. When the organization's president refused to cede the microphone, "four of us," Arthur MacEwan recalled, "jumped on the stage." MacEwan then read "a Condemnation Statement" denouncing mainstream economists as "the sycophants of inequality, alienation, destruction of environment, imperialism, racism, and the subjugation of women . . . the priests and prophets of an unjust society."[96]

Scientists could be disruptive as well. By 1969, a few had become quite radicalized, especially after encountering censorship when they tried to publish critiques of their fields in the learned societies' journals or make presentations at their annual meetings.[97] Their most notorious action took place at the 1970 annual meeting of the American Association for the Advancement of Science (AAAS) that had banned distribution of a Science for the People manifesto. A group of activists disrupted a panel to present the conservative physicist Edward Teller with the "Dr. Strangelove Award," a small wood and chrome statue of a police officer in the act of shooting that was engraved with the words: "I am just following orders." Teller, who had brought bodyguards to the session, likened the demonstrators to Nazis, as did the head of the AAAS. Still, despite the storm of hostility, the radicals did get the attention they sought.[98]

Most of the time, however, the left-wingers behaved. The political scientists did not disrupt their annual meetings, nor did the historians, despite Jesse Lemisch's call for the radicals to "come on very tough" at the American Historical Association's 1969 meeting.[99] Usually, the leftists staffed literature tables, recruited members, asked provocative questions at official panels, and presented papers at the mainstream sessions as well as at their own counter-conferences.[100] They also offered resolutions. Lots and lots of them. Ones opposing the Vietnam War were ubiquitous, although the texts varied and over time became increasingly more radical and specific. By the time Nixon invaded Cambodia in 1970, the learned societies, which only a few years before had refused to take a position on the conflict, called for immediate withdrawal, and by 1972 some actually sponsored rallies against the war.[101] By then, as well, the learned societies were dealing with—and usually passing—resolutions about women's issues.[102] And, by 1970, if not before, some of the disciplinary organizations were responding to the radicals' demands to do something about the incipient job crises in their fields.

The caucuses also submitted resolutions geared specifically to their particular areas of research. Thus, for example, the CCAS, besides offering a detailed proposal about Vietnam, also called for action with regard to the US-Japan Security Treaty and America's official hostility to the Chinese revolution.[103] The radical anthropologists pressed for a code of ethics that would include a ban on classified research as well as transparency about the source of research funding. MLA's radicals wanted to end the association's collaboration with a federal program of publishing notable American authors that they claimed reeked of elitism.[104]

Business meetings now tended to be hotly contested, sometimes lasting for hours. Factions organized in advance. Fearing that "a small caucus" might pack the American Historical Association's 1969 business meeting, Richard Hofstadter sent a letter to dozens of colleagues to urge them "to do something most of us rarely trouble to do—attend the business meeting" and make their wishes felt.[105] As they fought to block politicization, the leaders of the learned societies struggled to keep the radicals' resolutions off the meetings' agendas, usually by ruling that such questions had to be submitted to the entire membership in a mail ballot.[106] But even a plebiscite could create controversy, as when the MLA's official mailing on the referendum to move its future meetings from Chicago to protest what happened at the 1968 Democratic National Convention contained seriously misleading, and thus biased, information.[107]

Similar proposals to boycott Chicago turned up at many learned societies—with differing results.[108] In 1968 the canny China scholar John Fairbank, then president of the American Historical Association, avoided controversy altogether by convincing the AHA's ruling council to preemptively move its forthcoming meeting to New York from Chicago. Fairbank saw the decision, he explained, "as a practical, administrative matter, for the health of the annual meeting." Moreover, since the conference would simply move from one Hilton hotel to another, it would not incur a big expense.[109]

The AHA, however, could not avoid controversy the following year when its radical caucus ran Staughton Lynd for president. Despite the fears of Hofstadter and his establishment colleagues, the radicals, as the AHA president C. Vann Woodward told his daughter-in-law, "screamed & ranted a good bit but observed most of the amenities."[110] Lynd's candidacy was part of a campaign to democratize the AHA, as was a struggle against proposals to require mail ballots for the elections of officers and other measures clearly designed to avoid a left-wing takeover. That takeover did not occur. Lynd and his colleagues had gone too far, proposing their own constitutional revisions that included a code of ethics "prohibiting research for the military, the CIA, AID, etc." Widely criticized on the left as well as on the right as interfering with academic freedom, the proposed code of ethics did not fly.[111] Nor did the antiwar resolution or Lynd's presidential bid, which was defeated at the business meeting by a 1,040–396 vote.[112]

Other radical caucuses also took the electoral route. In 1969 the Caucus for a New Political Science ran a slate of candidates for the American Political Science Association's ruling council that combined a group of younger radicals with a few more established scholars who wanted to lessen the hold of behavioralism on the field and pay more attention to political theory and real-world policy issues. Only one member of that slate won—and he had been supported by the APSA leadership anyhow.[113] Despite its poor showing, the CNPS continued to run candidates for the next few years, including (unsuccessfully in 1970) the antiwar international relations specialist Hans Morgenthau for president. By then, however, the radicals who had formed the caucus had abandoned it. In a quest for respectability, its moderate members had added the Nixon adviser Daniel Moynihan and the Chicago sociologist Morris Janowitz to the steering committee. The CNPS, as far as its left-wing founders were concerned, had sold out; it was no longer engaged in "the task of creating a political science oriented to the Movement nor to radical social criticism."[114]

The radicals had more electoral success within the American Sociological Association. In 1973, they ran the venerable Alfred McClung Lee for president as a write-in candidate and won. Though he did manage to expand the scope of panels at the annual meeting, Lee recalled, "persistent opposition—even sabotage—from the strongly proestablishment Council and office staff" blocked all serious efforts at change.[115] Louis Kampf and Florence Howe, the two insurgent presidents of the MLA, were similarly hamstrung by the association's other elected officials and bureaucrats.[116] Such failures and limited successes bolstered those radicals who had long opposed working within the societies. Even at the height of the Left's success, some of them were already asking whether it was worth it to "spend our time 'reforming' the MLA. . . . Is it not diversionary for us to be engaged to a dinosaur?"[117]

Beyond the Learned Societies: The Radical Caucuses on Campus and in the Community

For many, if not most, of these dissident academics, it was as important—if not more so—to operate at the local, as well as the national, level. Both the NUC and the radical caucuses encouraged their supporters to form chapters focusing on local issues at their home institutions and in their regions. Thus, for example, Science for the People's Madison Collective produced a 118-page exposé of the university's recently bombed Army Mathematics Research Center.[118] At Columbia, the Committee of Concerned Asian Scholars chapter discovered that the School of International Affairs had received a grant from the State Department to explore the "economic rehabilitation of Vietnam"; it then pressured the university to reevaluate its entire program of research contracts.[119] The Union for Radical Political Economics was active in New England, where it organized a series of regional conferences. Attendees recalled an URPE 1971 conference at the Yale Law School on "Women and Economics" as eye-opening.[120] The Psychologists for a Democratic Society encouraged local campaigns around such issues as open admissions, curricular reform, and, of course, opposition to the war in Vietnam.[121]

Many of these faculty radicals also wanted to engage with a broader audience outside the academy. The activists in Science for the People, for example, were quite explicit about their desire for the "demystification of science and technology." In the group's founding manifesto, "Towards a Science for the People," Bart Meyers and his coauthors specifically dedicated the new organization to removing "the false mystery surrounding science and technology" and destroying "the hold of experts on decision making. . . . Understandable information can be made available to all those for whom it is pertinent."[122]

Outreach was also central to the mission of the Committee of Concerned Asian Scholars.[123] Its Boston chapter published a weekly column in the local underground paper; Washington University's Mark Selden had a similar gig at radio station KDNA in St. Louis. CCAS chapters at Berkeley, Stanford, the University of Michigan, and elsewhere organized conferences, supplied speakers, and distributed packets of information about Vietnam. They also taught—both official courses and unofficial ones.[124] URPE did the same. Besides publishing a scholarly journal, the radical economists also put out *Dollars & Sense*, a still-extant popular magazine founded by its Boston chapter. In a similar vein, the sociologists at Washington University, who had formed what was for a short time the most explicitly left-wing sociology department in the United States, started the publication *Transaction* to bring the insights of sociology to lay as well as academic readers.[125] Radical historians also looked for a broader audience. In the abortive draft constitution that they wrote up for the American Historical Association in 1969, they had designed a position for someone "to oversee the publication of Association books, periodicals, films, radio and television programs, etc., that develop and present the work of historians to the profession and to the public."[126]

Many of these radicals were also eager to connect with educators outside the university. The CCAS created classroom materials on Vietnam specifically for high school teachers, while activists from Science for the People worked directly with those from K–12.[127] The MLA caucus wanted to reach out to high school English teachers in the hope of encouraging them to expand the canon beyond the works of the traditional white, male authors. Some radicals even fantasized about requiring all future English teachers to know Black, women's, and working-class literature.[128]

International contacts also mattered. China, Cuba, and Vietnam all beckoned, and the radicals actively pursued direct connections with those revolutionary regimes. The New University Conference, for example, not only conducted drives to send scholarly books to Cuba, but, as the first academic delegation to receive an official invitation, it began to sponsor trips there.[129] The Committee of Concerned Asian Scholars' visits to China were even more pathbreaking. In the summer of 1971, a CCAS-linked delegation of Hong Kong–based language students and researchers became one of the very first groups of Americans to go to the People's Republic of China since the Chinese revolution. A second contingent went the following year. URPE and Science for the People also sent delegations to China in the early seventies.[130]

A few academic radicals also went to Vietnam, though most of these people traveled as individuals and were either antiwar activists like Chomsky, Zinn, and the international law scholar Richard Falk or else left-wing scientists and physicians who could supply useful expertise.[131] The CCAS and Science for the People along with other radical groups organized book drives for Hanoi, providing up-to-date scientific and technical journals as well as medications and other supplies. CCAS members also worked with the Japanese peace movement and supported US military defectors.[132]

At the same time, these academics also educated themselves.[133] Everyone, it seemed, belonged to a study group. In almost every field, people gathered to read *Das Kapital*, as well as the latest left-wing literature.[134] When Albert Szymanski took on the editorship of *The Insurgent Sociologist*, he put out a call for "good radical reading lists. . . . Short critical reviews of bad books. . . . Short reviews of good books to inform others what's being published."[135] At the University of Texas, the radical graduate students in sociology formed the Gerrard Winstanley Memorial Caucus (named after a seventeenth-century English revolutionary), and in the aftermath of a massive student strike in May 1970, one member recalled, they "transformed the Sociology Department into one vast study group . . . . [that] debated revolutionary strategy and tactics handed down from the masters like Lenin, Trotsky, Mao, Luxemburg, Gramsci, Guevara, Ho Chi Minh, and Vo Nguyen Giap."[136]

Like good New Leftists, the academic radicals also paid attention to the personal side of their political work. The European historian Mary Nolan recalled the collectives of the Middle Atlantic Radical Historians Association as "a support network for how people would operate day to day as graduate students, as junior faculty."[137] From the start, the founders of URPE sought to "ward . . . off professional loneliness." As one of them, Samuel Bowles, explained, "If you're isolated and not within the dominant paradigm, you will get discouraged or become a crank."[138] Accordingly, the organization adopted a model pioneered by the early SDS: it held annual summer conferences at rustic camps. These legendary retreats soon attracted between three and four hundred people who came for several days of intense intellectual and political discussions along with softball, swimming, and lots and lots of music. "It was like an extended family," participants recalled, "a party" with "all these really nice, smart people talking about radical economics." They also held more formal sessions on "poverty, imperialism, economic development for poor countries" and similar topics. There were also "endless" business meetings.[139]

Radicals in other fields also recognized the value of community. Before the Committee of Concerned Asian Scholars folded in the early 1970s, it, too, held summer retreats, designed, its newsletter explained, to enable members "to exchange ideas, to make some decisions, but above all, to get to know each other better and to build solidarity away from the rush and crush of meetings in some big city." The radical sociologists seem to have had at least one such get-together.[140] And when a group of New York–based historians sought to rejuvenate the AHA's radical caucus in the early 1970s, they planned to sponsor "parties, social gatherings and outings in the country" as well as study groups and public forums. It worked. As Michael Wallace recalled, "We sure had a good time. And part of this was that music and dancing and, dare I say it, illegal substances . . . were very much part of the culture from the beginning."[141]

"THE FIELD IS TO SOME EXTENT OURS"

Radicals Rethink the Disciplines

Whether or not the American Historical Association officially condemned the war in Vietnam probably had less impact on higher education than the emergence of social history within the profession. Such was the case as well within most of the humanities and social sciences, where radical scholars not only questioned the underlying assumptions of their disciplines, but also developed new interpretations and new areas of research. They did not always succeed. Nonetheless, the radicals' scholarship as well as their broader critiques may well have constituted their movement's main contribution to American intellectual life.

Whatever their disciplines, these scholars often asked more or less the same questions and shared similar insights. They all came to view higher education and their own profession as guardians of the status quo who cloaked their collaboration with the powers that be in the mantle of "objectivity." Whether these radicals expressed that understanding in the withering polemics of Martin Nicolaus's attack on "Fat Cat Sociology" or in the more measured analyses of the literary scholars Louis Kampf, Paul Lauter, and Richard Ohmann, the indictment was the same: the academic establishment was a deeply corrupt bulwark of a predatory and duplicitous ruling class. The Sociology Liberation Movement's Nicolaus pulled no punches. He identified his fellow sociologists as "a kind of spy." They

> stand guard in the garrison and report to its masters on the movements of the occupied populace. The more adventurous sociologists

don the disguise of the people and go out to mix with the peasants in the "field," returning with books and articles that break the protective secrecy in which a subjugated population wraps itself, and make it more accessible to manipulation and control. . . .

The honored sociologist, the big-status sociologist, the jet-set sociologist, the fat-contract sociologist, the book-a-year sociologist, the sociologist who always wears the livery, the suit and tie, of his masters . . . sets the tone and the ethic of the profession, and . . . is nothing more or less than a house servant in the corporate establishment, a white intellectual Uncle Tom.[1]

For the literary radicals, their field performed a similar function within the realm of culture. An "English department's work," Ohmann explained, was "as a sorter-out of elites and domesticator of the rest."[2] Kampf and Lauter agreed. They put together a collection of essays on the politics of literature in 1970 that allowed them and their contributors to amplify their critique. As they saw it, the university and its required English courses sought to inculcate the masses of ordinary students with the high culture of the upper classes, a tactic designed "to preserve the cultural hegemony of the elite and to delegitimize" that of the working class, the marginalized, and the powerless.[3]

Radicals in political science similarly blasted their field as a "handmaiden to the counterrevolutionary reflex of America in its policies at home and abroad."[4] Anthropologists agreed. As Kathleen Gough Aberle, a leading radical, explained, anthropology was "a child of Western capitalist imperialism" whose current practitioners "are increasingly being caught up in struggles between the powers that fund them and many of the people they are wont to study." They can work for the oppressors, withdraw into triviality, or resist and face discrimination or worse.[5] The historical establishment also sided with power. "Our history has been written from elite sources and has been, naturally enough, favorable to the elite," was the way the gadfly Jesse Lemisch summed up its orientation, while revealing in detail how enthusiastically the AHA's leaders endorsed Cold War anti-communism at home and abroad.[6]

A 1973 manifesto produced by Science for the People, though directed against mainstream science, sums up the radicals' case against the entire academic profession as they urge their fellow scientists

> to understand . . . how the structure and ideology of science itself serve to perpetuate the present social and economic order. How the specialization and professionalism within science lead to fragmented and myopic thinking. How the competition and hierarchy reinforce individualism and non-collective attitudes. How the myth of scientific neutrality makes scientists the unwitting instruments of political power. How the technocratic mentality (that of scientific, nonpolitical decision making) is at best undemocratic and at worst fascistic. How the propagation of elitism and elitist attitudes serve only to deny the people power over their own lives. How the philosophy and methodology of a positivistic science, when applied to the social sciences, means only social manipulation and control.[7]

Mystification, positivism, elitism, professionalism, individualism, specialization, manipulation: these terms suffuse the rhetoric of the academic Left. Central to their indictments was their fields' refusal to abandon so-called "value-neutrality." Issues that by definition demanded moral considerations were all too often ruled out of bounds as subjects for scholarly investigation. As a result, according to the 1968 "Call to Action" of the Sociology Liberation Movement, "we have failed [to help] the poor, the powerless or the unorganized."[8]

As many radicals saw it, one reason why the academy's moderate and liberal leaders avoided controversial issues was because exploring America's internal conflicts threatened to undermine their fields' theoretical underpinnings, especially in the social sciences. During the 1950s, most of them had embraced pluralism and the end-of-ideology consensus. Formulated most cogently by Daniel Bell and Robert Dahl, it contended that the United States had essentially solved all its major social and economic problems, leaving to the realm of politics only the pluralistic process of eradicating the nation's few remaining defects by means of negotiations among legitimate interest groups.[9] The radicals rejected that interpretation. Besides its serious empirical

defects, they attacked it as giving the academic establishment an intellectually respectable justification for ignoring such supposedly "ideological" issues as racism, imperialism, and economic inequality.[10]

As the radicals saw it, an additional reason for the academic establishment's adhesion to "value-neutrality" was its fear of a political
backlash. The nation's leading scholars had all lived through the 1950s
when McCarthyism had disrupted the academy. Yet, even as the activists in the Committee of Concerned Asian Scholars acknowledged the
particularly traumatic impact of the witch hunt on their field, their
angst about Vietnam impelled them to denounce their elders' "timid
political position."[11] "What is a profession like," they asked,

> in which many of the senior men who experienced the McCarthyite
> horror, in fear of appearing un-American, assume one must play it
> safe? The result has been a frozen silence by much of the profession
> on critical issues, while a veritable deluge of Cold War studies have
> been produced to tacitly or explicitly justify American Asian policy.[12]

The scholarship in other fields was also distorted. Physicists, for
example, absorbed, perhaps unknowingly, a mindset about the apolitical nature of their field that made it possible for them to work on
weapons.[13] Philosophers, whose discipline had the highest percentage of members under attack, became reluctant to explore ethical
issues that might cause political problems. They turned instead to
the abstractions of logical positivism—"finding intellectual respectability for their political prudence," as one critic put it. "One way
to indicate that one was not a Communist, or a fellow traveler, or a
sympathizer (and so on) was to engage in a quasi-scientific pursuit
of truth."[14]

A similar drive for a more rigorous and scientific methodology
emerged among social scientists even in fields that were relatively unscathed by McCarthyism.[15] A 1955 survey of more than 2,400 social
scientists at 165 large and small institutions revealed that "teachers
avoided not only particular subjects, but also discussion of considerably broader areas, such as 'political and economic problems,' 'any
criticism of the status quo,' and 'explorations of the merits of dis-

sent.'"[16] No wonder, then, that establishment social scientists stressed the unbiased nature of their work, seeking to emulate the natural sciences by adopting their quantifiable and presumably more objective methodology.

This is not to say that McCarthyism caused the turn toward quantification. There were genuine intellectual advantages to be gained by the manipulation of large amounts of data. After all, quite a few radical economists, sociologists, political scientists, and even historians were themselves "quants." Or, as the economist Michael Meeropol explained, "one could be rigorous and mathematical and still be a Marxist."[17]

Even so, they realized, as did a number of moderate and highly respected social scientists—like Kenneth Galbraith, James Tobin, and Theodore Lowi—that the mainstream's emphasis on methodology induced researchers to focus even more narrowly on metrics at the expense of issues that resisted quantification. According to the political scientist Christian Bay, "Political scientists have worked manfully to develop their own quantifiable key concepts, but it seems that they have advanced toward increasing exactness only at the expense of increasing triviality." In fact, the field had become so obsessed with the pursuit of the quantifiable that Berkeley's department not only abandoned its program in political theory, but, as a group of radical graduate students complained, also restricted their research to statistical analyses of existing behavior, attitudes, and institutions.[18]

Economics was even more dominated by numbers. Ever since World War II, the profession had become increasingly concerned with mathematical models. As long as the Keynesianism of its leading practitioners coincided with the goals of the nation's leaders, which at that time emphasized growth and stability, it did deal with some real-world issues. But subjects that questioned that political consensus or could not be easily quantified simply disappeared from view.[19]

The Union for Radical Political Economics' Samuel Bowles recalled his perplexity when the Southern Christian Leadership Conference organizers of Martin Luther King Jr.'s Poor People's Campaign contacted him and his group of radical Harvard economists in 1968 for background information about poverty in the United States.

I looked at the questions and didn't have a clue how to answer them. I had a PhD in economics, but I didn't know where to start about inequality and moving to less inequality in general. There were questions like the suburbanization of jobs, what should be the role of compensatory education in eliminating poverty. . . . My training [in economics] was inadequate.[20]

Ultimately, Bowles and his radical colleagues reeducated themselves and their students. "Liberal Keynesian reforms were seen as inadequate responses to the severe defects of capitalist economies," Michigan's Thomas Weisskopf explained. Instead, he noted, URPE members

often analyzed phenomena that standard economic theorizing had difficulty explaining, e.g. situations where the logic of individual self-interested behavior and free-market equilibrium fails. We typically worked on issues where the functioning of a capitalist economy was found wanting, seeking to show how fundamental changes in economic and political institutions would be necessary for improving outcomes.[21]

Yet, even when they applied orthodox economic tools to questions of poverty, racism, and militarism, the URPE academics remained on the margins of their discipline. In the eyes of conventional economists (especially after the field moved to the right in the 1970s and rejected Keynes for neoliberalism), the questions the radicals raised belonged to other disciplines—political science, history, sociology, or anthropology.[22]

Unlike the radicals in other fields, the historians did not challenge the methodology of the mainstream. This may well have been, as Carl Schorske noted, because history was "such an intellectually loose discipline" that it essentially had no methodology to challenge.[23] Almost everybody—left, right, and mainstream—subscribed to a consensus about what good work was: that is, well-written narratives with coherent generalizations based on careful archival research. As a result, a moderately conservative professor like Columbia's Fritz Stern, though deploring the radical politics of one of his graduate students, could, nonetheless, successfully recommend her to his equally conservative colleagues at Harvard.[24]

Still, the radical historians had plenty of complaints. They focused on what the mainstream omitted from the field—the books not assigned, the interpretations not taught, and the subjects not studied. Marxism, working-class history—forget about it. Radicals challenged the dominant narrative of America as a benign self-correcting liberal polity by pointing to the nation's unresolved conflicts. Antiwar scholars in diplomatic history, for example, followed the trail of William Appleman Williams and brought imperialism back into the mix. Others rejected the field's traditional focus on "Great White Men," promoting instead what came to be called "history from the bottom up," an approach that granted historical agency to such under-represented populations as workers, people of color, and women.

The literary left undertook a similar mission. They viewed their "major task" as "reconstructing the canon of what is studied and taught," seeking alternatives, in other words, to the "Dead White Men" of English 101.[25] The correspondence and newsletters of literary radicals are replete with requests for and suggestions of new texts by women, Blacks, and other un- and under-represented groups.[26] Florence Howe established the Feminist Press to resuscitate the oeuvre of forgotten female writers, while other scholars put together anthologies that included the work of African American, ethnic, and working-class authors as well as women. Such a mission also countered the hierarchical ranking of literary "masterpieces" and the narrowly proscribed and apolitical approach that "removed from the range of 'legitimate' or 'important' discussion fundamental political, ideological, or cultural alternatives to bourgeois capitalism." So constricted was the canon, one former graduate student at the University of Wisconsin recalled, that "teaching assistants of Freshman Composition were under strict orders to not touch on subjects in any way relating to 'sex, religion, or politics.'"[27] The mainstream's individualistic emphasis was equally deleterious, creating obstacles to a collective attempt to create a more meaningful and just society. As Louis Kampf pointed out, "The narcissistic obsession of modern literature for the self, the critical cant concerning the tragic isolation of the individual—these are notions which tie our hands and keep us from the communion necessary for meaningful action."[28]

The radical literary scholars particularly disagreed with the New Criticism that dominated their field in the 1940s and 1950s. That approach insisted on the autonomy of the text, using the method of close reading to, in Richard Ohmann's words, "pry the words loose from their social origins." By emphasizing "irony, ambiguity, tension, and paradox," the New Critics reinforced an attitude of passivity, thus enabling readers to distance themselves from real-world problems. That many of the leading New Critics were also political conservatives did not endear them to Ohmann and his radical colleagues.[29]

Other leftists were similarly critical of their disciplines. Even before Edward Said popularized the term "orientalism," members of the Committee of Concerned Asian Scholars had identified it as their field's dominant tradition—that is, the study of Asia through Western eyes that denied its cultures and societies an identity apart from their "response to the West." These young scholars sought instead to "develop a humane and knowledgeable understanding of Asian societies and their efforts to maintain cultural integrity and to confront such problems as poverty, oppression, and imperialism."[30] To do so, they decided, it was first necessary to critique both the US relationship with Asia as well as their own field's scholarship. They organized a two-summer research seminar at Harvard that produced a collection of essays that could, in the words of its editors, Edward Friedman and Mark Selden, help "change our relation to Asia" so that "we would be open to learning much from Asian people that could help us create a more decent and just society in the United States."[31]

Radical psychologists were similarly critical of their discipline. Activists in the Psychologists for Social Action denounced the professional psychologists who worked for the military. They were also distressed by the mainstream's attempts to catalog the personality traits of student activists. For social scientists like Richard Flacks, such a project raised fears that it might exploit that research "to detect, control, and neutralize the growth of radical beliefs among American youth." In addition, as one radical psychologist noted, there was something "intellectually dishonest" about the field's medicalization of dissent and its emphasis on the "individual causes of insanity and neuroses when whole societies also acted in irrational, even insane ways."[32] By the late 1960s, these dissident psychologists were also, along with colleagues in Science for the People, speaking out against the new field of sociobiology and its proclivity for a renewed genetic determinism that could bolster racism and sexism.[33]

Professionalism and Scholarship

The academic radicals identified a common enemy in the debilitating professionalism that had distorted higher education. That professionalization, as the MLA's leftists saw it, produced "the bourgeois fragmentation of the disciplines," as well as the narrowness of their own field, its "retreat into specialization," and its unimaginative organization by "the iron laws of chronology and genre."[34] Even mainstream scholars, David Riesman most prominently, were beginning to echo these complaints (albeit for different reasons).[35] The most distressing conclusion of that analysis—at least for the radicals—was that the increased emphasis on professionalism almost inevitably led to co-optation.

So pervasive were the pressures for disciplinary professionalization that even idealists who hoped to change the world could not avoid contamination. Surveying their field, the radical sociologists David Colfax and Jack L. Roach, complained:

> Those who entered graduate school with the intention of acquiring skills to deal with *social* issues found themselves obligated instead to deal with scholastically derived *sociological* issues; those who were motivated by a sense of *social* responsibility found themselves being socialized into a coterie in which *professional* obligations claimed precedence.[36]

Sociology was not unique; graduate training was, after all, designed to turn students into professionals. To be a successful sociologist or literary critic or economist, the fledgling practitioner had to jettison his or her big dreams and instead produce a tidy, publishable project that filled a specified niche and didn't challenge the mainstream. To do otherwise, unless someone was a certified genius, invited marginalization or worse.

Accordingly, radical scholars sought to break out, to offer new approaches and wider perspectives, while creating what they hoped could become models of a more humane and socially responsible scholarship. The MLA's radicals, for example, had long been chafing under the "isolation of literary study." Besides embracing insights from outside their field, they also sought to broaden the canon, looking to sources beyond the conventional literary texts. A student of Dickens's *Hard Times*, Kampf and Lauter suggested, might profit from considering Friedrich Engels's study of the English working class.[37] At the same time, other literary scholars began to explore different forms of expression—movies, museums, and popular culture, among them.[38]

Radical economists adopted a similarly inclusive perspective. According to Thomas Weisskopf, their research "was often more interdisciplinary than that of mainstream economists, drawing on sociological, political, historical, even psychological analysis."[39] So, too, with historians. In 1973 the Middle Atlantic Radical Historians Organization (MARHO) hosted forums that offered presentations not only by left-wing historians but also by sociologists, anthropologists, literary critics, and filmmakers. Gay history, sports history, Latin American history, working-class history, not to mention the pioneering work by Immanuel Wallerstein on the world systems of the seventeenth century—all came within the purview of the radical historians.[40]

Moreover, as E. P. Thompson's multiple appearances at MARHO forums indicated, the academic Left welcomed contacts with likeminded intellectuals from abroad. It would be hard to overestimate the importance of European Marxists on the development of radical thought within the American academy. When, for example, MARHO published a collection of interviews with leading left historians, onethird of the interviewees were Europeans.[41]

Thompson was especially influential. As simultaneously a pathbreaking historian, an activist, and a Marxist, Thompson was a triple role model for the young radicals who were looking for intellectual and political mentors. In the early 1970s, as the Vietnam War wound down and the New Left imploded, many academic rebels began to leave the streets for the library. They hunkered down on their campuses and tried to understand what was happening. Dissatisfied with mainstream scholarship, they began to explore Marxism. They did not find much American work. During the 1950s and early 1960s, Marxism had been pushed out of the academy that treated it, Harvard's John Womack explained, with "about as much respect from teachers and students as astrology."[42] In response, graduate students and young faculty members in disciplines ranging from literature to economics felt compelled to educate themselves. As one MARHO activist recalled, "Marxist study groups are all over the place among this set of people in the early to mid-'70s." They read *Das Kapital*, as well as the current, usually European, Marxist literature.[43]

Of course, not all of this Marxism was necessarily sophisticated. There was some posturing and sectarianism, identified by the sociologist David Colfax as the uncritical acceptance of "a largely spurious, ahistorical, and uncritical Marxism . . . reminiscent of those of earlier decades when sloganeering and textual exegesis displaced analysis and practices." Most of the serious new Marxist and *marxisante* scholars, while jettisoning the traditional faith in the preordained triumph of a working-class revolution, found, Colfax explained, "a Marxist class-analysis of contemporary society holds the greatest promise for the transformation of sociological and social consciousness."[44]

Radical economists employed Marx's insights. Admittedly, most rejected the orthodox Marxism that relied upon the labor theory of value and the inevitable collapse of capitalism. Instead, as URPE's Thomas Weisskopf explained:

More of us saw ourselves as "neo-Marxian," drawing somewhat eclectically on Marx's political and philosophical writings for an overall framework in which to analyze capitalist and alternative economic systems, and making use of mainstream economic tools as well as insights from Marx and later Marxist social scientists and philosophers. We rejected orthodox Marxism and were influenced as much by Marx's work on alienation as by his work on the economics of capitalism.

At the same time, however, Weisskopf and his URPE colleagues were definitely radical.

> All of us sought to draw a sharp line between the approach of radical economists and that of liberal as well as conservative mainstream economists. Liberal Keynesian reforms were seen as inadequate responses to the severe defects of capitalist economies; such "non-revolutionary reforms" were to be rejected in favor of "revolutionary reforms," if not revolution itself.[45]

Red or Expert? The Radicals' Dilemma

And revolution was in the air. More and more activists increasingly embraced the notion that the capitalist system was so defective that no amount of tinkering could produce a just and humane society. Ultimately, it would have to be replaced.[46] At the same time, most of them also realized that such an eventuality was far in the future. The dilemma they faced, thus, was how to pursue their revolutionary goals while still maintaining their foothold within the decidedly non-revolutionary institutions of higher education. Obviously, if the revolution was imminent, then, as one sociologist noted, "the lectern is the wrong barricade to be behind." But for the long haul, they would have to find some way to reconcile their political activism with their academic work.[47]

As the CCAS's Orville Schell put it, any attempt to meld movement work and an academic career created "a severe case of schizophrenia: one's life becomes divided between two essential human functions, namely thinking and acting."[48] Attempts to bridge that divide not only led to serious psychological and moral dilemmas for individuals, but also tore more than a few organizations apart. Since some activists came to consider academic life, by definition, antithetical to serious political work, even working within the radical caucuses or pursuing radical scholarship could be viewed as an insufficient commitment to the cause . . . or worse. As one particularly militant sociologist put it, bourgeois radical scholarship "can legitimate reactionary modes of intellectual involvement in the name of radicalism."[49]

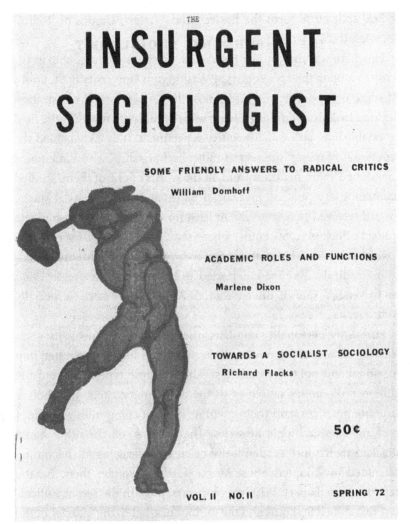

FIGURE 15.1. *The Insurgent Sociologist* (Spring 1972), now *Critical Sociology.* © Courtesy of the Tamiment Library, New York University.

Radical sociologists, perhaps because of their direct engagement with the nation's social problems, seemed particularly prone to agonizing over their personal politics, as seen in early issues of *The Insurgent Sociologist.*[50] Should sociologists try to transform their field, or simply drop out and join the working class?[51] The Sociology Liberation Movement actually splintered within a year of its formation when a number of younger scholars who considered it insufficiently radical split off to form the Eastern and Western Unions of Radical Sociologists.[52]

Nowhere was the conflict between activism and scholarship as intense as among the sociologists at Washington University in St. Louis. At some point during the mid-1960s, the university's administration decided to cash in on the growing wave of radicalism within the field by establishing an explicitly leftist department. It quickly gained the reputation of being "the seat of radical scholarship" whose members abandoned value-neutrality and, in the words of one of them, studied "contemporary political and social issues and took a critical stance toward received perspectives." At least for a while, left-wing graduate students flocked to St. Louis, where they gained power over faculty appointments and hired about half a dozen of their field's most fiery young radicals. "We were expected to be original, imaginative and controversial," one of them recalled. And so they were—especially controversial.[53]

Fueled by personality conflicts, the Washington University sociologists' debates about politics and scholarship soon degenerated into "personal and political vendettas." The scholarly types criticized the militants' disruptive activities in the community, their unorthodox teaching practices, and their attempts to form communes and adopt working-class or hippie lifestyles. The activists, on the other hand, attacked their more academically oriented colleagues for becoming "alienated and coopted 'house Marxist[s].'" No wonder, then, that the department fell apart. Within a few years, most of the senior radicals had abandoned St. Louis and the junior ones, left to the mercies of the traditional sociologists who remained, were all kicked out.[54]

Similar, though less lethal, struggles wracked the Committee of Concerned Asian Scholars. Formed explicitly to advance the larger campaign against the conflict in Southeast Asia, the CCAS was above all an antiwar group, even as it attacked the Asian studies establishment's failure to oppose the Vietnam War and its hostile treatment of the Chinese revolution. Like the other radical academics, the group exhibited some of the ideological turbulence that characterized the late New Left. "Vietnam," Marilyn Young recalled, "was making us crazy." They were also influenced by the hyper-egalitarianism of the Cultural

Revolution in China that some of them viewed as an inspiration of sorts. Thus, for example, Mark Selden questioned the group's name. For its members to call themselves "scholars," he thought, smacked of elitism. In a like vein, when a group of CCAS graduate students published an antiwar collection of essays, *The Indochina Story: A Fully Documented Account*, they did so anonymously.[55]

The CCAS's radicals also organized a quixotic campaign to boycott the Asian studies establishment and the foundations and government agencies that funded it. Even Young ran afoul of the group's demand for purity. She had delivered a paper at the 1970 Association for Asian Studies annual conference—and was criticized for doing so. A few years later, she was again under attack for participating in a conference on women in China sponsored by the Social Science Research Council. Since just about every promising Asian scholar had received support from a foundation or government agency, the boycott was about as unrealistic a political tactic as could be imagined.[56]

Such conflicts occurred among the radical economists as well. "What bothered me about URPE," one member recalled, "was arguments about whether you were more Marxist than others, which meant you were more radical, so we had debates about what Marxists were and what was more Marxist."[57] Perhaps because of URPE's particularly tolerant political culture, these sometimes ferocious disagreements did not pull the organization apart.

But other radical caucuses had more trouble. Some of Science for the People's most militant activists split off after demanding that the organization turn itself into a Leninist organization led by members of the working class.[58] Similar sectarian pressures emerged within Columbia's New University Conference chapter, where the Progressive Labor Party tried to encourage it to organize workers at General Electric.[59] At the same time, the appeal of the counterculture also diverted people from serious political activities. Louis Kampf recalls his disenchantment at an NUC summer workshop that seemed more focused on personal liberation via drugs, alcohol, and "screwing around," than radical politics.[60]

And, as within the NUC, the burgeoning women's liberation movement created conflicts within the caucus movement.[61] "We wanted to inject gender into URPE," Heidi Hartmann, one of that organization's leading feminists, explained. After the group ignored the demands of its Women's Caucus for greater representation within the leadership, the women marched out. The men capitulated, going so far as to rule that at URPE meetings and panels, chairs had to call on a woman or person of color after every time a white male spoke. But tensions over "white male privilege" never fully disappeared.[62] Radical female sociologists encountered similar sexism. Quite a few of their male colleagues were overtly hostile to feminism. Not only did they consider it a "bourgeois deviation," but they also refused to publish pro-feminist pieces.[63]

Nor were the radical feminists themselves unified. By the early 1970s, as the movement grew and struggled to gain a foothold within the academy, it also began to splinter.[64] On one side were what Marlene Dixon called the "wildcats" who were anti-male, and on the other were the leftists who viewed the wildcats "as hopelessly a-political and counterrevolutionary."[65] Left-wing academic feminists struggled to balance their commitment to the women's liberation movement with their embrace of political radicalism.[66] The historian Renate Bridenthal, for example, had assumed that her original Marxist-feminist group would do a class analysis of gender, but instead it ended up delving into its members' own family histories. In response, she and a few others formed their own reading group. But for a while, she coped with the conflict by "running from the radical caucus to the women's caucus."[67] And when the academic Left took its scholarly turn by the mid-1970s, she ended up collaborating on a pioneering volume of essays for the new field of women's history.[68]

Not surprisingly, since so many of the founders of women's studies came out of the radical academic world, much of the structure and content of the field reflected the concerns of faculty radicals in other areas. Like their male colleagues, these feminist academics questioned objectivity as a constructed and ideological concept. After all, their goal, as one historian put it, "was not merely to study women's position in the world but to change it." Despite the skepticism and hostility of senior male professors, the enormous student demand for courses on women's issues encouraged administrations and foundations to provide resources for the new field.[69] But it took decades.

Student demand also brought Black studies onto the campus. Its most radical academic proponents faced problems that were both similar to and wildly different from those confronting the pioneers of women's studies. Like the academic feminists, they represented a broader movement. Many were Black Power activists who sought to develop strong ties to the African American community. For the field's most radical practitioners, assimilation was no longer acceptable. "Integration has traditionally meant that blacks should try to be like whites," the sociologist Charles Hamilton asserted. "It has implied that black people were being done a favor by whites. This is what the black students are rejecting, and they believe that the institutions of higher learning have been and are insensitive to this."[70] Instead, these students and their faculty mentors sought programs specifically designed to promote political and cultural autonomy. In a proposal submitted to a Carnegie Foundation–funded survey in the early 1970s, the anonymous author was quite explicit about the program's political function: "It will provide the educational resources for the positive maintenance of a black family, and the eventual building of a black nation."[71]

The militant students and their faculty mentors also called for Black teachers for the Black studies courses. They simply did not believe that even the most well-meaning white academics, with only a tiny handful of exceptions, were sufficiently knowledgeable about, let alone attuned to, the Black American experience to provide relevant instruction. Though the feminist academics of the late 1960s had to create their field from scratch, well-trained Black scholars like Lawrence Reddick and St. Clair Drake had been doing high-quality research for decades, only to be ignored by an obtuse and bigoted white establishment. No wonder then, as the Spelman historian Vincent Harding explained in 1968, the student protesters were unwilling to "submit their Black Studies programs to the wisdom of the faculties. They know that these are the same faculties who had never heard of Horace Mann Bond, Charles W. Chestnutt, Martin Delany, or Charlie

Parker five years ago, who never thought the black experience was worth one course three years ago."[72]

Such demands, including some for separate sections for Black students, encountered immediate opposition, especially within the faculties of majority-white institutions. Not only would this restore segregation, they argued, but, by bringing in poorly trained instructors simply because of their race, they would also undermine the quality of the faculty. The mainstream Black scholars who had long worked within the integrationist paradigm also opposed what they saw as the separatist thrust of the radical Black activists. Not only would it divert promising young Black men and women from the struggle for equal rights, but, they insisted, it would exemplify all the racial stereotypes about the inferiority of African Americans. The eminent sociologist Kenneth Clark was so upset by the development of a separate Black studies program at Antioch College that he resigned from its board of directors. "To encourage or endorse a separate black program not academically equivalent to the college curriculum generally," Clark explained, "indeed, to endorse any such program is to reinforce the Negro's inability to compete with whites for the real power of the real world."[73]

Despite such determined opposition, hundreds of Black studies programs were created, often with foundation funding and the support of top administrators who hoped they would pacify their campuses. But once the threat of a Black student uprising evaporated and a backlash gained steam, the foundations moved on, leaving most of those Black studies programs in the lurch. Within a few years, the faculty members who staffed the remaining programs adapted to the status quo, behaving more as conventional academics than community activists. Like the feminists who developed women's studies, they had been co-opted. Yet Black studies, like women's studies, remained as a not entirely symbolic outpost of the initial movement for social change. Ultimately, its eventual legitimation did, in fact, make it possible for future generations of scholars in the field to transform the curricula and research agendas of the academic mainstream in significant ways, even if they could not achieve the liberatory goals of the 1960s radicals.[74]

Co-optation, Decline, and Impact

The difficulties that the young radical scholars encountered increased by the end of the sixties. To begin with, they were getting older. No longer did they have the time or energy to devote themselves as fully as they once had to the movement. This was especially the case because the demands of the academy had increased. For the first time since the late 1950s, financial constraints curtailed the expansion of American higher education. No longer could graduate students assume that they would be able to choose between several job offers. There were not enough academic positions to go around. In addition, tenure was no longer a sure thing. Junior faculty members would have to pay serious attention to their research if they wanted to remain academically employed.

Radicals were particularly vulnerable within this newly straitened landscape. They all too often lost their jobs for political reasons and sometimes could not find another. For those radicals already disillusioned with academic life, these pressures reinforced a decision to drop out. Many, if not most, were probably the victims of covert political purges, but even people with secure positions left the university.[75]

The sociologist and NUC activist Howard Ehrlich was one of the latter. By his own account, he was "a model young professional" at the University of Iowa who "published two books and placed articles in all the right journals." He had "tenure, a light teaching load, a good salary, graduate research fellows and assistants, even a part-time secretary." But as he became increasingly alienated by his university's collaboration with the war machine, he explained:

> I became an insurgent sociologist organizing students and faculty for the coming revolution. I felt that I could no longer comfortably pursue a professional career. I traded in my three-piece tweed suit for drawstring pants. They may have both been uniforms, but certainly my new one was more comfortable. By the time I left the university my hair was down to my shoulder blades and I carried a bag on my shoulder, usually filled with leaflets and posters and paraphernalia to hang them.

When political opposition almost blocked his promotion to full professor in 1971, Ehrlich decided to leave the academy. His colleagues thought he was crazy. He moved to Baltimore, where he and a few associates established an independent research center to provide sociological expertise to movement activists. He published pamphlets as well as scholarly articles and soon broadened his activities to include a program on National Public Radio, a peer-reviewed academic journal *Social Anarchism*, and an alternative adult school.[76]

Some CCAS activists also left academic life. For several years, the former student of John Fairbank Tom Englehardt had been urging his comrades to give up academic careers. Along with Jim Peck and Orville Schell, he abandoned his graduate work to collaborate with Franz Schurmann in a short-lived independent research center.[77] Englehardt and Peck then signed on as editors at Pantheon Books, André Schiffrin's left-wing publishing house. Schell became a journalist, ultimately returning to the academy many years later as the dean of Berkeley's School of Journalism. Other CCAS people switched into different fields or abandoned higher education altogether.

Radical scientists followed a somewhat different trajectory. In 1969, James Shapiro—who along with Jonathan Beckwith and another colleague were the first biologists to isolate a gene—announced during an interview with Barbara Walters on the *Today* show:

> I am dropping out of science because it is simply being exploited by the people who run this country to serve their own ends. To work in a laboratory is futile at the present time. The only useful mode of life I can imagine now is to challenge the present political system.

He went to Cuba to teach science for two years before becoming disillusioned with that system. He returned to the United States and, abandoning politics, joined the University of Chicago. Other Science for the People activists dropped out of academic life to take blue-collar jobs.[78]

The Brooklyn College psychologist Bill Zimmerman also left higher education. He experienced "the defining moral crisis of my life" when he and his colleague Bart Meyers got a request for reprints of their articles about psychopharmacology from scientists at Fort Detrick, the army's main chemical and biological warfare laboratory. Unwilling to allow their research to be used by the military, the two activists agonized for months before deciding to give up research altogether. They publicized their decision, urging other like-minded scientists to take the same step. Meyers gave back his grants and closed his laboratory. Zimmerman, who unlike Meyers did not have tenure, decided to abandon the academy to become a full-time political organizer. His first job: running the Boston chapter of Science for the People.[79]

Other radicals seem to have given up or dropped out for a variety of reasons, burnout included. The chaos that swirled around the disintegration of the New Left after 1969 alienated even someone as stalwart as Staughton Lynd, who simply could not bring himself to call policemen "pigs."[80] By 1970, Charles Haynie, then at SUNY Buffalo, also found himself so estranged by the "rapidly spreading macho male model," of the splintering movement, its drugs and rhetorical embrace of violence, that he simply withdrew.[81] Others embraced the counterculture. One of Beckwith's top postdoctoral students, for example, turned down an assistant professorship at Harvard, changed his name to Sundance, and went to live in a tepee in Northern California. A few people left the country, some to avoid the draft in Canada and others emigrating to more hospitable venues.[82]

The most common response, however, was to focus more intensively on the academic side of the scholar/activist dichotomy. As campuses quieted down after the massive protests against the invasion of Cambodia and the Kent State shootings in the spring of 1970, faculty activism petered out as well. Many members of the radical caucuses retreated to their libraries and offices.[83] And began to write. As a result, in the 1970s, radical scholarship took root.[84] Its impact on the different disciplines varied, greater in fields like sociology and literary studies, less so in political science and psychology.

In history, their work was often absorbed into the mainstream. The social history that the Marxists pioneered flowered. Dissertations in women's, Black, working-class, and ethnic history quadrupled between 1958 and 1978.[85] In fact, radical historians had become so respectable that three of them—Eugene Genovese, William Appleman

Williams, and the feminist Gerda Lerner—eventually served as presidents of the Organization of American Historians. Its publication, the *Journal of American History*, not only published radical scholarship, but it also borrowed MARHO's "notion of reviewing films and museum exhibits and stuff like that" and moved such innovations into the mainstream.[86] Still, as Peter Novick noted, the radicals did lose their political edge and, except in a few areas, like labor history, were never to set the agendas of their discipline.[87]

That was not the case with sociology. As Richard Flacks noted in retrospect, "The field is to some extent ours." Expecting to be purged, they found themselves

> coopted into leadership roles in the ASA, . . . [and] the perspectives we passionately contrasted with the established paradigms would soon become dominant rather than underground. Even more ironically, what we could not have foreseen was that the achievement of many of our hopes would be possible without the transformation of either the society or the university.

"What we lost," Flacks lamented, was the "hope for a community of radical intellectuals engaged in a collective effort to remake sociology so that it might begin to be a vehicle of human enlightenment."[88]

There was a similarly disconcerting element in the intellectual success of the MLA's radicals—at least for them. Although their demands for the inclusivity and their espousal of interdisciplinarity were taken up by the establishment, the political thrust of their efforts got lost in the postmodern turn that had originally built upon their movement. Ostensibly progressive European theories replaced New Criticism's focus on isolated texts. But their incomprehensibility served only to intensify the depoliticization and narrow professionalization of the field, just at a moment when, due to systemic economic change, the role of literature and the humanities within higher education was about to shrink.[89] According to the anthropologist Leith Mullings, the same kind of transformation occurred in her field when "poststructuralism undercut the activism and critical edge that developed with the emphasis on political economy" among the radicals during the late 1960s and 1970s.[90]

It is hard to generalize about the impact of the radical academics on their disciplines. Political turmoil within American society was already forcing the academic community to reform itself. It is unlikely that the American Political Science Association jettisoned its refusal to deal with current political and social problems as a response to the hardly radical demands of the Caucus for a New Political Science. After all, even the nation's leading political scientists recognized that their field's pluralist ideology could not account for what was going on both on and off the campus. However, such a realization did not empower the field's small and marginalized cohort of leftists.

Nor, despite URPE's organizational stability and intellectual achievements, did its scholarship make much of an impact as the field of economics turned to the right under the influence of neoliberalism during the 1970s and '80s. The radicals' work had a greater impact on sociologists than on their colleagues. Even now, as some mainstream economists have taken up the issues of "social injustice, inequality, discrimination, market failure, and economic crisis," that research did not, Thomas Weisskopf admitted, "draw much on contributions by radical economists."[91]

So, as we assess the impact of the academic Left, we find a mixed picture. There was opposition and repression, but there was also acceptance and co-optation. There were reforms. Faculty hiring practices changed. Radicals got their scholarship published. A few departments—sociology at Washington University, the University of California, Santa Barbara, and Livingston College at Rutgers; history at Wisconsin, Rochester, and Northern Illinois; and economics at the University of Massachusetts and the New School, as well as the Braudel Center at SUNY Binghamton—housed significant concentrations of radicals, at least for a while. New and overlooked areas of concern developed in women's and Black studies, as well as the subfield of science, technology, and society.[92] And some individual leftists even made it to the top of their disciplines.

Nonetheless, the radicals' dream of a liberated university that would somehow contribute to the remaking of American society did not materialize. Though professors were more liberal than the rest of society, they did not want to make radical changes in their profession. The culture of academe, like that of the rest of the nation, was too bound up in the struggle for individual advancement to give alternative visions a chance. And without a strong social movement in the rest of society to press for radical change, the efforts of the left-wing academics of the 1960s and early 1970s to revolutionize higher education were doomed to fail.

16

"CAUSE FOR CONCERN"

*Violations of Academic Freedom during
the Late Sixties and Early Seventies*

We don't know exactly how many men and women were dismissed or otherwise penalized for political reasons during the 1960s and early 1970s. No official tally exists. The AAUP did not publicize every complaint the organization received and only issued reports on about fifty political violations of academic freedom between 1960 and 1974.[1] But even a cursory glance reveals many more such cases. One study claims (without documentation, alas) that about 160 college teachers faced sanctions for political reasons during the 1960s and early 1970s, one-third were fired, the rest suffered other forms of punishment.[2] But that figure seems low, since it may not include the thirty or so people fired or denied tenure as a result of the faculty strike at San Francisco State or those faculty radicals who, having little faith in what they considered the academic community's bourgeois procedures, did not lodge formal complaints with the AAUP or their own institutions. Finally, it probably does not account for all the men and women who, recognizing that they were politically unacceptable at their institutions, took the hint, found other positions, and did not protest or publicize their departure.[3]

Significantly, however, only a few of the young radicals who lost their jobs during those turbulent times were explicitly fired for political reasons. The rest could not prove that their troubles stemmed from their unorthodox politics or unconventional lifestyles. If they were given a reason, it was almost always an ostensibly professional one. Whether it was poor teaching, inadequate research, insufficient progress on their dissertations, or simply that "we can find somebody better," it was easy to craft an academic justification for a negative personnel decision.[4] In fact, as an American Economic Association committee pointed out:

> It must be candidly said that if political factors did enter, say in evaluation of research or of teaching, it would require only the slightest skill on the part of administrators or departments to conceal the fact. Indeed it might require no skill at all because the factors may well be operating at an unconscious level.[5]

Moreover, not all of the denials of tenure and non-reappointments of left-wing activists were bogus. After all, not every radical was a competent teacher or productive scholar. As a result, the historical record is messy. Still, it seems clear that it was not uncommon for institutions to divest themselves of their most politically unorthodox faculty members. However, because of the expansion of higher education and its concomitant demand for warm bodies with graduate training, it was possible for radical faculty members to remain employed within the academic community even if they had been fired for disruptive behavior.[6]

Thus, for example, when the historian M. L. Michael Kay was summarily sacked in 1968 for participating in an anti-ROTC demonstration at Alfred University in upstate New York, he got another job at West Chester State College in Pennsylvania. A year later, he was severed from that institution ostensibly because he had not told the authorities there about his earlier troubles at Alfred. Then, even after being explicitly not hired at Western Illinois University for the same reason, he still managed to find yet another academic job.[7] The Tulane University mathematician Edward Dubinsky, also fired for disrupting an ROTC ceremony, went to Canada for a year and then took a series of temporary jobs before he, too, found a permanent position—albeit, as was often the case, at a less prestigious institution.[8]

Of Gadflies and Blacklists

A few people were, in fact, forced out of academic life, but they were among the profession's squeakiest wheels, incendiary radicals who viewed themselves more as revolutionaries than scholars and teachers. Though some voluntarily abandoned their academic careers after they were fired, others encountered rejection after rejection.[9] The cases of political scientist Michael Parenti, the literary scholar Bruce Franklin, and the historian Staughton Lynd indicate the boundaries of acceptability within the academic world. No matter how talented—all three had major-league credentials and were considered gifted teachers and scholars—professors who advocated civil disobedience, participated in unruly student demonstrations, and openly defied the norms of academic life could expect trouble.

Parenti had the hardest time. A dedicated Marxist, he was a visiting associate professor at the main campus of the University of Illinois. In the spring of 1970, Parenti supported the students' attacks on the university's complicity with the war machine. A fiery speaker, he was a fixture at protests and was already considered a troublemaker before he called for a campus strike at a mass rally the day after the Kent State killings. Disorders broke out the next day, especially after a garbage truck began to back into a student demonstration. As Parenti and others argued with the authorities about the incident, several dozen local police and highway patrolmen charged the crowd. They zeroed in on Parenti, beating him so badly that he needed a dozen stitches. Then they arrested him, for the "aggravated battery" of a state trooper and more. At his trial in October, a hostile judge blamed him for the campus unrest. He then sentenced the rather small political scientist to two years' probation, a fine of $250, and court costs for the unlikely crime of assaulting a large and well-protected officer of the law.[10]

The academic community meted out a more serious punishment. Parenti had been hired by the University of Vermont a few months before his arrest. Although the university's entire academic establishment, from the political science department on up to, and including, the president, strongly supported the renewal of his contract, the trustees rejected it. It was, they claimed, necessary "to protect the image of the university." A blacklist followed. Parenti recalled:

Despite the fact that I had by then published four books and some 50 articles, including ones in the leading political science and sociology journals, and had a Ph.D. from Yale, glowing recommendations from two former presidents of the American Political Science Association and from other leading members of the profession, and top evaluations as a classroom teacher, I repeatedly was passed over for less qualified, but politically safer and politically inactive candidates at scores of colleges and universities to which I applied. Time and again I heard from sympathetic political scientists who were privy to recruitment procedures in their departments that I was rejected because of my leftist views and political activism. In several instances, when a particular department manifested interest in making an offer, my candidacy was squelched by administrators.[11]

With the exception of a two-year stint at SUNY Albany and a few one-year gigs, Parenti was never again to hold a full-time academic job. He managed to support himself as a public intellectual, giving speeches and writing popular texts for left-wing publishers and journals.[12]

Unlike Parenti, Bruce Franklin did find academic employment after his dismissal from Stanford—but not until he spent several years in purgatory as the only tenured professor to have been fired for his politics from a major research university. He had been something of a golden boy at Stanford, but by the time he was fired, Franklin was by far the most notorious radical on the faculty. Equally militant off campus, he was active in a variety of San Francisco Bay Area Maoist and multiracial revolutionary outfits that, among other things, emulated the Black Panthers' espousal of "urban guerrilla war" and "armed self-defense" against the repressive forces of the state. He also belonged to the New University Conference (NUC), playing a conspicuous role in the events at the Modern Language Association's meeting in 1968.[13]

In early 1971, after an unruly confrontation at the computer center, Stanford's president Richard Lyman decided the incendiary English professor had to go. His "incitement" of student disruptions had become, Lyman believed, a serious threat to the institution.[14] Surprisingly, Franklin took the university's judicial proceedings seriously. On January 21, 1971, he wrote to Lyman, whom he called "the Chief Designated Agent of the Board of Trustees of Leland Stanford Junior University, Heirs of the Family Who Stole this Land and the Labor of those Who Built their Railroad, War Profiteers and Rulers of the U.S.

Empire," demanding "as public a hearing and as close to a semblance to a fair trial as I can get." And he got it. For six weeks, an elected faculty committee heard from a hundred people, as Franklin, acting as his own lawyer, cross-examined witnesses, while contesting the university's procedural lapses.[15]

One of the main reasons why the committee voted 5–2 to recommend dismissal was the conviction that Franklin was too committed a revolutionary to ever be "rehabilitated." The ousted literary scholar fought back. Not only did he appeal the decision through the university's procedures, but, assisted by the Northern California branch of the ACLU, two Stanford law professors, and the then-liberal Alan Dershowitz, he also went to court, charging the university with violating his First Amendment rights.[16]

It took eight years until the appeals process finally wound down, during some of which time Franklin was confronting a blacklist. He had, he recalled, "applied to almost every department in the country," receiving form letters or silence in reply. Occasionally he would be offered jobs, only to have them disappear when the higher authorities vetoed them. Eventually an Old Left professor, who had kept his head down for years, became chair of the English department at Rutgers-Newark and deployed his accumulated academic capital to bring Franklin onto the faculty as a full professor.[17]

The equally charismatic and uncompromising antiwar activist Staughton Lynd had no such luck. A promising early American historian, Lynd had joined the faculty at Yale in 1964 after leaving Atlanta's Spelman College to protest the firing of his colleague and comrade Howard Zinn. Although the equally radical Zinn had managed to land a tenured position at Boston University, Lynd was not reappointed at Yale.

Whether or not he could have remained at such a selective institution as Yale, where junior faculty members did not automatically get tenure, the university was, in Lynd's words, "beginning to lose its enthusiasm for me." His highly publicized trip to Hanoi with Herbert Aptheker in December 1965 produced such a storm of alumni protest that President Kingman Brewster felt compelled to denounce it as giving "aid and comfort to a government engaged in hostilities with

American forces."[18] Officially advised by his chair a few months later that his appointment would probably be terminal, Lynd spent the following academic year of 1966–67 as a visiting professor at Roosevelt University while unsuccessfully looking for a faculty position in the Chicago area.[19]

The history departments at both the University of Illinois at Chicago Circle and Northern Illinois University voted unanimously to hire Lynd, only to be overruled by their administrations. Finally, in late April 1967, he got an "official offer" from the dean of Chicago State College. But Illinois's Board of Governors of State Colleges and Universities refused to honor that commitment. "We in no way quarreled with Dr. Lynd's right to dissent," a board member explained. "But he went beyond dissent—engaging in and supporting unlawful activity." Worse yet, another trustee pointed out, his "unhealthy" views "might indirectly influence students."[20]

Lynd pressed the AAUP and its Committee A on Academic Freedom and Tenure to open an official investigation.[21] But the organization kept putting him off.[22] Meanwhile, a group of Chicago-area historians circulated a statement of support for Lynd signed by dozens of eminent academics and others—Arthur Schlesinger Jr., Martin Luther King Jr., Henry Steele Commager, Norman Thomas, Irving Howe, Richard Hofstadter, David Riesman, Daniel Berrigan, and C. Vann Woodward among them.[23]

Nothing worked. While Lynd sued Chicago State, AAUP staff members claimed that they were authorizing an investigation, but warned Lynd and his supporters not to discuss it publicly. They cited the technical difficulties presented by a case of non-appointment, rather than outright dismissal, as well as their own qualms about opening an investigation while a lawsuit was in progress.[24] No investigation ensued. The following year, after the president of Roosevelt University refused to let the history department hire Lynd, he and his supporters again pressed the AAUP for a formal investigation. Instead, the organization sent a contingent of "consultants"—not an official investigating committee. Though admitting that Roosevelt's president "should have accepted the judgment of the History Department and the Dean of the College of Arts and Sciences in the matter of Professor

FIGURE 16.1. Resistance rally on Boston Common, April 3, 1968; Staughton Lynd speaking, Noam Chomsky (*second from right*) waiting onstage. © Peter Simon Collection, Special Collections and University Archives, University of Massachusetts Amherst Libraries.

Lynd's fitness," the AAUP's representatives did not recommend further action. Along with some staff members, they believed that the Roosevelt president's reservations about Lynd's "judgment" did not provide enough evidence "beyond a reasonable doubt" of a violation of academic freedom.[25]

Shocked, Lynd and his supporters refused to drop the case.[26] Finally, in the beginning of 1970, the AAUP's staff presented the case to the organization's National Council and its Committee A on Academic Freedom and Tenure. But since both groups were as seriously divided about the dissident historian as the staff had been, there was to be no investigation. In a letter informing Lynd's most energetic champion that he believed "the file on Professor Lynd's case should be closed," the AAUP's general secretary noted in early July 1970, "I know of no other case during my years with the Association in which the question of investigation has been so exhaustively considered. . . . Out of all this consideration, plus that of the staff, has come no firm consensus in favor of investigation."[27] By then, Lynd had given up his academic job hunt and entered law school.

"Atrocity of the Week": Firing Activists in the Sixties

The travails of Parenti, Franklin, and Lynd got national attention. Those of less well-known individuals at second- and third-tier schools did not. The activities that led to an overtly political dismissal varied considerably, depending not only on the activities but also on the type of institution and its political culture. Not surprisingly, those academic dissenters who transgressed the boundaries between speech and actions encountered severe consequences. Participation in the forms of civil disobedience that led to sanctions against undergraduates and graduate students could end a junior faculty member's career. Robert Wolfe, for example, never got back on the tenure track after he was arrested, convicted, and sent to prison for taking over the New York University computer in the spring of 1970. Along with a group of SDS students, Wolfe, a self-identified revolutionary and assistant professor of European history, had not only invaded the building housing the computer, but had also carried in some homemade napalm and threatened to ignite it if NYU did not fork over $100,000 for the Black Panthers' defense fund.[28] While Wolfe (who did later get some adjunct appointments) may have been the most extreme faculty dissident of that turbulent era, dozens of others were arrested for participating in building occupations and similar acts of civil disobedience—and often experienced academic repercussions.[29]

Jack Stauder at Harvard was one of them. The young anthropologist was already notorious for sponsoring a controversial SDS-led experimental course, "Radical Perspectives on Social Change," even before he became one of the very few faculty members arrested during the occupation of University Hall in 1969. Although he had not played a major role in the action, Stauder was grilled by a special committee of trustees and professors, barred from teaching for a semester, demoted from lecturer to instructor, and handed a serious pay cut. He also did not get his contract renewed, but since so few junior faculty members at Harvard made it to tenure, this was no surprise. In any event, he soon found another job.[30]

A similar case involved the "Faculty Four" at the University of Connecticut. Sociologists David Colfax, John Leggett, and Jack Roach plus Charles Brover of the English department were among the most radical members of the faculty. After their arrests during a student protest against a Dow Chemical Company recruiter in October 1968, the university began disciplinary proceedings against them. A month later, Colfax and Roach were arrested at another antiwar demonstration. The trustees put the four on probation, while alerting Leggett and, later, Brover to the prospect that they would not be reappointed. Although Colfax was recommended for tenure by his department, he, too, was nixed by the trustees. He then returned to Washington University, from which he had taken a leave of absence to teach at UConn. When he was denied tenure there as well, he left the academy. As for Roach, who did have tenure, and who had apparently scandalized the locals by giving state troopers the finger during the November melee, the authorities obtained an injunction specifically preventing him from taking over buildings or "making noise or commotion calculated to disrupt, impede, or impair lawful activities on University premises . . . or encouraging others to do" the same. He remained at UConn and, with the help of the ACLU, was able to quash the injunction on First Amendment grounds.[31]

Less radical dissenters at smaller, less turbulent institutions could also lose their jobs if they drew unwanted attention. Luis Serron, a tenured assistant professor of sociology at East Tennessee State University, for example, was fired because he participated in the local observance of the national Moratorium to End the War in Vietnam on October 15, 1969, and was misquoted in the local newspaper as endorsing a Vietcong victory. Even the governor called for action against Serron. The administration dismissed him for "insubordination." Because of the moratorium, he had failed to attend his department's regular faculty meeting, missing a discussion about buying a coffee pot and raising money for the United Fund. Even the AAUP was shocked. It investigated the case and censured the university.[32]

The AAUP was equally shocked by Indiana State University's treatment of Scott Chisholm. Chisholm had been warned by the administration in March 1967 that he would probably not get tenure because his unorthodox teaching methods and the profanity in some of his reading assignments had caused "embarrassment" to the university.

A month later, during a class discussion about "symbolic language," Chisholm burned an American flag. The conflagration spread quickly as parents, the local press, veterans' groups, and the area's congressman demanded action—and got it. The administration suspended the controversial writing instructor. A faculty committee investigated, declared that Chisholm had been "unprofessional," and recommended a reprimand. Instead, the president and board of trustees fired him. The AAUP again voted to censure the institution.[33]

It also censured Ohio State for dismissing David Green, a popular first-year assistant professor of American history. On the day after Martin Luther King Jr. was killed, Green devoted an entire class to discussing the assassination and then burned his draft card. At first the authorities held back; they already had their hands full with the university's militant Black students. Still, Green had violated federal law; although the dean did not think it merited dismissal, he was considering some kind of scolding and a salary freeze. A committee of senior professors criticized Green's "serious lack of judgment," and recommended censure and probation. But the president, under pressure from the trustees, planned to terminate him when his contract expired. The trustees, however, voted unanimously to fire him at once.[34]

The dismissals of Serron, Chisholm, and Green typified the reprisals academic dissenters could expect. During the early 1960s, as we have seen, the most blatant such incidents targeted critics of white supremacy at southern colleges and universities, both Black and white. But as student unrest spread throughout higher education, antiwar and other political activists in all parts of the country were disproportionately let go or denied tenure.[35] Yet almost invariably, when reasons were given for firing these faculty members, they were portrayed as routine professional decisions. Certainly, people did lose their jobs because of academic inadequacies. But the circumstantial evidence for a political purge is strong. By 1969, the NUC's leaders formed a defense committee to collect information about probable political dismissals. As it explained:

> The Committee's working assumption is that, while in most individual cases the discriminatory institution can plausibly allege academic

or personal grounds for its action, a statistical summary of the difficulties experienced by radical scholars in securing employment and promotion would be difficult for academia to brush aside.[36]

More than a few other (and less radical) observers had reached a similar conclusion. "There is cause for concern about the state of academic freedom within the profession," the 1974 report of the AHA's Committee on the Rights of Historians concluded.

> Despite the fact that there can be no sure knowledge of the absolute level of infringement on the rights of historians nor any firm basis for knowing whether the trend is up or down, there are many allegations of unfair treatment and there is ample evidence that a significant proportion of the profession perceives injustices being done.[37]

A committee of the American Economic Association reached a similar conclusion.[38]

Such injustices were especially common among the leaders of the radical caucuses and the NUC.[39] Richard Flacks and Jesse Lemisch at Chicago;[40] Bert Garskof, another NUC activist and a mainstay of the Psychology Liberation Movement at Michigan State;[41] the labor studies scholar Wells Keddie at Penn State; the radical biologist Richard Levins at the University of Puerto Rico;[42] Paul Lauter at the University of Maryland, Baltimore County.[43] Other NUC casualties included Kenneth Megill at the University of Florida, James Cockcroft at the University of Wisconsin–Milwaukee, John McDermott at Long Island University, Steve Shapiro at the University of California, Irvine, and Eileen van Tassell at Michigan State.[44] In fact, the dismissals and nonreappointments of radicals became so common that the *NUC Newsletter* began to run a feature called "Atrocity of the Week," chronicling political discrimination against its members.

Defying Pedagogical and Intellectual Orthodoxy

Even when political considerations were clearly involved, there could still be ostensibly legitimate academic reasons for eliminating an institution's gadflies. After all, many of them did not play by the same rules as their more moderate colleagues. In some cases, their teaching and research violated academic norms. Allen Krebs at Hofstra assigned only one reading, *The Communist Manifesto*, in all of his sociology courses and gave every class the same short-answer final exam. At Brooklyn College, when the psychologist Bill Zimmerman announced that he would no longer conduct research under a capitalist system, his seriously divided colleagues denied him reappointment.[45] Although in retrospect it seems that such radicals were behaving outrageously, at the time many believed themselves to be operating within the parameters of the society they hoped to create. They viewed their teaching and scholarship as part of their political work.[46]

Grades were especially fraught. Ever since the rank-list controversy of the mid-1960s, radical academics had been questioning their profession's traditional practices.[47] One NUC stalwart, for whom "the grading system is a horror," called on his tenured comrades "to subvert this system openly." Because grades "rationalize existing exploitive relationships," to stop using them would be, he explained, "a revolutionary act."[48] Even without tenure, quite a few radical academics embarked upon that revolutionary venture.[49]

For example, when the historian Katherine Kish Sklar realized that her students at Eastern Michigan University might be drafted if they got poor grades, she decided to give them all A's. It was, she thought, an "innocuous" strategy, "but some colleagues started shunning me, people stopped speaking to me."[50] Other radicals lost their jobs for their unorthodox grading policies.[51] In the summer of 1968, an untenured assistant professor of sociology at the University of Wisconsin announced that he would no longer grade his students. He had been hoping to spark a debate about the issue; instead he got attacked for violating the norms of "good colleagueship." No surprise, his contract was not renewed. Six other Madison sociologists also revamped their grading policies. Maurice Zeitlin, for example, held a discussion in his 400-student class that resulted in a decision to give everyone an A. As the only tenured member of the six, Zeitlin could not be fired.

But Wisconsin's regents specifically denied him a raise—though the faculty and administration forced them to rescind that action.[52]

Meanwhile, at Harvard, Samuel Bowles and a group of radical economists who had organized an experimental course, "The Capitalist Economy," petitioned the administration to let them teach it without forcing their students into the "alienated labor" of competing for grades. "Needless to say," Bowles explained, "the university didn't agree with this." A few years later, Bowles discussed the issue with his classes at the University of Massachusetts, ultimately deciding to allocate grades in the Marxist manner: "to each according to his or her need." Bill Zimmerman, then teaching temporarily at the University of Chicago, did the same, though he warned his students that he needed a respectable distribution of A's, B's, and C's to keep the administration from cracking down on him. Radicals elsewhere were often refusing to submit grades or simply letting students grade themselves.[53]

But it was not Bowles's challenge to the Harvard grading system that led to his highly publicized tenure denial in 1972–73. It was his research. His more conservative senior colleagues believed that his work on education did not belong within their field. Bowles and his fellow Marxist and neo-Marxist economists were increasingly marginalized within their discipline. Their research on such issues as inequality, poverty, and racism was considered "negligible" in the words of the Harvard chair. Except for those academics who managed to establish radical economics departments at places like the University of Massachusetts, the New School, and (temporarily) CCNY, left-wing economists risked isolation at best.[54]

The rejection of radical scholarship was especially pronounced within economics, but it was not unknown elsewhere. Such opposition was particularly serious for the radicals who were trying to gain acceptance for the emerging fields of women's and Black studies and whose presence within the faculty was in large part a response to the student pressure for so-called "relevant" courses. Their fields' unconventional—and contested—origins ensured that, from the start, these scholars encountered intense resistance from within the professoriate, even though foundations and administrations supported them in the hope it would pacify their campuses.[55]

Not only did these pioneering scholars have to overcome the academy's long-standing legacies of sexism and racism, but they also had to deal with what may well have been the genuine inability of so many senior professors to recognize the quality of their teaching and scholarship. With only a few exceptions, the men and women working in such unorthodox areas as Black and women's studies encountered discrimination that prevented them from gaining the accoutrements of the academic establishment. They did not publish in the mainstream journals, hold office in the leading professional associations, or belong to the old-boy networks. And, of course, most were political activists as well.[56]

Many of the scholars who established the new programs in these fields during the 1960s and 1970s were already ensconced in the academy—just not as regular faculty members at prestigious institutions. The women were often faculty wives with good academic credentials holding part-time and non-tenure-track positions, while the African American professors taught in the historically Black colleges and universities.[57] As they moved into more mainstream positions, both groups encountered discrimination along with the charge that they were lowering standards.[58] Their fates soon diverged, however, primarily because of the female scholars' demographic advantage. There were a lot more of them—and more students eager to take their courses. As one women's studies pioneer put it, "we have the numbers." Moreover, since women, unlike African Americans, made up a near majority of most undergraduate student bodies, the field's enrollments grew steadily.[59]

Such was not the case with Black studies. The perceived inadequacy of the pipeline for Black faculty members led to complaints by white academics that they were being compelled to hire inferior candidates—a situation that for years gave the field a poor reputation.[60] And some of the early programs were less than adequate, containing what one Black foundation official described as "hastily conceived and academically unsound courses designed to stave off disaster rather than remedy curriculum deficiencies."[61] In addition, many institutions that had rushed to put those programs together failed to supply the necessary resources for them to succeed, especially after the initial foundation grants dried up. As a result, many of the over five hundred such programs, departments, and institutes that were created between 1968 and 1971 simply disappeared. And of the programs that did survive, almost all shed their Black Power roots and activist agendas.[62] A similar evolution occurred in women's studies. As they gained acceptance, faculty members in the field stressed its intellectual accomplishments rather than its revolutionary aspirations, abandoning courses in automobile repair in favor of more traditional offerings in traditional disciplines.[63]

Conflicts—Cultural, Generational, and Structural

Sometimes it was hard to tell whether the violations of academic freedom during the late 1960s and early 1970s were examples of political repression or a reflection of the cultural and generational tensions that accompanied the massive expansion of higher education. Clearly, the academy was changing in ways that many of its older inhabitants were unprepared for, and they felt increasingly uncomfortable with the social and cultural, not to mention political, baggage that the influx of younger scholars brought to their campuses.

Because some of these younger scholars were also pressing for higher academic standards and a broader national, rather than local, orientation to the academic community, they could be seen as demeaning the achievements of their colleagues who had built their careers in less demanding times. This so-called "Academic Revolution," chronicled by Christopher Jencks and David Riesman in their influential 1968 volume of that name, took place throughout the 1960s as a surprisingly broad range of colleges and universities joined the competition for academic prestige.[64]

It is common to view the conflicts that this supposed revolution precipitated as occurring primarily at the kind of institution an Iowa State professor disparagingly called an "island in a sea of corn."[65] The story is familiar: the hirsute young ABD from Berkeley, Columbia, or the Big Ten shows up at North Podunk State only to find his unconventional lifestyle, innovative scholarship and pedagogy, and left or left-liberal politics so unacceptable to his senior colleagues, not to mention the local elites, that he is soon eased out, if he doesn't flee first. But, in fact, similarly fierce cultural-cum-intellectual conflicts took place at quite a few major universities and urban institutions, among others, the University of Wisconsin, Stanford, and the City College of New York.

Admittedly, at the smaller, less well-known schools, the atrocities were sometimes so obvious that even the AAUP was willing to take a stand. While most of its reports during the late 1960s and early 1970s focused on procedural abuses like the failure to conduct faculty hearings, many also described clashes between the politics and values of the ousted teachers and the folkways of their institutions and communities. Quite a few young faculty members, hired explicitly to introduce modern methodologies and up-to-date scholarship to the institutions that hired them, were terminated because they didn't fit in.

Rupert Koeninger was actually told, when he was fired from Sam Houston State Teachers College in May 1961, that he was "out of place" and should "return to Minnesota."[66] Frank Kosik's dismissal from Northern State College in Aberdeen, South Dakota, occurred eleven days after he began teaching there in August 1966. According to the AAUP's investigators, he was ousted because his left-wing politics "exceeded the limits of what the local community found tolerable" and were "not compatible with what was expected here."[67] Brent Davis had a similar experience at Arkansas A&M, where he was summarily fired near the beginning of the term in October 1965. The poster of Malcolm X in his office, as well as his religious agnosticism and opposition to the war in Vietnam, was more than his senior colleagues and the community could handle. Pressed to fire Davis by the board of trustees, the president reluctantly let the young speech instructor go. "I had no alternative," he explained. "When a question arises which balances the good of this college against an individual, I know what stand I will always take."[68]

Trustees and administrators were not the only individuals carrying out these dismissals. Senior faculty did, as well.[69] That seems to have been what happened to the historians Paul Faler and Malcolm Sylvers at the University of Wisconsin–Stout. Although the school's administration claimed to be eager for innovations, telling the two that "we were precisely the type of new faculty that were needed at Stout," they were informed in the beginning of 1970 that their contracts would not be renewed because their teaching was at fault. Not only were they guilty of "left-wing propagandizing in the classroom," but they also did not require attendance and gave essay exams rather than multiple-choice ones. As Faler and Sylvers saw it, they upset the conservative senior professors who "wish to maintain the high school atmosphere which has so characterized Stout. . . . They seek to shelter Stout students and protect them from new ideas."[70]

Perhaps the most extreme attempt to foist conformity upon an influx of new recruits took place in February 1970 at the University of Georgia, where the chair of the history department announced that in all future tenure decisions the

> criteria for retention will be the individual's total contribution to the Department and the University, based upon COMPATIBILITY as well as teaching and research.
>
> . . . It is felt that individuals who are unhappy with the circumstances of their professional environment, and who are unable to resolve these problems over a period of years, cannot satisfactorily carry out the requirements of their appointments. It is no service either to the individual concerned or to the University to encourage such persons to protract their stay at Georgia.

Even moderates were appalled, especially after the administration granted promotions to two lackluster, but loyal, historians, while denying them to three more qualified candidates. Although the public outcry against the compatibility requirement was so intense that it was soon rescinded, the department did not recover. Within a few years, if they could find new jobs, almost all of the recently hired historians, including those with tenure, were gone.[71]

The History Wars at CCNY

Unfortunately, there were dozens of such conflicts.[72] When these cultural and intellectual battles occurred during a serious political crisis, the situation could become especially toxic—as it did among the historians at the City College of New York. The publicity that CCNY's struggles received not only fed the conservative and even liberal opposition to the Black demands for open admissions, but also contributed to the growing public disapproval of faculty members' supposedly feckless behavior. Because of its broader implications for public higher education and affirmative action, the CCNY history department's internecine struggle demands our attention.[73]

When the department met in early May 1969 to elect a new chair, it had already failed twice to agree on a candidate. As the seriously polarized professors began deliberating yet again, they could smell the smoke from an attempted arson elsewhere in the building. City College was in turmoil. A coalition of Black and Puerto Rican students had taken over CCNY's South Campus. Their "Five Demands" echoed those made by minority-group students elsewhere: a school of Black and Puerto Rican studies, an undergraduate-run orientation program for Black and Hispanic students, required Spanish courses for education majors as well as ones in African American and Puerto Rican history, more student control over the remedial SEEK program, and—the most important demand—"that the racial composition of the entering freshman class be racially reflective of the high school population." That final demand reflected City College's anomalous situation. Located in the heart of Harlem, its student body contained few members of the surrounding community. An earlier attempt to upgrade the institution had actually reduced its cohort of Black students to 4 percent and Puerto Ricans to 5 percent. Even CCNY's most conservative professors understood that something had to change.[74]

CCNY's president Buell Gallagher, like the similarly liberal administrators at Buffalo and San Francisco State, hoped to calm the campus by closing the school and negotiating seriously with the protesters. But the media sensationalized the situation and outside politicians intervened, escalating the conflict. When the conservative mayoral candidate Mario Procaccino got a court order to reopen the campus, Gallagher simply gave up. "My own functions as a reconciler of differences and a catalyst for constructive change have become increasingly difficult to carry out," he explained. "And with the intrusion of politically motivated forces in recent days, it has become impossible to carry on the processes of reason and persuasion."[75]

Already splintered by their own personal, political, and educational conflicts, City College's historians were also unable "to carry on the processes of reason and persuasion." The department's 13–11 vote for the medievalist Howard Adelson as chair over the pioneering women's historian Joan Kelly-Gadol solved nothing. While the New York City Board of Higher Education did manage to defuse the student crisis by acceding to most of the Black and Puerto Rican students' demands, its most important action—putting into immediate operation an open-admissions program it had planned to unveil in 1975—merely intensified the history department's warfare.[76] That warfare revealed how preexisting conflicts over such academic matters as hiring and curriculum contributed to the broader political struggles over the democratization of higher education.[77]

Admittedly, CCNY was a unique institution. Since its founding in 1847, it had offered New York City's upwardly mobile young men a completely free liberal arts education that would be, in the words of its founders, "in no way inferior to our other colleges." By the 1920s and 1930s, its student body was largely composed of ambitious and hard-working first- and second-generation working- and lower-middle-class Jews who had been excluded from more elite institutions by anti-Semitic quotas. These were the students who gave City College its mythical image as the "Jewish Harvard" teeming with future Nobel laureates and budding New York Intellectuals debating the finer points of socialist politics in the alcoves of the college lunchroom.[78] Within a generation, however, the postwar expansion of higher education and the waning of anti-Semitism, as well as the economic progress of New York's Jewish community, provided the college's traditional constituency with many more options for higher education. And they took them.[79] Though still a mecca for local strivers, by the 1960s CCNY had expanded so much that many of its older professors and alumni were bemoaning a supposed decline in quality. They looked back nostalgically to the age, when, in the ironic words of a future president, its "'Brilliant Student Superachievers,' . . . made City College a national phenomenon." Yet there were still plenty of "very sharp, very inquisitive" students who were "a pleasure to teach," as both new and old faculty members recalled. And because the institution's expansion could not keep up with the growing demand for free higher education, CCNY's entrance requirements actually rose dramatically during the 1960s, not only shutting out the poorly prepared graduates of the nearby Harlem high schools, but also large numbers of whites.[80]

CCNY's faculty was changing as well, but not without considerable resistance. Until the 1960s, the senior faculty of the inbred history department consisted primarily of City College graduates, barred by anti-Semitism from most other institutions of higher education. Eight of the department's thirteen full professors were, in fact, alumni with higher degrees from Columbia. These people had been socialized into the academic profession at a time when college teaching was less demanding. They did not try to keep up with the recent developments in their fields or adapt their teaching to an increasingly diverse student body.* Conflicts emerged in the 1960s, as the department responded to the college's growth by recruiting what a later CCNY president considered an impressive cluster of "generally younger, highly qualified and nationally recognized faculty."[81]

When these "sixties people," as one of them called his cohort, arrived at City College, they were shocked by the narrow perspectives of their older colleagues. The incoming teachers were expected to follow a curriculum that had been developed some thirty years before and teach exactly the same material in exactly the same way as their senior colleagues. Worse yet, the department would not let the junior people introduce modern scholarship. Year after year, one young Europeanist submitted proposals for offerings in social and cultural history only to have them ignored by the curriculum committee.[82]

The department's hiring practices were equally indefensible—if not corrupt. Instead of searching for teachers to satisfy student demands or cover unrepresented fields, Howard Adelson, the chair, sought to

---

* My late husband, a City College undergraduate in the late 1950s, described a rather brutal prank he and Robert Scheer pulled on a particularly retrograde history professor. They asked him his opinion of the latest work of the Belgian medievalist "Jacques Alvert." After a long pause, the professor explained that, despite its insights, he didn't think it measured up to Alvert's earlier scholarship. At that point, my late husband and Scheer stood up, announced to the rest of the class, "There is no Jacques Alvert," and walked out of the room.

replicate the status quo. One year, six of the nine new faculty hires were medievalists, most of them Adelson's students, who then had to teach courses on subjects for which they had no preparation. The disgruntled sixties people fought back, explicitly organizing themselves into a caucus that did manage to implement some curricular reforms. They eliminated a few requirements and developed courses to meet the needs of their newly expanded and less docile student body.[83]

There were political conflicts as well, exacerbated by the student protests of the late 1960s. The advent of open admissions in the fall of 1970 further tore the department apart. Adelson was a conservative who surfaced as the main spokesman for the faculty opponents of the new admissions policy. When the distinguished University of Rochester physicist and City College alumnus Robert Marshak took over as president to implement open admissions, Adelson declared war. He campaigned all over the city, speaking to synagogues and other Jewish groups and feeding tidbits to an all-too-receptive media, while claiming to champion the traditional academic standards of the "Proletarian Harvard." Having to deal with so many poorly educated Black and Puerto Rican students, he told the nationally syndicated conservative columnists Rowland Evans and Robert Novak, provided "indications that this college is finished as a learned institution." At one point in a debate with Marshak before the Bronx High School of Science PTA, Adelson actually urged his listeners to send their children to Queens College rather than CCNY.[84]

Open admissions was, in fact, flawed from birth. Although Joan Kelly-Gadol and many of the younger historians welcomed it as a long-delayed attempt to rectify the racial imbalance within higher education, they recognized that the panicky Board of Higher Education had rushed it into operation without the necessary preparation or funding to cope with a freshman class that at City College grew from 1,752 in 1969 to 2,742 in 1970. Even so, most of City College's historians tried with varying degrees of success to implement the program. Their opponents did not. Unwilling or unable to revise their syllabi or alter their teaching style, they simply flunked large numbers of the new undergraduates—most of whom, it must be noted, were neither Black nor Hispanic students but working-class white ethnics who had been unable to meet CCNY's previous admission standards.[85]

Additional conflicts arose over the allocation of opportunities to teach at the newly created City University of New York Graduate Center. Adelson controlled access to the PhD program and kept many of the qualified new faculty members from teaching in it.[86] As relations between the factions became increasingly bitter, department meetings degenerated into shouting matches, with a conservative cluster of five senior professors attacking their opponents as "Stalinists" and "Maoist scum" and accusing them of anti-Semitism. The leftists were almost as vituperative. Moreover, as the level of invective escalated, it became almost impossible to carry out even the most routine operations—let alone deal with such sensitive matters as changing the curriculum or hiring and promoting people.[87]

By 1971, the dysfunction had become so serious that Marshak brought in an outside committee to assess the department. Composed of three eminent historians under the chairmanship of Carl Schorske, then at Princeton, the committee began its official report by noting:

> The Department is wholly immobilized by division and dissension. The materials sent us by the members of the Department before our arrival prepared us for the manifestations of discord which marked our first visit, but not for the extent to which even the most imaginative, able and committed historians are frozen into ineffectiveness, and their Department paralyzed.

As the visitors saw it, what made the department's troubles "so unusual and so dangerous" was their connection to the problems caused by the open-admissions policy and the new PhD program. Schorske and his colleagues recommended that "a new chairman of established reputation should be chosen from outside."[88]

And so the groundbreaking labor historian Herbert Gutman, whom Marshak had known from the University of Rochester, came to City College with the support of the history department's liberals. Gutman's appointment, however, brought no peace. Adelson and his allies continued their public campaign against open admissions, citing their own department's troubles as evidence. They denigrated both the administration and their colleagues for subverting CCNY's educational quality, pointing to the early tenuring of Eric Foner, future Pulitzer Prize winner and president of the American Historical Association, as an example of the department's allegedly lowered standards. Gutman, unable to handle the conservatives' abuse, turned his attention to the Graduate Center, where he built up a major program in labor and working-class history.[89]

Meanwhile, the conflicts continued, even degenerating into a public shoving match between Kelly-Gadol and the most vituperative right-winger. The department, another outside arbitrator observed, had become "a political cesspool." A second investigating committee was formed, and then a third, both leaning toward the Kelly-Gadol group and even recommending sanctions against the conservative dissidents who had refused to cooperate with the investigators.[90] The warfare did not abate until New York City's 1975 fiscal crisis hit the City University, threatening massive dismissals. "In order to save the department," Gutman's successor as chair recalled,

> the Gadol people had to work with the other group because otherwise the department would be cut to pieces, we lost no one, we saved the department, we lost all our untenured people . . . but we were able to save the tenured people. . . . The crisis led people who hated each other to cooperate, the personal animosities were reduced and we were able to work together.[91]

Given the educational toll of the financial crisis—the abandonment of open admissions and the end of free tuition among other austerity measures—the denouement of CCNY's history wars could hardly be considered a victory for either side. The unfavorable publicity that those wars attracted was to contribute to the unwillingness of so many New York City politicians and other elites to protect their municipal college system.[92] Although City College's history wars were particularly extreme, the conflicts they exemplified plagued many a college and university. The public hostility that they engendered was similarly widespread. And it was not going to abate.

17

"REVOLT OF THE RATIONALLY COMMITTED"

Intellectuals and the Media Construct a Scenario of Student Unrest

As the CUNY Board of Higher Education deliberated over its open-admissions policy in the fall of 1969, a group of conservative City College professors, history department chair Howard Adelson in the lead, called on their colleagues to help them "protect our college" by joining the CCNY chapter of the University Centers for Rational Alternatives.[1] UCRA was the brainchild of the NYU philosopher and quintessential New York Intellectual Sidney Hook, who envisioned it as a national network that would push for a tough response to the campus troubles of the time. Hook launched the venture at the end of 1968 by inviting two thousand academics to become its "charter sponsors." Designed to "create a counterforce to extremism," UCRA would, Hook explained, lead a "revolt of the rationally committed" to expose the "terrorist tactics and multiple varieties of putschism" that threatened the university.[2]

The response was promising. Within weeks, Hook's letter had produced some two hundred recruits, half of whom volunteered to organize chapters at their schools. The group was elitist from the start. "We are frankly a leadership organization, as distinct from a mass organization or a check-off," one of its few staff members admitted.[3] By the end of the decade, its board of directors and list of sponsors read like a *Who's Who* of the academy's most outspoken opponents of the student movement. Besides campus activists like Adelson, John Bunzel and S. I. Hayakawa of San Francisco

FIGURE 17.1. Sidney Hook at the microphone, date unknown. © Sidney Hook Papers, Envelope A, Hoover Institution Library & Archives.

State,* Paul Seabury of Berkeley, and Paul Kurtz of SUNY Buffalo, there were several Nobel Prize winners including the Princeton physicist Eugene Wigner and the economists Milton Friedman and Herbert Simon as well as such eminent academics as Reinhard Bendix, Bruno Bettelheim, Daniel Boorstin, Zbigniew Brzezinski, Oscar Handlin, Samuel Huntington, Daniel Moynihan, W. V. Quine, John Roche, Robert Scalapino, and Edward Teller. European émigrés were over-represented as were refugees from Berkeley and Cornell—among them Walter Berns, Lewis Feuer, Walter Galenson, Nathan Glazer, Seymour Martin Lipset, and Thomas Sowell.[4]

Not every well-known academic conservative joined Hook's group. According to a colleague, Glazer and Lipset were initially wary, having "only a dim and not entirely reassuring impression."[5] And although David Riesman shared Hook's opinion of the students, he did not believe it necessary to create a new organization while groups like the ACLU and AAUP were active. The Harvard Russian historian Richard Pipes also opposed Hook's initiative. He felt that local organizations would be more effective than a national one. Harvard, he noted, already had a functioning conservative caucus of influential professors—as did, among others, San Francisco State, Berkeley, and the universities of Michigan and Massachusetts.[6]

In addition, he feared, as did Riesman and others, that the organization might be too conservative. In fact, despite its claim to represent professors of every political persuasion, UCRA's obsessive focus on student atrocities and its failure to confront what many academics considered the greater threat of a right-wing backlash was alienating potential supporters "of a moderate left position who," the hardly liberal Pipes explained, "might not wish to be publicly identified with some of the members of your organization."[7] As one disillusioned member who had fled from Berkeley explained in his 1973 resignation letter, he was "embarrassed" to be associated with the "smug, old-line conservatives" and "reactionaries" in UCRA's Yale chapter. And, he

---

* Bunzel was to quit Hook's board when Governor Ronald Reagan appointed him president of San Jose State College, as did S. I. Hayakawa when he took over as president of San Francisco State. They wanted to avoid the perception that UCRA was an administrative rather than faculty body. M. M. Todorovich to Oscar Handlin, January 25, 1969, box 27, Handlin Papers.

continued, the organization was "out of touch with events that now really matter . . . [and] is not and never has been a rallying point for us."[8]

Even so, the group had been able to publish an occasional newsletter, mount a few conferences, and obtain grants from the Mellon, Sloan, and Smith Richardson Foundations, as well as the National Endowment for the Humanities. It also got covert support from the Nixon White House, which pressed the IRS to grant it a tax exemption. Its CCNY chapter claimed to have been instrumental in torpedoing an administration proposal to allot 50 percent of the slots in incoming classes for "disadvantaged" students to residents from the city's Black and Puerto Rican neighborhoods. On other campuses—the University of Connecticut and SUNY Buffalo, among them—UCRA's most active members gathered hundreds of faculty signatures on petitions demanding a hard line against student protesters. UCRA also supported lawsuits against "weak and permissive" administrations at the University of Michigan and Washington University for failing to protect faculty members and students from violent demonstrations.[9] By the mid-1970s, however, as the campus unrest it was organized to counter faded away, the University Centers for Rational Alternatives began to run out of money and support.[10]

Nonetheless, its ideological campaign had considerable success, in large part because its clearly articulated, if wildly overdrawn, attack on the liberal campus expressed the views of what may well have been the silent majority of the professoriate. To be sure, there is no way to tell whether UCRA had much to do with the dissemination and popular acceptance of its interpretation of the academic crisis. After all, Hook and the others had plenty of intellectual capital of their own that they expended lavishly in opposing what they considered an existential threat to the nation's universities—if not to the democratic system itself.

These people had been writing about and analyzing academic issues since the Berkeley crisis, if not before. As the sociologist Charles Kadushin noted, "The very high prestige intellectuals were not only more likely to perceive culture and values as problems but to be interested in working in this area." Quite a few of them—Lewis Feuer, Nathan Glazer, and Seymour Martin Lipset, along with David Riesman and Daniel Bell—dedicated most of their literary output in the late 1960s and early 1970s to the crisis in academe. Bell stated quite explicitly in a September 1965 letter to Riesman that one of the main reasons he and NYU's Irving Kristol were starting the journal *Public Interest* was to "open up a continuing discussion of the American education scene." The prolific output of such people allowed them to dominate much of the public debate about the turmoil within the academic community and its cultural and political implications.[11] In the process, they legitimized the increasingly negative view of the university held by so many of their fellow citizens.

These intellectuals, as well as their lesser-known allies within the academic Right, did not agree on every issue. Some—Handlin, Scalapino, and Seabury, for example—supported the war in Vietnam; others, like Glazer and Riesman, opposed it. On the other hand, Riesman supported Harvard president Nathan Pusey's 1969 decision to call in the cops, while Glazer opposed it.[12] Similarly, some of these writers used polemical language, while others adopted a more moderate tone. The timing of their enlistment in the conservative academic movement also varied. As the campus unrest intensified during the 1960s, many initially moderate and liberal faculty members moved to the right, sloughing off their original support for political dissent as their antipathy toward the protests hardened.[13] Carl Schorske recalled how "the watershed in politics" kept

> shifting. . . . So people who were at one moment what you could generally characterize as a large left if the watershed begins to shift, many of the people who were in the large left become a large center, and the left becomes smaller, while the people in the center begin to move right.[14]

The historian C. Vann Woodward, for example, began the decade as a classic liberal and strong supporter of the Black freedom struggle, "more than happy," he told Riesman in 1960, "to uphold your hand in defending protest and dissent from the charge of irrationality." By 1967 he had turned against the war in Vietnam. But by then, he had also turned against the Left, describing "our Black Nationalists, or some of them at least" as "taking a decidedly Fascistic, racist and anti-intellectual line," while at the same time decrying antiwar students as "extremists" who "prolonged the war."[15]

Riesman underwent a similar conversion. He had originally aligned himself with the budding New Left. As an ardent proponent of nuclear disarmament, he welcomed an alliance with the emerging student peace movement of the early 1960s. He also espoused much of the same critique of America's consumerism and conformity as Tom Hayden and the early SDS. But he had been in Berkeley during the free speech crisis and, like Lipset and Glazer, was affronted by the students' civil disobedience.[16] His Harvard colleague H. Stuart Hughes followed a similar trajectory, turning against the students, though not the antiwar movement. Unable to stomach the young insurgents' coercive tactics, he claimed, like Riesman, to see "no alternative to calling the police to evict the occupants of University Hall" in 1969.[17]

The Blame Game

By the end of the 1960s, even as new issues emerged, Glazer, Lipset, and their allies were still deploying the same anti-student rhetoric they had used during the Free Speech Movement at Berkeley.[18] Whether their target was Mario Savio or Mark Rudd, most conservative (and some not-so-conservative) academics demonized the radicals, ignoring the diversity within the student movement and treating its members as completely irrational. They viewed the campus rebels as nihilists, seeking to destroy higher education by undermining the rational debate that constituted its core. As Charles Kadushin discovered, "Every professor who talked about university problems [save one] . . . was of the opinion that rationality was a main issue, and that the students opposed rationality."[19]

Emerging during the early debates about Berkeley in 1964–65, the term "rationality" gained even more purchase later in the decade as the academic opponents of the student movement claimed to see a devotion to rational discourse as *the* defining characteristic of the idealized university that the radicals allegedly sought to destroy. As Daniel

Bell, himself a major player during the Columbia troubles, put it, "We believe that without rational authority and civil discourse, a civilized society—and that is the ultimate model of the university—is impossible."[20] Accordingly, any students or faculty members who rejected rationality did not belong in that institution.[21]

The belief that the campus radicals were devoid of—if not hostile to—reason was pervasive.[22] Thus, for Irving Howe, the student movement was part of a "growing current of irrationalism . . . a worldwide cultural revolt" fueled by anti-intellectualism. And while quite a few unsympathetic professors recognized their best students among the demonstrators, they still believed that the protesters were driven, the Columbia historian Fritz Stern explained, by an "antagonism toward the process of education, toward 'mere' scholarship" as well as a "disdain [for] all nonpolitical learning." Other hostile academics, Lewis Feuer the most prominent, considered the students' unruly behavior to be a generational revolt whose adherents, one eminent psychologist explained, belonged to the "Spit-On-Daddy Club." Although, as contemporary social scientists like Kenneth Kenniston, Samuel Lubell, and Richard Flacks discovered, such was not the case, that interpretation received considerable attention.[23]

Other intellectuals pushed the notion that the protesters were immature thrill-seekers out for kicks and seeking some kind of transcendent communal experience. David Riesman claimed that they "wanted to be arrested" and got "enjoyment in . . . watching the liberals squirm." The University of Chicago historian and future Librarian of Congress Daniel Boorstin charged them with seeking power for its own sake while engaged in a "desperate quest for sensation." Self-absorbed and lazy, these "New Barbarians" were not genuine radicals, Boorstin explained.

> They do not care enough about the problems of their society to burn the midnight oil over them. Impatient to sate their egos with the sensations of "Direct Action," they are too indolent intellectually to do the hard work of exploring the problems to which they pretend a concern.

Other conservatives were equally negative, some even accusing the students of wanting to shut down their schools in order to avoid having to write papers or take exams.[24]

The same tropes recurred again and again. The students were mentally disturbed. They were out of touch with reality. They were manipulated by outsiders—with SDS or Maoist "revolutionaries" pulling the strings. Conservative professors at Chicago claimed to believe that the student rebels were using a supposed SDS manual on "how to organize insurrection, incite riot, and attack the power structure." Administrators at Howard University insisted that the unrest was the result of a "sinister Communist conspiracy" on the part of "unreasonable" students operating under the influence of "a Marxist view of shared authority in running a university." And, all maintained, such dissidents were determined to destroy their university or at least, in the Columbia literary critic Lionel Trilling's words, turn it into "some scruffy Latin-American university," where the students "are able to kick the chancellor out by having a protest movement."[25]

By propagating a blanket denunciation of the student movement as irrational and unthinkingly hostile to authority, its main academic critics trivialized the students' concerns, thus avoiding a serious engagement with them.[26] Nowhere, for example, in their examination of the troublemakers' motivations, did these conservatives mention the war in Vietnam. Even those academics, Sidney Hook included, who were willing to grant that universities, as well as the rest of society, did need to change, felt that the coercive behavior of the protesters overrode all other considerations. The students were simply too irrational to treat with respect.[27]

The defense of rationality, it seemed, brought its own flight from reason. Contemporary observers noted with consternation the hostility and irrationality of so many professors.[28] The literary scholar Wayne Booth, then a dean at the University of Chicago, recalled the "atrocious" behavior of some faculty members during the Marlene Dixon crisis. "One arrived at most meetings wearing his army uniform with all of his badges. Another suggested, before the students actually got in, that we leave some cash distributed about the office desks so that we could have students arrested for theft."[29] Perhaps Chicago was unique. Its faculty seems to have been more uniformly conservative than that at comparable schools. "Throughout the experience," Richard Flacks recalled,

> I was being continuously astonished by how quickly this privileged and secure faculty group could mirror a John Birch Society meeting in both temper and ideology. Lurid depictions of the student protesters' capabilities for violence and disorder—including repeated reference to the "smell" and slovenliness—enlivened department meetings. Repeated calls for law and order, including proposals that the faculty themselves prepare to physically engage the students, were made in meetings and in public press conferences.[30]

A similar antagonism emerged on other campuses as well. Although horrified by the incivility and foul language of the SDS activists and Black Power advocates, many faculty conservatives indulged in the same kind of name-calling.[31] Besides "extremists," the student dissidents and their faculty allies were "terrorists," "storm troopers," "gangsters," "barbarians," and "half-assed," if not "paranoid," "fanatical," "madmen," or "psychotics." As during the free speech crisis at Berkeley, analogies to Nazi youth groups flourished—especially among the European émigrés who had fled fascism three decades before and played an outsized role in demonizing the student Left.[32]

While the students' actions could perhaps be explained away by their youth, for many UCRA types, the actions of their colleagues who supported the student movement could not. They were as culpable as the undergraduate militants, if not more so. According to Boorstin, they were "opportunists," whose espousal of "unpopular or outlandish" opinions was designed to gain the "publicity [that] brings academic careers."[33] In an impassioned speech that electrified the Harvard faculty meeting after the University Hall bust in April 1969, the Russian-born economist Alexander Gerschenkron excoriated his more permissive colleagues as "middle-aged popularity kids who have done considerable damage to this university" because they feared that students will stop taking their classes. Not only did these "popularity kids" tolerate their students' flouting of authority, but they even asked them to call them by their first names![34] Gerschenkron was not alone. Conservative scholars on other campuses were equally antagonistic toward those of their colleagues who supported the students' demands.

Worse yet were those faculty members who actually joined the protests. As another eminent economist put it, "A university teacher who participates in coercive revolutionary organization and action is betraying—in a special and particular sense beyond his normal obligations as a citizen—his charge to act as a responsible teacher."[35] Yet more than the dereliction of duty was involved. Many conservatives off the campus (though not so many on it) actually blamed the faculty's radicals for the unrest. They assumed that students were much too gullible and immature to become radicalized on their own. Their leftist teachers must have led them astray. Or, as the Harvard Soviet expert Adam Ulam put it, "The American student is being exploited by middle-aged men who for their own purpose or profit propagandize him to become agitated and disturbed and to abandon that gaiety and ambition so appropriate to his age and so necessary to social progress." For San Francisco State's Hayakawa, the protesters were being taught the alienation that produced the campus violence "by professors in the liberal arts departments—the humanities, English, philosophy, sometimes in social science."[36]

But the true traitors, the worst of all, in the eyes of the conservative academics, were not the faculty radicals, but the moderate and liberal administrators and professors who closed their eyes to the mayhem and allowed their campuses to fall to the forces of unreason. For the "liberal in our midst," as the arch-conservative economist and Nobel laureate James Buchanan put it, "his is the job of feeding violence with concession."[37] Already an important part of the right-wing repertory since the Berkeley free speech crisis, the charge that well-meaning, but spineless, professors and administrators had sabotaged their universities became central to the campaign against the academic establishment. Torn by liberal guilt about race and their own careerist behavior, the academy's main leaders, so the conservatives claimed, were easy marks for the rampaging students. Willing to make "whatever sacrifices of principle are necessary to maintain peace," these liberals and moderates surrendered their legitimate authority.[38] "This is the classic pattern of appeasement, which is both morally intolerable and practically disastrous," Hook's recruitment letter for the UCRA explained. "At best, such policies merely repress symptoms without dealing with fundamental causes. More often, they enhance the power and whet the appetite of extremists."[39]

The events on troubled campuses gave plausibility to such an analysis. As we have seen, despite a strong consensus that the militants who took over buildings, blocked access to recruiters, and disrupted classes should face sanctions, most of the academic authorities who had to contend with that behavior could find no coherent or judicious way to discipline them.[40] Their confusion made it easy for conservative professors to blame them for the disarray. "Our failure to punish the wrong-doers in December is in my opinion directly responsible for the recent violence," the political scientist Carl J. Friedrich told President Pusey a few days after the Harvard bust. "I am still hoping that a majority of our faculty will decide to throw students out who will not respect the law nor the rights of people who differ with them."[41] To do otherwise was to "capitulate" and encourage further disorders. The word "capitulation" in the hands of an institution's conservative critics almost always denoted its refusal to crack down on its students.[42]

For such conservatives, Cornell's troubles in April 1969 exemplified the horrors of capitulation. Terrified by the prospect of racial violence and a massive student uprising, the administration had panicked. The faculty did, too, acceding to the president's request that it nullify its previous decision to reprimand Black students for earlier transgressions. Both may have been overreacting.[43] But Cornell's professors, as the legal scholar Milton Konvitz put it, believed that the university "stood on the brink. We could have a state of war." Konvitz changed his vote, supported amnesty, and felt awful about it, as did dozens, if not hundreds, of his colleagues. They had given in with an action "the world at large will construe . . . as a craven capitulation." And, so it did, thanks in part to the highly publicized barrage of criticism by professors like Konvitz.[44]

A few days later, the Harvard faculty's "appeasement"—that is, its vote to give the university's Black undergraduates power over a new Afro-American studies program—drew similarly sensationalized calumny. A few months earlier, the faculty had approved a proposal for a Black studies program designed by a student-faculty committee chaired by the widely respected former Berkeley economist and future Harvard dean, Henry Rosovsky. The core of the program consisted of a major that would combine work in a traditional discipline with courses on African American subjects.

On April 22, however, under new pressures from the Association of African and Afro-American Students, Harvard's professors junked that program. Instead, they supported the Black militants' demand for a separate Department of Afro-American Studies and gave them an unprecedented say over the department's design and the hiring and firing of its faculty. Terming this an "academic Munich" that would undermine the quality of Harvard's Black studies for years, Rosovsky noted that "the shadow of Cornell was spreading in Cambridge, Massachusetts." While he regretted that "we saw fit to make such fundamental changes so quickly and in the face of threats," he added, "I do not blame the black students. I blame the white faculty."[45]

So, too, did the traditionalist professors of UCRA.[46] They were deeply disturbed by the growing demand for student power and terrified that the academic establishment might give in to it—as, albeit with less passion, were many of their moderate and liberal colleagues. Though they agreed that it was fine for undergraduates to have a major say in such matters as dormitory regulations and dress codes, granting them control over curriculum and faculty appointments would destroy the university.[47] Relevance would reign, academic standards would fall, and a pall of left-wing orthodoxy would smother independent thought, forcing professors to tailor their courses to the students' demands, while grades would follow accordingly. Worse yet, as the Cornell political scientists Allan Sindler and Walter Berns warned, academic freedom would disappear, the victim of "an intransigent moralism promoting the cleansing of the campus of 'institutional racism' and of the 'military-industrial complex' [that] undercuts the freedom of inquiry and the profession of honest belief a faculty requires." In such an environment, Sindler later noted, faculty members will censor themselves, "play it safe, . . . teach students what they want to hear and will accept."[48]

Sindler's jeremiad was hardly unique. During the late sixties and early seventies, few concepts were brandished as promiscuously—and as vaguely—as academic freedom. At its most basic level, it was a professional perquisite that protected faculty members from outside interference with their teaching and research. Tenure provided the main institutional safeguard for that protection. Amid the tumult of the student movement, however, this traditional version of academic freedom, with its concomitant promise of lifetime employment and professional immunity, understandably came under attack.[49]

Both radicals and conservatives viewed academic freedom as a protection of the status quo—which they both claimed to detest. Both sides deployed surprisingly similar analyses of the concept's essentially elitist function. From the left, for example, Angela Davis thundered against academic freedom as "an empty concept that professors use to guarantee their right to work undisturbed by the real world, undisturbed by the real problems of this society."[50] While on the right, Irving Kristol considered it a device to protect mediocrity and allow academics to resist measures that might "cost the faculty anything—not money, not time, not power over their conditions of employment."[51]

Because academic freedom seemed to give faculty members special benefits, it was hard for them to defend it without hypocrisy. Obfuscation was the order of the day, as a young visiting professor at Cornell noted.

> Instead . . . of talking realistically about how they function, most faculty members either called up memories of the embattled leftist teachers of the McCarthy era or spun out images of some Newman-esque* university that Cornell never was, at least not in the years I have known it. Forced to define the conditions for academic freedom, faculty members fell back on elaborate abstractions which translated out as "whatever makes a faculty man comfortable."[52]

---

* Cardinal John Henry Newman, a nineteenth-century British theologian and educator, stressed the crucial role of higher education as a purely intellectual endeavor designed to inculcate rationality.

And, if nothing else, campus radicals did make their professors uncomfortable. Though the students clearly had no power to eliminate tenure, the prospect conjured up some seriously dystopic scenarios within the faculty. At Cornell, Sindler and his allies believed that it had become unsafe to criticize the Black militants, who

> politicized the teaching and study of racial issues to an extent that made honest discussion and analysis of such issues extremely difficult. Professors told of student "monitors" appearing in class, keeping their ears open to what was said about race.[53]

Even before the phrase "political correctness" entered mainstream American discourse, as one discomfited CCNY professor put it, "the threat of being labeled a bigot frightened at least some members of the faculty far more than any physical danger ever could have." With tenure supposedly at risk, such fears intensified.[54]

Even more discomfiting, because it was about to be implemented, was the specter of open admissions. At City College and elsewhere, agitated professors envisioned hordes of poorly prepared young people of color swarming onto their campuses—and then making trouble because they could not handle the work. Worse yet was the "propagandizing" thrust of the Black studies programs that these students demanded. Those programs were bound to become what one CCNY critic called "soul courses . . . sure to create a slum college producing scratchily educated B.A.'s full of resentment against the 'white power structure' which kept them out of the American mainstream."[55]

Talk about self-fulfilling prophecies. As these critics spread all-too-influential scare stories about the prospect of illiterate undergraduates and the erosion of academic standards, they also evinced a similar hostility to affirmative action programs designed to bring more Black and Puerto Rican scholars onto the faculty. Whether or not Howard Adelson and his fellow conservatives sincerely wanted to maintain the college's traditionally meritocratic standards by ensuring the right kind of open admissions and attracting the most qualified professors as they claimed, their widely disseminated disparagement of the university's compensatory programs and hiring policies could only have undermined them.[56]

Worse yet, the conservatives' campaign against the changes at CUNY exacerbated the growing challenge to the city's liberal polity exemplified by the concurrent conflict between Jewish teachers and the Black community in the Ocean Hill–Brownsville section of Brooklyn. As a result, within a few years, just as the city's finances imploded, the nation's most promising experiment in universal free higher education lost key political support and starved to death.[57]

Intellectual Rot—or Not

For many of the academic intellectuals who pontificated about the abysmal state of higher education in the late 1960s, the debacle had begun years before. As they saw it, the seeds of capitulation had been planted by the contemporary university's drive to become socially useful at the expense of its commitment to scholarship and teaching. The result—a disastrous decline in the quality of higher education. Not only had faculties and, especially, administrations watered down the curriculum and eliminated required courses, but they were adding more and more vocational courses, while abandoning the transmission of humanistic learning, rational discourse, and the values of Western civilization.[58] That assessment was not completely wrong, although the flight from the traditional liberal arts curriculum probably stemmed more from such factors as the rapid expansion of mass higher education in the 1950s and 1960s, the adoption of a research-driven academic model, and the rise of neoliberalism than it did from liberal guilt, woolly idealism, and faculty careerism.[59]

Clark Kerr was the designated villain here. His conception of the "multiversity" envisioned the university as the main component of America's "knowledge industry," which had become "the focal point for national growth."[60] It was a materialistic vision that traditional faculty members—and quite a few radicals—could not stomach. Walter Berns, for example, found it "absolutely disgusting," an indication that Kerr had "absolutely no sense of the noble role of the university."[61] Columbia's all-purpose public intellectual and former dean, Jacques

Barzun, was equally negative: the "deterioration" of the university stemmed from its "mistaken desire to enlarge its role through what it called public service."[62] In a widely circulated speech, the University of Chicago's president Edward Levi warned that relying "upon universities as handy agencies to solve immediate problems, remote from education, can only end in corruption of the universities."[63] Such complaints became common, providing ammunition for off-campus critics as well.

Few professors were as hostile to the non-academic mission of the multiversity as Berns and his like-minded colleagues at Cornell—the political scientists Allan Sindler, Allan Bloom, and Clinton Rossiter, in particular. They viewed their own president, James Perkins, and his desire to turn the university into a force for social good as even more reprehensible than Kerr's promotion of the multiversity. From their perspective, Perkins's brand of "liberal progressivism" lacked academic heft. And, in a strangely illogical leap of faith, his critics cited Perkins's failure to preserve "the distinct intellectual integrity of the university" as one of the main reasons why he collapsed in the face of the Black students' demands.[64]

Other academic traditionalists were equally contemptuous of those administrators and faculty who expanded their institutions into areas they were unequipped to deal with. According to Adam Ulam of Harvard, they were "arousing excessive expectations" by claiming that the university was

> not just one institution of many fulfilling an extremely important but of necessity limited function, but the master institution of modern society not only teaching and advancing knowledge, but being the seat of virtue and social wisdom, the vehicle for political reform.

Not only was such an extravagant mission doomed to fail, but it also undermined the institutional autonomy necessary for protecting the academic community from external interference.[65] By entering the public arena and, especially, by abandoning its political neutrality, colleges and universities subverted their own freedom while losing their raison d'être—or so many faculty conservatives believed.[66]

In his five years in the University of Wisconsin's English department, one younger professor recalled, "No question came up more often, or aroused more passion when it did, than the question of whether and when and how far the university or any of its organs, such as the department, should actively tangle in political affairs."[67] It seemed axiomatic to Berkeley's eminent European émigré, Carl Landauer, that the "university cannot at the same time be a forum for the combat of ideas and a party in that combat."[68] Significantly, it was not just conservatives who resisted attempts to politicize the academy. Seymour Martin Lipset and Evert Carll Ladd Jr. were surprised to find, in surveys in 1968 and 1972, that many professors who were radical with regard to national issues nonetheless refused to tamper with the traditional neutrality of their institutions.[69] As a 1968 University of Wisconsin report noted, although it was fine for individual academics to take a political position, "the burdens of explicit institutional commitment are for other organizations to bear, not because of academic indifference to this grave and urgent controversy, but because a university, by becoming a political actor, would threaten its reason for being."[70]

The problem, of course, was that what was seen as neutrality by one party was viewed as selling out by another. Only a few academic conservatives, like Ulam, rejected all collaboration with the state. Most others were willing to welcome defense-related research and the ROTC in the name of national security and academic freedom, while criticizing their left-leaning colleagues for seeking to use the university as "the base for their involvement (*cum* tenure) with the great social forces of our day."[71] Since so many issues in the 1960s seemed to be unacceptably polarizing, many, if not most, liberal and moderate faculty members believed that the seriously splintered academic community was simply too fragile and beleaguered from outside to endure internal warfare.[72] Unfortunately, they may have been right.

At Cornell, for example, one of the nation's most prominent antiwar academics feared that committing an institution to political action might create an opening for its enemies on the right. As a Southeast Asia scholar whose expertise helped to create the intellectual case against the Vietnam War, George M. Kahin argued persuasively from his own experience for the academic community's traditional avoidance of political involvement. The university's recent capitulation to its students was, he feared, "undermining" it as "a very special, protected and permissive environment" that enables its members to "operate in a context of freedom found in few other spots on this earth." He was particularly worried about the precedent that had been set for forces "longing to crack down on the freedom of the universities. . . . [T]hose forces can marshal immensely more power than you can. Do you really want to unleash them?"[73]

Kahin's fear of a political backlash reverberated within those sectors of the academic community that were just beginning to appreciate how serious such a backlash could be. From conservatives like Sidney Hook to the liberals of the AAUP, right-wingers and moderates predicted a devastating response from the general public to what was happening on their campuses.[74] The sociologist and future US senator Daniel Moynihan, then on leave from Harvard to serve in the Nixon White House, raged against his former colleagues' willingness to risk such repercussions. In a letter to Richard Hofstadter in September 1970, he noted:

> I am overwhelmed by what appears to me a stark incapacity within the ranks of higher education to recognize just how unpopular their institutions have become, and how exposed on that ground.
>
> To politicize the university in any situation would seem to me disastrous, but to do so at just the moment when there is the furthest possible distance between the politics of the nation and those of the campus seems to invite lean times at the very least.[75]

Berkeley's prescient Landauer pointed out the obvious:

> The pressure for relinquishing or limiting institutional neutrality comes at present from the political Left. Aside from all questions of principle, this pressure is a mistake on the part of those by whom it is exerted. Once the rule of institutional neutrality was abrogated, the political Right would be more effective than the Left in using the universities for its own purposes.[76]

As a result, if it was to fend off attacks from hostile politicians and other outsiders, the university, most academics believed, had to maintain its political neutrality. It would also have to take a tougher stand against the radicals on its campuses and perhaps even pay more attention to teaching.[77] Unfortunately, such nostrums were unrealistic. There was probably no way that liberal and moderate academics could have protected their institutions from outside intervention by policing themselves and their colleagues. The student uprising had rendered them too unpopular.

The Media and the Academic Crisis

The American public did not like what was happening on the nation's campuses. And hadn't ever since Mario Savio climbed onto the roof of a police car in the fall of 1964. The main public opinion polls revealed considerable hostility to the student movement—and support for cracking down on it. By the spring of 1969, according to a Gallup poll, 94 percent of the people it surveyed said they would "like to see college administrators take a stronger stand on student disorders," while 82 percent wanted all protesters expelled; and 52 percent of those answering a Harris poll that same spring opposed even peaceful campus demonstrations. A year later, during the troubles that followed the invasion of Cambodia and the Kent State shootings, 82 percent of Gallup's respondents strongly opposed "college students going on strike to protest the way things are run in this country." They also ranked "campus unrest" as the most important issue then facing the country, just as they did two years later—even though that unrest had largely subsided.[78]

No wonder, then, that Gallup's "educator of the year" in 1969 was San Francisco State's S. I. Hayakawa. He had become wildly popular for his willingness to physically confront demonstrators, as he did when he pulled the wires out of the striking students' sound truck a few days after Governor Reagan appointed him president of that troubled campus. He pulled no verbal punches either, especially when baiting the faculty, whose "twelve-hour teaching load," he explained, "is one of the nicest, softest jobs in the world." The media gobbled up

Hayakawa's provocations and, no doubt, would have done so even if they hadn't been enhanced by the efforts of the full-time press agent that a wealthy Chicago businessman supplied to the combative president. Hayakawa was simply too colorful to ignore. And higher education was too central to society to ignore, either.[79]

To what extent the media fed—or followed—the public's increasingly negative view of academia is hard to tell. Perhaps, if we are to subscribe to Richard Hofstadter's view of anti-intellectualism in American life, that hostility had always been there. Even at the height of the university's golden age in the early 1960s, George Wallace was not the only politician to grumble about overpaid college professors.[80] What was certainly apparent was the largely unsympathetic—and all too often sensationalized—coverage the most campus unrest received, as well as the way that coverage reinforced the charges of academic conservatives.[81] The problem was not so much an overt bias—although that certainly existed—as it was the standard operating procedures of the mainstream press and television networks, above all their need to attract an audience. Conflict rather than understanding dominated the news, as well as an emphasis on a readily comprehensible "story" rather than a more nuanced analysis of what that story meant. Because peaceful marches, informative lectures, and educational reforms were not considered newsworthy, how could ordinary citizens find out that most political protests on campus did not explode?[82]

Further contributing to the media's lopsided portrayal of what was happening was its embrace of the mythical standard of "objectivity" and "balance" that, as the social critic Todd Gitlin discovered, almost always gave as much play to a handful of right-wing counter-demonstrators as it did to thousands of peaceful marchers, while counterpoising the most outrageous slogans of revolutionary militants against "reasonable-sounding, fact-brandishing authorities." Moreover, just as activists, administrators, and faculty members faced unprecedented situations with no preexisting templates, so, too, journalists found themselves equally confused by the baffling events they had to report on. Nor, given the deadline-driven practices of their industry, did they have the time to do much about it.[83]

Still, bias did creep in. As individuals, reporters, like college professors, tended to be more liberal than the rest of society, but their superiors within the mainstream publications and networks were full-fledged members of the establishment. Accordingly, these journalists were constrained by the corporate media's unwillingness and even inability to examine—let alone challenge—the underlying allocation of power within society. There was, in addition, an unspoken fear of being seen as leftist that dated from the McCarthy era. Accordingly, as radical students and their allies questioned the normal patterns of academic life—and by extension those of the rest of society—the mainstream media's coverage not only sensationalized and/or trivialized the issues, but did so in a way that invited disapproval by a public already unnerved by racial unrest and the war in Vietnam.[84]

From the major networks to the small-town weeklies, the story was pretty much the same: student protesters and their faculty allies were seeking to destroy the system and had to be restrained. When Stanford's students heckled Vice President Hubert Humphrey in February 1966, a *Washington Post* editorial—entitled "Shame! Shame! Shame!"—excoriated the "roughnecks, rowdies, and storm troopers" who created "an environment where orderly discussion is not possible."[85]

Even a hardly radical cause like Berkeley's essentially liberal Free Speech Movement got a bad press. Some of the blame belonged to J. Edgar Hoover, who had been pursuing a vendetta against Clark Kerr and the University of California ever since a 1959 freshman placement exam at UCLA included an unwelcome question about "the dangers to a democracy of a national police organization like the FBI." As the free speech crisis developed, the Bureau, which was operating a secret "Mass Media Program" of leaks to friendly journalists, helped a reporter for the local Hearst paper write a three-part exposé, depicting the FSM as a communist plot to undermine the university.[86] That series and similar coverage "made it harder to operate," Kerr explained. "It was a situation in which the public was certainly ill at ease anyway, and then having exaggerated press reports about what was going on on-campus—the two together create a rather explosive situation." Not that the university's president had clean hands. At one point he intervened in the making of a CBS documentary on the FSM, apparently persuading the network's president to redo the piece and order its producer "to fly out to Berkeley and interview professors analyzing the revolt and saying things like, 'The kids are immature and impatient. It will all blow over,' that kind of thing."[87]

The *New York Times* was no better. Its San Francisco reporters drew most of their stories from the university's official spokesmen. They tended to stress the disruptive aspects of the struggle, ignoring the students' legitimate grievances as well as the provocations of the administration and local and state authorities.[88] Similarly misleading material about the campus upheavals appeared in the *Times* for the rest of the long sixties. Not only did its Sunday magazine feature the jeremiads of Sidney Hook et al., but it also presented disturbing accounts of troubles at schools like Wesleyan, the University of Connecticut, and San Francisco State.[89]

Particularly deleterious was the newspaper's treatment of Columbia's 1968 crisis. With hundreds of students occupying five classroom and administration buildings only a few subway stops from the newsroom, the *Times* flooded the campus with reporters. Every day the paper featured at least one front-page article chronicling the chaos, as well as other pieces purporting to offer background. On the day after the bust, there were three stories on the front page and nine more inside. Unfortunately, because of the *Times'* reputation for comprehensiveness and probity, its massive and largely negative coverage not only magnified the university's troubles, but also legitimized the public's growing antagonism to the rest of academe.[90]

No doubt the presence of the *Times'* publisher Arthur Ochs Sulzberger on Columbia's board of trustees had much to do with the excessive attention that his newspaper paid to official sources. One such article actually presented the administration's case for the proposed gymnasium in Morningside Park as if it had been specifically designed to benefit the Harlem community, while the *Times'* one-sided reporting of the bust stunned outsiders as well as protagonists.[91] Even when one of its own reporters was pushed down several staircases and beaten during the clearing of an occupied building, it refused to acknowledge the police violence that occurred. The only reference I found to the injured students, teachers, journalists, and bystanders noted, "There were students that were hurt and students who pretended they were hurt." Instead, its lead article by managing editor A. M. Rosenthal opened by quoting President Grayson Kirk's distress at the mess in his office: "My God, how could human beings do a thing like this?"[92] And, of course, the *Times*' editorials and most of its columnists left little doubt about which side the paper was on. With language about "hoodlum tactics," "Fascism of the left," and "the exaltation of irresponsibility over reason," these pieces recycled the indictments that the academic conservatives had been making ever since Berkeley.[93]

The *Times*' treatment of the Cornell crisis a year later further reinforced that narrative, although, to be fair, the iconic photographs of the armed Black students exiting the Willard Straight student center had even more power.[94] The *Times*' stories from Ithaca, however, did not favor the administration, but rather fleshed out the already ubiquitous scenario of weak administrators and compliant faculties kowtowing to campus thugs. "Armed Negro Students End 36-Hour Occupation After Cornell Capitulates" read the front-page headline, while the body of that piece and of the many that followed devoted considerable attention to the senior professors who opposed that "capitulation." Over the next few days, the *Times*' correspondents— especially its chief education reporter, Fred M. Hechinger, and the Pulitzer Prize–winning Homer Bigart—chronicled the faculty dissidents' openly acknowledged "counterattack" on Cornell's "surrender to intimidation." That coverage—replete with quotes about "the first stages of a totalitarian takeover" from the likes of Allan Bloom, Walter Berns, and Allan Sindler—highlighted these professors' resignations and threats to resign and their "intense and bitter propaganda battle" against their own administration and its supposedly wishy-washy treatment of the student unrest. That coverage was, in fact, so hostile and so damaging to the university that several years later the *Times*' publisher actually apologized to Cornell's former president James Perkins about Bigart's "lack of balance."[95]

Although a few of the journalists, most notably Tom Wicker, offered a more sympathetic account of the Black students' demands and the university's response to them, the overt messages from the *Times*' editorial pages reprised charges that campus conservatives had been making for years. What was necessary, a June 16 editorial announced, was "a renaissance of academic self-government" that would take on "the unhappy responsibility of isolating the destroyers and, if necessary, removing them from the campus." The alternative, as so many academics from Sidney Hook to George Kahin had been warning, was that less well-intentioned outsiders would intervene. As, of course, they did.[96]

EPILOGUE

Academic Reform and Political Backlash

The student unrest of the long sixties reached its apogee in the spring of 1970 and then subsided. Nixon's invasion of Cambodia and the killings at Kent State and Jackson State touched off a wave of strikes and other protests that affected about a third of the nation's twenty-five hundred colleges and universities. But when the new academic year began, campuses were surprisingly quiet. There were sporadic disruptions for a few more years, but never again would so much political dissent upend higher education.[1]

Nonetheless, the disturbances left a devastating legacy. As both liberal and conservative Cassandras had feared, hostile forces from outside the university moved in. Energized by the campus unrest, the enemies of the liberal academy attacked its ideological and financial underpinnings just when it was more internally divided than ever before. Moreover, even if the academy could have fended off the hostility of the Right, it would still have had to cope with the national economic crunch that brought an end to the seemingly unlimited expansion of the postwar years. Perhaps if there been no external campaign against it and the economy had been steadier, the university might have weathered the crisis. Despite facing an ultimately overwhelming political assault, the academic community was not entirely without the resources and the will to make changes that might have revived its prestige and authority, if not its promise to extend the benefits of higher education to anyone able to profit from them. Even so, bleak as the future of American higher education was to become, the legacy of the academy's long sixties did have its positive features.

Educational Reforms

A massive reform movement swept through academe that, despite its limitations, produced some genuine, if not earth-shaking, improvements. In trying to adapt their institutions to the newly competitive academic culture, university leaders sought to modernize their operations, revise governance structures, update the curriculum, and soften, if not eliminate, in loco parentis. Nothing unusual here—change was a constant within the academy. The pressures of the late 1960s for a more democratic campus simply speeded up the process. Successful or not—and many of the measures adopted to head off a seemingly existential crisis faded fast—they were ubiquitous. That almost every institution sought some kind of reform indicates how desperate the academic community had become. Unfortunately, however, many of the measures taken, while often useful, were naturally limited by the university's inability and, in some cases, unwillingness to handle the seemingly intractable social, political, and economic problems that precipitated the campus unrest. Not only did it lack the power to overcome those problems, but at times professors, students, and administrators could be—and were—irrational, dense, racist, sexist, and authoritarian.

Nonetheless, self-studies and special committees proliferated as faculties and administrations struggled to develop structural and educational fixes for their problems. Formed at every kind of public and private institution, these panels dealt with the main political challenges of the time—from outside recruiters and ROTC to Black studies and classified research. Governance reforms were nearly universal.[2] Among the most common—besides revamped judicial bodies, the elimination of in loco parentis restrictions, and the addition of a few students and faculty members to boards of trustees—were new organizations to give representation to the main constituencies on campus. Faculty senates were particularly popular. They were of such recent vintage that 85 percent of all such bodies in existence in 1974 had been established within the previous seven years.[3] Unions emerged as well, especially when administrations refused to recognize their faculty members' desire for control over the policies that affected them. By the end of 1974, professors at nearly 350 colleges and universities had adopted collective bargaining.[4]

Educational reforms were even more common than structural ones. Usually adopted without the warfare that ravaged CCNY's polarized history department, many schools eliminated or revised requirements—foreign languages, in particular, but also at institutions where it was compulsory ROTC and physical education. Pass/fail became a widespread option, as did freshman seminars and other types of more personalized instruction. Many administrations also sought to satisfy their students' demands for power by letting them evaluate their teachers—a reform that, not surprisingly, encountered considerable faculty opposition.[5]

More controversial, but almost as ubiquitous, were the educational experiments that flowered at the same time. Some were the product of serious planning on the part of committed faculty members, others sprouted as offshoots of the New Left or the counterculture. Many were top-down developments, created by administrators and funded by foundations to circumvent faculty resistance to innovations like interdisciplinary programs or Black and women's studies. Entire institutions—among them, Hampshire College in Massachusetts, Evergreen in Washington State, and SUNY Old Westbury on Long Island—sprang up as alternatives to traditional colleges and universities. They had flexible personnel policies, interdisciplinary offerings, and considerable student input with a whiff of hippie culture—at least in their early days.[6]

There were also experimental units within traditional universities; some like the University of Michigan's Residential College are still around, while others like SUNY Buffalo's pacifist-oriented Tolstoy College soon disappeared. There were experimental courses as well, designed to supply the relevance that so many students claimed to seek. At Harvard, the young leftists in the economics department taught "The Capitalist Economy," while the interdisciplinary offering "Social Change in America" that Jack Stauder headed became the largest class in the university. It had no set syllabus; the radical graduate and undergraduate students who led its more than forty sections could teach whatever they wanted to.[7]

Actually, just about every single institution that I looked at had some kind of experimental program or set of classes, often organized with the administration's blessing and foundation funding. San Francisco State pioneered this development when in the fall of 1965 a group of intellectually ambitious students, inspired by the Freedom Schools of the Mississippi Summer Project and the Berkeley Free Speech Movement, founded what may have been the earliest, but was certainly the most influential, experimental college. Within a year, it had over twelve hundred students taking seventy courses, some of them for credit. Classes consisted of a quintessential sixties mixture of countercultural, political, and vocational topics, "Zen Basketball" as well as the nation's first courses in Black studies at a four-year college. Anybody who wanted to could offer a class. Its unpaid faculty drew San Francisco State professors chafing at the disciplinary constraints of their departments, representatives of the local arts and activist communities, and more than a few hippies.[8]

The model caught on at once. By the end of the following school year, ten other California state colleges had similar programs, as did dozens of schools across the country. A few days after the Columbia bust, its Liberation School opened, with sympathetic faculty members, graduate students, and community people teaching outdoor "counter classes" on everything from the "Liberated Talmud" to "Economic Aspects of U.S. Imperialism" and "Guerrilla Film-making."[9] Even such an unlikely institution as the University of Alabama in Huntsville was hosting its Union College that offered fifteen courses to some 140 students with the standard mix of alternative subjects ranging from African art and existentialism to auto mechanics and the draft.[10]

Within a few years, that wave of educational experimentation had subsided. Co-optation occurred as departments absorbed such supposedly radical innovations as women's and African American studies. A few experiments survived as stand-alone adult education ventures of the Left, but most disappeared, as did the other reforms that swept through the academic community at the time. Some of the faculty senates and other representative bodies created to ward off disruption are still functioning. Others faded away; their student members and then their faculty ones losing interest in governance and failing to produce a quorum.[11] Academic unions are still around, but barely. The Supreme Court's 1980 *Yeshiva* decision wiped them out in private institutions, while its 2018 *Janus* one seriously undermines them in the public sector.[12] In any event, by the mid-1970s when financial exigency replaced student unrest as the academic community's main problem, none of the long sixties' educational or structural reforms could have restored its lost élan.

Political Opposition and Economic Crisis

Admittedly, I exaggerate. But it is clear that the academic community had been so demoralized by its internal struggles during the 1960s that it failed to protect itself from the conservative onslaught against it. As American society moved to the right in the 1970s, its political class abandoned public higher education. Not only did many leading local, state, and national politicians withdraw their support from the academy, but they attacked it—and had been doing so for years.

California led the way. Just as its 1960 Master Plan exemplified the ambitious drive to offer higher education to the masses, so, too, did the rise of Ronald Reagan reveal the political fragility of that promise's institutional base. Reagan began his ascent by demonizing Berkeley— and never stopped. Not only had he and his supporters on the board of regents thrown the University of California's liberal leadership on the defensive by ousting Clark Kerr in 1966, but they also intervened in other personnel and curricular matters. In 1968, for example, they moved to deny credit to a student-initiated course to be taught by the Black Panther leader Eldridge Cleaver. Two years later, they went after Angela Davis at UCLA.[13]

Nor was Reagan alone. The turmoil on campus had rendered the academic community so unpopular that politicians nationwide clamored to punish it. During its 1969 session alone, California's lawmakers considered as many as one hundred repressive measures directed against their colleges and universities. Even though we have no exact figure, it is likely that hundreds, and perhaps thousands, of similar proposals came before state legislatures during the late 1960s and early 1970s.[14] Most were not enacted, while many that did get passed were thrown out by the courts.[15] Still, by the middle of 1970, more than thirty states had some kind of law against campus disorders, with at least a dozen of them calling for criminal penalties against disruptive individuals.[16]

Most, however, copied a federal law that withdrew financial assistance from militant students. Since many institutions were unable to identify, let alone discipline, such students, the measure was essentially unenforceable. Nonetheless, ambitious state politicians took it up.[17] They were also concerned about radical teachers. A Wisconsin lawmaker expressed the views of his fellow politicians when, besides calling for the mass expulsion of student rioters, he stated, "If there are any faculty members involved, they should be fired."[18] For Florida legislators, no "if" was involved. "In nearly every instance of campus unrest," the report of that state's Select Committee on Campus Unrest and Drug Abuse asserted, "the leaders were for the most part being counseled, guided, and occasionally directed by faculty members." The co-chair of a similar Illinois committee considered abolishing tenure as a way to punish the "Communists" who were masterminding the disorders.[19]

Although much of this anti-academic rhetoric was simply bluster on the part of politicians designed to pacify their constituents who had been bombarding them with demands to crack down on the campus ever since the Berkeley Free Speech Movement hit the nightly news, their hostility to the academic community ultimately took a serious toll. Perhaps the clearest indication that the political weather had changed was the California legislature's vote in the summer of 1970 to deny faculty members in the University of California and California State College systems the automatic cost-of-living salary increase that went to all state employees. Within a few years, other states were taking similar action.[20]

The federal government starved the university as well. Richard Nixon's distaste for the academy is well known. He ended several research programs and evinced considerable hostility to elite universities and their faculties.[21] But it's unclear whether he actually intended to punish the entire academy when his administration decided to transfer its support for higher education from direct grants to institutions to individual student loans—a move that, along with the state legislatures' cutbacks, forced colleges and universities to rely ever more heavily on their students' tuitions than on the public purse.[22]

The Corporate Campaign against the Academic Mind

Besides the defunding of public higher education, there was another side to the backlash against the university. By the late 1960s, a well-financed campaign against the academy was seeking to undermine its position as a source of relevant knowledge and expertise. Worried that the combination of falling profits, increased regulation, and mounting inflation threatened the very survival of the system of free enterprise, an important sector of the business community embarked upon an ideological crusade to change American political culture.[23] Besides engaging more directly in electoral politics and taking on the media, this campaign zeroed in on higher education. As these corporate leaders and their intellectual allies saw it, it was essential to reverse the anti-capitalist message that the academy—its social scientists, in particular—had been disseminating to its students as well as to the rest of society. The language that campaign used and the arguments it relied upon to delegitimize the university could have come directly from Sidney Hook's University Centers for Rational Alternatives. And, in fact, some of it did.[24]

In 1971 when the prominent Virginia attorney and soon-to-be Supreme Court justice Lewis F. Powell Jr. was asked for advice by a friend who had just been appointed chair of the Chamber of Commerce's Education Committee, he dispatched a 34-page memorandum sketching out a blueprint for a campaign to create a business-friendly polity that would combat what he considered a threat to free enterprise. This so-called Powell Memorandum has become iconic, in large part because so many of its recommendations actually came to pass. Decrying the ideological "imbalance" of an institution that indoctrinates its "bright young men" with a hatred of the system that they then seek to destroy, Powell laid out "a long-range and difficult project" to reshape the university and with it the nation's political discourse. Eliminating radical faculty members was central to his scenario, but so, too, was creating a network of endowed professorships, right-wing journalists, think tanks, and public speakers to spread the business community's alternative message on campus and beyond.[25]

With the help of conservative foundations and sympathetic billionaires, Powell's Gramscian vision pushed free-market libertarianism into the intellectual mainstream. It took years, but the business community's campaign to shrink the public sector was to deprive the academy of the funding it had long relied upon. At the same time, that campaign also managed to undermine the university's reputation by promoting the so-called culture wars of the 1980s and 1990s that reprised the 1960s-era demonization of higher education as the abode of tenured radicals and spineless administrators.[26]

Perhaps the most influential example of that genre was the work of Allan Bloom, the former Cornell philosopher then ensconced at the University of Chicago. Subsidized by more than $3 million from the Olin Foundation, his 1987 rant against the current academic scene, *The Closing of the American Mind*, reached the top of the best-seller list. At the same time, other conservative writers pushed scenarios about the academy's so-called political correctness that, they claimed, forced both students and professors to conform to a leftist agenda.[27] Since, as Nancy MacLean points out in *Democracy in Chains* her magisterial account of that "stealth plan" to delegitimize the university, its promoters tried to conceal their objectives, we should not blame the academy for failing to recognize the threat it faced.[28]

Devastating as the corporate sector's campaign to destroy the influence and credibility of the liberal academy was, it was only one facet of the triple whammy that hit the campuses just as the long sixties ended. There was also the national economic crisis of the early 1970s, fueled by factors far beyond the academy's control that undermined its financial stability. And, finally, there was the popular backlash—

fueled by hostility to the unruly students as well to the timid roll-out of affirmative action—that denied higher education the political support it had once enjoyed.

The university's liberal moment had passed. Its formerly respected leaders were thrown onto the defensive by a wave of conservatism hostile to their moderate worldview. Lost in the turmoil of the sixties was the promise that the university could make the American dream come true. Attacked from both the left and the right, the splintered and demoralized academic community could not mount a cohesive defense of its progressive mission of providing a first-rate system of mass higher education.

A paradox emerged. Although a college degree had become essential for entrée into and survival within the middle class, the institutions that purveyed it had lost their aura. Where politicians and the public once showered colleges and universities with money and respect, those schools were now denounced.[29] The right-wing campaign against them has successfully convinced most ordinary citizens that American higher education was in the hands of out-of-touch elitists and over-the-top "snowflakes" who prowl for micro-aggressions, write incomprehensible prose, and only work twelve hours a week. Thus demonized, an increasingly powerless academic community was to find its intellectual authority under attack.

To a certain extent, the university's failure to counter the deleterious stereotypes undermining its credibility revealed the declining status of the institution. Not that the academic community of the so-called golden age had ever realized the postwar liberal vision of a more democratized system of higher education. Its complicity with the warfare state, along with its failure to honestly confront its own structural racism and sexism, had destroyed whatever trust an entire generation of left-liberal and radical academics had in the moral integrity of the educational institutions that housed them. The Left's critique of the university's sins, though largely valid, also—and unfortunately—helped to remove the veil that had shielded the academic community from the more disingenuous and destructive charges of the Right.

The politically active professors of the sixties are now emeriti. They have successors, but they no longer possess automatic respect because of their vocation—which is by no means a bad thing. Nor can they pursue academic careers without risking enormous economic insecurity. The job market tanked even before the sixties ended. The imposition of austerity in response to the fiscal crisis of the 1970s signaled, more than anything else, the loss of the public's previously unquestioning support for higher education.[30] Even as enrollments continued to rise, the academic community had been cut adrift. As legislators reduced the percentage of their universities' budgets they were willing to fund, the academy tightened its belt and sought new sources of support. Colleges and universities stopped replacing retiring professors, raised tuitions, and adopted corporate-style strategies designed to streamline their operations and attract paying customers.

Instead of making a case for a more democratic system that would offer all comers access to a high-quality system of universal higher education, the academy's leaders adopted the individualistic mantra of neoliberalism. They mouthed platitudes about the common good, while treating a college education as a personal benefit, rather than one that serves society as a whole. The result, as we well know, is the trillions of dollars of debt that blights the futures of so many students, limiting their current options and life chances. Wealthy undergraduates can major in art history; less affluent ones end up in accounting.

Besides its unaffordability, the most deleterious feature of the current university is a hollowed-out faculty in an increasingly hierarchical system. Inequality reigns—among both students and institutions. Except at the most selective brand-name colleges and universities that have the resources to offer an intellectually stimulating liberal education and whose students have the economic security to risk it, vocationalism and adjunctification hold sway. Composed largely of part-timers and people with short-term contracts, an academic precariat with no prospects for tenure now teaches more than 70 percent of all college and university classes. Most are skilled and committed teachers. But they earn an average of $2,700 a course. If they don't have outside employment, a trust fund, or an affluent mate, they must teach a brutal load of courses, often at several different institutions, and sometimes rely on food stamps. COVID-19 has only made their plight even more precarious. Unless they have the diminishing luxury of a union contract, they rarely have job security. Often hired at the very last minute, they can be fired at any time, for any reason, or for no reason at all. Talk about quality. Will they risk student complaints if they don't grade easily or water down their syllabi? Academic freedom—forget about it.[31]

Moreover, because of the financial pressures on their increasingly strapped students, these overloaded and seriously underpaid instructors are no longer teaching the courses in the humanities and social sciences that formed the core of the curriculum during the long sixties. Instead, they must offer the vocational training that today's students and their parents demand. Going, if not gone, is the traditional emphasis on the liberal arts that ideally exposes students to the broad range of cultures and ideas needed for understanding our complicated and changing world. In its place is what one scholar has called the "Instrumental University," an institution whose mission is to enable graduates to get a job.[32]

Since it is ever more obvious that the current academy functions primarily to replicate an increasingly inequitable status quo, it is hard to imagine how it could be restructured to serve a more democratic purpose without external pressure for something like universal free higher education. Whether or not the campus unrest of the long sixties and the still ongoing backlash against it aborted a promising effort to broaden access to that education is hard to tell. Perhaps the time has come to restore that earlier promise. If we do, however, we must heed the demand of the much-maligned sixties radicals for the academy to become relevant as well as accessible. If nothing else, the university of the twenty-first century must stimulate students to think critically. It's a cliché, to be sure. But open and well-trained minds are essential if we are to retain a democratic polity and—dare I say it—save the earth.

RESEARCHING THE ACADEMY IN THE LONG SIXTIES

A Bibliographic Essay

Perhaps I should have stuck to a narrower topic. At the end of the last millennium, while editing the AAUP's magazine *Academe*, I wrote what I thought would be a short overview of the then-current condition of academic freedom and higher education. But, as a historian, I could not look at a contemporary problem without examining its roots. Having studied the impact of McCarthyism on the university, I assumed that someone else must have done the same for the upheavals of the following decade and a half. Wrong. Not only was there little scholarly literature on academic freedom during the 1960s, but there was no general study of the transformation of the university during the most turbulent period in its history. It was clear that a broader investigation was needed not only to understand what the academic community experienced in the long sixties, but also to figure out how those experiences continue to shape higher education today.

Given a universe populated by over 2,500 institutions and a professoriate that grew from 236,000 to 450,000 between 1960 and 1970, it is no surprise that the resources available for research on the political history of higher education in the long sixties are so abundant. From scholarly monographs to personal interviews to contemporary journalism to official records to memoirs—the amount and variety of sources boggle the mind. And these are only those that exist in the print world that I mainly inhabit. As a relic of the twentieth century, I admit to insufficient knowledge of the amazing resources that exist on the web. This essay, thus, does not claim to be comprehensive. At best, it might introduce readers to some useful literature and point out areas others might want

456 * Researching the Academy in the Long Sixties

to explore. The specific items mentioned below, it must be noted, represent only the tiniest amount of the material that exists. I *know* that I have missed more than a few crucial sources. (For additional documentation beyond the endnotes, see www.ellenschrecker.com).

One factor that may account for the wealth of resources is that this study deals with a population that writes a lot. Academics did considerable navel-gazing during and after the long sixties. Would any other professional group have produced anywhere near the number of memoirs, monographs, and journalistic essays about its own experiences? Significantly, some of the most prominent public intellectuals of the period—Seymour Martin Lipset, David Riesman, and Daniel Bell, for example—devoted much of their output during the 1960s and 1970s to studying higher education. Their work is valuable not only for the information it conveys, but also for what it shows about the attitudes and assumptions these influential writers held.

Among the most useful sources for this study have been the contemporary publications that were pouring out of commercial and scholarly presses in the late 1960s and early 1970s. Produced by scholars who were living through the events they were writing about, collections of essays by academics about their universities proved indispensable, like the volume covering sixteen institutions edited by David Riesman and Verne A. Stadtman in 1973, *Academic Transformation*. Similar compilations dealt with individual universities, among them the ones on Cornell by Cushing Strout and David I. Grossvogel, *Divided We Stand* (1970); the University of Wisconsin by Philip G. Altbach, Robert S. Laufer, and Sheila McVey, *Academic Supermarkets* (1971); and San Francisco State by Arlene Kaplan Daniels, Rachel Kahn-Hut, and Associates, *Academics on the Line* (1970). Besides books about individual institutions, there were collections of essays about various aspects of the academic scene, among them those by Julian Foster and Durward Long, *Protest! Student Activism in America* (1970); Howard S. Becker, *Campus Power Struggle* (1970); and Daniel Bell and Irving Kristol, *Confrontation* (1969). There was also the pathbreaking series of "antitextbooks" published by the Pantheon editor André Schiffrin. Edited by such left-wing academics as Louis Kampf and Paul Lauter, *The Politics of Literature* (1972), Barton

J. Bernstein, *Towards a New Past* (1968); Edward Friedman and Mark Selden, *America's Asia* (1971); and Theodore Roszak, *Dissenting Academy* (1967), they contained essays designed to introduce readers to the new radical scholarship within the disciplines.

Equally useful are the monographs on higher education sponsored by such organizations as the Carnegie Commission on Higher Education and the Ford Foundation, which benefited from their authors' access to the people whose institutions they were studying. Among the most informative of these institutional surveys are E. Alden Dunham's 1969 account of the second-tier public colleges and universities, *Colleges of the Forgotten Americans*; John Millett's 1978 discussion of the structural reforms of the long sixties in *New Structures of Campus Power*; and Earl Cheit's 1971 survey of the financial crisis of the early 1970s, *The New Depression in Higher Education*.

Another type of publication that may be peculiar to the academic community consists of hybrid collections of essays put together in the 1990s and beyond that combine personal recollections of the sixties with scholarship. Most—like Paul Buhle's 1990 volume of writings, *History and the New Left*, by and about the radical students and historians at the University of Wisconsin—focus on a single institution or discipline. Reginald Zelnik's exemplary account of the Berkeley faculty's response to the free speech crisis is the highlight of the book that he and Robert Cohen co-edited in 2002, *The Free Speech Movement*. There are similarly valuable essays in the 1991 compilation *Radical Sociologists and the Movement* by Martin Oppenheimer, Martin J. Murray, and Rhonda F. Levine.

Nonetheless, for all the important scholarship about universities in the long sixties, no one has yet produced a comprehensive survey of the academy as a whole during those years. The closest approximation— even though it deals only with the main research universities—is Roger Geiger's institutional study, *Research and Relevant Knowledge* (1993), probably the single most thorough analysis of the post–World War II academy. While there are other fine studies, they tend to be narrower in scope.

As for monographs—some topics receive considerable attention, others little or none. Given their importance in inspiring the antiwar movement, it seems odd, for example, that the scholarly literature contains no serious study of the teach-ins, though there is a nice website at http://michiganintheworld.history.lsa.umich.edu/antivietnamwar/ and a useful collection of essays and documents in *Teach-Ins* by Louis Menashe and Ronald Radosh (1967). And despite useful articles on individual disciplines by the likes of Marlene Kim, "URPE at Fifty" (2018), and Tiago Mata, "Migrations and Boundary Work" (2009), there is no general study of the members of the academic Left and their organizations. Another lacuna is academic freedom. Since both left and right were claiming its protection, it seems a topic worthy of attention.

Among the topics that attracted some fine recent scholarship are the Black Power and Black studies controversies and the ethical issues facing scientists. Martha Biondi's *Black Revolution on Campus* (2012) presents a fairly broad picture, while the work of other scholars offers insights into the Black Power movement and its connection to Black studies, including Peniel E. Joseph's edited volume *The Black Power Movement* (2006), Fabio Rojas's *From Black Power to Black Studies* (2007), Noliwe M. Rooks's *White Money/Black Power* (2006), William L. Van Deburg's *New Day in Babylon* (1992), David A. Varel's *The Scholar and the Struggle* (2020), Ibram H. Rogers [Kendi]'s *The Black Campus Movement*, and Joy Ann Williamson's *Radicalizing the Ebony Tower* (2008), among others. Also exemplary is the scholarship about scientists. Particularly helpful are Stuart W. Leslie's *The Cold War and American Science* (1993), Rebecca S. Lowen's *Creating the Cold War University* (1997), Kelly Moore's *Disrupting Science* (2008), Sarah Bridger's *Scientists at War* (2015), Paul Rubinson's *Redefining Science* (2016), and Margaret Pugh O'Mara's *Cities of Knowledge* (2005).

There is, of course, a vast literature on individual schools. Ranging from official and unofficial histories to a wide variety of monographs, journalism, documentary collections, and memoirs, it's a body of work that sometimes treats the long sixties in detail and sometimes just refers to it in passing. Among the particularly useful first-person accounts are those by administrators at two of the most troubled campuses—SUNY Buffalo's Richard Siggelkow, *Dissent and Disruption* (1991), and San Francisco State's Robert Smith, Richard Axen, and DeVere Pentony, *By Any Means Necessary* (1970). There are also helpful chronicles by student journalists, especially the volumes on Columbia by Jerry L. Avorn et al., *Up Against the Ivy Wall* (1968), and on Harvard by Lawrence E. Eichel et al., *The Harvard Strike* (1970). There are dozens, if not hundreds, of memoirs and historical studies of these and other institutions. Some typical monographs include Morton Keller and Phyllis Keller's *Making Harvard Modern* (2001); Matthew Levin on the University of Wisconsin–Madison, *Cold War University* (2013); Mary Ann Wynkoop on Indiana University, *Dissent in the Heartland* (2002); Bruce M. Stave on the University of Connecticut, *Red Brick in the Land of Steady Habits* (2006); Donald Downs's *Cornell '69* (1999); Thomas M. Grace's *Kent State* (2016); and the excellent sociological study of the University of Chicago by Donald Light Jr. and John Spiegel, *The Dynamics of University Protest* (1977). Also useful are a number of works like Kenneth J. Heineman's *Campus Wars* (1993) and Richard M. Freeland's *Academia's Golden Age* (1992) that look at a select handful of schools.

The memoirs vary enormously, though even the most deplorable contain tidbits of useful information about specific institutions or organizations. Beside the Smith and Siggelkow works cited above, some other helpful ones are Bruce Dancis's *Resister* (2014) and Charles Haynie's *A Memoir of the New Left* (2009) on Cornell; Richard Lyman's *Stanford in Turmoil* (2009); Robert E. Marshak's *Academic Renewal in the 1970s* (1982) on CCNY; Warren Bennis's *The Leaning Ivory Tower* (1973) on SUNY Buffalo; Wayne Booth's *My Many Selves* (2006) on the University of Chicago; John Morton Blum's *A Life with History* (2004) and William Sloane Coffin Jr.'s *Once to Every Man* (1978) on Yale; Mickey Flacks and Dick Flacks's *Making History, Making Blintzes* (2018) on the University of Chicago and University of California, Santa Barbara; J. Stanley Marshall's *The Tumultuous Sixties* (2006) on Florida State University; and, among the few such memoirs by women, Florence Howe's *A Life in Motion* (2011) and Roberta Salper's *Domestic Subversive* (2014), on the New University Conference and women's studies.

Disciplines got attention as well, both at the time and later. Some examples include, beside the work on Black studies cited above: Michael A. Bernstein's *A Perilous Progress* (2001) on economics, Peter

Novick's *That Noble Dream* (1988) on history, Fabio Lanza's *The End of Concern* (2017) on East Asian studies, and Marilyn Boxer's *When Women Ask the Questions* (1998) on women's studies. Because so much was happening both on and off campus during the long sixties, it was necessary to consult scholarship on dozens of related topics in order to make sense of the broader picture. Among the most useful works were those by Seth Rosenfeld, *Subversives: The FBI's War on Student Radicals, and Reagan's Rise to Power* (2012); David Schalk, *War and the Ivory Tower: Algeria and Vietnam* (1991); Lawrence M. Baskir and William A. Strauss, *Chance and Circumstance: The Draft, the War, and the Vietnam Generation* (1978); and Marjorie Heins, *Priests of Our Democracy: The Supreme Court, Academic Freedom, and the Anti-Communist Purge* (2013).

The range of primary sources is similarly wide. The many fine contemporary collections of relevant documents were particularly helpful. Seymour Martin Lipset and Sheldon Wolin (1965) produced an early compendium, *The Berkeley Student Revolt*, while Immanuel Wallerstein and Paul Starr (1971) put out the two-volume *University Crisis Reader*. There was also the previously mentioned 1967 book of documents on the teach-ins by Menashe and Radosh. Recently, collections of dozens, if not hundreds, of relevant documents have been posted on the internet, often by students as well as professors. For an example of such a collection, see the archive of materials about Bruce Franklin at Stanford on the website a3mreunion.org.

Interviews were crucial for this work. I conducted them with about 130 academics both in person and over the phone. Most, but not all, were radicals who had been involved in one way or another with the civil rights and antiwar movements and/or the dissent on their campuses and within their disciplines. These interviews—with men and women like Renate Bridenthal, Louis Kampf, Paul Lauter, John McDermott, Joan Wallach Scott, Allan Silver, Walter Struve, and Leon Wofsy—were particularly useful in providing background information about these people's careers and political activities that would have been otherwise unavailable. I would have liked to have interviewed more conservatives as well, but they had usually been senior professors and administrators—and few were still around. Fortunately, however, many of their stories and those of other academics were recorded at the time or later by oral historians and deposited in institutional archives and, in many cases, made available online.

Columbia's pioneering Oral History Project began interviewing professors and administrators within a few weeks of the university's 1968 crisis. Its collection of more than forty transcripts is an invaluable trove of information about the behavior and attitudes of the university's leaders and faculty members during that crisis. The interviews with Richard Hofstadter, Peter Kenen, Walter Metzger, and Immanuel Wallerstein were particularly revealing. The Bancroft Library at Berkeley conducted a similar set of interviews several decades later. Though they focused on the Free Speech Movement, they actually covered a longer period than the ones at Columbia and, thus, proved even more rewarding. Among the most valuable were those with Charles Muscatine, Robert Scalapino, Howard Schachman, Carl Schorske, Neil Smelser, and Kenneth Stampp. Other archives, at Ohio State and San Francisco State, for example, also contain oral histories with faculty leaders that add significantly to the available resources for a study of these and other troubled institutions. There is a plethora of similarly relevant oral histories in the archives of other colleges and universities and on the internet.

And then there are the archives themselves, the repositories of the official records of institutions and their top leaders, as well as those of other groups and the personal papers of faculty members. Since I wanted to examine as wide a range of colleges and universities as possible, I had to be selective about which institutions I would cover, since even an exhaustive investigation of one university's records would have taken months. Most of the collections I looked at were professionally organized; others were still works in progress. Among the official archives I explored were those of SUNY Buffalo, the University of California, Berkeley, and San Francisco State, Vassar College, CCNY, Fordham University, and the Universities of Chicago, Connecticut, and Massachusetts Amherst. I also looked at the records of such organizations as the AAUP at George Washington University, the New University Conference at the Wisconsin Historical Society, and RESIST at Trinity College, Hartford.

The private papers of individual professors deposited in their university's archives were an invaluable source. Harvard's Pusey Library harbored many of the most useful collections, among them those of John King Fairbank, Oscar Handlin, Robert McCloskey, and David Riesman. McCloskey's papers were so poorly organized—two boxes containing folders labeled "A, B, C, D, etc."—that it was only due to serendipity and chutzpah that I opened an unmarked manila envelope to find a 1967 exchange of letters about Vietnam between a group of Harvard heavyweights and the president of the United States. There was a similar correspondence between LBJ and an equally eminent contingent from Columbia in the papers of Richard Hofstadter at that university. The papers of Robert S. Browne in Swarthmore College's Peace Collection contained massive amounts of material on the early antiwar movement. Serendipity was important; someone's personal papers sometimes contained materials from unexpected correspondents or now-forgotten organizations. For example, the papers collected by a little-known radical political scientist named Robert Winston, now housed in the archives at UMass Amherst, contain a veritable trove of documents about the radical caucus within his discipline.

Individual academics also offered me access to their own personal papers. The most valuable, by far, considering the disorganized condition of the AAUP's still-to-be-processed case records, were the files of Alfred F. Young in the possession of NYU's Robert Cohen, which contained the correspondence of the American Historical Association's special committee investigating violations of academic freedom within the historical profession. Other scholars were equally generous with their papers. Paul Lauter allowed me to look at his files a few years before he gave them to Trinity College, while Joseph Esherick loaned me his papers full of useful documents from the Committee of Concerned Asian Scholars.

In short, as I hope this brief overview of the available resources reveals, there is an enormous amount of material available for any researcher interested in looking at the political history of higher education between the mid-1950s and the mid-1970s. I only began to scratch the surface.

ACKNOWLEDGMENTS

This book is the inadvertent middle volume of a trilogy that deals with the politics of American higher education in the last half of the twentieth century. I didn't plan it that way. *No Ivory Tower* (1986), my study of McCarthyism and the universities, looked at the late 1940s and 1950s, while *The Lost Soul of Higher Education* (2010) surveyed the academic scene in the early twenty-first century.[1] Accordingly, although I started work on this book about ten years ago, it rests upon deeper foundations—and my debts stretch back into the late 1970s.

My main one, by far, is more recent. It belongs to my incomparable editor, Timothy Mennel. Not only did his initial enthusiasm for what was an embarrassingly inchoate proposal buoy me up when so many other publishers understandably found that proposal confusing, but his devotion to the project never flagged—even as due date after due date came and went. He read early drafts, suggested bibliography, and encouraged me to keep on working. Then, after we both recognized that the final manuscript was too long to be publishable, he did the necessary surgery—brilliantly. I am in awe of his literary sensitivity and ability to pare away unnecessary verbiage, without distorting either my ideas or my prose. I am still, of course, solely responsible for the book, but it has been much improved by Tim's diligence and by the advice and assistance of many others.

I have accumulated immense debts over the years to colleagues, archivists, friends, and, especially, to the more than 130 academics who generously let me interview them. Some—Ernst Benjamin, Renate Bridenthal, Carolyn Eisenberg, Joseph Esherick, Bruce Franklin, Michael Frisch, William Herbert, David Kettler, Paul Lauter, the late Jesse Lemisch, Ngo Vinh Long, Richard Mann, the late Marshall Sahlins, Stuart Schaar, David Schalk, George Schwab, and the late Judith Stein and Leon Wofsy—also gave me access to their personal papers or sent manuscripts and other materials. Robert Cohen deserves special thanks, not only for providing me with copies of Alfred F. Young's files on academic freedom in the historical profession, but also for his willingness to read some of the manuscript and sharing his deep knowledge of higher education in the 1960s. Other research assistance came from Zachary Natan Cohen and my student at Yeshiva College, Eliot Friedman.

I have been fortunate in finding other colleagues willing to offer advice as well as critique all or part of this book. Molly Nolan and Dick Ohmann were particularly generous in their comments on a much-too-long manuscript. The thoughtful reports from my outside readers, Joy Rohde and Jeremy Varon, not only cheered me up, but also offered invaluable suggestions for revising the book as well as much-needed bibliographical assistance. Among the other friends and scholars who provided helpful advice and encouragement, sometimes without realizing it, were Clyde Barrow, Renate Bridenthal, Chandler Davis, the late William Gamson, Todd Gitlin, Van Gosse, Erica Harth, Kevin Y. Kim, Frances Maher, John McDermott, Henry Reichman, Lise Vogel, and the late Marilyn Young. I am grateful, as well, for the useful comments I received when presenting early portions of the manuscript at an MLA Panel on the 1960s, Columbia's University Seminar on 20th Century Politics and Society, and the Tamiment Library's Center for the Study of the United States and the Cold War.

Because I taught at a small institution that lacked the facilities for serious research in my field, I could not have written this book without the long-term institutional support of the Tamiment Library and Robert H. Wagner Labor Archives at New York University's Bobst Library. For more than a decade, I enjoyed the status of a visiting scholar with access to the major research library and a congenial place to work. I am particularly grateful for the wisdom and encouragement of Michael Nash, the Tamiment's late and irreplaceable head curator, as well as the assistance of his successors, Timothy Naftali and Tim Johnson. Though handicapped by the COVID shutdown, the Tamiment's current head Shannon O'Neill and her fellow curator Michael Koncewicz have continued to perform miracles, especially in working with the Dean and Director of Special Collections Charlotte Priddle to maintain my visiting scholar status and then to find illustrations for the book.

Archivists elsewhere have also aided my work enormously. Especially during the COVID crisis when I was looking for visual materials at a time when most depositories were closed to the public, some of these people personally searched their collections to come up with the pictures I needed. Among them were Jocelyn Wilk at Columbia; Mary Jo Orzech at SUNY Brockport; Sarah Patton at the Hoover Institution; Michael Lange at the Bancroft Library, University of California, Berkeley; Wendy Chiemelewski at the Swarthmore College Peace Collection; and Catherine Powell at San Francisco State University. In the pre-COVID era, some of these archivists were also helpful during on-site visits as were Sydney Van Ort at CCNY, Tanya Hollis and Meredith Eliassen at San Francisco State, Anne Coleman at the University of Alabama at Huntsville, Tom Frusciano at Rutgers University, and William Offhaus at the State University at Buffalo. Thanks also to my literary agent, Sandra Dijkstra, and her associate, Elise Capron, as well as to the patient and helpful folks at the University of Chicago Press, Susannah Engstrom and Erin DeWitt.

Then, there are all the people "without whom" this book could not have been written. Some were the friends and relatives who put me up during my archival visits: Ernst Benjamin and Judith McCombs, Michael Frisch, Linda Gordon and Allen Hunter, Frances Maher and John McDermott, Morton Paley and Gunnel Tottie, Margaret Power, and David and Michaelene Zipser. My stepdaughter Eva Braiman literally rescued me by tracking down and obtaining the permissions for the illustrations. Because my late husband suffered from a particularly nasty form of Alzheimer's during much of the time I was working on this book, I could not have managed without the expert and loving care he received from Lindsay Spence, Musa Tunkara, and, especially, Maurice Yapp, his wife Carmel, and his angelic son Connor, who brought cheer into all our lives. I also owe a lot to Morgana Tessler and Melissa Gutierrez, who kept me vertical; Freddie Riviera, who kept the lights on; as well as to the members of both my warmly supportive "Not Sissies" and later book groups.

Judy and Norman Stein, as well as my brother and sister-in-law, Tony and Mary Alice Wolf, and sister and brother-in-law, Mary and Howard Hurtig, provided much-needed respite throughout, as did my sons, Michael and Daniel Schrecker, and their wives, Karina Goldrajch-Schrecker and Sair Goldenberg. Michael and Dan also supplied the technological assistance that their computer-challenged mother could not have survived without, while my granddaughters, Pazit, Ila, and April, contributed nothing but joy. The main collateral benefit I received from this project was to interview Mark Selden, who then entered my life a few years later and never left it. His belief in the value of my work, as well as his calm good sense, sly humor, and willingness to chop garlic and ginger has made it possible for me to finish the book without too much sturm and drang.

NOTES

Introduction

1. Leonard Kriegel, *Working Through: A Teacher's Journey in the Urban University* (New York: Saturday Review Press, 1972), 192.

2. Richard M. Freeland, *Academia's Golden Age: Universities in Massachusetts, 1945–1970* (New York: Oxford University Press, 1992). See also Roger L. Geiger, *Research and Relevant Knowledge: American Research Universities since World War II* (1st ed., Oxford University Press, 1993; New Brunswick, NJ: Transaction, 2004), 198, a study that remains the most intelligent overall treatment of the academic community after World War II.

3. The conception of "the long sixties" owes a debt to the taxonomy developed by Jacqueline Dowd Hall in "The Long Civil Rights Movement and the Political Uses of the Past," *Journal of American History* 91, no. 4 (March 2005): 1233–63.

4. Nicholas Kristof, "We're No. 28! And Dropping!" *New York Times*, September 10, 2020.

5. For a similar periodization by an astute observer, if not a successful administrator, see the foreword by the ill-starred University of California president Clark Kerr in Everett Carll Ladd Jr. and Seymour Martin Lipset, *Professors, Unions, and American Higher Education* (Berkeley: Carnegie Foundation for the Advancement of Teaching, 1973), x–xi.

6. Bruce Jackson, "Buffalo English: Literary Glory Days at UB," *Buffalo Beat*, February 26, 1999, https://www.acsu.buffalo.edu/~bjackson/englishdept.htm (accessed September 10, 2020): "The key thing about those years was the war in Southeast Asia. It touched nearly everything we did: how we taught our classes, the lives of our students, our conversations. Faculty argued on both sides of the war issue for years. I didn't realize it then, but that argument made us a community as nothing else has since. Even in arguing against one another, we met people we would not otherwise have met, engaged in conversations we would not otherwise have had, dealt with ethical issues that transcended the ordinary politics of the campus."

7. Michael Walzer, *Political Action: A Practical Guide to Movement Politics* (Chicago: Quadrangle Books, 1971), 15.

8. Geiger, *Research and Relevant Knowledge*, 249; Nancy Weiss Malkiel, *"Keep the Damned Women Out": The Struggle for Coeducation* (Princeton, NJ: Princeton University Press, 2016).

Chapter One

1. E. Alden Dunham, *Colleges of the Forgotten Americans: A Profile of State Colleges and Regional Universities* (New York: McGraw-Hill, 1969), 7–11.

2. Dunham, *Colleges of the Forgotten Americans*, 8–18.

3. John R. Thelin, *A History of American Higher Education* (Baltimore: Johns Hopkins University Press, 2004), 293, 322.

4. Dunham, *Colleges of the Forgotten Americans*, 142–43; Robert E. Marshak, *Academic Renewal in the 1970s: Memoirs of a City College President* (Washington, DC: University Press of America, 1982), 11–12; Leonard Kriegel, "Surviving the Apocalypse: Teaching at City College," *Change* 4, no. 6 (Summer 1972): 60; Arthur K. Bierman, "Oral History," 51, interviewed by Peter Carroll, January 14, 17, 28, 1992, Labor Archives and Research Center, San Francisco State University.

5. John D. Millett, *New Structures of Campus Power* (San Francisco: Jossey-Bass, 1978), 82–83; Thelin, *A History of American Higher Education*, 264; John Walsh, "Stanford's Search for Solutions," in *Academic Transformation: Seventeen Institutions under Pressure*, ed. David Riesman and Verne A. Stadtman (New York: McGraw-Hill, 1973), 303.

6. Jack H. Schuster and Martin J. Finkelstein, *The American Faculty: The Restructuring of Academic Work and Careers* (Baltimore: Johns Hopkins University Press, 2006), 39; Richard M. Freeland, *Academia's Golden Age: Universities in Massachusetts, 1945–1970* (New York: Oxford University Press, 1992), 88.

7. Magali Sarfatti Larson, "Master Plan, Master Failure," in *Academics on the Line: The Faculty Strike at San Francisco State*, ed. Arlene Kaplan Daniels, Rachel Kahn-Hut, and Associates (San Francisco: Jossey-Bass, 1970), 66.

8. Dunham, *Colleges of the Forgotten Americans*, 51–56; Thelin, *A History of American Higher Education*, 286–89.

9. Robert S. Fisk and William C. Puffer, "Public University System: State University of New York," in *Faculty Unions and Collective Bargaining*, ed. E. D. Duryea, Robert S. Fisk, and Associates (San Francisco: Jossey-Bass, 1973), 133.

10. Marshak, *Academic Renewal*, 5–6.

11. Marshak, *Academic Renewal*, 48.

12. Roger L. Geiger, *Research and Relevant Knowledge: American Research Universities since World War II* (1st ed., Oxford University Press, 1993; New Brunswick, NJ: Transaction, 2004), 138.

13. Christopher J. Adams, "An Historical Documentation on the Origins and Es-

tablishment of Faculty Collective Bargaining at Hofstra University" (EdD diss., Hofstra University, 2005), 53.

14. Morton Keller and Phyllis Keller, *Making Harvard Modern: The Rise of America's University* (Cary, NC: Oxford University Press, 2001), 295.

15. Geiger, *Research and Relevant Knowledge*, 217.

16. Walsh, "Stanford's Search for Solutions," in *Academic Transformation*, ed. Riesman and Stadtman; J. Stanley Marshall, *The Tumultuous Sixties: Campus Unrest and Student Life at a Southern University* (Tallahassee: Sentry Press, 2006), 305.

17. Thelin, *A History of American Higher Education*, 289; Neil J. Smelser, "Berkeley in Crisis and Change," in *Academic Transformation*, ed. Riesman and Stadtman, 54; University of California, Berkeley Academic Senate, *Education at Berkeley: Report of the Select Committee on Education*, March 1966, 13 (hereafter "Muscatine Report").

18. Dunham, *Colleges of the Forgotten Americans*, 81.

19. Claudia Goldin and Lawrence F. Katz, *The Race between Education and Technology* (Cambridge, MA: Harvard University Press, 2008), 89.

20. Thelin, *A History of American Higher Education*, 262–67; Geiger, *Research and Relevant Knowledge* 40–42; Freeland, *Academia's Golden Age*, 73–74.

21. On the value of college education, see Goldin and Katz, *The Race between Education and Technology*.

22. Matthew Johnson, *Undermining Racial Justice: How One University Embraced Inclusion and Inequality* (Ithaca, NY: Cornell University Press, 2020), 10.

23. Kelly Moore, *Disrupting Science: Social Movements, American Scientists, and the Politics of the Military, 1945–1975* (Princeton, NJ: Princeton University Press, 2008), 51; Sarah Bridger, *Scientists at War: The Ethics of Cold War Weapons Research* (Cambridge, MA: Harvard University Press, 2015), 61.

24. Margaret Pugh O'Mara, *Cities of Knowledge: Cold War Science and the Search for the Next Silicon Valley* (Princeton, NJ: Princeton University Press, 2005), 97–141; Rebecca S. Lowen, *Creating the Cold War University: The Transformation of Stanford* (Berkeley: University of California Press, 1997), 73–88, 109–10, 124; Alvin Weinberg, head of the Oak Ridge Atomic Laboratory, quoted in Stuart W. Leslie, *The Cold War and American Science: The Military-Industrial-Academic Complex at MIT and Stanford* (New York: Columbia University Press, 1993), 141; Freeland, *Academia's Golden Age*, 141.

25. Bridger, *Scientists at War*, 17; Geiger, *Research and Relevant Knowledge*, 174.

26. George Kistiakowsky, *A Scientist at the White House: The Private Diary of President Eisenhower's Special Assistant for Science and Technology* (Cambridge, MA: Harvard University Press, 1976), viii; Charles S. Maier, "Introduction," in *A Scientist at the White House*, by Kistiakowsky, xxix–lix.

27. Daniel J. Kevles, *The Physicists: The History of a Scientific Community in Modern America*, 2nd ed. (1977; Cambridge, MA: Harvard University Press, 1995), 394–97; Freeland, *Academia's Golden Age*, 141; Moore, *Disrupting Science*, 32;

Bridger, *Scientists at War*, 17–20; Ann Finkbeiner, *The Jasons: The Secret History of Science's Postwar Elite* (New York: Viking, 2006), 26, 61.

28. For the relationship between the government and the economics profession, see Michael A. Bernstein, *A Perilous Progress: Economists and Public Purpose in Twentieth-Century America* (Princeton, NJ: Princeton University Press, 2001).

29. Contemporaries noted this transformation and often decried it. The sociologist David Riesman was perhaps the most influential of those who sought to analyze the changes in higher education. Christopher Jencks and David Riesman, *The Academic Revolution* (New York: Doubleday, 1968). See also Freeland, *Academia's Golden Age*, 5–7; and Harold L. Hodgkinson, *Institutions in Transition: A Profile of Change in Higher Education* (New York: McGraw-Hill, 1971).

30. For an overview of how the South's most prestigious private universities adapted to the pressures for integration, see Melissa Kean, *Desegregating Private Higher Education in the South: Duke, Emory, Rice, Tulane, and Vanderbilt* (Baton Rouge: Louisiana State University Press, 2008). Marshall, *The Tumultuous Sixties*, 13, reveals a similar drive for status at Florida State University. See also Eddie R. Cole, *The Campus Color Line: College Presidents and the Struggle for Black Freedom* (Princeton, NJ: Princeton University Press, 2020), 29, 156–97; and William J. Billingsley, *Communists on Campus: Race, Politics, and the Public University in Sixties North Carolina* (Athens: University of Georgia Press, 1999), 108–68.

31. Smelser, "Berkeley in Crisis and Change," in ed. Riesman and Stadtman, *Academic Transformation*, 54.

32. Thelin, *A History of American Higher Education*, 310.

33. Schuster and Finkelstein, *The American Faculty*, 39.

34. Geiger, *Research and Relevant Knowledge*, 138.

35. Walsh, "Stanford's Search for Solutions," in *Academic Transformation*, ed. Riesman and Stadtman, 304–5; Adams, "Hofstra," 53.

36. Dunham, *Colleges of the Forgotten Americans*, 96.

37. Riesman, "Commentary and Epilogue," in *Academic Transformation*, ed. Riesman and Stadtman, 413.

38. For a full treatment of the experiences of these refugee scholars in the segregated South, see Gabrielle Simon Edgcomb, *From Swastika to Jim Crow: Refugee Scholars at Black Colleges* (Malabar, FL: Krieger, 1993). See also Wilma Iggers and Georg Iggers, *Two Lives in Uncertain Times: Facing the Challenges of the 20th Century as Scholars and Citizens* (New York: Berghahn Books, 2006).

39. John Morton Blum, *A Life with History* (Lawrence: University Press of Kansas, 2004), 62.

40. Herbert G. Gutman, "Learning about History," in *History and the New Left: Madison, Wisconsin, 1950–1970*, ed. Paul Buhle (Philadelphia: Temple University Press, 1990), 49.

41. Though his future colleagues didn't know it, Dowd was also Jewish, or at least

his mother was. Doug Dowd, *Blues for America: A Critique, a Lament, and Some Memories* (New York: Monthly Review Press, 1997), 61.

42. Blum, *A Life with History*, 103.

43. "Carl Bridenbaugh," American Historical Society, http://www.historians.org/about-aha-and-membership/aha-history-and-archives/presidential-addresses/carl-bridenbaugh (accessed August 5, 2015).

44. Carl E. Schorske, *Intellectual Life, Civil Libertarian Issues, and the Student Movement at the University of California, Berkeley, 1960–1969*, 13, interviews conducted by Ann Lage in 1996, 1997, Regional Oral History Office, Bancroft Library, University of California, Berkeley, 2000, http://digitalassets.lib.berkeley.edu/rohoia/ucb/text/intelllifecivilooschorich.pdf (hereafter Schorske, Bancroft Oral History).

45. David A. Varel, *The Scholar and the Struggle: Lawrence Reddick's Crusade for Black History and Black Power* (Chapel Hill: University of North Carolina Press, 2020); Adam Fairclough, *A Class of Their Own: Black Teachers in the Segregated South* (Cambridge, MA: Harvard University Press, 2007).

46. John Hope Franklin, *Mirror to America: The Autobiography of John Hope Franklin* (New York: Farrar, Straus and Giroux, 2005), 167–69.

47. Margaret W. Rossiter, *Women Scientists in America before Affirmative Action, 1940–1972* (Baltimore: Johns Hopkins University Press, 1995), xvi and passim.

48. Nancy Topping Bazin, "The Gender Revolution," in *The Politics of Women's Studies: Testimony from Thirty Founding Mothers*, ed. Florence Howe (New York: Feminist Press, 2000), 62; Varel, *The Scholar and the Struggle*, 57; Gerda Lerner, "Women among the Professors of History: The Story of a Process of Transformation," in *Voices of Women Historians: The Personal, the Political, the Professional*, ed. Eileen Boris and Nupur Chaudhuri (Bloomington: Indiana University Press, 1999), 1–10.

49. Mimi Reisel Gladstein, "The Deodorant of Success," 122; Barbara W. Gerber, "Moving from the Periphery to the Center," 73; Annis Pratt, "Imploding Marginality," 82; and Mary Anne Ferguson, "Awakening," 172: all in *The Politics of Women's Studies*, ed. Howe.

50. Schorske, Bancroft Oral History, 70.

51. D. W. Light Jr., L. R. Mardson, and T. C. Corl, *The Impact of the Academic Revolution on Faculty Careers* (Washington, DC: American Association for Higher Education, 1973), 5, 2.

52. Geiger, *Research and Relevant Knowledge*, 221–24; Lowen, *Creating the Cold War University*, 152–53, 158–59.

53. Thelin, *A History of American Higher Education*, 280–81.

54. Geiger, *Research and Relevant Knowledge*, 217–24; Lowen, *Creating the Cold War University*, 158.

55. Rossiter, *Women Scientists in America before Affirmative Action*.

56. Martin Oppenheimer, telephone interview with the author, March 21, 2014.

57. Allan Silver, interview with the author, June 19, 2013, New York City.

58. William Tabb, interview with the author, August 26, 2013, New York City;

Thomas Mayer, telephone interview with the author, January 23, 2015; Kate Ellis, interview with the author, June 17, 2013, New York City.

59. Troy Duster, *An Oral History with Troy Duster*, 29, interviews conducted by Richard Cándida Smith and Nadine Wilmot in 2002, 2003, Regional Oral History Office, Bancroft Library, University of California, Berkeley 2012, https://digitalassets.lib.berkeley.edu/roho/ucb/text/duster_troy_public.pdf.

60. Renate Bridenthal, interview with the author, May 23, 2013, New York City; Carl Riskin, interview with the author, November 4, 2014, New York City; Linda Gordon, interview with the author, January 29, 2015, New York City.

61. Moss Roberts, interview with the author, June 19, 2014, New York City.

62. Saul Slapikoff, interview with the author, August 15, 2015, Hawley, MA.

63. William M. Chace, *100 Semesters: My Adventures as Student, Professor, and University President and What I Learned along the Way* (Princeton, NJ: Princeton University Press, 2006), 57–58.

64. Mary Ann Wynkoop, *Dissent in the Heartland: The Sixties at Indiana University* (Bloomington: Indiana University Press, 2002), 163.

65. Chace, *100 Semesters*, 60; Geiger, *Research and Relevant Knowledge*, 221–26.

66. "Muscatine Report," 167–68.

67. Geiger, *Research and Relevant Knowledge*, 223–26.

68. John Womack, interview with the author, April 1, 2013, Cambridge, MA.

69. Geiger, *Research and Relevant Knowledge*, 224; "Muscatine Report," 170.

70. Emily K. Abel, *Terminal Degrees: The Job Crisis in Higher Education* (New York: Praeger, 1984), 60; Light, Mardson, and Corl, *The Impact of the Academic Revolution on Faculty Careers*, 35; Ronald Grele, interview with the author, January 22, 2015, New York City.

71. Marjorie Heins, *Priests of Our Democracy: The Supreme Court, Academic Freedom, and the Anti-Communist Purge* (New York: New York University Press, 2013), 316n45.

72. Schorske, Bancroft Oral History, 70; Blum, *A Life with History*, 157.

73. *The Letters of C. Vann Woodward*, ed. Michael O'Brien (New Haven, CT: Yale University Press, 2013), xxxiii.

74. Jules Chametzky, interview with the author September 19, 2014, Amherst, MA.

75. Abel, *Terminal Degrees*, 3.

76. Jencks and Riesman, *Academic Revolution*, 241.

77. Staughton Lynd, telephone interview with the author, June 23, 2014.

78. Bill Zimmerman, *Troublemaker: A Memoir from the Front Lines of the Sixties* (New York: Doubleday, 2011), 100–101.

79. Mayer, interview, January 23, 2015.

80. Chace, *100 Semesters*, 118.

81. Light, Mardson, and Corl, *The Impact of the Academic Revolution on Faculty Careers*, 11, 3.

82. Jencks and Riesman, *Academic Revolution*, 175; Freeland, *Academia's Golden Age*, 118.

83. Johnson, *Undermining Racial Justice*, 2.

84. David R. Goddard and Linda C. Koons, "A Profile of the University of Pennsylvania," in *Academic Transformation*, ed. Riesman and Stadtman, 232–33.

85. Marshak, *Academic Renewal*, 46.

86. Dunham, *Colleges of the Forgotten Americans*, 51, 59.

87. Lowen, *Creating the Cold War University*, 75.

88. Jencks and Riesman, *Academic Revolution*, 17.

89. David Riesman, "Commentary," in Dunham, *Colleges of the Forgotten Americans*, 167–75.

90. Jencks and Riesman, *Academic Revolution*.

91. Jencks and Riesman, *Academic Revolution*, 273; Geiger, *Research and Relevant Knowledge*, 202; Howard Schachman, interview with the author, January 3, 2014, Berkeley, CA; Jonathan Beckwith, interview with the author, April 2, 2013, Boston, MA.

92. Clark Kerr, *The Uses of the University* (Cambridge, MA: Harvard University Press, 1963), 59.

93. Seymour Martin Lipset and David Riesman, *Education and Politics at Harvard* (New York: McGraw Hill, 1975), 167–68.

94. Geiger, *Research and Relevant Knowledge*, 80.

95. James Axtell, *The Making of Princeton University: From Woodrow Wilson to the Present* (Princeton, NJ: Princeton University Press, 2006), 90–94.

96. Riesman, "Commentary," in Dunham, *Colleges of the Forgotten Americans*, 230–35.

97. Freeland, *Academia's Golden Age*, 167.

98. Leon Wofsy, *Professor Emeritus in Immunology, Political Activist*, 6, interviews conducted by Lisa Rubens in 1999, Regional Oral History Office, Bancroft Library, University of California, Berkeley, 2008, https://digitalassets.lib.berkeley.edu/roho/ucb/text/wofsy_leon_2008.pdf.

99. William J. McGill, *The Year of the Monkey: Revolt on Campus, 1968–69* (New York: McGraw-Hill, 1982), 63, 48; H. Stuart Hughes, *Gentleman Rebel: The Memoirs of H. Stuart Hughes* (New York: Ticknor & Fields, 1990), 298.

100. Lowen, *Creating the Cold War University*, 88, 131–34; O'Mara, *Cities of Knowledge*, 97–141.

101. Lowen, *Creating the Cold War University*, 73, 15. I have relied heavily on Lowen's brilliant study of Stanford's ascent during the postwar era. Roger Geiger's *Research and Relevant Knowledge* and Stuart W. Leslie's *The Cold War and American Science* offer a similar portrayal of Terman and the rise of Stanford.

102. Warren Bennis, *The Leaning Ivory Tower* (San Francisco: Jossey-Bass, 1973), 114; italics in original.

103. Nicholas Dagen Bloom, *How States Shaped Postwar America: State Government and Urban Power* (Chicago: University of Chicago Press, 2019), 149–70.

104. Bennis, *Leaning Ivory Tower*, 125.

105. Bruce Jackson, "Buffalo English: Literary Glory Days at UB," *Buffalo Beat*, February 26, 1999, http://www.acsu.buffalo.edu/~bjackson/englishdept.htm (accessed August 24, 2015).

106. Bennis, quoted in Richard A. Siggelkow, *Dissent and Disruption: A University under Siege* (Buffalo: Prometheus Books, 1991), 83.

107. Dunham, *Colleges of the Forgotten Americans*, 98.

108. Bennis, *Leaning Ivory Tower*, 139.

109. Bierman, "Oral History," 24.

Chapter Two

1. For an overview of the impact of McCarthyism on the academic community, see Ellen Schrecker, *No Ivory Tower: McCarthyism and the Universities* (New York: Oxford University Press, 1986).

2. Paul Lazarsfeld and Wagner Thielens Jr., *The Academic Mind* (Glencoe, IL: Free Press, 1958).

3. Seth Rosenfeld, *Subversives: The FBI's War on Student Radicals, and Reagan's Rise to Power* (New York: Farrar, Straus and Giroux, 2012), 37, 77, 88, 189, 210–14, 227–41, 252; James Kirkpatrick Davis, *Assault on the Left: The FBI and the Sixties Antiwar Movement* (Westport, CT: Praeger, 1997); Jeff Woods, *Black Struggle, Red Scare; Segregation and Anti-Communism in the South, 1948–1968* (Baton Rouge: Louisiana State University Press, 2004).

4. For an overview of Jencks's travails during the 1950s, see Ellen Schrecker, *Many Are the Crimes: McCarthyism in America* (New York: Little, Brown, 1998), 309–58. See also Raymond Caballero, *McCarthyism vs. Clinton Jencks* (Norman: University of Oklahoma Press, 2019).

5. Clinton Edward Jencks, Hearing before the Committee on Un-American Activities, House of Representatives, 86th Cong., 1st sess., July 22, 1959, 1093–101.

6. Memo, Baumgardmer to Belmont, May 15, 1959; SAC SF to Dir., May 26, 1959: both in Clinton Jencks, Headquarters File, 100039680 (hereafter Jencks, FBI file).

7. Memo, M. A. Jones to DeLoach, October 2, 1959, #146; report [name deleted], San Francisco, May 25, 1960, #148; J. F. Bland to W. C. Sullivan, April 17, 1962, #155; report [name deleted], San Francisco, October 27, 1964, #189; and report [name deleted], San Diego, December 19, 1965, #200: all in Jencks, FBI File.

8. Doug Dowd, *Blues for America: A Critique, a Lament, and Some Memories* (New York: Monthly Review Press, 1997), 95–96; Leon Wofsy, *Professor Emeritus in Immunology, Political Activist*, interviews conducted by Lisa Rubens in 1999, Regional Oral History Office, Bancroft Library, University of California, Berkeley, 2008, https://digitalassets.lib.berkeley.edu/roho/ucb/text/wofsy_leon _2008.pdf (hereafter Wofsy, Bancroft Oral History).

9. Most of the information here about the Lowell Tech firings comes from the official report of the AAUP's Committee A on Academic Freedom and Tenure, "Academic Freedom and Tenure: Lowell Technological Institute," *AAUP Bulletin* 45, no. 4 (December 1959): 550–67.

10. Elias Snitzer, testimony, in "Investigation of Communist Activities in the New

England Area," Hearings before the Committee on Un-American Activities, House of Representatives, 85th Cong., 2nd sess., Part III, 2345.

11. AAUP's Committee A, "Academic Freedom and Tenure: Lowell Technological Institute," *AAUP Bulletin* 45, no. 4; Elias Snitzer, Oral History, interview conducted by Joan Bromberg, August 6, 1984, Cambridge, MA, American Institute of Physics, https://www.aip.org/history-programs/niels-bohr-library/oral-histories/5057 (accessed September 28, 2015).

12. "Academic Freedom and Tenure: The George Washington University," *AAUP Bulletin* 48, no. 3 (September 1962): 240–47.

13. Paul Sporn, testimony, April 29, 1964, in "Communist Activities in the Buffalo, N.Y. Area," Hearings before the Committee on Un-American Activities, House of Representatives, 88th Cong., 2nd sess., April 29 and 30, 1964, 1569–99; Marjorie Heins, *Priests of Our Democracy: The Supreme Court, Academic Freedom, and the Anti-Communist Purge* (New York: New York University Press, 2013), 201, 316n45.

14. Schrecker, *No Ivory Tower*, 205–7; Statement by C. C. Furnas to Members of the Faculty, May 26, 1964, accession 5/4/304, box 7, Office of Chancellor/President: Central Files, Permanent Files—Paul Sporn, 1964–65, University Archives, University at Buffalo, The State University of New York (hereafter Paul Sporn File).

15. Heins, *Priests of Our Democracy*, 201–2; Press Release, June 8, 1964, J. Lawrence Murray to Paul Sporn, June 8, 1964: both in Paul Sporn File.

16. Paul Sporn to Dear Colleague, n.d.; Alexander Meiklejohn et al. to Clifford Furnas, May 31, 1964; Isaac Alcabes and 119 other SUNY Buffalo faculty members to Furnas, n.d.; Philip Morrison to Furnas, June 6, 1964; Meyer Schapiro to Furnas, June 14, 1964; Flyer for Protest Meeting, June 10, 1965; and Richard Lipsitz to Furnas, June 11, 1964: all in Paul Sporn File.

17. Louis M. Hellman to Samuel Gould, and attached, October 27, 1964, in Paul Sporn File.

18. Clipping, *ACLU News* (SF), October 1964, in AAUP Committee A Case Files—1974, box 24, folder: University of California–Berkeley, AAUP Records, Special Collections Research Center, Gelman Library, George Washington University, Washington, DC.

19. Wofsy, Bancroft Oral History, 10–14; Bluma Goldstein, interview by the author, February 7, 2014, Berkeley, CA.

20. Howard Schachman, *UC Berkeley Professor of Molecular Biology: On the Loyalty Oath Controversy, the Free Speech Movement, and Freedom in Scientific Research*, interviews conducted by Ann Lage in 2000–2001, Regional Oral History Office, Bancroft Library, University of California, Berkeley, 2007, https://digitalassets.lib.berkeley.edu/roho/ucb/text/schachman_howard.pdf (hereafter Schachman, Bancroft Oral History); Neil J. Smelser, "Berkeley in Crisis and Change," in *Academic Transformation: Seventeen Institutions under Pressure*, ed. David Riesman and Verne A. Stadtman (New York: McGraw-Hill, 1973), 56–57.

21. "Academic Freedom and Tenure: The University of California at Los Angeles," *AAUP Bulletin* 57, no. 3 (September 1971): 382–420 (hereafter *AAUP Bulletin*, UCLA). I have relied heavily on this lengthy and detailed report by the AAUP's committee that investigated Davis's case.

22. For a good overview of Angela Davis's travails, see Mike Davis and Jonathan Wiener, *Set the Night on Fire: L.A. in the Sixties* (London: Verso, 2020), 522–38; National United Committee to Free Angela Davis, "A Political Biography," in *If They Come in the Morning: Voices of Resistance*, ed. Angela Y. Davis et al. (New York: Third Press, 1971), 171–76; Rosenfeld, *Subversives*, 485; Davis, *Assault on the Left*, 171.

23. "Report of Chancellor Young's Ad Hoc Committee," in *AAUP Bulletin*, UCLA, 405–12.

24. Regent Coblentz in *AAUP Bulletin*, UCLA, 397.

25. "Texas Technological College," *AAUP Bulletin* 44, no. 1 (March 1958): 170–87; Joy Ann Williamson-Lott, "The Battle over Power, Control, and Academic Freedom at Southern Institutions of Higher Education, 1955–1965," *Journal of Southern History* 79, no. 4 (November 2013): 900–902.

26. "Academic Freedom and Tenure: Allen University and Benedict College," *AAUP Bulletin* 46, no. 1 (March 1960): 87–104; Williamson-Lott, "The Battle over Power, Control, and Academic Freedom," 890–97.

27. For an overview of the Arkansas membership-list legislation, see Jeff Woods, "'Designed to Harass': The Act 10 Controversy in Arkansas," *Arkansas Historical Quarterly* 56, no. 4 (Winter 1997): 443–60.

28. Ralph F. Fuchs, "The Association and the Desegregation Controversy," *AAUP Bulletin* 48, no. 2 (June 1962): 167–69; Woods, "'Designed to Harass'"; "Aid to the Arkansas Professors," *AAUP Bulletin* 46, no. 1 (March 1960); "Academic Freedom and Tenure: University of Arkansas," *AAUP Bulletin* 49, no. 4 (December 1963): 344–51; *Shelton v. Tucker*, 364 U.S. 479, 81 S. Ct. 247, 5 L. Ed. 2d 231 (1960).

29. Jo Ann Gibson Robinson, *The Montgomery Bus Boycott and the Women Who Started It: The Memoir of Jo Ann Gibson Robinson* (Knoxville: University of Tennessee Press, 1987).

30. Robert Van Waes, "Academic Freedom and Tenure: Alabama State College," *AAUP Bulletin* 47, no. 4 (December 1961): 303–9; Carol Polsgrove, *Divided Minds: Intellectuals and the Civil Rights Movement* (New York: Norton, 2001), 117–31; Robinson, *Montgomery Bus Boycott*, 173; David A. Varel, *The Scholar and the Struggle: Lawrence Reddick's Crusade for Black History and Black Power* (Chapel Hill: University of North Carolina Press, 2020), 127–52.

31. Robert Cohen, "'Two, Four, Six, Eight, We Don't Want to Integrate': White Student Attitudes toward the University of Georgia's Desegregation," *Georgia Historical Quarterly* 80, no. 3 (Fall 1996): 631; Calvin Trillin, *An Education in Georgia: The Integration of Charlayne Hunter and Hamilton Holmes* (New York: Viking, 1964), 65.

32. Joy Ann Williamson, *Radicalizing the Ebony Tower: Black Colleges and the*

Black Freedom Struggle in Mississippi (New York: Teachers College Press, 2008), 57, 76.

33. Nadine Cohodas, *The Band Played Dixie: Race and the Liberal Conscience at Ole Miss* (New York: Free Press, 1997), 91–101; "The University of Mississippi Situation: A Review of the Association's Interest and Action," *AAUP Bulletin* 48, no. 4 (December 1962): 317–20.

34. Cohodas, *The Band Played Dixie*, 107; "Academic Freedom in Mississippi: A Report of a Special Committee," *AAUP Bulletin* 51, no. 3 (September 1965): 341–56.

35. James W. Silver, "Mississippi: The Closed Society," *Journal of Southern History* 30, no. 1 (February 1964): 3–34.

36. Cohodas, *The Band Played Dixie*, 111–12; Polsgrove, *Divided Minds*, 211–29.

37. Michael Sletcher, "The Loyalty of Educators and Public Employees: Opposition to Loyalty Oaths in Twentieth-Century Massachusetts and the U.S. Supreme Court," *Massachusetts Historical Review* 12, no. 1 (2010): 39–45.

38. Heins, *Priests of Our Democracy*, 189; Peter Radcliff, "Oral History," interview by Harvey Schwartz, May 31, 2000, rev. 2015, Labor Archives and Research Center, San Francisco State University; John McDermott, interview with the author, August 2, 2013, Truro, MA.

39. For the most recent account of the California Loyalty Oath controversy, see Bob Blauner, *Resisting McCarthyism: To Sign or Not to Sign California's Loyalty Oath* (Stanford, CA: Stanford University Press, 2009). See also David P. Gardner, *The California Oath Controversy* (Berkeley: University of California Press, 1967).

40. Richard Ohmann, "English and the Cold War," in *The Cold War and the University: Toward an Intellectual History of the Postwar Years*, by Noam Chomsky et al. (New York: New Press, 1997), 89.

41. Kenneth M. Stampp, *Historian of Slavery, the Civil War, and Reconstruction, University of California, Berkeley, 1946–1983*, 83–85, interviews conducted by Ann Lage in 1996, Regional Oral History Office, Bancroft Library, University of California, Berkeley, 1998, https://digitalassets.lib.berkeley.edu/rohoia/ucb/text/historianslaveryoostamrich.pdf (hereafter Stampp, Bancroft Oral History); Schachman, Bancroft Oral History.

42. Stampp, Bancroft Oral History, 85.

43. Sheldon Wolin, telephone interview with the author, February 13, 2014; Steve Batterson, *Stephen Smale: The Mathematician Who Broke the Dimension Barrier* (Providence, RI: American Mathematical Society, 2000), 70; Howard Schachman, interview with the author, January 3, 2014, Berkeley, CA.

44. For an overview of the legislation, see Wayne Urban, *More than Science and Sputnik: The National Defense Education Act of 1958* (Tuscaloosa: University of Alabama Press, 2010).

45. Jessica Wang, *American Science in an Age of Anxiety: Scientists, Anticommunism, and the Cold War* (Chapel Hill: University of North Carolina Press, 1999), 256–59.

46. Bentley Glass and William P. Fidler, "Disclaimer Affidavit Requirement: Association Officers Express Disapproval of Title X, Section 1001 (f) (1) of the National Defense Education Act of 1958," *AAUP Bulletin* 44, no. 4 (December 1958): 769–72; "Disclaimer Affidavit: Non-Participating and Disapproving Colleges and Universities," *AAUP Bulletin* 48, no. 4 (December 1962): 331; Urban, *More than Science and Sputnik*, 185–89; Heins, *Priests of Our Democracy*, 186.

47. John F. Kennedy, "The Loyalty Oath—An Obstacle to Better Education," *AAUP Bulletin* 45, no. 1 (March 1959): 26–27; Morton Keller and Phyllis Keller, *Making Harvard Modern: The Rise of America's University* (Cary, NC: Oxford University Press, 2001), 207.

48. Howard Zinn to Winston Ehrmann, May 17, 1964, box 310, Spelman College, Howard Zinn, AAUP Committee A Case Files—1974, in AAUP Records, George Washington University. John McDermott lost his job at Long Island University because he refused to sign the Feinberg affidavit. McDermott, interview, August 2, 2013.

49. Wofsy, Bancroft Oral History, 7–14.

50. Wofsy, Bancroft Oral History, 7–14.

51. Blauner, *Resisting McCarthyism*, 219; N. M. Mundell to Thomas Cunningham, June 21, 1965; Cunningham to Roger W. Heyns, October 1, 1965; *Aronson et al. vs. the Regents of the University of California*, 1967: all in University of California, President, Permanent Files 1958–75, CU-5, series 8, box 27, folder 3, University Archives, University of California, Berkeley.

52. John E. Landon to John A. Perkins, October 17, 1973, University of California, President, Permanent Files 1958–75, CU-5, series 8, box 27, folder 5, University Archives, University of California, Berkeley.

53. *Baggett v. Bullitt*, 377 U.S. 360 (1964); Heins, *Priests of Our Democracy*, 180–91.

54. I have relied heavily for my treatment of the *Keyishian* case on Heins's magisterial *Priests of Our Democracy*.

55. Heins, *Priests of Our Democracy*, 186–222.

56. Heins, *Priests of Our Democracy*, 194, 196.

57. *Keyishian v. Board of Regents*, 385 U.S. 589 (1967).

58. Heins, *Priests of Our Democracy*, 250.

59. Sletcher, "The Loyalty of Educators and Public Employees," 35–68; Joseph Pedlosky, telephone interview with the author, September 9, 2015.

60. Pedlosky, interview, September 9, 2015.

61. Sletcher, "The Loyalty of Educators and Public Employees," 52–53; "The Bowles Campaign," *Harvard Crimson*, March 24, 1966; Jonathan Fuerbringer, "Corporation Plans Not to Oppose Court Action Reinstating Bowles," *Harvard Crimson*, March 17, 1966.

62. Mark Bollotin, "Loyalty Oath Fund Aids Protest," *The Tech* [MIT], May 17, 1966.

63. Sletcher, "The Loyalty of Educators and Public Employees," 51; "Court Postpones Firing of Bowles," *Harvard Crimson*, March 19, 1966; Bowles statement

in Carlos Torres Alberto, *Education, Power, and Personal Biography: Dialogues with Critical Educators* (New York: Routledge, 1998), 52–53.

64. Richard A. Siggelkow, *Dissent and Disruption: A University under Siege* (Buffalo: Prometheus Books, 1991), 22–32; Gary Murrell, *"The Most Dangerous Communist in the United States": A Biography of Herbert Aptheker* (Amherst: University of Massachusetts Press, 2015), 157, 367; William J. Billingsley, *Communists on Campus: Race, Politics, and the Public University in Sixties North Carolina* (Athens: University of Georgia Press, 1999), 208–9.

65. Mary Ann Wynkoop, *Dissent in the Heartland: The Sixties at Indiana University* (Bloomington: Indiana University Press, 2002), 43–44; Carl E. Schorske, *Intellectual Life, Civil Libertarian Issues, and the Student Movement at the University of California, Berkeley, 1960–1969,* 28–29, interviews conducted by Ann Lage in 1996, 1997, Regional Oral History Office, Bancroft Library, University of California, Berkeley, 2000, http://digitalassets.lib.berkeley.edu/rohoia/ucb/text/intelllifecivilooschorich.pdf (hereafter Schorske, Bancroft Oral History).

66. Murrell, *"The Most Dangerous Communist in the United States,"* 153–57.

67. Schrecker, *No Ivory Tower,* 89–93.

68. Robert Cohen, "The Many Meanings of the FSM," in *The Free Speech Movement: Reflections on Berkeley in the 1960s,* ed. Robert Cohen and Reginald E. Zelnik (Berkeley: University of California Press, 2002), 14; Billingsley, *Communists on Campus,* xv; Kenneth J. Heineman, *Campus Wars: The Peace Movement at American State Universities in the Vietnam Era* (New York: New York University Press, 1993), 84.

69. Reginald E. Zelnik, "On the Side of the Angels: The Berkeley Faculty and the FSM," 266–67; Waldo Martin, "Holding One Another: Mario Savio and the Freedom Struggle in Mississippi and Berkeley," 98; and Henry Mayer, "A View from the South: The Idea of a State University," 158: all in *Free Speech Movement,* ed. Cohen and Zelnik. Rosenfeld, *Subversives,* 189.

70. Stampp, Bancroft Oral History, 130; Schorske, Bancroft Oral History, 28–33.

71. W. J. Rorabaugh, *Berkeley at War: The 1960s* (New York: Oxford University Press, 1989), 15.

72. "The Seventh Alexander Meiklejohn Award," *AAUP Bulletin* 50, no. 2 (June 1964): 185–87.

73. "Ohio State Trustees Uphold New Gag Rule," *Harvard Crimson,* October 17, 1951, http://www.thecrimson.com/article/1951/10/17/ohio-state-trustees-uphold-new-gag/ (accessed November 12, 2015); Billingsley, *Communists on Campus,* 17–18.

74. Murrell, *"The Most Dangerous Communist,"* 161–64; Jeff Schwartz, "Oral History," 14–22, interview by Bill Shkurti, November 16, 2012, Ohio State University Archives, https://kb.osu.edu/bitstream/handle/1811/54598/ARV_Schwartz_Jeff_Transcript.pdf?sequence=4&isAllowed=y; David Kettler, interview with the author, December 12, 2016, Rhinebeck, NY.

75. Cohodas, *The Band Played Dixie,* 44–46.

76. "Academic Freedom and Tenure: The University of Mississippi," *AAUP Bulletin* 56, no. 1 (Spring 1970): 75–86.

77. The main source for this discussion of the North Carolina 1963 speakers law is William J. Billingsley's fine monograph, *Communists on Campus*.

78. Billingsley, *Communists on Campus*, 182, 189.

79. Billingsley, *Communists on Campus*, 218.

80. Billingsley, *Communists on Campus*, 197–98; Murrell, "The Most Dangerous Communist," 181–84.

81. Gary S. Sprayberry, "Student Radicalism and the Antiwar Movement at the University of Alabama," in *Rebellion in Black and White: Southern Student Activism in the 1960s*, ed. Robert Cohen and David J. Snyder (Baltimore: Johns Hopkins University Press, 2013), 167.

Chapter Three

1. Edward R. Cain, "The Legion Invades a Campus," *The Nation*, September 9, 1961; "The Professor as Citizen: The Brockport Incident: An Item of Unfinished Business," *AAUP Bulletin* 48, no. 2 (June 1962): 170–72.

2. "Prof Profiles: Dr. Cain," *The Stylus*, March 9, 1962, http://nyshistoricnewspapers.org/lccn/np00060001/1962-03-09/ed-1/seq-2/ (accessed November 18, 2015). I owe the use of the term "pre-sixties" to Michael Schudson, *The Rise of the Right to Know: Politics and the Culture of Transparency, 1945–1975* (Cambridge, MA: Harvard University Press, 2015), 101.

3. Rebecca S. Lowen, *Creating the Cold War University: The Transformation of Stanford* (Berkeley: University of California Press, 1997), 208.

4. Evan Stark, "In Exile," in *History and the New Left: Madison, Wisconsin, 1950–1970*, ed. Paul Buhle (Philadelphia: Temple University Press, 1990), 166–74. I have relied heavily on Buhle's valuable collection of memoirs by former Wisconsin students and faculty members.

5. Buhle, "Madison: An Introduction," 17; Saul Landau, "From the Labor Youth League to the Cuban Revolution," 107–10; and Jeffry Kaplow, "Parentheses: 1952–1956," 62: all in *History and the New Left*, ed. Buhle.

6. Joan Wallach Scott, interview with the author, December 16, 2014, New York City.

7. Just about every essay in Paul Buhle's valuable collection of memoirs describes the culture of Wisconsin's student Left. See especially Nina Serrano, "A Madison Bohemian," 73–82; Bertell Ollman, "From Liberal, to Social Democrat, to Marxist: My Political Itinerary through Madison in the Late 1950s," 102–5; and James B. Gilbert, "The Intellectuals and the First New Left," 119–21: all in *History and the New Left*, ed. Buhle.

8. Elizabeth Ewen, "A Way of Seeing," in *History and the New Left*, ed. Buhle, 150.

9. James Weinstein, "Studies on the Left," 115; and Warren Susman, "The Smoking Room School of History," 46: both in *History and the New Left*, ed. Buhle. See

also Matthew Levin, *Cold War University: Madison and the New Left in the Sixties* (Madison: University of Wisconsin Press, 2013), 79–88.

10. Herbert G. Gutman, "Learning About History," 49; William Preston, "WASP and Dissenter," 52; Landau, "From the Labor Youth League to the Cuban Revolution," 108–10; Harriet Tanzman, "Civil Rights and History," 142–46; and Ewen, "A Way of Seeing," 150, 164: all in *History and the New Left*, ed. Buhle. John Womack, interview with the author, April 1, 2013, Cambridge, MA.

11. Levin, *Cold War University*, 81.

12. George Mosse, "New Left Intellectuals/New Left Politics," in *History and the New Left*, ed. Buhle, 238.

13. Buhle, "Madison: An Introduction," in *History and the New Left*, ed. Buhle, 25.

14. *Studies on the Left* 1, no. 1 (1960).

15. Kevin Mattson, "Between Despair and Hope: Revisiting *Studies on the Left*," in *The New Left Revisited*, ed. John McMillian and Paul Buhle (Philadelphia: Temple University Press, 2003), 30–34.

16. Susman, "The Smoking Room School of History," 45.

17. William A. Williams, "My Life in Madison," in *History and the New Left*, ed, Buhle, 270.

18. Mattson, "Between Despair and Hope," 40.

19. Michael Walzer, interview with the author, May 13, 2013, New York City; Scott, interview, December 16, 2014; Evan Stark, "Talking Sociology: A Sixties Fragment," in *Radical Sociologists and the Movement: Experiences, Lessons, and Legacies*, ed. Martin Oppenheimer, Martin J. Murray, and Rhonda F. Levine (Philadelphia: Temple University Press, 1991), 54–58.

20. Stephen J. Whitfield, "A Radical in Academe: Herbert Marcuse at Brandeis," *Journal for the Study of Radicalism* 9, no. 2 (Fall 2015): 93–124, https://muse.jhu.edu/journals/journal_for_the_study_of_radicalism/v009/9.2.whitfield.html (accessed November 23, 2015).

21. Philip Morrison, interview with the author, December 22, 1977, Cambridge, MA.

22. Charles Haynie, *A Memoir of the New Left: The Political Autobiography of Charles A. Haynie*, ed. Aeron Haynie and Timothy S. Miller (Knoxville: University of Tennessee Press, 2009), 3, 28–29.

23. Doug Dowd, *Blues for America: A Critique, a Lament, and Some Memories* (New York: Monthly Review Press, 1997), 135.

24. For an illuminating discussion of the University of Michigan's social science tradition, see David A. Hollinger, *Science, Jews, and Secular Culture: Studies in Mid-Twentieth-Century American Intellectual History* (Princeton, NJ: Princeton University Press, 1996), 121–54.

25. William Gamson, telephone interview with the author, May 10, 2013; Zelda F. Gamson, "Michigan Muddles Through: Luck, Nimbleness, and Resilience in Crisis," in *Academic Transformation: Seventeen Institutions under Pressure*, ed. David Riesman and Verne A. Stadtman (New York: McGraw-Hill, 1973), 173–97.

26. Gamson, "Michigan Muddles Through," in *Academic Transformation*, ed. Riesman and Stadtman; Michael Zweig, interview with the author, May 12, 2015, New York City.

27. Ernst Benjamin, interview with the author, June 27, 2013, Silver Spring, MD; Kelly Moore, *Disrupting Science: Social Movements, American Scientists, and the Politics of the Military, 1945–1975* (Princeton, NJ: Princeton University Press, 2008), 96–109.

28. Jonathan Beckwith, interview with the author, April 2, 2013, Boston; Womack, interview, April 1, 2013; Ethan Signer, interview with the author, February 2, 2015, New York City; Paul Rubinson, *Redefining Science: Scientists, the National Security State, and Nuclear Weapons in Cold War America* (Amherst: University of Massachusetts Press, 2016); Sarah Bridger, *Scientists at War: The Ethics of Cold War Weapons Research* (Cambridge, MA: Harvard University Press, 2015), 89.

29. Betty Medsger, *The Burglary: The Discovery of J. Edgar Hoover's Secret FBI* (New York: Knopf, 2014), 12, 439; Thompson Bradley, oral history interview, November 2, 2014, in Black Liberation 1969 Archive, Swarthmore College, http://blacklib1969.swarthmore.edu/items/show/1189.

30. See, for example, Donald Fleming and Bernard Bailyn, eds., *The Intellectual Migration: Europe and America, 1930–1960* (Cambridge, MA: Harvard University Press, 1969). On the lives of the Frankfurt school scholars in the United States, see Stuart Jeffries, *Grand Hotel Abyss: The Lives of the Frankfurt School* (London: Verso, 2016).

31. My main source for the story of the émigré scholars in the South is Gabrielle Simon Edgcomb, *From Swastika to Jim Crow: Refugee Scholars at Black Colleges* (Malabar, FL: Krieger, 1993); Georg Iggers and Wilma Iggers, *Two Lives in Uncertain Times: Facing the Challenges of the 20th Century as Scholars and Citizens* (New York: Berghahn Books, 2006); Georg Iggers and Wilma Iggers, interview with the author, Amherst, NY, May 22, 2015.

32. Temma Kaplan, "My Way," in *Becoming Historians*, ed. James M. Banner Jr. and John R. Gillis (Chicago: University of Chicago Press, 2009), 213–14.

33. Roz Baxandall, "Another Madison Bohemian," 136–37; and Stuart Ewen, "The Intellectual New Left," 180: both in *History and the New Left*, ed. Buhle. Norma Stoltz Chincilla, "Critical Sociologists: Born or Made?" in *Radical Sociologists*, ed. Oppenheimer, Murray, and Levine, 135.

34. Donna Murch, *Living for the City: Migration, Education, and the Rise of the Black Panther Party in Oakland, California* (Chapel Hill: University of North Carolina Press, 2010), 75–80.

35. Jack Zipes, telephone interview with the author, March 8, 2013.

36. Hester Eisenstein, interview with the author, April 7, 2015, New York City.

37. John Womack interview, in *Visions of History*, ed. Henry Abelove, Betsy Blackmar, Peter Dimock, and Jonathan Schneer (New York: Pantheon, 1983), 258; Bertell Ollman, interview with the author, January 19, 2015, New York City.

38. Eric Foner, "My Life as a Historian," in *Historians and Race: Autobiography*

and the Writing of History, ed. Paul A. Cimbala and Robert F. Himmelberg (Bloomington: Indiana University Press, 1996), 98.

39. Joan Wallach Scott, "Finding Critical History," 32–33; Linda Gordon, "History Constructs a Historian," 88; and John R. Gillis, "Detours," 161, 164: all in *Becoming Historians*, ed. Banner and Gillis.

40. Carl Schorske, *Intellectual Life, Civil Libertarian Issues, and the Student Movement at the University of California, Berkeley, 1960–1969*, 26–28, interviews conducted by Ann Lage in 1996, 1997, Regional Oral History Office, Bancroft Library, University of California, Berkeley, 2000, http://digitalassets.lib .berkeley.edu/rohoia/ucb/text/intelllifecivilooschorich.pdfs; Seth Rosenfeld, *Subversives: The FBI's War on Student Radicals, and Reagan's Rise to Power* (New York: Farrar, Straus and Giroux, 2012), 77–78.

41. David Kotelchuck, interview with the author, May 7, 2014, New York City; Haynie, *Memoir*, 31.

42. "Petition to the House of the 87th Congress," *Washington Post*, January 2, 1961.

43. Arthur Bierman to Maxwell Keith, July 2, 1959; Bierman to Helen Miller, July 21, 1959; Bierman to Hans Rosenhaupt, July 3, 1959: all in Arthur Bierman Papers, box 2, folder 4, San Francisco State University Archives.

44. Rosenfeld, *Subversives*, 77–87.

45. Richard Flacks, telephone interview with the author, February 22, 2013; Haynie, *Memoir*, 26; Eric Foner, interview with the author, March 26, 2013, New York City; Gordon, "History Constructs a Historian," in *Becoming Historians*, ed. Banner and Gillis, 85 ; Serrano, "A Madison Bohemian," in *History and the New Left*, ed. Buhle 82; Martin Oppenheimer, telephone interview with the author, March 21, 2014; Bluma Goldstein, interview with the author, February 7, 2014, Berkeley, CA; Zweig, interview, May 12, 2015; Eddie R. Cole, *The Campus Color Line: College Presidents and the Struggle for Black Freedom* (Princeton, NJ: Princeton University Press, 2020), 132–33.

46. Richard Falk, telephone interview with the author, February 16, 2015; Foner, "My Life as a Historian," in *Historians and Race*, ed. Cimbala and Himmelberg, 95; Ray Franklin, interview with the author, January 3, 2014, New York City.

47. Oppenheimer, interview, March 21, 2014; Richard D. Mann, "The Ann Arbor Teach-In and Beyond: An Oral History," 2, manuscript in the author's possession; Richard Mann, telephone interview with the author, November 14, 2014.

48. Stark, "Talking Sociology," in *Radical Sociologists*, ed. Oppenheimer, Murray, and Levine, 61; Ewen, "A Way of Seeing," 50 and Stark, "In Exile," 169: both in *History and the New Left*, ed. Buhle.

49. Thomas Mayer, telephone interview with the author, January 23, 2015; Ruth Misheloff, interview with the author, October 30, 2014, New York City; Carl Riskin, interview with the author, November 4, 2014, New York City.

50. Kenneth M. Stampp, *Historian of Slavery, the Civil War, and Reconstruction, University of California, Berkeley, 1946–1983*, 131, interviews conducted by Ann Lage in 1996, Regional Oral History Office, Bancroft Library, University of California, Berkeley, 1998, https://digitalassets.lib.berkeley.edu/rohoia/

ucb/text/historianslaveryoostamrich.pdf (hereafter Stampp, Bancroft Oral History).

51. Charles Sellers, interview with the author, February 3, 2014, Berkeley, CA.

52. Haynie, *Memoir*, 38–76.

53. William Sloane Coffin Jr., *Once to Every Man: A Memoir* (New York: Atheneum, 1978), 151–69.

54. Robert Cohen, ed., *Howard Zinn's Southern Diary: Sit-Ins, Civil Rights, and Black Women's Student Activism* (Athens: University of Georgia Press, 2018), 48–49.

55. Alice Lynd and Staughton Lynd, *Stepping Stones: Memoir of a Life Together* (Lanham, MD: Lexington Books, 2009), 65–66; Martin Duberman, *Howard Zinn: A Life on the Left* (New York: New Press, 2012), 40; Carol Polsgrove, *Divided Minds: Intellectuals and the Civil Rights Movement* (New York: Norton, 2001), 115.

56. Kotelchuck, interview, May 7, 2014; Jeffrey A. Turner, "The Rise of Black and White Student Protest in Nashville," in *Rebellion in Black and White: Southern Student Activism in the 1960s*, ed. Robert Cohen and David J. Snyder (Baltimore: Johns Hopkins University Press, 2013), 140; John R. Salter Jr., *Jackson, Mississippi: An American Chronicle of Struggle and Schism* (Hicksville, NY: Exposition Press, 1979).

57. William M. Chace, *100 Semesters: My Adventures as Student, Professor, and University President and What I Learned along the Way* (Princeton, NJ: Princeton University Press, 2006), 90; Jack Nelson and Jack Bass, *The Orangeburg Massacre* (New York: World, 1970), 5–6; Cole, *The Campus Color Line*, 293.

58. For a classic (and devastating) assessment of the situation of Black academics in the South, see E. Franklin Frazier, *Black Bourgeoisie: The Rise of a New Middle Class* (New York: Free Press, 1965).

59. Robert J. Norrell, *Reaping the Whirlwind: The Civil Rights Movement in Tuskegee* (New York: Knopf, 1985).

60. Jo Ann Gibson Robinson, *The Montgomery Bus Boycott and the Women Who Started It: The Memoir of Jo Ann Gibson Robinson* (Knoxville: University of Tennessee Press, 1987).

61. Cohen, ed., *Howard Zinn's Southern Diary*, 48–49.

62. David A. Varel, *The Scholar and the Struggle: Lawrence Reddick's Crusade for Black History and Black Power* (Chapel Hill: University of North Carolina Press, 2020), 123.

63. Joy Ann Williamson-Lott, "Student Free Speech on Both Sides of the Color Line in Mississippi and the Carolinas," 67; Dan T. Carter, "Deep South Campus Memories and the World the Sixties Made," xiii; Cleveland L. Sellers Jr., "Black Power and the Freedom Movement in Retrospect," 295; and Turner, "The Rise of Black and White Student Protest in Nashville": all in *Rebellion in Black and White*, ed. Cohen and Snyder, 134. Joy Ann Williamson, "Black Colleges and Civil Rights: Organizing and Mobilizing in Jackson, Mississippi," in *Higher Education and the Civil Rights Movement: White Supremacy, Black Southerners,*

and College Campuses, ed. Peter Wallenstein (Gainesville: University Press of Florida, 2007), 123–24; James W. Silver, "Mississippi: The Closed Society," *Journal of Southern History* 30, no. 1 (February 1964): 3–34; Joy Ann Williamson, *Radicalizing the Ebony Tower: Black Colleges and the Black Freedom Struggle in Mississippi* (New York: Teachers College Press, 2008).

64. Adam Fairclough, *A Class of Their Own: Black Teachers in the Segregated South* (Cambridge, MA: Harvard University Press, 2007), 337–40, 352, 377–420; Cole, *The Campus Color Line*, 16–69; Cohen, ed., *Howard Zinn's Southern Diary*; Joy Ann Williamson, *Radicalizing the Ebony Tower: Black Colleges and the Black Freedom Struggle in Mississippi* (New York: Teachers College Press, 2008).

65. Stampp, Bancroft Oral History, 130–31; John Hope Franklin, *Mirror to America: The Autobiography of John Hope Franklin* (New York: Farrar, Straus and Giroux, 2005), 238.

66. "Prospectus for a Summer Freedom School Program in Mississippi," December 1963, Mississippi Freedom School Curriculum, http://www .educationanddemocracy.org/FSCfiles/B_05_ProspForFSchools.htm (accessed January 14, 2016).

67. Howard Zinn, *You Can't Be Neutral on a Moving Train: A Personal History of Our Times* (1994; repr., Boston: Beacon Press, 2002), 81–82.

68. Florence Howe, *A Life in Motion* (New York: Feminist Press, 2011), 115–18.

69. Lynd and Lynd, *Stepping Stones*, 67–72; William L. Van Deburg, *New Day in Babylon: The Black Power Movement and American Culture, 1965–1975* (Chicago: University of Chicago Press, 1992), 49–50, 59.

70. For the classic work on the relationship between the civil rights movement and second-wave feminism, see Sara Evans, *Personal Politics: The Roots of Women's Liberation in the Civil Rights Movement and the New Left* (New York: Vintage, 1980).

71. For an overall look at the early scientists' movement, see Alice Kimball Smith, *A Peril and a Hope: The Scientists' Movement in America, 1945–47* (Chicago: University of Chicago Press, 1965).

72. Smith, *A Peril and a Hope*, 85; Jessica Wang, *American Science in an Age of Anxiety: Scientists, Anticommunism, and the Cold War* (Chapel Hill: University of North Carolina Press, 1999); Eugene Rabinowitch, in Lawrence S. Wittner, *One World or None: A History of the World Nuclear Disarmament Movement through 1953* (Stanford, CA: Stanford University Press, 1993), 59–62.

73. Wang, *American Science in an Age of Anxiety*, 53–84; Moore, *Disrupting Science*, 61.

74. Wang, *American Science in an Age of Anxiety*, 275–76; Thomas Hager, *Force of Nature: The Life of Linus Pauling* (New York: Simon and Schuster, 1995), 380–90; Wayne Reynolds, "Interview with Linus Pauling," in *Linus Pauling: Scientist and Peacemaker*, ed. Clifford Mead and Thomas Hager (Corvallis: Oregon State University Press, 2001), 41.

75. Bridger, *Scientists at War*, 2–4.

76. Moore, *Disrupting Science*, 56.

77. Moore, *Disrupting Science*, 56–57, 72; Bridger, *Scientists at War*, 100–101.

78. Moore, *Disrupting Science*, 55, 75.

79. Paul Lauter, interview with the author, August 21, 2013, New York City; Oppenheimer, interview, March 21, 2014; Jules Chametzky, interview with the author, September 19, 2014, Amherst, MA; Robin Dizard, interview with the author, September 19, 2015, Amherst, MA; Dan T. Carter, "Reflections of a Reconstructed White Southerner," in *Historians and Race*, ed. Cimbala and Himmelberg, 42.

80. Moore, *Disrupting Science*, 83, 101–2; Michael Egan, *Barry Commoner and the Science of Survival: The Remaking of American Environmentalism* (Cambridge, MA: MIT Press, 2007), 51–52.

81. Hager, *Force of Nature*, 445–48, 461, 465–72, 496.

82. Reynolds, "Interview with Linus Pauling," in *Linus Pauling*, ed. Mead and Hager, 42–43; Hager, *Force of Nature*, 477.

83. Moore, *Disrupting Science*, 112; Hager, *Force of Nature*, 481–82.

84. Egan, *Barry Commoner*, 58–62; Moore, *Disrupting Science*, 78–79, 88, 125.

85. Egan, *Barry Commoner*, 68–72; "The Baby Tooth Survey," *The Pauling Blog*, June 1, 2011, https://paulingblog.wordpress.com/tag/committee-for-nuclear-information/ (accessed December 17, 2015).

86. For a useful overview of the organization, see Milton S. Katz, *Ban the Bomb: A History of SANE, the Committee for a Sane Nuclear Policy, 1957–1985* (Westport, CT: Greenwood Press, 1986), 21–92. Berenice A. Carroll, "Three Faces of Trevia: Identity, Activism, and Intellect," in *Voices of Women Historians: The Personal, the Political, the Professional*, ed. Eileen Boris and Nupur Chaudhuri (Bloomington: Indiana University Press, 1999), 18; Arthur K. Bierman, "Oral History," 34, interviewed by Peter Carroll, January 14, 17, 28, 1992, Labor Archives and Research Center, San Francisco State University; Haynie, *Memoir*, 31.

87. Smith, *A Peril and a Hope*, 72.

88. Bridger, *Scientists at War*, 22–23, 40, 46–48, 58–62; Rubinson, *Redefining Science*.

89. Bridger, *Scientists at War*, 84; Rubinson, *Redefining Science*.

Chapter Four

1. William Scranton et al., *The Report of the President's Commission on Campus Unrest* (New York: Arno Press, 1970), x, 22 (hereafter "Scranton Report"); Garth Buchanan and Joan Brackett, assisted by Alease M. Vaughn, *Survey of Campus Incidents as Interpreted by College Presidents, Faculty Chairmen, and Student Body Presidents* (Washington, DC: Urban Institute, 1971).

2. The amount of material—monographs, memoirs, oral histories, documentary collections—available on the Free Speech Movement in print and on the web is overwhelming. Probably the single most useful discussion of the faculty's role in the FSM is the late Reginald E. Zelnik's "On the Side of the Angels: The

Berkeley Faculty and the FSM," in *The Free Speech Movement: Reflections on Berkeley in the 1960s*, ed. Robert Cohen and Reginald E. Zelnik (Berkeley: University of California Press, 2002). Just as useful have been the oral history transcripts of faculty members that were produced by the University of California's Bancroft Library: https://www.lib.berkeley.edu/libraries/bancroft-library/oral-history-center/search-oral-histories (accessed February 2, 2021).

3. "Scranton Report," 22.

4. "Scranton Report," 22.

5. Roger L. Geiger, *Research and Relevant Knowledge: American Research Universities since World War II* (1st ed., Oxford University Press, 1993; repr., New Brunswick, NJ: Transaction, 2004), 74–80.

6. Clark Kerr, *The Uses of the University* (Cambridge, MA: Harvard University Press, 1963).

7. Bundy statement as quoted from memory by Henry Rosovsky, telephone interview with the author, May 15, 2013.

8. Robert Scalapino, *Free Speech Movement Oral History Project*, 31, interviews conducted by Lisa Rubens in 2000, Regional Oral History Office, Bancroft Library, University of California, Berkeley, 2014, https://digitalassets.lib.berkeley.edu/roho/ucb/text/scalapino_robert_2014.pdf (hereafter Scalapino, Bancroft Oral History).

9. William M. Chace, *100 Semesters: My Adventures as Student, Professor, and University President and What I Learned along the Way* (Princeton, NJ: Princeton University Press, 2006), 99.

10. Earl F. Cheit, *Professor, Vice Chancellor, Dean, Vice President, Athletic Director, Advisor, Trustee. University of California, 1957–2002*," interviews conducted by Germaine LaBerge in 1999–2001, Regional Oral History Office, Bancroft Oral History, University of California, Berkeley, 2002, https://digitalassets.lib.berkeley.edu/rohoia/ucb/text/earlfrankivepresoocheirich.pdf (hereafter Cheit, Bancroft Oral History); Neil Smelser, *Distinguished Sociologist, University Professor and Servant to the Public*," 176, interviews conducted by Jess McIntosh and Lisa Rubens in 2011–2012, Regional Oral History Office, Bancroft Oral History, University of California, Berkeley, 2013, https://digitalassets.lib.berkeley.edu/roho/ucb/text/smelser_neil.pdf (hereafter Smelser, Bancroft Oral History); Scalapino, Bancroft Oral History, 31.

11. For the most recent treatment of the loyalty oath conflict, see Bob Blauner, *Resisting McCarthyism: To Sign or Not to Sign California's Loyalty Oath* (Stanford, CA: Stanford University Press, 2009).

12. Henry Mayer, "A View from the South: The Idea of a State University," 151–62; and Robert Cohen, "The Many Meanings of the FSM," 13–15: both in *Free Speech Movement*, ed. Cohen and Zelnik; Charles Sellers, "Memoirs of Charles G. Sellers, Jr., Part II," 5, http://nature.berkeley.edu/~c-merchant/Sellers/memoirs/2.pdf; Max Heirich and Sam Kaplan, "Yesterday's Discord," in *The Berkeley Student Revolt: Facts and Interpretations*, ed. Seymour Martin Lipset and Sheldon S. Wolin (Garden City, NY: Doubleday, 1965), 30.

13. Charles Sellers, interview with the author, February 3, 2014, Berkeley, CA; Lawrence W. Levine, *Historian of American Culture, Professor at Berkeley, 1962–1994*, 268–70, interviews conducted by Ann Lage in 2004–2005, Regional Oral History Office, Bancroft Library, University of California, Berkeley, 2014, https://digitalassets.lib.berkeley.edu/roho/ucb/text/levine_lawrence_2014.pdf (hereafter Levine, Bancroft Oral History); John Leggett, *Free Speech Movement Oral History Project*, interviews conducted by Lisa Rubens in 2001, Regional Oral History Office, Bancroft Library, University of California, Berkeley, 2014, https://digitalassets.lib.berkeley.edu/roho/ucb/text/leggett_john_2014.pdf (hereafter Leggett, Bancroft Oral History).

14. Carl Schorske, *Intellectual Life, Civil Libertarian Issues, and the Student Movement at the University of California, Berkeley, 1960–1969*, 27–28, interviews conducted by Ann Lage in 1996, 1997, Regional Oral History Office, Bancroft Library, University of California, Berkeley, 2000, http://digitalassets.lib.berkeley.edu/rohoia/ucb/text/intelllifecivilooschorich.pdf (hereafter Schorske, Bancroft Oral History); Kenneth M. Stampp, *Historian of Slavery, the Civil War, and Reconstruction, University of California, Berkeley, 1946–1983*, 230–31, interviews conducted by Ann Lage in 1996, Regional Oral History Office, Bancroft Library, University of California, Berkeley, 1998, https://digitalassets.lib.berkeley.edu/rohoia/ucb/text/historianslaveryoostamrich.pdf (hereafter Stampp, Bancroft Oral History).

15. Waldo Martin, "Holding One Another: Mario Savio and the Freedom Struggle in Mississippi and Berkeley," 88–89; Zelnik, "On the Side of the Angels," 266–70: both in *Free Speech Movement*, ed. Cohen and Zelnik.

16. Zelnik, "On the Side of the Angels," 268–70; Seth Rosenfeld, *Subversives: The FBI's War on Student Radicals, and Reagan's Rise to Power* (New York: Farrar, Straus and Giroux, 2012), 82–85; Lincoln Constance, *Versatile Berkeley Botanist: Plant Taxonomy and University Governance*, 253–54, interviews conducted by Ann Lage in 1986, Regional Oral History Office, Bancroft Library, University of California, Berkeley, 1987, https://archive.org/details/versatilebotanistooconsrich/page/n9/mode/2up (hereafter Constance, Bancroft Oral History).

17. Zelnik, "On the Side of the Angels," 269–70.

18. Cheit, Bancroft Oral History, 131; Scalapino, Bancroft Oral History, 37; Charles Muscatine, *The Loyalty Oath, the Free Speech Movement, and Education Reforms at the University of California, Berkeley*, 28, interviews conducted by Germaine LaBerge in 2000, Regional Oral History Office, Bancroft Library, University of California, Berkeley, 2004, https://archive.org/details/loyaltyoathoomuscrich/page/n5/mode/2up (hereafter Muscatine, Bancroft Oral History); Schorske, Bancroft Oral History, 30.

19. Lewis S. Feuer, "Rebellion at Berkeley," *New Leader* 47, no. 26 (December 21, 1964): 3.

20. Cohen, "The Many Meanings of the FSM," in *Free Speech Movement*, ed. Cohen and Zelnik, 23.

21. Edward W. Strong, *Philosopher, Professor, and Berkeley Chancellor, 1961–1965*, 345, interviews conducted by Harriet Nathan in 1988, Regional Oral History Office, Bancroft Library, University of California, Berkeley, 1992, https://digitalassets.lib.berkeley.edu/rohoia/ucb/text/stringedwphiloprooostrorich.pdf (hereafter Strong, Bancroft Oral History).

22. Smelser, Bancroft Oral History, 185; Schorske, Bancroft Oral History, 44–45; Henry F. May, *Professor of American Intellectual History, University of California, Berkeley, 1952–1980*, 122, interviews conducted by Ann Lage in 1998, Regional Oral History Office, Bancroft Library, University of California, Berkeley, 1999, https://archive.org/details/profamintelloomayhrich/page/n5/mode/2up (hereafter May, Bancroft Oral History); Nathan Glazer, *Remembering the Answers: Essays on the American Student Revolt* (New York: Basic Books, 1970), 87. For a more extensive discussion of the Eli Katz case, see chapter 2, supra.

23. Rosenfeld, *Subversives*, 87; Clark Kerr, "Fall of 1964 at Berkeley: Confrontation Leads to Reconciliation," in *Free Speech Movement*, ed. Cohen and Zelnik; Stampp, Bancroft Oral History, 231; Sellers, interview, February 3, 2014.

24. "The Seventh Alexander Meiklejohn Award," *AAUP Bulletin* 50, no. 2 (June 1964): 185–87.

25. Sheldon S. Wolin and John H. Schaar, "A Special Supplement: Berkeley and the Fate of the Multiversity," *New York Review of Books*, March 11, 1965.

26. Martin, "Holding One Another," 90–91; Jo Freeman, "From Freedom Now! to Free Speech: The FSM's Roots in the Bay Area Civil Rights Movement," 73–77; and Zelnik, "On the Side of the Angels," 266–67: all in *Free Speech Movement*, ed. Cohen and Zelnik,; John Leggett, Bancroft Oral History, 54; Neil J. Smelser, *Reflections on the University of California: From the Free Speech Movement to the Global University* (Berkeley: University of California Press, 2010), 58–59.

27. Strong, Bancroft Oral History, 295; Kerr, "Fall of 1964," in *Free Speech Movement*, ed. Cohen and Zelnik, 373.

28. Nathan Glazer, "What Happened at Berkeley," *Commentary*, January 1965, reprinted in Glazer, *Remembering the Answers*, 88; Kerr, "Fall of 1964," 392.

29. For useful narratives of the crisis, see Editors of the *California Monthly*, "Chronology of Events: Three Months of Crisis," in *The Berkeley Student Revolt*, ed. Lipset and Wolin, 99–198; and Max Heirich, *The Spiral of Conflict: Berkeley 1964* (New York: Columbia University Press, 1971).

30. Freeman, "From Freedom Now! to Free Speech," in *Free Speech Movement*, ed. Cohen and Zelnik, 80.

31. *Daily Californian*, October 1, 1965.

32. Sellers, "Memoirs, Part II," 6.

33. Leggett, Bancroft Oral History, 58–60; Zelnik, "On the Side of the Angels," 328; Hal Draper, "FSM: Freedom Fighters or Misguided Rebels," speech on KPFA, January 9, 1965, in *The Berkeley Student Revolt*, ed. Lipset and Wolin, 331.

34. Edward Strong, statements, September 30 and October 1, in *Daily Californian*, October 1, 2, 1964, http://newsprint.dailycal.org/issues/1964/10/01/#1, http://newsprint.dailycal.org/issues/1964/10/02/#1.

35. Rosenfeld, *Subversives*, 193–95; Kerr, "Fall of 1964," 382.
36. Glazer, "What Happened at Berkeley," *Commentary*, January 1965, 91; Seymour Martin Lipset, *Rebellion in the University* (1971; repr., Chicago: University of Chicago Press, 1976), xvi–xvii; Stampp, Bancroft Oral History, 30.
37. Rosovsky, interview, May 15, 2013; Zelnik, "On the Side of the Angels," 272–73; Smelser, Bancroft Oral History, 175–76; Heirich, *Spiral of Conflict*, 181–82.
38. Cheit, Bancroft Oral History, 121.
39. Editors of the *California Monthly*, "Chronology of Events," in *The Berkeley Student Revolt*, ed. Lipset and Wolin, 134.
40. Editors of the *California Monthly*, "Chronology of Events," in *The Berkeley Student Revolt*, ed. Lipset and Wolin, 117–18; Zelnik, "On the Side of the Angels," 272–73; Rosenfeld, *Subversives*, 195–97; Ira Michael Heyman, *Chancellor, 1980–1990, Vice Chancellor, and Professor of Law, UC Berkeley; and Secretary, the Smithsonian Institution, 1994–1999*, 39, interviews conducted by Harriet Nathan in 1995–2001, Regional Oral History Office, Bancroft Library, University of California, Berkeley, 2004, https://archive.org/details/heymaniramchancooheymrich/page/n5/mode/2up (hereafter Heyman, Bancroft Oral History).
41. Zelnik, "On the Side of the Angels," 275; Cheit, Bancroft Oral History, 123–24; Strong, Bancroft Oral History, 329–30.
42. For a thoughtful discussion of the First Amendment issues involved, see Robert Post, "Constitutionally Interpreting the FSM Controversy," in *Free Speech Movement*, ed. Cohen and Zelnik, 401–21; Zelnik, "On the Side of the Angels," 283–88.
43. Kerr, "Fall of 1964," 364.
44. Glazer, "What Happened at Berkeley," 92; Cheit, Bancroft Oral History, 124–26.
45. Muscatine, Bancroft Oral History, 41; Reginald Zelnik, "Carl Schorske and Berkeley's Time of Troubles," in Schorske, Bancroft Oral History, xi; Martin Edward Malia, *Historian of Russian and European Intellectual History*, 136, interviews conducted by David Engerman in 2003, Regional Oral History Office, Bancroft Library, University of California, Berkeley, 2005, https://digitalassets.lib.berkeley.edu/roho/ucb/text/MaliaBook.pdf (hereafter Malia, Bancroft Oral History); Sellers, interview, February 3, 2014.
46. Besides Muscatine, its "most stable presences," according to Reginald Zelnik, were Sellers, Schorske, Stampp, Selznick, Lowenthal, Wolin, Schachman, and the political scientists Jacobus ten Broek and Herbert McClosky. Zelnik, "On the Side of the Angels," 290–93; Howard Schachman, interview with the author, January 3, 2014, Berkeley, CA. Schorske's recollections of the group's membership also included William Kornhauser and Henry Nash Smith. Schorske, Bancroft Oral History, 101; Leon Wofsy, "When the FSM Disturbed the Faculty Peace," in *Free Speech Movement*, ed. Cohen and Zelnik, 346; Levine, Bancroft Oral History; Martin Roysher, "Recollections of the FSM," in *Free Speech Movement*, ed. Cohen and Zelnik, 149.

47. Zelnik, "On the Side of the Angels," 271, 279; Lawrence W. Levine, "From the Big Apple to Berkeley: Perspectives of a Junior Faculty Member," 342; and Steve Weissman, "Endgame, How the Berkeley Grads Organized to Win," 177: all in *Free Speech Movement*, ed. Cohen and Zelnik. Malia, Bancroft Oral History, 137; Smelser, Bancroft Oral History, 172.

48. Kerr, "Fall of 1964," 383.

49. May, Bancroft Oral History, 125; Glazer, "What Happened at Berkeley," 297.

50. Heirich, *Spiral of Conflict*, 275–78; Matthew Dallek, *The Right Moment: Ronald Reagan's First Victory and the Decisive Turning Point in American Politics* (New York: Free Press, 2000), 84–88; Editors of the *California Monthly*, "Chronology of Events," in *The Berkeley Student Revolt*, ed. Lipset and Wolin, 162–69.

51. Steve Batterson, *Stephen Smale: The Mathematician Who Broke the Dimension Barrier* (Providence, RI: American Mathematical Society, 2000), 88–89; Leggett, Bancroft Oral History, 62–66; Zelnik claimed that no faculty members were arrested. Zelnik, "On the Side of the Angels," 322.

52. Sellers, interview, February 3, 2014; Robert H. Cole, "December 1964: Some Reflections and Recollections," in *Free Speech Movement*, ed. Cohen and Zelnik, 427; Heirich, *Spiral of Conflict*, 282.

53. Morton Paley, interview with the author, June 4, 2013, New York City; Paley, telephone interview, January 15, 2018.

54. May, Bancroft Oral History, 121; Schorske, Bancroft Oral History, 98.

55. Zelnik, "On the Side of the Angels," 303.

56. Scalapino, Bancroft Oral History, 36.

57. Heirich, *Spiral of Conflict*, 280–82.

58. Heirich, *Spiral of Conflict*, 281–84; Zelnik, "On the Side of the Angels," 303–7.

59. Malia, Bancroft Oral History, 134; Lewis Feuer, *The Conflict of Generations: The Character and Significance of Student Movements* (New York: Basic Books, 1969), 75; Heirich, *Spiral of Conflict*, 282.

60. Smelser, Bancroft Oral History, 177.

61. Zelnik, "On the Side of the Angels," 285.

62. May, Bancroft Oral History, 125–27.

63. Zelnik, "On the Side of the Angels," 308.

64. Stampp, Bancroft Oral History, 235–36; Sellers, interview, February 3, 2014.

65. Text of the Committee of 200's drafts in *Daily Californian*, December 8, 9, 1964.

66. Weissman, "Endgame," in *Free Speech Movement*, ed. Cohen and Zelnik, 177.

67. Zelnik, "On the Side of the Angels," 311; Heirich, *Spiral of Conflict*, 292; May, Oral History, 127.

68. May, Bancroft Oral History, 127; Wofsy, "When the FSM Disturbed the Faculty Peace," 347.

69. Delmer M. Brown, *Professor of Japanese History, University of California, Berkeley, 1946–1977*, 153, interviews conducted by Ann Lage in 1995, Regional Oral History Office, Bancroft Library, University of California, Berkeley, 2000, https://archive.org/details/profjaphistoobrowrich/page/n5/mode/2up (here-

after Brown, Bancroft Oral History); Sheldon Wolin, telephone interview with the author, February 13, 2014; Muscatine, Bancroft Oral History, 42; Cheit, Bancroft Oral History, 133; Wofsy, "When the FSM Disturbed the Faculty Peace," 347.

70. Heirich, *Spiral of Conflict*, 315; May, Bancroft Oral History, 128.

71. Heirich, *Spiral of Conflict*, 304–5, 309–10; Lewis S. Feuer, "A Reply," *New Leader* 48, no. 1 (January 4, 1965): 17.

72. Heirich, *Spiral of Conflict*, 307–8; Brown, Bancroft Oral History, 155; Cheit, Bancroft Oral History, 137–38; Glazer, "What Happened at Berkeley," 300.

73. Malia, Bancroft Oral History, 137–38.

74. Cheit, Bancroft Oral History, 121.

75. Smelser, Bancroft Oral History, 180.

76. Zelnik, "On the Side of the Angels," 313.

77. Brown, Bancroft Oral History, 145–56; "Election of the Emergency Executive Committee," n.d., in Schorske, Bancroft Oral History, 172–74.

78. Malia, Bancroft Oral History, 139–40; Cheit, Bancroft Oral History, 141; Zelnik, "Carl Schorske and Berkeley's Time of Troubles," in Schorske, Bancroft Oral History, xii; Zelnik, "On the Side of the Angels," 318–19.

79. Schorske, Bancroft Oral History, 40; Cheit, Bancroft Oral History, 142; Zelnik, "On the Side of the Angels," 319–20; Heirich, *Spiral of Conflict*, 318; Stampp, Bancroft Oral History, 237.

80. Schorske, Bancroft Oral History, 42; Philip Selznick, "Reply to Glazer," in *The Berkeley Student Revolt*, ed. Lipset and Wolin, 303–12.

81. Stampp, Bancroft Oral History, 237, 241; Rosenfeld, *Subversives*, 214.

82. Zelnik, "On the Side of the Angels," 319–20; Cheit, Bancroft Oral History, 143–44; Malia, Bancroft Oral History, 142.

83. Heirich, *Spiral of Conflict*, 319; Zelnik, "On the Side of the Angels," 320.

84. Cheit, Bancroft Oral History, 150–52; Cole, "December 1964," in *Free Speech Movement*, ed. Cohen and Zelnik, 429. For the text of the Cole memo, see Lipset and Wolin, *The Berkeley Student Revolt*, 273–80.

85. Heirich, *Spiral of Conflict*, 319.

86. Martin Meyerson, Statements, January 3, 13, 1965, in *The Berkeley Student Revolt*, ed. Lipset and Wolin, 379–86.

87. Wolin and Schaar, "Berkeley and the Fate of the Multiversity," *New York Review of Books*, March 11, 1965.

88. Kerr, "Fall of 1964," 377, 395.

89. Cohen, "The Many Meanings of the FSM," 5–7; and Margot Adler, "My Life in the FSM: Memories of a Freshman," 128: both in *Free Speech Movement*, ed. Cohen and Zelnik.

90. Clark Kerr, "A Message to Alumni," February 1965, in *The Berkeley Student Revolt*, ed. Lipset and Wolin, 250.

91. Henry Nash Smith, "Why Has the Berkeley Faculty Failed to Condemn Violations of the Law by Students?" in *The Berkeley Student Revolt*, ed. Lipset and Wolin, 255–56.

92. Roysher, "Recollections of the FSM," 143; Schorske, Bancroft Oral History, 31; David A. Hollinger, "A View from the Margins," in *Free Speech Movement*, ed. Cohen and Zelnik, 182. For a useful discussion of the motivations of the non-radical students in the FSM, see Robert Cohen, "This Was *Their* Fight and *They* Had to Fight It: The FSM's Nonradical Rank and File," in *Free Speech Movement*, ed. Cohen and Zelnik, 227–63.

93. Kerr, "Fall of 1964," 366, 372; Rosovsky, interview, May 15, 2013.

94. Cohen, "The Many Meanings of the FSM," 24–26; Rosenfeld, *Subversives*, 210–11.

95. Robert Cohen, *Freedom's Orator: Mario Savio and the Radical Legacy of the 1960s* (New York: Oxford University Press, 2008), 219.

96. Kerr, "Fall of 1964," 374, 382–84; Stampp, Bancroft Oral History, 242; Smelser, Bancroft Oral History, 186; Cohen, "This Was *Their* Fight," 246; Constance, Bancroft Oral History, 278.

97. Heirich, *Spiral of Conflict*, 314.

98. Glazer, "What Happened at Berkeley," 286; Lipset, *Rebellion in the University*, xix; William Petersen, "What Is Left at Berkeley," in *The Berkeley Student Revolt*, ed. Lipset and Wolin, 384.

99. Morton Keller and Phyllis Keller, *Making Harvard Modern: The Rise of America's University* (Cary, NC: Oxford University Press, 2001), 319; Rosovsky, interview, May 15, 2013.

100. Stampp, Bancroft Oral History, 239–40; Schorske, Bancroft Oral History, 109; David Landes, "To the Editor," *New York Times*, December 29, 1964.

101. Smelser, Bancroft Oral History, 201.

102. Lipset, *Rebellion in the University*, xviii; Stampp, Bancroft Oral History, 237.

103. Ellen Sewell and William Sewell, *Free Speech Movement Oral History Project*, 20–21, interviews conducted by Lisa Rubens in 2000, Regional Oral History Office, Bancroft Library, University of California, Berkeley, 2014, https://digitalassets.lib.berkeley.edu/roho/ucb/text/sewell_william_and_ellen_2014.pdf (hereafter Ellen Sewell, Bancroft Oral History).

104. Rosovsky, interview, May 15, 2013.

105. Smelser, Bancroft Oral History, 201; Petersen, "What Is Left at Berkeley," 379, 382, 385.

106. Schorske, Bancroft Oral History, 107.

107. Schorske, Bancroft Oral History, 133–34.

108. May, Bancroft Oral History, 129–30.

109. Cheit, Bancroft Oral History, 150; Rosenfeld, *Subversives*, 248–51, 330–31.

110. Brown, Bancroft Oral History, 145–46; Schorske, Bancroft Oral History, 37–38; May, Bancroft Oral History, 129–30.

111. May, Bancroft Oral History, 129–30.

112. Malia, Bancroft Oral History, 150; Schorske, Bancroft Oral History, 19–23, 130.

113. Scalapino, Bancroft Oral History, 35.

114. Smelser, Bancroft Oral History, 125; Petersen, "What Is Left at Berkeley," 379.

115. Smelser, Bancroft Oral History, 173, 201.

116. Mike Rogin, *Free Speech Movement Oral History Project*, 39, interviews

conducted by Lisa Rubens in 2000, Regional Oral History Office, Bancroft Library, University of California, Berkeley, 2014, https://digitalassets.lib.berkeley.edu/roho/ucb/text/rogin_mike_2014.pdf (hereafter Rogin, Bancroft Oral History), 3; Scalapino, Bancroft Oral History, 39.

117. Norman Jacobson, *Professor of Political Theory*, 13–14, interviews conducted by Lisa Rubens in 1999, Regional Oral History Office, Bancroft Library, University of California, Berkeley, 2007, https://digitalassets.lib.berkeley.edu/roho/ucb/text/jacobson_norman.pdf (hereafter Jacobson, Bancroft Oral History).

118. Jacobson, Bancroft Oral History, 15; Schorske, Bancroft Oral History, 21–22.

119. Rogin, Bancroft Oral History, 16.

120. Wolin, interview, February 13, 2014; Jacobson, Bancroft Oral History, 8, 18; Rogin, Bancroft Oral History, 8.

121. Neil J. Smelser, "Berkeley in Crisis and Change," in *Academic Transformation: Seventeen Institutions under Pressure*, ed. David Riesman and Verne A. Stadtman (New York: McGraw-Hill, 1973), 64.

122. Nobel Prize–winning economist James Buchanan, credited with providing much of the intellectual infrastructure for the market-oriented scenario of the conservative movement, relied on Lipset's analysis of the student movement in his 1970 attack on the academic community. James M. Buchanan and Nicos E. Devletoglou, *Academia in Anarchy: An Economic Diagnosis* (New York: Basic Books, 1970), 97.

123. Wolin, interview, February 13, 2014; Searle quoted in Cohen, *Freedom's Orator*, 220; Seymour Martin Lipset and Paul Seabury, "The Lesson of Berkeley," in *The Berkeley Student Revolt*, ed. Lipset and Wolin, 340.

124. Feuer, "Rebellion at Berkeley"; Richard Abrams, "The Student Rebellion at Berkeley," 385–95; and Marshall Windmiller, "Berkeley Revolt," 414–20: both in *The Berkeley Student Revolt*, ed. Lipset and Wolin. Hal Draper, "The 'New Left' Uprising at Berkeley," 19.

125. Zelnick, "On the Side of the Angels," 322; Wolin, interview, February 13, 2014.

126. Muscatine, Bancroft Oral History, 37.

127. Selznick, "Reply to Glazer," in *The Berkeley Student Revolt*, ed. Lipset and Wolin, 311.

128. Herbert McClosky, "Statement on Academic Senate Resolution of December 8, 1964," in *The Berkeley Student Revolt*, ed. Lipset and Wolin, 261; Paul Jacobs, "Dr. Feuer's Distortions," *New Leader* 48, no. 1 (January 4, 1965): 10; Wolin and Schaar, "Berkeley and the Fate of the Multiversity"; Seymour Martin Lipset, "University Student Politics," in *The Berkeley Student Revolt*, ed. Lipset and Wolin, 4.

129. Cohen, "This Was *Their* Fight," 227–63.

130. Wolin and Schaar, "Berkeley and the Fate of the Multiversity"; Cohen, "This Was *Their* Fight," 244; Jeff Lustig, "The FSM and the Vision of a New Left," in *Free Speech Movement*, ed. Cohen and Zelnik.

131. Chace, *100 Semesters*, 100; Schorske, Bancroft Oral History, 104.

132. Cheit, Bancroft Oral History, 127; Smelser, Bancroft Oral History, 184, 198;

Stampp, Bancroft Oral History; Lipset and Seabury, "The Lesson of Berkeley," in *The Berkeley Student Revolt,* ed. Lipset and Wolin, 341; Albert Lepawsky quoted in Heirich, *Spiral of Conflict,* 310; Thomas Cushman and John Rodden, "Sociology and the Intellectual Life: An Interview with Lewis S. Feuer," *American Sociologist* 28, no. 4 (Winter 1997): 73–74.

133. Wofsy, "When the FSM Disturbed the Faculty Peace," 347.

134. Constance, Bancroft Oral History, 255.

135. Scalapino, Bancroft, Oral History, 37.

136. Constance, Bancroft Oral History, 267.

137. May, Bancroft Oral History, 122.

138. Glazer, "What Happened at Berkeley," 298; Brown, Bancroft Oral History.

139. William Petersen, quoted in Heirich, *Spiral of Conflict,* 313; Petersen, "What Is Left at Berkeley," 382; Feuer, *Conflict of Generations,* 418; John R. Searle, *The Campus War: A Sympathetic Look at the University in Agony* (New York: World, 1971), 3, 57.

140. Feuer, "Rebellion at Berkeley," 8; Feuer, *Conflict of Generations,* 453.

141. Lipset, "University Student Politics," *Free Speech Movement,* ed. Cohen and Zelnik, 3–4.

142. May, Bancroft Oral History, 119.

143. Clark Kerr, Statement, December 3, 1964, in *The Berkeley Student Revolt,* ed. Lipset and Wolin, 246; Rosovsky, interview, May 15, 2013.

144. Searle, *Campus War,* 121.

145. Lipset, "University Student Politics," 5.

146. Feuer, *Conflict of Generations,* viii; Feuer, "Rebellion at Berkeley," 7.

147. Lipset, "University Student Politics," 5.

148. Cheit, Bancroft Oral History, 127; Kenneth Keniston, "What's Bugging the Students?" in *Perspectives on Campus Tensions: Papers Prepared for the Special Committee on Campus Tensions,* ed. David C. Nichols (Washington, DC: American Council on Education, 1970), 47–67; Richard Flacks, "Who Protests: The Social Bases of the Student Movement," in *Protest! Student Activism in America,* ed. Julian Foster and Durward Long (New York: William Morrow, 1970), 134–57; Samuel Lubell, "That 'Generation Gap,'" in *Confrontation: The Student Rebellion and the Universities,* ed. Daniel Bell and Irving Kristol (New York: Basic Books, 1969), 58–66.

149. Feuer, "Rebellion at Berkeley," 10, 12.

150. Kerr, "A Message to Alumni," in *The Berkeley Student Revolt,* ed. Lipset and Wolin, 249.

151. Cohen, "The Many Meanings of the FSM," 21; Adler, "My Life in the FSM," 123; Doug Rossinow, "Mario Savio and the Politics of Authenticity," in *Free Speech Movement,* ed. Cohen and Zelnik, 546.

152. Rosenfeld, *Subversives,* 210.

153. On Sherriffs and the FBI, see Rosenfeld, *Subversives,* 189–91, 210–11; Strong, Bancroft Oral History, 298.

154. Constance, Bancroft Oral History, 265.

155. Rosenfeld, *Subversives*, 210.

156. Glazer, "What Happened at Berkeley," 292.

157. Weissman, "Endgame," in *Free Speech Movement*, ed. Cohen and Zelnik, 173.

158. Smelser, Bancroft Oral History, 184, 197.

159. Malia, Bancroft Oral History, 137.

160. Cheit, Bancroft Oral History, 127; Stampp, Bancroft Oral History.

161. Weissman, "Endgame," 174.

162. Scalapino, Bancroft Oral History, 32.

163. Petersen, "What Is Left at Berkeley," in *The Berkeley Student Revolt*, ed. Lipset and Wolin, 371.

164. Glazer, "What Happened at Berkeley," 301.

165. Henry Stapp, "Reflections on the Crisis at Berkeley," 266; Petersen, "What Is Left at Berkeley," 372, 379; Nathan Glazer, "Reply to Selznick": all in *The Berkeley Student Revolt*, ed. Lipset and Wolin, 314.

166. Kerr, *Uses of the University*.

167. Kerr, *Uses of the University*, 64, 104, 110.

168. Cohen, "The Many Meanings of the FSM," 16–18.

169. Wolin and Schaar, "Berkeley and the Fate of the Multiversity"; Feuer, "Rebellion at Berkeley," 3–4.

170. Wolin and Schaar, "Berkeley and the Fate of the Multiversity"; Glazer, "What Happened at Berkeley," 294; Adler, "My Life in the FSM," 115; Rossinow, "Mario Savio and the Politics of Authenticity," in *Free Speech Movement*, ed. Cohen and Zelnik, 542.

171. Glazer, "What Happened at Berkeley," 295; Ellen Sewell, Bancroft Oral History, 4.

172. A. H. Raskin, "The Berkeley Affair: Mr. Kerr vs. Mr. Savio & Co.," *New York Times Magazine*, February 14, 1965, in *The Berkeley Student Revolt*, ed. Lipset and Wolin, 424.

173. Paul Goodman, "Thoughts on Berkeley," *New York Review of Books*, January 14, 1965, in *The Berkeley Student Revolt*, ed. Lipset and Wolin, 316–17; Wolin, interview, February 13, 2014.

174. Schorske, Bancroft Oral History, 87; Kerr, "Fall of 1964," 375.

175. Lloyd Ulman, *An Oral History*, 198, interviews conducted by Riyad Koya in 2011, Regional Oral History Office, Bancroft Library, University of California, Berkeley, 2013, https://digitalassets.lib.berkeley.edu/roho/ucb/text/ulman_lloyd_2013.

176. Mervin D. Field, "The UC Student Protests: California Poll," in *The Berkeley Student Revolt*, ed. Lipset and Wolin 199–98.

Chapter Five

1. C. Vann Woodward to Richard Hofstadter, February 16, 1959, in Woodward, *The Letters of C. Vann Woodward*, ed. Michael O'Brien (New Haven, CT: Yale University Press, 2013), 85.

2. Van Gosse, *Where the Boys Are: Cuba, Cold War America, and the Making of a New Left* (London: Verso, 1993), 55, 77, 108–18.

3. Gosse, *Where the Boys Are*, 124–25.

4. Gosse, *Where the Boys Are*, 155–57; Carol Polsgrove, *Divided Minds: Intellectuals and the Civil Rights Movement* (New York: Norton, 2001), 125–35. Marvin Gettleman was my late husband, but I could not interview him for this book because he had dementia. Over the years, however, he had often talked about how impressed he had been by much, though not all, of what he saw in Cuba.

5. Among the other academics who engaged in this political sightseeing were David Kotelchuck, James Gilbert, Paul Baran, Lee Baxandall, Ruth Misheloff, and James Weinstein. William Tabb, interview with the author, August 26, 2013, New York City; Louis Menashe, interview with the author, June 12, 2013, Brooklyn, NY.

6. Gosse, *Where the Boys Are*, 157.

7. Saul Landau, "From the Labor Youth League to the Cuban Revolution," in *History and the New Left: Madison, Wisconsin, 1950–1970*, ed. Paul Buhle (Philadelphia: Temple University Press, 1990), 111.

8. "The Cuban Revolution: The New Crisis in Cold War Ideology," *Studies on the Left* 1, no. 3 (1960): 1–2.

9. C. Wright Mills, *Listen, Yankee: The Revolution in Cuba* (New York: McGraw-Hill, 1960).

10. Gosse, *Where the Boys Are*, 182–83.

11. Gosse, *Where the Boys Are*, 160; Maurice Zeitlin, telephone interview with the author, January 28, 2014; Ray Franklin, interview with the author, January 3, 2014, New York City.

12. "Academic Freedom and Tenure: The University of Arizona," *AAUP Bulletin* 49, no. 4 (December 1963): 336–41; "Academic Freedom and Tenure: Lincoln College (Ill.)," *AAUP Bulletin*, September 1964.

13. Gosse, *Where the Boys Are*, 209; Thomas Mayer, telephone interview with the author, January 23, 2015.

14. Zeitlin, interview, January 28, 2014; Ray Franklin, interview, January 3, 2014.

15. Gosse, *Where the Boys Are*, 257; Steve Batterson, *Stephen Smale: The Mathematician Who Broke the Dimension Barrier* (Providence, RI: American Mathematical Society, 2000), 70.

16. Michael Marcus, interview with the author, October 6, 2015, New York City.

17. Gosse, *Where the Boys Are*, 210–11.

18. Gosse, *Where the Boys Are*, 203.

19. Gosse, *Where the Boys Are*, 213, 217.

20. "Professors Sign Protest of U.S. Policy in Cuba," *Harvard Crimson*, May 5, 1961; "Times' Ad Blasts Kennedy on Cuba," *Harvard Crimson*, May 11, 1961; Gosse, *Where the Boys Are*, 225.

21. Carl E. Schorske, *Intellectual Life, Civil Libertarian Issues, and the Student Movement at the University of California, Berkeley, 1960–1969*, 25, interviews conducted by Ann Lage in 1996, 1997, Regional Oral History Office, Ban-

croft Library, University of California, Berkeley, 2000 http://digitalassets.lib
.berkeley.edu/rohoia/ucb/text/intelllifecivilooschorich.pdf (hereafter Schorske, Bancroft Oral History); Reginald B. Zelnik, "Introduction," in Schorske,
Bancroft Oral History, xi, http://oskicat.berkeley.edu/record=b10389141~S52
(accessed February 11, 2016).

22. Gosse, *Where the Boys Are*, 225; "Administration's Cuban Policy Criticized by
Faculty Members," *Daily Princetonian* 85, no. 71 (May 16, 1961).

23. "Professors Sign Protest of U.S. Policy in Cuba," *Harvard Crimson*, May 5, 1961.

24. Gosse, *Where the Boys Are*, 231–33.

25. Gosse, *Where the Boys Are*, 241.

26. Batterson, *Stephen Smale*, 76.

27. Jonathan Beckwith, interview with the author, April 2, 2013, Boston; Alice
Lynd and Staughton Lynd, *Stepping Stones: Memoir of a Life Together* (Lanham,
MD: Lexington Books, 2009), 66; "Academic Freedom and Tenure: Lincoln
College (Ill.)."

28. Charles Kleinhans, Skype interview with the author, June 9, 2015.

29. Anthony Hiss, "Cuba Protest Meeting," *Harvard Crimson*, October 25, 1962.

30. H. Stuart Hughes, *Gentleman Rebel: The Memoirs of H. Stuart Hughes* (New
York: Ticknor & Fields, 1990), 251, 256.

31. Tom Wells, *The War Within: America's Battle over Vietnam* (Berkeley: University of California Press, 1994), 17–18.

32. Staughton Lynd, telephone interview with the author, June 23, 2014.

33. Dorothy Fall, *Bernard Fall: Memories of a Soldier-Scholar* (Washington, DC:
Potomac Books, 2006), 100–104.

34. Mary Hershberger, *Traveling to Vietnam: American Peace Activists and the War*
(Syracuse, NY: Syracuse University Press, 1998), xvi.

35. John McDermott, email to the author, May 5, 2016.

36. Robert Scigliano and Guy H. Fox, *Technical Assistance in Vietnam: The Michigan State University Experience* (New York: Praeger, 1965), 34, 63.

37. Robert S. Browne to editor, *New York Herald Tribune*, August 27, 1963, Browne
Papers, box 1, folder: Correspondence, 1962–1963, in Swarthmore College
Peace Collection, McCabe Library, Swarthmore College (hereafter Browne
Papers).

38. Fall, *Bernard Fall*, 100–104.

39. See, for example, "A Crisis and a Turning Point Approaches in Vietnam,"
I. F. Stone's Bi-Weekly 11, no. 25 (December 23, 1963), http://www.ifstone.org/
weekly/IFStonesWeekly-1963dec23.pdf (accessed March 10, 2016)

40. Joseph G. Morgan, *The Vietnam Lobby: The American Friends of Vietnam,
1955–1975* (Chapel Hill: University of North Carolina Press, 1997), 11.

41. Most of the information about the MSU project comes from a quasi-official
report by two former members, Robert Scigliano and Guy H. Fox, *Technical
Assistance in Vietnam*.

42. Scigliano and Fox, *Technical Assistance in Vietnam*, 8.

43. Stanley K. Sheinbaum, "Introduction," in Warren Hinckle with Sol Stern and

Robert Scheer, "The University on the Make," *Ramparts Magazine*, April 1966, 13; Scigliano and Fox, *Technical Assistance in Vietnam*, 11, 34.

44. Mai Elliott, *RAND in Southeast Asia: A History of the Vietnam War Era* (Los Angeles: RAND Corporation, 2010), viii–ix, 24, http://site.ebrary.com/lib/nyulibrary/detail.action?docID=10383242 (accessed March 14, 2016).

45. Scigliano and Fox, *Technical Assistance in Vietnam*, 51–54; Gerald C. Hickey, *Window on a War: An Anthropologist in the Vietnam Conflict* (Lubbock: Texas Tech University Press, 2002), 66.

46. Wesley R. Fishel, "Vietnam's One-Man Democratic Rule," *New Leader*, November 2, 1959, 10–13.

47. Marc Pilisuk, "The First Teach-In: An Insight into Professional Activism," in *Teach-Ins: U.S.A. Reports, Opinions, Documents*, ed. Louis Menashe and Ronald Radosh (New York: Praeger, 1967), 10.

48. Much of the following discussion of Fall and Morgenthau comes from the memoir of Fall's widow, Dorothy Fall, *Bernard Fall*, 100–104, and an unnecessarily adulatory account of Morgenthau's opposition to the war, in Louis B. Zimmer, *The Vietnam War Debate* (Lanham, MD: Lexington Books, 2011), 63.

49. Fall, *Bernard Fall*, 76.

50. Fall, *Bernard Fall*, 154, 159.

51. Fall, *Bernard Fall*, 195–200.

52. McDermott, email, May 5, 2016.

53. Zimmer, *Vietnam War Debate*.

54. David L. Schalk discusses the move toward a moralistic critique of the United States in Vietnam throughout his book *War and the Ivory Tower: Algeria and Vietnam* (New York: Oxford University Press, 1991); see, especially, 112–61. See also Robert Tomes, *Apocalypse Then: American Intellectuals and the Vietnam War, 1954–1975* (New York: NYU Press, 1998), 118.

55. Carl Degler to Howard Zinn, November 19, 1965, Howard Zinn Papers, box 1, folder: 10, Tamiment Library and Robert F. Wagner Labor Archives, Bobst Library, New York University.

56. Neil Jumonville, *Henry Steele Commager: Midcentury Liberalism and the History of the Present* (Chapel Hill: University of North Carolina Press, 1999), 165–66.

57. Richard Falk, telephone interview with the author, February 16, 2015.

58. Joseph Esherick, interview with the author, February 17, 2016, Berkeley, CA.

59. Geoffrey Kabaservice, *The Guardians: Kingman Brewster, His Circle, and the Rise of the Liberal Establishment* (New York: Henry Holt, 2004), 237–41; Penny Lewis, *Hardhats, Hippies, and Hawks: The Vietnam Antiwar Movement as Myth and Memory* (Ithaca, NY: Cornell University Press, 2013), 68. For a thoughtful look at the dilemma of some of the government's top scientific advisers, see Sarah Bridger, *Scientists at War: The Ethics of Cold War Weapons Research* (Cambridge, MA: Harvard University Press, 2015), 115–54.

60. Milton S. Katz, *Ban the Bomb: A History of SANE, the Committee for a Sane Nuclear Policy, 1957–1985* (Westport, CT: Greenwood Press, 1986), 94.

61. Stanley Millet, "Terror in Vietnam: An American's Ordeal at the Hands of Our 'Friends,'" *Harper's Magazine*, September 1, 1962, 31–39.

62. Morgan, *The Vietnam Lobby*, 60–98.

63. Carl Degler to Howard Zinn, June 29, 1965, Zinn Papers, box 1, folder 10.

64. See the dozens of invitations in Browne's Papers, box 1, folders: Writings/speeches/statements; Correspondence, 1962–1963; Correspondence, 1964; and Correspondence, 1965 (January–May).

65. Lewis, *Hardhats, Hippies, and Hawks*, 60.

66. Helen Lamb to Robert Browne, March 21, 1963, Browne Papers, box 1, folder: Correspondence, 1962–1963.

67. Fred Halstead, *Out Now! A Participant's Account of the American Movement Against the Vietnam War* (New York: Monad Press, 1978), 7–8.

68. Hughes, *Gentleman Rebel*, 281.

69. Katz, *Ban the Bomb*, 94–95.

70. Sanford Gottlieb to Robert Browne, July 17, 1964, and text of petition, in Browne Papers, box 3, folder: Involvement with Ad Hoc Group of 5000 College and University Professors for Vietnam, 1964.

71. Gottlieb to Browne, July 17, 1964.

72. Justin Jackson, "Kissinger's Kidnapper: Eqbal Ahmad, the U.S. New Left, and the Transnational Romance of Revolutionary War," *Journal for the Study of Radicalism* 4, no. 1 (Spring 2010): 90.

73. C. Vann Woodward to S. Douglass Cater, September 10, 1964, in Woodward, *Letters*, 241.

74. Elinor Langer, "After the Pentagon Papers: Talk with Kistiakowsky and Wiesner," *Science*, n.s., 174, no. 4012 (November 26, 1971): 923, http://www.jstor.org/stable/1732753 (accessed November 15, 2016).

75. "Statement of Faculty Committee against Goldwater," Gerald Braunthal Papers, box 2, folder 22, University of Massachusetts Archives, UMass Amherst.

76. Lynd, interview, June 23, 2014.

77. Charles Haynie, *A Memoir of the New Left: The Political Autobiography of Charles A. Haynie*, ed. Aeron Haynie and Timothy S. Miller (Knoxville: University of Tennessee Press, 2009), 79–80.

78. Eugene D. Genovese, "American Imperialism Confronts a Revolutionary World," in *Teach-Ins*, ed. Menashe and Radosh, 228.

Chapter Six

1. Howard Brick, *Age of Contradiction: American Thought and Culture in the 1960s* (New York: Twayne, 1998), 28–29, calls this line of thought "a rhetoric of 'responsibility.'" For a good example of this kind of rhetoric, see William Appleman Williams, "Our Leaders Are Following the Wrong Rainbow," in *Teach-Ins: U.S.A. Reports, Opinions, Documents*, ed. Louis Menashe and Ronald Radosh (New York: Praeger, 1967), 48.

2. Morgenthau quoted in Louis B. Zimmer, *The Vietnam War Debate* (Lanham, MD: Lexington Books, 2011), 63; Bruce Franklin, interview with the author, February 3, 2013, Montclair, NJ.

3. David L. Schalk, *War and the Ivory Tower: Algeria and Vietnam* (New York: Oxford University Press, 1991), 48.

4. Paul Lyons, *The People of This Generation: The Rise and Fall of the New Left in Philadelphia* (Philadelphia: University of Pennsylvania Press, 2003), 28.

5. Frederick Crews, telephone interview with the author, May 12, 2014.

6. Leon Wofsy, *Professor Emeritus in Immunology, Political Activist*, 33, interviews conducted by Lisa Rubens in 1999, Regional Oral History Office, Bancroft Library, University of California, Berkeley, 2008, https://digitalassets.lib.berkeley .edu/roho/ucb/text/wofsy_leon_2008.pdf (hereafter Wofsy, oral history).

7. William Gamson, telephone interview with the author, May 10, 2013.

8. Marshall Sahlins, "The Teach-Ins: Anti-War Protest in the Old Stoned Age," *Anthropology Today* 25 (2009).

9. Milton S. Katz, *Ban the Bomb: A History of SANE, the Committee for a Sane Nuclear Policy, 1957–1985* (Westport, CT: Greenwood Press, 1986), 96.

10. "Vietnam: America Must Decide between a Full Scale War and a Negotiated Truce," *New York Times*, February 19, 1965, 21.

11. "Open Letter to President Johnson," *New York Times*, February 28, 1965, Robert S. Browne Papers, Swarthmore College Peace Collection, McCabe Library, Swarthmore College (hereafter Browne Papers).

12. Morton Paley, interview with the author, June 4, 2013, New York City.

13. The following information about the genesis of the Michigan teach-in comes from William A. Gamson, "Commitment and Agency in Social Movements," *Sociological Forum* 6, no. 1 (March 1991): 27–50; Gamson, interview, May 10, 2013; Richard Mann, telephone interview with the author, November 14, 2014; Anatol Rapoport, "Dialogue or Monologue?"; and Marc Pilisuk, "The First Teach-In: An Insight into Professional Activism": both in *Teach-Ins*, ed. Menashe and Radosh.

14. There is a discussion of the political culture of Michigan's social scientists in chapter 3.

15. William Gamson, "Afterword," in *Rhyming Hope and History: Academics and Social Movement Scholarship*, ed. David Croteau, William Hoynes, and Charlotte Ryan (Minneapolis: University of Minnesota Press, 2005).

16. Gamson, interview, May 10, 2013; Mann, interview, November 14, 2014.

17. Gamson, "Commitment and Agency," 29.

18. Subcommittee to Investigate the Administration of the Internal Security Act and other Internal Security Laws to the Committee on the Judiciary, United States Senate, *The Anti-Vietnam Agitation and the Teach-In Movement: The Problem of Communist Infiltration and Exploitation, A Staff Study* (Washington: US Government Printing Office, 1965), 18 (hereafter Senate Internal Security Subcommittee, *Anti-Vietnam Agitation*).

19. Schalk, *War and the Ivory Tower*, 49.
20. Pilisuk, "The First Teach-In," 8–10; Gamson, "Commitment and Agency," 31–32; Gamson, interview, May 10, 2013.
21. Pilisuk, "The First Teach-In."
22. Gamson, "Commitment and Agency," 34; Roger Rapoport, "Protest, Learning, Heckling Spark Viet Rally," *Michigan Daily*, March 26, 1965, in *Teach-Ins*, ed. Menashe and Radosh, 15–16.
23. Pilisuk, "The First Teach-In," 11.
24. Charles Austin, "Hudson Valley Teach-In on Vietnam," in *Teach-Ins*, ed. Menashe and Radosh, 36–38.
25. Among the organizations that put on the early teach-ins were the Michigan State University Faculty Committee for Peace in Vietnam, Columbia's Ad Hoc Teach-In Committee on Vietnam, Rutgers's New Jersey Chapter of the Committee on the Problems of War and Peace, Wisconsin's Committee to End the War in Vietnam, the University Committee on Vietnam of UCLA, the Stanford Committee for Peace in Vietnam, Berkeley's Faculty Peace Committee, NYU's Ad Hoc Committee for a Teach-In on Vietnam, the Nashville Committee to End the War in Viet Nam, Indiana University's Ad Hoc Faculty Committee on Viet Nam—to name a few.
26. Mitchel Levitas, "Vietnam Comes to Oregon U.," in *Teach-Ins*, ed. Menashe and Radosh, 17.
27. Richard Flacks, telephone interview with the author, February 22, 2013.
28. Rapoport, "Dialogue or Monologue?," in *Teach-Ins: U.S.A.*, ed. Menashe and Radosh, 7.
29. Richard Mann to Members of the National Board, n.d., Browne Papers, box 1, folder: Involvement with Inter-University Committee for Debate on Foreign Policy 1965 (cont.).
30. Anatol Rapoport to Robert Browne, May 27, 1965, Browne Papers, box 1, folder: Involvement with Inter-University Committee for Debate on Foreign Policy 1965.
31. Gamson, interview, May 10, 2013.
32. Stanley Diamond to Dear Colleague, n.d., Browne Papers, box 3, folder: Involvement with Inter-University Committee for Debate on Foreign Policy 1965 (cont.); Joe Griffith to Executive Council, January 6, 1966, Browne Papers, box 3, folder: Involvement with Inter-University Committee for Debate on Foreign Policy, 1966.
33. Charles Haynie, *A Memoir of the New Left: The Political Autobiography of Charles A. Haynie*, ed. Aeron Haynie and Timothy S. Miller (Knoxville: University of Tennessee Press, 2009), 83–84.
34. Anatol Rapoport, "Dialogue or Monologue? (Part 2)," in *Teach-Ins*, ed. Menashe and Radosh, 174; Gamson, "Commitment and Agency," 32.
35. Webster Schott, "The Teach-In: New Forum for Reason," in *Teach-Ins*, ed. Menashe and Radosh, 29.
36. Marshall Windmiller to Robert Browne, September 3, 1965, Browne Papers,

box 3, folder: Involvement with Inter-University Committee for Debate on Foreign Policy 1965.

37. Michael W. Miles, "Forum Speakers Disagree on Policy in Vietnam War," *Daily Princetonian*, May 6, 1965.

38. Kenneth J. Heineman, *Campus Wars: The Peace Movement at American State Universities in the Vietnam Era* (New York: New York University Press, 1993), 49.

39. Joseph G. Morgan, *The Vietnam Lobby: The American Friends of Vietnam, 1955–1975* (Chapel Hill: University of North Carolina Press, 1997), 112.

40. Steve Batterson, *Stephen Smale: The Mathematician Who Broke the Dimension Barrier* (Providence, RI: American Mathematical Society, 2000), 101.

41. Fred Halstead, *Out Now! A Participant's Account of the American Movement Against the Vietnam War* (New York: Monad Press, 1978), 55.

42. Halstead, *Out Now!*, 54; Robert A. Scalapino, "The Teach-In at the University of California (Berkeley): A Refusal to Attend," in *Teach-Ins*, ed. Menashe and Radosh, 25; Senate Internal Security Subcommittee, *Anti-Vietnam Agitation*, 22.

43. Haynie, *Memoir*, 85.

44. McCandlish Phillips, "Now the Teach-In," *New York Times*, March 27, 1965.

45. Vicki A. Alberti, "The Genovese Affair: Prologue to 'The Sixties'" (PhD diss., Drew University, Madison, NJ, 2009), 61.

46. Alberti, "The Genovese Affair," 71.

47. Ronald Grele, interview with the author, January 22, 2015, New York City; Alice Kessler-Harris, interview with the author, New York City, n.d.; Alberti, "The Genovese Affair," 64–65.

48. Eugene D. Genovese, "American Imperialism Confronts a Revolutionary World," in *Teach-Ins*, ed. Menashe and Radosh, 225.

49. For a contemporary account of the Genovese affair, see Arnold Beichman, "Study in Academic Freedom," in *Teach-Ins*, ed. Menashe and Radosh, 235–42. See also Alberti, "The Genovese Affair."

50. Dean Rusk, quoted in *Teach-Ins*, ed. Menashe and Radosh, 118.

51. Tom Wells, *The War Within: America's Battle over Vietnam* (Berkeley: University of California Press, 1994), 28.

52. McGeorge Bundy, "The Invitation Refused: Reply by McGeorge Bundy to the Invitation of April 10," in *Teach-Ins*, ed. Menashe and Radosh, 141–43.

53. Wells, *War Within*, 29.

54. Wells, *War Within*, 34–35.

55. For an account of his experiences by one of the truth team members, see Thomas F. Conlon, "The 'Truth-Teams': A View from the Podium," and for the mainstream press reports on the Wisconsin incident in the *New York Times* and *Time* magazine, see Donald Janson, "Sit Down and Shut Up," and "The Black-Banders": all in *Teach-Ins*, ed. Menashe and Radosh, 128–37. Halstead, *Out Now!*, 49–51.

56. Batterson, *Stephen Smale*, 103.

57. Mann, interview, November 14, 2014; Zimmer, *Vietnam War Debate*, 67; Wells,

War Within, 31; Rapoport, "Dialogue or Monologue? (Part 2)," in *Teach-Ins: U.S.A.,* ed. Menashe and Radosh, 175–76.

58. Rapoport, "Dialogue or Monologue? (Part 2)," in *Teach-Ins: U.S.A.,* ed. Menashe and Radosh, 177.

59. Senate Internal Security Subcommittee, *Anti-Vietnam Agitation,* 156–57.

60. Rapoport, "Dialogue or Monologue? (Part 2)," 176.

61. Zimmer, *Vietnam War Debate,* 135; Wells, *War Within,* 33; Robert Scalapino, *Free Speech Movement Oral History Project,* interviews conducted by Lisa Rubens in 2000, Regional Oral History Office, Bancroft Library, University of California, Berkeley, 2014, https://digitalassets.lib.berkeley.edu/roho/ucb/text/scalapino_robert_2014.pdf.

62. Mann, interview, November 14, 2014; Rapoport, "Dialogue or Monologue? (Part 2)," 180–82.

63. Marshall Windmiller to Robert Browne, September 3, 1965, in Browne Papers, box 3, folder: Involvement with Inter-University Committee for Debate on Foreign Policy 1965; Mann, interview, November 14, 2014; Stanley Diamond, "The TV Debate," in *Teach-Ins,* ed. Menashe and Radosh, 209.

64. Mary Wright to Robert Browne et al., November 16, 1965; and Joe Griffith to Robert Browne, n.d.: both in Browne Papers, box 3, folder: Involvement with Inter-University Committee for Debate on Foreign Policy 1965 (cont.).

65. Dowd, quoted by Wells, *War Within,* 92.

66. Joe Griffith to Robert Browne, n.d. (1965), in Browne Papers, box 3, folder: Involvement with Inter-University Committee for Debate on Foreign Policy 1965 (cont.).

67. Haynie, *Memoir,* 85.

68. Penny Lewis, *Hardhats, Hippies, and Hawks: The Vietnam Antiwar Movement as Myth and Memory* (Ithaca, NY: Cornell University Press, 2013), 61; Wells, *War Within,* 17–18.

69. Alice Lynd and Staughton Lynd, *Stepping Stones: Memoir of a Life Together* (Lanham, MD: Lexington Books, 2009), 89; Staughton Lynd, telephone interview with the author, June 23, 2014.

70. Martin Duberman, *Howard Zinn: A Life on the Left* (New York: New Press, 2012), 122.

71. Noam Chomsky, interview with the author, September 13, 2013, Cambridge, MA; Robert F. Barsky, *Noam Chomsky: A Life of Dissent* (Cambridge: MIT Press, 1997), 121.

72. John McDermott, interview with the author, August 2 and 3, 2013, Truro, MA; *Viet-Report* 1, no. 1 (July 1965), http://archives.lib.uconn.edu/islandora/object/20002%3A859951519#page/1/mode/1up (accessed April 7, 2016).

73. Martin Nicolaus, "Viet-Report (1965–1968)," *My Soapbox,* http://nicolaus.com/mn/2011/09/viet-report/ (accessed April 7, 2016); McDermott, interview, August 2 and 3, 2013.

74. John McDermott, manuscript, "Chapter 2: Interpreting 'the 60s,'" in the author's possession; McDermott, email to the author, May 5, 2016.

75. John McDermott, list of college appearances, in the author's possession.

76. McDermott, interview, August 2 and 3, 2013.

77. "Colonialism and Liberation in America," *Viet-Report* 3, nos. 8–9 (summer 1968); Carol Brightman, "The 'Weed Killers' and the University at the Front: Projects 'Spicerack' and 'Summit' at the University of Pennsylvania," *Viet-Report* 2, nos. 4–5 (June/July 1966); "The University and Secret Research," *Viet-Report* 3, no. 3.

78. Robert Wolfe, "The Vietnam Anthologies," *Viet-Report* 2, no. 1 (January 1966).

79. Louis Menashe, interview with the author, June 12, 2013, Brooklyn, NY.

80. Marvin E. Gettleman, ed., *Viet Nam: History, Documents, and Opinions on a Major World Crisis* (New York: Fawcett, 1965). Its current edition is Gettleman, Jane Franklin, Marilyn B. Young, and H. Bruce Franklin, eds., *Vietnam and America: A Documented History*, 2nd ed. (New York: Grove, 1995).

81. Bernard B. Fall and Marcus Raskin, eds., *The Viet-Nam Reader: Articles and Documents on American Foreign Policy and the Viet-Nam Crisis* (New York: Basic Books, 1965).

82. Haynie, *Memoir*, 84–85.

83. Leon Wofsy, "When FSM Disturbed the Faculty," manuscript in the author's possession, 8; Franz Schurmann, Peter Dale Scott, and Reginald Zelnik, *The Politics of Escalation in Vietnam* (Boston: Beacon Press, 1966).

84. Crews, interview, May 12, 2014.

85. Scalapino, "The Teach-In at the University of California (Berkeley)," in *Teach-Ins*, ed. Menashe and Radosh, 29.

86. McDermott, interview, August 2 and 3, 2013.

87. Mary Hershberger, *Traveling to Vietnam: American Peace Activists and the War* (Syracuse, NY: Syracuse University Press, 1998), 9–11.

88. Lynd had originally invited the SNCC leader Robert Moses, who, though interested, backed out—perhaps because he did not want to expose his organization to the Red-baiting he feared the journey might produce.

89. Hershberger, *Traveling to Vietnam*, 35–49; Gary Murrell, *"The Most Dangerous Communist in the United States": A Biography of Herbert Aptheker* (Amherst: University of Massachusetts Press, 2015), 168–80; Carl Mirra, *The Admirable Radical: Staughton Lynd and Cold War Dissent, 1945–1970* (Kent, OH: Kent State University Press, 2010), 99–115.

90. Joe Griffith to Marshall Windmiller, December 29, 1965, Browne Papers, box 3, folder: Involvement with Inter-University Committee for Debate on Foreign Policy 1965 (cont.).

91. Mirra, *Admirable Radical*, 101.

92. Murrell, *"The Most Dangerous Communist in the United States,"* 174–76; Hershberger, *Traveling to Vietnam*, 149.

93. Hershberger, *Traveling to Vietnam*, 52, 38; Mirra, *Admirable Radical*, 115.

94. Lynd and Lynd, *Stepping Stones*, 83; Lynd, telephone interview, June 23, 2014.

95. Geoffrey Kabaservice, *The Guardians: Kingman Brewster, His Circle, and the Rise of the Liberal Establishment* (New York: Henry Holt, 2004), 256–57.

96. Ann Davidon to Louis Green, April 13, 1966, in William and Ann Davidon Papers, Series D—Vietnam, box 29, folder: Saigon Trip of W. Davidon, A. J. Muste, et al. (1966–1967), Swarthmore College Peace Collection, McCabe Library, Swarthmore College (hereafter Davidon Papers).

97. Hershberger, *Traveling to Vietnam*, 56–61. Davidon press conference, April 24, 1966; Nat Hentoff, "Letters to the Times," clipping, n.d.; Jack Lloyd, "Saigon Greeted Group Warmly, Davidon Says," *Philadelphia Inquirer*, April 24, 1966, clipping; and "Davidon Loses Post as Head of Department," *Main Line Times*, May 26, 1966, clipping: all in Davidon Papers, Series D—Vietnam, box 29, folder: Saigon Trip of W. Davidon, A.J. Muste, et al. (1966–1967).

98. Hershberger, *Traveling to Vietnam*, 54.

99. Hershberger, *Traveling to Vietnam*, 91–93; J. B. Neilands in James W. Clinton, *The Loyal Opposition: Americans in North Vietnam, 1965–1972* (Niwot: University Press of Colorado, 1995), 69–70.

100. Carl Degler to Howard and Roz Zinn, April 26, June 29, 1965, box 1, folder 10, Howard Zinn Papers; TAM.542; Tamiment Library/Robert F. Wagner Labor Archives, New York University.

101. Press Release, Wm. Fitts Ryan, August 12, 1965, Browne Papers, box 1, folder: Speaking Engagements; Otto Feinstein to Dear Colleagues, July 12, 1965, Browne Papers, box 3, folder: Involvement with Inter-University Committee for Debate on Foreign Policy 1965.

102. U.S. Policy with Respect to Mainland China: Hearings before the United States Senate Committee on Foreign Relations, Eighty-Ninth Congress, 2nd sess., on March 8, 10, 16, 18, 21, 28, 30, 1966; Wells, *War Within*, 68–69; Arthur M. Schlesinger Jr., To the Children, February 21, 1966, in *The Letters of Arthur Schlesinger, Jr.*, ed. by Andrew Schlesinger and Stephen Schlesinger (New York: Random House, 2013), 308.

Chapter Seven

1. Everett Carll Ladd, "American University Teachers and Opposition to the Vietnam War," *Minerva* 8, no. 4 (October 1970); Kenneth J. Heineman, *Campus Wars: The Peace Movement at American State Universities in the Vietnam Era* (New York: New York University Press, 1993), 32–75.

2. Roger Rapoport, "Protest, Learning, Heckling Spark Viet Rally," in *Teach-Ins: U.S.A. Reports, Opinions, Documents*, ed. Louis Menashe and Ronald Radosh (New York: Praeger, 1967), 14–15.

3. David L. Schalk, *War and the Ivory Tower: Algeria and Vietnam* (New York: Oxford University Press, 1991), 113; Tom Wells, *The War Within: America's Battle over Vietnam* (Berkeley: University of California Press, 1994), 69–70.

4. Louis B. Zimmer, *The Vietnam War Debate* (Lanham, MD: Lexington Books, 2011), 92; "Experts Reply to Critics of United States," in *Teach-Ins*, ed. Menashe and Radosh, 110–11.

5. One study of random faculty members at seventeen Boston institutions in 1966,

shows that 15 percent supported immediate withdrawal, 46 percent wanted to stop bombing North Vietnam, and 66 percent felt that the United States shouldn't have gone into Vietnam. William R. Morgan, "Faculty Mediation in Campus Conflict," in *Protest! Student Activism in America*, ed. Julian Foster and Durward Long (New York: William Morrow, 1970), 365–66; Joseph G. Morgan, *The Vietnam Lobby: The American Friends of Vietnam, 1955–1975* (Chapel Hill: University of North Carolina Press, 1997), 104; Wells, *War Within*, 146–48.

6. Ernest Van Der Haag, "American Intervention Minimizes Violence," in *Teach-Ins*, ed. Menashe and Radosh, 77–83; C. Vann Woodward to David Riesman, April 23, 1975, in *The Letters of C. Vann Woodward*, ed. Michael O'Brien (New Haven, CT: Yale University Press, 2013), 312; Fred Halstead, *Out Now! A Participant's Account of the American Movement Against the Vietnam War* (New York: Monad Press, 1978), 299.

7. Samuel Beer and Paul Seabury, quoted in Zimmer, *Vietnam War Debate*, 83.

8. C. Vann Woodward to Charles A. Barker, October 8, 1968, in *Letters of C. Vann Woodward*, 268–69; John Morton Blum, *A Life with History* (Lawrence: University Press of Kansas, 2004), 183–85.

9. H. Stuart Hughes, *Gentleman Rebel: The Memoirs of H. Stuart Hughes* (New York: Ticknor & Fields, 1990), 283–84.

10. Arthur Schlesinger Jr. to Philip Potter, March 23, 1966, in *The Letters of Arthur Schlesinger, Jr.*, ed. Andrew Schlesinger and Stephen Schlesinger (New York: Random House, 2013), 318.

11. Arthur Schlesinger Jr. to Oscar Sachs, March 10, 1966, in *Letters of Arthur Schlesinger, Jr.*, 311; "Editors' Introduction," in *Teach-Ins*, ed. Menashe and Radosh, 44; Schlesinger statement in *Authors Take Sides on Vietnam*, ed. Cecil Woolf and John Bagguley (New York: Simon and Schuster, 1967), 67–68.

12. Carl Degler to Howard Zinn, November 19, 1965, Howard Zinn Papers, box 1, folder 10, Tamiment Library and Robert F. Wagner Labor Archives, Bobst Library, New York University.

13. Daniel Bell, Alexander Dallin, Herbert Deane, Wolfgang Friedman, Richard Hofstadter, William Leuchtenberg, Robert Merton, Henry L. Roberts, Fritz Stern, and David B. Truman to Lyndon Johnson, May 18, 1966, and Johnson to Bell et al., June 16, 1966 (underlined in original), in Hofstadter Papers, box 2, Rare Book and Manuscript Library, Butler Library, Columbia University; David S. Brown, *Richard Hofstadter: An Intellectual Biography* (Chicago: University of Chicago Press, 2006), 170.

14. Franklin Ford et al., to the President, August 3, 1967; Lyndon B. Johnson to Robert G. McCloskey, September 5, 1967; and Franklin Ford to the President, October 13, 1967: all in Robert McCloskey Papers, box 1, Harvard University Archives, Nathan M. Pusey Library, Cambridge, MA.

15. Morgan, "Faculty Mediation in Campus Conflict," in *Protest!*, ed. Foster and Long, 366.

16. Milton S. Katz, *Ban the Bomb: A History of SANE, the Committee for a Sane Nuclear Policy, 1957–1985* (Westport, CT: Greenwood Press, 1986), 96–102.

17. Hughes, *Gentleman Rebel*, 280–81.

18. Schalk, *War and the Ivory Tower*, 117.

19. On early antiwar activities, see chapter 5, supra. News Release, December 14, 1964, "Open Letter on Vietnam to the President of the United States," in Ann and William Davidon Papers, box 30, folder: Misc. Printed Material, 1964– 1965, Swarthmore College Peace Collection, McCabe Library, Swarthmore College (hereafter Davidon Papers).

20. Schalk, *War and the Ivory Tower*, 116–17, 216–17.

21. Ladd, "American University Teachers and Opposition to the Vietnam War," 543–44.

22. Richard Ohmann, interview with the author, February 7, 2013, New York City.

23. James Rowe to Lyndon Johnson, May 17, 1967, in Wells, *War Within*, 143.

24. Wells, *War Within*, 135; Halstead, *Out Now!*, 291; Nancy Zaroulis and Gerald Sullivan, *Who Spoke Up? American Protest Against the War in Vietnam, 1963– 1975* (Garden City, NY: Doubleday, 1984), 118.

25. Schalk, *War and the Ivory Tower*, 114, 153; Heineman, *Campus Wars*, 209–10; Wells, *War Within*, 546; C. Vann Woodward to Wallace Notestein, June 4, 1967, *Letters of C. Vann Woodward*, 259.

26. Ladd, "American University Teachers and Opposition to the Vietnam War," 544; Stephen H. Wheeler, "'Hell No—We Won't Go, Y'all': Southern Student Opposition to the Vietnam War," in *The Vietnam War on Campus: Other Voices, More Distant Drums*, ed. Marc Jason Gilbert (Westport, CT: Praeger, 2001), 154; Noam Chomsky, "To All Signers of Boston Area Faculty Committee Ads," n.d.; and Robert S. Cohen to "Dear Colleague," n.d. [spring 1966]: both in David Schalk, personal papers, in possession of the author.

27. Jonathan Beckwith, interview with the author, April 2, 2013, Boston; Beckwith, *Making Genes, Making Waves: A Social Activist in Science* (Cambridge, MA: Harvard University Press, 2002), 47–48.

28. Halstead, *Out Now!*, 100; Katz, *Ban the Bomb*, 96; Thomas Maier, *Dr. Spock: An American Life* (New York: Harcourt Brace, 1998), 247–50; SANE Leaflet "March on Washington for Peace in Vietnam," in Schalk, personal papers.

29. Leon Wofsy, "The Faculty Peace Committee," from Bancroft Library Symposium: FSM and the Legacy of Social Protest, April 13–14, 2001, Panel: Vietnamization of the Berkeley Campus, 1965–1970, manuscript in possession of the author; Troy Duster, telephone interview with the author, May 1, 2013; Frederick Crews, telephone interview with the author, May 12, 2014.

30. Halstead, *Out Now!*, 84–85.

31. Seth Rosenfeld, *Subversives: The FBI's War on Student Radicals, and Reagan's Rise to Power* (New York: Farrar, Straus and Giroux, 2012), 268–73; Wells, *War Within*, 50; Gerard J. De Groot, "The Limits of Moral Protest and Participatory Democracy: The Vietnam Day Committee," *Pacific Historical Review* 64, no. 1 (February 1995): 95–119.

32. Steve Batterson, *Stephen Smale: The Mathematician Who Broke the Dimension Barrier* (Providence, RI: American Mathematical Society, 2000), 108, 112.

33. Morton Paley, interview with the author, June 4, 2013, New York City.
34. Batterson, *Stephen Smale*, 121–22, 127.
35. Zaroulis and Sullivan, *Who Spoke Up?*, 90.
36. Wells, *War Within*, 78.
37. Wells, *War Within*, 92.
38. Wells, *War Within*, 59–60, 93–95.
39. Mary Ann Wynkoop, *Dissent in the Heartland: The Sixties at Indiana University* (Bloomington: Indiana University Press, 2002), 42.
40. Sue Schwartz, "Community Politics," *Peace and Freedom News*, no. 26 (May 16, 1966), in Ephemera Collection, Tamiment Library and Robert F. Wagner Labor Archives, Bobst Library, New York University.
41. Michael Walzer, *Political Action: A Practical Guide to Movement Politics* (Chicago: Quadrangle Books, 1971).
42. All these facts, dare I say it, came from Wikipedia.
43. Hughes, *Gentleman Rebel*, 251.
44. Hughes, *Gentleman Rebel*, 256–60.
45. Douglas Dowd, "Foreword," in Charles Haynie, *A Memoir of the New Left: The Political Autobiography of Charles A. Haynie*, ed. Aeron Haynie and Timothy S. Miller (Knoxville: University of Tennessee Press, 2009), xi; Haynie, *Memoir*, 37–38; Doug Dowd, *Blues for America: A Critique, a Lament, and Some Memories* (New York: Monthly Review Press, 1997), 135.
46. C. Vann Woodward to S. Douglass Cater, September 10, 1964, in *Letters of C. Vann Woodward*, 241; Maier, *Dr. Spock*, 229; Haynie, *Memoir*, 79–80; Halstead, *Out Now!*, 188.
47. Halstead, *Out Now!*, 133, 188; "The Peace Candidates," *Peace and Freedom News*, no. 30 (July 26, 1966).
48. Katz, *Ban the Bomb*, 100.
49. Stanley Aronowitz, "'Peace' at the Polls," *Viet-Report* 2, nos. 4–5 (June–July 1966).
50. Peter Richardson, *A Bomb in Every Issue: How the Short, Unruly Life of Ramparts Magazine Changed America* (New York: New Press, 2009), 59–63; Serge Lang, *The Scheer Campaign* (New York: W. A. Benjamin, 1967).
51. Richardson, *A Bomb in Every Issue*, 58–59.
52. Wynkoop, *Dissent in the Heartland*, 42; Haynie, *Memoir*, 88–89; Maier, *Dr. Spock*, 261; "60,000 Peace Votes Cast in N.Y. Primary," *Peace and Freedom News*, no. 29, July 15, 1966; "To the National Board," n.d., Robert S. Browne Papers, box 3, folder: Involvement with Inter-Univ. Committee for Debate on Foreign Policy, 1966, in Swarthmore College Peace Collection, McCabe Library, Swarthmore College (hereafter Browne Papers); Mike Klare, "Scheer East: A Profile of the Cook Campaign," *Peace and Freedom News*, no. 31 (August 12, 1966); "Cook Seeks Giamo's Congressional Seat," *Yale Daily News*, April 26, 1966; Richard Wolff, telephone interview with the author, January 23, 2014; Mary Lee Morrison, *Elise Boulding: A Life in the Cause of Peace* (Jefferson, NC: McFarland, 2005), 82–83; Thomas Mayer, telephone interview with the author, January 23, 2015.

53. Richard Mann, telephone interview with the author, November 14, 2014.

54. Halstead, *Out Now!*, 161; "Cornell Referendum," *Cornell Daily Sun* 84, no. 45 (November 7, 1967); "Ithacans Vote Ceasefire, Withdrawal," *Cornell Daily Sun* 84, no. 46 (November 8, 1967), http://cdsun.library.cornell.edu/cgi-bin/cornell?a=d&d=CDS19671107.2.20 (accessed July 27, 2016); William Galeota, "Peace Petition Defeated," *Harvard Crimson*, November 29, 1967, http://www.thecrimson.com/article/1967/11/29/peace-petition-defeated-pthe-cambridge-neighborhood/ (accessed July 27, 2016); Patrick M. Quinn, "Radicalization in 1960s Madison, Wisconsin: One Participant's Reflection," Solidarity-US.org, https://www.solidarity-us.org/site/node/3545 (accessed July 26, 2016); Maurice Zeitlin, telephone interview with the author, September 8, 2016.

55. Halstead, *Out Now!*, 292–93; William M. Kutik, "Vietnam Summer Evolves from Phone Call to Nation-Wide Organizing Project," *Harvard Crimson*, May 4, 1967, http://www.thecrimson.com/article/1967/5/4/vietnam-summer-evolves-from-phone-call/?page=2 (accessed July 27, 2016).

56. Wells, *War Within*, 138, 168–69; Wendy Chiemielski, "Introduction to Finding Aid," Vietnam Summer Records, 1967, Swarthmore College Peace Collection, McCabe Library, Swarthmore College, https://www.swarthmore.edu/library/peace/DG051-099/dg067vietnamsum.html (accessed July 27, 2016); Michael Walzer, interview with the author, May 13, 2013, New York City.

57. Maier, *Dr. Spock*, 283–87; Zaroulis and Sullivan, *Who Spoke Up?*, 128.

58. Dowd, *Blues for America*, 156–57; Ronald Grele, interview with the author, January 22, 2015, New York City; Michael Marcus, interview with the author, October 6, 2015, New York City.

59. George Rising, *Clean for Gene: Eugene McCarthy's 1968 Presidential Campaign* (Westport, CT: Praeger, 1997), 53–63.

60. Blum, *A Life with History*, 188; Arthur Schlesinger to Kenneth Galbraith, September 26, 1967, in *Letters of Arthur Schlesinger, Jr.*, 340; John Kenneth Galbraith, *A Life in Our Times: Memoirs* (Boston: Houghton Mifflin, 1981), 486–506.

61. *Valley Peace Center Newsletter*, January 12, 1968, Valley Peace Center Papers, box 2, folder 6, Special Collections and University Archives, W. E. B. Du Bois Library, University of Massachusetts Amherst (hereafter Valley Peace Center Papers).

62. Blum, *A Life with History*, 187–88.

63. Martin Edward Malia, *Historian of Russian and European Intellectual History*, 149, interview conducted by David Engerman in 2003, Regional Oral History Office, Bancroft Library, University of California, Berkeley, 2005, https://digitalassets.lib.berkeley.edu/roho/ucb/text/MaliaBook.pdf; Bruce Dancis, *Resister: A Story of Protest and Prison during the Vietnam War* (Ithaca, NY: Cornell University Press, 2014), 144.

64. "Against Withholding Class Rank," in *The University Crisis Reader*, ed. Immanuel Wallerstein and Paul Starr, vol. 1, *The Liberal University under Attack*

(New York: Random House, 1971), 208–9; John Coatsworth, interview with the author, July 28, 2016, New York City.

65. Lawrence M. Baskir and William A. Strauss, *Chance and Circumstance: The Draft, the War, and the Vietnam Generation* (New York: Knopf, 1978), 36.

66. Dan T. Carter, "Deep South Campus Memories and the World the Sixties Made," in *Rebellion in Black and White: Southern Student Activism in the 1960s*, ed. Robert Cohen and David J. Snyder (Baltimore: Johns Hopkins University Press, 2013), xiii.

67. William Gamson, "Afterward," 2009, manuscript in the author's possession, 4.

68. Donald W. Light Jr., "Directed Resistance: The Structure of Tactics in Student Protest," in *The Dynamics of University Protest*, ed. Donald Light Jr. and John Spiegel (Chicago: Nelson-Hall, 1977), 93n24, 110; Carolyn Eisenberg, interview with the author, September 23, 2013, Brooklyn, NY. "Feldman Report," August 15, 1966, and "Special Report: Student Demonstration": both in Campus Unrest Collection, Accession No. 33, RG 3/5/1, box 3, no. 3/5/897, folder 4: Dow Chemical Co. Controversy 1967, University of Buffalo Archives, Capen Hall, University at Buffalo (hereafter Buffalo, "Feldman Report").

69. Grayson Kirk to William A. M. Burden, February 18, March 7, 1966, in Series I: Central Files, 1895–1971—Office of the President, box 593, file 1.1.983 Selective Service—Class Ranking in Columbia University Archives, Rare Book and Manuscript Library, Butler Library, Columbia University; Summary of the Meeting of May 7, 1966, Buffalo, "Feldman Report."

70. *Peace and Freedom News*, no. 26 (May 27, 1966).

71. Heineman, *Campus Wars*, 129; W. J. Rorabaugh, *Berkeley at War: The 1960s* (New York: Oxford University Press, 1989), 114–15.

72. Beverly Woodward, letter to the dean, in "WSP Resigns Professor's Job over Grades—Draft Issue," *Peace and Freedom News*, no. 26 (May 16, 1966).

73. Baskir and Strauss, *Chance and Circumstance*, 16–17.

74. Michael S. Foley, *Confronting the War Machine: Draft Resistance during the Vietnam War* (Chapel Hill: University of North Carolina Press, 2003), 59.

75. Buffalo, "Feldman Report"; Research of Dean G. Pruitt and James Gahagan, 1967–1972, 1975, box 3, #3/5/897, folder 4: Dow Chemical Co. controversy 1967, in Campus Unrest Collection, University at Buffalo Archives, Capen Hall, State University of New York, Amherst.

76. Kenneth M. Dolbeare, "Faculty Power," in *Academic Supermarkets: A Critical Case Study of a Multiversity*, ed. Philip G. Altbach, Robert S. Laufer, and Sheila McVey (San Francisco: Jossey-Bass, 1971), 165–66.

77. "An Educators' Statement of Principle on Selective Service, May 1966," in *The University Crisis Reader*, ed. Wallerstein and Starr, 1:207–8.

78. Resolution of the Academic Senate, San Francisco State College, April 26, 1966, http://archive.lib.msu.edu/DMC/AmRad/nationalvietnamexam.pdf (accessed September 2, 2016).

79. Geoffrey Kabaservice, *The Guardians: Kingman Brewster, His Circle, and the Rise of the Liberal Establishment* (New York: Henry Holt, 2004), 301.

80. Richard A. Siggelkow, *Dissent and Disruption: A University under Siege* (Buffalo: Prometheus Books, 1991), 53.

81. Joseph Dorinson, interview with the author, June 11, 2013, Brooklyn, NY.

82. Michael Ferber and Staughton Lynd, *The Resistance* (Boston: Beacon Press, 1971), 40.

83. Gamson, "Afterward," 4–6; William Gamson, telephone interview with the author, May 10, 2013; Mann, interview, November 14, 2014.

84. Richard Flacks, telephone interview with the author, February 22, 2013; Light, "Directed Resistance" in *The Dynamics of University Protest*, ed. Light and Spiegel, 84; Eisenberg, interview, September 23, 2013; Jesse Lemisch, interview with the author, February 5, 2013, New York City. The thoughtful case study of the Chicago takeover by the sociologist Donald W. Light Jr. was particularly helpful here. It contained excerpts from interviews with Chicago faculty members on all sides of the issue, although it would have been even more helpful for a historian if he had named names.

85. Christopher Chandler, "Professors Decry Use of Grades in Drafting," *Chicago Sun-Times*, April 21, 1966, in Davidon Papers, series D, Vietnam, box 29, folder: Students and the Draft (1965–67).

86. Light, "Directed Resistance," 82–86; Clifford Furnas, "Statement," in Buffalo, "Feldman Report"; Gregory J. Nigosian, "Regents Respond to Crisis," in *Academic Supermarkets*, ed. Altbach, Laufer, and McVey, 98; "Dates Set for Administering of Optional Draft Exams," *Yale Daily News*, March 8, 1966.

87. Furnas, "Statement," in Buffalo, "Feldman Report."

88. Wells, *War Within*, 82–83; Halstead, *Out Now!*, 168; "Fourth Draft Test to Be Offered, *The Campus* (CCNY), May 10, 1966; "National Vietnam Examination," box 4, folder 48, Valley Peace Center Papers; Baskir and Strauss, *Chance and Circumstance*, 23. For a copy of the exam, see http://archive.lib.msu.edu/DMC/AmRad/nationalvietnamexam.pdf.

89. Evan Stark, "Talking Sociology: A Sixties Fragment," in *Radical Sociologists and the Movement: Experiences, Lessons, and Legacies*, ed. Martin Oppenheimer, Martin J. Murray, and Rhonda F. Levine (Philadelphia: Temple University Press, 1991), 68; Evan Stark, "In Exile," in *History and the New Left: Madison, Wisconsin, 1950–1970*, ed Paul Buhle (Philadelphia: Temple University Press, 1990), 174; Dancis, *Resister*, 48; Wilma Iggers and Georg Iggers, *Two Lives in Uncertain Times: Facing the Challenges of the 20th Century as Scholars and Citizens* (New York: Berghahn Books, 2006), 112.

90. Light, "Directed Resistance," 88, 107–8; Lemisch, interview, February 5, 2013; Dancis, *Resister*; Foley, *Confronting the War Machine*, 57–58; Kirkpatrick Sale, *SDS* (New York: Random House, 1973), 111–16.

91. Light, "Directed Resistance," 84.

92. *The Campus* (CCNY), May 18, 1966; *Peace and Freedom News*, no. 26 (May 27, 1966); Amy Kesselman, "Reflections on a Sit-In," *Peace and Freedom News*, no. 31 (August 12, 1966).

93. Dancis, *Resister*, 46.

94. Siggelkow, *Dissent and Disruption*, 52–59.
95. Richard W. Lyman, *Stanford in Turmoil: Campus Unrest, 1966–1972* (Stanford, CA: Stanford General Books, 2009), 36.
96. Light, "Directed Resistance," offers the most coherent account I have seen of the Chicago 1966 sit-in.
97. Stark, "Talking Sociology," in *Radical Sociologists*, ed. Oppenheimer, Murray, and Levine, 68; Stark, "In Exile," in *History and the New Left*, ed. Buhle, 174; David Maraniss, *They Marched into Sunlight: War and Peace, Vietnam and America, October 1967* (New York: Simon and Schuster, 2003), 104.
98. Dancis, *Resister*, 50.
99. Stark, "Talking Sociology," in *Radical Sociologists*, ed. Oppenheimer, Murray, and Levine, 68–69; Stark, "In Exile," 175; Joan Scott, interview with the author, December 16, 2014, New York City; Coatsworth, interview, July 28, 2016.
100. Light, "Directed Resistance," 81–87; Lemisch, interview, February 5, 2013; Milton Friedman and Rose D. Friedman, *Two Lucky People: Memoirs* (Chicago: University of Chicago Press, 1998) 212, 343; Bill Zimmerman, *Troublemaker: A Memoir from the Front Lines of the Sixties* (New York: Doubleday, 2011), 85–86.
101. Donald Light Jr., "The Dynamics of Faculty Response to Student Protest," in *The Dynamics of University Protest*, ed. Light and Spiegel, 97–137.
102. Light, "Directed Resistance," 87, 92n22.
103. Friedman and Friedman, *Two Lucky People*, 378; Zaroulis and Sullivan, *Who Spoke Up?*, 105–6.
104. Matthew Levin, *Cold War University: Madison and the New Left in the Sixties* (Madison: University of Wisconsin Press, 2013), 134; Maraniss, *They Marched into Sunlight*, 104; Stark, "Talking Sociology," in *Radical Sociologists*, ed. Oppenheimer, Murray, and Levine, 68; James B. Gilbert, "The Intellectuals and the First New Left," in *History and the New Left*, ed. Buhle, 123.
105. Nigosian, "Regents Respond to Crisis," in *Academic Supermarkets*, ed. Altbach, Laufer, and McVey, 98–99.
106. Coatsworth, interview, July 28, 2016.
107. Summary of the Meeting of May 7, 1966, Buffalo, "Feldman Report"; Zelda F. Gamson, "Michigan Muddles Through: Luck, Nimbleness, and Resilience in Crisis," in *Academic Transformation: Seventeen Institutions under Pressure*, ed. David Riesman and Verne A. Stadtman (New York: McGraw-Hill, 1973), 182.
108. Gamson, "Michigan Muddles Through," in *Academic Transformation*, ed. Riesman and Stadtman, 181.
109. *The Campus* (CCNY), November 22, 1966; Dancis, *Resister*, 50.
110. Heineman, *Campus Wars*, 133.
111. Lyman, *Stanford in Turmoil*, 40.
112. *The Campus* (CCNY), November 22, 1966.
113. Dancis, *Resister*, 50.
114. Joanne Grant, *Confrontation on Campus: The Columbia Pattern for the New Protest* (New York: New American Library, 1969), 35.
115. Robert Samuelson, "Ford Says Faculty Probably Won't Discuss Draft Again

This Month," *Harvard Crimson,* December 8, 1966; Foley, *Confronting the War Machine,* 59.

116. Light, "Dynamics of Faculty Response," 119.
117. Buffalo, "Feldman Report"; Heineman, *Campus Wars,* 166–67; Siggelkow, *Dissent and Disruption,* 59–62.
118. Eric Solomon, "Oral History," 12, interviewed by Peter Carroll, February 2, 1992, Labor Archives and Research Center, San Francisco State University (hereafter LARC, SFSU); Robert Smith, Richard Axen, and DeVere Pentony, *By Any Means Necessary: The Revolutionary Struggle at San Francisco State* (San Francisco: Jossey-Bass, 1970), 12–14; Peter Radcliff, "Oral History," 17–20, interviewed by Harvey Schwartz, May 31, 2000, rev. 2015, LARC, SFSU.

Chapter Eight

1. John Raines, interview with the author, March 20, 2014, Philadelphia.
2. William Sloane Coffin Jr., *Once to Every Man: A Memoir* (New York: Atheneum, 1978), 231.
3. Bruce Dancis, *Resister: A Story of Protest and Prison during the Vietnam War* (Ithaca, NY: Cornell University Press, 2014), 127; Sherry Gershon Gottlieb, *Hell No, We Won't Go! Resisting the Draft during the Vietnam War* (New York: Viking, 1991), 141.
4. Thomas B. Wenzl to RESIST, May 5, 1968, in box 6-1, RESIST Records, Watkinson Library and Trinity College Archives, Raether Library, Trinity College, Hartford, CT (hereafter RESIST Records, Trinity).
5. Lawrence M. Baskir and William A. Strauss, *Chance and Circumstance: The Draft, the War, and the Vietnam Generation* (New York: Knopf, 1978), 9; John Trumpbour, "Harvard, the Cold War, and the National Security State," in *How Harvard Rules: Reason in the Service of Empire,* ed. John Trumpbour (Boston: South End Press, 1989), 112; Gottlieb, *Hell No, We Won't Go!,* 200, 217.
6. Charles Freehof, interview with the author, December 27, 2012, New York City.
7. David Schalk, interview with the author, December 17, 2013, New York City.
8. Baskir and Strauss, *Chance and Circumstance,* 37–41.
9. Gottlieb, *Hell No, We Won't Go!,* 252; *Valley Peace Center Newsletter,* February 3, 1968, in box 2, folder 6, Valley Peace Center Records, Special Collections and University Archives, W. E. B. Du Bois Library, University of Massachusetts Amherst (hereafter Valley Peace Center Records); Kenneth J. Heineman, *Campus Wars: The Peace Movement at American State Universities in the Vietnam Era* (New York: New York University Press, 1993), 184–85; Alice Lynd and Staughton Lynd, *Stepping Stones: Memoir of a Life Together* (Lanham, MD: Lexington Books, 2009), 90, 85–86.
10. Paul Lauter, interviews with the author, April 13, 2008, August 21, 2013, New York City. For the text of the "Guide," see http://www.sds-1960s.org/Guide-to-CO.pdf.

11. David L. Schalk, *War and the Ivory Tower: Algeria and Vietnam* (New York: Oxford University Press, 1991), 207n92; Schalk, interview, December 17, 2013.

12. Georg Iggers, "History and Social Action Beyond National and Continental Borders," manuscript in possession of the author.

13. Wilma Iggers and Georg Iggers, *Two Lives in Uncertain Times: Facing the Challenges of the 20th Century as Scholars and Citizens* (New York: Berghahn Books, 2006), 128–29; Georg Iggers, telephone interview with the author, December 9, 2014; George and Wilma Iggers, interview with the author, May 22, 2015, Amherst, NY.

14. Richard Falk, telephone interview with the author, February 16, 2015; Baskir and Strauss, *Chance and Circumstance*, 39–41.

15. Bill Zimmerman, *Troublemaker: A Memoir from the Front Lines of the Sixties* (New York: Doubleday, 2011), 164–65.

16. Doug Dowd, *Blues for America: A Critique, a Lament, and Some Memories* (New York: Monthly Review Press, 1997), 140.

17. Michael Ferber and Staughton Lynd, *The Resistance* (Boston: Beacon Press, 1971), 277–78; Michael S. Foley, *Confronting the War Machine: Draft Resistance during the Vietnam War* (Chapel Hill: University of North Carolina Press, 2003), 46–67.

18. For first-person accounts of the student resistance movement, see Dancis, *Resister*; David Harris, *Dreams Die Hard: Three Men's Journey through the Sixties* (New York: St. Martin's Press, 1982); and Ferber and Lynd, *The Resistance*, 2.

19. Form letter, Kay Boyle et al. to Dear Colleague, March 5, 1965, in David Schalk Papers, in possession of the author; Ferber and Lynd, *The Resistance*, 116–17; Carl Mirra, *The Admirable Radical: Staughton Lynd and Cold War Dissent, 1945–1970* (Kent, OH: Kent State University Press, 2010), 94.

20. Mirra, *Admirable Radical*, 90–97.

21. Lynd and Lynd, *Stepping Stones*, 95–96.

22. Schalk, *War and the Ivory Tower*, 59–60; Text of Open Letter, in Letter to Mr. W. Walter Boyd from Herbert Sonthoff, March 28, 1967, https://collection1 .libraries.psu.edu/cdm/singleitem/collection/transaction/id/17162 (accessed August 29, 2016).

23. Morris Kaplan, "Writers Protest Vietnam War Tax," *New York Times*, September 17, 1967; text of the ad in http://archives.nwtrcc.org/history/writers-and -editors-names.php (accessed September 3, 2016). Among the signers of the Writers and Editors petition were such writers, academics, and intellectuals as James Baldwin, Eric Bentley, Carol Brightman, Daniel and Philip Berrigan, Noam Chomsky, Jules Chametzky, Frederick Crews, Stanley Diamond, Martin Duberman, Leslie Fiedler, Eugene Genovese, Louis Kampf, Staughton Lynd, Norman Mailer, John McDermott, Frances Fox Piven, Anatol Rapoport, Marshall Sahlins, Robert Scheer, Peter Dale Scott, Susan Sontag, Benjamin Spock, and Howard Zinn, along with dozens of editors, journalists, poets, and novelists.

24. Robert Lange, interview with the author, September 12, 2013, Cambridge, MA.
25. *Valley Peace Center Newsletter*, February 3, 1968, in box 2, folder 6, Valley Peace Center Records; Richard Ohmann, interview with the author, February 7, 2013, New York City; Sarah Bridger, *Scientists at War: The Ethics of Cold War Weapons Research* (Cambridge, MA: Harvard University Press, 2015), 146, 347.
26. Robert F. Barsky, *Noam Chomsky: A Life of Dissent* (Cambridge, MA: MIT Press, 1997), 124, 126.
27. Schalk, *War and the Ivory Tower*, 57–60; Philip Nobile, *Intellectual Skywriting: Literary Politics and the New York Review of Books* (New York: Charterhouse, 1974), 41–42.
28. Noam Chomsky, "The Responsibility of Intellectuals," *New York Review of Books*, February 23, 1967.
29. Frederick Crews, telephone interview with the author, May 12, 2014.
30. Francine du Plessix Gray, *Divine Disobedience* (New York: Knopf, 1970), 135–40; Dowd, *Blues for America*, 136; Dancis, *Resister*.
31. Nathan Tarcov, "Four Crucial Years at Cornell," in *Confrontation: The Student Rebellion and the Universities*, ed. Daniel Bell and Irving Kristol (New York: Basic Books, 1969), 136; Tom Bell, "Organizing Draft Resistance," in *We Won't Go: Personal Accounts of War Objectors*, ed. Alice Lynd (Boston: Beacon Press, 1966), 212–13; Dowd, *Blues for America*, 136; Dancis, *Resister*, 68, 90–93.
32. *Cornell Sun*, December 14, 1966; Dancis, *Resister*, 104.
33. Dancis, *Resister*, 99–102.
34. Lynd, *We Won't Go*, xi, 87. Texts of some "We Won't Go" statements are on 203–5.
35. Ohmann, interview, February 7, 2013.
36. Crews, interview, May 12, 2014.
37. Noam Chomsky, "On Resistance," *New York Review of Books*, December 7, 1967.
38. Robert Zevin, interview with the author, September 18, 2016, Cambridge, MA.
39. Richard Ohmann, interview with the author, March 15, 2013, New York City.
40. Martin Duberman, *Howard Zinn: A Life on the Left* (New York: New Press, 2012), 139–40.
41. Robert Greenblatt to "Dear Friends," May 3, 1967, box 6-1, RESIST Records, Trinity.
42. Ferber and Lynd, *The Resistance*, 119–20; Zevin, interview, September 18, 2016.
43. Denise Levertov, "The Intellectuals and the War Machine," *North American Review*, January 1968; Schalk, *War and the Ivory Tower*, 146; Jessica Mitford, *The Trial of Dr. Spock, The Reverend William Sloane Coffin, Jr., Michael Ferber, Mitchell Goodman, and Marcus Raskin* (1969; repr., New York: Vintage, 1970), 20, 31.
44. "Declaration of Conscience," *Daily Californian*, May 25, 1967.
45. Noam Chomsky, interview with the author, September 21, 2016, Cambridge, MA.
46. Mitford, *The Trial of Dr. Spock*, 48–50.

47. Ferber and Lynd, *The Resistance*, 120–23; Noam Chomsky, Donald Kalish, Marc Raskin, Arthur Waskow, and Robert Zevin, to "Dear Friend," August 3, 1967, box 6-1, RESIST Records, Trinity. The collection of RESIST materials donated by Paul Lauter to the Trinity College (Hartford) Library contains dozens of these fundraising letters as well as hundreds of signed statements sent to the RESIST office by academics from all over the United States.

48. Copies of this document abound on the internet. Here's one: http://coursesa .matrix.msu.edu/~hst306/documents/resist.html (accessed September 16, 2016). Of the original 158 signers, only nine were women: Denise Levertov, Grace Paley, Muriel Rukeyser, Susan Sontag, Inge Powell Bell, Louisa Calder, Jean Davidson, Barbara Guest, and Elizabeth Sutherland.

49. Levertov, "The Intellectuals and the War Machine"; Schalk, *War and the Ivory Tower.*

50. Mitford, *The Trial of Dr. Spock*, 32–34.

51. Schalk, *War and the Ivory Tower*, 141; Tom Wells, *The War Within: America's Battle over Vietnam* (Berkeley: University of California Press, 1994), 192.

52. Levertov, "The Intellectuals and the War Machine"; Coffin, *Once to Every Man*, 240; Mitford, *The Trial of Dr. Spock*, 32–34.

53. Minutes, Organizational Meeting of RESIST, October 2, 1967, box 6-1, RESIST Records, Trinity; Lauter, interview, August 21, 2013: Louis Kampf, interview with the author, April 3, 2013, Cambridge, MA; Crews, interview, May 12, 2014.

54. Kampf, interview, April 3, 2013.

55. Schalk, *War and the Ivory Tower*, 44; Foley, *Confronting the War Machine*, 94; Mitford, *The Trial of Dr. Spock*, 65. Again, the sources disagree about the number of signers. Signed petitions came into the RESIST office for months after the "Call to Resist" was originally published. I found one fifty-page undated document in the RESIST files with a list of 1,756 names. Jessica Mitford claims the "Call" attracted 28,000 signers. There is agreement, however, about the fact that most of them were academics.

56. Mitford, *Trial of Dr. Spock*, 28; Foley, *Confronting the War Machine*, 107–8.

57. Harris, *Dreams Die Hard*, 192.

58. Dancis, *Resister*, 128.

59. Foley, *Confronting the War Machine*, 131–32; Ohmann, interview, March 15, 2013. There is quite a discrepancy in the figures I've seen for the numbers of draft cards delivered to the Department of Justice. Michael Foley gives the figure of 992, Levertov, 600, and the indictment lists 357.

60. Coffin, *Once to Every Man*, 247.

61. Mitford, *The Trial of Dr. Spock*, 40–44.

62. Levertov, "The Intellectuals and the War Machine"; Ferber and Lynd, *The Resistance*, 151–54; Coffin, *Once to Every Man*, 253–54; Foley, *Confronting the War Machine*, 134–41.

63. Wells, *War Within*, 230–36; Foley, *Confronting the War Machine*, 232.

64. Mitford, *The Trial of Dr. Spock*, 5.

65. Mitford, *The Trial of Dr. Spock*, 66.

66. Crews, interview, May 12, 2014.

67. Mitford, *The Trial of Dr. Spock*, 77, 209.

68. Ohmann, interview, March 15, 2013; Zevin, interview, September 18, 2016; Foley, *Confronting the War Machine*, 194–97.

69. Geoffrey Kabaservice, *The Guardians: Kingman Brewster, His Circle, and the Rise of the Liberal Establishment* (New York: Henry Holt, 2004), 320.

70. Leonard Glantz, "Good Morning, FBI," *The Informer*, October 8, 1968, in Howard Zinn Papers, box 22, folder 13, Tamiment Library and Robert F. Wagner Labor Archives, Bobst Library, New York University (hereafter Zinn Papers); Foley, *Confronting the War Machine*, 310–21.

71. Michael Albert, *Remembering Tomorrow: From SDS to Life after Capitalism* (New York: Seven Stories Press, 2006), 41; Noam Chomsky, interview with the author, September 13, 2013, Cambridge, MA.

72. "News From the Chapters," *NUC Newsletter* 1, no 3 (October 4, 1968), in Paul Lauter Papers, Watkinson Library and Trinity College Archives, Raether Library, Trinity College, Hartford, CT, (hereafter Lauter Papers); Richard Mumma, "More on Sanctuary," *RESIST Newsletter*, October 14, 1968, in Gerard Braunthal Papers, box 2, folder 17, Special Collections and University Archives, W. E. B. Du Bois Library, University of Massachusetts Amherst (hereafter Gerard Braunthal Papers); Conor Tomás Reed, "'What We Are Part of' Teaching at CCNY: 1968–1974: Adrienne Rich, Part II," in *Lost and Found*, series 4, no. 3, part 2 (Fall 2013): 42, http://freeuniversitynyc.org/files/2014/02/Adrienne -Rich-SEEK-CCNY-social-movements.pdf (accessed October 2, 2016); Foley, *Confronting the War Machine*, 317–21.

73. Betty Medsger, *The Burglary: The Discovery of J. Edgar Hoover's Secret FBI* (New York: Knopf, 2014), 15.

74. Zevin, interview, September 18, 2016; Lauter, interview, August 21, 2013.

75. Fred Halstead, *Out Now! A Participant's Account of the American Movement Against the Vietnam War* (New York: Monad Press, 1978), 68; Homer Bigart, "264 Seized Here in Draft Protest," *New York Times*, December 6, 1967. See clippings (many undated and unidentified) in Ann and William Davidon Papers, series D, Vietnam, box 28, folder: Protests, Rallies and Forums (1965– 1966), in Swarthmore College Peace Collection, McCabe Library, Swarthmore College.

76. Chomsky, interview with the author, September 13, 2013.

77. Jesse Lemisch, interview with the author, February 5, 2013, New York City; Thomas Mayer, telephone interview with the author, January 23, 2015.

78. Chomsky, interview, September 13, 2013; Norman Mailer, *Armies of the Night* (New York: Signet, 1968), 203.

79. Zevin, interview, September 18, 2016; Michael Novak, *Writing from Left to Right: My Journey from Liberal to Conservative* (New York: Image, 2013), 61; Jules Chametzky, interview with the author, September 19, 2014, Amherst, MA.

80. Francine du Plessix Gray, *Divine Disobedience*, 157.

81. Wells, *War Within*, 503.

82. Carolyn Eisenberg, interview with the author, September 23, 2013, Brooklyn, NY.

83. Gray, *Divine Disobedience*, 116–30; James H. Forest, "Daniel Berrigan: The Poet and Prophet as Priest," in *Witness of the Berrigans*, ed. Stephen Halpert and Tom Murray (New York: Doubleday, 1972), 103.

84. For a riveting account of the Media, PA, break-in, see Medsger, *The Burglary*.

Chapter Nine

1. Joel Aber, Jules Benjamin, and Robin Martin, *Germ Warfare Research for Vietnam* (Philadelphia: Philadelphia Area Committee to End the War in Vietnam, n.d.), 5, https://collections.mun.ca/digital/collection/radical/id/30223/ (accessed January 19, 2021); Jonathan Goldstein, "Agent Orange on Campus: The Summit-Spicerack Controversy at the University of Pennsylvania, 1965–1967," in *Sights on the Sixties*, ed. Barbara L. Tischler (New Brunswick, NJ: Rutgers University Press, 1992); Carol Brightman, "The 'Weed Killers' and the University at the Front: Projects 'Spicerack' and 'Summit' at the University of Pennsylvania," *Viet-Report* 2, nos. 4–5 (June/July 1966); Sol Stern, "The War Catalogue of the University of Pennsylvania," *Ramparts Magazine*, August 1966, 31–40; Paul Lyons, *The People of This Generation: The Rise and Fall of the New Left in Philadelphia* (Philadelphia: University of Pennsylvania Press, 2003), 116–20; Fred Halstead, *Out Now! A Participant's Account of the American Movement Against the Vietnam War* (New York: Monad Press, 1978), 217–19.

2. Goldstein, "Agent Orange on Campus"; Brightman, "The 'Weed Killers.'"

3. "Protest March Is Scheduled," *Daily Pennsylvanian*, October 11, 1965, http://dparchives.library.upenn.edu/ (accessed October 18, 2016).

4. Stephen H. Klitzman, "Vietnam Critics Charge Institute with Germ Warfare Research," *Daily Pennsylvanian*, October 11, 1965; Aber, Benjamin, and Martin, *Germ Warfare*.

5. Brightman, "The 'Weedkillers,'" 12–13, 33–34, 44–45; Goldstein, "Agent Orange on Campus," 46; Margaret Pugh O'Mara, *Cities of Knowledge: Cold War Science and the Search for the Next Silicon Valley* (Princeton, NJ: Princeton University Press, 2005), 50–51.

6. Goldstein, "Agent Orange on Campus," 46, 50; Denis Wilen, "Faculty Members Clash on ICR, Gas and Germ Warfare Research," *Daily Pennsylvanian*, October 13, 1965; Wilen, "ICR Director Upholds Research, Calls Gas, Germ Warfare 'Defensive,'" *Daily Pennsylvanian*, October 12, 1965; "An Embarrassed Administration," *Daily Pennsylvanian*, November 3, 1965.

7. Klitzman, "Vietnam Critics Charge," *Daily Pennsylvanian*, October 11, 1965; David R. Goddard and Linda C. Koons, "A Profile of the University of Pennsylvania," in *Academic Transformation: Seventeen Institutions under Pressure*, ed. David Riesman and Verne A. Stadtman (New York: McGraw-Hill, 1973), 243.

8. Richard Shapiro and Elliot Werner, "Physics Faculty, Senate Chairman Oppose University Classified Research," *Daily Pennsylvanian*, October 21, 1965.

9. Denis Wilen, "Faculty Senate Asks Administration to Halt Secret Campus Studies," *Daily Pennsylvanian*, November 4, 1965.

10. Brightman, "The 'Weedkillers,'" 44; Julius Wishner and William F. Baxter, "Classified Research," *AAUP Bulletin* 54, no. 4 (December 1968): 453–61.

11. Don Morrison, "Faculty Reaction Mixed on Secret Study Vote," *Daily Pennsylvanian*, November 5, 1965.

12. Lyons, *The People of This Generation*, 119–21.

13. Michael S. Neiberg, *Making Citizen-Soldiers: ROTC and the Ideology of American Military Service* (Cambridge, MA: Harvard University Press, 2000), is a good study of the ROTC. I drew heavily on it. John R. Thelin, *A History of American Higher Education* (Baltimore: Johns Hopkins University Press, 2004), 75–81. For the full text of the Morrill Act, see https://www .ourdocuments.gov/doc.php?doc=33&page=transcript (accessed October 31, 2016).

14. Daniel J. Kevles, *The Physicists: The History of a Scientific Community in Modern America*, 2nd ed. (1977; Cambridge, MA: Harvard University Press, 1995), 288; Carol S. Gruber, *Mars and Minerva: World War I and the Uses of Higher Learning in America* (Baton Rouge: Louisiana State University Press, 1975), 118–62.

15. Tevi Troy, *Intellectuals and the American Presidency: Philosophers, Jesters, or Technicians* (Lanham, MD: Rowman and Littlefield, 2002), 6–8.

16. Rebecca S. Lowen, *Creating the Cold War University: The Transformation of Stanford* (Berkeley: University of California Press, 1997), 43–50; Sarah Bridger, *Scientists at War: The Ethics of Cold War Weapons Research* (Cambridge, MA: Harvard University Press, 2015), 156.

17. Kelly Moore, *Disrupting Science: Social Movements, American Scientists, and the Politics of the Military, 1945–1975* (Princeton, NJ: Princeton University Press, 2008), 24–27.

18. Kevles, *The Physicists*, 304–20.

19. Thomas Hager, *Force of Nature: The Life of Linus Pauling* (New York: Simon and Schuster, 1995), 249, 257.

20. David Milne, *America's Rasputin: Walt Rostow and the Vietnam War* (New York: Hill and Wang, 2008), 32.

21. Michael A. Bernstein, *A Perilous Progress: Economists and Public Purpose in Twentieth-Century America* (Princeton, NJ: Princeton University Press, 2001), 73–90.

22. Bernstein, *A Perilous Progress*, 114–19.

23. Roger L. Geiger, *Research and Relevant Knowledge: American Research Universities since World War II* (1st ed., Oxford University Press, 1993; New Brunswick, NJ: Transaction, 2004), 7–11; Paul Forman, "Beyond Quantum Electronics: National Security as Basis for Physical Research in the United

States, 1940–1960," *Historical Studies in the Physical and Biological Sciences* 18, no. 1 (1987): 155, 178; Lowen, *Creating the Cold War University*, 95.

24. Geiger, *Research and Relevant Knowledge*, 187.
25. Daniel Bell, "Columbia and the New Left," in *Confrontation: The Student Rebellion and the Universities*, ed. Daniel Bell and Irving Kristol (New York: Basic Books, 1969), 74; William Gamson, telephone interview with the author, May 10, 2013; Kenneth J. Heineman, *Campus Wars: The Peace Movement at American State Universities in the Vietnam Era* (New York: New York University Press, 1993), 201; James Rowen, "Politics of University Research," in *Academic Supermarkets: A Critical Case Study of a Multiversity*, ed. Philip G. Altbach, Robert S. Laufer, and Sheila McVey (San Francisco: Jossey-Bass, 1971), 121–27; Moore, *Disrupting Science*, 52.
26. Forman, "Beyond Quantum Mechanics," 178; Geiger, *Research and Relevant Knowledge*, 18–25; Lowen, *Creating the Cold War University*, 96; Moore, *Disrupting Science*, 18.
27. R. C. Lewontin, "The Cold War and the Transformation of the Academy," in *The Cold War and the University: Toward an Intellectual History of the Postwar Years*, by Noam Chomsky et al. (New York: New Press, 1997), 18–19.
28. Geiger, *Research and Relevant Knowledge*, 67; Forman, "Beyond Quantum Electronics," 156; Bridger, *Scientists at War*, 156–67.
29. Berkeley, Caltech, Case Institute of Technology, Chicago, Columbia, MIT, Princeton, Stanford, Tulane, and the Universities of Pennsylvania, Illinois, and Michigan; list in Bell, "Columbia and the New Left," in *Confrontation*, ed. Bell and Kristol, 74.
30. Bridger, *Scientists at War*, 21; Moore, *Disrupting Science*, 149.
31. Ann Finkbeiner, *The Jasons: The Secret History of Science's Postwar Elite* (New York: Viking, 2006), 44.
32. Finkbeiner, *The Jasons*, xxix; Kevles, *The Physicists*, 402.
33. Martin L. Perl, "The Scientific Advisory System: Some Observations," *Science*, September 24, 1971, 1215.
34. Moore, *Disrupting Science*, 149; Finkbeiner, *The Jasons*, 107.
35. Stuart W. Leslie, *The Cold War and American Science: The Military-Industrial-Academic Complex at MIT and Stanford* (New York: Columbia University Press, 1993), 58; Perl, "Scientific Advisory System," 1215.
36. Silvan Schweber, quoted in Leslie, *The Cold War and American Science*, 148; Geiger, *Research and Relevant Knowledge*, 66–67.
37. Forman, "Beyond Quantum Electronics," 221.
38. Stuart Leslie quoted in Moore, *Disrupting Science*, 31.
39. Thomas Jundt, *Greening the Red, White, and Blue: The Bomb, Big Business, and Consumer Resistance in Postwar America* (New York: Oxford University Press, 2014), 127–33.
40. Lowen, *Creating the Cold War University*, 88, 131–34.
41. O'Mara, *Cities of Knowledge*, 64–73 and especially chap. 3, 97–141.

42. Leslie, *The Cold War and American Science*, 63–71; O'Mara, *Cities of Knowledge*, 217; Forman, "Beyond Quantum Electronics," 160–66; Bridger, *Scientists at War*, 158–60.

43. Geiger, *Research and Relevant Knowledge*, 193; NACLA, "Project Themis Grants for 1969," https://nacla.org/article/project-THEMIS-grants-1969 (accessed November 23, 2016); Heineman, *Campus Wars*, 18, 35; Moore, *Disrupting Science*, 29.

44. Geiger, *Research and Relevant Knowledge*, 69; Lowen, *Creating the Cold War University*, 201–5; Bridger, *Scientists at War*, 157; Kai Bird, *The Color of Truth: McGeorge Bundy and William Bundy: Brothers in Arms* (New York: Simon and Schuster, 1998), 139.

45. Stern, "War Catalogue of the University of Pennsylvania," 39–40.

46. Bernstein, *A Perilous Progress*, 94–101.

47. James Hershberg, *James B. Conant: Harvard to Hiroshima and the Making of the Nuclear Age* (New York: Knopf, 1993) 412–13; Joy Rohde, *Armed with Expertise: The Militarization of American Social Research during the Cold War* (Ithaca, NY: Cornell University Press, 2013), 14–15.

48. John Trumpbour, "Harvard, the Cold War, and the National Security State," in *How Harvard Rules: Reason in the Service of Empire*, ed. John Trumpbour (Boston: South End Press, 1989), 53; Bird, *Color of Truth*, 138.

49. For a more detailed discussion of the Michigan State involvement with Vietnam, see chapter 4, 125–28. See also Robert Scigliano and Guy H. Fox, *Technical Assistance in Vietnam: The Michigan State University Experience* (New York: Praeger, 1965); and Heineman, *Campus Wars*, 22–23.

50. For a fine overview of SORO's operations, see Rohde, *Armed with Expertise*, 4–89.

51. Rohde, *Armed with Expertise*, 4–89.

52. Irving Louis Horowitz, ed., *The Rise and Fall of Project Camelot* (Cambridge, MA: MIT Press, 1967); Rohde, *Armed with Expertise*, 63–89.

53. Forman, "Beyond Quantum Electronics," 208; Lowen, *Creating the Cold War University*, 141–42.

54. Howard Schachman and Cyril M. Kay, *John Tileston Edsall, 1902–2002, A Biographical Memoir*, (Washington, DC: National Academy of Sciences, 2010), http://www.nasonline.org/publications/biographical-memoirs/memoir-pdfs/edsall-john.pdf (accessed June 29, 2015), 14–15.

55. Hershberg, *Conant*, 397–98.

56. Richard M. Freeland, *Academia's Golden Age: Universities in Massachusetts, 1945–1970* (New York: Oxford University Press, 1992), 82.

57. Leslie, *The Cold War and American Science*, 95; Forman, "Beyond Quantum Electronics," 222; Lowen, *Creating the Cold War University*, 140.

58. Killian, quoted in Freeland, *Academia's Golden Age*, 141; Lowen, *Creating the Cold War University*, 96–99.

59. Forman, "Beyond Quantum Electronics," 216–19; Lowen, *Creating the Cold War University*, 141–43.

60. Lowen, *Creating the Cold War University*, 143.

61. Lowen, *Creating the Cold War University*, 149.
62. Lowen, *Creating the Cold War University*, 143; Wishner and Baxter, "Classified Research," *AAUP Bulletin,* 458.
63. Eric F. Goldman, *The Tragedy of Lyndon Johnson* (New York: Knopf, 1969), 9.
64. For an overview of the impact of McCarthyism on American science, see Jessica Wang, *American Science in an Age of Anxiety: Scientists, Anticommunism, and the Cold War* (Chapel Hill: University of North Carolina Press, 1999); see also Freeland, *Academia's Golden Age*, 110.
65. Hofstadter, quoted in Troy, *Intellectuals and the American Presidency*, 11.
66. Troy, *Intellectuals and the American Presidency*, 2.
67. Troy, *Intellectuals and the American Presidency*, 21.
68. Troy, *Intellectuals and the American Presidency*, 21–25; John Kenneth Galbraith, *A Life in Our Times: Memoirs* (Boston: Houghton Mifflin, 1981), 385; Carl Kaysen, recorded interview by Joseph E. O'Connor, July 15, 1966, 4, John F. Kennedy Library Oral History Program, https://docs.google.com/viewerng/viewer?url=https://archive2.jfklibrary.org/JFKOH/Kaysen,+Carl/JFKOH-CK-02/JFKOH-CK-02-TR.pdf (accessed October 16, 2016) (hereafter Kaysen, Oral History).
69. Troy, *Intellectuals and the American Presidency*, 26–47; Bird, *Color of Truth*, 150–52.
70. Goldman, *The Tragedy of Lyndon Johnson*, 427, 440–505; Troy, *Intellectuals and the American Presidency*, 57, 74.
71. Leslie Gelb, interview with the author, n.d., New York City.
72. Galbraith, *A Life in Our Times*, 462–79.
73. For a thoughtful discussion of the influence (or lack thereof) of top scientists within the government, see Paul Rubinson, *Redefining Science: Scientists, the National Security State, and Nuclear Weapons in Cold War America* (Amherst: University of Massachusetts Press, 2016).
74. Bird, *Color of Truth*.
75. W. W. Rostow, *The Stages of Economic Growth: A Non-Communist Manifesto* (Cambridge: Cambridge University Press, 1960).
76. Milne, *America's Rasputin*.
77. Troy, *Intellectuals and the American Presidency*, 80–112; Michael Koncewicz, *They Said No to Nixon: Republicans Who Stood Up to President's Abuses of Power* (Berkeley: University of California Press, 2018), 72–101.
78. Perl, "Scientific Advisory System," 1213; Joel Primack and Frank von Hippel, *Advice and Dissent: Scientists in the Political Arena* (New York: Basic Books, 1974), 42–45, 62–71; Bridger, *Scientists at War*, 18–19.
79. Perl, "Scientific Advisory System," 1215; Rubinson, *Redefining Science*.
80. Hager, *Force of Nature*, 497; Bridger, *Scientists at War*, 32–88.
81. Elinor Langer, "After the Pentagon Papers: Talk with Kistiakowsky and Wiesner," *Science*, n.s., 174, no. 4012 (November 26, 1971): 925–28, http://www.jstor.org/stable/1732753 (accessed November 15, 2016); Primack and von Hippel, *Advice and Dissent*, 60–71.

82. Bridger, *Scientists at War*, 63–70.

83. Finkbeiner, *The Jasons*, 64.

84. Bridger, *Scientists at War*, 119.

85. Langer, "After the Pentagon Papers," 925.

86. Finkbeiner, *The Jasons*, 67–68; Bridger, *Scientists at War*, 129–30.

87. Finkbeiner, *The Jasons*, 67–68.

88. Bridger, *Scientists at War*, 121–24.

89. Finkbeiner, *The Jasons*, 69, 76–77.

90. Bridger, *Scientists at War*, 227.

91. Finkbeiner, *The Jasons*, 73–89.

92. Bridger, *Scientists at War*, 131–42; Primack and von Hippel, *Advice and Dissent*, 104.

93. Berkeley SESPA (Scientists and Engineers for Social and Political Action), "Science Against the People," December 1972, http://science-for-the-people .org/wp-content/uploads/2014/02/science-against-the-people_1972.pdf (accessed January 20, 2021).

94. Finkbeiner, *The Jasons*, 89; Langer, "After the Pentagon Papers," 927.

95. Primack and von Hippel, *Advice and Dissent*, 102–4; Rubinson, *Redefining Science*.

96. Bridger, *Scientists at War*, 142–49.

97. Bridger, *Scientists at War*, 132.

98. Kevles, *The Physicists*, 405–6.

99. Bridger, *Scientists at War*, 148.

100. Langer, "After the Pentagon Papers," 927–28; Moore, *Disrupting Science*, 36.

101. Primack and von Hippel, *Advice and Dissent*, 42–45; Jundt, *Greening the Red, White, and Blue*, 156–57.

102. Bernstein, *A Perilous Progress*, 150–55; Kaysen, Oral History, 76–77.

103. Bernstein, *A Perilous Progress*, 152–55; Lawrence S. Lifschultz, "Could Karl Marx Teach Economics in the United States?" in *How Harvard Rules*, ed. Trumpbour, 284.

104. Primack and von Hippel, *Advice and Dissent*, 103.

105. Woods Hole Summer Studies, Standard Practices and Procedures for Security, n.d., in Owen Chamberlain Papers, carton 14, folder 8, BANC MSS 2002/345z, Bancroft Library, University of California, Berkeley; Langer, "After the Pentagon Papers," 927–28.

106. Wiesner quoted in Langer, "After the Pentagon Papers," 923, 928. For a well-informed overview of the deleterious effects of official secrecy, see Daniel Patrick Moynihan, *Secrecy: The American Experience* (New Haven, CT: Yale University Press, 1998).

107. Primack and von Hippel, *Advice and Dissent*, 33–35, 107; Perl, "The Scientific Advisory System," 1213–15.

108. Langer, "After the Pentagon Papers," 926.

109. Finkbeiner, *The Jasons*, 91–92.

110. Primack and von Hippel, *Advice and Dissent*, 71; Bridger, *Scientists at War*, 136, 143.

111. Primack and von Hippel, *Advice and Dissent*, 9–27; Langer, "After the Pentagon Papers," 927.

112. Joyce Purnick, "Columbia Profs Defend Role in Jason Program," *New York Post*, April 28, 1972; and Malvin Ruderman and Henry M. Foley, "A Statement on Jason by two members," n.d. [probably April 1972], mimeograph: both in Renate Bridenthal, personal papers.

113. Matthew Meselson, telephone interview with the author, January 28, 2015; Primack and von Hippel, *Advice and Dissent*, 145–47.

114. Primack and von Hippel, *Advice and Dissent*, 74–75, 146; Bridger, *Scientists at War*, 72–74.

115. Bridger, *Scientists at War*, 81, 88–89; Meselson, interview, January 28, 2015; Bill Zimmerman, *Troublemaker: A Memoir from the Front Lines of the Sixties* (New York: Doubleday, 2011), 159; Arthur W. Galston, "Falling Leaves and Ethical Dilemmas: Agent Orange in Vietnam," in *New Dimensions in Bioethics: Science, Ethics, and the Formulation of Public Policy*, ed. Arthur W. Galston and Emily G. Schurr (New York: Springer, 2001).

116. Bridger, *Scientists at War*, 90–97; Primack and von Hippel, *Advice and Dissent*, 147–48.

117. Bridger, *Scientists at War*, 97–99.

118. Primack and von Hippel, *Advice and Dissent*, 157; Meselson, interview, January 28, 2015.

119. Meselson, interview, January 28, 2015.

Chapter Ten

1. Bill Zimmerman, Len Radinsky, Mel Rothenberg, and Bart Meyers, "Towards a Science for the People," in *Science for the People: Documents from America's Movement of Radical Scientists*, ed. Sigrid Schmalzer, Daniel S. Chard, and Alyssa Botelho (Amherst: University of Massachusetts Press, 2018), 22–23 (also available at https://www.ocf.berkeley.edu/~schwrtz/SftP/Towards.html; accessed January 20, 2021).

2. Kelly Moore, *Disrupting Science: Social Movements, American Scientists, and the Politics of the Military, 1945–1975* (Princeton, NJ: Princeton University Press, 2008), 131.

3. Sarah Bridger, *Scientists at War: The Ethics of Cold War Weapons Research* (Cambridge, MA: Harvard University Press, 2015), 194–207.

4. Murray Eden, "Historical Introduction," in *March 4: Scientists, Students, and Society*, ed. Jonathan Allen (Cambridge, MA: MIT Press, 1970), vii–xxiii; Bridger, *Scientists at War*, 163–68.

5. Eden, "Historical Introduction," in *March 4*, ed. Allen, viii; Moore, *Disrupting Science*, 138–45, 247–48. There are dozens of flyers with teach-in programs

in the Campus Unrest Collection, Accession No. 33, RG 3/5/1, box 1, folder: Teach-ins, Spring 69, February 28–March 5, 1969, University at Buffalo Archives, Capen Hall, State University of New York, Amherst, NY (hereafter Buffalo, Campus Unrest Collection).

6. Statement of President Howard W. Johnson, to special faculty meeting, November 3, 1969, in *The University Crisis Reader*, ed. Immanuel Wallerstein and Paul Starr, vol. 1, *The Liberal University under Attack* (New York: Random House, 1971), 243–44.

7. Bridger, *Scientists at War*, 171–90; Noam Chomsky, interview with the author, September 13, 2013, Cambridge, MA; Howard Wesley Johnson, *Holding the Center: Memoirs of a Life in Higher Education* (Cambridge, MA: MIT Press, 1999), 168–74, 191–95.

8. Moore, *Disrupting Science*, 50–51; Joanne Grant, *Confrontation on Campus: The Columbia Pattern for the New Protest* (New York: New American Library, 1969), 34–35; Jeffry Kaplow, interview, May 13, 1968, 6, Columbia Oral History Project, Columbia Crisis of 1968 Project, Rare Book and Manuscript Library, Butler Library, Columbia University (hereafter COHP); Daniel Bell, "Columbia and the New Left," in *Confrontation: The Student Rebellion and the Universities*, ed. Daniel Bell and Irving Kristol (New York: Basic Books, 1969), 74.

9. Moore, *Disrupting Science*, 50–51; Grant, *Confrontation on Campus*, 34–35; Kaplow, COHP, 6.

10. Steven V. Roberts, "31 at Princeton Held in Protest," *New York Times*, October 24, 1967, 1.

11. Paul Sigmund, "Princeton in Crisis and Change," in *Academic Transformation: Seventeen Institutions under Pressure*, ed. David Riesman and Verne A. Stadtman (New York: McGraw-Hill, 1973), 254–56. Much of the information about Princeton and the IDA comes from the student newspaper, the *Daily Princetonian*, October 12, 13, 16, 24, 27, November 1, 21, and 28, 1967, http://theprince.princeton.edu/princetonperiodicals/cgi-bin/princetonperiodicals?a=d&d=Princetonian19671012-01&e=-------en-20--1--txt-txI (accessed March 23, 2017).

12. *Daily Princetonian*, October 12, 13, 16, 24, 27, November 1, 21, and 28, 1967.

13. *Daily Princetonian*, November 28, 1967; Sigmund, "Princeton in Crisis and Change," in *Academic Transformation*, ed. Riesman and Stadtman, 255–54.

14. Seymour Martin Lipset and David Riesman, *Education and Politics at Harvard* (New York: McGraw Hill, 1975), 212–13; Maurice Zeitlin, telephone interviews with the author, January 29, 2014, September 8, 2016.

15. David Maraniss, *They Marched into Sunlight: War and Peace, Vietnam and America, October 1967* (New York: Simon and Schuster, 2003), 70, 486; Robert Smith, Richard Axen, and DeVere Pentony, *By Any Means Necessary: The Revolutionary Struggle at San Francisco State* (San Francisco: Jossey-Bass, 1970), 28; Kenneth J. Heineman, "American Schism: Catholic Activists, Intellectuals, and Students Confront the Vietnam War," in *The Vietnam War on Campus: Other Voices, More Distant Drums*, ed. Marc Jason Gilbert (Westport, CT: Praeger, 2001), 102–3; Bridger, *Scientists at War*, 163; Frederick W. Obear, "Stu-

dent Activism in the Sixties," in *Protest! Student Activism in America*, ed. Julian Foster and Durward Long (New York: William Morrow, 1970), 20; Jeffrey A. Turner, *Sitting In and Speaking Out: Student Movements in the American South, 1960–1970* (Athens: University of Georgia Press, 2010), 233.

16. Richard A. Siggelkow, *Dissent and Disruption: A University under Siege* (Buffalo: Prometheus Books, 1991), 65; Ralph Hanson to William. Sewell, Nov. 8, 1967, in University of Wisconsin, Archives, Chancellor William H. Sewell Records, 4/20/1 General Subject File, box 19, folder: Student Demonstrations, UW-Madison Archives, Madison, Wisconsin (hereafter Sewell Records).

17. Morton Keller and Phyllis Keller, *Making Harvard Modern: The Rise of America's University* (Cary, NC: Oxford University Press, 2001), 310.

18. Immanuel Wallerstein and Frederick Starr, "Recruiting on Campus: Can Some Recruiters Be Banned," in *The University Crisis Reader*, ed. Wallerstein and Starr, 1:245.

19. "Complete Text of Report on Recruiting Policy," *Columbia Daily Spectator* 112, no. 32 (November 13, 1967), http://spectatorarchive.library.columbia.edu/cgi -bin/columbia?a=d&d=cs19671113-01.2.38&e=-------en-20--1--txt-txIN------ (accessed April 6, 2017).

20. Maraniss, *They Marched into Sunlight*, 137–38.

21. Bridger, *Scientists at War*, 173–77, 183–85.

22. Minutes, Faculty Senate special meeting, November 13, 1967, Buffalo, Campus Unrest Collection, box 1, folder: Faculty Senate Minutes, Resolutions, etc., October 1967–1969.

23. "The Issue Is Academic Freedom," letter from Dr. Bill B. May to President Kenneth Pitzer of Stanford, April 15, 1969, in *The University Crisis Reader*, ed. Wallerstein and Starr, 1:231–34.

24. "Corporation and Government Recruiters on the College Campus," statement by American Civil Liberties Union, February 19, 1968, in *The University Crisis Reader*, ed. Wallerstein and Starr, 1:247.

25. Howard Zinn, "Dow Shalt Not Kill," in *The University Crisis Reader*, ed. Wallerstein and Starr, 1:248–55.

26. Henry Steele Commager, "The University as Employment Agency," *New Republic*, February 24, 1968, in *The University Crisis Reader*, ed. Wallerstein and Starr, 1:255–62.

27. One contemporary survey of faculty attitudes toward the student demonstrations at over one hundred schools found that only 5 percent of the faculty supported the takeovers. William R. Morgan, "Faculty Mediation in Campus Conflict," in *Protest!*, ed. Foster and Long, 468.

28. Siggelkow, *Dissent and Disruption*, 71; Smith, Axen, and Pentony, *By Any Means Necessary*, 27; Bell, "Columbia and the New Left," in *Confrontation*, ed. Bell and Kristol, 68–69.

29. On Meyerson's leadership at Berkeley, see Neil J. Smelser, *Reflections on the University of California: From the Free Speech Movement to the Global University* (Berkeley: University of California Press, 2010), 11–55; Warren Bennis,

The Leaning Ivory Tower (San Francisco: Jossey-Bass, 1973), 42–43; Kenneth J. Heineman, *Campus Wars: The Peace Movement at American State Universities in the Vietnam Era* (New York: New York University Press, 1993), 35.

30. Matthew Levin, *Cold War University: Madison and the New Left in the Sixties* (Madison: University of Wisconsin Press, 2013), 154; Bernard Sklar, "Corporate Recruitment on Campus," in *Academic Supermarkets: A Critical Case Study of a Multiversity*, ed. Philip G. Altbach, Robert S. Laufer, and Sheila McVey (San Francisco: Jossey-Bass, 1971), 137; Durward Long, "Wisconsin: Changing Styles of Administrative Response," in *Protest!*, ed. Foster and Long, 252.

31. Maraniss, *They Marched into Sunlight*, 120.

32. Maraniss, *They Marched Into Sunlight*, 137; Siggelkow, *Dissent and Disruption*, 73–75; Philip G. Altbach, Robert S. Laufer, and Sheila McVey, "Prologue: The Multiversity in Crisis," in *Academic Supermarkets*, ed. Altbach, Laufer, and McVey, 18–19.

33. Maraniss, *They Marched into Sunlight*, 432–40; Levin, *Cold War University*, 156–57; Tom Bates, *Rads: The 1970 Bombing of the Army Math Research Center at the University of Wisconsin and Its Aftermath* (New York: HarperCollins, 1992), 91.

34. Siggelkow, *Dissent and Disruption*, 71. Minutes, Faculty Senate special meeting, November 13, 1967; and Minutes, faculty meeting, December 14, 1967: both in Buffalo, Campus Unrest Collection, box 1, folder: Faculty Senate Minutes, Resolutions, etc. October 1967–1969.

35. "The Dow Chemical and CIA Crisis, December 1967," mimeograph (n.d., probably by Dean G. Pruitt), Buffalo, Campus Unrest Collection, Research of Dean G. Pruitt and James Gahagan, 1967–1972, 1975, box 3, folder 5—Dow Chemical Co. controversy 1967 (hereafter Pruitt and Gahagan Research, University at Buffalo Archives).

36. Lipset and Riesman, *Education and Politics at Harvard*, 214; Keller and Keller, *Making Harvard Modern*, 310.

37. David S. Brown, *Richard Hofstadter: An Intellectual Biography* (Chicago: University of Chicago Press, 2006), 171.

38. Allan Silver, interview with the author, June 19, 2013, New York City; Archibald Cox et al., *Crisis at Columbia: Report of the Fact-Finding Commission Appointed to Investigate the Disturbances at Columbia University in April and May 1968* (New York: Vintage, 1968), 67; Bell, "Columbia and the New Left," 69; "Complete Text of Report on Recruiting Policy," *Columbia Daily Spectator*, November 13, 1967.

39. Bruce M. Stave, *Red Brick in the Land of Steady Habits: Creating the University of Connecticut, 1881–2006* (Hanover, NH: University Press of New England, 2006), 123–27.

40. Minutes, Faculty Senate, November 30, 1967, Gerard Braunthal Papers, box 2, folder 16, Special Collections and University Archives, W. E. B. Du Bois Library, University of Massachusetts Amherst (hereafter Braunthal Papers, UMass Amherst).

41. Matthew W. Finkin, "The Hershey Letter," *AAUP Bulletin* 53, no. 4 (December 1967): 412–13.

42. University of Connecticut, Provost's Office Records, Series III—General Correspondence Edward V. Gant, box 12, folder: Draft, clipping, *New Republic*, April 6, 1968, in Archives and Special Collections at the Thomas J. Dodd Research Center, University of Connecticut Libraries, University of Connecticut, Storrs.

43. "Text of Kirk Statement," *Columbia Daily Spectator* 112, no. 36 (November 22, 1967), http://spectatorarchive.library.columbia.edu/cgi-bin/columbia?a=d&d=cs19671122-01.2.11&e=-------en-20--1--txt-txIN------ (accessed April 7, 2017).

44. Oren Root, "Columbia Ends Temporary Ban on Campus Military Recruiting," *Columbia Daily Spectator* 112, no. 57 (January 11, 1968), http://spectatorarchive.library.columbia.edu/cgi-bin/columbia?a=d&d=cs19680111-01.2.8&e=-------en-20--1--txt-txIN------ (accessed April 7, 2017).

45. Paul Lyons, *The People of This Generation: The Rise and Fall of the New Left in Philadelphia* (Philadelphia: University of Pennsylvania Press, 2003), 199; Morgan, "Faculty Mediation in Campus Conflict," in *Protest!*, ed. Foster and Long, 377.

46. Joseph F. Kauffman, Dean of Student Affairs to Sewell, November 17, 1967; Sewell to F. Jas. Sensenbrenner, Jr., December 6, 1967, Sewell Records, box 19, folder: Student Demonstrations.

47. Roger L. Geiger, *Research and Relevant Knowledge: American Research Universities since World War II* (1st ed., Oxford University Press, 1993; New Brunswick, NJ: Transaction, 2004), 193; Heineman, *Campus Wars*, 19; Elinor Langer, "THEMIS: DOD Plan to Spread the Wealth Raises Questions in Academe," *Science*, n.s., 156, no. 3771 (April 7, 1967): 48–50, http://www.jstor.org/stable/1720917 (accessed April 6, 2017); Theodore Kruse to Charles Brower, May 9, 1967, James P. Begin Papers, R-MC 048, box 1, folder 3, Special Collections and University Archives, Alexander Library, Rutgers University, New Brunswick (hereafter Begin Papers, Rutgers); J. Stanley Marshall, *The Tumultuous Sixties: Campus Unrest and Student Life at a Southern University* (Tallahassee: Sentry Press, 2006), 90.

48. Bridger, *Scientists at War*, 244.

49. Michael S. Neiberg, *Making Citizen-Soldiers: ROTC and the Ideology of American Military Service* (Cambridge, MA: Harvard University Press, 2000), 18–26, 36; Jack Nusan Porter, *Student Protest and the Technocratic Society: The Case of ROTC* (Chicago: Adams Press, 1971, 1973), 115; "Charge to the Committee," n.d., in William F. Field Papers, RG 30/2 F5, box 2, folder 688, Special Collections and University Archives, W. E. B. Du Bois Library, University of Massachusetts Amherst (hereafter Field Papers, UMass Amherst).

50. Neiberg, *Making Citizen-Soldiers*, 31–40.

51. Professor [Arthur] Sutherland, in Minutes of Special Meeting of the Faculty of Arts and Sciences, Harvard University, February 4, 1969, in *The University Crisis Reader*, Wallerstein and Starr, 1:284.

52. Minutes, Board of Governors meeting, October 9, 1970, box 10, folder 1, Begin Papers, Rutgers.

53. Shlomo Swirski, "Four Decades of Activism," in *Academic Supermarkets*, ed. Altbach, Laufer, and McVey; Minutes, Faculty Senate, November 14, 1961, box 2, folder 688, in Field Papers, UMass Amherst.

54. Lyons, *The People of This Generation*, 199; Heineman, "American Schism," in *The Vietnam War on Campus*, ed. Gilbert; Martha Biondi, *The Black Revolution on Campus* (Berkeley: University of California Press, 2012), 36; Turner, *Sitting In and Speaking Out*, 81; Dwain Sachs, "Oppressive Conditions at SMS," clipping from unknown student paper, April 18, 1969, in box 6-1, RESIST Records, Watkinson Library and Trinity College Archives, Raether Library, Trinity College, Hartford, CT (hereafter RESIST Records, Trinity).

55. Neiberg, *Making Citizen-Soldiers*, 50–58; Allan Brick, "The Campus Protest Against ROTC," mimeographed pamphlet, n.d., in box 7, Robert Winston Papers, Special Collections and University Archives, W. E. B. Du Bois Library, University of Massachusetts Amherst; Keller and Keller, *Making Harvard Modern*, 208.

56. Brick, "Campus Protest Against ROTC"; Neiberg, *Making Citizen-Soldiers*, 58.

57. Neiberg, *Making Citizen-Soldiers*, 111, 114.

58. Porter, *Student Protest and the Technocratic Society*, 115.

59. Neiberg, *Making Citizen-Soldiers*, 75–77, 103.

60. Neiberg, *Making Citizen-Soldiers*, 142–44.

61. Neiberg, *Making Citizen-Soldiers*, 70–73, 105; Martin J. Mead to Reverend Michael Walsh, February 10, 1970, Martin Walsh Papers, box 2, folder: Demonstration, November 12, 1969, Archives and Special Collections, Fordham University Library, Bronx, NY (hereafter Walsh Papers).

62. John Morton Blum, *A Life with History* (Lawrence: University Press of Kansas, 2004), 202.

63. Neiberg, *Making Citizen-Soldiers*, 102, 105, 123–24; Brick, "Campus Protest Against ROTC"; Blum, *A Life with History*, 204; Rogers Albritton in Minutes of Special Meeting of the Faculty of Arts and Sciences, Harvard University, February 4, 1969, in *The University Crisis Reader*, ed. Wallerstein and Starr, 1:278–79.

64. Brick, "Campus Protest Against ROTC"; Seth Rosenfeld, *Subversives: The FBI's War on Student Radicals, and Reagan's Rise to Power* (New York: Farrar, Straus and Giroux, 2012), 78, 364–65.

65. Saul Landau, "From the Labor Youth League to the Cuban Revolution," 111; Lee Baxandall, "New York Meets Oshkosh," 132; and Roz Baxandall, "Another Madison Bohemian," 139: all in *History and the New Left: Madison, Wisconsin, 1950–1970*, ed. Paul Buhle (Philadelphia: Temple University Press, 1990). "Partial Agenda of Resist to End of Semester," mimeograph, n.d. [1969], box 6-1, RESIST Records, Trinity; "Bulletin: A Week to Confront Campus Militarism," April 5, 1969, Gerald Braunthal Papers, box 2, folder 19; Rosenfeld, *Subversives*, 78, 364–65.

66. Nadine Cohodas, *The Band Played Dixie: Race and the Liberal Conscience at Ole Miss* (New York: Free Press, 1997), 137.

67. Mead to Walsh, February 10, 1970, in Walsh Papers; Porter, *Student Protest and the Technocratic Society*, 57–58.

68. "Academic Freedom and Tenure: Alfred University (New York)," *AAUP Bulletin* 56, no. 1 (March 1970): 87–93.

69. "Academic Freedom and Tenure: Tulane University," *AAUP Bulletin* 56, no. 4 (December 1970): 424–35; Turner, *Sitting In and Speaking Out*, 255–56.

70. Marshall, *Tumultuous Sixties*, 98; Robert Cohen, "Prophetic Minority versus Recalcitrant Majority: Southern Student Dissent and the Struggle for Progressive Change in the 1960s," in *Rebellion in Black and White: Southern Student Activism in the 1960s*, ed. Robert Cohen and David J. Snyder (Baltimore: Johns Hopkins University Press, 2013), 25; Biondi, *Black Revolution on Campus*, 36.

71. Turner, *Sitting In and Speaking Out*, 228; Bates, *Rads*, 20; Keller and Keller, *Making Harvard Modern*, 319; Siggelkow, *Dissent and Disruption*, 111.

72. Minutes, faculty meeting, May 18, 1970, box 10, folder 1, Begin Papers, Rutgers.

73. Neiberg, *Making Citizen-Soldiers*, 107, 109.

74. Memorandum by U.S. Army ROTC Instructor Group, Harvard University, December 4, 1968, in *The University Crisis Reader*, ed. Wallerstein and Starr, 1:265.

75. Fred Glimp to Nathan Pusey, February 14, 1989, in *The University Crisis Reader*, ed. Wallerstein and Starr, 1:289–90; Neiberg, *Making Citizen-Soldiers*, 146.

76. Neiberg, *Making Citizen-Soldiers*, 123.

77. Arthur K. Bierman, "Oral History," 68, interviewed by Peter Carroll, January 14, 17, 28, 1992, Labor Archives and Research Center, San Francisco State University.

78. Porter, *Student Protest and the Technocratic Society*, 61.

79. Minutes of Special Meeting of the Faculty of Arts and Sciences, Harvard University, February 4, 1969, in *The University Crisis Reader*, ed. Wallerstein and Starr, 1:278–86; Blum, *A Life with History*, 204; Minutes, Faculty Senate, November 20, 1969, in Field Papers, UMass Amherst, box 2, folder 688.

80. Smith, Axen, and Pentony, *By Any Means Necessary*, 46–47.

81. Neiberg, *Making Citizen-Soldiers*, 127.

82. Minutes, Faculty Senate meeting, November 6, 1969, Field Papers, UMass Amherst, box 2, folder 688.

83. Neiberg, *Making Citizen-Soldiers*, 125; Meade to Walsh, February 10, 1970, Walsh Papers.

84. Neiberg, *Making Citizen-Soldiers*, 125.

85. Report of Ad Hoc Committee on ROTC, March 14, 1970, box 5, folder 2, Pruitt and Gahagan Research, University at Buffalo Archives; Turner, *Sitting In and Speaking Out*, 261.

86. Turner, *Sitting In and Speaking Out*, 255; Minutes, Faculty Senate meeting, November 6, 1969, Field Papers, UMass Amherst, box 2, folder 688.

87. Keller and Keller, *Making Harvard Modern*, 324; Neiberg, *Making Citizen-Soldiers*, 126.

88. William Scranton et al., *The Report of the President's Commission on Campus Unrest* (New York: Arno Press, 1970), x, 22, 18.

89. Lipset and Riesman, *Education and Politics at Harvard*, 219; Keller and Keller, *Making Harvard Modern*, 313–14; Franklin Ford to Nathan Pusey, February 11, 1969, in *The University Crisis Reader*, ed. Wallerstein and Starr, 1:286–88.

90. Brick, "Campus Protest Against ROTC."

91. Minutes, Board of Governors meeting, November 19, 1971, box 10, folder 1, Begin Papers, Rutgers.

92. Minutes, Board of Trustees meeting, May 29, 1970, box 2 folder 688, in Field Papers, UMass Amherst.

93. Neiberg, *Making Citizen-Soldiers*, 149–50.

94. Minutes, Board of Trustees meeting, April 4, 1973, box 2, folder 688, Field Papers, UMass Amherst; Minutes, Board of Governors meeting, May 12, 1972, box 10, folder 1, Begin Papers, Rutgers.

Chapter Eleven

1. Morton Keller and Phyllis Keller, *Making Harvard Modern: The Rise of America's University* (Cary, NC: Oxford University Press, 2001), 306; Seymour Martin Lipset and David Riesman, *Education and Politics at Harvard* (New York: McGraw Hill, 1975), 215–16; William H. Orrick Jr., *Shut It Down! A College in Crisis: A Report to the National Commission on the Causes and Prevention of Violence* (Washington, DC: National Commission on the Causes and Prevention of Violence, 1969), 18; Henry Rosovsky, telephone interview with the author, May 15, 2013; Adam Ulam, *The Fall of the American University* (LaSalle, IL: Library Press, 1972), 129.

2. Donald W. Light Jr., "Directed Resistance: The Structure of Tactics in Student Protest," in *The Dynamics of University Protest*, ed. Donald Light Jr. and John Spiegel (Chicago: Nelson-Hall, 1977), 81–82; John W. Boyer, *The University of Chicago: A History* (Chicago: University of Chicago Press, 2015), 380–84.

3. Richard E. Peterson, *The Scope of Organized Student Protest in 1967–1968* (Princeton, NJ: Educational Testing Service, 1968), is particularly useful here.

4. Martha Biondi, *The Black Revolution on Campus* (Berkeley: University of California Press, 2012), offers a broad view of that "revolution," as does Ibram H. Rogers [Kendi], *The Black Campus Movement: Black Students and the Racial Reconstitution of Higher Education, 1965–1972* (New York: Palgrave Macmillan, 2012).

5. Jeffrey A. Turner, *Sitting In and Speaking Out: Student Movements in the American South, 1960–1970* (Athens: University of Georgia Press, 2010).

6. Peterson, *The Scope of Organized Student Protest*, 33; Joy Ann Williamson-Lott, "Student Free Speech on Both Sides of the Color Line in Mississippi and

the Carolinas," in *Rebellion in Black and White: Southern Student Activism in the 1960s*, ed. Robert Cohen and David J. Snyder (Baltimore: Johns Hopkins University Press, 2013).

7. Fred Halstead, *Out Now! A Participant's Account of the American Movement Against the Vietnam War* (New York: Monad Press, 1978), 22.

8. John Walsh, "Stanford's Search for Solutions," in *Academic Transformation: Seventeen Institutions under Pressure*, ed. David Riesman and Verne A. Stadtman (New York: McGraw-Hill, 1973), 310.

9. Frederick W. Obear, "Student Activism in the Sixties," in *Protest! Student Activism in America*, ed. Julian Foster and Durward Long (New York: William Morrow, 1970), 20; Lipset and Riesman, *Education and Politics at Harvard*, 212–13.

10. Light, "Directed Resistance," in *The Dynamics of University Protest*, ed. Light and Spiegel, 85.

11. Light, "Directed Resistance," 89; James Axtell, *The Making of Princeton University: From Woodrow Wilson to the Present* (Princeton, NJ: Princeton University Press, 2006), 353.

12. Jerry L. Avorn, with Andrew Crane, Mark Jaffe, Oren Root Jr., Paul Starr, Michael Stern, and Robert Stulberg, *Up Against the Ivy Wall: A History of the Columbia Crisis* (New York: Atheneum, 1968), 11, 17.

13. Matthew Levin, *Cold War University: Madison and the New Left in the Sixties* (Madison: University of Wisconsin Press, 2013), 157; Philip G. Altbach, Robert S. Laufer, and Sheila McVey, "Prologue: The Multiversity in Crisis," in *Academic Supermarkets: A Critical Case Study of a Multiversity*, ed. Philip G. Altbach, Robert S. Laufer, and Sheila McVey (San Francisco: Jossey-Bass, 1971); John Coatsworth, interview with the author, July 28, 2016, New York City.

14. Donna Murch, *Living for the City: Migration, Education, and the Rise of the Black Panther Party in Oakland, California* (Chapel Hill: University of North Carolina Press, 2010), 71–75, 97–116, 135.

15. Robert Cohen, "Prophetic Minority versus Recalcitrant Majority: Southern Student Dissent and the Struggle for Progressive Change in the 1960s," in *Rebellion in Black and White*, ed. Cohen and Snyder, 6; William L. Van Deburg, *New Day in Babylon: The Black Power Movement and American Culture, 1965–1975* (Chicago: University of Chicago Press, 1992), 67.

16. Biondi, *Black Revolution on Campus*, 22.

17. Peniel E. Joseph, "Black Studies, Student Activism, and the Black Power Movement," in *The Black Power Movement: Rethinking the Civil Rights–Black Power Era*, ed. Peniel E. Joseph (New York: Routledge, 2006), 35; Turner, *Sitting In and Speaking Out*, 181, 198.

18. Joseph, "Black Studies," 269; Murch, *Living for the City*, 10, 88–96.

19. Joy Williamson, *Black Power on Campus: The University of Illinois, 1965–1975* (Urbana: University of Illinois Press, 2003), 74–75, 85, 94–96; Nick Aaron Ford, *Black Studies: Threat-or-Challenge* (Port Washington, NY: Kennikat

Press, 1973), 98; William H. Friedland and Harry Edwards, "Confrontation at Cornell," in *Campus Power Struggle*, ed. Howard S. Becker (Piscataway, NJ: Transaction Books, 1970), 81.

20. Jack Nelson and Jack Bass, *The Orangeburg Massacre* (New York: World, 1970), 97–98; Robert J. Norrell, *Reaping the Whirlwind: The Civil Rights Movement in Tuskegee* (New York: Knopf, 1985), 174.

21. Joy Ann Williamson, *Radicalizing the Ebony Tower: Black Colleges and the Black Freedom Struggle in Mississippi* (New York: Teachers College Press, 2008), 39–57; Turner, *Sitting In and Speaking Out*, 175–79; Robert Cohen, "Mentor to the Movement," in *Howard Zinn's Southern Diary: Sit-Ins, Civil Rights, and Black Women's Student Activism*, ed. Robert Cohen (Athens: University of Georgia Press, 2018), 23.

22. Williamson, *Black Power on Campus*, 12–13.

23. Williamson, *Black Power on Campus*, 14.

24. Paul Sigmund, "Princeton in Crisis and Change," in *Academic Transformation*, ed. Riesman and Stadtman, 251; Friedland and Edwards, "Confrontation at Cornell," in *Campus Power Struggle*, ed. Becker, 80; Donald Alexander Downs, *Cornell '69: Liberalism and the Crisis of the American University* (Ithaca, NY: Cornell University Press, 1999), 4.

25. Biondi, *Black Revolution on Campus*, 4; Mary Ann Wynkoop, *Dissent in the Heartland: The Sixties at Indiana University* (Bloomington: Indiana University Press, 2002), 120–21; Harry Edwards, *The Struggle That Must Be: An Autobiography* (New York: Macmillan, 1980), 158.

26. Biondi, *Black Revolution on Campus*, 81.

27. Keller and Keller, *Making Harvard Modern*, 285; Stefan M. Bradley, *Harlem vs. Columbia University: Black Student Power in the Late 1960s* (Urbana: University of Illinois Press, 2009), 10.

28. Williamson, *Black Power on Campus*, 35.

29. Altbach, Laufer, and McVey, "Prologue: The Multiversity in Crisis," 21; Philip G. Altbach, "The Champagne University in the Beer State," in *Academic Transformation*, ed. Riesman and Stadtman, 398; Wynkoop, *Dissent in the Heartland*, 119.

30. Nathan Glazer, "City College," in *Academic Transformation*, ed. Riesman and Stadtman, 84; E. Alden Dunham, *Colleges of the Forgotten Americans: A Profile of State Colleges and Regional Universities* (New York: McGraw-Hill, 1969), 52; Biondi, *Black Revolution on Campus*, 43; George S. Rothbart, "Ivory Tower or Modern Building," in *Academics on the Line: The Faculty Strike at San Francisco State*, by Arlene Kaplan Daniels, Rachel Kahn-Hut, and Associates (San Francisco: Jossey-Bass, 1970), 89; Orrick, *Shut It Down!*, 75.

31. Rogers [Kendi], *The Black Campus Movement*, 22–26; Bruce M. Stave, *Red Brick in the Land of Steady Habits: Creating the University of Connecticut, 1881–2006* (Hanover, NH: University Press of New England, 2006), 152–53; Williamson, *Black Power on Campus*, 16–22, 61; Bradley, *Harlem vs. Columbia University*, 10–11, 140; Edwards, *Struggle*, 111; Thomas M. Grace, *Kent State:*

Death and Dissent in the Long Sixties (Amherst: University of Massachusetts Press, 2016), 26; Eddie R. Cole, *The Campus Color Line: College Presidents and the Struggle for Black Freedom* (Princeton, NJ: Princeton University Press, 2020), 70–118.

32. The information was in a message to the Amherst College Class of 1959 at their sixtieth reunion, information courtesy of Mark Selden; Biondi, *Black Revolution on Campus*, 82.

33. Ford, *Black Studies*, 98–99; Rita James Simon and James Carey, "The Phantom Racist," in *Campus Power Struggle*, ed. Becker, 101; Biondi, *Black Revolution on Campus*, 81.

34. Wynkoop, *Dissent in the Heartland*, 116–23; Roger Rapoport and Laurence J. Kirshbaum, *Is the Library Burning?* (New York: Random House, 1969), 27; Williamson, *Black Power on Campus*, 26–32.

35. Rapoport and Kirshbaum, *Is the Library Burning?*, 25; Lawrence E. Eichel, "The Founding of the Afro-American Studies Department: The Crisis of 1969," in *Blacks at Harvard: A Documentary History of African-American Experience at Harvard and Radcliffe*, ed. Werner Sollors, Caldwell Titcomb, and Thomas A. Underwood (New York: New York University Press, 1993), 380–81; Harry Edwards, *Black Students* (New York: Free Press, 1970), 64–67; Keller and Keller, *Making Harvard Modern*, 286; Biondi, *Black Revolution on Campus*, 18–20.

36. Biondi, *Black Revolution on Campus*, 14, 82; Ford, *Black Studies*, 101.

37. Keller and Keller, *Making Harvard Modern*, 285; Geoffrey Kabaservice, *The Guardians: Kingman Brewster, His Circle, and the Rise of the Liberal Establishment* (New York: Henry Holt, 2004), 328; Downs, *Cornell '69*, 4; Richard McCormick, "Rutgers, the State University," in *Academic Transformation*, ed. Riesman and Stadtman, 275; Harold L. Hodgkinson, *Institutions in Transition: A Profile of Change in Higher Education* (New York: McGraw-Hill, 1971), 78, 173; Rapoport and Kirshbaum, *Is the Library Burning?*, 104–5; Wayne Glasker, *Black Students in the Ivory Tower: African American Activism at the University of Pennsylvania, 1967–1990* (Amherst: University of Massachusetts Press, 2002), 20; Williamson, *Black Power on Campus*, 58.

38. Benson Snyder, "Change Despite Turmoil at MIT," in *Academic Transformation*, ed. Riesman and Stadtman, 164; Martin Kilson, "Harvard and the Small-Towner," in *Blacks at Harvard*, ed. Sollors, Titcomb, and Underwood, 492. Wayne Glasker cites similar figures in *Black Students in the Ivory Tower*, 45.

39. Van Deburg, *New Day in Babylon*, 67; Biondi, *Black Revolution on Campus*, 4.

40. Edwards, *Black Students*, 74–119; Rogers, *The Black Campus Movement*, 86; Williamson, *Black Power on Campus*, 36–38, 47–49; Wynkoop, *Dissent in the Heartland*, 12–21.

41. George Nash, *The University and the City: Eight Cases of Involvement* (New York: McGraw-Hill, 1973), 5, 76; Noliwe M. Rooks, *White Money/Black Power: The Surprising History of African American Studies and the Crisis of Race in Higher Education* (Boston: Beacon Press, 2006), 36.

42. Glasker, *Black Students in the Ivory Tower*, 58–59.

43. C. Vann Woodward to James W. Silver, December 28, 1962, in *The Letters of C. Vann Woodward*, ed. Michael O'Brien (New Haven, CT: Yale University Press, 2013), 233.

44. Kabaservice, *The Guardians*, 328; Wynkoop, *Dissent in the Heartland*, 119; Conor Tomás Reed, "'What We are Part of' Teaching at CCNY: 1968–1974, Adrienne Rich, Part II," in *Lost and Found*, Series 3, #3, Part 2, Fall 2013, 56–58, http://freeuniversitynyc.org/files/2014/02/Adrienne-Rich-SEEK-CCNY-social-movements.pdf (accessed October 2, 2016). For a devastating critique of how white liberal administrations failed to provide for Black students at the University of Michigan, see Matthew Johnson, *Undermining Racial Justice: How One University Embraced Inclusion and Inequality* (Ithaca, NY: Cornell University Press, 2020).

45. Williamson, *Black Power on Campus*, 80.

46. Stave, *Red Brick*, 147–49.

47. Hodgkinson, *Institutions in Transition*, 172–74; Biondi, *Black Revolution on Campus*, 51, 82, 115; Stephen J. Whitfield and Jonathan B. Krasner, "Jewish Liberalism and Racial Grievance in the Sixties: The Ordeal of Brandeis University," *Modern Judaism* 35, no. 1 (February 2015): 23, https://muse.jhu.edu/journals/modern_judaism/v035/35.1.whitfield.html (accessed June 30, 2017); Williamson, *Black Power on Campus*, 64–72; McCormick, "Rutgers," in *Academic Transformation,* ed. Riesman and Stadtman, 275; Glasker, *Black Students in the Ivory Tower*, 93; Nash, *The University and the City*, 43–46.

48. Robin Dizard, interview with the author, Amherst, MA, September 19, 2015; Murch, *Living for the City*, 7–8.

49. Johnson, *Undermining Racial Justice*, 34–39, 131.

50. Hodgkinson, *Institutions in Transition*, 173–76; Theodore Kroeber, "Confronting Irreconcilable Issues," in *Academics on the Line*, ed. Daniels, Kahn-Hut et al., 123; Biondi, *Black Revolution on Campus*, 138; Wynkoop, *Dissent in the Heartland*, 86; Downs, *Cornell '69*, 47.

51. Biondi, *Black Revolution on Campus*, 44; Rogers, *The Black Campus Movement*, 93–97; Joseph Shoben Jr., Philip Werdell, and Durward Long, "Radical Student Organizations," in *Protest!*, ed. Foster and Long, 218–19.

52. Rogers, *The Black Campus Movement*, 114–18; Tom Bates, *Rads: The 1970 Bombing of the Army Math Research Center at the University of Wisconsin and Its Aftermath* (New York: HarperCollins, 1992), 98; Rapoport and Kirshbaum, *Is the Library Burning?*, 66–67; Sigmund, "Princeton in Crisis and Change," 259; Fabio Rojas, *From Black Power to Black Studies: How a Radical Social Movement Became an Academic Discipline* (Baltimore: Johns Hopkins University Press, 2007), 70.

53. Glasker, *Black Students in the Ivory Tower*, 118.

54. Van Deburg, *New Day in Babylon*, 68–69.

55. Altbach, "The Champagne University in the Beer State," in *Academic Transformation*, ed. Riesman and Stadtman, 399; Bates, *Rads*, 113.

56. Friedland and Edwards, "Confrontation at Cornell," in *Campus Power Struggle*, ed. Becker, 81; Downs, *Cornell '69*, 57–69. See "Harambee House" for a discussion about Wellesley's peaceful establishment of its Black student center: https://www.wellesley.edu/harambee/about (accessed February 10, 2018).

57. Downs, *Cornell '69*, 58.

58. Gerald Grant, "A Network of Antiochs," in *Academic Transformation*, ed. Riesman and Stadtman, 30; Glasker, *Black Students in the Ivory Tower*, 88–89; Van Deburg, *New Day in Babylon*, 72–73; Kabaservice, *The Guardians*, 327–29; Stave, *Red Brick*, 147.

59. Glasker, *Black Students in the Ivory Tower*, 54; Williamson, *Black Power on Campus*, 72–73.

60. Zelda Gamson, "Michigan Muddles Through," in *Academic Transformation*, ed. Riesman and Stadtman, 186–87; Wynkoop, *Dissent in the Heartland*, 123; Glasker, *Black Students in the Ivory Tower*, 56; Williamson, *Black Power on Campus*, 60.

61. Johnson, *Undermining Racial Justice*, 113.

62. Downs, *Cornell '69*, 48.

63. Cole, *The Campus Color Line*, 71.

64. Cole, *The Campus Color Line*, 83, 118.

65. On the role of the University of Chicago in gentrifying its neighborhood in a way that intensified the city's already serious residential segregation in the 1950s, see Cole, *The Campus Color Line*, 70–118, and Arnold R. Hirsch, *Making the Second Ghetto: Race and Housing in Chicago, 1940–1960* (Cambridge: Cambridge University Press, 1983), 135–70. See also Nash, *The University and the City*, 9, 11–24; Howard S. Becker, "The Struggle for Power on the Campus," in *Campus Power Struggle*, ed. Becker, 13; Boyer, *University of Chicago*, 343–54; and Hanna Holborn Gray, *An Academic Life: A Memoir* (Princeton, NJ: Princeton University Press, 2018), 177.

66. Glasker, *Black Students in the Ivory Tower*, 48–49; Margaret Pugh O'Mara, *Cities of Knowledge: Cold War Science and the Search for the Next Silicon Valley* (Princeton, NJ: Princeton University Press, 2005), 154–68; Ted Asregadoo, "'A Bulwark Against Radicalism': Protest Movements at the University of Pennsylvania and the Struggle for Reform, 1965–1969," *Peace and Change* 42, no. 3 (July 2017): 410–35.

67. Lawrence E. Eichel, Kenneth W. Jost, Robert D. Luskin, and Richard M. Neustadt, *The Harvard Strike* (Boston: Houghton Mifflin, 1970), 67–68; Jonathan Beckwith, *Making Genes, Making Waves: A Social Activist in Science* (Cambridge, MA: Harvard University Press, 2002), 50–51; Jonathan Beckwith, interview with the author, April 2, 2013, Boston; Eichel, "The Founding of the Afro-American Studies Department," 387; Bradley, *Harlem vs. Columbia University*, 139–42; Jack Nusan Porter, *Student Protest and the Technocratic Society: The Case of ROTC* (Chicago: Adams Press, 1971, 1973), 16, 50; "Wayne-

in-Exile," in *The University Crisis Reader*, ed. Immanuel Wallerstein and Paul Starr, vol. 1, *The Liberal University under Attack* (New York: Random House, 1971), 167–68.

68. Bradley, *Harlem vs. Columbia University*, 28–32; Avorn et al., *Up Against the Ivy Wall*, 13.

69. Daniel Bell, "Columbia and the New Left," in *Confrontation: The Student Rebellion and the Universities*, ed. Daniel Bell and Irving Kristol (New York: Basic Books, 1969), 70.

70. Bradley, *Harlem vs. Columbia University*, 20–62; Avorn et al., *Up Against the Ivy Wall*, 18–20, 84–86.

71. Bell, "Columbia and the New Left," in *Confrontation*, ed. Bell and Kristol, 83.

72. Bradley, *Harlem vs. Columbia University*, 131.

73. Rogers, *The Black Campus Movement*, 131–38; Everett Carll Ladd Jr. and Seymour Martin Lipset, *The Divided Academy: Professors and Politics* (New York: McGraw-Hill, 1975), 218.

74. Rogers, *The Black Campus Movement*, 99–100; David A. Varel, *The Scholar and the Struggle: Lawrence Reddick's Crusade for Black History and Black Power* (Chapel Hill: University of North Carolina Press, 2020); Martin White, "The Black Studies Controversy at Reed College, 1968–1970," *Oregon Historical Quarterly* 119, no. 1 (Spring 2018).

75. Ladd and Lipset, *The Divided Academy*, 218.

76. Porter, *Student Protest and the Technocratic Society*, 49; Kenneth J. Heineman, *Campus Wars: The Peace Movement at American State Universities in the Vietnam Era* (New York: New York University Press, 1993), 67.

77. Corydon Ireland, "Harvard's Long-Ago Student Risings," *Harvard Gazette*, April 19, 2012, https://news.harvard.edu/gazette/story/2012/04/harvards-long-ago-student-risings/ (accessed June 17, 2018).

78. Nelson and Bass, *Orangeburg Massacre*, 5–6; Turner, *Sitting In and Speaking Out*, 25–27; Howard Zinn to Board of Trustees (Spelman College) et al., in AAUP Committee A Case Files—1974, box 310, Spelman College, Howard Zinn, in AAUP Records, Special Collections Research Center, Gelman Library, George Washington University, Washington, DC.

79. Beth Bailey, *Sex in the Heartland* (Cambridge, MA: Harvard University Press, 1999), 200–202.

80. Stave, *Red Brick*, 120.

81. On pre–World War II restrictions, see Paula Fass, *The Damned and the Beautiful: American Youth in the 1920s* (New York: Oxford University Press, 1977); Grace, *Kent State*, 25, 79.

82. Cohen, "Mentor to the Movement," *Howard Zinn's Southern Diary*, ed. Cohen, 20; Bailey, *Sex in the Heartland*, 88–89.

83. Rapoport and Kirshbaum, *Is the Library Burning?*, 10; Eichel et al., *Harvard Strike*, 16–17.

84. Nelson and Bass, *Orangeburg Massacre*, 5–6; Heineman, *Campus Wars*, 23; Tom Hurwitz, "The Smartest Kids I'd Ever Met: Memories of a Columbia

Rebel," in *A Time to Stir: Columbia '68*, ed. Paul Cronin (New York: Columbia University Press, 2018), 126–27.

85. James S. Turner, "Ohio State: Free Speech and Student Power," in *Protest!*, ed. Foster and Long, 346.

86. Seth Rosenfeld, *Subversives: The FBI's War on Student Radicals, and Reagan's Rise to Power* (New York: Farrar, Straus and Giroux, 2012), 78, 189.

87. Williamson-Lott, "Student Free Speech," in *Rebellion in Black and White*, ed. Cohen and Snyder, 66–69.

88. "Academic Freedom and Tenure: Troy State University," *AAUP Bulletin* 54, no. 3 (September 1968): 299–300; "Academic Freedom and Tenure: Southeastern Louisiana College," *AAUP Bulletin*, September 1969, 372.

89. Williamson-Lott, "Student Free Speech," in *Rebellion in Black and White*, ed. Cohen and Snyder, 70.

90. Stacy Braukman, *Communists and Perverts under the Palms: The Johns Committee in Florida, 1956–1965* (Gainesville: University Press of Florida, 2012), 144–56; Karen L. Graves, *And They Were Wonderful Teachers: Florida's Purge of Gay and Lesbian Teachers* (Urbana: University of Illinois Press, 2009), 59–61; Judith G. Poucher, *State of Defiance: Challenging the Johns Committee's Assault on Civil Liberties* (Gainesville: University Press of Florida, 2014), 120–33; "Academic Freedom and Tenure: University of South Florida," *AAUP Bulletin*, March 1964.

91. "Academic Freedom and Tenure: Armstrong State College [Georgia]," *AAUP Bulletin*, September 1969.

92. J. Stanley Marshall, *The Tumultuous Sixties: Campus Unrest and Student Life at a Southern University* (Tallahassee: Sentry Press, 2006), 21–22.

93. "Academic Freedom and Tenure: The University of Illinois," *AAUP Bulletin* 49, no. 1 (March 1963): 25–43.

94. Dowd, *Cornell '69*, 37–38; Smith, Axen, and Pentony, *By Any Means Necessary*, 6, 14, 23–25.

95. Cohen, "Mentor to the Movement," 5.

96. Marshall, *The Tumultuous Sixties*, 21–28.

97. Christopher A. Huff, "Conservative Student Activism at the University of Georgia," 171–75; Gary S. Sprayberry, "Student Radicalism and the Antiwar Movement at the University of Alabama," 148–49: both in *Rebellion in Black and White*, ed. Cohen and Snyder.

98. "Report on Troy State University," *AAUP Bulletin*, September 1968, 299–300.

99. Most of the information about the Richard Bernstein case comes from the *Yale Daily News*, spring 1965.

100. Among the schools where students demonstrated to restore the positions of fired teachers were Boston University, Brooklyn College, Catholic University, Howard University, Northern Illinois University, Queensborough Community College, San Francisco State, South Carolina State College, Southeastern Massachusetts University, University of Chicago, University of Hawaii, Vassar College, Wayne State College (Nebraska), and Yale.

101. Victor C. Chen, "The Book on Richard J. Bernstein," *Yale Daily News*, March 2, 1965.

102. James Adams, "Students Begin 3-Day Vigil," *Yale Daily News*, March 2, 1965; Frank Clifford et al., "Professors to Join Tenure Discussion," *Yale Daily News*, March 4, 1965; "Vigil Ends on High Note," *Yale Daily News*, March 5, 1965.

103. Albert La Valley, quoted in Frank Berliner and James Adams, "Yale Professors Back Students at Debate," *Yale Daily News*, March 3, 1965.

104. "Committee May Reconsider," and "Professors, Students Propose End of US Military Aid to Vietnam," both in *Yale Daily News*, March 5, 1965.

105. Kabaservice, *The Guardians*, 225–26; Victor C. Chen, "Department Votes Down Bernstein," *Yale Daily News*, March 8, 1965; Blum, *A Life with History*, 181.

106. Nelson and Bass, *Orangeburg Massacre*, 5–6; Turner, *Sitting In and Speaking Out*, 183–84.

107. Turner, *Sitting In and Speaking Out*, 256.

108. Zimmerman, *Troublemaker*, 166.

109. The scholarly literature on the student unrest at the University of Chicago is sparse. The most useful source is the collection of essays edited (and largely written) by Donald Light Jr. and John Spiegel, *The Dynamics of University Protest* (Chicago: Nelson-Hall, 1977), but, unfortunately, it does not deal with the Dixon case.

110. Rapoport and Kirshbaum, *Is the Library Burning?*, 47; Joan Wallach Scott, interview with the author, December 16, 2014, New York City; Richard Flacks, telephone interview with the author, February 22, 2013; Boyer, *University of Chicago*, 374–76; Gray, *An Academic Life*, 191–93; Supriya Sinhababu, "The Sit-In 40 Years Later," *Chicago Maroon*, December 2, 2008, https://www.chicagomaroon.com/2008/12/02/the-sit-in-40-years-later/.

111. Boyer, *University of Chicago*, 377; Gray, *An Academic Life*, 193.

112. Student Committee on Faculty Firing to Vassar Students, April 26, 1971, Vassar College, 1971 Sit-In Collection, box 1, folder 1, Archives and Special Collections Library, Vassar College.

113. Joseph Illick, in College of Ethnic Studies, 40th Anniversary Conference, October 8, 2009, San Francisco State University, https://diva.sfsu.edu/collections/coes/bundles/189539 (accessed June 10, 2018); Herbert Wilner, "Zen Basketball, etc., at State," in *Academics on the Line*, ed. Daniels, Kahn-Hut et al., 15–32; Arthur K. Bierman, "Oral History," 72, interviewed by Peter Carroll, January 14, 17, 28, 1992, Labor Archives and Research Center, San Francisco State University (hereafter LARC, SFSU); Eric Solomon, "Oral History," 4, interviewed by Peter Carroll, February 2, 1992, LARC, SFSU.

114. There has been quite a lot written about the events at San Francisco State in the 1960s. The memoir of a former president and two of his top aides is particularly useful: Robert Smith, Richard Axen, and DeVere Pentony, *By Any Means Necessary: The Revolutionary Struggle at San Francisco State* (San Francisco: Jossey-Bass, 1970). Some other useful works are Biondi, *Black Revolu-*

tion on Campus, 43–78; Orrick, *Shut It Down!*; and Daniels, Kahn-Hut et al., *Academics on the Line*.

115. Biondi, *Black Revolution on Campus*, 51. Magali Sarfatti Larson, "Master Plan, Master Failure," 71–74; and George S. Rothbart, "Ivory Tower or Modern Building," 89: both in *Academics on the Line*, ed. Daniels, Kahn-Hut et al., 89.

116. Dikran Karagueuzian, *Blow It Up! The Black Student Revolt at San Francisco State College and the Emergence of Dr. Hayakawa* (Boston: Gambit, 1971), 54, 73–83; James Benét, "Interpretation and Objectivity in Journalism," in *Academics on the Line*, ed. Daniels, Kahn-Hut et al., 114–15; Kay Boyle, *The Long Walk at San Francisco State and Other Essays* (New York: Grove Press, 1970), 51–52.

117. Biondi, *Black Revolution on Campus*, 54; Rachel Kahn-Hut, "Going Radical," in *Academics on the Line*, ed. Daniels, Kahn-Hut et al., 39; Orrick, *Shut It Down!*

118. Smith, Axen, and Pentony, *By Any Means Necessary*, 42–64; Karagueuzian, *Blow It Up!*, 54–67; Boyle, *Long Walk*, 52.

119. Smith, Axen, and Pentony, *By Any Means Necessary*, 5–6; Bierman, "Oral History," 69; Orrick, *Shut It Down!*

120. Biondi, *Black Revolution on Campus*, 35–36; Lawrence B. de Graaf, "Howard: The Evolution of a Black Student Revolt," in *Protest!*, ed, Foster and Long, 328.

121. Smith, Axen, and Pentony, *By Any Means Necessary*, 97–137.

122. The strike demands are reprinted in (among many collections) Immanuel Wallerstein and Paul Starr, eds., *The University Crisis Reader*, vol. 2, *Confrontation and Counterattack* (New York: Random House, 1971), 389–90. See also Helene Whitson, "Strike! . . . Concerning the 1968–69 Strike at San Francisco State College," *FoundSF*, n.d., http://www.foundsf.org/index.php?title =STRIKE! . . . _Concerning_the_1968-69_Strike_at_San_Francisco_State _College (accessed June 14, 2018).

123. Karagueuzian, *Blow It Up!*, 105–13; Smith, Axen, and Pentony, *By Any Means Necessary*, 145, 159.

124. Smith, Axen, and Pentony, *By Any Means Necessary*, 256.

125. Smith, Axen, and Pentony, *By Any Means Necessary*, 87–201.

126. Smith, Axen, and Pentony, *By Any Means Necessary*, 208; Arlene Kaplan Daniels, "Making of the President, 1969," in *Academics on the Line*, ed. Daniels, Kahn-Hut et al., 186–97; Warren Bennis, *The Leaning Ivory Tower* (San Francisco: Jossey-Bass, 1973), 59.

127. James McEvoy and Abraham Miller, "The Crisis at San Francisco State," in *Campus Power Struggle*, ed. Becker, 76.

128. Wallerstein and Starr, eds., *The University Crisis Reader*, 2:389–90. See also Whitson, "Strike!"

129. Julian Foster, "Student Protest," in *Protest!*, ed. Foster and Long, 413.

130. Bell, "Columbia and the New Left," 82; Friedland and Edwards, "Confrontation at Cornell," in *Campus Power Struggle*, ed. Becker, 90–92; Donald Light Jr., "The Dynamics of Faculty Response to Student Protest," in *The Dynamics of University Protest*, ed. Light and Spiegel, 123.

131. Stanley Ofsevit, "Politics of Justice," 214–26; and Rachel Kahn-Hut, "Which

Side Are You On?," 162: both in *Academics on the Line*, ed. Daniels, Kahn-Hut et al.; Karagueuzian, *Blow It Up!*, 193–94.

132. Eichel et al., *Harvard Strike*, 73.

133. Rapoport and Kirshbaum, *Is the Library Burning?*, 24–26.

134. Cohen, "Prophetic Minority versus Recalcitrant Majority," in *Rebellion in Black and White*, ed. Cohen and Snyder, 3.

135. Bruce Dancis, *Resister: A Story of Protest and Prison during the Vietnam War* (Ithaca, NY: Cornell University Press, 2014), 49–50.

136. Wayne C. Booth, *My Many Selves: The Quest for a Plausible Harmony* (Logan: Utah State University Press, 2006), 194.

137. Altbach, Laufer, and McVey, "Prologue: The Multiversity in Crisis," in *Academic Supermarkets*, ed. Altbach, Laufer, and McVey, 12.

138. Robert Friedman, "Introduction," in Avorn et al., *Up Against the Ivy Wall*, 21.

139. de Graaf, "Howard," in *Protest!*, ed. Foster and Long, 326–30.

140. Eichel et al., *Harvard Strike*, 32–34.

141. Rapoport and Kirshbaum, *Is the Library Burning?*, 78–79.

142. Gray, *An Academic Life*, 188; Obear, "Student Activism in the Sixties," in *Protest!*, ed. Foster and Long, 14–17; Downs, *Cornell '69*, 3–14, 87; Cushing Strout, "A Personal Narrative of a Rude Awakening," in *Divided We Stand: Reflections on the Crisis at Cornell*, ed. Cushing Strout and David I. Grossvogel (Garden City, NY: Doubleday, 1970), 54.

143. Wallerstein, interview in the *Columbia Spectator*, June 25, 1968, in Wallerstein, Columbia Oral History Project, 72, Rare Books and Manuscripts Library, Butler Library, Columbia University; Avorn et al., *Up Against the Ivy Wall*, 161; Bennett Gershman, "In the Spirit of Reconciliation," in *A Time to Stir*, ed. Cronin, 79–82.

144. Sprayberry, "Student Radicalism," in *Rebellion in Black and White*, ed. Cohen and Snyder, 165–66; Richard A. Siggelkow, *Dissent and Disruption: A University under Siege* (Buffalo: Prometheus Books, 1991), 97–98; Heineman, *Campus Wars*, 217.

145. Flacks, interview, February 22, 2013.

146. Rapoport and Kirshbaum, *Is the Library Burning?*, 152, 250.

147. Smith, Axen, and Pentony, *By Any Means Necessary*, 85; de Graaf, "Howard," 324, 327–30; Biondi, *Black Revolution on Campus*, 38–39.

Chapter Twelve

1. Michael Frisch, telephone interview with the author, May 19, 2015; Richard A. Siggelkow, *Dissent and Disruption: A University under Siege* (Buffalo: Prometheus Books, 1991), 204.

2. Siggelkow, *Dissent and Disruption*, 203–7.

3. Statement of Edward Doty, March 18, 1970, in Axelrod to Interested Colleagues, April 21, 1970, in Campus Unrest: Research of Dean G. Pruitt and

James Gahagan, 1967–1972, 1975, box 3, #3/5/897, folder 12—Faculty 45, March 15, 1970, Campus Unrest Collection, University Archives, Capen Hall, University at Buffalo, State University of New York (hereafter Pruitt and Gahagan Research, University at Buffalo Archives).

4. Georg Iggers, interview with the author, May 22, 2015, Amherst, NY.
5. Statement of Henry E. Urbanski, March 18, 1970, Press Release, March 15, 1970, in Axelrod to Interested Colleagues, April 21, 1970, box 3, #3/5/897, folder 12—Faculty 45, March 15, 1970, Pruitt and Gahagan Research, University at Buffalo Archives; Siggelkow, *Dissent and Disruption*, 203–5, 210.
6. "A Note on the Disposition of the Faculty 45 Case," n.d., in box 3, folder 12—Faculty 45, March 15, 1970, Pruitt and Gahagan Research, University at Buffalo Archives; Siggelkow, *Dissent and Disruption*, 211–18.
7. Siggelkow, *Dissent and Disruption*, 212.
8. Siggelkow, *Dissent and Disruption*, 80–83.
9. Siggelkow, *Dissent and Disruption*, 20, 80–81, 129; Michael Frisch, telephone interview with the author, July 19, 2013; Warren Bennis, *The Leaning Ivory Tower* (San Francisco: Jossey-Bass, 1973), 112–28. Bennis, an eminent administrator, had been recruited to Buffalo by Meyerson. His memoir provides a disillusioned insider's view of the crisis.
10. Siggelkow, *Dissent and Disruption*, 112; Bennis, *Leaning Ivory Tower*, 43; Kenneth J. Heineman, *Campus Wars: The Peace Movement at American State Universities in the Vietnam Era* (New York: New York University Press, 1993), 33–35, 68, 271.
11. Interview with Robert Watson of the BSU-PODER-OAAA Negotiating team by Jim Gahagan December 17, 1969, box 3, folder 7—Medical School Crisis, November 1969, Pruitt and Gahagan Research, University at Buffalo Archives.
12. Siggelkow, *Dissent and Disruption*, 59, 64–68, 99–101, 111; Peter Regan to University Community, November 10, 1969, box 3, folder 7—Medical School Crisis, November 1969, Pruitt and Gahagan Research, University at Buffalo Archives.
13. Siggelkow, *Dissent and Disruption*, 59.
14. Minutes, Faculty Senate special meeting, November 13, 1967, box 1, folder: Faculty Senate Minutes, Resolutions, etc., October 1967–1969; Richard Siggelkow to the Faculty Senate, December 6, 1967, box 1, folder: Faculty Senate Minutes, Resolutions, etc., October 1967–1969; handwritten memo, n.d.: all in Pruitt and Gahagan Research, University at Buffalo Archives. See also box 3, folder 4—Dow Chemical Co. controversy 1967, Campus Unrest Collection, Accession No. 33, RG 3/5/1, University at Buffalo Archives; Siggelkow, *Dissent and Disruption*, 69–71.
15. Minutes, Executive Committee, Faculty Senate, December 13, 1967, May 14, 1968, July 19, 1968, September 30, 1968; and Minutes of Faculty meeting, December 14, 1967: all in box 1, folder: Faculty Senate Minutes, Resolutions, etc., October 1967–1969, Pruitt and Gahagan Research, University at Buffalo

Archives. Handwritten chronology, December 1969, box 3, folder 7, Medical School Crisis, November 1969, Pruitt and Gahagan Research, University at Buffalo Archives.

16. There are two full folders of materials from the March 1969 teach-ins. Some samples: Authorized Statements from S.U.N.Y.A.B., n.d.; Memorandum to All Department Heads, March 3, 1969; mimeograph, "Teach-In Schedule for Wednesday" (March 5); "Proposed Agenda for Law School Faculty-Student Convocation on Friday, March 7, 1969, 10 A.M.; Bennis, Welch et al., memorandum, March 10, 1969; Teach-in Schedule for Thursday (March 6); memo, Dean Franklin M. Zweig to All Students and Faculty, March 4, 1969; leaflet from Dental School Students, n.d., box 1, folder: Teach-ins, Spring '69, February 28–March 5, 1969; list, Department of Mechanical Engineering, n.d.; mimeograph, Information Regarding the Day's Events, March 6, 1969; Teach-in Schedule, March 7, 1969, box 1, folder: Teach-in Spring '69, March 6–12, 1969: all in Campus Unrest Collection, Accession No. 33, RG 3/5/1, University at Buffalo Archives.

17. Siggelkow, *Dissent and Disruption*, 64–68, 97–99, 103; Bennis, *Leaning Ivory Tower*, 142.

18. Statement by Martin Meyerson, April 18, 1969, in box 1, folder: Faculty Senate Minutes, Resolutions, etc., October 1967–1969, Campus Unrest Collection, Accession No. 33, RG 3/5/1, University at Buffalo Archives.

19. Siggelkow, *Dissent and Disruption*, 141–46. Bill Vaccaro, "February 25, 1970: A History," 1993; and Spectrum Retrospect, mimeograph, "STRIKE DEMANDS," n.d.: both in scrapbook in Michael Frisch, personal papers (hereafter Frisch scrapbook).

20. "A Report to the University: A Reconstruction with Commentary of Critical Events on Wednesday, February 26, 1970," March 7, 1970. The Campus Unrest Collection in the University of Buffalo Archives contains numerous copies of this document, the so-called Greiner Report, named after the investigating committee's chair, law professor Charles Greiner. The one I photocopied came from the collection's Individual Collection, box 2, folder 7: Wilma Rizzo, Campus Handouts.

21. Bennis, *Leaning Ivory Tower*, 90; Siggelkow, *Dissent and Disruption*, 156–57; interview with James McGavern, March 14, 1972, box 37, folder 2: Faculty Interviews, Pruitt and Gahagan Research, University at Buffalo Archives.

22. "A Note on the Peace Patrol," n.d., box 5, folder 4: Peace Patrol, Pruitt and Gahagan Research, University at Buffalo Archives.

23. "The Crisis at the State University of New York at Buffalo: A Summary of Events and a Recommendation for Action," Executive Committee, SUNY/B Chapter, AAUP, April 5, 1970, in Frisch scrapbook.

24. *State University of N.Y. v. Denton*, November 5, 1970, 35 A.D.2d 176 (1970), https://www.leagle.com/decision/197021135ad2d1761164 (accessed July 1, 2018).

25. Siggelkow, *Dissent and Disruption*, 172; "A Note on the Peace Patrol," n.d.,

box 5, folder 4: Peace Patrol, Pruitt and Gahagan Research, University at Buffalo Archives.

26. Bennis, *Leaning Ivory Tower*, 44; Siggelkow, *Dissent and Disruption*, 137, 164; memo, Dean Franklin M. Zweig to All Students and Faculty, March 4, 1969, box 1, folder: Teach-ins, Spring '69, February 28–March 5, 1969; interview with William Baumer, August 25, 1970, and interview with Tom Connolly, May 24, 1971, box 3, folder 1: Faculty Interviews; Position Statement of the Council of the State University of New York at Buffalo, March 6, 1970, box 5, folder 2: all in Pruitt and Gahagan Research, University at Buffalo Archives.

27. Interview w. David Hayes [*sic*], n.d., box 5, folder 4: Peace Patrol, Pruitt and Gahagan Research, University at Buffalo Archives.

28. Baumer, interview, August 26, 1970; and Connolly, interview, May 24, 1971: both in box 3, folder 1: Faculty Interviews, Pruitt and Gahagan Research, University at Buffalo Archives.

29. For some examples, see Council of Deans and Chairs to Acting President Regan, March 8, 1970; Richard H. Cox and Robert Scigliano to Dear Colleague, March 2, 1970; French Department, memo, March 9, 1970; School of Management, memo, March 3, 1970, box 4, folder 13: Faculty Handouts: all in Pruitt and Gahagan Research, University at Buffalo Archives.

30. Peter Regan to Dear Colleagues, March 8, 1970, box 4, folder 13: Faculty Handouts, Pruitt and Gahagan Research, University at Buffalo Archives.

31. Peter Regan to Commissioner Frank N. Felicetta, March 7, 1970, box 5, folder 1, Pruitt and Gahagan Research, University at Buffalo Archives; leaflet, "Repression at the State University of New York at Buffalo," n.d., Frisch scrapbook; To Acting President Regan, 3/8/70, box 4, folder 13: Faculty Handouts, Pruitt and Gahagan Research, University at Buffalo Archives.

32. Walter Bennis to "Dear Peter," March 9, 1970; and "History Boycotts Classes," clipping, *Midnight Oil*, March 12, 1970: both in Frisch scrapbook. See also Minutes, Psychology Department faculty meeting, March 9, 1970, box 4, folder 13: Faculty Handouts, Pruitt and Gahagan Research, University at Buffalo Archives.

33. Michael Frisch, interview with the author, May 19, 2015, Buffalo, NY.

34. Minutes, Faculty Senate meeting, March 11, 1970, box 5, folder 1: Tentative Proposal for Consideration, March 15, 1970, 9 A.M., box 5, folder 10: University Survival Group, 1970, Pruitt and Gahagan Research, University at Buffalo Archives.

35. Bennis, *Leaning Ivory Tower*, 46, 50.

36. Minutes, Faculty Senate special meeting, March 17, 1970, box 5, folder 1, Pruitt and Gahagan Research, University at Buffalo Archives.

37. Siggelkow, *Dissent and Disruption*, 200. Interview with Tom Connolly, May 24, 1971, box 3, folder 1: Faculty Interviews; and "History of the University Survival Group," News Release, March 17, 1970, box 5, folder 10: University Survival Group, 1970: both in Pruitt and Gahagan Research, University at Buffalo Archives.

38. Handwritten note, report on meeting with Albany legislators, March 19, 1970, box 5, folder 9: University Survival Group, 1970, Pruitt and Gahagan Research, University at Buffalo Archives.

39. Bennis, *Leaning Ivory Tower*, 46–52, 129–36; Siggelkow, *Dissent and Disruption*, 227; Frisch, interview, July 19, 2013.

40. For a useful overview of faculty attitudes toward student unrest, see Everett Carll Ladd Jr. and Seymour Martin Lipset, *The Divided Academy: Professors and Politics* (New York: McGraw-Hill, 1975), 203–18; Neil J. Smelser, "Berkeley in Crisis and Change," in *Academic Transformation: Seventeen Institutions under Pressure*, ed. David Riesman and Verne A. Stadtman (New York: McGraw-Hill, 1973), 64.

41. Lawrence E. Eichel, Kenneth W. Jost, Robert D. Luskin, and Richard M. Neustadt, *The Harvard Strike* (Boston: Houghton Mifflin, 1970), 170.

42. Molly Levin and John Spiegel, "Point and Counterpoint in the Literature on Student Unrest," in *The Dynamics of University Protest*, ed. Donald Light Jr. and John Spiegel (Chicago: Nelson-Hall, 1977), 39; John Spiegel, "The Group Psychology of Campus Disorders" in *The Dynamics of University Protest*, ed. Light and Spiegel, 146, 148; Daniel Bell, "Columbia and the New Left," in *Confrontation: The Student Rebellion and the Universities*, ed. Daniel Bell and Irving Kristol (New York: Basic Books, 1969), 68.

43. Peter Stamberg, "From College Walk to the Stonewall Inn," in *A Time to Stir: Columbia '68*, ed. Paul Cronin (New York: Columbia University Press, 2018), 351; Reminiscences of Immanuel Wallerstein, May 17, 1968, 8, 16, in Columbia Oral History Project, Columbia Crisis of 1968 Project, Rare Books and Manuscripts Library, Butler Library, Columbia University (hereafter COHP).

44. The most useful single sources on the Columbia and Harvard crises are books by groups of student journalists: Jerry L. Avorn, with Andrew Crane, Mark Jaffe, Oren Root Jr., Paul Starr, Michael Stern, and Robert Stulberg, *Up Against the Ivy Wall: A History of the Columbia Crisis* (New York: Atheneum, 1968); and Eichel et al. *The Harvard Strike*.

45. Donald W. Light Jr., "Directed Resistance: The Structure of Tactics in Student Protest," in *The Dynamics of University Protest*, ed. Light and Spiegel, 85; Faculty Committee to Investigate the Dow Incident of Indiana University, "Indiana: The Anatomy of Violence," in *Protest! Student Activism in America*, ed. Julian Foster and Durward Long (New York: William Morrow, 1970), 230–33; Julian Foster, "Student Protest," in *Protest!*, Foster and Long, 409; Joy Williamson, *Black Power on Campus: The University of Illinois, 1965–1975* (Urbana: University of Illinois Press, 2003), 85–88.

46. Michael Garrett, "Attempting to Hold the Center at Columbia, 1968," in *A Time to Stir*, ed. Cronin, 65.

47. William R. Morgan, "Faculty Mediation in Campus Conflict," in *Protest!*, ed. Foster and Long, 376–77; on Columbia's decision not to prosecute, see Bennett Gershman, "In the Spirit of Reconciliation," in *A Time to Stir*, ed. Cronin; Michael Albert, *Remembering Tomorrow: From SDS to Life after Capitalism* (New

York: Seven Stories Press, 2006), 106–8; and Eichel et al., *The Harvard Strike*, 60–62.

48. Bernard Sklar, "Corporate Recruitment on Campus," in *Academic Supermarkets: A Critical Case Study of a Multiversity*, ed. Philip G. Altbach, Robert S. Laufer, and Sheila McVey (San Francisco: Jossey-Bass, 1971), 152–53.

49. Reminiscences of Richard Hofstadter, May 15, 1968, COHP, 28.

50. Eichel et al., *The Harvard Strike*, 167; Morton Keller and Phyllis Keller, *Making Harvard Modern: The Rise of America's University* (Cary, NC: Oxford University Press, 2001), 311; Spiegel, "The Group Psychology of Campus Disorders," in *Dynamics of University Protest*, ed. Light and Spiegel, 169; Peter Brooks, "Panther and Bulldog: Recalling May Day 1970," *Yale Review* 101, no. 3, 57.

51. Roger Rapoport and Laurence J. Kirshbaum, *Is the Library Burning?* (New York: Random House, 1969), 120, 127; Noam Chomsky, interview with the author, September 13, 2013, Cambridge, MA; Matthew Levin, *Cold War University: Madison and the New Left in the Sixties* (Madison: University of Wisconsin Press, 2013), 66–67; Allan Silver, interview with the author, June 19, 2013, New York City.

52. Eichel et al., *The Harvard Strike*, 58. For a response by other radical and antiwar professors, see Richard W. Lyman, *Stanford in Turmoil: Campus Unrest, 1966–1972* (Stanford, CA: Stanford General Books, 2009), 62.

53. Even at Berkeley, before police actions became more common, professors like Nathan Glazer and Henry Rosovsky begged Clark Kerr not to bring in the police. Henry Rosovsky, telephone interview with the author, May 15, 2013; Reminiscences of Walter Metzger, May 15, 1968, COHP, 2.

54. Reminiscences of Peter Kenen, May 16, 1968, COHP, 38; Eichel et al., *The Harvard Strike*, 161–64, 169; Avorn et al., *Up Against the Ivy Wall*, 70.

55. Morgan, "Faculty Mediation in Campus Conflict," in *Protest!*, ed. Foster and Long, 372.

56. On the media, see Todd Gitlin, *The Whole World Is Watching: Mass Media in the Making and Unmaking of the New Left* (Berkeley: University of California Press, 1980).

57. Noliwe M. Rooks, *White Money/Black Power: The Surprising History of African American Studies and the Crisis of Race in Higher Education* (Boston: Beacon Press, 2006), 34; Arlene Kaplan Daniels, "From Lecture Hall to Picket Line," in *Academics on the Line: The Faculty Strike at San Francisco State*, ed. Arlene Kaplan Daniels, Rachel Kahn-Hut, and Associates (San Francisco: Jossey-Bass, 1970), 44.

58. Avorn et al., *Up Against the Ivy Wall*, 181–98; Jeffrey A. Turner, *Sitting In and Speaking Out: Student Movements in the American South, 1960–1970* (Athens: University of Georgia Press, 2010), 210.

59. Eichel et al., *Harvard Strike*, 131; Gary Sprayberry, "Student Radicalism and the Antiwar Movement at the University of Alabama," in *Rebellion in Black and White: Southern Student Activism in the 1960s*, ed. Robert Cohen and David J. Snyder (Baltimore: Johns Hopkins University Press, 2013), 148–49, 163; Barry

Gottehrer, *The Mayor's Man: One Man's Struggle to Save Our Cities* (Garden City, NY: Doubleday, 1975), 179.

60. Sprayberry, "Student Radicalism," 165–66; Heineman, *Campus Wars*, 62; Turner, *Sitting In and Speaking Out*, 228; Ward Churchill and Jim Vander Wall, *The COINTELPRO Papers: Documents from the FBI's Secret Wars Against Domestic Dissent* (Boston: South End Press, 1990), 222–23, 226; Aaron J. Leonard with Conor A. Gallagher, *Heavy Radicals: The FBI's Secret War on America's Maoists, the Revolutionary Union/Revolutionary Communist Party, 1968–1980* (Winchester, UK: Zero Books, 2014), 68–69.

61. Rooks, *White Money/Black Power*, 34; Tom Bates, *Rads: The 1970 Bombing of the Army Math Research Center at the University of Wisconsin and Its Aftermath* (New York: HarperCollins, 1992); William H. Orrick Jr., *Shut It Down! A College in Crisis: A Report to the National Commission on the Causes and Prevention of Violence* (Washington, DC: National Commission on the Causes and Prevention of Violence, 1969), 380–89.

62. Donald Alexander Downs and Ilia Murtazashvili, *Arms and the University: Military Presence and the Civic Education of Non-Military Students* (New York: Cambridge University Press, 2012), 135, 140; Mary Ann Wynkoop, *Dissent in the Heartland: The Sixties at Indiana University* (Bloomington: Indiana University Press, 2002), 113; Paul Sigmund, "Princeton in Crisis and Change," in *Academic Transformation*, ed. Riesman and Stadtman, 264; Seth Rosenfeld, *Subversives: The FBI's War on Student Radicals, and Reagan's Rise to Power* (New York: Farrar, Straus and Giroux, 2012), 432–36.

63. William J. Bouwsma, *Historian of European Culture in the Early Modern Era, University of California, Berkeley, 1956–1991*, 166, interviews conducted by Ann Lage in 2000, Regional Oral History Office, Bancroft Library, University of California, Berkeley, 2008, https://digitalassets.lib.berkeley.edu/roho/ucb/text/bouwsma_william.pdf (hereafter Bouwsma, Bancroft Oral History); David R. Goddard and Linda C. Koons, "A Profile of the University of Pennsylvania," in *Academic Transformation*, ed. Riesman and Stadtman.

64. Rapoport and Kirshbaum, *Is the Library Burning?*, 25; Goddard and Koons, "A Profile of the University of Pennsylvania," in *Academic Transformation*, ed. Riesman and Stadtman, 235.

65. Rosenfeld, *Subversives*, 436–37; Williamson, *Black Power on Campus*, 97; Stephen J. Whitfield and Jonathan B. Krasner, "Jewish Liberalism and Racial Grievance in the Sixties: The Ordeal of Brandeis University," *Modern Judaism* 35, no. 1 (February 2015): 28, https://muse.jhu.edu/journals/modern_judaism/v035/35.1.whitfield.html (accessed June 30, 2017).

66. Nancy Zaroulis and Gerald Sullivan, *Who Spoke Up? American Protest Against the War in Vietnam, 1963–1975* (Garden City, NY: Doubleday, 1984), 238; Robert Smith, Richard Axen, and DeVere Pentony, *By Any Means Necessary: The Revolutionary Struggle at San Francisco State* (San Francisco: Jossey-Bass, 1970), 226. Rosenheim to "Dear alumnus," n.d., box 127, folder 3; and G. L. Lee Jr. to Earl J. McGrath, November 20, 1970, box 121, folder 14: both in Office

of the President, Levi Administration Records, Department of Special Collections, University of Chicago Library (hereafter Office of the President, Levi Administration Records).

67. Eichel et al., *The Harvard Strike*, 279; Keller and Keller, *Making Harvard Modern*, 317; William M. Chace, *100 Semesters: My Adventures as Student, Professor, and University President and What I Learned along the Way* (Princeton, NJ: Princeton University Press, 2006), 149.

68. Donald Alexander Downs, *Cornell '69: Liberalism and the Crisis of the American University* (Ithaca, NY: Cornell University Press, 1999), 69, 214; Martin Lipset to David Riesman, January 31, 1969, in David Riesman Papers, box 17, HUG (FP) 99.12, Harvard University Archives, Nathan M. Pusey Library, Cambridge, MA.

69. Siggelkow, *Dissent and Disruption*, 126.

70. Sprayberry, "Student Radicalism," 155.

71. Gordon Fellman, interview with the author, September 12, 2013, Waltham, MA; Whitfield and Krasner, "Jewish Liberalism and Racial Grievance"; Richard Flacks, telephone interview with the author, June 20, 2013; Martha Biondi, *The Black Revolution on Campus* (Berkeley: University of California Press, 2012), 84–85.

72. Jack Zipes, telephone interview with the author, March 8, 2013; News Bureau, NYU, "The Disruptions at Loeb, Courant, and Kimball: A report to the New York University community on the occupation of three University buildings at Washington Square during the Cambodian crisis period of May 1970," Collection: NYU in the 1970s, New York University Archives, Elmer Holmes Bobst Library, New York University; Lyman, *Stanford in Turmoil*, 181–84; David R. Seager, "Repression in Academia: New Left and Antiwar College Teachers and Political Dissent in the Vietnam War Era, 1964–1975" (PhD diss., University of Maine, 1995), 12–13.

73. Leon Wofsy, "When the FSM Disturbed the Faculty Peace," in *The Free Speech Movement: Reflections on Berkeley in the 1960s*, ed. Robert Cohen and Reginald E. Zelnik (Berkeley: University of California Press, 2002), 353–54; Siggelkow, *Dissent and Disruption*, 213; "Conference on Southern Illinois Vietnamese Studies Center, October 23–24, 1970," *CCAS Newsletter*, November 1970, in Joseph Esherick, personal papers.

74. Douglas Dowd, "Whose Academic Freedom?" Statement to the Committee on Academic Freedom and Tenure of the Cornell Constituent Assembly, May 1969, in *The University Crisis Reader*, ed. Immanuel Wallerstein and Paul Starr, vol. 2, *Confrontation and Counterattack* (New York: Random House, 1971), 64.

75. Flacks, interview, June 20, 2013; Jesse Lemisch, interview with the author, February 5, 2013, New York City; Troy Duster, telephone interview with the author, May 1, 2013; Bill Zimmerman, *Troublemaker: A Memoir from the Front Lines of the Sixties* (New York: Doubleday, 2011), 169; Seager, "Repression in Academia," 98, 113–14; William J. McGill, *The Year of the Monkey: Revolt on Campus, 1968–69* (New York: McGraw-Hill, 1982), 60; Bruce M. Stave,

Red Brick in the Land of Steady Habits: Creating the University of Connecticut, 1881–2006 (Hanover, NH: University Press of New England, 2006), 128; Jeff Kaye, "DHS Says FBI 'Possibly Funded' Terrorist Group," ShadowProof, February 20, 2013, https://shadowproof.com/2013/02/20/dhs-says-fbi-possibly-funded-terrorist-group/ (accessed November 23, 2019); Ward Churchill and Jim Vander Wall, *Agents of Repression: The FBI's Secret War Against the Black Panther Party and the American Indian Movement* (Boston: South End Press, 1988), 182.

76. William Sloane Coffin Jr., *Once to Every Man: A Memoir* (New York: Atheneum, 1978), 258–59.

77. Bob Feldman, "A People's Prehistory of Columbia, 1968," in *A Time to Stir*, ed. Cronin, 52.

78. Avorn et al., *Up Against the Ivy Wall*, 89, 96, 101; Zimmerman, *Troublemaker*, 164–65; Metzger, COHP, 15; Silver, interview, June 19, 2013; Allan Silver, in *A Time to Stir*, dir. Paul Cronin, 2018. This massive documentary may never be publicly shown because of copyright, not to mention length, issues. I saw a special screening of portions at Columbia in 2018 and took notes.

79. Cushing Strout and David I. Grossvogel, eds., *Divided We Stand: Reflections on the Crisis at Cornell* (Garden City, NY: Doubleday, 1970), 20.

80. Thomas M. Grace, *Kent State: Death and Dissent in the Long Sixties* (Amherst: University of Massachusetts Press, 2016), 99, 139, 158–59; Heineman, *Campus Wars*, 37, 175–76; Julian Foster and Durward Long, "The Dynamics of Institutional Response," in *Protest!*, ed. Foster and Long, 433.

81. Rapoport and Kirshbaum, *Is the Library Burning?*, 66–67.

82. Eichel et al., *The Harvard Strike*, 87–89; Avorn et al., *Up Against the Ivy Wall*, 55–77; Foster, "Student Protest," 415–16.

83. Rosenfeld, *Subversives*, 425; Robert J. Norrell, *Reaping the Whirlwind: The Civil Rights Movement in Tuskegee* (New York: Knopf, 1985), 192–94; Rapoport and Kirshbaum, *Is the Library Burning?*, 146; Turner, *Sitting In and Speaking Out*, 187; "The Tuskegee Revolt: SNCC, Black Power, the Legacy of Booker T. Washington and the Assassination of M.L.K., Jr.," interview with Alashe Michael Oshooshi, by Brian Jones, 2016, oshoosi.com/Tuskegee-movement-sncc.html (accessed July 12, 2018); Strout and Grossvogel, *Divided We Stand*, 13; Smith, Axen, and Pentony, *By Any Means Necessary*, 128; Biondi, *Black Revolution on Campus*, 39–40.

84. Eichel et al., *The Harvard Strike*, 287.

85. Avorn et al., *Up Against the Ivy Wall*, 62; Raymond M. Brown, in *A Time to Stir*, dir. Cronin; Wallerstein, COHP, 34; Gene Slater, "Uniters," in *A Time to Stir*, ed. Cronin, 326.

86. Arthur K. Bierman, "Oral History," 87, interviewed by Peter Carroll, January 14, 17, 28, 1992, Labor Archives and Research Center, San Francisco State University (hereafter LARC, SFSU); Duster, interview, May 1, 2013; Biondi, *Black Revolution on Campus*, 70; Brian Glick, *War at Home: Covert Action Against U.S. Activists and What We Can Do about It* (Boston: South End Press, 1989), 16–18; Churchill and Vander Wall, *The COINTELPRO Papers*, 130–33; Mike

Davis and Jon Wiener, *Set the Night on Fire: L.A. in the Sixties* (London: Verso, 2020).

87. Downs, *Cornell '69*, 178; Strout and Grossvogel, *Divided We Stand*, 24–25; William H. Friedland and Harry Edwards, "Confrontation at Cornell," in *Campus Power Struggle*, ed. Howard S. Becker (Piscataway, NJ: Transaction Books, 1970), 89.

88. Zelda Gamson, "Michigan Muddles Through," in *Academic Transformation*, ed. Riesman and Stadtman, 84; McGill, *Year of the Monkey*, 127; Karla Spurlock-Evans, "Forming Community, Forging Commitment: A Hamilton Hall Story," in *A Time to Stir*, ed. Cronin, 343.

89. Robert W. Hanning, "The Great Morningside Rising," 108; and Slater, "Uniters," 326: both in *A Time to Stir*, ed. Cronin,; Robert A. McCaughey, *Stand, Columbia: A History of Columbia University in the City of New York, 1754–2004* (New York: Columbia University Press, 2003), 442.

90. Metzger, COHP, 9–11; Silver, interview, June 19, 2013.

91. Wallerstein, COHP, 47–49; Wayne Glasker, *Black Students in the Ivory Tower: African American Activism at the University of Pennsylvania, 1967–1990* (Amherst: University of Massachusetts Press, 2002), 51.

92. Dikran Karagueuzian, *Blow It Up! The Black Student Revolt at San Francisco State College and the Emergence of Dr. Hayakawa* (Boston: Gambit, 1971), 54, 73–83, 177; James Benét, "Interpretation and Objectivity in Journalism," in *Academics on the Line*, ed. Daniels, Kahn-Hut et al., 114–15; Kay Boyle, *The Long Walk at San Francisco State and Other Essays* (New York: Grove Press, 1970), 51–52; Orrick, *Shut It Down!*, 137–38; Smith, Axen, and Pentony, *By Any Means Necessary*, 123, 226–27.

93. Lawrence E. Eichel, "The Founding of the Afro-American Studies Department: The Crisis of 1969," in *Blacks at Harvard: A Documentary History of African-American Experience at Harvard and Radcliffe*, ed. Werner Sollors, Caldwell Titcomb, and Thomas A. Underwood (New York: New York University Press, 1993), 386.

94. Raymond M. Brown, "Race and the Specter of Strategic Blindness," 15, 23–24 and Jay Kriegel, "Getting Back to 'Life as Normal,'": both in *A Time to Stir*, ed. Cronin, 179–83.

95. Rosenfeld, *Subversives*, 433; Siggelkow, *Dissent and Disruption*, 127.

96. Smith, Axen, and Pentony, *By Any Means Necessary*, 145–46.

97. Eric Foner, interview with the author, March 26, 2013, New York City; Eric Foner, "My Life as a Historian," in *Historians and Race: Autobiography and the Writing of History*, ed. Paul A. Cimbala and Robert F. Himmelberg (Bloomington: Indiana University Press, 1996), 99; Dan T. Carter, "Deep South Campus Memories and the World the Sixties Made," in *Rebellion in Black and White*, ed. Cohen and Snyder, xiii.

98. Bierman, "Oral History," 96–97, LARC, SFSU.

99. Durward Long, "Black Protest," in *Protest!*, ed. Foster and Long, 474.

100. John H. Bunzel, "Black Studies at San Francisco State," in *Confrontation*, ed.

Bell and Kristol, 23–43; Bierman, "Oral History," 109, LARC, SFSU; Smith, Axen, and Pentony, *By Any Means Necessary*, 132–33, 259, 302.

101. Eichel et al., *Harvard Strike*, 219–20; Seymour Martin Lipset and David Riesman, *Education and Politics at Harvard* (New York: McGraw Hill, 1975), 231.

102. Leaflet, n.d., and Chas. D. O'Connell to Edward Levi, John T. Wilson, February 2, 1971, box 121, folder 14, Office of the President, Levi Administration Records; *Measure*, no. 7, March 1970, in Oscar Handlin Papers, box 27, Harvard University Archives, Nathan M. Pusey Library, Cambridge, MA; Marshall W. Meyer, "After the Bust: Student Politics at Harvard, 1969–1972," in *Academic Transformation*, ed. Riesman and Stadtman, 135.

103. Brooks, "Panther and Bulldog: Recalling May Day 1970"; Downs, *Cornell '69*, 240–42.

104. Nick Aaron Ford, *Black Studies: Threat-or-Challenge* (Port Washington, NY: Kennikat Press, 1973), 160; Long, "Black Protest," in *Protest!*, ed. Foster and Long, 479; Smith, Axen, and Pentony, *By Any Means Necessary*, 41–42.

105. Foner, "My Life as a Historian," 99; Foner, interview, March 26, 2013.

106. Carter, "Deep South Campus Memories," in *Rebellion in Black and White*, ed. Cohen and Snyder, xiii.

107. Long, "Black Protest," 478–79.

108. Harry Edwards, *The Struggle That Must Be: An Autobiography* (New York: Macmillan, 1980), 170–71; Jelani Favors, "North Carolina A&T Black Power Activists and the Student Organization for Black Unity," in *Rebellion in Black and White*, ed. Cohen and Snyder, 270.

109. Williamson, *Black Power on Campus*, 86; Cushing Strout, "A Personal Narrative," in *Divided We Stand*, ed. Strout and Grossvogel, 49.

110. Zimmerman, *Troublemaker*, 168; Turner, *Sitting In and Speaking Out*, 190; Biondi, *Black Revolution on Campus*, 119–20.

111. Kenen, COHP, 12.

112. Sklar, "Corporate Recruitment on Campus, in *Academic Supermarkets*, ed. Altbach, Laufer, and McVey, 136–37; Rapoport and Kirshbaum, *Is the Library Burning?*, 60–61.

113. Kenneth M. Dolbeare, "Faculty Power," in *Academic Supermarkets*, ed. Altbach, Laufer, and McVey, 168; Algo Henderson, "San Francisco State College," in *Academic Transformation*, ed. Riesman and Stadtman, 298–300; Faculty Committee, "Indiana: The Anatomy of Violence," in *Protest!*, ed. Foster and Long, 244; American Council on Education, Report of the Special Committee on Campus Tensions, Sol. M. Linowitz, Chair, text in *Chronicle of Higher Education*, April 27, 1970, in box 21, folder 21, Office of the President, Levi Administration Records.

114. Bouwsma, Bancroft Oral History, 74; Carl E. Schorske, *Intellectual Life, Civil Libertarian Issues, and the Student Movement at the University of California, Berkeley, 1960–1969*, 47, interviews conducted by Ann Lage, in 1996, 1997, Regional Oral History Office, Bancroft Library, University of California, 2000,

http://digitalassets.lib.berkeley.edu/rohoia/ucb/text/intelllifecivilooschorich
.pdf.

115. Howard S. Becker, "Introduction: The Struggle for Power on the Campus," in *Campus Power Struggle*, ed. Becker, 9–10.

116. William Leuchtenberg, in *A Time to Stir*, dir. Cronin.

117. Avorn et al., *Up Against the Ivy Wall*, 139–41; Kenen, COHP, 21; Bell, "Columbia and the New Left," 81.

118. John Blum considered Staughton Lynd "excessively emotional, hyperbolically emotional, not subject to rational discourse about either urban racial issues or/and the war in Vietnam." Geoffrey Kabaservice, *The Guardians: Kingman Brewster, His Circle, and the Rise of the Liberal Establishment* (New York: Henry Holt, 2004), 256–57. See also Reminiscences of Polykarp Kusch, May 17, 1968, COHP, 3; Charles Kadushin, *The American Intellectual Elite* (New York: Little, Brown, 1974), 277–79.

119. Martin Edward Malia, *Historian of Russian and European Intellectual History*, interviews conducted by David Engerman in 2003, Regional Oral History Office, Bancroft Library, University of California, Berkeley, 2005, https:// digitalassets.lib.berkeley.edu/roho/ucb/text/MaliaBook.pdf; John Hope Franklin, statement February 7, 1969, box 127, folder 4, Office of the President, Levi Administration Records.

120. Robert E. Marshak, *Academic Renewal in the 1970s: Memoirs of a City College President* (Washington DC: University Press of America, 1982), 14; Smith, Axen, and Pentony, *By Any Means Necessary*, 193.

121. Wynkoop, *Dissent in the Heartland*, 59; Lyman, *Stanford in Turmoil*, 40; Morgan, "Faculty Mediation in Campus Conflict," in *Protest!*, ed. Foster and Long, 372.

122. Siggelkow, *Dissent and Disruption*, 101–4, 190–91.

123. Lyman, *Stanford in Turmoil*, 104.

Chapter Thirteen

1. Matthew Levin, *Cold War University: Madison and the New Left in the Sixties* (Madison: University of Wisconsin Press, 2013), 154–57.

2. Everett Carll Ladd Jr. and Seymour Martin Lipset, *The Divided Academy: Professors and Politics* (New York: McGraw-Hill, 1975), 108–22, 137–44, 189–97.

3. Ronald Grele, interview with the author, January 22, 2015, New York City; David Kettler to Bob Ross, August 5, 1968, box 3, file 6, New University Conference Papers, Wisconsin Historical Society, Madison (hereafter NUC Papers, WHS); David Kettler, "Oral History," interview by Kevlin Haire, 2011, Ohio State University Archives, https://kb.osu.edu/handle/1811/48370; Kenneth M. Dolbeare, "Faculty Power," in *Academic Supermarkets: A Critical Case Study of a Multiversity*, ed. Philip G. Altbach, Robert S. Laufer, and Sheila McVey (San Francisco: Jossey-Bass, 1971), 160–63; Paul Mangelsdorf Jr., "Swarthmore

Knocks on Wood," in *Academic Transformation: Seventeen Institutions under Pressure*, ed. David Riesman and Verne A. Stadtman (New York: McGraw-Hill, 1973), 334; William J. Bouwsma, *Historian of European Culture in the Early Modern Era, University of California, Berkeley, 1956–1991*, 81, interviews conducted by Ann Lage in 2000, Regional Oral History Office, Bancroft Library, University of California, Berkeley, 2008, https://digitalassets.lib.berkeley.edu/roho/ucb/text/bouwsma_william.pdf (hereafter Bouwsma, Bancroft Oral History); American Council on Education, Report of Special Committee on Campus Tensions, Sol. M. Linowitz, chair, text in *Chronicle of Higher Education*, April 27, 1970, in Office of the President, Levi Administration Records, box 21, folder 21, University of Chicago Archives, Department of Special Collections, University of Chicago Library (hereafter Office of the President, Levi Administration Records).

4. Dolbeare, "Faculty Power," 64; Sheila McVey, "Departmental Clashes," in *Academic Supermarkets*, ed. Altbach, Laufer, and McVey, 162, 229; Arthur K. Bierman, "Oral History," 24–25, interviewed by Peter Carroll, January 14, 17, 28, 1992, Labor Archives and Research Center, San Francisco State University (hereafter LARC, SFSU); David Kettler to Bob Ross, August 5, 1968, box 3, file 6, NUC Papers, WHS; E. Alden Dunham, *Colleges of the Forgotten Americans: A Profile of State Colleges and Regional Universities* (New York: McGraw-Hill, 1969), 23, 139–44; Lawrence B. de Graaf, "Howard: The Evolution of a Black Student Revolt," in *Protest! Student Activism in America*, ed. Julian Foster and Durward Long (New York: William Morrow, 1970), 321–22, 328–29; testimony of James B. Jones, November 3, 1967, in "Riots, Civil and Criminal Disorders," Hearings before the Permanent Subcommittee on Investigations of the Committee on Government Operations, US Senate, 90th Cong., 1st sess., November 1, 2, 3, 6, 1967 (Washington, DC: US Government Printing Office, 1967), 261–72.

5. Bruce Franklin, interview with the author, February 14, 2013, Montclair, NJ.

6. Richard Mann, telephone interview with the author, November 14, 2014.

7. Allan Silver, interview with the author, June 19, 2013, New York City.

8. Minutes, Committee of the Council, October 7, 1968; A. A. Albert to Committee of the Council, February 21, 1969; and Minutes, Council of the University Senate, January 14, 1969: all in box 106, folder 3, Office of the President, Levi Administration Records.

9. John Womack, interview with the author, April 1, 2013, Cambridge, MA; Frederick A. Siegler, "Comments on Several Issues," box 121, folder 14, Office of the President, Levi Administration Records; Sheila Delaney, interview with the author, March 29, 2016, New York City.

10. American Council on Education, Report of the Special Committee on Campus Tensions, Sol. M. Linowitz, chair, text in *Chronicle of Higher Education*, April 27, 1970, box 21, folder 21, Office of the President, Levi Administration Records.

11. William R. Morgan, "Faculty Mediation in Campus Conflict," in *Protest!*, ed. Foster and Long, 374.

12. Donald Light Jr., "The Dynamics of Faculty Response to Student Protest," in *The Dynamics of University Protest*, ed. Donald Light Jr. and John Spiegel (Chicago: Nelson-Hall, 1977), 101.

13. Jerry L. Avorn with Andrew Crane, Mark Jaffe, Oren Root Jr., Paul Starr, Michael Stern, and Robert Stulberg, *Up Against the Ivy Wall: A History of the Columbia Crisis* (New York: Atheneum, 1968), 69–77; Reminiscences of Immanuel Wallerstein, May 17, 1968, 36, 75, Columbia Oral History Project, Columbia Crisis of 1968 Project, Rare Books and Manuscripts Library, Butler Library, Columbia University (hereafter COHP); Eric Foner, interview with the author, March 26, 2013, New York City.

14. Benson Snyder, "Change Despite Turmoil at MIT," in *Academic Transformation*, ed. Riesman and Stadtman, 169; Cushing Strout and David I. Grossvogel, eds., *Divided We Stand: Reflections on the Crisis at Cornell* (Garden City, NY: Doubleday, 1970), 69, 222; W. V. Quine, quoted in Richard A. Siggelkow, *Dissent and Disruption: A University under Siege* (Buffalo: Prometheus Books, 1991), 130; Adam Ulam, *The Fall of the American University* (LaSalle, IL: Library Press, 1972), 140; Fran Geteles, interview with the author, February 17, 2014, New York City; "Extraordinary Meeting of the Academic Senate," n.d. [1966], box 121, folder 14, in Office of the President, Levi Administration Records; Council minutes, February 17, 1969, box 127, folder 3, Office of the President, Levi Administration Records.

15. McVey, "Departmental Clashes," in *Academic Supermarkets*, ed. Altbach, Laufer, and McVey, 254.

16. Eric Solomon, "Oral History," interviewed by Peter Carroll, February 2, 1992, 9, LARC, SFSU; see also Rachel Kahn-Hut, "Going Radical," in *Academics on the Line: The Faculty Strike at San Francisco State*, ed. Arlene Kaplan Daniels, Rachel Kahn-Hut, and Associates (San Francisco: Jossey-Bass, 1970), 36–37.

17. Bouwsma, Bancroft Oral History, 71, 94.

18. Carol Smith, interview with the author, date unknown, New York City; Walter Daum, interview with the author, January 10, 2018, New York City; Howard Adelson, Morris Ettenberg, Marnin Feinstein, Lloyd Gartner, Louis Heller, Benjamin Klebaner, and Gerard Sorkin, leaflet, n.d. [October 1969], in Jacob Rothenberg Papers, box 5, folder: History Department Minutes, 1969, CCNY Archives and Special Collections, Cohen Library, City College of New York, City University of New York.

19. Michael Walzer, interview with the author, May 13, 2013, New York City; Lawrence E. Eichel, Kenneth W. Jost, Robert D. Luskin, and Richard M. Neustadt, *The Harvard Strike* (Boston: Houghton Mifflin, 1970), 159–64.

20. Donald Alexander Downs, *Cornell '69: Liberalism and the Crisis of the American University* (Ithaca, NY: Cornell University Press, 1999), 218–19.

21. Dolbeare, "Faculty Power," 63–64; and Bernard Sklar, "Anatomy of Faculty

Conflict," 190–209: both in *Academic Supermarkets*, ed. Altbach, Laufer, and McVey.

22. Donald Light Jr., "Directed Resistance," in *The Dynamics of University Protest*, ed. Light and Spiegel, 86.

23. Wallerstein, COHP, May 17, 1968; Doug Dowd, *Blues for America: A Critique, a Lament, and Some Memories* (New York: Monthly Review Press, 1997), 161.

24. Avorn et al., *Up Against the Ivy Wall*, 140, 161; Reminiscences of Richard Hofstadter, COHP, May 15, 1968, 5–7; Reminiscences of Walter Metzger, COHP, May 15, 1968, 17–20; Light, "Dynamics of Faculty Response," 111, 114.

25. Avorn et al., *Up Against the Ivy Wall*, 163; Silver, interview, June 19, 2013.

26. Evan Stark, "Talking Sociology: A Sixties Fragment," in *Radical Sociologists and the Movement: Experiences, Lessons, and Legacies*, ed. Martin Oppenheimer, Martin J. Murray, and Rhonda F. Levine (Philadelphia: Temple University Press, 1991), 68; Light, "Dynamics of Faculty Response," 106. For an extended discussion of the views of right-wing faculty members about their more liberal colleagues, see chapter 17.

27. Avorn et al., *Up Against the Ivy Wall*, 172; Barry Gottehrer, *The Mayor's Man: One Man's Struggle to Save Our Cities* (Garden City, NY: Doubleday, 1975), 163–68; Reminiscences of Polykarp Kusch, COHP, 12.

28. Warren Bennis, *The Leaning Ivory Tower* (San Francisco: Jossey-Bass, 1973), 42.

29. Avorn et al., *Up Against the Ivy Wall*, 232.

30. John R. Searle, *The Campus War: A Sympathetic Look at the University in Agony* (New York: World, 1971), 116–17.

31. Geoffrey Kabaservice, *The Guardians: Kingman Brewster, His Circle, and the Rise of the Liberal Establishment* (New York: Henry Holt, 2004), 353–54. MIT was another institution that maintained reasonable relationships with its radicals. See Michael Albert, *Remembering Tomorrow: From SDS to Life after Capitalism* (New York: Seven Stories Press, 2006), 78–79, 93, 102–3; Noam Chomsky, interview with the author, September 13, 2013, Cambridge, MA; Snyder, "Change Despite Turmoil at MIT," in *Academic Transformation*, ed. Riesman and Stadtman, 156–59.

32. Archibald Cox et al., *Crisis at Columbia: Report of the Fact-Finding Commission Appointed to Investigate the Disturbances at Columbia University in April and May 1968* (New York: Vintage, 1968), 34, 50–51, 68 (hereafter Cox Report).

33. Gottehrer, *Mayor's Man*, 179.

34. Dan Pellegrom, "Silence Is Compliance," in *A Time to Stir: Columbia '68*, ed. Paul Cronin (New York: Columbia University Press, 2018), 244.

35. Avorn et al., *Up Against the Ivy Wall*, 12, 148.

36. Avorn et al., *Up Against the Ivy Wall*, 119; Cox Report, 49.

37. Avorn et al., *Up Against the Ivy Wall*, 22, 78–79, 102, 132, 144, 149, 156.

38. Avorn et al., *Up Against the Ivy Wall*, 43–44.

39. Avorn et al., *Up Against the Ivy Wall*, 170–71.

40. Reminiscences of Peter Kenen, May 16, 1968, COHP, 18.

41. Kabaservice, *The Guardians*, 351.

42. Avorn et al., *Up Against the Ivy Wall*, 167, 199.

43. Cox Report, 122.

44. Metzger, COHP, 16–18; Wallerstein, COHP, 86–89; Avorn et al., *Up Against the Ivy Wall*, 108–9, 134–35; Cox Report, 148–53.

45. Kusch, COHP, 7; Hofstadter, COHP, 7–10; Kenen, COHP, 35.

46. Cox Report, 195–96.

47. Eichel et al., *The Harvard Strike*, 43; Morton Keller and Phyllis Keller, *Making Harvard Modern: The Rise of America's University* (Cary, NC: Oxford University Press, 2001), 310; Richard M. Freeland, *Academia's Golden Age: Universities in Massachusetts, 1945–1970* (New York: Oxford University Press, 1992), 174.

48. Albert, *Remembering Tomorrow*, 100–101; Faculty Committee to Investigate the Dow Incident of Indiana University, "Indiana: The Anatomy of Violence," 230–31; and Morgan, "Faculty Mediation in Campus Conflict," 370, both in *Protest!*, ed. Foster and Long.

49. Eichel et al., *The Harvard Strike*, 109–10; Julian Foster and Durward Long, "The Dynamics of Institutional Response," in *Protest!*, ed. Foster and Long, 430.

50. Kabaservice, *The Guardians*, 384; Eichel et al., *Harvard Strike*, 38–39.

51. Eichel et al., *The Harvard Strike*, 10, 156, 173–75; Seymour Martin Lipset and David Riesman, *Education and Politics at Harvard* (New York: McGraw Hill, 1975), 220–21; Keller and Keller, *Making Harvard Modern*, 327–35.

52. Robert Smith, Richard Axen, and DeVere Pentony, *By Any Means Necessary: The Revolutionary Struggle at San Francisco State* (San Francisco: Jossey-Bass, 1970); Light, "Dynamics of Faculty Response," 101; Rachel Kahn-Hut, "Which Side Are You On?" in *Academics on the Line*, ed. Daniels, Kahn-Hut et al., 165.

53. Smith, Axen, and Pentony, *By Any Means Necessary*, 238–71; Solomon, "Oral History," 27–37, LARC, SFSU.

54. The most useful and detailed, though hardly unbiased, account of the Cornell crisis is Downs, *Cornell '69*, 222–29. See also the essays in Strout and Grossvogel, *Divided We Stand*, as well as William H. Friedland and Harry Edwards, "Confrontation at Cornell," in *Campus Power Struggle*, ed. Howard S. Becker (Piscataway, NJ: Transaction Books, 1970), 79–99. A useful chronology can be found in Strout and Grossvogel, *Divided We Stand*, 3–33.

55. Betty Mills and Richard M. Warshauer, "Faculty Takes Controversial Stand," *Cornell Daily Sun*, April 22, 1969.

56. Tom Jones, quoted in Downs, *Cornell '69*, 240.

57. Strout and Grossvogel, *Divided We Stand*, 32–33; Eldon Kenworthy, "The Non-Militant Students," in *Divided We Stand*, ed. Strout and Grossvogel, 84; Downs, *Cornell '69*, 233–37, 247–48.

58. George McT. Kahin, "Address in Barton Hall, April 25, 1969," in *Divided We Stand*, ed. Strout and Grossvogel, 39; Howard M. Feinstein, "April 1969: A Celebration of the Mass," in *Divided We Stand*, ed. Strout and Grossvogel, 105.

59. Downs, *Cornell '69*, 259.

60. Feinstein, "April 1969," in *Divided We Stand*, ed. Strout and Grossvogel, 90.

61. Milton R. Konvitz, "Why One Professor Changed His Vote," *New York Times*, May 18, 1969.

62. Among the émigrés besides Bloom, Kagan, Sindler, and Berns were David Brian Davis and Thomas Sowell. Clinton Rossiter, who had proposed the nullification resolution at the second faculty meeting, committed suicide about a year later.

63. Downs, *Cornell '69*, 265.

64. Downs, *Cornell '69*, 271–72.

65. Downs, *Cornell '69*, 93.

66. Downs, *Cornell '69*, 282; Homer Bigart, "Cornell Bears Scars of Conflict; Faculty Is Divided Over Perkins," *New York Times*, May 28, 1969, 1, 30.

67. Nathan Glazer, "City College," in *Academic Transformation*, ed. Riesman and Stadtman, 87–88; Philip Barnett, Judy Connorton, William Gibbons, and Sydney Van Nort, "Five Demands: The Student Protest and Takeover of 1968," pamphlet, n.d. [c. 2009], CCNY Archives and Special Collections, Cohen Library, City College of New York; Robert E. Marshak, *Academic Renewal in the 1970s: Memoirs of a City College President* (Washington, DC: University Press of America, 1982), 14–19.

68. C. Vann Woodward to Tom Kahn, May 12, 1970, in *The Letters of C. Vann Woodward*, ed. Michael O'Brien (New Haven, CT: Yale University Press, 2013), 282.

69. Kingman Brewster to John Perry Miller, April 6, 1969, box 121, folder 14, Office of the President, Levi Administration Records; Kabaservice, *The Guardians*, 352–57.

70. Hester Eisenstein, interview with the author, April 7, 2015, New York City; Peter Brooks, "Panther and Bulldog: Recalling May Day 1970," *Yale Review* 101, no. 3, 59.

71. Dan Georgakas and Marvin Surkin, *Detroit: I Do Mind Dying: A Study in Urban Revolution* (New York: St. Martin's Press, 1975), 57–73; Ernst Benjamin, interview with the author, June 27, 2013, Silver Spring, MD.

72. William H. Exum, *Paradoxes of Protest: Black Student Activism in a White University* (Philadelphia: Temple University Press, 1985), 62–77. For other schools that seemed to avoid serious trouble, see Thomas H. Eliot to Edward Levi, January 6, 1969 (Washington University, St. Louis); and William Trombley, "Student Power," *Los Angeles Times*, May 12, 1969 (Antioch): both in box 126, folder 9, Office of the President, Levi Administration Records.

73. Freeland, *Academia's Golden Age*, 232; Stephen J. Whitfield and Jonathan B. Krasner, "Jewish Liberalism and Racial Grievance in the Sixties: The Ordeal of Brandeis University," *Modern Judaism* 35, no.1 (February 2015), 28, https://muse.jhu.edu/journals/modern_judaism/v035/35.1.whitfield.html (accessed June 30, 2017); Gordon Fellman, interview with the author, September 12, 2013, Waltham, MA; Robert A. Jordan and William A. Davis, "Blacks End Brandeis Sit-In; Win Amnesty in Compromise," *Boston Globe*, January 19, 1969, clipping in box 126, folder 9, Office of the President, Levi Administration Records.

74. "Boston U. Gives In," *Chicago Tribune*, April 25, 1969, clipping in box 121, folder 14, Office of the President, Levi Administration Records; de Graaf, "Howard," in Foster and Long, eds., *Protest!*, 337–38; Orville Schell, Vice Chair Board of Trustees, November 1, 1969, in Black Studies Sit-In Records (1966–1974), box 3, folder 1, Vassar College Archives; James A. Rubenstein, "Williams Take-Over Ceases; Non-Negotiable Demands Met," *Vassar Miscellany*, April 7, 1969.

75. Office of Public Information, Chronology of Events Concerning the Nonreappointment of Mrs. Marlene Dixon to the Faculty of the University of Chicago, January 30, 1969; and Chronology, February 10, 1969: both in box 127, folder 4, Office of the President, Levi Administration Records. For a sample of these statements, see Alan Gewirth, "Open Letter to the Sit-Inners," February 10, 1969; Statement from Faculty of Graduate School of Education, February 13, 1969; Charles Huggins to Edward Levi, February 14, 1969; and O. J. Kleppa, statement, February 5, 1969: all in Levi Administration Records, box 125, folder 1; John Hope Franklin, statement February 7, 1969, box 127, folder 4, Office of the President, Levi Administration Records.

76. Bruce Norton, "Faculty Holds Vigil Against Discipline," *Maroon*, April 15, 1969, clipping in box 125, folder 1, Office of the President, Levi Administration Records.

77. Philip Meyer, "Campus Officials Flunk Big Test, Says Sociologist," *Detroit Free Press*, April 27, 1969, clipping in box 123, folder 1; and Wm. Benton to Edward Levi, April 29, 1969, box 126, folder 2: both in Office of the President, Levi Administration Records.

78. Kingman Brewster to John Perry Miller, April 6, 1969, box 121, folder 14, Office of the President, Levi Administration Records.

79. John Kendall and George Kannar, "Disciplining on Campus Tougher than Believed," *Los Angeles Times*, June 23, 1969, clipping in box 124, folder 1, Office of the President, Levi Administration Records; Albert, *Remembering Tomorrow*, 102–3.

80. Martin J. Meade to Michael Walsh, February 10, 1970, box 2, folder: Demonstration, November 12, 1969, Fr. Walsh Papers (Reverend Michael Walsh), Archives and Special Collections, Fordham University Library, Fordham University, Bronx, NY.

Chapter Fourteen

1. Noam Chomsky, Frederick Crews, Richard Ohmann, Paul Lauter, and Louis Kampf, "To the Editors," *New York Review of Books*, December 19, 1968.

2. Louis Kampf and Paul Lauter, "Introduction," in *The Politics of Literature: Dissenting Essays on the Teaching of English*, ed. Kampf and Lauter (New York: Pantheon, 1972), 3–54, offers the most accessible account of what happened at the 1968 MLA conference. See also New University Conference of the Modern Language Association, *Newsletter*, no. 1, January 1969, in Paul Lauter Papers

(hereafter Lauter Papers). Over the years, I have been able to consult Paul Lauter's personal files, both in his office at Trinity College and later after he donated them to the Trinity College archives. As a result, some of the citations here are sketchier than others, since many refer to materials that I accessed before they were professionally processed. In addition, many of the documents I cite here and elsewhere I found in other repositories as well as in other people's personal papers.

3. Kampf and Lauter, "Introduction," in *The Politics of Literature*, ed. Kampf and Lauter, 34–37; Florence Howe, "What Success at the MLA?," box 13, folder 5, New University Conference Papers, Wisconsin Historical Society, Madison (hereafter NUC Papers, WHS); Richard Ohmann, interview with the author, March 15, 2013, New York City.

4. "NUC at the MLA," *Newsletter*, no. 1, January 1969, box 13, folder 5, NUC Papers, WHS; Kampf and Lauter, "Introduction," 35–38.

5. Israel Shenker, "Language Forum Hears Protests," *New York Times*, December 28, 1968; Florence Howe, Paul Lauter, Richard Ohmann, Louis Kampf to A. H. Raskin, January 1, 1969, Lauter Papers.

6. Kampf and Lauter, "Introduction," 34–39; Florence [Howe] to Bob [Ross], n.d., box 5, folder 9, NUC Papers, WHS; Howe, Lauter, Ohmann, Kampf to A. H. Raskin, January 1, 1969, Lauter Papers; Florence Howe, *A Life in Motion* (New York: Feminist Press, 2011), 240; Harland G. Bloland and Sue M. Bloland, *American Learned Societies in Transition: The Impact of Dissent and Recession* (New York: McGraw-Hill, 1974), 70.

7. Howe, "What Success at the MLA?"

8. Jonathan Beckwith, *Making Genes, Making Waves: A Social Activist in Science* (Cambridge, MA: Harvard University Press, 2002), 51–53.

9. The most influential discussion of the evolution of academic culture during this period was Christopher Jencks and David Riesman, *The Academic Revolution* (New York: Doubleday, 1968). See also Theodore Roszak, "Introduction: On Academic Delinquency," in *Dissenting Academy*, ed. Roszak (New York: Pantheon, 1967), 23.

10. Ira Eli Wessler, "The Political Resolutions of American Learned Societies" (PhD diss., NYU, 1973), 7. For information about Black historians, see August Meier and Elliott Rudwick, *Black History and the Historical Profession, 1915–1980* (Urbana: University of Illinois Press, 1986).

11. Roszak, "Introduction: On Academic Delinquency," in *The Dissenting Academy*, ed. Roszak, 16. For an overview of the learned societies in the mid-1960s, see Bloland and Bloland, *American Learned Societies in Transition*, especially chapters 2 and 3.

12. Richard Ohmann, *English in America: A Radical View of the Profession*, 2nd ed. (1976; Middleton, CT: Wesleyan University Press, 1996), 32.

13. Bloland and Bloland, *American Learned Societies*, 10.

14. For a discussion of the early adoption of objectivity, see, for example, Mary O. Furner, *Advocacy and Objectivity* (Lexington: University Press of Kentucky,

1975); Thomas Haskell, *The Emergency of Professional Social Science* (Urbana: University of Illinois Press, 1977); Burton J. Bledstein, *The Culture of Professionalism* (New York: Norton, 1976); and Peter Novick, *That Noble Dream: The "Objectivity Question" and the American Historical Profession* (Cambridge: Cambridge University Press, 1988).

15. Bloland and Bloland, *American Learned Societies*, 18; Charles Cell, "The AAS at Work: Or How to Avoid Critical Issues," *CCAS Newsletter*, May–June 1971, in Joseph Esherick, personal papers; Kelly Moore, *Disrupting Science: Social Movements, American Scientists, and the Politics of the Military, 1945–1975* (Princeton, NJ: Princeton University Press, 2008), 12–13.

16. David Riesman to Philip Altbach, November 21, 1967, in David Riesman Papers, box 1, HUG (FP) 99.12, Harvard University Archives, Nathan M. Pusey Library, Cambridge, MA.

17. Paul Buhle, "Madison: An Introduction," in *History and the New Left: Madison, Wisconsin, 1950–1970*, ed. Buhle (Philadelphia: Temple University Press, 1990), 26; James Weinstein, "Studies on the Left," in *History and the New Left*, ed. Buhle, 116–17; Mickey Flacks and Dick Flacks, *Making History, Making Blintzes: How Two Red Diaper Babies Found Each Other and Discovered America* (New Brunswick, NJ: Rutgers University Press, 2018), 253; John McDermott, "NUC as Cadre," *NUC Newsletter* 3, no. 3 (January 20, 1970), in Lauter Papers; Robert Ross, interview with the author, April 3, 2013, Worcester, MA.

18. Program of the First Annual Socialist Scholars Conference at Columbia University, September 11–12, 1965, Tamiment Ephemera Collection, PE .036, box 92, folder: Socialist Scholars Conference, Tamiment Library, NYU (hereafter Socialist Scholars Conference, Tamiment Ephemera).

19. Vicki A. Alberti, "The Genovese Affair: Prologue to 'The Sixties'" (PhD diss., Drew University, Madison, NJ, 2009), 108.

20. David Mermelstein, interview with the author, May 2, 2013, New York City; Louis Menashe, interview with the author, June 12, 2013, Brooklyn, NY; Menashe to Dear Colleague, December 6, 1965, in Socialist Scholars Conference, Tamiment Ephemera; Frederic S. Lee, "History and Identity: The Case of Radical Economics and Radical Economists, 1945–70," *Review of Radical Political Economics* 36, no. 2 (Spring 2004): 185.

21. Program of the Second Annual Socialist Scholars Conference at Hotel Commodore, September 9–11, 1966, Socialist Scholars Conference, Tamiment Ephemera.

22. On the so-called "Ap-Flap," see Michael O'Brien, "Introduction," *The Letters of C. Vann Woodward*, ed. O'Brien (New Haven, CT: Yale University Press, 2013), xxxv–xxxix.

23. Program of the Third Annual Socialist Scholars Conference, New York Hilton, September 9 and 10, 1967, in Socialist Scholars Conference, Tamiment Ephemera; Mermelstein, interview, May 2, 2013.

24. Steering Committee to Dear Participant, August 14, 1968; Program of the Fourth Annual Socialist Scholars Conference, "The Socialist Perspective in the

Advanced Countries," Rutgers University, September 6, 7, 8, 1968; Program of the Fifth Annual Socialist Scholars Conference, "Aspects of Socialist Culture," September 5, 6, 7, 1969; and leaflet, "Blacklisting," October 1969: all in Socialist Scholars Conference, Tamiment Ephemera.

25. Eric Foner, interview with the author, March 26, 2013, New York City.

26. Fred L. Pincus and Howard J. Ehrlich, "The New University Conference: A Study of Former Members," *Critical Sociology* 15, no. 2 (Summer 1988): 145–47.

27. Louis Kampf, interview with the author, April 3, 2013, Cambridge, MA; Bart Meyers, interview with the author, April 14, 2008, Woodstock, NY; John McDermott, interview with the author, May 3, 2008, New York City; Ross, interview, April 3, 2013.

28. Irwin Unger, "The 'Long March Through the Institutions': Movement for a Democratic Society and the New University Conference," in *A Master's Due: Essays in Honor of David Herbert Donald*, ed. William J. Cooper Jr., Michael F. Holt, and John McCardell (Baton Rouge: Louisiana State University Press, 1985), 248.

29. Barbara Haber and Al Haber, "Getting by with a Little Help from Our Friends," in *Radicals in the Professions, Selected Papers*, October 1967.

30. Michael Goldfield, "Report on the Conference," in *Radicals in the Professions, Selected Papers*, October 1967.

31. Michael Zweig, "The Radical in the Academy," in *Radicals in the Professions, Selected Papers*; Ross, interview, April 3, 2013; Jesse Lemisch, interview with the author, February 5, 2013, New York City; John McMillian, "Love Letters to the Future: REP, *Radical America*, and New Left History," *Radical History Review*, no. 77 (2000): 49.

32. Richard Rothstein to Arthur Waskow, December 4, 1969, box 5, folder 8, NUC Papers, WHS. A similar position was taken by the chair of the NUC's radical caucuses committee; see Neil Resnikoff, "Progress Report from the Chairman of the National Committee's Subcommittee on Professional Organizing," January 30, 1970, in Lauter Papers.

33. Zweig, "The Radical in the Academy."

34. Martin Oppenheimer, quoted in Unger, "The 'Long March Through the Institutions,'" in *A Master's Due*, ed. Cooper et al., 248.

35. Flacks and Flacks, *Making History, Making Blintzes*, 254.

36. Richard Flacks to Fellow Sociologists, August 1, 1968, box 5, folder 10, NUC Papers, WHS; McDermott, interview, May 3, 2008.

37. Boldface in original; New University Conference, "A Call to Action," in *The Movement toward a New America*, ed. Mitchell Goodman (New York: Knopf, 1970). There is a somewhat different (and undated) draft in the NUC Papers, WHS. Tom Hayden et al., "A Declaration of Belief," n.d., in New University Conference Papers, Tamiment Library and Robert F. Wagner Labor Archives, Bobst Library, NYU (hereafter NUC Papers, Tamiment); Unger, "The 'Long March Through the Institutions,'" in *A Master's Due*, ed. Cooper, Holt, and McCardell, 256.

38. "Interim Committee—New University Conference Statement," Draft #2, October 1968, NUC Papers, Tamiment.

39. Novick, *That Noble Dream*, 429.

40. Flacks and Flacks, *Making History, Making Blintzes*, 253–55; Unger, "The 'Long March Through the Institutions,'" 256–58; McDermott, interview, May 3, 2008.

41. Jesse Lemisch, interview, February 5, 2013; Lemisch, "Who Will Write a Left History of Art While We Are Putting Our Balls on the Line?," *Journal of American History* 76, no. 2 (September 1989): 485–86. For a more detailed discussion of the debate between Lynd and Lemisch, see Jim O'Brien, "'Be Realistic, Demand the Impossible': Staughton Lynd, Jesse Lemisch, and a Committed History," *Radical History Review*, no. 82 (Winter 2002): 65–90.

42. Norman Birnbaum, "New University Conference: The Dilemmas of Resistance," *The Nation*, April 22, 1968.

43. McDermott, interview, May 3, 2008; Kampf, interview, April 3, 2013.

44. Kirkpatrick Sale, *SDS* (New York: Random House, 1973), 413.

45. Memo to "All NUC Chapter Contacts, Executive Committee, 1970–71 Staff," April 12, 1970, in Lauter Papers.

46. Memo to "All NUC Chapter Contacts, Executive Committee, 1970–71 Staff," April 12, 1970, in Lauter Papers; Rue Wallace, "Some Notes: Executive Committee Women Discussing Structure," *Women's Caucus Newsletter*, no. 5 (January 1971), in Renate Bridenthal, personal papers; Kampf, interview, April 3, 2013; Pincus and Ehrlich, "The New University Conference," in *Critical Sociology* (Summer 1988): 146.

47. NUC leaflet, "Open Up the Schools," n.d. [late 1969 or 1970], box 9, folder 4, NUC Papers, WHS.

48. Anon. [probably Paul Lauter] to Bob, October 21, 1968, in Lauter Papers.

49. Sale, *SDS*, 528; NUC leaflet, "The War Comes Home," [late 1969?], box 9, folder 4, NUC Papers, WHS. Many of the people I interviewed recalled that the author of the felicitous phrase "in, around, and in spite of institutions of higher education" was Michelle Russell, one of the few African Americans in the NUC's leadership.

50. Richard Flacks, telephone interview with the author, February 22, 2013; Bertell Ollman, interview with the author, January 19, 2015, New York City.

51. NUC of University of Maryland–Baltimore County to All Faculty and staff, December 15, 1969, in Lauter Papers.

52. "Pre-Election Recess Program in Brooklyn College," October 20–November 2, 1970[?], in Bridenthal, personal papers; Conference Program, "An End to Racism in Higher Education in Maryland," April 11, 1970, in Lauter Papers.

53. Ann Marie Taylor, Comments on draft by [Ken] Megill, n.d., box 9, folder 4, NUC, WHS. Bob Klawitter to Paul Booth, July 20, 1969; Wells Keddie to Rinda [West], December 2, 1970; and Taylor to N[ational] O[ffice], December 1970: all in box 4, file 4, NUC, WHS. Rita Lavery, "NUC—NRA," n.d. [probably 1971], box 9, folder 4, NUC Papers, WHS; Paul Lauter to Grover Furr, February 3, [1969?], in Lauter Papers.

54. "BC-NUC Summer 1970 Internal Education Reading List," in Bridenthal, personal papers.

55. "News from the Chapters," *NUC Newsletter* 1, no. 3 (October 4, 1968); NYU chapter of the New University Conference, "A Rational Inquiry into the Roles Played by Dr. Ivan L. Bennett, Jr. and New York University in the Utilization and Development of Technical and Human Resources for the U.S. Government's Chemical Biological Weapons Program and Military Policies," 1970, NUC Papers, Tamiment.

56. Michele [Russell] memo to Exec. Comm., March 13, 1970, source unknown.

57. Marlene Dixon and Naomi Weisstein, "A Reply to One Editor's View of the Women's Caucus," *NUC Newsletter* 1, no. 3 (October 4, 1968), in Lauter Papers.

58. "Women's Caucus Perspective," adopted at the National Convention of NUC, June 1969, in Bridenthal, personal papers.

59. Roberta Salper, *Domestic Subversive: A Feminist's Take on the Left, 1960–1976* (Tucson: Anaphora Literary Press, 2014), 86, 10; Mark Ritchey to John Root, November 2, 1970, box 5, folder 8, NUC Papers, WHS.

60. NUC leaflet, "Women's Liberation," n.d., box 9, folder 4, NUC Papers, WHS.

61. Salper, *Domestic Subversive*, 86–87, 91.

62. Paul Lauter to Comrades, May 25, [1973?], Lauter Papers; Peninsula Women's Caucus, "'OUTS' and the Virginia Women's Caucus," *NUC Women's Caucus Newsletter*, fall 1971, in Bridenthal, personal papers.

63. Salper, *Domestic Subversive*, 91, 101.

64. Louis Kampf, interview with the author, April 3, 2013, Cambridge, MA.

65. Kampf, interview, April 3, 2013; Press Release, February 9, 1970 and Richie [Rothstein] to NUC Executive Committee, March 16, 1970: both in Lauter Papers. Will Watson to Rich, February 11, 1970, box 5, folder 8, NUC Papers, WHS.

66. Memo, to Executive Committee Members and Regional Organizing Groups, April 21, 1970, Lauter Papers.

67. Ann Arbor Steering Committee Meeting of the New University Conference, May 24–26, 1968, in Bridenthal, personal papers; "Political Repression, Workshop Draft," n.d., Lauter Papers.

68. *NUC Newsletter* 3, no. 10 (January 15, 1970); and Wells Keddie to EC Members and Staff, August 9, 1971: both in Lauter Papers; Keddie, Statement, April 6, 1972, box 9, folder 4, NUC Papers, WHS.

69. Paul Lauter to [Ken] Megill, August 7, 1971, Lauter Papers. David Yale, "The NUC Tracking System," n.d. [probably December 1970 or January 1971]; and Memo, Tom Hecht to The Membership of NUC, January 4, 1971: both in Bridenthal, personal papers.

70. For an example of such a position, see that of the American Sociological Association in J. David Colfax and Jack L. Roach, "Introduction: The Roots of Radical Sociology," in *Radical Sociology*, ed. Colfax and Roach (New York: Basic Books, 1971), 8.

71. Ross, interview, April 3, 2013.

72. Martin Oppenheimer, "Introduction," in *Radical Sociologists and the Movement: Experiences, Lessons, and Legacies*, ed. Oppenheimer, Martin J. Murray, and Rhonda F. Levine (Philadelphia: Temple University Press, 1991), 7.

73. For an early discussion of radical professional organizing outside of the academic core, see *Radicals in the Professions, Selected Papers*, October 1967; Ibram H. Rogers [Kendi], *The Black Campus Movement: Black Students and the Racial Reconstitution of Higher Education, 1965–1972* (New York: Palgrave Macmillan, 2012), 154.

74. Wessler, "The Political Resolutions of American Learned Societies," 131–34, 159–60.

75. Bloland and Bloland, *American Learned Societies*, 44; Marshall Windmiller, "The New American Mandarins," in *Dissenting Academy*, ed. Roszak, 122; Marvin Surkin and Alan Wolfe, "Introduction," in *An End to Political Science: The Caucus Papers*, ed. Surkin and Wolfe (New York: Basic Books, 1970), 3.

76. Martin Surkin, interview with the author, February 2, 2015, New York City; Bloland and Bloland, *American Learned Societies*, 44–46.

77. Colfax and Roach, "Introduction: The Roots of Radical Sociology," in *Radical Sociology*, ed. Colfax and Roach, 8; Richard Flacks, "The Sociology Liberation Movement: Some Legacies and Lessons," in *Radical Sociologists*, ed. Oppenheimer, Murray, and Levine, 17.

78. Flacks to Fellow Sociologists, August 1, 1968, box 5, folder 10, NUC Papers, WHS.

79. Flacks to Fellow Sociologists; Flacks and Flacks, *Making History, Making Blintzes*, 266–70; Carol A. Brown, "The Early Years of the Sociology Liberation Movement," in *Radical Sociologists*, ed. Oppenheimer, Murray, and Levine, 44–45; Colfax and Roach, "Introduction: The Roots of Radical Sociology," in *Radical Sociology*, ed. Colfax and Roach, 10; Wessler, "The Political Resolutions of American Learned Societies," 209.

80. Brown, "Early Years," in *Radical Sociologists*, ed. Oppenheimer, Murray, and Levine, 46; Richard Flacks, "'Radical Caucuses' Shake the Disciplines," *NUC Newsletter* 1, no. 3 (October 4, 1968), in Lauter Papers.

81. "Radical Economics: The Union for Radical Political Economics," *Radicals in the Professions Newsletter*, fall 1968; Marlene Kim, "URPE at Fifty: Reflections on a Half Century of Activism, Community, Debate (and a Few Crazy Moments)," *Review of Radical Political Economics* 50, no. 3 (2018), offers a good overview of the organization. See also Lee, "History and Identity."

82. The recent monograph by Fabio Lanza, *The End of Concern: Maoist China, Activism, and Asian Studies* (Durham, NC: Duke University Press, 2017), deals with the CCAS but underplays its founders' overriding "concern" with the Vietnam War.

83. The CCAS mission statement was published in every issue of the organization's main publication, the *Bulletin of the Concerned Asian Scholars*.

84. Lanza, *The End of Concern*, 18; Carl Riskin, interview with the author, November 4, 2014, New York City; Joseph Esherick, interview with the author, February 17, 2016, Berkeley, CA.

85. The entire issue of the *Bulletin of the Concerned Asian Scholars* 3, no. 2, is devoted to the Vietnamese Studies Center at Southern Illinois. See also *CCAS Newsletter*, November 1970, February 1971, and "Statement on Center for Vietnamese Studies and Programs at Southern Illinois University," October 23, 1970: all in Esherick, personal papers. Others besides the CCAS were involved in opposing the SIU Center; see Doug Dowd, *Blues for America: A Critique, a Lament, and Some Memories* (New York: Monthly Review Press, 1997), 208–9. For information about a similar venture at Columbia, see *CCAS Newsletter*, March 1972, in Esherick, personal papers.

86. See, for example, Edward Friedman and Mark Selden, eds., *America's Asia: Dissenting Essays on Asian-American Relations* (New York: Pantheon, 1971); and The Committee of Concerned Asian Scholars, *The Indochina Story: A Fully Documented Account* (New York: Pantheon, 1970).

87. Sarah Bridger, *Scientists at War: The Ethics of Cold War Weapons Research* (Cambridge, MA: Harvard University Press, 2015), 198.

88. Beckwith, *Making Genes*, 16, 66; Moore, *Disrupting Science*, 37.

89. R. Hobart Ellis, "APA Debates Whether to Take Positions on Public Issues," *Physics Today*, 21, 3, 81, 1968; Charles Schwartz, interview with the author, February 4, 2014, Berkeley, CA; Charles Schwartz, interview by Patrick Catt, July 19, 1995, University of California, Berkeley, http://science-for-the-people.org/wp-content/uploads/2015/07/CattInterview_Schwartz1.pdf; Bridger, *Scientists at War*, 195–99.

90. Moore, *Disrupting Science*, 130.

91. Moore, *Disrupting Science*, 158–88, 254–55; Sigrid Schmalzer, Daniel S. Chard, and Alyssa Botelho, "Introduction," in *Science for the People: Documents from America's Movement of Radical Scientists*, ed. Schmalzer, Chard, and Botelho (Amherst: University of Massachusetts Press, 2018), 2–3.

92. Moore, *Disrupting Science*, 159–63; Howe, Lauter, Ohmann, Kampf to A. H. Raskin, January 1, 1969, in Lauter Papers.

93. Berenice Carroll to Arthur Waskow, December 5, 1969; and Ralph Desmarais [?] to Arthur Waskow, n.d. [fall 1969(?)]: both in box 5, folder 8, NUC Papers, WHS.

94. Brown, "Early Years," in *Radical Sociologists*, ed. Oppenheimer, Murray, and Levine, 47; Colfax and Roach, "Introduction: The Roots of Radical Sociology," in *Radical Sociology*, ed. Colfax and Roach, 11.

95. *Insurgent Sociologist* 2, no. 1 (1971); Martin Oppenheimer, "Pages from a Journal of the Middle Left," in *Radical Sociologists*, ed. Oppenheimer, Murray, and Levine, 123.

96. Kim, "URPE at Fifty," *Review of Radical Political Economics* 50, no. 3 (2018): 472–73.

97. Bill Zimmerman, Len Radinsky, Mel Rothenberg, and Bart Meyers, "Towards a Science for the People," in *Science for the People*, ed. Schmalzer, Chard, and Botelho, 22–23 (also available at https://www.ocf.berkeley.edu/~schwrtz/SftP/Towards.html); Meyers, interview, April 14, 2008; Bill Zimmerman, *Troublemaker: A Memoir from the Front Lines of the Sixties* (New York: Doubleday, 2011), 190–91; Bridger, *Scientists at War*, 203–5.

98. Bridger, *Scientists at War*, 207–9; Moore, *Disrupting Science*, 131, 158–68; Walter Sullivan, "Strike to Protest 'Misuse' of Science," *New York Times*, February 6, 1969, clipping in Lauter Papers; Zimmerman, *Troublemaker*, 190–95.

99. O'Brien, "'Be Realistic, Demand the Impossible,'" 72.

100. Zimmerman, *Troublemaker*, 190; Flacks, "'Radical Caucuses' Shake the Disciplines," *NUC Newsletter* 1, no. 3 (October 4, 1968); Colfax and Roach, "Introduction: The Roots of Radical Sociology," 10; Agenda, New University Conference Program for the Midwest Modern Language Association Convention, October 23–25, 1969, St. Louis, box 13, folder 5, NUC Papers, WHS; Waskow to Dear Friends, n.d. [fall 1969], box 5, folder 8, NUC Papers, WHS; John Berninghausen for Stanford Chapter, "ccas participation in the 1970 aas convention: scholarly cooperation or political cooptation?," in Esherick, personal papers.

101. Tom Wells, *The War Within: America's Battle over Vietnam* (Berkeley: University of California Press, 1994), 560.

102. Colfax and Roach, "Introduction: The Roots of Radical Sociology," 10; Alfred McClung Lee, "Steps Taken toward Liberating Sociologists," in *Radical Sociologists*, ed. Oppenheimer, Murray, and Levine, 36; Kenneth M. Stampp, *Historian of Slavery, the Civil War, and Reconstruction, University of California, Berkeley, 1946–1983*, 140–41, interviews conducted by Ann Lage in 1996, Regional Oral History Office, Bancroft Library, University of California, Berkeley, 1998, https://digitalassets.lib.berkeley.edu/rohoia/ucb/text/historianslaveryoostamrich.pdf; Resolution for MLA 1969 Annual Meeting, box 13, folder 5, NUC Papers, WHS.

103. Richard Flacks to Fellow Sociologists, August 1, 1968, box 5, folder 10, NUC Papers, WHS; "Committee of Concerned Asian Scholars: Statement of Purpose" n.d., in Esherick, personal papers.

104. Moore, *Disrupting Science*, 164; Kampf and Lauter, "Introduction," in *The Politics of Literature*, ed. Kampf and Lauter, 39.

105. Richard Hofstadter to Dear Colleague, December 1, 1969, Hofstadter Papers, box 1, Rare Book and Manuscript Library, Butler Library, Columbia University.

106. Kampf and Lauter, "Introduction," 39; Cell, "The AAS at Work" *CCAS Newsletter*, May–June 1971; Moore, *Disrupting Science*, 164; Colfax and Roach, "Introduction: The Roots of Radical Sociology," 11; Philip M. Hauser, "On Actionism in the Craft of Sociology," in *Radical Sociology*, ed. Colfax and Roach, 430; Bloland and Bloland, *American Learned Societies*, 64; Caucus for a New Political Science, *Newsletter*, November 1969, in Robert Winston Papers, box 4,

Special Collections and University Archives, W. E. B. Du Bois Library, UMass Amherst (hereafter Winston Papers, UMass Amherst); Ann Gordon, interview with the author, January 4, 2019, Newark, NJ; Alan Wolfe, "The Professional Mystique," in *An End to Political Science*, ed. Surkin and Wolfe, 293.

107. "CHICAGO, 1969 and the MLA," n.d., mimeograph; "What Happened at the MLA, NUC at the MLA," *Newsletter* no. 1, January 1969; and Howe, "What Success at the MLA?": all in box 13, folder 5, NUC Papers, WHS.

108. Colfax and Roach, "Introduction: The Roots of Radical Sociology," 10; Flacks, "Radical Caucuses Shake the Disciplines"; Bloland and Bloland, *American Learned Societies in Transition*, 53; Jack Sawyer, "Toward a Psychology with Conscious Values," *American Psychologist*, July 1970, in box 13, folder 4, NUC Papers, WHS; Moore, *Disrupting Science*, 152.

109. Minutes of the meeting of the Council of the AHA, September 28, 1968; John K. Fairbank to Ward, January 23, 1969, box 3, Fairbank Papers, 12.17; and Fairbank to AHA Council Members, September 23, 1968, box 2, Fairbank, 12.10: all in John King Fairbank Papers, Harvard University Archives, Nathan M. Pusey Library, Cambridge, MA.

110. C. Vann Woodward to Susan Woodward, January 1, 1970, in *The Letters of C. Vann Woodward*, 279.

111. Ann Gordon et al. to Historians who signed up as radicals, September 1969; To Brothers and Sisters, October 8, 1969; Berenice Carroll to Arthur Waskow, December 5, 1969; and Richard Kagan to Arthur Waskow, December 10, 1969: all in box 5, folder 8, NUC Papers, WHS.

112. Carl Mirra, *The Admirable Radical: Staughton Lynd and Cold War Dissent, 1945–1970* (Kent, OH: Kent State University Press, 2010), 156–61; Constance Myers to NUC, n.d. (received January 8, 1970), box 5, folder 8, NUC Papers, WHS.

113. Henry Raymont, "Political Science Association Faces Young Dissidents' Attack," *New York Times*, September 4[?], 1969, in box 4, Winston Papers, UMass Amherst; Surkin, interview, February 2, 2015.

114. Bloland and Bloland, *American Learned Societies*, 49–53, 64; Raymont, "Political Science Association Faces Young Dissidents' Attack"; Surkin, interview, February 2, 2015; Flacks, "'Radical Caucuses' Shake the Disciplines"; Alan Wolfe, "Unthinking about the Thinkable: Reflections on the Failure of the Caucus for a New Political Science," *Politics and Society*, May 1971, 393–406.

115. Lee, "Steps Taken toward Liberating Sociologists," in *Radical Sociologists*, ed. Oppenheimer, Murray, and Levine, 37–38.

116. Howe, *A Life in Motion*, 256–57; Ohmann, *English in America*, 50.

117. Neal Resnikoff, Progress Report, January 30, 1970, box 13, folder 4, NUC Papers, WHS; Howe, "What Success at the MLA?"

118. Science for the People Madison Collective, *The AMRC Papers: An Indictment of the Army Mathematics Research Center* (1973), in *Science for the People*, ed. Schmalzer, Chard, and Botelho, 71–75.

119. *CCAS Newsletter*, March 1972, in Esherick, personal papers.

120. Kim, "URPE at Fifty," 477; Thomas Weisskopf, "Reminiscences on the Early Years of URPE," *Review of Radical Political Economics* 50, no. 3 (2018): 584–85.

121. Meyers, interview, April 14, 2008; Rothstein to Waskow, December 13, 1969, box 5, folder 8, NUC Papers, WHS.

122. Zimmerman et al., "Towards a Science for the People," in *Science for the People*, ed. Schmalzer, Chard, and Botelho, 22–23.

123. Mark Selden, interview with the author, February 18, 2015; Mark Selden, "What's in a Name?," *CCAS Newsletter*, January 1971, in Esherick, personal papers.

124. Berkeley CCAS to Local Chapter Heads, n.d. [1969–70]; and *CCAS Newsletter*, October 1, 1971: both in Esherick, personal papers.

125. Kim, "URPE at Fifty," 481; Henry Etzkowitz, "The Contradictions of Radical Sociology: Ideological Purity and Dissensus at Washington University," 78; and Evan Stark, "Talking Sociology: A Sixties Fragment," 60–61: both in *Radical Sociologists*, ed. Oppenheimer, Murray, and Levin.

126. Staughton Lynd and Arthur Waskow, draft constitution, December 10, 1969, in Fairbank Papers, box 3, HUG (FP) 12.17; *MARHO Newsletter* 1, no. 2 [probably 1973].

127. *CCAS Newsletter*, October 1, 1971, March 1972, in Esherick, personal papers; Moore, *Disrupting Science*, 182–83.

128. Neal Resnikoff to Doris Gunderson, November 12, 1969, box 5, folder 10, NUC Papers, WHS; anon., "Response to NUC actions at CCC and to proposals on p. 265, this issue," box 13, folder 5, NUC Papers, WHS.

129. Ruth Misheloff, "Break the Blockade," *NUC Newsletter* 3, no. 10 (January 15, 1970), in Lauter Papers; Salper, *Domestic Subversive*, 102, 111.

130. Moore, *Disrupting Science*, 176; Kim, "URPE at Fifty," 482; Lanza, *The End of Concern*, 136.

131. James W. Clinton, *The Loyal Opposition: Americans in North Vietnam, 1965–1972* (Niwot: University Press of Colorado, 1995); Mark Ptashne, interview with the author, December 12, 2014, New York City.

132. *CCAS Newsletter*, October 1971, in Esherick, personal papers; Selden, interview, February 18, 2015; Zimmerman, *Troublemaker*, 217–19.

133. "Internal Education," n.d.; and Paul Lauter to "NUC members and friends," n.d.: both in Lauter Papers.

134. Kim, "URPE at Fifty," 476; Letter to Dear Comrades, April 22, 1970, Lauter Papers; Caucus for a New Political Science, *Newsletter*, November 1969, in box 4, Winston Papers, UMass Amherst; *MARHO Newsletter* 1, no. 6, Tamiment Ephemera.

135. Al Szymanski, "Insurgent Sociologist," *NUC Newsletter* 5, no. 2, October 1–16, 1971, in Bridenthal, personal papers.

136. Martin J. Murray, "Building Fires on the Prairie," in *Radical Sociologists*, ed. Oppenheimer, Murray, and Levine, 109.

137. "A Conversation about the Radical History Review: Former and Current Collective Members Reminisce," Andor Skotnes, moderator and editor, *Radical History Review*, no. 79 (Winter 2001): 17.

138. Kim, "URPE at Fifty," 475.

139. Kim, "URPE at Fifty," 477–78.

140. *CCAS Newsletter*, July–August 1971, in Esherick, personal papers; Powder Hill Conference of Radical Sociologists, July 7–8, 1969, box 13, folder 4, NUC Papers, WHS.

141. MARHO, *Newsletter* 1, no. 4 [1973?]; Michael Wallace, in "A Conversation about the Radical History Review," 41.

Chapter Fifteen

1. Martin Nicolaus, "Fat-Cat Sociology," in *Radical Sociologists and the Movement: Experiences, Lessons, and Legacies*, ed. Martin Oppenheimer, Martin J. Murray, and Rhonda F. Levine (Philadelphia: Temple University Press, 1991), 251–54.

2. Richard Ohmann, *English in America: A Radical View of the Profession*, 2nd ed. (1976; Middleton, CT: Wesleyan University Press, 1996), 231.

3. Louis Kampf and Paul Lauter, "Introduction," in *The Politics of Literature: Dissenting Essays on the Teaching of English*, ed. Kampf and Lauter (New York: Pantheon, 1972), 23–25; Ellen Cantarow, "Why Teach Literature: An Account of How I Came to Ask That Question," in *The Politics of Literature*, ed. Kampf and Lauter, 99.

4. Marvin Surkin and Alan Wolfe, "Introduction," in *An End to Political Science: The Caucus Papers*, ed. Surkin and Wolfe (New York: Basic Books, 1970), 4.

5. Kathleen Gough, "World Revolution and the Science of Man," in *The Dissenting Academy*, ed. Theodore Roszak (New York: Pantheon, 1968), 136, 139, 149; Neal Resnikoff, Progress Report, January 30, 1970, box 13, folder 4, New University Conference Papers, Wisconsin Historical Society, Madison (hereafter NUC Papers, WHS).

6. Jesse Lemisch, quoted in John McMillian, "Love Letters to the Future: REP, *Radical America*, and New Left History," *Radical History Review* 77 (2000): 41; Jesse Lemisch, *On Active Service in War and Peace: Politics and Ideology in the American Historical Profession* (Toronto: New Hogtown Press, 1975).

7. "Call to AAAS Actions," *Science for the People* 5, no. 1 (January 1973), in *Science for the People: Documents from America's Movement of Radical Scientists*, ed. Sigrid Schmalzer, Daniel S. Chard, and Alyssa Botelho (Amherst: University of Massachusetts Press, 2018), 60.

8. Marshall Windmiller, "The New American Mandarins," in *Dissenting Academy*, ed. Roszak, 113; Text of the "Call to Action," in Carol A. Brown, "The Early Years of the Sociology Liberation Movement," in *Radical Sociologists*, ed. Oppenheimer, Murray, and Levine, 45.

9. Daniel Bell, *The End of Ideology: On the Exhaustion of Political Ideas in the Fifties* (Glencoe, IL: Free Press, 1960); Robert Dahl, *Who Governs?* (New Haven, CT: Yale University Press, 1961); Sumner M. Rosen, "Keynes without Gadflies," 74–87; and Christian Bay, "The Cheerful Science of Dismal Politics," 209: both in *Dissenting Academy*, ed. Roszak.

10. Michael Parenti, "Power and Pluralism: A View from the Bottom," in *The End of Political Science*, ed. Surkin and Wolfe, 111–43.

11. Richard Kagan, "McCarran's Legacy: The Association for Asian Studies," *Bulletin of Concerned Asian Scholars* 1, no. 4 (May 1969); Edward Friedman and Mark Selden, "Introduction," in *America's Asia: Dissenting Essays on Asian-American Relations*, ed. Friedman and Selden (New York: Pantheon, 1971), ix–x. See my own account of academic McCarthyism in *No Ivory Tower: McCarthyism and the University* (New York: Oxford University Press, 1986).

12. See also the Columbia CCAS, "The American Asian Studies Establishment," and Moss Roberts, "Some Problems Concerning the Structure and Direction of Contemporary Chinese Studies—A Reply to Professor Fairbank," *Bulletin of Concerned Asian Scholars* 3, nos. 3–4 (Summer–Fall 1971, double issue).

13. Paul Rubinson, *Redefining Science: Scientists, the National Security State, and Nuclear Weapons in Cold War America* (Amherst: University of Massachusetts Press, 2016), 3–7.

14. John McCumber, *Time in the Ditch: American Philosophy and the McCarthy Era* (Evanston, IL: Northwestern University Press, 2001), 25, 45–46; John Wilkinson, "The Civilization of the Dialogue," in *Dissenting Academy*, ed. Roszak, 168.

15. In my own work on McCarthyism and the universities, I was surprised to find how few social scientists actually lost their jobs, compared to, say, English professors or philosophers. I could not find more than three or four economists, plus Stanford's Paul Baran, whose salary was frozen. This may have been the result of an earlier attack on social scientists in the beginning of the twentieth century that essentially defanged many of those fields' most eminent practitioners.

For information about the earlier attacks on social scientists, see Mary O. Furner, *Advocacy and Objectivity* (Lexington: University Press of Kentucky, 1975); Thomas Haskell, *The Emergence of Professional Social Science* (Urbana: University of Illinois Press, 1977); Burton J. Bledstein, *The Culture of Professionalism* (New York: Norton, 1976); Peter Novick, *That Noble Dream: The "Objectivity Question" and the American Historical Profession* (Cambridge: Cambridge University Press, 1988); and Richard Hofstadter and Walter P. Metzger, *The Development of Academic Freedom in the United States* (New York: Columbia University Press, 1955).

16. Paul Lazarsfeld and Wagner Thielens Jr., *The Academic Mind* (Glencoe, IL: Free Press, 1958), 198ff.

17. Richard Flacks, telephone interview with the author, February 22, 2013; William Tabb, interview with the author, August 26, 2013, New York City; Thomas E. Weisskopf, "Reflections on 50 Years of Radical Political Economy," *Review of Radical Political Economics* 46, no. 4 (2014): 437–47; Michael Meeropol, "How URPE Helped This 'Tenured Radical' Thrive in a Non-Radical Economics Department," *Review of Radical Political Economics* 50, no. 3 (2018): 459; J. David Colfax and Jack L. Roach, "Critiques of Radicalism in Sociology," in *Radical Sociology*, ed. Colfax and Roach (New York: Basic Books, 1971), 422–23; Surkin and Wolfe, "Introduction," in *An End to Political Science*, ed. Surkin and Wolfe, 4.

18. Evan Stark, "Talking Sociology: A Sixties Fragment," in *Radical Sociologists*, ed. Oppenheimer, Murray, and Levine, 66; Surkin and Wolfe, *An End to Political Science*, 243; Bay, "The Cheerful Science of Dismal Politics," in *Dissenting Academy*, ed. Roszak, 209; David Underhill, "Death at a Later Age: Political Science versus the Columbia Rebellion," in *The End of Political Science*, ed. Surkin and Wolfe, 283; Graduate Association of Students of Politics, "The Situation at Berkeley," in Caucus for a New Political Science, *Newsletter*, May 1970, in box 4, Robert Winston Papers, Special Collections and University Archives, University of Massachusetts Amherst (hereafter Winston Papers, UMass Amherst).

19. For a discussion of the rise of quantification within economics, see Michael A. Bernstein, *A Perilous Progress: Economists and Public Purpose in Twentieth-Century America* (Princeton, NJ: Princeton University Press, 2001). See also Robert M. Solow, "How Did Economics Get That Way and What Way Did It Get?," in *American Academic Culture in Transformation*, ed. Thomas Bender and Carl E. Schorske (Princeton, NJ: Princeton University Press, 1998), 66.

20. Samuel Bowles quoted in Marlene Kim, "URPE at Fifty: Reflections on a Half Century of Activism, Community, Debate (and a Few Crazy Moments)," *Review of Radical Political Economics* 50, no. 3 (2018): 470.

21. Weisskopf, "Reflections," *Review of Radical Political Economics* 46, no. 4 (2014): 437–47.

22. Bernstein, *A Perilous Progress*, 124.

23. Carl E. Schorske, *Intellectual Life, Civil Libertarian Issues, and the Student Movement at the University of California, Berkeley, 1960–1969*," 130, interviews conducted by Ann Lage, 1996, 1997, Regional Oral History Office, Bancroft Library, University of California, Berkeley, 2000, http://digitalassets.lib.berkeley.edu/rohoia/ucb/text/intelllifecivilooschorich.pdf.

24. Mary Nolan, interview with the author, January 7, 2019, New York City.

25. Kampf and Lauter, "Introduction," 10.

26. Fred Whitehead, "The Discipline of Literary Study," box 13, folder 5, NUC Papers, WHS; "Nineteenth Century Working Class Poetry," box 13, folder 5, NUC Papers, WHS.

27. Eleanor Hakim, "The Tragedy of Hans Gerth," in *History and the New Left*:

Madison, Wisconsin, 1950–1970, ed. Paul Buhle (Philadelphia: Temple University Press, 1990), 255.

28. Kampf and Lauter, "Introduction," 25, 14; Sheila Delaney, "Up Against the Great Tradition,", 11; Kampf, "The Scandal of Literary Scholarship," 56–57: all in *The Politics of Literature*, ed. Kampf and Lauter.

29. Richard Ohmann, "Teaching and Studying Literature at the End of Ideology," 134–41; and Bruce Franklin, "The Teaching of Literature in the Highest Academies of the Empire," 113–14: both in *The Politics of Literature*, ed. Kampf and Lauter.

30. "Committee of Concerned Asian Scholars: Statement of Purpose," n.d., in Joseph Esherick, personal papers; Fabio Lanza, *The End of Concern: Maoist China, Activism, and Asian Studies* (Durham, NC: Duke University Press, 2017), 25–26.

31. Friedman and Selden, eds., *America's Asia*, vii.

32. Jack Sawyer, "Does Military Psychology Promote Human Welfare?" August 1969; and Sawyer, "Establishing the Right to Be Heard: The Development of a Program Takeover," n.d. [probably 1969 or 1970]: both in box 13, folder 4, NUC Papers, WHS; Bill Zimmerman, *Troublemaker: A Memoir from the Front Lines of the Sixties* (New York: Doubleday, 2011), 120; Radical Caucus at the American Psychiatric Association Annual Convention, box 13, folder 4, NUC Papers, WHS; Underhill, "Death at a Later Age," in *The End of Political Science*, ed. Surkin and Wolfe, 251–56; D[ale] Johnson, "Counter-insurgent Study of Students Protested," *The Insurgent Sociologist* 1, no. 4 (April 1971).

33. Kelly Moore, *Disrupting Science: Social Movements, American Scientists, and the Politics of the Military, 1945–1975* (Princeton, NJ: Princeton University Press, 2008), 176–77; Zimmerman, *Troublemaker*, 162, 181; Jonathan Beckwith, *Making Genes, Making Waves: A Social Activist in Science* (Cambridge, MA: Harvard University Press, 2002), 52–57, 99–114.

34. Kampf and Lauter, "Introduction," 18, 28; "Tact and Tactics, or Something Important Happened that Sunday Night," n.d., anon. DY [probably David Yale], box 13, folder 5, NUC Papers, WHS; "Statement of Principles," *MARHO Newsletter* 1, no. 6 (1974).

35. Christopher Jencks and David Riesman, *The Academic Revolution* (New York: Doubleday, 1968), offers an influential contemporary critique of academic professionalism by mainstream authors.

36. J. David Colfax and Jack L. Roach, "Introduction: The Roots of Radical Sociology," in *Radical Sociology*, ed. Colfax and Roach, 7.

37. Kampf and Lauter, "Introduction," in *Politics of Literature*, ed. Kampf and Lauter, 18.

38. Leonard Henny, "Films as Weapons in the Struggle to Liberate the American Mind," *The Insurgent Sociologist* 1, no. 2 (April 1970): 5.

39. Weisskopf, "Reflections," *Review of Radical Political Economics* 46, no. 4 (2014).

40. *MARHO Newsletter* 1, nos. 3, 4.

41. Bertell Ollman and Edward Vernoff, "Introduction," in *The Left Academy: Marxist Scholarship on American Campuses*, ed. Ollman and Vernoff (New York: McGraw-Hill, 1982), 8; Henry Abelove, Betsy Blackmar, Peter Dimock, and Jonathan Schneer, eds., *Visions of History* (New York: Pantheon, 1983); Jesse Lemisch, "The American Revolution Bicentennial and the Papers of Great White Men," *AHA Newsletter*, 1971, in "History at Yale in the Dark Ages, 1953–76," History News Network, January 6, 2007, http://hnn.us/article/33300 (accessed September 16, 2013); Joan Wallach Scott, "Finding Critical History," 32–35; Linda Gordon, "History Constructs a Historian," 88; and John R. Gillis, "Detours," 164: all in *Becoming Historians*, ed. James M. Banner Jr. and John R. Gillis (Chicago: University of Chicago Press, 2009). Eric Foner, "My Life as a Historian," in *Historians and Race: Autobiography and the Writing of History*, ed. Paul A. Cimbala and Robert F. Himmelberg (Bloomington: Indiana University Press, 1996), 98.

42. John Womack, in *Visions of History*, ed. Abelove et al., 258.

43. Meeropol, "How URPE Helped This 'Tenured Radical,'" *Review of Radical Political Economics* 50, no. 3 (2018): 457–67; Trent Schroyer, "A Reconceptualization of Critical Theory," in *Radical Sociology*, ed. Colfax and Roach, 132–48; Roy Rosenzweig, in "A Conversation about the Radical History Review: Former and Current Collective Members Reminisce," Andor Skotnes, moderator and editor, *Radical History Review*, no. 79 (winter 2001), 33; J. David Colfax, "Varieties and Prospects of 'Radical Scholarship' in Sociology," in *Radical Sociology*, ed. Colfax and Roach, 84; Lanza, *The End of Concern*, 64–65; Renate Bridenthal, interview with the author, June 4, 2013, New York City.

44. Colfax, "Varieties and Prospects of 'Radical Scholarship' in Sociology," 84.

45. Weisskopf, "Reflections," *Review of Radical Political Economics* 46, no. 4 (2014): 439.

46. Howard Wachtel quoted in Weisskopf, "Reflections," 438; "Science for the People at Ann Arbor," *Science for the People* 2, no. 2 (August 1970). Howard J. Ehrlich, "Notes from an Anarchist Sociologist: May 1989," 235; Robert J. S. Ross, "At the Center and the Edge: Notes on a Life in and out of Sociology and the New Left," 201: both in *Radical Sociologists*, ed. Oppenheimer, Murray, and Levine.

47. Albert Syzmanski, "Toward a Radical Sociology," 106; and Ehrlich, "Notes from a Radical Social Scientist, February 1970," 203: both in *Radical Sociology*, ed. Colfax and Roach.

48. Pfeffer and Schell, quoted in Lanza, *The End of Concern*, 79, 93.

49. Rothstein to Waskow, December 4, 1969, box 5, folder 8, NUC Papers, WHS; Colfax, "Varieties and Prospects of 'Radical Scholarship' in Sociology," in *Radical Sociology*, ed. Colfax and Roach, 85.

50. See, for example, the pieces by Albert Szymanski, Mike Ducey, Irwin Sperber, Sue Jacobs, and Carol Brown, in *The Insurgent Sociologist* 1, no. 3 (August 1970).

51. Brown, "Early Years," in *Radical Sociologists*, ed. Oppenheimer, Murray, and Levine, 48.

52. Colfax and Roach, "Introduction: The Roots of Radical Sociology," 10; Joel C. Edelstein, Western Caucus for a New Polit. Science at the Western Political Science Association meeting, n.d., box 4, Winston Papers, UMass Amherst.

53. Henry Etzkowitz, "The Contradictions of Radical Sociology: Ideological Purity and Dissensus at Washington University," in *Radical Sociologists*, ed. Oppenheimer, Murray, and Levine, 74–95, offers a useful, though admittedly biased, overview.

54. Stark, "Talking Sociology" in *Radical Sociologists*, ed. Oppenheimer, Murray, and Levine, 60–61; Jeff Shevitz, "The Irving Show Goes Sour in St. Louis," *The Insurgent Sociologist* 1, no. 3 (August 1970).

55. Mark Selden, "What's in a Name?" *CCAS Newsletter*, January 1971, in Esherick, personal papers; Committee of Concerned Asian Scholars, *The Indochina Story: A Fully Documented Account* (New York: Pantheon Books, 1970); Marilyn Young, interview with the author, May 9, 2013, New York City; Lanza, *The End of Concern*, 94.

56. Young, interview, May 9, 2013; Moss Roberts, interview with the author, June 19, 2014, New York City; Lanza, *The End of Concern*, 82, 88–89, 137–38.

57. Kim, "URPE at Fifty," *Review of Radical Political Economics* 50, no. 3 (2018): 479.

58. Beckwith, *Making Genes*, 95; Moore, *Disrupting Science*, 184.

59. Rich Rothstein to NUC Exec. Comm. December 5, 1969, Lauter Papers.

60. Kampf, interview, April 3, 2013.

61. Moore, *Disrupting Science*, 182–84.

62. Kim, "URPE at Fifty," 479; Julie Matthaei, "URPE, Radical Political Economics, Social Movements, and Revolution—From Identity Politics to Solidarity Economics: Looking Backward, Looking Forward on the Occasion of URPE's Fiftieth Anniversary," *Review of Radical Political Economics* 50, no. 3 (2018): 504–21.

63. Brown, "Early Years," 50–51; Norma Stoltz Chincilla, "Critical Sociologists: Born or Made?," 138; and Lynda Ann Ewen, "Coming Home: A Sociological Journey," 148: all in *Radical Sociologists*, ed. Oppenheimer, Murray, and Levine, 148; Margaret Strobel, "The Academy and the Activist," in *The Politics of Women's Studies: Testimony from Thirty Founding Mothers*, ed. Florence Howe (New York: Feminist Press, 2000), 159.

64. Scholars have paid considerable attention to the women's liberation movement and the rise of women's studies. See, for example, *The Politics of Women's Studies*, ed. Howe; and Marilyn Jacoby Boxer, *When Women Ask the Questions: Creating Women's Studies in America* (Baltimore: Johns Hopkins University Press, 1998).

65. Marlene Dixon, "On Women's Liberation," in *Radical Sociology*, ed. Colfax and Roach, 380.

66. See Alice Echols, *Daring to Be Bad: Radical Feminism in America, 1967–1975* (Minneapolis: University of Minnesota Press, 1989); and *The Feminist Memoir Project*, ed. Rachel DuPlessis Blau and Ann Snitow (New York: Three Rivers Press, 1998), especially the pieces by Jo Freeman and Barbara Epstein about the conflicts between political radicalism and radical feminism.

67. Bridenthal, interview, June 4, 2013.

68. Renate Bridenthal and Claudia Koonz, *Becoming Visible: Women in European History* (Boston: Houghton Mifflin, 1977).

69. Gerda Lerner, "Women among the Professors of History: The Story of a Process of Transformation," in *Voices of Women Historians: The Personal, the Political, the Professional*, ed. Eileen Boris and Nupur Chaudhuri (Bloomington: Indiana University Press, 1999), 5–7.

70. Martha Biondi, *The Black Revolution on Campus* (Berkeley: University of California Press, 2012), 21.

71. Nick Aaron Ford, *Black Studies: Threat-or-Challenge* (Port Washington, NY: Kennikat Press, 1973), 62. Unfortunately for future historians, Nick Aaron Ford, the chair of the Morgan State English department who conducted an invaluable survey of one hundred Black studies programs in the early 1970s, rendered all of his respondents and their institutions anonymous.

72. Ford, *Black Studies*, 5; David A. Varel, *The Scholar and the Struggle: Lawrence Reddick's Crusade for Black History and Black Power* (Chapel Hill: University of North Carolina Press, 2020).

73. Ford, *Black Studies*, 99; Fabio Rojas, *From Black Power to Black Studies: How a Radical Social Movement Became an Academic Discipline* (Baltimore: Johns Hopkins University Press, 2007), 34; Ibram H. Rogers [Kendi], *The Black Campus Movement: Black Students and the Racial Reconstitution of Higher Education, 1965–1972* (New York: Palgrave Macmillan, 2012), 138–40.

74. Rojas, *From Black Power to Black Studies*, 130–66.

75. Novick, *That Noble Dream*, 458–59; Lanza, *The End of Concern*, 80, 146.

76. Ehrlich, "Notes from an Anarchist Sociologist," in *Radical Sociologists*, ed. Oppenheimer, Murray, and Levine, 233–43; Dana Williams and Jeffrey Shantz, "An Anarchist in the Academy, a Sociologist in the Movement: The Life, Activism, and Ideas of Howard J. Ehrlich," *Journal for the Study of Radicalism* 10, no. 2 (2016): 101–22.

77. Lanza, *The End of Concern*, 80, 115.

78. Beckwith, *Making Genes*, 58; Jonathan Beckwith, interview with the author, April 2, 2013, Boston.

79. Zimmerman, *Troublemaker*, 156–63, 203, 217; Bart Meyers, interview with the author, April 14, 2008, Woodstock, NY.

80. Alice Lynd and Staughton Lynd, *Stepping Stones: Memoir of a Life Together* (Lanham, MD: Lexington Books, 2009), 90.

81. Charles Haynie, *A Memoir of the New Left: The Political Autobiography of Charles A. Haynie*, ed. Aeron Haynie and Timothy S. Miller (Knoxville: University of Tennessee Press, 2009), 128.

82. Malcolm Sylvers, "Memories from the Periphery," in *History and the New Left*, ed. Buhle, 187.
83. Leith Mullings, interview with the author, February 11, 2019, New York City; Clyde Barrow, "The Political and Intellectual Origins of the New Political Science," *New Political Science* 39, no. 4 (2017); Brown, "Early Years," in *Radical Sociologists*, ed. Oppenheimer, Murray, and Levine, 51.
84. Ollman and Vernoff, *The Left Academy*; "A Conversation about the Radical History Review: Former and Current Collective Members Reminisce," Andor Skotnes, moderator and editor, *Radical History Review*, no. 79 (winter 2001): 33.
85. Novick, *That Noble Dream*, 440.
86. Roy Rosenzweig in "A Conversation about the Radical History Review," ed. Skotnes, 33.
87. Novick, *That Noble Dream*, 458–59.
88. Richard Flacks, "The Sociology Liberation Movement: Some Legacies and Lessons," in *Radical Sociologists*, ed. Oppenheimer, Murray, and Levine, 25–27.
89. Ohmann, *English in America*, 224–26; Thomas Bender and Carl E. Schorske, eds., *American Academic Culture in Transformation* (Princeton, NJ: Princeton University Press, 1998), 42.
90. Mullings, interview, February 11, 2019.
91. Bernstein, *A Perilous Progress*, 91; Weisskopf, "Reflections," *Review of Radical Political Economics* 46, no. 4 (2014).
92. Sigrid Schmalzer, Daniel S. Chard, and Alyssa Botelho, "Introduction," in *Science for the People*, ed. Schmalzer, Chard, and Botelho, 6–7.

Chapter Sixteen

1. "Academic Freedom and Tenure: Indiana State University," *AAUP Bulletin*, March 1970; "Arkansas Agricultural and Mechanical College," *AAUP Bulletin* 53, no. 4 (December 1967): 385–90. Bill Denham to Douglas H. McCay, May 8, 1968, box 6-1; and Sallie Blake to Dorothy Wertz, April 15, 1968, box 6-2: both in RESIST Records, Watkinson Library and Trinity College Archives, Raether Library, Trinity College, Hartford, CT (hereafter RESIST Records).
2. David R. Seager, "Repression in Academia: New Left and Antiwar College Teachers and Political Dissent in the Vietnam War Era, 1964–1975" (PhD diss., University of Maine, 1995), 89–90.
3. David Kettler to Bob Ross, August 5, 1968, D.O. Chambers to Judy [Longley], January 25, 1969, box 3, file 6, New University Conference Papers, Wisconsin Historical Society, Madison (hereafter NUC Papers, WHS); Nancy McDermid, "Strike Settlement," in *Academics on the Line: The Faculty Strike at San Francisco State*, by Arlene Kaplan Daniels, Rachel Kahn-Hut, and Associates (San Francisco: Jossey-Bass, 1970), 234.
4. Everett C. Frost, typewritten memo, n.d., box 9, folder 5, NUC Papers, WHS; Carl E. Schorske, *Intellectual Life, Civil Libertarian Issues, and the Student*

Movement at the University of California, Berkeley, 1960–1969, 16, interviews conducted by Ann Lage, 1996, 1997, Regional Oral History Office, Bancroft Library, University of California, Berkeley, 2000, http://digitalassets.lib.berkeley .edu/rohoia/ucb/text/intelllifecivilooschorich.pdf; Michael Parenti, "Struggles in the Temple of Knowledge," in *Guarding the Ivory Tower: Repression and Rebellion in Higher Education*, ed. Philip J. Meranto, Oneida J. Meranto, and Matthew R. Lippman (Denver: Lucha Publications, 1985), 71.

5. Tiago Mata, "Migrations and Boundary Work: Harvard, Radical Economists, and the Committee on Political Discrimination," *Science in Context* 22, no. 1 (2009): 133.

6. "Fraser Holds Job for Leggett," *Hartford Times*, March 27, 1969, in Homer D. Babbidge Papers, Series II Campus Unrest, box 167, University of Connecticut Archives, University of Connecticut Library, Thomas J. Dodd Research Center, University of Connecticut, Storrs.

7. Seager, "Repression in Academia," 73; "Academic Freedom and Tenure: Alfred University," *AAUP Bulletin*, March 1970. Memo case of M. L. Michael Kay, n.d.; "Dr. Marvin L. Michael Kay's Statement"; "Western Illinois University and M.L. Michael Kay" [probably by Merrill Hough], December 1971; John T. Bernhard to James R. Conner, June 9, 1970; Michael Kay to Alfred Young, October 14, 1971: all in Alfred Young Papers, courtesy of Robert Cohen (hereafter Young Papers). Alfred Young was a historian at Northern Illinois University who essentially created the official American Historical Association's Committee on the Rights of Historians. I was unable to find anything on many of the cases in Young's papers in the official records of the AHA at the Library of Congress.

8. "Academic Freedom and Tenure: Tulane University," *AAUP Bulletin* 56, no. 4 (December 1970); Edward Dubinsky, telephone interview with the author, May 13, 2019.

9. Bill Zimmerman, *Troublemaker: A Memoir from the Front Lines of the Sixties* (New York: Doubleday, 2011), 203.

10. Parenti, "Struggles in the Temple of Knowledge," in *Guarding the Ivory Tower*, ed. Meranto, Meranto, and Lippman, 55–72; Carl Boggs, "Reflections on Politics and Academia: An Interview with Michael Parenti," *New Political Science*, June 2012; Berenice A. Carroll, "Three Faces of Trevia: Identity, Activism, and Intellect," in *Voices of Women Historians: The Personal, the Political, the Professional*, ed. Eileen Boris and Nupur Chaudhuri (Bloomington: Indiana University Press, 1999), 24; Winton U. Solberg, telephone interview with the author, June 30, 2014.

11. Parenti, "Struggles in the Temple of Knowledge," 65–68; Michael Miles, "The Triumph of Reaction," *Change* 4, no. 10 (Winter 1972/1973): 33; "Teacher Backed by U. of Vermont," *New York Times*, December 6, 1970, clipping in Young Papers.

12. Boggs, "Reflections"; Clyde Barrow, "The Political and Intellectual Origins of the New Political Science," *New Political Science* 39, no. 4 (2017).

13. Bruce Franklin, interview with the author, February 15, 2013, Montclair, NJ;

Aaron J. Leonard with Conor A. Gallagher, *Heavy Radicals: The FBI's Secret War on America's Maoists, the Revolutionary Union/Revolutionary Communist Party, 1968–1980* (Winchester, UK: Zero Books, 2014), 30–102.

14. Richard W. Lyman, *Stanford in Turmoil: Campus Unrest, 1966–1972* (Stanford, CA: Stanford University Press, 2009), 179–84.

15. Bruce Franklin to Richard Lyman, January 21, 1971, http://a3mreunion.org/ archive/1971-1972/71-72_franklin/files_71-72_franklin_firing/71-72Franklin _Franklin_to_Lyman_1_21.pdf; Franklin to Lyman, February 25, 1971, http:// a3mreunion.org/archive/1971-1972/71-72_franklin/files_71-72_franklin_firing/ 71-72 Franklin_Franklin_to_Lyman_2_25_p_1.pdf (both accessed August 11, 2019); Donald Kennedy, *Academic Duty* (Cambridge, MA: Harvard University Press, 1997), 132–34; Stanford University News Service, Press Release, November 16, 1971, http://a3mreunion.org/archive/1971-1972/71-72_franklin _advisory/files_71-72_advisory/71-72FranklinBoard_Press_9.pdf (accessed August 11, 2019).

16. Franklin, interview, February 15, 2013; Lyman, *Stanford in Turmoil*, 191; Meranto, Meranto, and Lippman, eds., *Guarding the Ivory Tower*, 92; "The Stanford Rehabilitation Movement," leaflet, n.d., http://www.a3mreunion.org/ archive/1971-1972/71-72_franklin_srm/files_71-72_srm/71-72FranklinSRM _SRM.pdf (accessed August 11, 2019).

17. Franklin, interview, February 15, 2013.

18. Alice Lynd and Staughton Lynd, *Stepping Stones: Memoir of a Life Together* (Lanham, MD: Lexington Books, 2009), 82–84, 89; Staughton Lynd, telephone interview with the author, June 23, 2014; John Morton Blum, *A Life with History* (Lawrence: University Press of Kansas, 2004), 183–85; Geoffrey Kabaservice, *The Guardians: Kingman Brewster, His Circle, and the Rise of the Liberal Establishment* (New York: Henry Holt, 2004), 256–58.

19. It is not clear whether or not the history department chair John Blum told Lynd that financial constraints dictated his non-reappointment. In any event, he seems to have believed that Lynd's scholarship would not have gotten him tenure anyhow. C. Vann Woodward was equally unenthusiastic about what he called Lynd's "mushy-mindedness, obscurantism, and anti-intellectualism." See Blum, *A Life with History*, 184–85; C. Vann Woodward to Charles A. Barker, October 8, 1968, *The Letters of C. Vann Woodward*, ed. Michael O'Brien (New Haven, CT: Yale University Press, 2013), 268–69.

20. Milton Byrd to Board of Governors, July 12, 1967; Committee on Academic Freedom in Illinois, "Fact Sheet on the Staughton Lynd Case," July 27, 1967; Irwin Suloway, Dean Arts and Sciences, Illinois Teachers College, Chicago-South to Lynd, April 24, 1967: all in box 30, AAUP Committee A Case Files—1974, Chicago State College, AAUP Records, Special Collections Research Center, Gelman Library, George Washington University, Washington, DC (hereafter AAUP, Chicago State College); "Roosevelt University: Report on the Visit of Association Consultants in the Matter of Professor Staughton Lynd," October 9, 1968, in Young Papers.

21. Clipping, Donald Janson, "Lynd Appointment to Chicago State College Is Rejected by Illinois Board of Governors," *New York Times*, July 18, 1967; and Staughton Lynd to Bertram Davis, July 23, 1967: both in AAUP, Chicago State College.

22. Bertram Davis to Richard Nelson, August 7, 1967; William Fidler to James Miller, September 11, 1967; and Miller to Fidler, September 18, 1967: all in AAUP, Chicago State College.

23. Alfred Young to Bertram Davis, September 2, 1967, in AAUP, Chicago State College; "A National Statement on the Staughton Lynd Case," October 1967, in Young Papers. C. Vann Woodward to Richard Hofstadter, October 3, 1967; and Hofstadter to Woodward, October 9, 1967: both in box 9, Richard Hofstadter Papers, Rare Book and Manuscript Library, Butler Library, Columbia University.

24. David Fellman to William P. Fidler, July 21, 1967; Fidler to James Miller, September 28, 1967; and Fidler to Professor Robert Shiffman et al., September 29, 1967: all in AAUP, Chicago State College.

25. "Roosevelt University: Report on the Visit of Association Consultants in the Matter of Professor Staughton Lynd," October 9, 1968; and Bertram Davis to Alfred Young, October 31, 1968: both in Young Papers. Jordan Kurland, telephone interview with the author, June 25, 2013.

26. Staughton Lynd to Bertram Davis, April 25, 1969; Alfred Young to Davis, January 25, 1970; and Davis to Young, January 28, 1970: all in Young Papers.

27. Bertram H. Davis to Alfred Young, July 8, 1970, in Young Papers.

28. News Bureau, NYU, "The Disruptions at Loeb, Courant, and Kimball: A report to the New York University community on the occupation of three University buildings at Washington Square during the Cambodian crisis period of May 1970"; "NYU in the 1970s"; and Leslie Oelsner, "2 Indicted in Raid on NYU Center," *New York Times*, July 30, 1970, clipping in Bio File, "Wolfe, Robert": all in New York University Archives, Bobst Library, New York University. (When I examined them, these archives were not well organized.) Robert Wolfe, interview with the author, August 13, 2015, New York City; Jack Zipes, telephone interview with the author, March 8, 2013.

29. Marshall Windmiller and John Gerassi, "Trouble at San Francisco State: An Exchange," in *The University Crisis Reader*, ed. Immanuel Wallerstein and Paul Starr, vol. 2, *Confrontation and Counterattack* (New York: Random House, 1971), 341–69; Paul Kleinberger, "Questionnaire on Discrimination in Employment and Promotion of Left Academics," n.d., box 9, folder 5, NUC Papers, WHS.

30. Lawrence E. Eichel, Kenneth W. Jost, Robert D. Luskin, and Richard M. Neustadt, *The Harvard Strike* (Boston: Houghton Mifflin, 1970), 48, 305–6; Jack Stauder, telephone interview and email with the author, November 3, 2014.

31. Bruce M. Stave, *Red Brick in the Land of Steady Habits: Creating the University of Connecticut, 1881–2006* (Hanover, NH: University Press of New England, 2006), 128–39; Temporary Injunction, Superior Court, Tolland County [Con-

necticut], February 5, 1969, box 9, folder 5, NUC Papers, WHS; Sociology
Liberation Movement, "To all radical sociologists," n.d. [early 1969?], box 5,
folder 10, NUC Papers, WHS; David Colfax, Charles Brover, John Leggett,
Jack Roach to Dear Colleagues and Friends, March 22, 1969, box 3, file 6, NUC
Papers, WHS; Len Krimerman, interview with the author, October 21, 2015,
Storrs, CT.
32. "Academic Freedom and Tenure: East Tennessee State University," *AAUP Bulletin*, March 1973.
33. "Academic Freedom and Tenure: Indiana State University," *AAUP Bulletin*, September 1972.
34. "Academic Freedom and Tenure: Ohio State University," *AAUP Bulletin,* March 1970; David Kettler to Bob Ross, August 5, 1968, box 3, file 6, NUC Records, WHS; William J. Shkurti, *The Ohio State University in the Sixties* (Columbus: Ohio State University Press, 2016), 246–47.
35. Joy Williamson-Lott, "The Battle for Academic Freedom at Southern Institutions of Higher Education, 1955–1965," *Journal of Southern History* 79 (November 2013): 879–920; Nadine Cohodas, *The Band Played Dixie: Race and the Liberal Conscience at Ole Miss* (New York: Free Press, 1997), 111–12; "Academic Freedom and Tenure: University of Arkansas," *AAUP Bulletin* 49, no. 4 (December 1963); James W. Silver, "Mississippi: The Closed Society," *Journal of Southern History* 30, no. 1 (February 1964): 3–34; Everett Carll Ladd Jr. and Seymour Martin Lipset, *The Divided Academy: Professors and Politics* (New York: McGraw-Hill, 1975). There is a lot of information about the particularly blatant firing of Howard Zinn at Spelman College in 1963. See, in particular, Martin Duberman, *Howard Zinn: A Life on the Left* (New York: New Press, 2012); *Howard Zinn's Southern Diary: Sit-Ins, Civil Rights, and Black Women's Student Activism*, ed. Robert Cohen (Athens: University of Georgia Press, 2018); and Howard Zinn, *You Can't Be Neutral on a Moving Train: A Personal History of Our Times* (1994; repr., Boston: Beacon Press, 2002).
36. Elizabeth Blum, "Questionnaire on Discrimination Against Left Academics," March 1969, box 9, folder 5, NUC Papers, WHS; Miles, "The Triumph of Reaction," *Change* 4, no. 10 (Winter 1972/1973): 34.
37. "Report of the American Historical Association Ad Hoc Committee on the Rights of Historians," March 5, 1974, in Young Papers.
38. Mata, "Migrations and Boundary Work," *Science in Context* 22, no. 1 (2009): 133.
39. Memo to "All NUC Chapter Contacts, Executive Committee, 1970–71 Staff," April 12, 1970, Paul Lauter Papers. (Paul Lauter collected an enormous amount of material. I originally saw some of it in his personal possession before he gave it to the library at Trinity College, Hartford, CT. As a result, although his papers are now accessible to researchers, my citation will be of little help in directing them to find specific documents in the official Lauter Papers.)

As the sociologist Martin Oppenheimer observed, by the mid-1970s "a creeping purge of the left in academia was underway." Martin Oppenheimer, "Pages from a Journal of the Middle Left," in *Radical Sociologists and the Movement: Experiences, Lessons, and Legacies*, ed. Martin Oppenheimer, Martin J. Murray, and Rhonda F. Levine (Philadelphia: Temple University Press, 1991), 126.

40. Richard Flacks, telephone interview with the author, February 22, 2013.

41. Richard Rothstein to Neil Resnikoff, October 14, 1969, box 5, folder 10, NUC Papers, WHS; Psychology Liberation Movement Program, draft, November 1969, box 13, folder 4, NUC Papers, WHS; Kenneth J. Heineman, *Campus Wars: The Peace Movement at American State Universities in the Vietnam Era* (New York: New York University Press, 1993), 52–53; *NUC Newsletter* 2, no. 3 (May 1969), in Lauter Papers.

42. Richard Levins, "Questionnaire on Discrimination in Employment and Promotion of Left Academics," n.d., box 9, folder 5, NUC Papers, WHS; Paul Lauter, interview with the author, August 21, 2013, New York City.

43. Lauter, interview with the author, August 21, 2013.

44. Union for Social Action, leaflet, n.d., box 9, folder 5; Colfax, Brover, Leggett, Roach to Dear Colleagues and Friends, March 22, 1969, box 3, file 6; and Ad Hoc Committee to Reinstate Kent, Brannan, Shapiro to Daniel Aldrich, Chancellor, UC Irvine, February 1969, box 3, file 6: all in NUC Papers, WHS; Heineman, *Campus Wars*, 260; Carol A. Brown, "The Early Years of the Sociology Liberation Movement," in *Radical Sociologists*, ed. Oppenheimer, Murray, and Levine, 47.

45. Lawrence Wittner, telephone interview with the author, April 21, 2018. Committee for Justice in the Novack Case to students and former students of David Novack, April 14, 1970; and Open Letter to the President et al., April 27, 1970: both in Vassar College, 1971 Sit-In, box 1.1, Archives and Special Collections Library, Vassar College Library, Poughkeepsie, NY. "Academic Freedom and Tenure: Adelphi University," *AAUP Bulletin* 53, no. 3, September 1967 (Autumn Issue): 278–91; Zimmerman, *Troublemaker*, 160–67; Bill Zimmerman, "Questionnaire on Discrimination Against Left Academics," n.d., box 9, folder 5, NUC Papers, WHS.

46. Sheila McVey, "Departmental Clashes," in *Academic Supermarkets: A Critical Case Study of a Multiversity*, ed. Philip G. Altbach, Robert S. Laufer, and Sheila McVey (San Francisco: Jossey-Bass, 1971), 247; Richard Flacks, "The Sociology Liberation Movement: Some Legacies and Lessons," in *Radical Sociologists*, ed. Oppenheimer, Murray, and Levine, 25.

47. Richard Mann, telephone interview with the author, November 14, 2014; Henry Mayer to Committee on the Rights of Historians, October 1, 1971, Young Papers.

48. William Doyle, "An Effective Politics for Professional Activists," n.d. [probably 1969–70]; and NUC leaflet "Open Up the Schools," n.d. [late '69 or '70]: both in box 9, folder 4, NUC Papers, WHS.

49. Josephine Donovan, "A Cause of Our Own," in *The Politics of Women's Studies: Testimony from Thirty Founding Mothers*, ed. Florence Howe (New York: Feminist Press, 2000), 101.

50. Kathryn Kish Sklar, "The Women's Studies Moment: 1972," in *The Politics of Women's Studies*, ed. Howe, 135; "Living US Women's History: An Oral History Interview with Sklar, Kathryn Kish," Melanie Gustafson interviewer, Brackney, Penn, 5 and 6, October 2000, *Women and Social Movements in the United States* 23, no. 1 (March 2019), http://womhist.alexanderstreet.com (accessed August 23, 2019), 62–63; Hester Eisenstein, interview with the author, April 7, 2015, New York City.

51. Kathleen Gough, "World Revolution and the Science of Man," in *The Dissenting Academy*, ed. Theodore Roszak (New York: Pantheon, 1968), 157; Alan Wolfe, "The Professional Mystique," in *An End to Political Science: The Caucus Papers*, ed. Marvin Surkin and Alan Wolfe (New York: Basic Books, 1970), 295.

52. Edward T. Silva, "Faculty Images of Power and Knowledge," in *Academic Supermarkets*, ed. Altbach, Laufer, and McVey, 170–77.

53. Wolfe, interview, August 13, 2015; Marvin Surkin, interview with the author, February 2, 2015, New York City; *NUC Newsletter* 2, no. 3 (May 1969), in Lauter Papers; Jack Zipes, telephone interview with the author, March 8, 2013; Marlene Kim, "URPE at Fifty: Reflections on a Half Century of Activism, Community, Debate (and a Few Crazy Moments)," *Review of Radical Political Economics* 50 no. 3 (2018): 480; Zimmerman, *Troublemaker*, 191–93; Eisenstein, interview, April 7, 2015.

54. Kim, "URPE at Fifty," *Review of Radical Political Economics* 50, no. 3 (2018): 482; Mata, "Migrations and Boundary Work," 115–43.

55. Philip G. Altbach, "The Champagne University in the Beer State," in *Academic Transformation: Seventeen Institutions under Pressure*, ed. David Riesman and Verne A. Stadtman (New York: McGraw-Hill, 1973), 399; Zimmerman, *Troublemaker*, 167; Harry Edwards, *The Struggle That Must Be: An Autobiography* (New York: Macmillan, 1980), 244–45; Boris and Chaudhuri, *Voices of Women Historians*; Howe, *The Politics of Women's Studies*.

56. Gerda Lerner, "Women among the Professors of History: The Story of a Process of Transformation," in *Voices of Women Historians*, ed. Boris and Chaudhuri, 4–10; David A. Varel, *The Scholar and the Struggle: Lawrence Reddick's Crusade for Black History and Black Power* (Chapel Hill: University of North Carolina Press, 2020).

57. Peniel E. Joseph, "Black Studies, Student Activism, and the Black Power Movement," in *The Black Power Movement: Rethinking the Civil Rights–Black Power Era*, ed. Joseph (New York: Routledge, 2006), 251.

58. Annette Kolodny, "A Sense of Discovery, Mixed with a Sense of Justice," in *The Politics of Women's Studies*, ed. Howe, 285; Marilyn Jacoby Boxer, *When Women Ask the Questions: Creating Women's Studies in America* (Baltimore: Johns Hopkins University Press, 1998), 191, 199.

59. Boxer, *When Women Ask the Questions*, 2. Mary Jo Buhle, "Introduction," xv–xvi; Elizabeth Lapovsky Kennedy, "Dream of Social Justice: Building Women's Studies at the State University of New York, Buffalo," 245–46; and Donovan, "A Cause of Our Own," 99: all in *The Politics of Women's Studies*, ed. Howe.

60. Nick Aaron Ford, *Black Studies: Threat-or-Challenge* (Port Washington, NY: Kennikat Press, 1973), 45–46, 97–98, 160; Kenneth M. Stampp, *Historian of Slavery, the Civil War, and Reconstruction, University of California, Berkeley, 1946–1983*, 139, interviews conducted by Ann Lage in 1996, Regional Oral History Office, Bancroft Library, University of California, Berkeley, 1998, https://digitalassets.lib.berkeley.edu/rohoia/ucb/text/historianslaveryoostamrich.pdf; Matthew Johnson, *Undermining Racial Justice: How One University Embraced Inclusion and Inequality* (Ithaca, NY: Cornell University Press, 2020), 132–34.

61. Noliwe M. Rooks, *White Money/Black Power: The Surprising History of African American Studies and the Crisis of Race in Higher Education* (Boston: Beacon Press, 2006), 17–21, 67–68.

62. Nellie Y. McKay, "Charting a Personal Journey: A Road to Women's Studies," in *The Politics of Women's Studies*, ed. Howe, 211; Sundiata Keita Cha-Jua, "Black Studies in the New Millennium: Resurrecting Ghosts of the Past," *Souls* 2 (Summer 2000): 44–49; Ford, *Black Studies*, 145; Joseph, "Black Studies," in *The Black Power Movement*, ed. Joseph, 251–77.

63. Kennedy, "Dream of Social Justice," 262–63; Myra Dinnerstein, "A Political Education," 294: both in *The Politics of Women's Studies*, ed. Howe

64. Christopher Jencks and David Riesman, *The Academic Revolution* (New York: Doubleday, 1968); Warren Bennis, *The Leaning Ivory Tower* (San Francisco: Jossey-Bass, 1973), 123–27, 134–40.

65. Ed Allaire to Louis [Kampf], January 16, 1968, box 6-1, RESIST Records.

66. "Academic Freedom and Tenure: Sam Houston State Teachers College," *AAUP Bulletin*, March 1963.

67. "Academic Freedom and Tenure: Northern State College (South Dakota)," *AAUP Bulletin*, September 1968.

68. "Academic Freedom and Tenure: Arkansas Agricultural and Mechanical College," *AAUP Bulletin*, December 1967. For similar cases, see "Academic Freedom and Tenure: The University of Illinois" and "Academic Freedom and Tenure: Arkansas State Teachers College," both in *AAUP Bulletin* 49, no. 1 (March 1963).

69. Kenneth M. Dolbeare, "Faculty Power," in *Academic Supermarkets*, ed. Altbach, Laufer, and McVey, 162–63; Ronald Grele, interview with the author, January 22, 2015, New York City. On the early non-reappointment of one of the University of Wisconsin's most conspicuous radicals, see McVey, "Departmental Clashes," 229–30, 246–51; and David Evett, "Travail of a Department," 260: both in *Academic Supermarkets*, ed. Altbach, Laufer, and McVey.

70. Paul Faler and Malcolm Sylvers, "Statement on the firing of Paul Faler and Malcolm Sylvers, 1970," in both the Young Papers and box 9, folder 5, NUC Papers, WHS.

71. Text of memo by Dr. R. G. McPherson, February 25, 1970, in student newspaper [U. Ga.?], March 5, 1970; Alfred Young, memo, n.d.; Robert Griffith, "Georgia's 'Compatibility' Oath," *Change*, October 1971; and Chas. Crowe to Young, June 4, 1972: all in Young Papers.

72. Alfred Young, memo, "Case: Richard Stremski and others, University of Alabama, Huntsville," August 17, 1972; "Preliminary Hearing Committee Report to the Faculty Appeals Committee on Dr. Richard Stremski's Appeal," n.d.; Memo, "Factors accounting for the nonretention of Dr. Dennis S. Nordin, Assistant Professor of History, Chicago State College," n.d.; Nordin to Sheldon Hackney, September 17, 1971; and Paul Faler and Malcolm Sylvers, "Statement on the firing of Paul Faler and Malcolm Sylvers, 1970": all in Young Papers.

73. See Philip Kay, "'Guttersnipes' and 'Eliterates': City College in the Popular Imagination" (PhD diss., Columbia University, 2011), for a particularly intelligent depiction of the City College crises of the 1960s and 1970s.

74. "The Five Demands," CUNY Digital History Project, cdha.cuny.edu (accessed October 28, 2019). Philip Barnett, Judy Connorton, William Gibbons, and Sydney Van Nort, "Five Demands: The Student Protest and Takeover of 1968," pamphlet, n.d. [c. 2009]; and Barbara Gutfreund Arfa, "History Department Controversy," *City College Alumnus*, April 1975: both in CCNY Archives and Special Collections, Cohen Library, City College of New York.

75. Barnett et al., "Five Demands"; Martha Biondi, *The Black Revolution on Campus* (Berkeley: University of California Press, 2012), 123–41; Nathan Glazer, "City College," in *Academic Transformation*, ed. Riesman and Stadtman, 71–90.

76. Robert E. Marshak, *Academic Renewal in the 1970s: Memoirs of a City College President* (Washington DC: University Press of America, 1982), 17–20.

77. Arfa, "History Department Controversy"; Glazer, "City College," in *Academic Transformation*, ed. Riesman and Stadtman, 88–90.

78. Kay, "Guttersnipes," 10, 206.

79. Sidney Ditzion, Acting Chair, to Copeland, May 26, 1969, in Office of the President, Papers, 1967–1969, box 4, folder, New York, City College, Dept of History, Correspondence 1967–1969, CCNY Archives.

80. Marshak, *Academic Renewal*, 56; George Schwab, interview with the author, February 11, 2014, New York City; Walter Struve, interview with the author, January 29, 2014, Tarrytown, NY; Kay, "Guttersnipes," 280; Leonard Kriegel, "Surviving the Apocalypse: Teaching at City College," *Change* 4, no. 6 (summer 1972): 60.

81. Marshak, *Academic Renewal*, 53, 103–4; Struve, interview, January 29, 2014.

82. Irwin Yellowitz, interview with the author, March 19, 2013, New York City; "Report on the Department of History of the City College, to President's Visiting Review Committee, March 1971"; and Martin Waldman, memo, n.d.: both in box 5, folder: Reports of History Department Investigation, 1971–1975, Jacob Rothenberg Papers, CCNY Archives. Struve, interview, January 29, 2014.

83. Folder: History Department Investigation: Correspondence, 1971–73, box 5; and folder: Reports of History Department Investigation, 1971–1975, box 5: both in Rothenberg Papers, CCNY Archives. Joan [Kelly-]Gadol, Report on European (Western) History, n.d., box 7, Irwin Yellowitz Papers, CCNY Archives; Arfa, "History Department Controversy"; Struve, interview, January 29, 2014.

84. Rowland Evans and Robert Novak, "The Wrecking of a College," *New York Post*, December 29, 1970; Marshak, *Academic Renewal*, 80; Yellowitz, interview, March 19, 2013; Kay, "Guttersnipes," 5; Judith Stein, interview with the author, December 13, 2013, New York City; Struve, interview, January 29, 2014.

85. Schwab, interview, February 11, 2014; Marshak, *Academic Renewal*, 48–51; Glazer, "City College," in *Academic Transformation*, ed. Riesman and Stadtman, 71–98.

86. Struve, interview, January 29, 2014.

87. "Report on the Department of History of the City College, to President's Visiting Review Committee, March 1971," box 5, folder: Reports of Hist. Department Investigation, 1971–1975, Rothenberg Papers, CCNY Archives.

88. Felix Gilbert, Edmund S. Morgan, and Carl E. Schorske to President Robert E. Marshak, May 18, 1971, in box 7, Irwin Yellowitz Papers, CCNY Archives.

89. Stein, interview, December 13, 2013; Schwab, interview, February 11, 2014.

90. Joseph W. Wildebush, "Award of Arbitrator," August 1, 1973, in "Case of Professor Henry Friedlander," George Schwab Personal Papers; Yellowitz, interview, March 19, 2013; Stein, interview December 18, 2013; Resolution of Censure, Special Meeting of the History Department, March 23, 1972, box 5, folder: History Department Investigation: Correspondence 1971–73, Rothenberg Papers, CCNY.

91. Yellowitz, interview, March 19, 2013.

92. On the fiscal crisis, see Kim Phillips-Fein, *Fear City: New York's Fiscal Crisis and the Rise of Austerity Politics* (New York: Metropolitan Books, 2017), 241–55.

Chapter Seventeen

1. Anon., "The Future of City College of New York?" and "Dear Colleague," December 8, 1969, both in box 5, folder: "History Department Minutes, 1969," Jacob Rothenberg Papers, CCNY Archives and Special Collections, Cohen Library, City College of New York.

2. I found copies of this letter, Sidney Hook to [name inserted], December 16, 1968, in the papers of several academics, including, among others Carl Friedrich: box 77, Carl J. Friedrich Papers, HUG(FP) 17.14, Harvard University Archives, Nathan M. Pusey Library, Harvard University, Cambridge, MA (hereafter Friedrich Papers).

3. Edward Chalfant to Oscar Handlin, August 18, 1970, box 27, Oscar Handlin Papers, Harvard University Archives.

4. Among the other well-known academics who joined UCRA were Gardner Ackley (Michigan), A. A. Berle (Columbia), Cleanth Brooks (Yale), Alexander Gerschenkron (Harvard), Gertrude Himmelfarb (Brooklyn College), Chalmers Johnson (Berkeley), Howard Mumford Jones (Harvard), Jeane Kirkpatrick (Georgetown), Milton Konvitz (Cornell), Paul Otto Kristeller (Columbia), Samuel Lubell (Columbia), Fritz Machlup (Princeton), Robert A. Nisbet

(Berkeley), R. R. Palmer (Yale), I. Milton Sacks (Brandeis), John Searle (Berkeley), and Martin Trow (Berkeley). These names came from the letterheads of Sidney Hook telegram to William Scranton, August 25, 1970, in box 170, folder 2; Hook to Arthur Singer, Jr., November 23, 1977, box 170, folder 3; Press Release, May 17, 1969, box 170, folder 1: all in Sidney Hook Papers, Hoover Institution Library and Archives, Stanford, CA (hereafter Hook Papers).

5. Marvin Meyers to Sidney Hook, March 6, 1969, and April 10, 1969, box 170, folder 1, Hook Papers.

6. Miro Todorovich to David Riesman, September 24, 1969; Riesman to Todorovich, September 30, 1969; and Richard Pipes to Sidney Hook, March 17, 1969: all in box 170, folder 1, Hook Papers. Memo from Executive Committee, Faculty Renaissance, January 8, 1969, San Francisco State Strike Collection, box: Faculty Renaissance, folder 106, Labor Archives and Research Center, University Archives, San Francisco State University (hereafter LARC, SFSU); Harry Girvetz to William French Smith, July 9, 1970, CU-5, series 8, box 27, folder 6, University of California, President, Permanent Files 1958–75, University of California Archives, Bancroft Library, University of California, Berkeley; *Measure*, Emergency Supplements, no. 2, May 12, 1970; and Arthur R. Hercz to Sidney Hook, April 20, 1970: both in box 27, Handlin Papers.

7. Riesman to Todorovich, September 31, 1969; and Richard Pipes to Sidney Hook, March 17, 1969: both in box 170, folder 1, Hook Papers.

8. Jacob Finkelstein to Miro Todorovich, October 23, 1973; and Sidney Hook to Arthur Singer Jr., November 23, 1977: both in box 170, folder 3, Hook Papers.

9. Morton J. Tenzer to Sidney Hook, February 4, 1969, box 170, folder 1, Hook Papers; Hook to Arthur Singer Jr., November 23, 1977, box 170, folder 3, Hook Papers; John Andrew III, *Power to Destroy: The Political Uses of the IRS from Kennedy to Nixon* (Chicago: Ivan R. Dee, 2002), 222; Lloyd P. Gartner, "Five Demands at City College of New York," *Midstream* 15, no. 8 (October 1969): 24–29. Arthur R. Hercz to Sidney Hook, April 20, 1970; and Miro Todorovich to Hercz, April 22, 1970: both in box 27, Handlin Papers.

10. Anon., "Should UCRA Continue?" n.d.; and Abba Lerner, Sidney Hook, and Miro Todorovich to All members of the Board of Directors, September 29, 1972: both in box 27, Handlin Papers.

11. Daniel Bell to David Riesman, September 13, 1965, box 1, David Riesman Papers, HUG (FP) 99.12, Harvard University Archives, Nathan M. Pusey Library, Harvard University (hereafter Riesman Papers); Charles Kadushin, *The American Intellectual Elite* (New York: Little, Brown, 1974), 237–47; Sidney Hook, "Academic Freedom and the Rights of Students," *New York Times Magazine*, January 3, 1965 [original title: "Freedom to Learn but Not Freedom to Riot"]; John Searle, "A Foolproof Scenario for Student Revolts," *New York Times Magazine*, December 29, 1968; Edward Fiske to Leonard R. Sussman, September 8, 1975, box 8, Handlin Papers.

12. Nathan Glazer to David Riesman, April 28, 1969, box 13, Riesman Papers; Riesman to Seymour Martin Lipset, April 23, 1969, box 28, Riesman Papers;

Fabio Lanza, *The End of Concern: Maoist China, Activism, and Asian Studies* (Durham, NC: Duke University Press, 2017), 202; Glazer to Hubert Humphrey, October 23, 1967, box 13, Riesman Papers.

13. John R. Searle, *The Campus War: A Sympathetic Look at the University in Agony* (New York: World, 1971), 124.

14. Carl E. Schorske, *Intellectual Life, Civil Libertarian Issues, and the Student Movement at the University of California, Berkeley, 1960–1969*, 37, interviews conducted by Ann Lage, 1996, 1997, Regional Oral History Office, Bancroft Library, University of California, Berkeley, 2000, http://digitalassets.lib .berkeley.edu/rohoia/ucb/text/intelllifecivilooschorich.pdf (hereafter Schorske, Bancroft Oral History).

15. C. Vann Woodward to David Riesman, June 7, 1960, April 23, 1975; Woodward to Wallace Notestein, June 4, 1967; Woodward to Wilma Dykeman Stokely, June 3, 1968; and Woodward to Eugene Genovese, June 21, 1969: all in *The Letters of C. Vann Woodward*, ed. Michael O'Brien (New Haven, CT: Yale University Press, 2013), xl, 211, 259, 266, 272, 312.

16. I am relying here on Daniel Geary, "Children of *The Lonely Crowd*: David Riesman, the Young Radicals, and the Splitting of Liberalism in the 1960s," *Modern Intellectual History* 10, no. 3 (November 2013): 603–33.

17. H. Stuart Hughes, *Gentleman Rebel: The Memoirs of H. Stuart Hughes* (New York: Ticknor & Fields, 1990), 284–85.

18. See chapter 4, for a discussion of the opposition to the Free Speech Movement at Berkeley.

19. Kadushin, *American Intellectual Elite*, 279; L. G. Heller, *The Death of the American University* (New Rochelle, NY: Arlington House, 1973), 53.

20. Reminiscences of Polykarp Kusch, May 17, 1968, 3, in Columbia Oral History Project, Rare Books and Manuscripts Library, Butler Library, Columbia University (hereafter COHP); Kadushin, *American Intellectual Elite*, 277–79; Daniel Bell and Irving Kristol, "Introduction," in *Confrontation: The Student Rebellion and the Universities*, ed. Bell and Kristol (New York: Basic Books, 1969), xi.

21. John Blum considered Staughton Lynd "excessively emotional, hyperbolically emotional, not subject to rational discourse about either urban racial issues or/and the war in Vietnam." Geoffrey Kabaservice, *The Guardians: Kingman Brewster, His Circle, and the Rise of the Liberal Establishment* (New York: Henry Holt, 2004), 256–57.

22. Martin Edward Malia, *Historian of Russian and European Intellectual History*, interviews conducted by David Engerman in 2003, Regional Oral History Office, Bancroft Library, University of California, Berkeley, 2005, https:// digitalassets.lib.berkeley.edu/roho/ucb/text/MaliaBook.pdf; John Hope Franklin, statement, February 7, 1969, box 127, folder 4, Office of the President, Levi Administration Records, University of Chicago Archives, Special Collections Research Center, University of Chicago Library (hereafter Office of the President, Levi Administration Records).

23. Irving Howe, "The Agony of the Campus," in *The University Crisis Reader*, ed. Immanuel Wallerstein and Paul Starr, vol. 2, *Confrontation and Counterattack* (New York: Random House, 1971), 437 (originally in *Dissent*, September–October 1969); Geary, "Children of *The Lonely Crowd*," 625; Fritz Stern, "Reflections on the International Student Movement," *American Scholar* 40, no. 1 (Winter 1970–71): 134; Kenneth Keniston, "What's Bugging the Students?" in *Perspectives on Campus Tensions: Papers Prepared for the Special Committee on Campus Tensions*, ed. David C. Nichols (Washington, DC: American Council on Education, 1970), 47–67; Richard Flacks, "Who Protests: The Social Bases of the Student Movement," in *Protest! Student Activism in America*, ed. Julian Foster and Durward Long (New York: William Morrow, 1970), 134–57; Samuel Lubell, "That 'Generation Gap,'" in *Confrontation*, ed. Bell and Kristol, 58–66.

24. Geary, "Children of *The Lonely Crowd*," 625; Searle, *Campus War*, 49; Daniel J. Boorstin, "The New Barbarians," *Esquire* 70, no. 4 (October 1, 1968): 159, 263; Heller, *Death of the American University*, 44–45.

25. Jerry L. Avorn with Andrew Crane, Mark Jaffe, Oren Root Jr., Paul Starr, Michael Stern, and Robert Stulberg, eds. *Up Against the Ivy Wall: A History of the Columbia Crisis* (New York: Atheneum, 1968), 70, 143–44; Donald Light Jr., "The Dynamics of Faculty Response to Student Protest," 121; and Light, "Directed Resistance," 88: both in *The Dynamics of University Protest*, ed. Donald Light Jr. and John Spiegel (Chicago: Nelson-Hall, 1977). Martha Biondi, *The Black Revolution on Campus* (Berkeley: University of California Press, 2012), 45.

26. For a representative view of the notion that students are flouting authority, see Searle, *Campus War*.

27. Sidney Hook, "Academic Freedom and the Rights of Students," in *The Berkeley Student Revolt: Facts and Interpretations*, ed. Seymour Martin Lipset and Sheldon S. Wolin (Garden City, NY: Doubleday, 1965), 440; Sidney Hook, letter to [name inserted], December 16, 1968. On the need for reforms, see Stern, "Reflections on the International Student Movement," *American Scholar* 40, no. 1 (Winter 1970–71): 131.

28. John Spiegel, "The Group Psychology of Campus Disorders," 142–43; and Light, "Dynamics of Faculty Response," 115: both in *The Dynamics of University Protest*, ed. Light and Spiegel.

29. Wayne C. Booth, *My Many Selves: The Quest for a Plausible Harmony* (Logan: Utah State University Press, 2006), 195.

30. Richard Flacks, "The Sociology Liberation Movement: Some Legacies and Lessons," in *Radical Sociologists and the Movement: Experiences, Lessons, and Legacies*, ed. Martin Oppenheimer, Martin J. Murray, and Rhonda F. Levine (Philadelphia: Temple University Press, 1991), 22–23.

31. S. J. Kline to Pro Tem California Group, June 9, 1969, box 170, folder 4, Hook Papers; Heller, *Death of the American University*, 105–6.

32. Press Release, May 17, 1969, box 170, folder 1, Hook Papers; Ernest Nagel to Leo [Rosten], October 28, 1968, box 163, folder 4, Hook Papers; Searle, *Cam-*

pus War, 121; Milorad M. Drachkovitch and Lewis H. Gann to Sidney Hook, March 17, 1969, in box 170, folder 1, Hook Papers; Spiegel, "The Group Psychology of Campus Disorders," in *The Dynamics of University Protest*, ed. Light and Spiegel, 141, 149, 169; Stern, "Reflections on the International Student Movement," 134; Paul Oskar Kristeller to Hook, February 21, 1971, box 170, folder 1, Hook Papers; Eldon Kenworthy, "The Non-Militant Students," in *Divided We Stand: Reflections on the Crisis at Cornell*, ed. Cushing Strout and David I. Grossvogel (Garden City, NY: Doubleday, 1970), 85; Nicholas Dawidoff, *The Fly Swatter: How My Grandfather Made His Way in the World* (New York: Pantheon, 2002), 312 (this is a biography of Alexander Gerschenkron); Gartner, "Five Demands," 19–20; Sidney Hook, "The Trojan Horse in American Higher Education," *Educational Record*, Winter 1969, in *The University Crisis Reader*, ed. Wallerstein and Starr, 2:403; O. J. Kleppa, statement, February 5, 1969, box 125, folder 1, Office of the President, Levi Administration Records.

33. Daniel Boorstin, "Goodbye, Mr. Chips: The Dissenting Professors," syndicated by AP, cited in Jesse Lemisch, *On Active Service in War and Peace: Politics and Ideology in the American Historical Profession* (Toronto: New Hogtown Press, 1975), 106.

34. Dawidoff, *Fly Swatter*, 303, 316–17.

35. Charles Hitch, quoted in Steve Shapiro, "UC AFT Conference," *NUC Newsletter* 3, no. 6 (April 18, 1970), in Paul Lauter Papers. (Paul Lauter collected an enormous amount of material. I originally saw some of it in his personal possession before he gave it to the library at Trinity College, Hartford, CT. As a result, although his papers are now accessible to researchers, my citation will be of little help in directing them to find specific documents in the Lauter Papers.)

36. S. I. Hayakawa, "Alienation Is Being Taught by Professors," in *The University Crisis Reader*, ed. Wallerstein and Starr, 2:441; Adam Ulam, *The Fall of the American University* (LaSalle, IL: Library Press, 1972), 142.

37. James M. Buchanan and Nicos E. Devletoglou, *Academia in Anarchy: An Economic Diagnosis* (New York: Basic Books, 1970), 138.

38. Searle, *Campus War*, 139.

39. Hook to [name to be inserted], December 16, 1968; and Hook quoted in Martin L. Gross, "Professor May Yet Save Campuses from Extinction," *Los Angeles Times*, June 30, 1969, clipping: both in box 170, folder 4, Hook Papers; Heller, *Death of the American University*, 50; Stern, "Reflections on the International Student Movement," 132; Searle, *Campus War*, 128; Hook, "The Trojan Horse in American Higher Education," in *The University Crisis Reader*, ed. Wallerstein and Starr, 2: 398–404.

40. Reminiscences of Polykarp Kusch, COHP, 29; Heller, *Death of the American University*, 50.

41. Carl J. Friedrich to Nathan Pusey, April 13, 1969, box 27, folder: Student revolts, etc. 1969, Friedrich Papers.

42. For comments about capitulation, see, for example, Buchanan and Devleto-glou, *Academia in Anarchy*, 80.

43. Strout and Grossvogel, eds., *Divided We Stand*; Donald Alexander Downs, *Cornell '69: Liberalism and the Crisis of the American University* (Ithaca, NY: Cornell University Press, 1999), 236–37, 254–65.

44. Milton R. Konvitz, "A Letter from Cornell: Why One Professor Changed His Vote," *New York Times*, May 18, 1969; Bruce Dancis, *Resister: A Story of Protest and Prison during the Vietnam War* (Ithaca, NY: Cornell University Press, 2014), 245–69.

45. Henry Rosovsky, "Black Studies at Harvard: Personal Reflections Concerning Recent Events," *American Scholar* 38, no. 4 (Autumn 1969): 562–72.

46. Dumas Malone to Richard Hofstadter, May 2, 1969, in box A, Richard Hof-stadter Papers, Rare Book and Manuscript Library, Butler Library, Columbia University (hereafter Hofstadter Papers).

47. Light, "Dynamics of Faculty Response," in *The Dynamics of University Protest*, ed. Light and Spiegel, 112; T. R. McConnell, "Faculty Interests in Value Change and Power Conflicts," *AAUP Bulletin* 55, no. 3 (September 1969, Autumn Issue): 346; Minutes of meeting of UCRA National Board, April 19, 1970, box 170, folder 4, Hook Papers; Ralph S. Brown Jr., "Upholding Professional Standards in the 70s," *AAUP Bulletin* 56, no. 2 (Summer 1970): 120.

48. Allan Sindler and Walter Berns, quoted in Downs, *Cornell '69*, 265; Sindler, paper presented at APSA annual meeting, 1969, in Kenworthy, "The Non-Militant Students," in *Divided We Stand*, ed. Strout and Grossvogel, 87.

49. For a useful discussion of academic freedom, see Matthew W. Finkin and Robert C. Post, *For the Common Good: Principles of American Academic Freedom* (New Haven, CT: Yale University Press, 2011).

50. Angela Davis, quoted in "Academic Freedom and Tenure: The University of California at Los Angeles," *AAUP Bulletin* 57, no. 3 (September 1971): 410.

51. Irving Kristol, "A Different Way to Restructure the University," in *Confrontation*, ed. Bell and Kristol, 146–47.

52. Kenworthy, "The Non-Militant Students," in *Divided We Stand*, ed. Strout and Grossvogel, 87; Edward T. Silva, "Faculty Images of Power and Knowledge," in *Academic Supermarkets: A Critical Case Study of a Multiversity*, ed. Philip G. Altbach, Robert S. Laufer, and Sheila McVey (San Francisco: Jossey-Bass, 1971), 170–189.

53. Downs, *Cornell '69*, 94.

54. Heller, *Death of the American University*, 104.

55. Gartner, "Five Demands," 17–18; Downs, *Cornell '69*, 129.

56. Heller, *Death of the American University*, 87–88.

57. Kim Phillips-Fein, *Fear City: New York's Fiscal Crisis and the Rise of Austerity Politics* (New York: Metropolitan Books, 2017), 241–55.

58. Dawidoff, *Fly Swatter*, 317; Howard Levant (Pepperdine U.) to Sidney Hook, October 22, 1973, box 170, folder 3, Hook Papers; Conference Program, Sep-

tember 21–22, 1973, and clipping from *Time*, October 8, 1973, box 170, folder 4, Hook Papers; Nathan Tarcov, "Four Crucial Years at Cornell," in *Confrontation*, ed. Bell and Kristol, 134.

59. For an influential assessment of that transformation, see Christopher Jencks and David Riesman, *The Academic Revolution* (New York: Doubleday, 1968); Cushing Strout, "A Personal Narrative of a Rude Awakening," in *Divided We Stand*, ed. Strout and Grossvogel, 54; Buchanan and Devletoglou, *Academia in Anarchy*, 120, 129; Downs, *Cornell '69*, 306.

60. Clark Kerr, *The Uses of the University* (Cambridge, MA: Harvard University Press, 1963).

61. Downs, *Cornell '69*, 28.

62. Jacques Barzun, "The Danger of 'Public Service,'" in *The University Crisis Reader*, ed. Immanuel Wallerstein and Paul Starr, vol. 1, *The Liberal University under Attack* (New York: Random House, 1971), 124.

63. John W. Boyer, *The University of Chicago: A History* (Chicago: University of Chicago Press, 2015), 372.

64. David I. Grossvogel, "The University in Transition," in *Divided We Stand*, ed. Strout and Grossvogel, 132–36, 141–42; Downs, *Cornell '69*, 7–8, 12, 19, 215, 236; Walter LaFeber, telephone interview with the author, November 12, 2008.

65. Ulam, *Fall of the American University*, 10.

66. Buchanan and Devletoglou, *Academia in Anarchy*, 141.

67. David Evett, "Travail of a Department," in *Academic Supermarkets*, ed. Altbach, Laufer, and McVey, 264.

68. Carl Landauer, "Further Comments on Institutional Neutrality," *AAUP Bulletin* 56, no. 2 (Summer 1970): 123.

69. Everett Carll Ladd Jr. and Seymour Martin Lipset, *The Divided Academy: Professors and Politics* (New York: McGraw-Hill, 1975), 218.

70. Joel Silbey, quoted in Downs, *Cornell '69*, 137; Richard Hofstadter, transcript of Commencement speech, June 4, 1968, https://exhibitions.library.columbia .edu/exhibits/show/1968/item/9566 (accessed February 8, 2021); "'Majority Statement,' Report of the Ad Hoc Committee on Mode of Response to Obstruction, Interview Policy, and Related Matters," University of Wisconsin–Madison campus, March 13, 1968, in *The University Crisis Reader*, ed. Wallerstein and Starr, 1:61; R. Stephen Berry et al., to Members of the University Faculties, May 13, 1970, box 121, folder 14, Office of the President, Levi Administration Records.

71. Ulam, *Fall of the American University*, 12–13; Gartner, "Five Demands," 35; Rosovsky, "Black Studies at Harvard," 568.

72. Winton U. Solberg, "On Institutional Neutrality," *AAUP Bulletin* 56, no. 1 (Spring 1970): 11–13; Lincoln S. Gordon, "Statement on 'Vietnam Moratorium' Proposal," September 30, 1969, box 38, folder 6, Office of the President, Levi Administration Records.

73. George McT. Kahin, "Address in Barton Hall, April 25, 1969," in *Divided We Stand*, ed. Strout and Grossvogel, 39–40.

74. Hook, "The Trojan Horse in American Higher Education," in *The University Crisis Reader*, ed. Wallerstein and Starr, 2: 398–404; Brown, "Upholding Professional Standards in the 70s," *AAUP Bulletin* 56, no. 2 (Summer 1970): 118–22; Glazer to Riesman, September 30, 1965, box 13, Riesman Papers.

75. Daniel P. Moynihan to Richard Hofstadter, September 12, 1970, box A, Hofstadter Papers.

76. Landauer, "Further Comments on Institutional Neutrality"; Brown, "Upholding Professional Standards in the 70s," 124. See also the similar warning from Herbert Deane at Columbia, in Avorn et al., *Up Against the Ivy Wall*, 290.

77. Brown, "Upholding Professional Standards in the 70s," 118–24; Hofstadter, transcript of Commencement speech, June 4, 1968; "The University as a Sanctuary of Academic Freedom," April 21, 1969, ad signed by over 800 Columbia faculty members, in *The University Crisis Reader*, ed. Wallerstein and Starr, 2:61–62; Lemisch, *On Active Service in War and Peace*, 103–4; Evett, "Travail of a Department," in *Academic Supermarkets*, ed. Altbach, Laufer, and McVey, 264.

78. Ladd and Lipset, *The Divided Academy*, xi, 35; Tom Wells, *The War Within: America's Battle over Vietnam* (Berkeley: University of California Press, 1994), 299.

79. Roger Rapoport and Laurence J. Kirshbaum, *Is the Library Burning?* (New York: Random House, 1969), 44; Robert Smith, Richard Axen, and DeVere Pentony, *By Any Means Necessary: The Revolutionary Struggle at San Francisco State* (San Francisco: Jossey-Bass, 1970), 248–51; Arlene Kaplan Daniels, "Making of the President, 1969," 186–97; and Magali Sarfatti Larson, "Master Plan, Master Failure," 190–96: both in *Academics on the Line: The Faculty Strike at San Francisco State*, by Arlene Kaplan Daniels, Rachel Kahn-Hut, and Associates (San Francisco: Jossey-Bass, 1970); Ladd and Lipset, *The Divided Academy*, 1.

80. Richard Hofstadter, *Anti-Intellectualism in American Life* (New York: Knopf, 1963); Eddie R. Cole, *The Campus Color Line: College Presidents and the Struggle for Black Freedom* (Princeton, NJ: Princeton University Press, 2020), 122–23, 218.

81. William Scranton et al., *The Report of the President's Commission on Campus Unrest* (New York: Arno Press, 1970), 28 (hereafter "Scranton Report"); Richard A. Siggelkow, *Dissent and Disruption: A University under Siege* (Buffalo: Prometheus Books, 1991), 67–68.

82. On the media, see Todd Gitlin, *The Whole World Is Watching: Mass Media in the Making and Unmaking of the New Left* (Berkeley: University of California Press, 2003), 4, 48, 163, and especially chapters 1–4; Lammers, "Tactics and Strategies Adopted by University Authorities," in *Dynamics of University Protest*, ed. Light and Spiegel, 187.

83. "Scranton Report," 28.

84. Gitlin, *The Whole World Is Watching*, 76.

85. Richard W. Lyman, *Stanford in Turmoil: Campus Unrest, 1966–1972* (Stanford, CA: Stanford General Books, 2009), 7.

86. Seth Rosenfeld, *Subversives: The FBI's War on Student Radicals, and Reagan's Rise to Power* (New York: Farrar, Straus and Giroux, 2012), 64–67, 76, 107, 212–13.

87. Robert Cohen, "The Many Meanings of the FSM," 26; and Martin Roysher, "Recollections of the FSM," 64–64: both in *The Free Speech Movement: Reflections on Berkeley in the 1960s*, ed. Robert Cohen and Reginald E. Zelnik (Berkeley: University of California Press, 2002); Gitlin, *The Whole World Is Watching*, 64–65.

88. Schorske, Bancroft Oral History, 46, 92; Henry Mayer, "A View from the South: The Idea of a State University," in *The Free Speech Movement*, ed. Cohen and Zelnik, 165.

89. Evan Hill, "The Revolution (Cont.): At the University of Connecticut," *New York Times Magazine*, February 23, 1969; John H. Bunzel, "'The War of the Flea' at San Francisco State," *New York Times Magazine*, November 9, 1969; Thomas Sowell, "A Black Professor Says . . . ," *New York Times Magazine*, December 13, 1970; Richard J. Margolis, "The Two Nations at Wesleyan University," *New York Times Magazine*, January 18, 1970.

90. Barry Gottehrer, *The Mayor's Man: One Man's Struggle to Save Our Cities* (Garden City, NY: Doubleday, 1975), 179.

91. Peter Millones, "Gym Controversy Began in Late 50's"; and B. Drummond Ayres Jr., "A Target of Campus Protest Is a 'Think Tank'": both *New York Times*, April 26, 1968. Michael T. Kaufman, "Students at Battlements in 5 Buildings," *New York Times*, April 27, 1968; John Kifner, "Many Thousands in Damage Reported," *New York Times*, May 1, 1968; Gotteherer, *Mayor's Man*, 17.

92. A. M. Rosenthal, "Combat and Compassion at Columbia: Combat and Compassion Mark Night of Many Moods as Police Move in at Campus," *New York Times*, May 1, 1968; Gotteherer, *Mayor's Man*, 17; Avorn et al., *Up Against the Ivy Wall*, 190; Neil Hurwitz, "The Essence of Spirit Is Freedom," in *A Time to Stir: Columbia '68*, ed. Paul Cronin (New York: Columbia University Press, 2018), 124; David Underhill, "Death at a Later Age: Political Science versus the Columbia Rebellion," in *An End to Political Science: The Caucus Papers*, ed. Marvin Surkin and Alan Wolfe (New York: Basic Books, 1970), 248–49.

93. "Hoodlumism at Columbia," *New York Times*, April 25, 1968; "The Campus Militants," *New York Times*, April 26, 1968.

94. Dancis, *Resister*, 269; Downs, *Cornell '69*, 281–84.

95. John Kifner, "Armed Negroes End Seizure: Cornell Yields: Armed Negro Students End 36-Hour Occupation after Cornell Capitulates," *New York Times*, April 21, 1969; Fred M. Hechinger, "Cayuga's Muddy Water: Cornell Crisis Brings Faculty Attacks Against Administration as Too Liberal," *New York Times*, April 22, 1969; Homer Bigart, "Cornell Faculty Reverses Itself on Negroes," *New York Times*, April 24, 1969; Bigart, "Faculty Revolt Upsets Cornell: Charges of Sellout Made—Many Won't Teach until Assured Guns Are Gone," *New York Times*, April 25, 1969; Fred M. Hechinger, "Faculty Falters in Leadership Role," *New York Times*, April 27, 1969; Bigart, "Perkins Denounces Black Separatism: Concedes Cornell Paid a High Price for Negro Peace Talks," *New*

York Times, April 28, 1969; Bigart, "Cornell's Stance and Future Are Debated Bitterly," *New York Times*, April 29, 1969.

96. John Kifner, "Cornell Negro Plan begun in '65," *New York Times*, April 22, 1969; editorial, "Guns on Campus," *New York Times*, April 22, 1969; C. Gerald Fraser, "Negroes at Cornell Call Black Studies Minimal," *New York Times*, April 26, 1969; Tom Wicker, "The Real Issue Is How Men Live," *New York Times*, April 27, 1969; Wicker, "In the Nation: Humanity vs. Principle at Cornell," *New York Times*, April 27, 1969; editorial, "Freedom of the Campus," *New York Times*, June 16, 1969.

Epilogue

1. William Scranton, *The Report of the President's Commission on Campus Unrest* (New York: Arno Press, 1970) (hereafter "Scranton Report"); Marshall W. Meyer, "After the Bust: Student Politics at Harvard, 1969–1972," in *Academic Transformation: Seventeen Institutions under Pressure*, ed. David Riesman and Verne A. Stadtman (New York: McGraw-Hill, 1973), 132; Paul Sigmund, "Princeton in Crisis and Change," in *Academic Transformation*, ed. Riesman and Stadtman, 265; John D. Millett, *New Structures of Campus Power* (San Francisco: Jossey-Bass, 1978), 88.

2. Verne A. Stadtman, "Constellations in a Nebulous Galaxy," in *Academic Transformation*, ed. Riesman and Stadtman, 1–11. The most useful work on the reforms of academic governance in the 1960s and early 1970s is by a former president of Miami University of Ohio: Millett, *New Structures of Campus Power*.

3. Millett, *New Structures of Campus Power*, xii.

4. Robert K. Carr and Daniel K. Van Eyck, *Collective Bargaining Comes to the Campus* (Washington, DC: American Council on Education, 1973) 21; James P. Begin, Theodore Settle, and Paula Alexander, *Academics on Strike* (New Brunswick, NJ: Institute of Management and Labor Relations University Extension Division, Rutgers, State University of New Jersey, 1975), 1.

5. James Axtell, *The Making of Princeton University: From Woodrow Wilson to the Present* (Princeton, NJ: Princeton University Press, 2006), 230; University of California, Berkeley Academic Senate, *Education at Berkeley: Report of the Select Committee on Education*, March 1966 (otherwise known as the "Muscatine Report"), 57–59; "Students to Have Pass-Fail Option in Fall," *Exponent*, July 1, 1970, in Archives and Special Collections, M. Louis Salmon Library, University of Alabama at Huntsville; L. G. Heller, *The Death of the American University* (New Rochelle, NY: Arlington House, 1973), 86; Morton Keller and Phyllis Keller, *Making Harvard Modern: The Rise of America's University* (Cary, NC: Oxford University Press, 2001), 298–99.

6. John A. Dunn Jr. "Old Westbury I and Old Westbury II," in *Academic Transformation*, ed. Riesman and Stadtman, 199–224.

7. Marlene Kim, "URPE at Fifty: Reflections on a Half Century of Activism, Community, Debate (and a Few Crazy Moments)," *Review of Radical Political*

Economics 50, no. 3 (2018): 480; Thomas E. Weisskopf, "Reflections on 50 Years of Radical Political Economy," *Review of Radical Political Economics* 46, no. 4 (2014): 437–47; Jack Stauder, telephone interview with the author, November 3, 2014; Keller and Keller, *Making Harvard Modern*, 312–13.

8. There is a huge collection of documents on the Experimental College and similar programs in the Experimental College Collection as well as the SFSU Strike Collection in the Labor Archives and Research Center, Special Collections, J. Paul Leonard Library, San Francisco State University. See, for example, "Experimental College Developments in the California State Colleges, November 1969," Experimental College Collection, box 2, folder: "Experimental Colleges within CSC"; and in the San Francisco State Strike Collection, Russell Bass, "Some Notes on the Experimental College," October 1967, box: SFSU—Related Organizations, EXPERIMENTAL COLLEGE, folder: Bass, Russell (hereafter, LARC, SFSU).

9. Joanne Grant, *Confrontation on Campus: The Columbia Pattern for the New Protest* (New York: New American Library, 1969), 138–39.

10. "Union College: A Good Start," December 10, 1969, "Union College in Full Swing for Spring Term," April 8, 1970, both in *Exponent*, Archives and Special Collections, University of Alabama in Huntsville.

11. Millett, *New Structures of Campus Power*, 354–55; Reminiscences of Polykarp Kusch, May 17, 1968, Columbia Crisis of 1968 Project, Columbia Oral History Project, Rare Books and Manuscript Library, Butler Library, Columbia University (hereafter COHP); "William J. Bouwsma: Historian of European Culture in the Early Modern Era, University of California, Berkeley, 1956–1991," interview conducted by Ann Lage in 2000, Regional Oral History Office, Bancroft Library, University of California, Berkeley, 2008, 71.

12. NLRB v. Yeshiva Univ., 444 U.S. 672 (1980); Janus v. American Federation of State, County, and Municipal Employees, 585 U.S. ___ (2018).

13. Matthew Dallek, *The Right Moment: Ronald Reagan's First Victory and the Decisive Turning Point in American Politics* (New York: Free Press, 2000); Seth Rosenfeld, *Subversives: The FBI's War on Student Radicals, and Reagan's Rise to Power* (New York: Farrar, Straus and Giroux, 2012); Neil J. Smelser, "Berkeley in Crisis and Change," in *Academic Transformation*, ed. Riesman and Stadtman 62–65; Julie A. Reuben, "The Limits of Freedom: Student Activists and Educational Reform at Berkeley in the 1960s," in *The Free Speech Movement: Reflections on Berkeley in the 1960s*, ed. Robert Cohen and Reginald E. Zelnik (Berkeley: University of California Press, 2002), 485–88; Roger Rapoport and Laurence J. Kirshbaum, *Is the Library Burning?* (New York: Random House, 1969), 38–40; W. J. Rorabaugh, *Berkeley at War: The 1960s* (New York: Oxford University Press, 1989), 83–84; William J. McGill, *The Year of the Monkey: Revolt on Campus, 1968–69* (New York: McGraw-Hill, 1982), 11–19.

14. John Kendall and George Kannar, "Disciplining on Campus Tougher than Believed," *Los Angeles Times*, June 23, 1969, clipping, in box 124, folder 1, Office of the President, Levi Administration Records, University of Chicago Archives,

Special Collections Research Center, University of Chicago Library; Nancy McDermid, "Assessments," in *Academics on the Line: The Faculty Strike at San Francisco State,* by Arlene Kaplan Daniels, Rachel Kahn-Hut, and Associates (San Francisco: Jossey-Bass, 1970), 238–39.

15. Herman Orentlicher, "*Haverford College v. Reeher,* a Landmark Decision on Campus Surveillance and Academic Freedom," *AAUP Bulletin* 57, no. 3 (September 1971): 420; Union for Social Action, leaflet, box 9, folder 5, New University Conference Papers, Wisconsin Historical Society, Madison (hereafter NUC Papers, WHS); William J. Billingsley, *Communists on Campus: Race, Politics, and the Public University in Sixties North Carolina* (Athens: University of Georgia Press, 1999), 225.

16. "Scranton Report," 40; Richard E. Peterson and John A. Bilorusky, *May 1970: The Campus Aftermath of Cambodia and Kent State* (Berkeley: Carnegie Commission on Higher Education, 1971), 81.

17. Mary Ann Wynkoop, *Dissent in the Heartland: The Sixties at Indiana University* (Bloomington: Indiana University Press, 2002), 79.

18. Bernard Sklar, "Corporate Recruitment on Campus," in *Academic Supermarkets: A Critical Case Study of a Multiversity,* ed. Philip G. Altbach, Robert S. Laufer, and Sheila McVey (San Francisco: Jossey-Bass, 1971), 146.

19. J. Stanley Marshall, *The Tumultuous Sixties: Campus Unrest and Student Life at a Southern University* (Tallahassee: Sentry Press, 2006), 9; "Fact Sheet on Illinois Special Legislative Commission to Investigate Campus Disturbances," box 9, folder 5, NUC Papers, WHS.

20. William Trombley, "California Falls Further Behind as Other Colleges Boost Pay," *Los Angeles Times,* July 12, 1970, clipping, in box: United Professors of California, folder 154, LARC, SFSU; Earl F. Cheit, *The New Depression in Higher Education: A Study of Financial Conditions at 41 Colleges and Universities* (New York: McGraw-Hill, 1971), 17.

21. H. R. Haldeman, *The Haldeman Diaries: Inside the Nixon White House* (New York: Putnam, 1994), 159–60; Michael Koncewicz, *They Said No to Nixon: Republicans Who Stood Up to the President's Abuses of Power* (Berkeley: University of California Press, 2018), 72–79.

22. Sheila Slaughter and Larry L. Leslie, *Academic Capitalism: Politics, Policies, and the Entrepreneurial University* (Baltimore: Johns Hopkins University Press, 1998), 72–73.

23. David Vogel, *Fluctuating Fortunes: The Political Power of Business in America* (New York: Basic Books, 1989), esp. 213–27.

24. Tom Wells, *The War Within: America's Battle over Vietnam* (Berkeley: University of California Press, 1994), 464; John Lawrence to Sidney Hook, April 20, 1970, box 170, folder 2, Sidney Hook Papers, Hoover Institution Library and Archives, Stanford, CA.

25. Nancy MacLean, *Democracy in Chains: The Deep History of the Radical Right's Stealth Plan for America* (New York: Viking, 2017), is the key text here. See also Jane Mayer, *Dark Money: The Hidden History of the Billionaires*

Behind the Rise of the Radical Right (New York: Anchor Doubleday, 2016), and Kim Phillips-Fein, *Fear City: New York's Fiscal Crisis and the Rise of Austerity Politics* (New York: Metropolitan Books, 2017). For a copy of the Powell memo, see http://www.thwink.org/sustain/articles/017_PowellMemo/ PowellMemoReproduction.pdf.

26. John J. Miller, *A Gift of Freedom: How the John M. Olin Foundation Changed America* (San Francisco: Encounter Books, 2006); Ellen Messer-Davidow, "Manufacturing the Attack on Liberalized Higher Education," *Social Text*, no. 36 (Autumn 1993): 40–80; Ellen Schrecker, *The Lost Soul of Higher Education: Corporatization, the Assault on Academic Freedom, and the End of the American University* (New York: New Press, 2010).

27. Allan Bloom, *The Closing of the American Mind: How Higher Education Has Failed Democracy and Impoverished the Souls of Today's Students* (New York: Simon and Schuster, 1987). For other examples of the genre, see Roger Kimball, *Tenured Radicals: How Politics Has Corrupted Our Higher Education* (New York: Harper & Row, 1990), and Dinesh D'Souza, *Illiberal Education: The Politics of Race and Sex on Campus* (New York: Free Press, 1991).

28. MacLean, *Democracy in Chains*, 178–84.

29. On the connection between higher education and economic equality (or the lack thereof), see Claudia Goldin and Lawrence F. Katz, *The Race between Education and Technology* (Cambridge, MA: Harvard University Press, 2008); and Christopher Newfield, *Unmaking the Public University: The Forty-Year Assault on the Middle Class* (Cambridge, MA: Harvard University Press, 2008).

30. Robert S. Fisk and William C. Puffer, "Public University System: State University of New York," in *Faculty Unions and Collective Bargaining*, ed. E. D. Duryea, Robert S. Fisk, and Associates (San Francisco: Jossey-Bass, 1973), 133.

31. Adrianna J. Kezar, Thomas DePaola, and Daniel T. Scott, *The Gig University: Mapping Labor in the Neoliberal University* (Baltimore: Johns Hopkins University Press, 2019), 45; Jane Mok and Victoria Tereschenko, "The Graduate Student Strike Explained," *Columbia Spectator*, March 18, 2021.

32. Ethan Schrum, *The Instrumental University: Education in Service of the National Agenda after World War II* (Ithaca, NY: Cornell University Press, 2019). There is a large and depressing body of scholarship on the problems that austerity has created for the contemporary university. For a useful recent example, see Christopher Newfield, *The Great Mistake: How We Wrecked Public Universities and How We Can Fix Them* (Baltimore: Johns Hopkins University Press, 2016).

Acknowledgments

1. Ellen Schrecker, *No Ivory Tower: McCarthyism and the Universities* (New York: Oxford University Press, 1986); Schrecker, *The Lost Soul of Higher Education: Corporatization, the Assault on Academic Freedom, and the End of the American University* (New York: New Press, 2010).

INDEX

Abel, Lionel, 32
Aberle, David, 142
Aberle, Kathleen Gough, 374
Abernathy, Ralph, 74
Abram, Morris, 338, 339
academic careers, 5, 26–30, 32, 34, 40, 346, 350–52, 391–93, 399, 453
academic freedom, 5, 7, 21, 34–35, 37–46, 48–50, 52, 54, 59–61, 70, 87–88, 127, 146–47, 184, 199, 225–26, 246, 335–37, 367, 397–409, 411–13, 431–32, 435–37, 454–55, 458; Angela Davis case, 39–40, 55, 203, 448; concept of, 50, 59–60, 199, 246, 432, 435, 437; lack of, 7, 21, 44, 454; loyalty oaths and, 45–46, 48–50; tenure and, 432–33; violations of and political dismissals, 34–43, 45–46, 48–50, 54, 59–61, 72, 87–88, 120, 225–26, 246, 323, 335, 397–409, 411–13, 431–33, 454–55, 458. *See also* American Association of University Professors
Academic Revolution, 411
Ackley, Gardner, 586–87n4
Adelson, Howard, 415–18, 420, 422, 433–34
admissions, 14, 23, 25, 28–29, 253, 287–88, 301–2, 321, 414–15, 417–19; Black students and, 275, 287–88, 301, 433–34; expansion of, and minorities, 288; open admissions, 14, 302, 321, 369, 414–15, 417–19, 433–34; selectivity, 28–29, 287
Advanced Research Projects Agency (ARPA), 220, 232
African Americans. *See* Black academics; Black students
Agent Orange, 236–38
Ahmad, Eqbal, 134, 202
Alabama, University of, 58, 75, 254–55, 282, 310
Alabama, University of, Huntsville, 447
Alabama State College, 42–43, 74, 389
Albany, State University of New York (SUNY), 19, 31, 33, 40
Alcorn A&M, 43, 280
Alfred University, 254, 398
Algeria, French opposition to war in, 202–3
Allen University, 41–42
Alperovitz, Gar, 177
American Anthropology Association, 360
American Association for the Advancement of Science (AAAS), 224, 238, 346, 365–66

Clergy and Laity Concerned About
Vietnam (CALCAV), 204–5
Closing of the American Mind, The, 451
Cloward, Richard, 155
Coatsworth, John, 189
Cobb, Charles, 76
Cockcroft, James, 407
Coetzee, John, 299
Coffin, William Sloane, 72, 175, 177, 193,
205–9, 312
Cohelan, Jeffrey, 176
Cohen, Robert, 101, 281–82, 462
Cohen, Wilbur, 360–61
Cole, Robert, 96, 100
Coleman, Henry, 313
Colfax, David, 381, 383, 404, 405
Colorado, University of, 28
Columbia University, 6, 71, 121, 166,
180, 190, 203, 217–19, 242, 244–
45, 264–65, 268, 280, 291, 293–95,
308–10, 312–15, 317–19, 322–23, 326,
328–31, 360, 416, 425–26, 434–35,
441–42; Black students at, 268–69,
308, 317; class-rank issue at, 180, 190;
crisis of 1968, 308–10, 312–15, 317–19,
326, 328–31; discipline, issue of, 328–
29; faculty response to student unrest
at, 308–9, 314; media coverage of,
441–42; military research at, 218–19,
242, 324; recruiters at, 244–45, 249–
50, 264–65; student protests at, 265,
291, 294–95, 308–10, 312–15, 317–19,
328 (*see also* crisis of 1968); urban renewal at, 276–77; violence at, 313–14
Commager, Henry Steele, 131, 246, 402
Commission on the Status of Women
(MLA), 345
Committee to Abolish HUAC, 69
Committee on Academic Freedom
(Berkeley), 95
Committee of Concerned Asian Scholars (CCAS), 361–62, 366, 370–71,
376, 380, 384, 386–87, 392, 396, 462,
566n83

Committee to End the War in Vietnam
(CEWV), 214–15
Committee for Non-Violent Action,
160
Committee for a Sane Nuclear Policy
(SANE), 82, 133–34, 138, 167, 170, 175
Commoner, Barry, 80–82, 143
Communist Party, 35, 37–38, 42
community colleges, 13, 17, 355
complicity statements, 197, 190, 200,
203
computers, 242, 311–12, 332, 338, 400,
404
Conant, James Bryant, 29–30, 224
Condon, E. U., 80
Congress of Racial Equality (CORE),
71–72, 139
Connecticut, University of, 272, 423,
404–5, 441
conscientious objectors, 194, 196. *See
also* draft
conservative academics, 95, 104–6, 112,
188, 190, 245, 284, 301, 307, 309, 312,
325, 329, 332, 378–80, 409, 413–14,
417–19, 420–38, 442–43; analysis of
campus unrest, 425–30, 442; attacks
on, 312, 316, 365–66. *See also* University Centers for Rational Alternatives
conservative politicians and public, 3,
19, 35, 39, 56, 59, 86, 87, 101, 112, 186,
281, 288, 337, 414, 436–38, 448–54;
punitive measures against universities, 448–50
Constance, Lincoln, 101, 108
Cook, Albert, 32
Cook, Robert, 182
Cornell University, 6, 20, 61, 65, 71–72,
121, 129, 143, 146, 157, 175, 181, 187,
200–201, 206, 240, 257, 264, 267, 275,
294, 311–15, 324–25, 333–37, 422, 430–
33, 435–37; antiwar activities at, 181,
187–89, 264, 292; Black students at,
267, 274–75 (*see also* crisis of 1969);
class-rank issue, at, 181, 184–90; crisis